ALSO BY PETER BOGDANOVICH

Movie of the Week (1999)

Who the Devil Made It (1997)

A Moment with Miss Gish (1995)

This Is Orson Welles (1992; expanded 1998), with Orson Welles

A Year and a Day Engagement Calendar (annually, 1991–98; a.k.a. *The White Goddess Engagement Diary,* based on works by Robert Graves; editor)

The Killing of the Unicorn: Dorothy Stratten 1960–1980 (1984)

Pieces of Time (1973; expanded 1985)

Allan Dwan: The Last Pioneer (1970)

Fritz Lang in America (1969)

John Ford (1967; expanded 1978)

The Cinema of Alfred Hitchcock (1963)

The Cinema of Howard Hawks (1962)

The Cinema of Orson Welles (1961)

WHO THE HELL'S
IN IT

WHO THE HELL'S IN IT

PORTRAITS AND CONVERSATIONS

Stella Adler • Humphrey Bogart • Marlon Brando
James Cagney • John Cassavetes • Charlie Chaplin
Montgomery Clift • Marlene Dietrich
Henry Fonda • Ben Gazzara • Lillian Gish
Cary Grant • Audrey Hepburn • Boris Karloff
Jack Lemmon • Jerry Lewis • Dean Martin
Sal Mineo • Marilyn Monroe • Anthony Perkins
River Phoenix • Sidney Poitier • Frank Sinatra
James Stewart • John Wayne

Peter Bogdanovich

Alfred A. Knopf   NEW YORK   2004

THIS IS A BORZOI BOOK
PUBLISHED BY ALFRED A. KNOPF

www.aaknopf.com

Owing to limitations of space, all acknowledgments to reprint previously
published material may be found preceding the index.

Library of Congress Cataloging-in-Publication Data

Bogdanovich, Peter, [date]
Who the hell's in it : portraits and conversations /
Peter Bogdanovich. — 1st ed.
p.   cm.
Includes index.
ISBN 0-375-40010-9 (alk. paper)
1. Motion picture actors and actresses—United States—Biography.
I. Title: Who the hell's in it.   II. Title.

PN1998.2.B64 2004
791.4302'8'092273—dc22
[B]   2003069494

Manufactured in the United States of America
FIRST EDITION

To the memory

of

Audrey Hepburn,

John Cassavetes,

Sal Mineo,

River Phoenix,

Madeline Kahn,

John Ritter,

and

Dorothy Stratten

Each gone from us

so much too soon

In pictures, personalities are it, you know. It isn't acting per se as it's known in the theater. You'd bring some kid in who just blazed off the screen—a girl or a fellow would hit you instantly. That's what we looked for—some photographic quality, some mysterious hidden thing certain people have. . . . The great movie stars learned the technique and a few mannerisms and a few moves and became sort of public idols. They couldn't do anything wrong, if you liked them—no matter what they did; it wasn't what they played. —ALLAN DWAN

Actors are like children. They must be coddled, and sometimes, spanked. —ALFRED HITCHCOCK

You and your directors! For me, it's all about the acting—movies are, you know. Pictures are ultimately about the performances. —ORSON WELLES

That's the great thing about the movies. . . . After you learn— and if you're good and Gawd helps ya and you're lucky enough to have a personality that comes across—then what you're doing is—you're giving people little . . . tiny pieces of time . . . *that they never forget.* —JAMES STEWART

Contents

WHO THE HELL'S
IN IT

Introduction

THE MAGICAL ART

Some thirty years ago, in Rome, Orson Welles and I were having a late-night drink in his suite at the Eden Hotel. We had spent a couple of hours taping our conversation for a book about his career. The tape machine, much to Orson's relief, was off now and stowed by the door. Of course, it was always at those times that Welles made the best comments. He had been going on about one of his favorite heresies—that directors, and indeed the whole job of directing, were highly overrated. For Orson, motion pictures were essentially about the performances.

When I remarked that a certain film was well directed but not well acted, Welles responded that he couldn't separate those qualities and if it wasn't well acted, then what good was it? Obviously, he said, he agreed that the highest level of great direction—with picturemakers he most admired, like Jean Renoir or John Ford, Ernst Lubitsch or Howard Hawks—certainly ranked among the fine arts. But that the average director, even some of the most successful, with long, distinguished careers, did not make the difference that really good performances do.

A little while later Orson cracked a disparaging remark about a popular contemporary stage and film star, ending with, "Well, you know—*actor!*" In show-biz circles, particularly among crews and production people, the use of the word "actor . . ." (said with just the slightest touch of contempt) reads as volumes of recorded experience. It is as much an expletive with or without a preceding "goddamn," and contains all the negative aspects behind the currently fashionable "diva," but none of the glitter or charm. "Actor," which can be hurled like a brick through a window or said under one's breath, carries a rather mundane connotation of a boringly self-involved, humorless and demanding person, often childish

*Orson Welles as Harry Lime in the Graham Greene–Carol Reed–
Alexander Korda thriller* The Third Man *(1949), the only movie
role Welles ever played without makeup. He also wrote the
famous "cuckoo clock" speech himself.*

and vain—in other words, tediously high-maintenance. None of this is
ever taken to imply that the actor is not a good one.

So I asked Orson, Well, if he thought acting was *it* in theater or film,
how could he so disparage "actors," and how did *he* himself behave when
he was acting? After all, he had done a great deal more of it than directing.
Welles replied, nodding boisterously once, *"Actor!"* We both laughed. Did
he mean that when he was acting, he behaved with all the unpleasant con-
notations behind the pejorative use of "Actor!"? Orson nodded, beaming,
almost proudly. "Yup—*actor*!" He laughed, loud and long.

This book repeatedly harks back to that essential paradox about actors,
male or female. To achieve what they often do so magically and with such
humanity, must there always be a childish or a childlike foundation? In

order perhaps to preserve some profound sense of innocent vulnerability? Acting does begin with play-acting. There was, in fact, an innocence on some level with all the star-players I met, and almost all actors, young or old. In their varying ways, at various points in their careers, as well, each of the actors in this book has on some level felt an unspoiled, selfless love for the work and the medium itself, whether on stage or screen (see, in particular, the Lillian Gish chapter).

During the old studio-system days (roughly from about 1915 until the early 1960s) star-players with beauty and peculiarities were the commodities most eagerly sought, most actively exploited, by the entire industry. With the relinquishing of contract talent, the business changed forever. No longer were the combined talents of the best directors, writers, producers and technical craftsmen in the world focused on making the contract players the best they could be. Everybody went on their own, actors preferred to be versatile rather than typed, and the studios—once factories that created entertainment and occasionally art, at the same time helping and mining the talent performing it—ended up having to go picture by picture and pay through the nose for the few stars that supposedly could "open" a movie in the now popular weekly top-ten box-office game, which never existed in the golden age. In the seventies, when the old studio way was already history, Howard Hawks once remarked to me that all through the twenties, thirties, forties, and into the fifties, there were more stars than ever in the history of the world. "And most of them," he said, "had very little to say about what they should play." It is a show-biz axiom that many actors and actresses are not necessarily the best judges of what they are best at. But most of the original movie stars had personalities and, as Allan Dwan* put it, they "just blazed off the screen."

As the gods and goddesses were for the Greeks, these stars formed a kind of twentieth-century mythology, created by the movies. They were no longer actors playing parts—because all their roles merged into one definitive character, one special folk hero, similar to but not necessarily identical with the original mortal. And this creation became, as director Fritz Lang* used to phrase it, a "valid dramaturgical element." Robert Aldrich,* who directed James Stewart in one sixties picture, admitted that he and his screenwriter decided to use for their script "what Stewart seems to be." The great film stars had an authenticity that transcended acting. They became real—not actors or even people playing themselves. They simply were: Cary Grant. John Wayne. Greta Garbo. Clark Gable. Marlene Dietrich.

*See chapter in *Who the Devil Made It.*

With normal fame and success intensified by virtual deification in the United States, of course, it became easy to forget integrity, lose all innocence; to sell out, succeed yet fail within. It is the typically American struggle in the *Golden Boy* syndrome (prizefighter vs. pianist): What shall it be, brute force or true passion? Money or poetry? The question itself now almost seems dated. But then *Faust* is an even older story. And as Faust learned, it is dangerous to ignore the immortal soul. This book, therefore, is dedicated to the spirits of all the brilliant players in it, long may they live.

Unlike my earlier work about directors, *Who the Devil Made It,* the chapters here are not arranged chronologically in order of the subjects' births, but rather in a more personal way: with the exception of the first two, and the last, these chapters are arranged roughly in the order that each person came into my life. Since my firsthand experiences with Lillian Gish and Marilyn Monroe were exceptionally brief—the latter not more than a glimpse—I have begun and ended with these two extraordinary women whom I wish I had gotten to know. Standing as vivid antipodes, both in career and character, the two represent the most traditional and archetypal—and most severely limiting—roles of women: virgin and whore. Because a truer understanding of female nature would radically improve relationships between the sexes all over the planet—and thus the planet—the continuing mythic power of Gish and Monroe seems appropriate to bookend these profiles of star power in a "man's world" ruled by personality.

My take on Bogart—which, as an *Esquire* article in 1964 (Bogie had died in 1957), heralded the beginnings of the Bogart cult—is the only other chapter that deals with someone I didn't actually know, even a little, or spend time with. The Bogart piece is also the most explicit look at the differences and similarities between the actual star-personality and the iconic image of them. The length of contact and levels of intimacy with the others, of course, vary greatly. From the briefest—with Montgomery Clift or Marlon Brando, to pretty brief with James Cagney, Henry Fonda or Charlie Chaplin—all the way to relationships that went on for nearly three decades, as with Cary Grant or James Stewart. Or, as is now for more than four decades, with Jerry Lewis. Portions of this material have appeared previously in other forms (noted either in the text or in the acknowledgments).

Résumé

Since the summer I turned sixteen, I've been working and living with professional actors. Actually, though hired as a glorified apprentice, I became one of their number within that first innocent summer, landing a lead role by the seventh week. But three years earlier, I had made my stage debut, doing the title part in our sixth grade (Collegiate School, on West 78th Street) production of the E. Y. Harburg–Burton Lane musical, *Finian's Rainbow.* My first line was "Eureka! Sharon, come quickly!" My dear mother became my first director when she heard me do a few lines and said, "You better work on that Irish accent."

Still, my earliest performances had been at some of my parents' intimate dinner parties in their New York apartments—either at 15 West 67th Street (from my infancy to nearly thirteen) or at 90th Street and Riverside Drive (until I was twenty-two)—where after the meal they would ask me to recite—poems like Poe's "Annabel Lee" or "The Raven," or Whitman's "O Captain! My Captain!" or Robert W. Service's "The Shooting of Dan McGrew"—or to read a short short story like Poe's "The Tell-Tale Heart."

In the same period, before I had turned thirteen, I produced and directed—and acted on—three or four radio productions made at home. This was just when dramatic and comic radio programs were fading from the scene; I had grown up on them, thought they were terrific. For Christmas my parents had given me a much-wished-for reel-to-reel Revere tape recorder, and with it I would tape a radio play (usually *Suspense*), then transcribe it word-for-word in longhand and type it out on my tiny portable typewriter. I would use my own selection of music with a little advice from my father or my uncle Fred Gandolfi and his extraordinary classical record collection (sections of Mussorgsky's *Night on Bald Mountain,* and Stravinsky's *Rite of Spring*). I played every part (including the women), and created all the sound effects by hand or vocally. When my sister Anna was born, I made a production of *Snow White and the Seven Dwarfs* for my mother and played it over the phone while she was in the hospital. I did all my own announcers, too, and had my own call letters: BTBC, Bogdanovich Tape Broadcasting Company.

Later that same year, having become a teenager, I went to see my first Broadway play (Henry Fonda in *Point of No Return* by Paul Osborn) and, thereafter, from 1952 to 1964, when I left New York for Los Angeles, I saw nearly every important show on or off Broadway. When I was sixteen or

*Edward Everett Horton in characteristic expression, flanked by
Katharine Hepburn and Jean Dixon in George Cukor's film of the
Philip Barry play* Holiday *(1938), starring Cary Grant.
Seventeen years later I was Horton's dresser.*

seventeen, my parents used some connections they had to arrange for me
to go backstage and meet Charles Laughton, who I believe was playing in
Shaw's *Don Juan in Hell* (which he also directed). He was quite heavy and
awfully nice in a slightly gruff yet self-deprecating way. When I told him I
wanted to be an actor he said, "Well, you should have no trouble—you're
a good-looking boy. *I've* looked like the hind end of an elephant since I
was twenty-one."

As a high school freshman (still at Collegiate), I was the youngest ever
to have the lead in the annual school production, playing the heavy in an
Agatha Christie–like suspense piece, *The Ninth Guest*, by Owen Davis. I
began cracking my knuckles as a character-thing and then couldn't stop
for about twenty years. All through my thirteen years at Collegiate, I was
nicknamed "Bugs," because of a popular impression I did of Bugs Bunny.

At other times, my nicknames fluctuated to Dean or Jerry, or Marlon, but Bugs prevailed. At fifteen, I started Saturday-morning teenage acting classes at the American Academy of Dramatic Arts, impressed the teacher, actress Eleanor Gould (especially with my Cyrano), and she invited me to become part of the children's theater and an apprentice with the main company for the summer of 1955 at the Cherry County Playhouse in Traverse City, Michigan.

The theater had a good resident company with actors from all over the country, especially New York, and each week a different star would come in, rehearse with us for a couple of days, then perform for a week, and move on. It was Star Summer Stock, lots of fun, and virtually gone today. I was more than a month shy of my sixteenth birthday when I left Manhattan (by train) and came back twelve weeks later, having played the lion in *The Wizard of Oz,* directed and written a kids' variety show, and done a (silent) butler in Maugham's *The Constant Wife* starring Sylvia Sidney. My birthday fell in that week and she gave me a real silent butler, with a handwritten card that read "Oh, you *are* the silent one!" A reference, I guess, to my being talkative. I wish now that I had talked less and asked more questions.

The sad truth is that within three years I would have known who each of those ten stars were, and what they had done *before* arriving in Traverse City, Michigan. Sylvia Sidney, for God's sake, had worked with Alfred Hitchcock,* Fritz Lang, King Vidor, Josef von Sternberg,* and Spencer Tracy, Henry Fonda and Cary Grant, among others. Did I know? No. When I finally met Sylvia Sidney again, about forty-five years later at a Hitchcock centennial celebration, I reminded her of her present and our brief association. Graciously, she pretended to remember. She was thin and fragile, had a hard time stepping up to the podium. Finally, her first words into the mike were: "Getting old is a bitch!" She died a few months later, those questions I would have asked never to be answered.

Nor, when I met Edward Everett Horton (I was his offstage dresser), had I even heard of all those great directors he'd worked with, whom I was so soon to revere (and in several cases, meet and befriend): Vidor, Sternberg, George Cukor,* Ernst Lubitsch* (five times!); and with Astaire and Rogers, Grant and Katharine Hepburn. Watching him from the wings every night, I learned how much you could get out of the smallest gesture if it was placed right. While holding someone at bay with a pistol, Horton at one point moved the wrist of his gun-hand very slightly and

*See chapter in *Who the Devil Made It.*

got a huge laugh. It was clearly his own moment, because he topped it by getting two more laughs with equally small hand gestures, plus a final "topper," which was the biggest laugh of the bunch. He may have been holding a gun but it was the audience he had in the palm of his hand. Horton died fifteen years later; I still recall—having helped him out of his dress coat and into a smoking jacket every night—the sharp yet musky smell of his cologne.

Others over that summer included Richard Arlen (unasked questions about Howard Hawks,* Sternberg, William Wellman, Gary Cooper); ZaSu Pitts (worked with Erich von Stroheim three times, Leo McCarey,* Douglas Fairbanks, Mary Pickford); Ilona Massey (the Marx Bros.). Veronica Lake got married for the second time during her days in Michigan—she was in Preston Sturges' *Sullivan's Travels,* shortly to become a favorite of mine. Ignorance may be bliss but you pay for it with recriminations.

My favorite role was in the seventh week, playing Signe Hasso's teenage son in Edward Mabley's comedy *Glad Tidings.* It was the juvenile lead and a terrific part to land while still an apprentice. And Signe—who, it would turn out, had also worked with Lubitsch, Cukor, Grant, C. B. DeMille, and Ronald Colman—gave me a still-treasured compliment when she said I got more laughs out of the role than anyone who had played it before, even on Broadway. She couldn't have been warmer or more kind. One afternoon, we went for a long lovely ride in her convertible. Actually, I saw her a number of times over the years, first in New York when she was doing an off-Broadway show, then in Hollywood, but somehow always at gatherings when we couldn't really speak. I rode uptown in a cab with her once soon after her beloved only son, also named Peter, had died in his twenties, over which she suffered terribly.

Signe, who was Swedish, was wonderful to have as my first mother in the theater, and not long before her death in 2002, I did phone her in Los Angeles a couple of times (I was back in N.Y.C. by then) and asked a few questions. "Cary was the most wonderful gentleman," she told me, and "DeMille was very underrated—he was very good, really." She adored Cukor, "a dear friend," and Lubitsch, "of course, was the best," acting out each part for every actor and "better than any of them. I used to tell him he was much better than me in my role as the French maid [in *Heaven Can Wait,* 1943]." Signe and I had planned to tape some of her reminiscences, but before we could she died suddenly in her eighty-fourth year.

*See chapter in *Who the Devil Made It.*

*Signe Hasso is the French maid who initiates teenager
Dickie Moore (who grows up to be Don Ameche) into the
mysteries of sex for Ernst Lubitsch's penultimate classic,*
Heaven Can Wait *(1943), a lovely human comedy, his first
in color. Spring Byington and Charles Coburn are
Dickie/Don's disapproving mother and approving uncle. At
the time, Moore was almost the same age as I was when
twelve years later Signe played my mother onstage.*

Another apprentice whom I met that summer advised me to study
with Stella Adler, by then already legendary as an actress/star-teacher, and
in the fall of 1955, having lied about my age (I said I was eighteen), I
entered into the beginner class she taught. For the next four falls, winters
and springs I took Stella's classes in the afternoons after school. I was also
briefly in the large cast of the Kurt Weill–Paul Green musical-drama
Johnny Johnson, which Stella directed off-Broadway. Those four years
with her were the solid foundation for all the directing and acting I
would ever do.

During June–September, 1956–58, I continued working in summer theaters: in Stratford, Connecticut, as an apprentice extra, bit player and understudy at John Houseman's American Shakespeare Festival (*King John, Measure for Measure, Taming of the Shrew*); and in Central Park at Joseph Papp's original New York Shakespeare Festival (*Othello, Twelfth Night*), trying out *Othello* for a week in Bala Cynwyd, Pennsylvania. My favorite summer of acting in stock was at Falmouth, Massachusetts, where (turning 19) I had a really good time playing fine parts in Shaw's *Major Barbara* (the stuffy son) and Arthur Koestler's *Darkness at Noon* (the Nazi-like main heavy), plus six comedy-part bits all in one farce (once, I followed myself on), using a different famous voice for each. After about the third entrance the audience figured out it was all the same actor and laughed every time I turned up.

Finally out of high school, I tried to get work in theater or in television. There were very few films made in New York at the time, and live dramatic TV was on its way out fast. I did bits on two of the last good ones: "Blast in Centralia No. 5" with Jason Robards, Jr., and Maureen Stapleton (directed by George Roy Hill for *Seven Arts Playhouse*), and "Fifty Grand," out of Hemingway, with Ralph Meeker (directed by Sidney Lumet* for *Kraft Television Theatre*). Auditioned twice and was turned down twice for the Actors Studio, did leads in a couple of showcases off-Broadway (Tennessee Williams' one-act *Talk to Me Like the Rain and Let Me Listen*), and in Westport, Connecticut (a new play by Michael Hastings, *Yes, and After*). I hated auditioning, and found the process humiliating and not a fair way to judge talent. Often, I would eventually discover, the best actors were not necessarily good auditioners, and good auditioners were not necessarily always as good once they had the role, the audition sometimes being the best you were going to get. When I started directing, my casting sessions were usually long because I tried to give the actors as much time as possible. The necessity of auditioning, however, is what propelled me away from acting as my primary career.

In the late fall of 1958, I suggested to a group of five students I was hanging out with at Stella's that I direct them in a scene from Clifford Odets' Hollywood drama, *The Big Knife*. We rehearsed for a week or so and then they performed it with great success during one of Stella's scene-classes. From this point on, my focus changed from acting to directing and by the end of the following year, in November 1959, I co-produced

*See chapter in *Who the Devil Made It*.

and directed an off-Broadway production of *The Big Knife,* which was a *succès d'estime.* I was twenty.

We had a good cast and everybody in it kept on working afterward, but the only one who became famous was Carroll O'Connor. I had cast him—it was only his second appearance in New York City, and his first leading role—as the movie-studio boss whose sanctimoniousness and hypocrisy were supposedly based largely on M-G-M's Louis B. Mayer. Carroll was superb in the part, received great notices, got his first agent from it, soon went to Hollywood, and never looked back. Ironically, in the Robert Aldrich film of *The Big Knife* (1957), Rod Steiger had played the studio boss and, years later, Carroll took another Steiger movie-role when he did the popular TV series based on *In the Heat of the Night.*

There occurred with O'Connor, shortly before we opened, one of those defining moments for a director. I was giving performance-notes to the cast after a run-through. One of them was a direction I had already given Carroll—repeatedly—and found repeatedly not being sufficiently heeded, so I said, without looking up from the clipboard, "And Carroll is still speaking quite often with the cigar in his mouth." I had pointed out earlier that his doing so made it difficult to understand the language, and that it *was* Clifford Odets, after all, whose brilliant idiosyncratic dialogue (as in the classic all-Odets-dialogued New York picture, *Sweet Smell of Success*) was perhaps the playwright's most often noted and praised attribute. Carroll now said in deliberate, irritated tones, "There's a lot more wrong with this production than my talking with the cigar in my mouth." I didn't look up. Nothing like this had ever happened to me before, of course, but clearly I knew I had to respond quickly and decisively to the challenge or I could lose control of the entire cast. After what seemed like an eternity in the atmosphere of that room, I said, keeping my head and voice down: "Yes, there *are* a lot of things wrong with this production." I looked up at him: "And *one* of them is that you talk with the cigar in your mouth. So don't do it anymore." He said nothing and I went on with the notes; we never spoke of it again, and he generally kept the cigar out of his mouth during his lines. What most amused me personally when seeing his decade-long, myth-making Archie Bunker of *All in the Family* was how often he spoke with a cigar in his mouth.

We saw each other only twice more before his death in 2001; at a political gathering (described below) and at the 1972 Golden Globes gala, where he won his first award for *All in the Family,* and had the final word on our moment of friction. I was seated directly below the winners' podium, having been nominated for directing and co-scripting *The Last Picture Show*. During Carroll's acceptance speech, he told about his having gotten his first important role from a young New York director who was "an arrogant son-of-a-bitch, and he's seated right below me here tonight." We hugged after the event, and spoke briefly. Not long after Carroll died, I ran into his one and only beloved wife Nancy, who told me that she and Carroll were so broke before *The Big Knife* that when I called him back to audition for a second time, Carroll was angry because they had to scrounge around and redeem pop-bottle deposits to make the subway fare.

When our *Big Knife* leading man (in his late thirties) announced his decision to do a Hollywood television film, I was so exhausted from the year-plus I had spent raising the money and then casting, directing, opening, advertising, promoting, I was simply too tired to look for, and direct all over again, a replacement in that crucial role for only the last two weeks of our run. I decided to play it myself. Orson Welles had done old men while in his teens, why couldn't I do fortyish at twentyish? This self-casting was generally deplored by the ensemble, but I ignored their objections, grayed my hair and played the doomed Charlie Castle for sixteen well-attended performances off-Broadway on Manhattan's East 30th Street, happily doing the role originated on Broadway by John Garfield, filmed with Jack Palance, directed on the Paris stage by Jean Renoir starring Daniel Gélin, and imagined by Odets himself when he wrote it (he told me) as Cary Grant. I loved every second of acting it, and the applause was as good as ever. I especially remember Carroll O'Connor's energy, precision, truth, and star-assurance; acting with him was easy because he gave you everything fully.

In the summer of 1961, I was the artistic director for a ten-week season of stock at the Phoenicia Playhouse in Phoenicia, in upstate New York, not far from Woodstock and Kingston (where I was born and lived for about three months). I also supervised the casting, chose several of the plays, directed four of them and acted in a couple. My own productions were the Moss Hart–George S. Kaufman Hollywood satire, *Once in a Lifetime,* Odets' rarely revived domestic drama *Rocket to the Moon,* Tennessee Williams' poetic allegory *Camino Real,* and Agatha Christie's classic whodunit, *Ten Little Indians.* Most of the actors and a couple of the directors who were just starting out with us that summer subsequently have had long careers: George Morfogen (who already was one of my closest friends), Anthony Zerbe, James Tolkin, Joanna Miles; directors Glenn Jordan, Michael Lindsay-Hogg, (actor-teacher) William Hickey; our costume designer was Polly Platt (who would become a prominent production designer and producer, my wife for eight years, and the mother of my two daughters). In 1964 (having started writing for *Esquire* magazine two years before), I directed and produced an ill-fated off-Broadway production of *Once in a Lifetime;* financial circumstances killed us, and within six months of its closing, I had moved to Los Angeles, where I lived and worked for most of the next thirty-two years.

Despite my career as a journalist, and my subsequent success as a film director, my roots obviously had been as an actor, although I acted infrequently after moving to California, yet most memorably: playing a lead role of the young director in my own first film as a director, *Targets* (1968), featuring a few scenes of me with Boris Karloff; acting a lead as another young film director, with Orson Welles directing and John Huston as an aging veteran filmmaker, in Welles' legendary last picture, *The Other Side of the Wind* (1970–1976), finally perhaps to be shown in 2005; playing a bit as myself with Gena Rowlands in the last scene of John Cassavetes' beautiful backstage drama, *Opening Night* (1977); acting the government-heavy opposite Ben Gazzara in Singapore for my own film version of Paul Theroux's novel, *Saint Jack* (1979); and, most famously, as the somewhat square but decent psychiatrist to psychiatrist Lorraine Bracco in David Chase's epoch-making HBO series, *The Sopranos* (1999–2005).

During my years directing pictures, I've been blessed with some magnificent casts and quite a few superb actors. Among these are many whom I was fortunate enough to introduce to the public in either their movie debut or their first notable role on the big screen: Sandy Baron, Timothy Bottoms, Eileen Brennan, Jeff Bridges, Sandra Bullock, Ellen Burstyn, Anthony Clark, Laura Dern, Burton Gilliam, John Hillerman, Madeline Kahn, Cloris Leachman, Tatum O'Neal, Randy Quaid, John Ritter, Cybill Shepherd, Eric Stoltz, and others. Apart from those who have a chapter of their own, I was also lucky to work with a number of illustrious, gifted, and in some cases, mythic stars (which is yet another book or two).

In the 1990s and into the twenty-first century, I have been acting more and more, usually in cameo roles, and often playing a movie director. It's called typecasting. To my eternal regret, I was unable to do a classic when Sydney Pollock kindly offered it to me—the director (Dabney Coleman did it) in *Tootsie.*

The Stars Party

The truth is that the acting life (especially in the movies) has a number of occupational hazards, high among them the emotional fallout from the repeated extraordinary closeness—of family-like proportions (known as production)—being summarily ended, most people rarely seen again. And so a sense of loss (or its ghost) pervades most phases of the actual work. The beautiful English author Rumer Godden once worked on a screen adaptation of a book of hers with Jean Renoir—to me (and to many others), the finest film director of the western world. Their collaboration, *The River,* shot entirely in India, is noted by all as one of his greatest triumphs. In a memoir (*A House with Four Rooms*), Godden ended her long and loving section on the making of that picture with this:

> When a film is over it is over. There seems to be an unwritten code that, when crew and actors part, you let them go. Maybe you will see them again in perhaps another film—as I have several times; then you pick up the threads where you left off but, meanwhile, you do not seek to keep contact. This sounds heartless but it is sense. How can professionals remember everyone they meet on a film?
>
> It is hard though for people outside the stage and film world to understand. They are often hurt by it. "We thought Renoir liked us," said the wife of the manager of the jute press in which we had filmed, and said it in bitterness. She felt they had been "used"—as they had. "We thought he liked us." They had sent Christmas cards, which were not reciprocated.
>
> "We did. He does." Which was true or would have been true if Jean had been reminded of them, but when the cards came he was probably in Italy or Mexico. "*The River?*" he would have said. "That's over long ago."

For actors, this sort of seesaw life leads to a somewhat bigger than natural need to unwind after a day's or week's or three months' intensive work.

Also, a lot of the moviemaking process is so boring for actors—the lighting usually takes a long time and repetitions of scenes from many angles, often necessitated by directorial uncertainty—that they often feel obliged to bust out for a night on the town. Or some awards presentation or special tribute (see below). Usually there's not much to do in Los Angeles at night: it's an early-rising company town. In the mid-1960s when I first got to Hollywood, an evening at a club called Whisky A Go Go was *the* place to be in California, or practically in the entire civilized world. By now, of course, much of the earth's nightlife is essentially the same experience as the one I had in 1965.

. . .

The Whisky had opened January 15, 1964, and at that moment was the hottest club in America. Jack Paar's *Tonight* show (Paar was before Johnny Carson and after Steve Allen) covered it and ABC-TV did a documentary on it, Johnny Rivers' records (he was singing there) were selling, and Whisky's four owners were doing fine. They had the furtive look of men who knew they were riding a wave, their eyes darting about, nervous to make it now because they might never get this kind of chance again.

But then, right then, everybody came. You'd see Loretta Young, and Jack Palance and his wife, Shelley Winters, Laurence Harvey, Sal Mineo. Fred Astaire came around one week. So did Bob Hope and Dean Martin. And the Beatles. They caused a riot on top of the usual one. Pierre Salinger (JFK's press secretary) was in one night. That blonde dancing wildly in the middle of the floor, a big black bow in her hair, that was Mamie Van Doren. Johnny Rivers was going with her at the time. And at the next booth were four of NASA's astronauts. That one in the middle was David Scott, who was rumored to be going to the moon (and did).

And the beatniks from Venice came (under some new moniker), and the arty crowd from UCLA and the hippies from New York and the squares from all over and the has-beens who wanted to be in on the action, and the in-crowd because they wanted to stay that way. There was a fellow with hair down to the middle of his back. And another with his hair cut like Shakespeare's. Quite a few mixed couples. Girls in the tightest possible Capri pants and high heels. Girls barefoot and covered with makeup. And boys covered with makeup. Men with beards and sunglasses. On the balcony, leaning against a pole, stood a surly young male prop in a goatee, staring down at the dance floor. He didn't move all night. No one could move much, the dancing mainly being various sexual gyrations, and the noise so deafening that conversations were not possible. In three cages suspended from the ceiling, three scantily-dressed young women moved about suggestively but with little excitement.

Meanwhile, the other clubs ran only half-filled or empty while the walls of the Whisky A Go Go shook and swelled from five times their comfortable capacity. Was it nicer? Better? Cheaper? No, dude, it was in.

The Stars Celebrate

On January 7, 1973, Paramount, the studio Adolph Zukor used to own, turned his hundredth birthday celebration into a glittering gala at the

Beverly Hilton Hotel, a benefit ($125 a plate) for the Variety Clubs of America, a major publicity blast for itself, and a tribute to the oldest founding father of the industry. Twelve hundred and fifty of Hollywood's finest turned up—a far better showing, in celebrities anyway, than the Oscars had been drawing in recent years. As Bob Hope unkindly put it, "If a bomb fell on this place, Troy Donahue would be back in business!" (In the twenty-first century, hardly anyone would get that joke.) Among the hundred or so on the three-tiered dais: Anne Baxter, Jack Benny, Michael Caine, Frank Capra, Bette Davis, Allan Dwan, Gene Hackman, Charlton Heston, Alfred Hitchcock, Rock Hudson, Danny Kaye, Gene Kelly, Dorothy Lamour, Mervyn LeRoy, Jerry Lewis, Fred MacMurray, Groucho Marx, Walter Matthau, Gregory Peck, George Raft, Buddy Rogers, Diana Ross, Gale Sondergaard, Barbara Stanwyck, George Stevens, Stella Stevens, James Stewart, Liv Ullmann, Jack Warner, William Wyler, not to mention the heads and key executives of all the major studios, and me. "A living wax museum," Hope called it.

When he was sixteen, so the story went, Zukor left Hungary and came to New York with $40 sewn into the lining of his coat. He eventually became a successful furrier, began investing in penny arcades and nickelodeons, finally exhibiting two-reelers, then the first feature film, *Queen Elizabeth,* Sarah Bernhardt's only movie, her "one chance for immortality," as she called it. A pretty bad picture then, it's unwatchable now except to meticulous archivists, but its success helped to promote Zukor's movie company, Famous Players (launched in 1912), into the big time. The firm's original formula, "Famous Players in Famous Plays," was actually not a good idea since it stuck to the idea of pictures as filmed theater—instead of moving in the direction Griffith and others were pointing: to a new art. Later Zukor merged with Jesse Lasky to form Famous Players–Lasky, which evolved, as movie companies did in those days, into the less cumbersomely named Paramount. ("If it's a Paramount Picture, it's the Best Show in Town" was the slogan for years.)

The mood of the evening was, What the hell, Zukor was one hundred years old and no one in pictures had ever made *that* before, so let's give him credit for everything! For Mary Pickford and Doug Fairbanks, for Gloria Swanson, Gary Cooper, Clara Bow, Hope and Crosby and Lamour, Dietrich too, and Veronica Lake, Alan Ladd, and Maurice Chevalier, and don't forget William S. Hart. If they didn't actually *say* he'd invented the movies, the implication was there, but after all it was for a good charity and no one really got hurt.

It was a show-biz night. Bob Hope came on with a string of nasty and brutally funny cracks—insults is the right word—but he was in his element. I hadn't heard him that good for years. No political jokes, no plugs for Vietnam, just a machine-gun barrage of one-liners and jokes that took the mickey out of everyone there, even himself. If he was a little cruel, at least he wasn't sanctimonious. He got a standing ovation, by the way—the only one of the evening except for Mr. Zukor when they finally wheeled him in at the end of the affair. But Hope's was spontaneous, while Zukor's was more or less mandatory. It was also difficult to *see* Mr. Zukor in that wheelchair behind the dais, so everyone remained standing for quite some time—long after they brought out the fourteen-foot birthday cake which looked plastic.

Before the start, the dais guests and assorted other VIPs and press assembled first in the Empire Room of the Hilton, surrounded by huge movie stills and a replica of the famous Paramount gates; drinks and canapés passed about by waiters, lots of business talk and gossip, not much real conversation, it was too crowded. Then the word went out for the dais people to gather in the next room for their entrance. I was talking with Jimmy and Gloria Stewart when Howard Koch, the producer of the gala (he also had done the last two Oscar shows), came over and said, pointing, "Hey, would you guys go in there and find your names and sit on them." He moved quickly away to the next group. Gloria turned to Jimmy. "What'd he say?"

Jimmy looked whimsical. "He said we should . . . he said would we find our names and *sit* on them."

"Oh," said Gloria. "Well, see you later, darling."

"Yeah," Jimmy said. "Well, I'm going to go find my name and *sit* on it."

The names were on little cardboard signs on rows of folding chairs. Much amusement and a little chaos in finding them: Stella Stevens browsing absent-mindedly through the B's; Hitchcock, launching into, for the benefit of Capra, Gene Hackman and Gene Kelly, his story of how he'd first worked for Mr. Zukor in England in 1920, though of course Mr. Zukor didn't know it at the time, Hitch being a lowly title-writer then. Before anyone could really sit down, we were being pulled to stage left for our entrances. Each of the hundred dais guests was announced separately, but also very quickly. Hardly enough time for a bow even, much less the applause to which some of them were accustomed and, indeed, entitled. But on they came at double time, except when the announcer got things screwed up (he introduced George Stevens, Sr., as George Stevens, Jr., and started to announce Mae West before someone could tell him she hadn't shown up) or there was a delay in finding someone who obviously hadn't found his name and sat on it.

After Hope and Jack Benny, came the "entertainment tribute," which was staged by Tommy Tune and Michael Stuart. It was an energetic display. Loud and fast and boisterous, lots of balloons, jets of smoke, strings of confetti. But I kept having the feeling—as various dancers came on impersonating Paramount stars Swanson and Bow and Dietrich and Betty Grable (I thought she was a Fox star), Veronica Lake and Mae West—that it was all really meant as a giant put-on. That Tommy Tune—who also starred on his stilt-like legs—had been stuck with this assignment and couldn't help but send it up in a kind of devilishly intense, almost sadistic fashion. I can't believe he really waxed sentimental about all those old stars he was "recapturing" for us, and indeed the whole performance—in fact, the whole evening—was strikingly bereft of sentiment or, strangely, even an honest stab at sentimentality. There was something coldly calculating about that stage show, and when, at the end of it, Tommy asked the audience to join him in counting out Mr. Zukor's one hundred years as the ensemble did a hundred high kicks, no one did. I guess the idea was for the thing to climax in cheering chaos with 1,250 voices blasting "one hundred," but the crowd didn't count; they just sat there watching.

Maybe they too couldn't help feeling the cold edge of derision behind it all. Otherwise, how to explain the culminating entrance of the real Dorothy Lamour, flanked by two small chimps whom she introduced as Bob and Bing? Add to this bit of weirdness the fact that the animals both misbehaved, shrieking chimp shrieks loudly to the delight of the crowd and the embarrassment of Miss Lamour, who handled it with the humor of a professional caught in a nightmare. I think she had really wanted to celebrate "Papa" Zukor's birthday—she's the only one who called him that all night—and felt sincerely warm toward him. Her remarks seemed completely genuine, but by that time it was too late. David Butler, the veteran director who had guided her and Hope and Crosby through one of the *Road* pictures, was sitting next to me. "Why didn't they give her a mike?" he said sadly. "She never had the greatest voice, you know, she needs a mike."

Oscars

Years ago, when Cary Grant and Dyan Cannon were getting divorced, a perhaps apocryphal story appeared in the scandal sheets: As an extreme example of Grant's supposed irrationality, Cannon cited to the judge

Cary's yearly habit of sitting in front of his television during the Academy Award ceremonies and sardonically abusing all the participants. This item, true or not, must have amused nearly everyone in Hollywood, since nearly everyone in Hollywood does pretty much the same thing. In fact, for those who avoid going to the actual telecast itself, having a TV dinner with friends while lacerating the presenters, winners and losers on the tube has become an almost eagerly awaited ritual.

The funny thing is that from all accounts, when the Academy Awards began in 1929, they were conducted in a similar spirit of irreverence, something that has practically disappeared from the event itself. "They used to have it down at the old Coconut Grove," Jimmy Stewart told me in the late seventies. "You'd have dinner and alawta drinks—the whole thing was . . . it was just . . . it was a *party.* Nobody took it all that seriously. I mean, it was swell if ya won because your friends were givin' it to you, but it didn't mean this big deal at the bawx office or anything. It was . . . it was just alawta friends gettin' together and tellin' some jokes and gettin' loaded and givin' out some little prizes—the things they handed out were a lot smaller those days. My gawsh, it was . . . there was no pressure or anything like that."

Cary Grant corroborated this to me: "It was a *private* affair, you see— no *tele*vision, of course, no *radio* even—just a group of friends giving each other a par-ty. Because, you know, there *is* something a little em*barra*ssing about all these wealthy people publicly con*grat*ulating each other. When it began, we *kid*ded ourselves: 'All right, Freddie March,' we'd say, 'we know you're making a *mil*lion dollars—now come on up and get your little *medal* for it!' "

The alleged origin of the award's now official nickname in itself indicates a certain inebriated lightness. Supposedly, the rear end of the statuette (for some reason it's a naked gent with a sword) reminded Bette Davis of the one on a boyfriend named Oscar, and she didn't mind loudly mentioning the resemblance. It was hard, therefore, to be entirely serious about a prize named after somebody's ass.

A lot of frivolous things have been turned into money, however, so the award that first went to the German star Emil Jannings (received for his performances in two silent films, *The Way of All Flesh* and *The Last Command*) has evolved into something not only treasured but deeply coveted. Actually, by the end of World War II, Jannings himself valued it more than when he received it. Having returned to Germany with the coming of sound in 1929, Jannings decided to stay there as part of Hitler's cultural scene. Evidently, when the Americans marched into Berlin, they encountered a rotund and pathetic figure meekly moving toward them down a bombed-out boulevard, clutching a brass statuette, holding it out to be recognized. "Please," he said, pointing to it desperately, "don't shoot—I vin Oscar."

Maybe there's only one place that does it right. Every year in Barcelona they give awards for poetry. The third prize is a silver rose, the second prize is a gold rose, and the first prize—the one for the best poem of all— is a real rose.

Stars and Politics

Long before Ronald Reagan became president, it was a commonplace that there was politics in show business and show business in politics. In 2001, Arthur Miller published a book-length essay, expanded from his Jefferson Lecture in Washington, D.C., *On Politics and the Art of Acting,* in which he dissects, examines and analyzes brilliantly this phenomenon as exemplified in the fractured 2000 election. I was present myself at three or four representative historical moments in the mix of politics and showbiz:

Nixon at San Clemente

In mid-1972, about a year before Watergate began to simmer, Mrs. Norman Taurog was on the phone (her husband had won an Oscar in 1931 for directing *Skippy*); being on the Committee to Re-elect the President, she was calling to find out how I was voting this year and whether I'd endorse Nixon. I told her I wasn't endorsing anyone.

"Don't you *like* our President?" she said.

"I don't know him."

"Would you like to meet him?"

"Sure."

That's how I happened to be invited to the August 27th reception for some four hundred Hollywood folk at the "Western White House" in San Clemente. I had got special permission to bring Cybill Shepherd, though she wasn't my wife. The check-in point was attended by Secret Service men, uniformed guards with walkie-talkies, and young Presidential aides (each wearing red, white and blue star-spangled ties) presided over by Los Angeles TV personality Johnny Grant, who looked a little overwhelmed by his job today. He leaned in, smilingly pretended to recognize us both but couldn't quite come up with names. Still, he seemed content to let us go, but the grim-faced official beside him, clipboard in hand, was less enthusiastic. He wanted the names, please. We were cleared and escorted to a receiving line. Debbie Reynolds was right ahead of us, Glen Campbell ahead of her, and Charlton Heston came up behind us, followed by Jim Brown. One of the aides told us the men should kindly precede the women.

"I thought you were a Democrat," I said to Heston.

"I was . . . well, I've always been an *Independent*," he answered, and then mumbled something about preferring Nixon this year.

At the end of the line, in the beam of a floodlight, the President and Mrs. Nixon were greeting their guests. Photographers were snapping away, aides stood around, Secret Service men scanned the line. Heston pointed out that they never look at the President but only at what is going on around him.

I turned to watch the President as a perspiring man lightly held my arm—I suppose to prevent me from jumping my cue. Mr. Nixon turned to me and the perspiring gentleman gave me a light push forward, at the same time supplying my name. I shook hands with the President and introduced Cybill to him and Mrs. Nixon.

"I've seen your name," the President said to me, waving one arm to indicate a movie screen, "on many *productions*." He made the word sound important.

I mumbled something or other. There was a pause. Some years before, a mutual friend of the Nixons and of my parents had given them a present of one of my late father's still lifes. Mrs. Nixon, however, had not liked it. "My mother met you some years back," I said. "She'd come to your apartment to pick up a painting of my father's."

I'm not at all sure that either the President or Mrs. Nixon remembered the incident, but Mr. Nixon shifted his look momentarily and nodded pleasantly.

"My father was a painter," I said.

"Of course I know your father is a painter," said Mr. Nixon, a little too genially.

There was another pause. The perspiring gentleman was not looking any better. We backed off. Mrs. Nixon kept right on smiling at us as the President turned to Heston.

More star-spangled ties indicated the way to the party where four hundred Hollywood people were talking, drinking, eating. There was Vince Edwards, Red Skelton, Zsa Zsa Gabor, Lawrence Welk, Jack Benny, Desi Arnaz, and Chuck Connors. Frank Sinatra flashed by, followed by several others, on the way to something urgent, from the look of the exit.

John Wayne waved and came over, puffing a small cigar. I told him my presence didn't mean I was a Republican. "*That's* OK," said Duke. Just then the music stopped and there was some applause; President Nixon had stepped onto the bandstand in front of a microphone. He looked smaller and thinner than he had before. "I am not going to impose on you another speech," he said, "after what many of you had to endure last week [at the convention] in terms of so many speeches." He then made a speech that lasted fourteen minutes. The emphasis was on movies:

"I would like to express appreciation as an individual, and also speaking as the President of the United States, for what you, the people of Hollywood, have done for America and have done for the world. I can speak with some feeling on this point. Let me begin by saying that my wife and I like movies. We like them on television. We fortunately now have our own projection set in the White House. [Laughter.] That is one of the reasons I ran again. [Another laugh.] I just can't stand those commercials on the *Late Show*. [Laughter.] But we have seen many movies. We haven't yet shown an X-rated movie in the White House. We had an 'R' one night, and I said, 'That is as far as you can go.' [Laughter.] But I like my movies made in Hollywood, made in America, and I don't mean that I can't appreciate a good foreign movie, or a foreign movie star or [slight pause, looking for a word] . . . or starlet. . . . In all the countries that my wife and I have visited, about eighty, I can assure you that Hollywood, in most of them, has been there before. We go along streets in the cities of Africa and Asia and Latin America, and everyplace, and on that marquee you will see the Hollywood names that we are so familiar with. It makes us feel at home as we see those names. . . ."

He was closing with an anecdote concerning a Harlem congressman named Charles Rangel; the President had called Rangel on the phone. "The congressman was somewhat overwhelmed by the call, and we talked a bit, and then he said, 'You know, Mr. President, when I was growing up in Harlem, if I had told my old man that someday I would be talking to the President of the United States, he would have told me I was crazy.' And I said, 'Well, Mr. Congressman, if when I was growing up, in Yorba Linda, I had told my old man that someday I would be talking to a congressman on the phone, he would have thought I was crazy.' [Laughter.] I will simply close my remarks tonight by saying . . . if I had told my old man when I was growing up in Yorba Linda that someday I would be talking to Jack Benny, he would have said I was crazy!"

He stepped down to laughter and applause, the band struck up again. We wandered around, taking in the sights: Clint Eastwood, Rhonda Fleming, Glenn Ford, Art Linkletter, Hugh O'Brian, Jack Warner, Richard Zanuck, Joanne Carson. Billy Graham was there, too, standing on a rise—overlooking the golf course, and surrounded by a bower of branches, with a kind of glow around him as he talked to several people. Then I noticed he was standing in a floodlight, too. Dr. Kissinger was as charming as ever, Jill St. John by his side. Jack Benny was trading jokes with George Burns, George Jessel, and Vice President Agnew, and when the opportunity came I said hello to Benny, who said that after the President's "plug," he'd calculated he had to be a Republican for "at *least* another eight years." Then Scatman Crothers sang with gusto a song about Nixon that he'd written for the occasion.

It was getting late. We worked our way through the crowd and came over to the President, still standing near the band, shaking hands with everyone as they were leaving. We stepped up.

"Well, thank you, Mr. President," I said as we shook hands. "I haven't been won over, but it's been a nice party."

He rode right over that—didn't hear it—but also didn't let go of my hand. "I had no idea you were so young," he said.

"It's my name—makes you think of an old fellow with a beard."

"Yes—*Bogdanovich*," he said as though to confirm agedness in the sound of it. He still held my hand, without awkwardness—not as though he couldn't find the right moment to let go, but just because he wanted to hold it, I guess. Certainly I wasn't going to pull it away. "But, you know," he said, "when you think of some of the great directors of the past—John Ford, for example—he started very young, didn't he?"

"He was twenty-two," I said. "I did a documentary about him."

He didn't seem to hear that, either—went right on with his thought— though he finally took his hand away to make a gesture. "You know, I ran a couple of his films the other day—*Apache* . . . ahm, *Fort Apache* and *She Wore a Yellow Ribbon*—was he twenty-two when he made those?"

"No—oh, no—that was later in his career. I guess he was around fifty when he did those." I was trying to get over the odd sensation of discussing one of my favorite directors with the President of the United States.

"Well," Mr. Nixon said pleasantly, "then you have a long time ahead of you, too."

I grinned. "You know, Mr. President," I said, "you were mentioned in a review of one of my pictures."

"Really?" he said, leaning his right ear closer, looking down. "What was that?"

"Well, this critic [it had been Pauline Kael in *The New Yorker*] said that the movie I'd made was one that 'even President Nixon would like.' "

He threw his head back and laughed. I believe he slapped his thigh. "Well!" he exclaimed, "you don't know if that's a compliment or not!"

"Yeah," I said, and laughed, too. "But, you know, Dr. Kissinger told me he thought you hadn't seen it."

"Well, I will," he said. "I will." He shook hands with Cybill and we started away. "You ought to put *her* in a picture!" he called after us.

"I did. That's the one you haven't seen."

"Oh?" He came after us and leaned in toward me confidentially. "What was the *name* of that production?"

"The Last Picture Show."

He looked up at me and there were several seconds of silence. He knitted his brow intently. "Ahm—the one in Texas?" he said tentatively.

"That's right."

"In—ahm—in black and white?"

"Yes."

"But I saw that! Why, that's a *remarkable* picture! We ran that at Camp David!" And to my amazement, he launched into a very flattering paragraph about the movie and the actors in it—Ben Johnson in particular—generally confirming Kael's prediction. Then he turned to Cybill, putting a hand on her arm. "And what part did *you* play?"

She said, "Jacy."

I said, "She was the one who stripped on the diving board."

The President paused. He looked at me, but kept his hand on Cybill's arm. "Well, *everyone* gave a remarkable performance in that film," he said, and then, still not looking at Cybill, but patting her arm as he spoke and with the barest flicker of a smile: "And, of course, I remember *you* very well now, my dear."

We said good-bye again, shook hands and left.

Carter at the Beverly Wilshire

Four years later, Warren Beatty was on the phone. "You wanna meet Carter?" he asked in a velvety whisper. "I'm having a few people over to meet him on Sunday—you and Cybill wanna come? Ask some tough questions."

As we walked into the Beverly Wilshire suite that Warren had hired for the cocktail party, guests were arriving in droves. The Secret Service was well represented, as were the caterers, but the crowd was still manageable enough for Warren to meet us at the door and at least take us into the main room.

In no time the place was packed. Art Buchwald, Carroll O'Connor,

James Caan and Tony Randall, Peter Falk, Diana Ross, Dinah Shore, Buck Henry and Paul Simon, Sidney Poitier, Hugh Hefner, all the non-Republican studio heads—precious few of those. Most of the Hollywood brass were over at Lew Wasserman's house where there had been a dinner party that same evening for Carter. Everyone at Warren's looked thrilled to be there. Movie people, used to leading fantasy lives, seem to always experience a special rush when exposed to the glamorous side of political power.

By the time Jimmy Carter got there, the crush in the room was so thick you could tell he had arrived only from the agitation of the crowd, and pretty soon, everyone was trying to have a private moment with the candidate. I turned to find him beside Cybill Shepherd and me. Confronted by his smiling visage, I couldn't think of anything relevant to say so I simply pointed out that we were both wearing the same suit. Gray herringbone. Carter looked at mine and said, "Indeed we are." His was adorned with one of those peanut campaign buttons he wore in the lapel. Cybill said, somewhat suggestively, "Ooo, I like your peanut." Carter grinned broadly at this and said he was glad to hear it. Cybill blushed. Carter blushed. Warren cut right in with Carroll O'Connor and our time in the sun was over.

Warren finally asked for quiet and eventually the din subsided so that he could be heard. With just the right edge of ironic mockery, he scored a few lightly irreverent jokes off Carter—who appeared to enjoy them as much as everyone else—and managed with some charm to combine an attitude of suave superiority and shit-kicking humility into precisely the right mix to fit the mood of the group. Just in case anyone was casting, Warren was doing a splendid audition for a swinging Secretary of State. At the appropriate moment, he stepped down and turned it over to Carter.

The future President's most appreciated remark had to do with his own bravery—considering his host's amorous reputation—in showing up at all for a Warren Beatty cocktail party. This not only got a big laugh but achieved the desired goal of putting him morally one-up on everybody in the room. When he went on to say that he had heard of everyone gathered about long before they had heard of him, I would guess he secured most of the available votes.

With some grace, he then moved casually into a more serious vein, explained some of his most popular positions and opened the scene to questions. Diana Ross asked very earnestly if Mr. Carter would tell why he thought he was qualified to be President, an obvious cue to recite one's résumé, which Carter patiently proceeded to do. Before long Jimmy Caan interrupted with a longish go-team speech in which he expressed his general enthusiasm for Carter, giving virtually no reasons, but plenty of boyish good-fellowship: "You've got *my* vote."

With some trepidation, I asked if Mr. Carter intended to do anything about secrecy in government, especially as it related to the maneuvers of the CIA and the FBI. He replied briskly that the heads of these agencies would be appointed from among people he knew and could trust and that they would be directly answerable to him. I don't know what response I had expected but I wasn't entirely happy. Possibly I'd hoped for something more rousing.

Then Carroll O'Connor was into his speech, expressing loud disapproval of Carter's then recent defense of the Russian author Solzhenitsyn. This caused consternation and embarrassment, since it was not a fashionable opinion around the room, and a lot of the looks that flashed around reflected the thought that maybe Carroll had been playing Archie Bunker too long. Carter, realizing that the question was unpopular, gave a short, succinct reply that left Carroll visibly dissatisfied and everyone else relieved.

At this point, Tony Randall launched into one of his favorite subjects—the need for greater government subsidy of the arts—in particular the formation of a national theater. Carter danced lightly around this for a time, speaking of all the fine cultural events he had observed in Georgia, allowing as how a good concert was a wonderful thing for folks to see. Tony was not to be easily appeased and he pressed for Carter's assurance that a national theater would become a reality during his term of office. Carter sidestepped with good humor, didn't answer yes or no or barely even maybe.

One could sense in the room a split vote for Tony as he continued with what was becoming a mini-filibuster on the subject of arts subsidy. Admittedly Carter was in a difficult position. He couldn't very well say what he might have been thinking: that he didn't give one damn about the arts when there were all these hungry people in the country, all this unemployment and all those headaches to deal with overseas. But a bunch of votes were at stake, so Jimmy Carter kept on smiling. Part of Randall's charm was in playing the scene so that the guest of honor *could* go on smiling and not seem silly. But the whole occasion ended without a satisfying exit for anyone.

There was a history of passivity and easy panic operating on Carter's side that evening. And show people have always been impressed with royalty—which the presidency has devolved into—the regal position being another the movies abdicated in their avid plunge toward everyday respectability. (Orson Welles used to say that one of the great steps downward for the acting profession came when theater star Henry Irving became the first actor to be knighted.) Artists, like presidents, are in the service of the people, though at their most valuable they lead the way. With a touch of the honest politician, an artist perhaps can be more successful in achieving his goals, just as a politician could use a touch of the artist.

Pop Mythology

In 1982, I was at the Kennedy Center in Washington on the night they honored five distinguished figures in the arts, among them Cary Grant. Our seats were directly in front of the stage, but none of the honorees ever left their places in the central area of the first balcony, so that all of us in the orchestra had to be satisfied with only a long-shot view of the principals. This had a strangely effective advantage: distanced so far and high above us, they retained some of their larger-than-life qualities—especially Grant, with whose face and voice and movements so many of us had grown up. When I turned along with the rest of the audience to watch attentively as the honored guests assembled, my eyes, like most of the others', remained on that tall, dashing figure we had admired and emulated for nearly half a century.

So when President Ronald Reagan entered last, and stood shaking hands with Cary Grant, I had for a moment quite a different vision of the event: surely if this were a scene from a picture, Cary would be playing the President and Ronald his tardy vice president, apologizing boyishly for his lateness. You could almost hear Cary saying: "That's awright, *Ron*nie, but try not to let it *hap*pen *again!*"

Personally, I had always hoped maybe Jimmy Stewart would be President one day—the Jimmy Stewart of *Mr. Smith Goes to Washington*—how comforting that would have been. Or Henry Fonda, who often played presidents or other important political figures, and was always absolutely convincing in the roles. Perhaps the greatest political team in history would have featured Stewart as President, Fonda as Secretary of State, and John Wayne as Chief of the Pentagon; Frank Capra would have been the director. For movie fans, Ronald Reagan never would have been first choice in the key role. Yet it was certainly difficult to argue that Reagan was President *not* because he had been a movie star. After watching Jimmy Carter win with the Capra approach, the Republicans must have figured they might as well try Hollywood themselves: if Carter was trying to do

Jimmy Stewart, why not have Reagan trying to do Jimmy Stewart; he certainly had more experience at it.

The pop-culture reverberations behind Reagan's election as leader of the free world resonated forward and backward through our history and confirmed unequivocally a suspicion many people have voiced about the great technological art form of the twentieth century (only five years older than the century itself), which had held the lively attention of the world for as many years as Ronald Reagan had been alive: the first movie-star president for a country unconsciously motivated by large shadows on a white screen. Could anyone refuse to take more seriously now the influence of the movies on our lives and times? Had we examined closely enough what exactly the picture-shows had been doing to us all these years?

The question had taken on a far more ironic, bizarre and ominous dimension in 1981. A hundred and fifteen years before, an actor had assassinated the President of the United States, but in the second year of the eighties, President Reagan, formerly an actor, was nearly assassinated by a movie fan. This person was inspired not by political motives, but rather by the machinations of a demented fictional character (Travis Bickle in Martin Scorsese's *Taxi Driver*) portrayed and glorified through the personality of another actor (Robert De Niro) who would, the day after the assassination attempt, win (for his role in Scorsese's *Raging Bull*) the Academy Award as best actor of the year. If somebody wrote that scenario for a picture, would anyone believe it? What had happened to the country, and to the movies?

Had we ever really agreed, though, on what movies were in the first place? There had always been those who'd called them trash, and those who'd called them art, and certainly we knew they often were both, but being the newest form of communication, it had been difficult gaining enough perspective to analyze what their most profound effect might be. Back in the mid-sixties, I'd written that film stars formed the basis for a kind of twentieth-century mythology, without realizing the largest implications of that statement.

When Fairbanks and Pickford and Chaplin made their tours of Europe in the twenties, they were greeted with a degree of adulation and deification unknown in history; the multitudes that welcomed them in Rome or London went beyond the most fervent hopes of a King or Pope or President. In truth, though "Little Mary" had been dubbed "America's Sweetheart," she and Fairbanks together became the only King and Queen the United States has ever had. It was less than happy for Doug and Mary, though, the crowds being so huge that the couple couldn't leave their hotel in Rome for several days, and though they had been anxious to tour the city, they never did. One night they managed to sneak out to a little pasta restaurant nearby, and as a result of that visit, "The Original" Alfredo's fettuccine became famous. Doug and Mary sent Alfredo a large serving spoon and fork, engraved with thanks and made of 24-karat gold. To this day, VIP customers of the restaurant are still allowed to eat with them.

Just a few years later, Dr. Goebbels, one of the chief architects of the Hitler regime, called film "the greatest medium for propaganda ever invented." When the Nazis took control of Germany, according to Fritz Lang—the country's leading director then—Goebbels personally asked him to head the newly reorganized film industry of the Third Reich. Lang told me he was polite and agreeable, went to his bank, drew out what funds he had, and that same day left his native land, not to return for nearly thirty years. His wife, screenwriter Thea von Harbou, with whom he had just made his best film (*M*), chose to stay and work for Hitler. There were many who remained, among them Leni Riefenstahl, who created *Triumph of the Will,* a devilishly well-directed and staged series of supposedly spontaneous pro-Hitler demonstrations of Wagnerian proportions, which helped (along with other similar films) to create out of the demonic little Führer an overwhelmingly powerful godlike figure—one to rival the sacred larger-than-life heroes of the ancient German sagas. We all know too well the consequences these movies helped to produce.

The advent of film had brought a new and very different dimension to the art of acting, one not sufficiently understood. Originally, remember, the key to real stardom in pictures had very little to do with the old theatrical concept of a well-crafted performance in a given role. We might speak of Burbage, Booth or Barrymore and their various interpretations of Hamlet, but what always distinguished the true film stars—until things began to change in the sixties—had been their ability to so totally eradicate an audience's disbelief that no question of artifice remained. They didn't seem to be playing a role at all but rather to be living out a given situation.

Though critics of the time spoke with reverence of fine screen performances from Olivier, Gielgud or Guinness, they would note disparagingly that John Wayne "always played himself." Yet it was Wayne's unique screen persona which captured and retained for close to forty years of his life a profound believability and trust in audiences over the entire world, one that has continued long after his death: an abiding faith, then, not in his acting, but in his actual being. The adventurousness and indestructibility of the Duke became as fondly familiar to the modern age as the exploits and character of Hercules had been to pre-Christian Europe. To many, his passing seemed strangely inconceivable: How could a god die? His vast continuing popularity into the twenty-first century confirms that he hasn't.

I knew pretty well the veteran director who made the picture in which Ronald Reagan gave probably his most genuinely likeable performance: in 1955, Allan Dwan did a little Western, based on a Bret Harte story, called *Tennessee's Partner.* Dwan had been directing since 1911; he died in 1982 at the age of ninety-five. I once asked him what kind of actor Reagan had been, and Allan said: "He was a fair actor who followed direction pretty well. One time I told him to ride his horse right by the camera, and as he passed I heard him talking to the horse: 'Whoa now,' he was saying, 'hold up now, damn it!' but the horse kept on going. We had to send a couple of cowboys to bring him back."

When Reagan was elected to the White House, I asked Dwan how it felt having one of his former actors as President of the country. Allan laughed and said: "Taught him everything he knows. . . ." By the time Reagan ran for governor of California, the studio factory-system which had created him had fallen apart and was in the process of disintegrating further; his last role was as the arch-villain in a violent thriller Don Siegel* made called *The Killers* (1964). The one time we ever spoke, at a Hollywood party after his governorship and before any serious moves toward national office, we talked about Allan Dwan. Reagan's eyes misted warmly; he was so glad to hear Allan was still alive and well. There was a melancholy smile on his face as we talked of pictures. A year before Dwan died, the Academy gave a special evening's tribute to this last pioneer, and President Reagan sent heartfelt congratulations.

The Republicans had eventually cast Reagan in the best role of his career, and his long experience in front of cameras served him exceptionally well in the age of television-politics—which John Kennedy had inaugurated in the election of 1960—the first leading-man political star elected to the White House. When Jack Kennedy went into politics, the movies lost a major possibility. Yet have we ever really concluded how good or bad this new TV-fashion of election has been for the country? Jimmy Stewart once expressed the worry to me in his own way: "I don't know 'bout all this TV all day long now; there's people *acting* all the

---

*See chapter in *Who the Devil Made It.*

time—they turn the thing on, somebody's there *acting* at them. I wonder if that's good for people—all this *acting*."

Maybe what he meant was that it was becoming difficult to separate reality from fiction, that even the news would inevitably begin to seem like just another show, that all this acting was in some way deadening people's reactions to genuine emotion, to real tragedy. Perhaps the Vietnam War in our living room, or the assassinations of the Kennedys or Martin Luther King, Jr., had not gained in resonance through accessibility, but had only lost a good portion of their horror by being reduced simply to another hour of TV. If we hadn't really understood the impact of the movies on our lives, how could we gauge the far more insidious effect of that friendly-seeming tube in the family room? If the giant size of the old screens played a major part in the creation of our pop mythology, couldn't the smaller-than-life proportions of television reduce reality and help to trivialize it?

The first star of pictures, the first screen deity, had been female: the lovely, euphoniously named Florence Lawrence. The earliest producers had hoped to keep their players anonymous in order to hold salaries down, but the public demand to know the identity of that beautiful girl of the nickelodeons became impossible to deny. Pickford followed, and Lillian Gish and Dorothy Gish, Theda Bara and Blanche Sweet, Mae Marsh and Gloria Swanson and Pola Negri, among the silents, and Garbo, who bridged the two eras. Not in the least coincidentally, within less than a decade after these early female stars became screen goddesses, women finally achieved the right to vote (first in Ireland, then England, then the United States). In the talkies, there were Dietrich, and Jean Harlow, Carole Lombard, Barbara Stanwyck, Kate Hepburn and Bette Davis, Joan Crawford, Veronica Lake, and Irene Dunne, Rita Hayworth, Ava Gardner and Audrey Hepburn and Grace Kelly. Since Marilyn Monroe died, there have been no love goddesses; virtually no female stars of equal impact to the males, though Streisand endured longer than most, due also (and initially) to her singing. Most of the girls of TV-land are variations on the Barbie-doll or *Playboy* image of women; there are fewer than ever female stars and none with the old mythic power.

The towering male stars of the golden age have been reduced to a mixed bag of TV stars sometimes straining for size, and serious or quasi-serious actors refusing to type themselves into mythic shape. Men of considerable talent and appeal like De Niro, Al Pacino and Tom Hanks have preferred versatility to the old kind of picture-stardom that required a certain consistency of character. Following Brando's lead, they have avoided a larger-than-life identity to the audience. More contemporary "old-fashioned" movie stars like Clint Eastwood or Bruce Willis have found few directors of myth-making ability to fully exploit their qualities, though Eastwood himself understood the principle well and learned to direct so effectively that he has essentially continued to create himself. Only a few other actors today (like Jack Nicholson), and one politician (Bill Clinton), have the really personal identity of the original movie stars with which this book deals.

Power of the Players

For Tuesday night, September 11, 2001, I had theater tickets to see Broadway's Tony-winning musical comedy revival, *42nd Street,* but of course that performance was canceled because of the catastrophe at the World Trade Center and the Pentagon. Following New York mayor Giuliani's plea for a return to some kind of normality in the face of the unthinkable, most Broadway shows reopened that Thursday evening. I went to see *42nd Street* the next night, the first weekend performance of an archetypically lightweight entertainment (based on several Warner Bros. film musicals of the early 1930s) only three days after an unprecedented, apocalyptical slaughter of American innocents. I have never seen or heard an audience so desperate for laughter and gaiety, so loudly and touchingly grateful for two hours of totally uncomplicated escape.

Sitting there, watching the huge cast of dancers, singers and actors doing their professional best, I wondered how many of them had been personally affected by deaths on September 11th. Though certainly this cataclysmic event bore out with a vengeance John Donne's famous poem about every person being an integral part of mankind—thus obviating any need to know "for whom the bell tolls," since "it tolls for thee." (France's newspaper *Le Monde* poignantly echoed that: *"Nous sommes tous les Americains."*) What struck me most, therefore, about that performance of *42nd Street* was the wonderful indomitability of show-business troupers, and why, after all, it *was* vitally important that "the show must go on."

Maybe that's part of what Orson Welles meant when he used to sign off his weekly radio shows: "I remain, as ever, obediently yours." He once told me that Marlene Dietrich had said to him that she found the phrase amusingly ironic. "It really isn't, Marlene," he responded, "I mean it."

That was surely the key emotion I felt during the star-studded two-hour telethon that was presented a week after the tragedy to raise money

*Joel McCrea as a famous movie director, and Veronica Lake
as a starlet, go off and live as hoboes in order to find out
what the world's really like in Preston Sturges'
comedy-drama* Sullivan's Travels *(1941). Fourteen years
later, I moved scenery for a play Lake starred in.*

for the victims' families. The single quality all the various performers had in common during their appearances was an extraordinary lack of ego. None of what they did was about them, but rather about the needs of the audience. Each artist contributed whatever he or she could to a cause far bigger than all of them put together, and you could feel their acute awareness of this. Wasn't that, finally, what art was meant to be? Clearly Bruce Springsteen's song on that occasion in four heartbreaking words summed up all New Yorkers' unspoken cry: "My city in ruins . . ." Springsteen's challenged artistry took us poetically in less than five minutes through the entire horror and tragedy of the experience and concluded with just the right sadly hopeful admonition: "Come on, rise up."

It is no coincidence, then, that during the bleak and crushing decade of the Great Depression, the movies' most singular and valuable contribution was the invention of the screwball comedy (*It Happened One Night, Bringing Up Baby, The Awful Truth,* etc.), or that with World War II looming (Europe already in the thick of it), Preston Sturges wrote in *Sullivan's Travels* a passionate testament to the crucial and uniquely human need for laughter. He told of a film director (played by Joel McCrea), noted for making ultra-light entertainment, who decides that he wants to create a meaningful social document about "life," about poverty and suffering. Out into the world he goes with a dime in his pocket to discover what being poor, homeless and on the run is all about. Eventually he finds himself in serious trouble on a horrific Southern chain gang where the only small respite for the miserable prisoners is the Sunday movies they're allowed to see at a run-down country church nearby. There he watches a silly Disney cartoon that gives him and his fellow convicts the only pleasure they've had all week. After he is rescued, flying back to Hollywood, his producers tell him they're now ready to back his serious film. But Sullivan explains that all he wants to do now is make comedies. "There's a lot to be said for making people laugh," he tells them. "Did you know that's all some people have. It isn't much but it's better than nothing in this cockeyed caravan. Boy!"

The most distressing aspect, finally, to the power of the players is how quickly it usually diminishes after their retirement or death. In directing a young actor in 1997, I mentioned as a way of encouraging him that he reminded me of James Cagney; the fellow had no idea who I was talking about. Toward the end of 2002, I told another actor in his twenties to handle the scene more lightly, "more Cary Grant," I said, and got a totally blank reaction. And these are actors!—people in show business whose job one would think is to be familiar with the great past achievements in their chosen field. The young American audience seems not only to be totally ignorant of these, but to have practically no interest in any film shot earlier than maybe 1980 or 1990. The classics of the twenties, thirties, forties and fifties might as well be in Sanskrit. Silent pictures are not even worth raising as a distant possibility. Black and white is anathema. The great names of the past—many of the players in this book—mean nothing to younger filmgoers. That they are missing untold pleasures, that there is an overflowing treasure of joyful, enriching, edifying experiences waiting for them doesn't seem to be within their realm of consciousness.

One of my hopes in compiling this book of encounters, conversations and observations around some of the eloquent stars of the past is to help make them human and accessible to potential new viewers. Also perhaps as something people of or around my generation can use to help pass along to children and friends some of their happiest enthusiasms and experiences. Most movies today simply aren't as good as pictures used to be, not by a long shot, but try telling that to youngsters who haven't even the slightest frame of reference by which they might compare the current output.

The modest goal here is to awaken a few so that maybe they'll look at what's out there just waiting to be discovered and relished. My father took me at age five to see Chaplin and Keaton movies at the Museum of Modern Art. I ran older pictures for my daughters starting at the same age; now in their thirties, they love them still. It is such a rich heritage that to allow its disappearance, its descent into obscurity, is to me a criminal deprivation of beauty and profound human achievement. To keep the past alive, then, is among my principal objectives. On the screen, many of these memorable players still breathe, still love, still elicit abundant laughter and tears. Why let their lights go out when they have so very much to give?

1

LILLIAN GISH

Forty-six years ago I saw Lillian Gish in person. It happened in the fall of 1958, I was still living with my parents in Manhattan, and had gone way uptown to the Museum of the City of New York to see a screening of one of D. W. Griffith's most popular films, *Way Down East*—among the biggest-grossing pictures of 1920; indeed, of the twenties—when pretty much everybody in the country went to the movies every week. That afternoon, thirty-eight years after its initial release, the crowd wasn't large and most of them were not especially impressed by the movie, which was represented by a fair 16mm print, projected none too brilliantly, with a spotty musical arrangement—from a number of records, I think it was—piped from a control booth. The audience laughed at the film numerous times—their attitude very superior to the dated social aspects of the hugely popular old Victorian stage melodrama on which the movie was based, about an innocent girl who gets tricked and ends up pregnant with no husband in a small and narrow-minded town.

I was bowled over by the ease and brilliance of the visual storytelling, and by the amazing performance Lillian Gish was giving, and irritated by the stupidity of the audience, which was judging the quality of the film through the mores and values of the current era instead of understanding the work in the context of its own time. Despite themselves they eventually got involved in Miss Gish's incandescent, mesmerizing performance, and held by the classic assurance of Griffith at his most confident—the father of movie narrative in his prime! Gish's extended close-up when she realizes her infant child has died in her arms is one of those unforgettable human moments of which only the screen is capable: a reaction shot that can haunt you forever.

Toward the end, the audience started getting superior again, chortling condescendingly over the much-imitated (from Griffith pictures) race-to-

Lillian Gish in one of her most popular roles, as sister to her blind sibling (played by real sister Dorothy Gish) for D. W. Griffith's French Revolution epic, Orphans of the Storm *(1922), which included a moving and famous ride-to-the-rescue—saving Gish from the guillotine*

the-rescue: Gish lying unconscious on an ice floe moving rapidly down the freezing Mamaroneck River, the hero desperately trying to save her, leaping from floe to floe to reach her before certain death at the waterfall. Largely also because the projection was too fast (as usual with silent films), the audience began laughing at this masterfully shot and edited action. The fellow running the museum's performance finally spoke out over the loudspeaker, saying angrily that the sequence they were watching was actually filmed at great peril on the Mamaroneck, that several people were injured and one person drowned during its making. Miss Gish, he went on hotly, had insisted on doing all the ice-floe shots herself, as well as on

*Lillian Gish herself lying on the ice floe as it careens down
the swift Mamaroneck River during the climactic sequence of
D. W. Griffith's* Way Down East *(1920)*

keeping one hand over the edge and in the freezing waters: to this day she
had not entirely recovered the feeling in that hand. The man's tight little
speech mercifully shut the audience up until the end of the picture.

This same fellow then introduced Lillian Gish to the startled crowd—
none of us had known she was there. Everyone applauded vigorously, to
make up for their rudeness and because her work had been genuinely
admired. Miss Gish, still beguiling at sixty-five, spoke briefly with
strength and eloquence. It was a little difficult to reconcile the luminous
larger-than-life young woman we had been watching for two hours with
the small and somewhat matronly figure before us. That her art had been
silent made hearing her speak disconcerting, too. Taking in Miss Gish

Lillian Gish as the doomed Mimi with her adoring artist-lover, played by the movies' top romantic lead, John Gilbert, in King Vidor's silent film based on the same stories as Puccini's opera La Bohème *(1926)*

required the past images to recede so that she could be brought into present-day focus.

For Lillian Gish had been the first virgin hearth goddess of the screen, as Audrey Hepburn was the last. It is no coincidence that for his huge epic of civilization through the ages, *Intolerance,* Griffith chose Gish to be the Hand at Home That Rocks the Cradle of Life. She remained a valiant and courageous symbol of fortitude and love through all distress: French Revolution in *Orphans of the Storm,* murderous bigotry in *The Scarlet Letter,* nature itself and man as predator in *The Wind.* Images of her in all these self-sacrificing roles—epitomized perhaps in her strong but dying waifs of *Broken Blossoms* and *La Bohème*—were what passed before me as the real woman stood there some thirty years later.

She spoke almost entirely about the sublime genius of D. W. Griffith, who had created *Way Down East* and other films so beautifully, and made it possible for her and all the actors to perform. Then, in conclusion, with great poise and certitude she said: "But, you know, when we were making pictures in those early days we weren't making them for the fame or for the money. We weren't even making them for Mr. Griffith. We were making them for *that . . .*" and she turned slightly and gestured with a sweep of her arm toward the screen behind her; meaning by this silent moment that all their work had been for the sacred ideal of the medium itself—which was not the cans of film in the booth, but rather the illusion that appeared on the screen.

I've never seen or heard a better description of the purity of a true artist's purpose. The spirit Miss Gish conveyed to me—now somewhat longer ago than the original release of *Way Down East* had been then—seems all the more poignant, and distant, in our current self-involved and hypercynical era of decadence. To recapture in the movies the love-innocence her remarks, gestures and enduring work speak toward is no small task. But what a precious goal!

Born Lillian Diana de Guiche, October 14, 1896, Springfield, OH; died February 27, 1993, New York, NY.

Selected starring shorts and features (with director):

1912: *An Unseen Enemy* (D. W. Griffith); *The Musketeers of Pig Alley* (Griffith)
1913: *The Mothering Heart* (Griffith)
1914: *The Battle at Elderbush Gulch* (Griffith); *Home Sweet Home* (Griffith)
1915: *The Birth of a Nation* (Griffith); *Enoch Arden* (Christy Cabanne)
1916: *An Innocent Magdalene* (Allan Dwan); *Intolerance* (Griffith)
1918: *Hearts of the World* (Griffith)
1919: *A Romance of Happy Valley* (Griffith); *Broken Blossoms* (Griffith); *True Heart Susie* (Griffith); *The Greatest Question* (Griffith)
1920: *Way Down East* (Griffith)

1922: *Orphans of the Storm* (Griffith)
1923: *The White Sister* (Henry King)
1924: *Romola* (King)
1926: *The Scarlet Letter* (Victor Sjöström); *La Bohème* (King Vidor)
1928: *The Wind* (Sjöström)
1933: *His Double Life* (Arthur Hopkins)
1943: *Commandos Strike at Dawn* (John Farrow)
1946: *Miss Susie Slagle's* (John Berry)
1947: *Duel in the Sun* (Vidor)
1948: *Portrait of Jennie* (William Dieterle)
1955: *The Cobweb* (Vincente Minnelli); *The Night of the Hunter* (Charles Laughton)
1960: *The Unforgiven* (John Huston)
1967: *The Comedians* (Peter Glenville)
1978: *A Wedding* (Robert Altman)
1987: *The Whales of August* (Lindsay Anderson)

2

HUMPHREY BOGART

At the start of the twenty-first century, the American Film Institute published the results of a poll taken to determine the greatest stars of the movies' golden age. Leading the list at number one was Humphrey Bogart. Nearly four decades earlier, in 1963—about seven years after Bogart's death—I had felt the urge to write a piece about him. I wanted to call it "An American Hero," and phoned Harold Hayes, *Esquire's* legendary editor, to suggest this.

He said, "*Humphrey* Bogart?"

I said, "Yeah."

He said, "But he's dead."

I said, "OK, forget it."

About six months later, there appeared in *Time* magazine a one-column news item reporting the popularity of Bogart films at Harvard and a kind of underground cult among students that had formed around the actor. At exam time, the local theater ran Bogart pictures. That same week, Hayes called me: "Hi, buddy!" (He was Southern.) "How'd you like to do a piece on Bogart?"

I said, "You read the thing in *Time*."

He said, "Do you want to do it or not?"

It is the only profile I've ever done on a person I did not see in person or get to know, and my main intention was to draw a line between how his friends remembered Bogart and how his films presented him—the difference between reality and myth. Because I felt that Howard Hawks had best captured "the Bogart character," which epitomized one's popular image of him, in *To Have and Have Not* (out of Hemingway via Faulkner) and *The Big Sleep* (Raymond Chandler, with Faulkner trimmings), I began with a light parody of Chandler's style:

*Humphrey Bogart as "Mad Dog" Roy Earle in the Sierra Mountains
for the climactic sequence of Raoul Walsh's tragic gangster
film* High Sierra *(1941), written by John Huston (from a novel
by W. R. Burnett). Playing older than his years, Bogart became a
top star because of this picture. He had received second billing
to star Ida Lupino but got the top position for every movie after
it. The film was a touching climax of, and conclusion to, the
thirties gangster genre at Warner Bros.*

Usually he wore the trench coat unbuttoned, just tied with the belt,
and a slouch hat, rarely tilted. Sometimes it was a captain's cap and a
yachting jacket. Almost always his trousers were held up by a cowboy belt.
You know the kind: one an Easterner waiting for a plane out of Phoenix
buys just as a joke and then takes a liking to. Occasionally, he'd hitch up
his slacks with it, and he often jabbed his thumbs behind it, his hands
ready for a fight or a dame.

Whether it was Sirocco or Casablanca, Martinique or Sahara, he was the only American around (except maybe for his buddy and the girl) and you didn't ask him how he got there, and he always worked alone—except for the fellow who thought he took care of him, the rummy, the piano player, the one *he* took care of, the one you didn't mess with. There was very little he couldn't do, and in a jam he could do anything: remove a slug from a guy's arm, fix a truck that wouldn't start. He was an excellent driver, knowing precisely how to take those curves or how to lose a guy that was tailing him. He could smell a piece of a broken glass and tell you right away if there'd been poison in it, or he could walk into a room and know just where the button was that opened the secret door. At the wheel of a boat, he was beautiful.

His expression was usually sour and when he smiled only the lower lip moved. There was a scar on his upper lip—maybe that's what gave him the faint lisp. He would tug meditatively at his earlobe when he was trying to figure something out and every so often he had a strange little twitch—a kind of backward jerk of the sides of his mouth coupled with a slight squinting of the eyes. He held his cigarette (a Chesterfield) cupped in his hand. He looked right holding a gun.

Unsentimental was a good word for him. "Leave 'im where he is," he might say to a woman whose husband has just been wounded, "I don't want 'im bleeding all over my cushions." And blunt: "I don't like you. I don't like your friends and I don't like the idea of her bein' married to you." And straight: "When a man's partner is killed he's supposed to do something about it. It doesn't make any difference what you thought of him. He was your partner and you're supposed to do something about it."

He was tough; he could stop you with a look or a line. "Go ahead, slap *me*," he'd say, or, "That's right, *go* for it," and there was in the way he said it just the right blend of malice, gleeful anticipation and the promise of certain doom. He didn't like taking orders. Or favors. It was smart not to fool around with him too much.

As far as the ladies were concerned, he didn't have too much trouble with them, except maybe keeping them away. It was the girl who said if he needed anything, all he had to do was whistle; he never said that to the girl. Most of the time he'd call her "angel," and if he liked her he'd tell her she was "good, awful good."

Whatever he was engaged in, whether it was being a reporter, a saloon-keeper, a gangster, a detective, a fishing-boat owner, a D.A. or a lawyer, he was impeccably, if casually, a complete professional. "You take chances," someone would say. "I get paid to," was his answer. But he never took himself too seriously. What was his job? a girl would ask. Conspiratorially, he'd lean in and say with the slightest flicker of a grin, "I'm a private dick on a case." He wasn't going to be taken in by Art either; he'd been to college, but he was a bit suspicious of the intellectuals. If someone mentioned Proust, he'd ask, "Who's he?" even though he knew.

Finally, he was wary of Causes. He liked to get paid for taking chances. He was a man who tried very hard to be Bad because he knew it was easier to get along in the world that way. He always failed because of an innate goodness which surely nauseated him. Almost always he went from belligerent neutrality to reluctant commitment. From "I stick my neck out for nobody" to "I'm no good at being noble, but it doesn't take much to see that the problems of three little people don't amount to a hill of beans in this crazy world." At the start, if the question was, "What are your sympathies?" the answer was invariably, "Minding my own business." But by the end, if asked why he was helping, risking his life, he might say, "Maybe 'cause I like you. Maybe 'cause I don't like them." Of course it was always "maybe" because he wasn't going to be that much of a sap, wasn't making any speeches, wasn't going to be a Good guy. Probably he rationalized it: "I'm just doing my job." But we felt good inside. We knew better.

In late 1963, the then very influential revival house, the New Yorker theater in Manhattan, ran the first U.S. retrospective of Humphrey Bogart movies—thirty of them (I helped to program it and wrote the accompanying notes). A one-day double bill of *The Big Sleep* and *To Have and Have Not* broke all the theater's attendance records. "I had two hundred people sitting on the floor," said Daniel Talbot, owner of the long-gone 830-seat theater on the Upper West Side, co-producer of the brilliant *Point of Order* (1964), and still the most distinguished exhibitor (Manhattan's Lincoln Plaza Cinemas) and distributor (New Yorker Films) of quality films in the country. "It was wild. I had to turn away a couple of hundred people. And that audience! First time Bogie appeared they applauded, and that was just the beginning. Any number of scenes got hands. And the laughs! Bogart is very hot right now," Talbot told me at the time. "It's more than a cult, it's something else, too. He's not consciously hip, but hip by default. You get the feeling that he lives up to the Code. Anyone who screws up deserves the fate of being rubbed out by Bogart. With Bogart you get a portrait of a patriot, a man interested in the landscape of America. I think he's an authentic American hero—more existential than, say, Gary Cooper, but as much in the American vein, and more able to cope with the present." Talbot paused and grinned. "Frankly, I just like to watch him at work. He hits people beautifully."

The French had a more intellectual, if nonetheless affectionate, approach to Bogart and the legend he left behind. As Belmondo stares mystically at a photo of Bogart in Godard's *Breathless* (1959), slowly exhaling cigarette smoke and rubbing his lip with his thumb, he murmurs wistfully, "Bogie . . ." and you can almost hear his director's thoughts, echoed, for instance, in the words of the late André Bazin, probably France's finest film critic. "Bogart is the man with a past," he wrote in *Cahiers du Cinéma* in 1957, a month after Bogart died. "When he comes into a film, it is already 'the morning after'; sardonically victorious in his macabre combat with the angel, his face scarred by what he has seen, and his step heavy from all he has learned, having ten times triumphed over his death, he will surely survive for us this one more time. . . . The Bogartian man is not defined by his contempt for bourgeois virtues, by his courage or cowardice, but first of all by his existential maturity which little by little transforms life into a tenacious irony at the expense of death."

"He satirized himself a great deal," said writer Betty Comden. Raymond Massey recalled an incident during the shooting of *Action in the North Atlantic* (1943): "The scene called for our doubles to jump from the bridge of a burning tanker into the water below, which was aflame with oil. Bogie turned to me and said, '*My* double is braver than yours.' I said that wasn't so, that *my* double was the braver man. Then Bogie looked at me and he said, 'The fact is I'm braver than you are.' I said that was nonsense. And the next thing I knew we did the damn stunt ourselves." Massey chuckled. "I burned my pants off and Bogie singed his eyebrows."

To Joseph L. Mankiewicz, who directed him in *The Barefoot Contessa* (1954), Bogart's toughness was a facade. "You'd be having dinner with him," he said, "and someone would come over and you could just see the tough guy coming on." And to Chester Morris: "He had a protective shell of seeming indifference. He wasn't, but he did a lotta acting offstage. He liked to act tough, liked to talk out of the side of his mouth." Writer-producer Nunnally Johnson said Bogart was convinced that people would have been disappointed if he didn't act tough with them. "A fan came over during dinner one time," said Johnson, "and Bogie told him to beat it. When the guy got back to his table I heard his companion say, quite happily, 'See, I told ya he'd insult you.' " Johnson reflected a moment. "But he was a lot tougher than I would be and a lot tougher than most people I know. I remember one time Judy Garland and her husband, Sid Luft,

"We'll always have Paris . . .": Humphrey Bogart with Ingrid Bergman in the Casablanca *(1943) flashback sequence, during which their brief, passionate romance is touchingly evoked. One of the great accidental masterpieces in movies, this is the picture that made Bogart a romantic lead.*

were at his home. Now Luft was a big alley fighter and a good deal broader than Bogart. But Bogie got annoyed about something or other and he walked right over to Luft, who also was a good head taller, and nodded at Judy. 'Would you take that dame out of this house,' he said, 'and never come back.' Luft kind of looked at him a moment and then he took her out." Johnson smiled. "Bogie took big risks."

Adlai Stevenson didn't find him that way. "He wasn't tough, not really," said the ambassador (and two-time nominee of the Democratic Party for President). "He was, to me, a nonconformist. He had a cynicism without being unhealthy. He had great curiosity and an arch kind of skepticism." And still another opinion: "He was a pushover," said Lauren Bacall.

"I never broke through his barrier," critic John McClain said. "I don't think anyone really got underneath. Bogart didn't unburden himself to men. He loved to be in love and with a woman. I think he came closer to

Bogie and Baby, as the press called them, at the happiest of their happy endings, as they walk off together to the jazz accompaniment of Hoagy Carmichael (on the piano) at the conclusion of Howard Hawks' To Have and Have Not *(1944), a sizzling romantic drama out of Hemingway (his novel) via Faulkner (he co-wrote the screenplay). Among the great American films.*

leveling with them than with anybody." Bogart married four women during his fifty-seven years, each of them an actress: Helen Menken (1926), Mary Philips (1928), Mayo Methot (1938), and, in 1945, Lauren Bacall. "I think once a person was out, they were really out," said Truman Capote, discussing the divorces. "He had emotional attachments."

The Bogart-Methot marriage was a stormy one. "Their neighbors were lulled to sleep," Dorothy Parker once said, "by the sounds of breaking china and crashing glass." Johnson recalled that Methot once had Bogart followed. "She was very jealous and positive that he was playing around. But Bogie never had a weakness for dames. The only weakness he ever had was for a drink and a talk." Johnson smiled. "Bogie soon found out a guy was tailing him, and he called up the fellow's agency. 'Hello, this is Humphrey Bogart,' he said. 'You got a man on my tail. Would you check with him and find out where I am.' "

The first time Bogart met Betty Bacall she was coming out of director Howard Hawks' office. She had made a test for Hawks, who had discovered her and first teamed the couple in *To Have and Have Not* (1945). "I saw your test," Bogart said to her. "We're gonna have a lotta fun together." It was with Bacall that he had his only children, a boy named Steve, which is what she called Bogart in that first movie, and a girl named Leslie Howard, after the actor who had insisted that Bogart be cast in the film version of *The Petrified Forest* (1936), the movie that really sparked his picture career. "He missed her when they were apart," Capote said. "He loved her. He used to talk a terrific line, but he was monogamous. Although that isn't entirely true—he fell in love with Bacall while he was still married to Mayo."

Bogart put it this way: "I'm a one-woman man and I always have been. I guess I'm old-fashioned. Maybe that's why I like old-fashioned women, the kind who stay in the house playing 'Roamin' in the Gloamin'.' They make a man think he's a man and they're glad of it."

The stories go that Bogart was a heavy drinker, but Nunnally Johnson thinks otherwise. "I don't think Bogie drank as much as he pretended to," he said. "Many's the time I was with him, the doorbell would ring, and he'd pick up his glass just to go answer the door. He couldn't have been as good at his job if he drank as much as he was supposed to have."

But Bogart did drink. "I think the whole world is three drinks behind," he used to say, "and it's high time it caught up." On one occasion he and a friend bought two enormous stuffed panda bears and took them as their dates to El Morocco. They sat them in chairs at a table for four and when an ambitious young lady came over and touched Bogart's bear, he shoved her away. "I'm a happily married man," he said, "and don't touch my panda." The woman brought assault charges against him, and when asked if he was drunk at four o'clock in the morning, he replied, "Sure, isn't everybody?" (The judge ruled that since the panda was Bogart's personal property, he could defend it.)

But Bogart didn't have to drink to start trouble. "He was an arrogant bastard," said Johnson, grinning. "It's kinda funny, this cult and everything. When he was alive, as many people hated him as loved him. I always thought of him as somewhat like Scaramouche." Johnson chuckled. "What was it? 'Born with the gift of laughter and the sense that the world was mad. . . .' He'd start a skirmish and then sit back and watch the consequences. Of course, there was nearly always something phony about the guy he was needling. Needle is the wrong word—howitzer would be

*Bogart as detective Sam Spade in the John Huston
adaptation of Dashiell Hammett's novel* The
Maltese Falcon *(1941), the first of six pictures
Bogart did with Huston, and perhaps their
most perfect and memorable*

more like it. The other fellow could use deflating, but it didn't take all
that artillery."

The original Holmby Hills Rat Pack, which Bogart initiated and
which died with him, sprang from this distaste for pretense. "What is a
Rat?" he once explained. "We have no constitution, charter or bylaws yet,
but we know a Rat when we see one. There are very few Rats in this town.
You might say that Rats are for staying up late and drinking lots of booze.
We're against squares and being bored and *for* lots of fun and being real
Rats, which very few people are, but if you're a real Rat, boy! Our slogan
is, 'Never rat on a Rat.' A first principle is that we don't care who likes us
as long as we like each other. We like each other very much."

John McClain tells of the yacht club Bogart belonged to and of the people who rented the large house next door for a summer. They were the Earls and they Dressed for Dinner. The members of the club (who were never invited) used to peer over their fence, watching the lush festivities. McClain had been invited to a Sunday dinner and had asked if he might bring Bogart along since they would be together on his yacht over the weekend. As they docked, McClain reminded Bogart to dress for the occasion and went off to get ready himself. Bogart went into the club for a drink or two. "After a while," McClain recalled, "Bogie announced to everyone in the club, 'My dear friends, the Earls,' he said, 'are having an open house and they want you all to come.' And into the Earl house comes Bogie followed by about thirty people, all wearing shorts and sport shirts and terrible sneakers." McClain laughed. "It was pretty funny, actually, but I was furious at the time."

"He could be very wrong, too," said Nathaniel Benchley. "One time at '21' I was standing at the bar with a couple of friends and Bogie got up from his table and came over. 'Are you a homosexual?' he said to one of them, just like that. The fellow looked rather taken aback and said he didn't see that it was any of his business. 'Well, *are* you?' said Bogie. 'Come on, we got a bet going at the table.' The fellow said, 'Since you ask, no.' I think Bogie could feel he'd been wrong and he turned to the other guy with us and asked him if *he* was a homosexual. The guy said no. He asked me and I said no and then he said, 'Well, *I* am,' and kinda minced away. He knew he'd been wrong."

A few weeks after Bogart's death, Peter Ustinov said, in a speech: "Humphrey Bogart was an exceptional character in a sphere where characters are not usually exceptional. To a visitor hot from the cold shores of England, he would put on an exaggerated Oxford accent and discuss the future of the 'British Empah' as though he wrong-headedly cared for nothing else in the wide world. His aim was to shake the newcomer out of his assumed complacency by insults that were as shrewdly observed as they were malicious. . . . The way into his heart was an immediate counterattack in a broad American accent, during which one assumed a complicity between him and his *bête noire*, Senator McCarthy, in some dark scheme. . . . It was in the character of the man that he smiled with real pleasure only when he had been amply repaid in kind."

Capote would go along with that: "The turning point in our friendship—the beginning really—was during *Beat the Devil* (1954). Bogie and John Huston and some others, they were playing that game—you know the one, what d'ya call it?—you take each other's hand across a table and try to push the other's arm down. Well, it just happens that I'm very good at that game. So, anyway, Bogie called over, 'Hey, Caposy.' That's what he called me, 'Caposy.' He said, 'C'mon, Caposy, let's see you try this.' And I went over and I pushed his arm down. Well, he looked at me . . . He had such a suspicious mind, he was sure that Huston had cut off my head and sewed it onto someone else's body. 'Let's see you do that again,' he said. And again I pushed his arm down. So he said, 'Once more,' and I said I would only if we bet a hundred dollars, which we did. I won again and he paid me, but then he came over and he started sort of semi-wrestling with me. It was something they did. He was crushing me and I said, 'Cut that *owat*,' and he said, 'Cut that *owat*.' I said, 'Well, do,' and he said, 'Why?' I said, 'Because you're hurting me.' But he kept right on squeezing, so I got my leg around behind him and pushed and over he went. He was flat on his can looking up at me. And from then on we were very good friends."

"Bogie's needling tactics were quite calculated," Johnson explained. "I had lunch with him and Betty at Romanoff's one time and she was giving him hell about some row at a party. He'd provoked it, of course. 'Someday somebody's gonna belt you,' she said, and he said, 'No, that's the art of it—taking things up to that point and then escaping.' "

In 1947, Bogart led a march to Washington to protest the investigations of the Un-American Activities Committee. Some people labeled him a pinko. He didn't like that. "I am an American," he said. Bogart's political freethinking was considered dangerous in Hollywood. In 1952, however, he campaigned most actively for Stevenson for President. "He never seemed to give a damn what people thought or said," Stevenson recalled. "And it was quite perilous in those days to be a Democrat, especially one partisan to me. He was disdainful about anybody trying to muscle about in a free country."

"He wasn't an extremist in anything," said Bacall, "except telling the truth. You had to admire Bogie. He always said what he thought. 'Goddamnit,' he used to say, 'if you don't want to hear the truth, don't ask me.' "

"That's true," Johnson said. "Everything he did was honest. He used to say, 'What's everybody whispering about? I've got cancer!' He'd say, 'For Christ's sake, it's not a venereal disease.' "

Bogart also said that the only point in making money is "so you can tell some big shot to go to hell." And: "I have politeness and manners. I was brought up that way. But in this goldfish-bowl life, it is sometimes hard to use them."

His widow thinks it was more than just good manners Bogart had. Finally, she'll tell you. "He was an old-fashioned man, a great romantic. And very emotional. He would cry when a dog died. You should have seen him at our wedding, tears streaming down his face. He told me that he started thinking about the meaning of the words. He was tough about life and totally uncompromising, but I remember he went to see Steve at nursery school and when he saw him sitting at his little desk, he cried."

Alistair Cooke met the Bogarts on the Stevenson campaign train and he remembered sitting with them one afternoon and saying that, of course, Stevenson wouldn't win. " 'What!?' said Bogie, astounded. 'Not a prayer, I'm afraid,' I said. 'Why, you son of a bitch,' Betty said, 'that's a fine thing to say.' 'Look,' I said, 'I'm a reporter. You're the lieutenants.' We bet ten dollars on it and when Stevenson lost he paid it to me. But he didn't really think I'd take it. You know what he said? 'It's a hell of a guy who bets against his own principles.' "

Cooke commented on this Bogart trait in an article he wrote for *The Atlantic Monthly* (May 1957): "A touchy man who found the world more corrupt than he had hoped . . . he invented the Bogart character and imposed it on a world impatient of men more obviously good. And it fitted his deceptive purpose like a glove. . . . From all . . . he was determined to keep his secret: the rather shameful secret, in the realistic world we inhabit, of being a gallant man and an idealist."

Other friends detected a similar quality in Bogart. Joe Mankiewicz called it, "A sadness about the human condition. He had a kind of eighteenth-century, Alexander Pope nature. I think he would have made a superb Gatsby. His life reflected Gatsby's sense of being an outsider." Stevenson found "a wistful note in him, as there often is in thinking people. He was much more profound than one might think." And Capote called him lost. "It was his outstanding single characteristic—that something almost pathetic. Not that he would ever ask for sympathy, far from it. It just always seemed to me as though he were permanently lonely. It gave him a rather poetic quality, don't you think?"

This secret inner world of Humphrey Bogart was reflected in his passion for sailing and his love for the *Santana*, his boat, on which he went off whenever he could, accompanied by a few friends. They used to drink Drambuies and play dominoes or just sail. He had learned early about the sea, having left school (at their request) at seventeen and joined the Navy. It was on the troopship *Leviathan* that he received the injury that permanently scarred his upper lip. "Sailing. That was the part of him no one could get at," Capote said. "It wasn't anything materialistic. It was some kind of inner soul, an almost mystical hideaway."

If the *Motion Picture Herald*'s annual Fame Poll of the Top Ten movie stars can be trusted, it appears that Bogart's peak years of popularity were 1943–1949, during and just after World War II. Cooke explained it this way: "He was . . . a romantic hero inconceivable in any time but ours. . . . When Hitler was acting out scripts more brutal and obscene than anything dreamed of by Chicago's North Side or the Warner Brothers, Bogart was the only possible antagonist likely to outwit him and survive. What was needed was no Ronald Colman, Leslie Howard or other knight of the boudoir, but a conniver as subtle as Goebbels. Bogart was the very tough gent required, and to his glory he was always, in the end, on our side." He didn't get his Oscar, however, until 1952 (for *The African Queen*), and popped up on the Top Ten again in 1955, just a little more than a year before he died.

Bogart said, "It took fifteen years to make us personalities. Gable and Cooper can do anything in a picture, and people would say, 'Oh, that's just good old Clark.' "

"His great basic quality," said Ustinov, "was a splendid roughness. Even when perfectly groomed, I felt I could have lit a match on his jaw. . . . He knew his job inside out, and yet it was impossible not to feel that his real soul was elsewhere, a mysterious searching instrument knocking at doors unknown even to himself. . . ."

Perhaps this is what Bogart's admirers sense. "There was something about him that came through in every part he played," said Bacall. "I think he'll always be fascinating—to this generation and every succeeding one. There was something that made him able to be a man of his own and it showed through his work. There was also a purity, which is amazing considering the parts he played. Something solid, too. I think as time goes by we all believe less and less. Here was someone who believed in something."

"Like all really great stars," said director George Cukor, "he had a secret." Cukor never worked with him, but they were friends. "You never really know him altogether. He also had boldness of mind, freedom of thought—a buccaneer. I think these young people haven't seen him," he went on, trying to explain the cult. "They're simply rediscovering him. After all, Bogie had class."

"The average college student would sooner identify with Bogart than, say, Sinatra, don't you think?" said Mankiewicz. "He had that rather intel-

*Bogart (with Gloria Grahame on bed) as the strangely mercurial
and occasionally violent screenwriter suspected of murder in Bogart's own
production,* In a Lonely Place *(1950), directed by Nicholas Ray;
writer-star Louise Brooks wrote that of all the actor's roles, this
one most reminded her of the Bogie she knew.*

lectual disrespect for authority. Also, I don't think anyone ever really
believed that Bogart was a gangster—that's what fascinated people. Bogart
never frightened them."

"It's angry youth," Chester Morris said. "They're cheering for the
heavy today. Everything must be nonconformist. They'd also like to do
the kind of things he did. He was a forerunner of James Bond." Benchley:
"He's a hero without being a pretty boy."

"Could it be anything as simple as sex appeal?" Cooke wondered. "He
had an image of sophisticated virility and he projected it remarkably well.
And with such humor. At last, he had such style that it doesn't wither, it
doesn't age, it doesn't date. Like Billie Holiday."

"I think Robin Hood has always been attractive," said Adlai Stevenson.

Before the adulation, there must be something to adulate. And this
must be created. "If a face like Ingrid Bergman's looks at you as though

you're adorable," Bogart once said, "everybody does. You don't have to act very much." Raymond Chandler thought otherwise: "All Bogart has to do to dominate a scene is to enter it." Evidently it wasn't always that way. In 1922, playing one of his first stage roles, he was reviewed by Alexander Woollcott: "His performance could be mercifully described as inadequate." But two years later, of another performance, Woollcott again: "Mr. Bogart is a young actor whose last appearance was recorded by your correspondent in words so disparaging that it is surprising to find him still acting. Those words are hereby eaten." It would figure that Bogart often used to quote the first review but never the second.

" 'Why, I'm a National Institution,' he used to say," Capote recalled. "He was very proud of his success and fame. But he was most serious about his acting. He thought of it as a profession, one that he was curious about, knew something about. After all, it was almost the sum total of his life. In the end, Bogart really was an artist. And a very selective one. All the gestures and expressions were pruned down and pruned down. One time I watched *The Maltese Falcon* with him and he sat there, muttering in that hoarse way, criticizing himself in the third person. 'Now he's gonna come in,' he'd say. 'Then he's gonna do this and that's where he does the wrong thing.' I gathered during the silences that he liked it. It was braggadocio through silence."

Richard Brooks, director-writer of a couple of Bogart films, told me, "Humphrey Bogart could never equate the money he was making with what he was doing. He was constantly mocking himself. And that's a good thing, you know what I mean?"

Howard Hawks directed Bogart in his two most archetypal roles, as Harry ("Steve") Morgan in *To Have and Have Not* and as Philip Marlowe in *The Big Sleep* (1946). "He was extremely easy to work with," Hawks said. "Really underrated as an actor. Without his help I couldn't have done what I did with Bacall. Not too many actors would sit around and wait while a girl steals a scene. But he fell in love with the girl and the girl with him, and that made it easy."

Bogart used to say that an audience was always a little ahead of the actor. "If a guy points a gun at you," he explained, "the audience knows you're afraid. You don't have to make faces. You just have to believe that you are the person you're playing and that what is happening is happening to you."

Ustinov acted with Bogart once, in a comedy called *We're No Angels* (1955). "Bogart had an enormous presence," he said, "and he carried the light of battle in his eye. He wished to be matched, to be challenged, to be teased. I could see a jocular and quarrelsome eye staring out of the character he was playing into the character I was playing—rather as an experienced bullfighter might stare a hotheaded bull to precipitate action."

"When the heavy, full of crime and bitterness," said Bogart, "grabs his wounds and talks about death and taxes in a husky voice, the audience is his and his alone."

This emotion, elicited so consciously from his movie audiences, ironically became a reality. His death was horribly, heartbreakingly in character. He died on January 14, 1957, of a cancer of the esophagus, and it had taken well over a year to kill him. "These days," he said, "I just sit around and talk to my friends, the people I like." Which is what he did.

"I went to see him toward the end," said Ambassador Stevenson. "He was very ill and very weak, but he made a most gallant effort to keep gay. He had an intolerance for weakness, an impatience with illness."

"I went a few times," Capote said. "Most of his friends went, some almost every day, like Sinatra. Some were very loyal. He seemed to bring out the best in them all. He looked so awful, so terribly thin. His eyes were huge and they looked so frightened. They got bigger and bigger. It was real fear and yet there was always that gay, brave self. He'd have to be brought downstairs on the dumbwaiter and he'd sit and wait and wait for his martini. He was only allowed one, I think, or two. And that's how we used to find him, smoking and sipping that martini."

During that time, his wife rarely left the house, though her friends and even Bogart urged her to go out more often. When someone asked why she had been out only six or seven times in ten months, Bogart replied: "She's my wife and my nurse. So she stays home. Maybe that's the way you tell the ladies from the broads in this town."

"He was quite a man, Bogart," Brooks said admiringly. He was genuinely tough and he was honest. I remember a couple of weeks before he died he was still having guests and seeing friends in the afternoon. I went out to see him one day and found him sitting there as usual, drink in hand. After a while, he had a terrible coughing fit and he started vomiting blood. It was an awful thing to see. I got up and started to leave the room till it was over. And Bogie looked up at me and said, 'What's a matter, Dick, can't you take it?' "

"He went through the worst and most agonizing pain any human can take," said Dr. Maynard Brandsma. "I knew this and when I'd see him I'd ask, 'How is it?' Bogie would always answer simply, 'Pretty rough.' He never complained and he never whimpered. I knew he was dying and during the last weeks I knew he knew it, too."

"I saw him twenty-three days before he died," said Cukor. "He

*Humphrey Bogart is detective Philip Marlowe, and Lauren Bacall plays
his client's daughter, whom he falls for, as Bogart did for Bacall, though
they were not yet married while making this mesmerizing 1946 Howard
Hawks adaptation (with script assistance by William Faulkner) of
Raymond Chandler's first novel,* The Big Sleep; *the quintessential
detective picture and among the three most archetypal Bogart performances.*

couldn't come downstairs anymore and he was heavily sedated. He kept
closing his eyes. Still he'd be telling jokes and asking to hear the gossip.
But his voice was the wonder. That marvelous voice. It was absolutely
alive. It was the last thing that died."

Upon his death, most of the newspaper reports were similar. Quite a
few of them told it this way: "Usually he kissed his wife Lauren Bacall and
said, 'Good night.' But according to Dr. Michael Flynn, this time he put
his hand on her arm and murmured in his familiar brusque fashion,
'Good-bye, kid.' " In other words, a Bogart death scene. He had walked
through seventy-five movie nights for the world, and it would be impossible now to change the image or alter a legend that had really just begun.

Forty years after I wrote most of that piece, Bogart is at the top of the list
of Hollywood legends. A couple of years ago when I sat down again with

Lauren Bacall, she would speak more intimately about Bogart, and it became clear that she was still as much in love with him as ever. The last time we had talked at any length was only seven years after Bogart had died, and she had smiled softly quite often with the slightly disconnected yet direct look in her eyes of stoic heartbreak—as though seven years had been no time at all. In 2002, as she spoke, forty-five years since his death didn't seem so long ago either.

Their love affair had begun with laughter between takes on *To Have and Have Not*. Bogart, being aware of her terrible nervousness on this first picture, would kid around with her, crack jokes to break her up. He succeeded. Before she felt any emotional attraction toward Bogart, she could laugh easily with him, and indeed credits this with making the "chemistry" between them even "more pronounced—it was terrific." That's an understatement; *To Have and Have Not* is unique by virtue of being the most vividly captured romantic connection between two stars—courtship to capitulation—in the sound era. (Only Greta Garbo and John Gilbert in the silent *Flesh and the Devil* come close.) The irony is that this is exactly what Howard Hawks had counted on by creating a character and molding an actress into what he would describe to me in the sixties as "an American Dietrich."* Hawks' notion was to take Bogart, the "most insolent" star on the screen, and put a young woman beside him who was "more insolent" than he was. As Bacall has said, her performance in the movie, the way she was presented, was all part of Hawks' fantasy. In his own way, Bacall came to realize, Hawks was shaping her to be his ideal woman and wanted also (though unstated) to have an afffair with her during the film. But the electricity he had bet on was so hot that Howard didn't have a prayer.

Bacall essentially confirmed all this in her own way. She said that it wasn't until around the fourth week of shooting that anything started, that it was Bogart who had "started," and that they had the greatest time with each other. Over the last two weeks of the movie, she thought only about him. No doubt a good deal of what happened resulted from their "playing scenes" for Hawks' picture. Bacall acknowledged the obvious "living the part" associations, but said that this certainly didn't happen "consciously." Bogart did not believe in living-the-part acting techniques. He used to tell Bacall she had to let the movie-work stay on the lot, and have a decent life at home. For Bogart, she said, what was crucial was being true to oneself and never lying.

*See Hawks chapter in *Who the Devil Made It*.

At first, Bacall's mother didn't like Bogart at all and tried to keep them apart. One night the phone rang at three in the morning and it was Bogart asking her to meet him in Beverly Hills. She leapt to go. Her mother was outraged, angrily exclaiming that he was married. Yes, he's been married *three* times, Bacall replied, and left to meet Bogart, standing with veteran character actor James Gleason, at a corner by the Beverly Wilshire Hotel. When she saw him she "just ran into his arms." Their period of "wooing" had been extraordinary. Bacall had been a virgin until Bogart.

For the actor, however, Bacall then being only nineteen plagued him, and her age continued to do so for years. Before their marriage, he would say that he was so much older she'd be gone within five years. His friend German actor Peter Lorre told him that five years was "better than nothing." Bogart countered that she was just starting out and he, at forty-five, was running down. Bacall reflected sadly that he did have only another twelve years.

Things became serious between Bogart and "Baby," as he called her (the press picked it up), during the summer after *To Have and Have Not* wrapped. One time at four a.m. he phoned asking her to meet him on Highway 101; he would be wearing a sunflower in his buttonhole. Again, despite her mother's objections, Bacall drove down and found Bogart as promised, walking alone down Highway 101, unshaven, wearing a large sunflower in a buttonhole, white slacks, blazer, espadrilles. Bacall could hardly believe the sight. He was "irresistible" "stunning"; Bogart "wooed better than anyone" she would ever know.

The two had a "fabulous" time, were "a great pair," Bacall said. Despite their twenty-five-year age difference, he often seemed considerably younger than her, had more energy than she did, and slept little. They would write letters to each other once a week. Bogart had partial duty with the U.S. Coast Guard (at the end of World War II), and one night a week they would meet at an agreed-upon spot, sit in his car for a half hour, exchange letters, and then she would have to leave. Bacall referred with affection to this romantic time as "kid stuff," very "collegiate," and said Bogart's letters were "flowery" and "wonderful." When she thought of those days, she noted that even though they happened so many years ago, "it's all so clear still."

Bogart was endlessly fascinating to Bacall because of his many-sided personality, his intelligence, his slightly cynical attitude. Yet she believes it was his essential integrity that is responsible for his ongoing popularity. He would not compromise his values—with movies or in life. What he cared about most, she said, was "doing good work." Bogart, she explained, never made the kind of money Cary Grant or Gary Cooper or many other stars made. Because studio head Harry Cohn knew how badly Bogart wanted to play Captain Queeg in *The Caine Mutiny*, the actor even cut his salary to be in it (and received another Oscar nomination). "But Bogie was a last-century boy," Bacall said, referring to Bogart's birth in 1899, he wasn't "a cheat," never fooled around, and did not behave like a movie star with an entourage of sycophants. He never kowtowed, always spoke his mind, and in pictures was always anxious to make the work "better."

Bacall described Bogart as extremely "generous" to act with, and in no way competitive. Because of his training and experience in the theater, Bogart was not simply a "personality," but an underrated, consummate actor, well educated and intelligent, an "avid reader," said Bacall. This was a surprise to her, his intelligence. After their marriage, she saw how much he would read, and here she herself had thought he was "one of those 'deez, dem, and doz' guys." Bogart was by nature "a worrier," with great anxieties about his work, fatherhood, things that were new to him, often "tense," which explained his love for the freedom of the sea and the boat where he would "unwind" and "relax," said Bacall. Not only was his bravery real, but he had great courage and "high standards of behavior" by which he himself lived. He would refer to "the luck of the draw," which might be "lousy" but simply had to be dealt with.

Bogart's fatal illness—he was to say he'd never been sick before in his life—lasted eleven long months, from the first terrible operation at the start of February 1956. Bacall remembered his amazing strength of character. Although there must have been strong feelings going on inside him, he never discussed them. There was no self-indulgence of any kind, she said; he acted as if all he had was "a cold." Bacall did not discuss the cancer with him because that was clearly his preference. While he slowly wasted away, those who dropped by to visit most often were Katharine Hepburn and Spencer Tracy; they came regularly as a couple. Tracy and Bogart had started in pictures together on the same film (John Ford's 1930 *Up the River*) and Hepburn and Bogart, of course, co-starred in John Huston's *The African Queen,* shot on tough locations in Africa, Bacall with them the whole time. Tracy and Hepburn were among the last to see him alive.

On the night before he lapsed into a coma from which he never revived, Bogart asked Bacall to sleep next to him above the covers. During that night, he woke up nearly every half hour, kept pushing on his chest from a feeling of suffocation. The next morning, a Sunday, they watched a musical on TV, Frank Sinatra came by on his way out of town, the doctor visited briefly and said Bogart's difficulties of the night before were not unexpected. Heading out for a quick trip to pick up their children from Sunday school, Bacall kissed him as usual, saying she'd be back right away, and returned to find him in a coma. Sensing the end, she "broke down." He was dead within twenty-four hours.

When watching him in a film, Bacall would remember all the fun they had shared, his wit, his "great sense of humor." He was "difficult," not at all an "easy man," but they "just happened to fit." Looking at a Bogart movie she thinks again how "unfair" and "terrible" it is that his life was cut so short, that he couldn't see his children grow up, especially because of his being such an "unusually good human being." And despite everything, the strength of his character prevailed. No one could possibly replace him, or be compared to him, in life or on the screen.

When I said that somehow even that *kind* of American didn't seem to exist anymore, Bacall shook her head. "No, it doesn't," she said. "And that kind of America doesn't exist either."

Humphrey DeForest Bogart, born December 25, 1899, New York, NY; died January 14, 1957, Los Angeles, CA.

Selected starring features (with director):

1930: *Up the River* (John Ford)
1936: *The Petrified Forest* (Archie Mayo)
1937: *Dead End* (William Wyler)
1938: *Angels with Dirty Faces* (Michael Curtiz)
1939: *The Roaring Twenties* (Raoul Walsh)
1940: *They Drive by Night* (Walsh)
1941: *High Sierra* (Walsh); *The Maltese Falcon* (John Huston)
1943: *Casablanca* (Curtiz)

1944: *To Have and Have Not* (Howard Hawks)
1946: *The Big Sleep* (Hawks)
1948: *The Treasure of the Sierra Madre*; *Key Largo* (both Huston)
1949: *Knock on Any Door* (Nicholas Ray)
1950: *In a Lonely Place* (Ray)
1951: *The African Queen* (Huston)
1954: *Beat the Devil* (Huston); *The Caine Mutiny* (Edward Dmytryk); *Sabrina* (Billy Wilder); *The Barefoot Contessa* (Joseph L. Mankiewicz)
1955: *The Desperate Hours* (Wyler)
1956: *The Harder They Fall* (Mark Robson)

3

MARLON BRANDO

The first and only star I ever asked for an autograph was Marlon Brando; he was also the first star I had met. It was around New Year's 1954, I was fourteen, and had just seen a matinee at New York's City Center starring José Ferrer in a heavy drama, *The Shrike.* Outside on the darkening winter sidewalk, I was looking at the posters proclaiming the production "a major cultural event" when I glanced up the street toward Seventh Avenue, and instantly from about a half-block away recognized the person coming toward me. My heart started beating faster as I quickly turned back to the poster. I felt I had to talk to him: it was Marlon Brando, for God's sake, and if I didn't get an autograph, no one would believe I had just seen him walking up 55th Street toward Sixth Avenue.

I knew Brando was in town shooting the longshoreman drama *On the Waterfront,* with Elia Kazan directing (and for which Brando would win his first Best Actor Oscar), but I didn't know until I saw the film eight months later that he was wearing his costume home: soon-to-be-familiar-to-the-world gray checkered jacket, work pants and motorcycle boots. I glanced again; when he was just a few feet away, absorbed in thought, hands shoved into the jacket's side pockets, I turned and approached him, saying, "Mr. Brando, may I have your autograph?"

He didn't alter his step a fraction, looked at me briefly, and just kept walking as he said, fairly deadpan, with that slightly nasal Midwestern twang, "Yeah." I fell in step with him, starting to search for a pad and pencil I knew I had somewhere, which is what I muttered. Brando looked over at me, still walking, and said, not unpleasantly, "You got a pen?"

I repeated that it was on me someplace and, to fill the moment, said enthusiastically that I had just seen José Ferrer in *The Shrike.* Had he seen it?

"Yeah," he said, "I thought it stunk."

*Marlon Brando in the costume he was wearing home the night I met him,
with the wonderful Eva Marie Saint, on location in Hoboken for Elia
Kazan's film* On the Waterfront *(1954), written by Budd Schulberg.
Although both Schulberg and Kazan had been willing witnesses who
named names before the House Un-American Activities Committee, the
revisionist view of the movie as a kind of apologia for informers was
certainly not the way the picture was perceived in its day, either by critics
or the public; it won a slew of Oscars, including Brando's first, after four
nominations in a row.*

I stammered something meek, finally found the pencil and small pad, handed them over. Still without hesitating or changing his stride, Brando signed his name lengthwise on the pad, first name above the second, then gave it and the pencil back to me. I thanked him and, still a bit thrown by his comment on the Ferrer production, couldn't really get it together for another remark, mind speeding the whole time to a kind of blurred blank. I would later recognize that same strange look of stasis on people asking for my autograph. The mind goes into overload—there is suddenly so much to talk about that no words at all can formulate themselves.

At this point in his career, Brando was already a kind of legend and yet he had appeared only in two successful Broadway plays (in the original *Life with Father* and in Kazan's production of Tennessee Williams' *A Streetcar Named Desire*) and five films, of which two (Fred Zinnemann's *The Men,* and Laslo Benedek's *The Wild One,* both produced by Stanley Kramer) had done poorly at the box office. When I ran into him on the street, I'd seen four of those five film performances more than once: seen him as Stanley Kowalski in Kazan's film version of *A Streetcar Named Desire* (Brando's first Oscar nomination); in the title role for Kazan's *Viva Zapata!,* written by John Steinbeck; as Marc Antony in the all-star Joseph Mankiewicz–John Houseman production of Shakespeare's *Julius Caesar;* and as the rebel biker in *The Wild One,* the first biker film, essentially the start of the modern Western.

After twelve years, Roger Corman had the first success in this genre with *The Wild Angels* (for which I wrote 80 percent of the final script and directed the second unit), making Peter Fonda a star and therefore setting the stage for *Easy Rider* three years later, which finally made the genre legitimate. And altered the Hollywood hierarchy radically for a while by inaugurating the brief Era of the Director in the United States, of which Brando himself would become an integral, indeed crucial, element with his 1972 performances in *The Godfather* and *Last Tango in Paris,* the wheel coming full circle.

Brando's first picture, *The Men,* had not been in circulation since its small initial 1950 release; Brando as a paraplegic was such a dud financially that when it was reissued (not until 1957, to cash in on Brando's extraordinary popularity in the mid-fifties) the title was changed to *Battle Stripe* to make it seem like a new war film. The public wasn't fooled and the movie fared no better. *The Wild One* (despite the success of *Streetcar* and moderate winners *Zapata* and *Caesar*) had recently opened in New York as the top half of a one-week double-bill, a sure sign that the studio didn't think it would work commercially.

Brando in the role that made him a star, first on Broadway, then on the screen: as Tennessee Williams' brutal Stanley Kowalski in A Streetcar Named Desire *(1951). Elia Kazan directed both, with the transfixing Vivien Leigh winning an Oscar as Blanche DuBois.*

Meanwhile, Brando is brilliant in both, and was already by this moment in time the hippest actor there was, the most influential, most imitated, most controversial, most respected by other actors. Since I wanted very much to be a professional actor, my awe in his presence essentially rendered me speechless though my mind was racing with all those many images of Brando I had already accumulated. The whole truth is that in those early teenage days I was a popular mimic at school, doing impressions of a number of stars, Brando prominent among them, and to such a degree that within a year or so some students started calling me Marlon.

By now, Brando and I had reached the corner of Sixth Avenue and 55th. The light was green so Brando kept going. I thanked him again as he moved off the curb and glanced at me to say, "So-long, kid." As he did I noticed one boot stepped into a pile of dog shit. I thought of advising him of what had happened but he continued on determinedly, hands shoved back into jacket pockets, and I flashed that my father had said stepping in dog shit was good luck. Certainly before I could figure out how to say, "You just stepped in dog shit," he was at the other side of the avenue, and soon disappearing into the darkness.

For years I treasured the little piece of paper with Brando's signature on it, carrying it in my wallet long into my twenties (though now it's lost). That evening, on the bus home, I felt a kind of magical sense of being special, of being among the chosen; why else would I be lucky enough to have had such an encounter? My inside pocket glowed like hot gold with the proof it contained of the miracle, the benediction. Certainly, I'd never felt anything like this before. Perhaps it's the sudden proximity to genius, talent or celebrity; the old thing about the spotlight falling on you because you're momentarily illuminated by the star's glow: reflected glory. I have felt it many times since that chance meeting with Brando but never again with the kind of intense mystery of the first experience.

Our second meeting was also by accident. It was four years later, the spring of 1958, and by then I had seen everything he had done since winning for *On the Waterfront* and becoming the most sought-after star in pictures, with his choices being just about everything that was out there. Brando had made four selections since we had met: as Napoleon in *Desirée,* a bizarre pick surely and a best-forgotten flop; as Sky Masterson in *Guys and Dolls,* the successful Mankiewicz–Samuel Goldwyn version of the hit Broadway musical, out of Damon Runyon by way of Frank Loesser; as a wise Okinawan for the film version of another Broadway smash, *The Teahouse of the August Moon,* Brando's first of numerous major associations with Asia and Asians; and as U.S. Army Lt. Gruber falling in love with a Japanese girl while stationed in Japan, for Joshua Logan's production of *Sayonara,* among the actor's biggest box-office successes.

Though I had admired the basic quality of all these performances, the ones I hadn't seen before receiving Brando's autograph, and now had seen more than once, were *The Men, On the Waterfront* and *Sayonara,* his most charming and refreshingly undisguised performance to that time, one which by now tended to dominate my own (and others') Brando impressions because the role seemed most like him in real life.

In the meantime, I had met many other actors and a few other stars, had worked in three seasons of summer stock, and had been studying acting for three years with Stella Adler, who was, of course, Marlon's own teacher. I had a regular girlfriend, and had auditioned for the Actors Studio and been rejected. I was walking from Fifth Avenue toward Madison and, passing the side windows of the famous F.A.O. Schwarz toy store (this is long before they moved), I looked at one of the displays in the shop window and saw Brando standing inside, leaning against a counter, looking at a stuffed animal. I turned on my heel and walked back to the entrance on Fifth. Brando was gazing quizzically at a different stuffed animal when I went over and said hello and told him my name, that I was a young actor and was working with Stella Adler.

Brando smiled. "Stella's great, isn't she?" I said she was amazing, and he grinned. "Yes, she's pretty amazin'," he said with an undertone of amusement and a lot of affection. I said I had learned everything from her, and he nodded: "So've I." Then I mentioned being friendly with a friend of his, television producer Joseph Cates (brother of film director Gilbert Cates). "Oh, yeah, how's Joe?" Brando asked fondly. I told him he was fine, but in my responses I could feel myself starting to fall into my Brando *Sayonara* impression. Fighting this reflexive impulse, I asked about the widely-read, controversial profile of him which Truman Capote had written and published recently as a long piece ("The Duke in His Domain") in *The New Yorker*. Had it bothered him? Since it seemed, I said, "kinda bitchy."

Brando looked off out the window in that characteristic way of his, reflecting a moment, then nodding slightly as he said, "Yeah, it was kinda bitchy." He pursed his lips. "But it doesn't *bother* me." He looked back at me. "I mean, there's been so much shit hittin' the fan, what the hell's a little more?" I started to say something but stopped myself before the Brando-sounding phrase could escape. My mind went blank and then I realized it was probably time to move on. Thanking him for his time, I said something about loving all his movies, reached out for his handshake, which was not that firm, and moved away with a wave. Outside when I passed the shop window again, Brando was still there, talking now to an attractive saleswoman.

Right afterward, I called Joe Cates to tell him what had happened. Not much later, I saw Joe and he said he'd spoken with Marlon, mentioned me, and that Marlon had remembered the encounter. "Oh, yeah, that crazy kid," Brando had said. Joe had told him I did a wicked Brando impression and he had responded, "I'd like to see it sometime." I can't remember how, but eventually I was given the phone number to his New York apartment and called him after a while. Brando still lived in Manhattan then, in the mid-Fifties on the West Side, with Wally Cox as his roommate. I had become a fan of Cox's from seeing him with Tony Randall on their *Mr. Peepers* television series, which seemed to me then a charming, dry and witty delight.

We spoke a few times over the next year or so but I can't recall much of what we said, except that he was funny and quite warm. After he moved permanently west I lost touch with him; as I did with Joe Cates, when I moved west. One time, maybe a year after F.A.O. Schwarz, Brando came briefly to a rehearsal of Stella Adler's off-Broadway production of *Johnny Johnson.*

Brando was known to have been the main backer, though he never took credit for it. Stella introduced him to the cast one afternoon and he sat on a table for a while, flipping his hat up and down in one hand, as he said a few words of praise for Stella, and wished us good luck.

Twenty years later, I was in Brando's longtime L.A. home on Mulholland Drive helping to celebrate a party he was holding in Stella Adler's honor. Cybill Shepherd and I were living together at the time, both of us having had a critical and popular success in 1971 with *The Last Picture Show.* Brando had virtually disappeared as a force by the end of the 1960s, then returned with the spectacular 1972 double-whammy of *The Godfather* and *Last Tango in Paris.* I had had two other successes, and Cybill had another on her own. It was the mid-seventies and everything seemed pretty great for all of us at this party for our Stella. I don't believe Marlon and I said anything to each other the whole night, the place being jammed with people.

The word on Marlon by this time was that he had virtually no interest or respect for any part of the movie business, or the art of acting, for that matter. I did remember something Stella had said about Brando way back in the late fifties. "When Marlon isn't acting," she told her class one afternoon, "it's Intermission!" Only the need for money to support himself and his ever-widening family (fourteen children) on a decently lavish scale kept him working after the personal and professional debacle of *One-Eyed Jacks,* released in 1961—only two pictures after *Sayonara.* (These were the World War II drama *The Young Lions,* with Brando riveting as a perhaps overly introspective Nazi; and brilliant with Anna Magnani in the Sidney Lumet film of Tennessee Williams' *The Fugitive Kind,* based on his play *Orpheus Descending.*)

Brando impressions always focused on his 1950s pictures (*Streetcar, Zapata, Caesar, Wild One, Waterfront, Guys and Dolls, Sayonara* were the most prevalent) and, until *The Godfather* in 1972 replaced most of these, *One-Eyed Jacks* was the last movie from which anybody imitated Brando. This was also the single one he had ever directed (and produced)—an unsuccessful and notoriously expensive, but nevertheless memorably original Technicolor Western drama with a terrific title. The two lines most

Marlon Brando's reading of the famous line "Friends, Romans, countrymen, lend me your ears" was surprising since he virtually threw it away as a shouted means of getting the people quiet for Antony's funeral oration in the film of Shakespeare's Julius Caesar *(1953), directed and adapted by Joseph L. Mankiewicz and with an all-star cast, including James Mason and John Gielgud.*

frequently mimicked were both evidently written by the ultra-hip novelist Calder Willingham, one of two credited screenplay writers (Guy Trosper is the other, adapted from Charles Neider's novel *The Authentic Death of Hendry Jones*). When asked why he had shot someone, Marlon's character replies, "He didn't give me no selection"; and, exploding at somebody else, he shouts in fury, "YOU scum-sucking pig!" Two uncredited fellows also worked on the script: Sam Peckinpah (before he had become a feature director) and Stanley Kubrick (post-*Spartacus*), who originally had been hired to direct. During a production conference when Brando supposedly gave everyone exactly three minutes to speak, upon being informed that his time was up, Kubrick told Marlon to "go fuck yourself," and soon afterward was replaced by the star who, Kubrick always maintained, had wanted to direct it himself all along. Brando was thirty-seven.

The shooting of *One-Eyed Jacks*—along the majestic coastline of the Monterey peninsula and in the Mexican desert (I can't recall another Western ever shot with views of the ocean)—took considerably longer than scheduled and cost a good deal more than budgeted, so the Paramount front office wasn't very happy by the time Brando was editing. They were even less happy with the picture they saw, which was three hours long and had an unhappy ending. Arguments ensued, ultimatums came, the conclusion was partially reshot, much was recut, deleted. No one, especially Brando, was really pleased with the compromised final version, which was halfheartedly released to tepid business. Brando's production company, Pennebaker (after his beloved mother's maiden name), which had had a great many plans, did only one or two other movies, and Marlon has never directed again.

Stella and all his other friends said that the experiences on this movie soured him forever on pictures and that the generally lackluster, increasingly less engaged (and not popular) work he did throughout most of the 1960s was the result of his gigantic disappointments with the making of *One-Eyed Jacks*. His spectacular 1972 twin comebacks on *The Godfather* and *Last Tango in Paris* were motivated by financial needs, and he acted in only three other films throughout the rest of the 1970s, two throughout the 1980s; and in the nineties, as he entered his seventies, neither quality nor interest returned, and physical, not emotional, weight took over.

So *One-Eyed Jacks* was perhaps the last time Brando acted out of a true commitment, an uncynical passion for the material, and he gives one of his very best performances as the outlaw betrayed by a friend (Karl Malden), seeking vengeance and finding love with the villain's stepdaughter. His direction is perceptive and effective—all the actors are uniformly excellent—evoking especially fine work from the newcomers, notably Piña Pellicer as the young woman who falls for him. Katy Jurado is fine as her mother; Malden, an old Brando friend and coworker (first in *Streetcar*, stage and screen), always good, is superbly ambiguous here; and Ben Johnson and Slim Pickens are wonderfully authentic. Ben told me that when Brando interviewed him for the role, he asked only one question: If

The film that seems to have broken his heart: Marlon Brando in his own production of the offbeat Western One-Eyed Jacks *(1961), the only picture the actor ever directed, and awfully well, too, but without commercial success. Old pal Karl Malden is the object of the Brando character's quite justifiable desire for revenge.*

Ben had been cast in the Jack Palance role (a killer who puts on gloves just prior to shooting someone) for George Stevens' Western, *Shane,* how would he have played it differently? Ben replied simply that if he were going to shoot somebody, he "sure as hell wouldn't wait to put on my gloves." Marlon told him he had the part.

At Stella's party in the mid-seventies, Brando was leaning over the back of his sofa, watching Cybill Shepherd as she walked away from him across the room. Her dress was not tight but it was clingy and therefore clear that she wasn't wearing any underwear. "Hey, Cybill!" Marlon called to her. She stopped, looked around, took a half-step back toward him and stopped. With a broad smile and a quick glance at me halfway across the room, he said, "Could you please come back here—and then turn around and walk away from me again?" Several people, including Cybill and me, laughed. She waved at him as if to say "silly boy," turned and continued out of the room, determinedly now weaving her hips (a little like the Lauren Bacall finish of *To Have and Have Not*). "Go on, hurt me like that," Brando said, grinning, and glanced at me mischievously again before turning back to the conversation he was having with the people on the couch. In Brando's own lingo and in how he played it, both Cybill and I understood the moment as a compliment (albeit a pretty macho one), both to Cybill and to my taste and good fortune. Which certainly was not the basic vibe either of us usually got about our relationship.

Only many years later did Cybill tell me that just before this moment, she had been sitting on the couch with Stella and Marlon and that Marlon had said, lifting a beer bottle, "If this girl"—meaning Cybill—"doesn't shut up, I'm gonna hit her on the head with this bottle." Cybill then thought, Better get out of here, got up and walked away. At which point, Marlon called out. So it was also an unspoken apology.

Over the years, his name has come up repeatedly for this or that picture project which I subsequently made or didn't make, and I always welcomed the idea, but for whatever reasons, it never worked out. In 2000, I was casting *The Cat's Meow,* one of the leading roles in which was publisher-producer William Randolph Hearst, and we were talking about the possibility of Brando's playing it, even though he was fourteen years older than Hearst was at the time the story takes place. We all agreed that he might be worth all the attendant problems that by now were legend in the business: his refusal to learn lines (they could be taped around the set, even on actors' faces, or piped into his ear via tiny speakers), his argumentativeness, his by now enormous weight and refusal to be shot below the waist. Nevertheless, we still all agreed he could be awfully interesting as Hearst; he certainly had Hearst's high voice. So we investigated through agents: Would Marlon work with Bogdanovich? Yes. Would he like to play William Randolph Hearst? No. With the quote—"please tell Peter" understood—that he didn't "want to go up against Orson Welles."

The reference, of course, was to the supposed performance of Hearst by Welles in *Citizen Kane.* The irony here was that Orson never really intended Kane to be a factual portrait, or an impersonation, of the real Hearst. In truth, the characterization is virtually nothing like Hearst was, and the actual character of Kane is a composite of a number of press lords, including a Midwestern one named Cyrus McCormick who actually did help found the Chicago Lyric Opera for his girlfriend "singer," as Kane famously does. Nevertheless, I knew what Brando meant. In the public's consciousness, he would be taking a look at a personage Welles had already on a certain level immortalized, and so he wanted no part of it.

Certainly the most influential actor of the last fifty years, Brando was the first star-personality in movies who possessed and exploited acting talent of an enormous versatility and range. Throughout his first decade in films, he challenged himself never to be the same from picture to picture, refusing to become the kind of film star the studio system had invented and thrived upon—the recognizable human commodity each new film was built around. Since his advent, actors labor most to prove their diversity and, with the final collapse of the old studio-contract days—ironically, right around the time of *One-Eyed Jacks*—the original star system has essentially disappeared, and personality-actors (like Clint Eastwood) are few and far between. The funny thing is that Brando's charismatic screen persona was vividly apparent despite the multiplicity of his guises. While today's stars are not ones easily mimicked, Brando always remained recognizable, a star-actor in spite of himself.

When Marlon died suddenly in the summer of 2004, the world was shocked, though with his enormous girth the last couple of decades it was amazing he had lived to be eighty. Nevertheless, the loss was palpable; the *New York Times* front page led national news with the story, its headline referring to Brando as "SCREEN GIANT OF ELECTRIC INTENSITY." The two photos next to this were from the films of *Streetcar* and *The Godfather*. Inside there was a full page and a half obituary with eight photographs, all but one (a small 1990 news shot) from work he had done before the end of the seventies. Other front pages ran shots from *The Wild One, Waterfront, Streetcar,* and *Godfather.* Had his death come twenty-five years earlier it felt as though the references about his professional legacy would not have been very different. (Only the tragic events of his family life—son involved in murder, daughter a suicide—would not have existed.) The reports and think pieces had the usual about "unfulfilled promise" as well as "greatest actor of his generation"; everyone agreed that in acting there was Before Brando and After Brando.

I thought of our first chance encounter exactly a half century before. *Streetcar, Wild One,* and most of *Waterfront* were all behind him even then. Over the years he repeatedly talked about how much he hated the acting profession, yet because he was a born actor, in essence wasn't he hating himself? To be so acclaimed for something you yourself hold in contempt is an unhappy place to live but that seems to have been much of Brando's life. According to Arthur Miller (see Monroe chapter), film stardom in the old Hollywood system (and Brando was at his peak in its final decade), by its very nature, placed one into "a culture of contempt." Indeed, Miller cites Brando as a good example of how someone could react, not unlike Monroe, by turning against himself.

But Marlon fired up actors, and acting, as no one ever has, and continues to, so despite his efforts to the contrary, the artist in him did prevail after all. And those brilliantly charged performances will endure both as inspiration for the art of acting, and as incisively crafted and often moving portraits of humanity.

Born Marlon Brando, Jr., April 3, 1924, Omaha, NE; died July 1, 2004, Los Angeles, CA.

Selected starring features (with director):

1950: *The Men* (Fred Zinnemann)
1951: *A Streetcar Named Desire* (Elia Kazan)
1952: *Viva Zapata!* (Kazan)
1953: *Julius Caesar* (Joseph L. Mankiewicz)
1954: *The Wild One* (Laslo Benedek); *On the Waterfront* (Kazan)
1955: *Guys and Dolls* (Mankiewicz)
1956: *The Teahouse of the August Moon* (Daniel Mann)
1957: *Sayonara* (Joshua Logan)
1958: *The Young Lions* (Edward Dmytryk)
1960: *The Fugitive Kind* (Sidney Lumet)

1961: *One-Eyed Jacks* (Marlon Brando)
1962: *Mutiny on the Bounty* (Lewis Milestone)
1963: *The Ugly American* (George Englund)
1966: *The Chase* (Penn)
1967: *A Countess from Hong Kong* (Charles Chaplin); *Reflections in a Golden Eye* (John Huston)
1969: *Burn!* (Gillo Pontecorvo)
1972: *The Godfather* (Francis Ford Coppola); *Last Tango in Paris* (Bernardo Bertolucci)
1976: *The Missouri Breaks* (Penn)
1979: *Apocalypse Now* (Coppola)
1990: *The Freshman* (Andrew Bergman)
1995: *Don Juan DeMarco* (Jeremy Levin)
2001: *The Score* (Frank Oz)

4

STELLA ADLER

Stella Adler wanted to be a movie star—so her oldest friends remember—but she acted only in three films, none of them particularly successful or really representative of the extraordinary presence and talent this amazing woman exhibited on the stage or in life. Ironically, as a teacher, how she taught acting led ultimately to the fall of the personality-star hierarchy to which she had once aspired. Her first movie and only starring vehicle, *Love on Toast* (1938), directed by E. A. Dupont, is actually quite a likeable little romantic comedy and Stella is brilliant in it. She plays the strong female lead with a knowing light touch, with the authority of a seasoned professional and the self-confidence of an established star. Of course, she had been a star on the New York stage since the late 1920s. When she and her brother Luther Adler opened on Broadway in *Success Story,* Stella used to say, in her grand mid-Atlantic accent, with very emphatic emphasis: "They said it was *genius,* darling! Genius! And *Luther* believed them." Her landmark portrait of the mother in Clifford Odets' *Awake and Sing!,* playing a broken-down Jewish New York tenement mother in her late fifties while she was still in her early thirties, is one of the fabled performances of the American theater.

Not entirely surprising, since Stella came from the famous acting family headed by Jacob Adler, who early in the twentieth century had established, and was the star of, Manhattan's first (and extremely popular) Yiddish Theater, downtown on Second Avenue. Stella had been in front of audiences since she was two, so to say that the theater was in her blood would be a considerable understatement—the theater *was* her blood. And she gave it everything she had, in several capacities, essentially altering in the process the way that America, and therefore the world, thought about actors and acting, in the theater and in pictures. As a teacher of acting from the late 1940s into the early 1990s, she left behind her a virtual wake

*At the peak of their Group Theatre glory, Stella Adler with her brother
Luther Adler (right) and playwright Clifford Odets in London on June 13,
1938. As is evident, Stella was the epitome of theatricality, believing that
you must be bigger than life in art, and she certainly was in life, too.*

of fine actors, and profoundly influential ones, from Marlon Brando to
Warren Beatty to Robert De Niro.

What is rarely mentioned is that Stella's difficulty in achieving movie-
stardom had a lot to do with the unspoken anti-Semitic attitude of the
country at that time. Stella's looks and name were considered "too Jewish." She reluctantly—and always a bit shamefacedly—allowed her billing
in *Love on Toast* to be "Stella Ardler." When Luther Adler, a superb,
underappreciated actor himself, was told that the Jewish studio heads
wanted to change her name, he suggested they just call her "Beverly
Wilshire" (a reference to the famous L.A. hotel), and added, "then they
can call *me* Bullocks Wilshire" (a then-popular department store).

In Brando's 1994 autobiography, *Songs My Mother Taught Me*, this
most famous of Stella's students wrote:

> Stella . . . left an astounding legacy. Virtually all acting in motion
> pictures today stems from her, and she had an extraordinary effect

on the culture of her time. I don't think audiences realize how much we are in debt to her.

The techniques she brought back to this country [from Stanislavski], and taught others, changed acting enormously. First she passed them on to the other members of the Group Theatre [of the 1930s], and then to actors like me who became her students. We plied our trade according to the manner and style she taught us; and since American movies dominate the world market, Stella's teachings have influenced actors throughout the world.

Stella always said no one could teach acting, but *she* could. . . . She could tell you not only *when* you were wrong, but *why*. . . . If I hit a sour note in a scene, she knew it immediately and said, "No, wait, wait, wait . . . that's wrong!" and then dug into her large reserve of intuitive intelligence to explain why my character would behave in a certain way based on the author's vision. Her instincts were unerring and extraordinary. . . . Because of Stella, acting changed completely during the '50s and '60s . . .

Although the Stanislavski "method" came to be associated with the Actors Studio, Lee Strasberg, Elia Kazan, and Brando, Stella Adler was the only American who actually ever worked and studied with the great Russian director himself. She spent considerable time in Paris with him and came back with voluminous notes. She shared these first with the Group Theatre—of which Strasberg, Kazan and director-teacher Robert Lewis were a part—and eventually with all her students through the years. Bobby Lewis wrote a best-selling actors' handbook, *Method—or Madness*, virtually all of it based on Stella Adler's notes.

Besides teaching choreographers such as Alvin Ailey and Jerome Robbins, actor-directors like Warren Beatty, Sydney Pollock, and me, and popular singers like Janis Ian and Diana Ross, Stella was most noted for having taught such other celebrated actors as James Coburn, Kevin Costner, Benicio Del Toro, Teri Garr, Harvey Keitel, Cloris Leachman, Karl Malden, Bette Midler, Matthew Modine, Anthony Quinn, John Ritter, Martin Sheen, Elaine Stritch, Leslie Uggams, Henry Winkler, Shelley Winters, and many more. The influence she had on stage and screen will endure as long as the art.

I entered this astonishing, inspiring and beautiful woman's studio when I was sixteen (having lied by two years to get in) and she became, over the next thirty-seven years until her death in 1992, my second mother, outliving my own mother by more than a decade. Though she never directed a movie, and directed only once or twice for the stage, Stella taught acting in such an inclusive way that she also was teaching directing. Not only because it's difficult to be a good director if you don't know or share in the actors' problems, but also because Stella taught a theater of "heightened reality"—seemingly *against* the very naturalism that movie acting generally encourages—but in keeping with the mythic proportions natural to the stage, to the theatrical-film medium, to the highest kind of artistic expression. Stella's truth insisted on dealing with something much more sizeable and weighty than a mere naturalistic representation of events; just as the greatest achievements of the stage and screen ultimately have been larger than life in their depiction of human archetypes.

Stella was one of the two most brilliant actors' directors I ever worked with, Orson Welles being the other. I only had the privilege with Stella for a short time on her striking, profoundly moving off-Broadway production of the Kurt Weill–Paul Green pacifist World War I musical drama, *Johnny Johnson*. The Group Theatre had premiered the play in the late thirties and Stella's off-Broadway revival in the mid-fifties was its first time back in New York. Stella was an extraordinarily specific director with the artistic eye of a hawk, and a vivid imagination. She rehearsed for months—as Stanislavski did—and since most of the cast were her students, no one thought of complaining or asking for money. She was so inspiring, brought such size, depth and resonance to everything. Sadly, she had to let me go while we were still in rehearsal. They had found out my real age and I was "too young" (as Stella put it) for them to afford me under Actors Equity rules and state laws about minors.

She fiddled with my bow tie as she broke the bad news to me one afternoon. "You're too young, darling," she said, sympathetically. And that's about all she said, however, forgetting, in her absentminded way, to explain that my age was a problem because of money and child-labor laws, not because I was too immature to play the role. (For an awfully long time, I didn't realize what she had meant, and it certainly did trouble me.) Although it was not a popular success, I saw two performances featuring a huge cast led by Matthew Broderick's talented father, James Broderick (who died young)—and it remains high among the most powerful theater experiences of my life.

There was another time, in class, that she said I was "too young," but this time she explained what she meant with one of the most brilliant acting images I've heard. Having seen the extraordinary Jason Robards, Jr.'s performance in the lead role of Eugene O'Neill's *The Iceman Cometh*—as it was revived very successfully by José Quintero in the fifties—I was so inspired by Robards' work that I memorized his character Hickey's famous final monologue, which ran for something like ten minutes, and performed it in Stella's class. I was seventeen. Afterward, she stood up, joined in the applause and then said to me, "Very good, darling, but you're too young for the part." She hesitated a beat, pursing her lips reflectively, and then went on, "You see, darling, when you walk down the street, you walk out near the curb . . ."—she paused a bit—"but this character does not. He walks close to the buildings." How many times over the years since have I noted where on the sidewalk I (or others) would unconsciously walk, as an indication of one's spiritual health. On other occasions, regarding age, she would say, "Never play your *own* age, darling. Either play younger than you are or older than you are. Playing your own age is *boring*!"

Age also was relative in the Adler family. Arthur Miller once told me that he had been at Stella's fiftieth birthday party and that her mother was there, too. Someone asked the elder Mrs. Adler her age and she said she was sixty-two. But, the person protested, how could that be—Stella being fifty? To which the mother replied, "That's *her* problem."

For four years I never missed a class Stella taught. And she was teaching *all* her famous ones then: the scene-breakdown class (where she would brilliantly analyze the text and style of the playwright, from Shakespeare, Wilde, Shaw and Ibsen, to Odets, Miller, Williams and Inge); the characterization class (in which she would work on the inner and outer features of a personality as revealed in the text); the crucial basics (sense-memory, handling invisible props, really looking at things and people, really listening).

Her very presence and intensity of focus were like pure oxygen, and equally intoxicating. You never knew what she was going to say. She would watch a scene, for example, with such palpable attention that she often got deeply into the emotions of the given material. You could see her over in the corner by stage right silently acting out all the parts, grasping her breast in agony, stifling a sob. She would shake her head or nod, or lean forward, or freeze except to purse her lips repeatedly, completely lost in the moment. One time a student was doing a really bad job on Hamlet's soliloquy ("To be or not to be"), but you couldn't tell from Stella's expression. We all felt he was murdering it, yet Stella just leaned farther forward, pursing her lips, occasionally shaking her head in sympathy, enthralled throughout. When he finished—as poorly as he had begun—Stella didn't speak for a long time. She sat, nodding quietly, thinking. Nobody moved. Finally, she shook her head and stood, saying, "Well . . ." and, looking beatific, said, "it's a great play!"

Stella's way of teaching was in direct contrast to Lee Strasberg's (in his book Brando heavily denigrates the Strasberg manner), which searched out "stage reality" from an actor's memory—especially memories that just by the touching of which could create the necessary emotions. For those actors who turned to this technique exclusively (which Stanislavski had in no way favored), Strasberg became a beacon. For others—although he was considered a brilliant analyst of what went on in scene-study classes (often dazzling guest playwrights and directors; see Marilyn Monroe chapter)—he wasn't really a very good teacher. Brando said he found unbearable Strasberg's focus on the actor's own underlying personality.

Adler insisted, rather, that an actor use imagination, concentrating on the specific character's situation and circumstances. As she saw it, much of the role was dictated by the text itself and the particular style of the playwright, rather than by the actor's personal emotional history. She would say, "You don't act with the same *style* in a play by Shakespeare as you do in a play by Oscar Wilde, or as you do in Tennessee Williams." She would say that "acting is 50 percent interior and 50 percent exterior." The two-time Tony winner Donna Murphy recently described the process she learned from Stella as the actor's becoming "a kind of sponge for humanity." Adler taught that clothes, accent, personal props, walk, stance, all of this, was certainly as important as the inner workings of emotion.

She believed in personal conviction: if the actor believed, the audience would. On stage once, she would relate, she had to open a drawer, take out a pistol and shoot someone, but this night the drawer was empty so she just reached in anyway, came out with her hand shaped like a gun, said "Bang!" very loudly, the other actor reacted and, she concluded triumphantly, "No one in the entire audience noticed!" She encouraged work on different accents and on taking characteristics from animals. I remember a hilarious impression she did of an addled kitten having been played with by a rambunctious child, or an amazingly accurate and funny take on English intellectuals—all brains and no grace. Certainly she believed in the ability of art to transform people and society by revealing essential human and poetic truths. The actor had to find this in himself, in his work. "Of course," she would say, as though it were self-evident, "you have to play *yourself*, darling. Who else can you play? But you have to find the character in yourself—we are all many people."

With Stella, it was never about fame or success. Though she wasn't the village-garret type of art-for-art's-sake revolutionary, she believed in artistic integrity and felt that in America, because it was such a young country, the tradition of culture and artistic morality was not very finely developed. "It takes more than two hundred years to become an American," was her roundabout way of saying that two hundred years was an awfully short time in the vast sweep of history and art that preceded America's formation, and that among the things not yet gained is a respect for tradition and a truly civilized culture. One of the plays she taught was Clifford Odets' *Golden Boy*—she and Odets, of course, were old friends and coworkers from the days of the Group. She broke the play down in riveting detail as the essential struggle between financial and artistic success, between brute force and poetic expression, between naturalism and spirituality. One afternoon, as Stella was discussing this drama, I was sitting on top of an old wardrobe trunk over at the left in her studio. I was seventeen, maybe eighteen by now. Suddenly, Stella pointed directly at me and said, loudly, "There he is! *There's* the Golden Boy!" Everyone looked at me. She added nothing more about me or why she had said that but went right on to connect Odets' play to the Faust legend.

I just sat there, trying to figure out what the hell she meant and wondering why I had been singled out. It took me several years to put it all together, and by then I'd already fallen prey, at least in part, to the dangers she warned against. Stella's lifelong injunctions to me of integrity—practically every time I saw or spoke with her—kept bringing me back to the right path more often than not. She would always refer to my parents as artists—she had been to their apartment for a dinner party or two; seen my father's paintings, my mother's gold-leaf frames. As she did with her own father—also a European artist transplanted to the United States—Stella held up my parents as examples of high quality and artistic purity.

Not that she had any aversion to money or luxury. She used to joke on the square: "I don't know what's the matter with young actresses these days—they're only interested in Chekhov. When I was starting out, actresses were only interested in *diamonds!*" Having acquired (for a while) a mansion in Bel Air and a vintage Silver Cloud Rolls-Royce, I found that Stella loved both. Taking a ride in the Rolls one time she said, "Darling, this is definitely the way an artist should live!" Certainly, as long as I knew Stella, she always lived in a grand fashion, with a large Fifth Avenue apartment, and comfortable rented houses in Los Angeles. She always dressed like a star of the theater.

Yet she never compromised for material success. In fact, she quit acting

Stella Adler (center) played twenty-five years older than she was in her most famous role, as the aging mother in Clifford Odets' acclaimed thirties drama, Awake and Sing!, *produced on Broadway by the Group Theatre in 1935, directed by Harold Clurman. Soon to be a movie star, Jules (later John) Garfield (standing) played her son. Others in the cast included brother Luther Adler (not pictured), Phoebe Brand (far right), and Art Smith (center).*

because she couldn't bear the competitive pressures of stardom and commercialization. All this was summed up in the way she responded to me when I asked her once why she had stopped performing. She shook her head slowly, looking very sad. "I couldn't anymore, darling." She shook her head again, as if to say the pain was too much, and repeated, "I couldn't anymore."

But she could teach, and she acted constantly in class—with such intuitive brilliance, with a technique so well tuned, it was beyond second nature. I believe she could transform herself into any character, any animal, any style, any period. She was kinder, generally speaking, to men than to women, but she could be brutal with either sex. In the mid-fifties, to one young actor who was playing a scene with all the mannerisms Brando had brought to his role in *A Streetcar Named Desire,* she shouted in the midst of the performance: "Stop it! Marlon isn't like that!" She asked another student and me to improvise two people in the woods, and after I said one line—something like "Should I get some firewood?"—she cried out, "Stop it! Don't write a bad play!" She could be equally brief and succinct if she liked what you had done. One exercise was to take a pop song or folk song and act out the lyrics rather than sing them. I chose, as purposely far from my own upbringing, a song Harry Belafonte had recently recorded called "I'm Just a Country Boy." When I finished, Stella only said, quietly, "Bravo, darling."

There were so many things Stella said that one carried forever, because you kept realizing at various ages how true they were, deepening as the years passed: A young actor, reacting to a criticism of Stella's, said, "But I *felt* it." Stella responded quickly and sharply: "It doesn't matter what *you* feel, darling, it's what the *audience* feels." Another time, another young actor said he didn't feel comfortable with some movement Stella had asked for. "The stage is no place to be *comfortable*. You're on a *platform*, darling, remember that."

She reacted similarly when I directed for the first time. I had rehearsed five of Stella's students in a long scene from Odets' *The Big Knife* (see Introduction). In her classes, normally scenes were never directed, and almost exclusively featured only two actors at a time. When ours was finished, Stella stood as though triumphant, and led the sizeable applause, then said: "But you've been *directed*! Who directed you!?" The actors, still on stage, all pointed toward the back of the studio where I was leaning against a wall and a couple said, "Peter." Stella looked proudly at me and said only three words: "Brilliant, darling! Bravo!" My first review as a director and still my favorite. This encouragement led straight to my directing (and co-producing) Odets' play off-Broadway as my first theater production, in November 1959. Stella came to see it and stayed seated in the middle of the theater until everyone had gone. She had been wiping her eyes, embraced me with seriousness and said of my humanist interpretation, "It's a bold and daring statement." My second favorite review.

The funny thing was that she sometimes watched movies or plays as though they were being presented in her scene class. When Brando's film *The Young Lions* was about to open, I was by then on the studios' screening lists for critics and tastemakers, and therefore invited to a special advance running at 20th Century–Fox's 57th Street projection room. Knowing Stella's fondness for Brando, I asked if she'd like to come with me. She said yes, and the two of us arrived when most of the other 250 guests were already seated. Brando's German officer doesn't appear in the movie for quite a while, during which time Dean Martin and Montgomery Clift as American soldiers are lengthily introduced. Stella tilted her head to me slightly: "Who's that?" I told her it was Dean Martin. A little later: "Who's that?" Montgomery Clift. The movie cross-cuts between these two for a while. "Who's that?" Dean Martin. "He's quite good," she said, and then, after a while, "Who's that?" Montgomery Clift. She shook her head. "He wasn't good there." All of this was fairly *sotto voce.* Finally, when Brando appeared in his Nazi uniform, blond hair and German accent, Stella gave no reaction for about two minutes and then, suddenly, in full voice she said, "My God, it's *Marlon!*" I would like to have sunk under my seat from then on because she was so absorbed by Brando that to her nobody else was there. "My God," she continued after a moment, still full voice, "he's so *German!*"

I could hear the man behind me whisper to his wife, "It's Stella Adler." Her comments only quieted slightly and continued throughout. I figured I would never be invited by Fox to a screening again but no one really seemed to mind. Stella was so thoroughly engrossed in the intricacies of the actual performances that she didn't really follow the plot and asked me a number of times what was happening. Toward the end, after Brando's character undergoes a kind of life-altering experience, she said, pretty loudly, "Something must have happened—that's the first time Marlon has walked like himself." But she knew exactly what was going on in the sequence during which the Americans are seen liberating a Nazi concentration camp. Stella just said, slowly, with a kind of angry sadness, "That is what they saw." And, after a moment or two, nodding her head, she repeated with finality, "That is what they saw."

The only other films I ever looked at in Stella's presence were a few of my own. Toward the end of *The Last Picture Show,* I remember seeing her put her hands over her eyes at a climactic moment, and after *Nickelodeon,* she sent me the loveliest note of congratulations (far more than the movie deserved). Following a screening of my film of Michael Frayn's theatrical farce, *Noises Off,* which had made her cry with laughter, I came over to her. She looked at me, still wiping her eyes, and demanded loudly, "Who directed that?" I said, "I did." She said, loudly, "You didn't!" I repeated, smiling, that I really did. She said again, louder, "You *didn't!*" Then she stood and embraced me, and said nothing else.

At the party I threw for her ninetieth birthday—the last one at my Bel Air residence—she arrived after most of the 200-plus guests (all handpicked by her). I ran out to the parking area and walked her in. She was a touch shaky but OK. As she entered the foyer, there were many of her friends clustered around anxiously—a lot of those in front were women—

and everyone applauded. Stella looked about in dismay and demanded, loudly, "Where are the MEN!?"

Over the years, I saw Stella with three of the men in her life, though never with stage director–author Harold Clurman—from all reports, the most explosive of her relationships—about whom I heard her tell a few anecdotes. The one I recall most vividly had to do with Clurman's cheating on her and, in retaliation, Stella's stepping onto a table at a party and demanding that the men she had slept with encircle her. "You see, Harold," she supposedly announced, "you have your girls—but I have my *men!*" (At my last party for her, Anthony Quinn told me with amusement that Stella had asked him quietly that night if the two of them had "ever done it." I believe he told her they had, though he left it ambiguous whether this was the truth.)

She had a longish affair with New York art dealer and poet Stanley Moss, a very tall and attractive man, perhaps twenty years her junior. I don't remember many details of the times I saw Stella with Stanley—they came at least twice to my parents' apartment on 90th Street and Riverside Drive in the mid-fifties—and I was over at Stella's apartment on Fifth Avenue a couple of times while she and Stanley were an item. But my impression was that Stella wasn't especially challenged intellectually by, or really terribly interested in, Stanley, who seemed almost like a trophy date—young, handsome, bright, and wealthy enough. On the other hand, I was pretty callow in those days, and could have misread things.

However, there was no mistaking her feelings about Mitchell Wilson, the scientist and novelist who combined his twin passions in the very successful novel *Meeting at a Far Meridian,* among others. Cybill Shepherd and I double-dated with Stella and Mitch in the seventies in Manhattan before and after they were married. Stella said to Cybill the first time she and Mitch met her (Cybill was about twenty-three at the time): "You're not really beautiful, are you?!" Cybill just kept smiling as Stella went right on with, for her, the triumphant ultimate compliment: "You *act* beautiful!"

We always had a great time: Mitch absolutely adored Stella and she was crazy about him, though she would occasionally give him a hard time. He was patience itself, to such a degree that it transcended patience and became an inherent saintliness, which Mitch possessed in spades. Such erudition (which he also had in abundance) combined with such a lack of either pomposity or academicism is rare in itself; then add self-effacing humor and ready wit, and a genuine interest in others, and you have an idea of what a special fellow Mitch Wilson was. His sudden death from a heart attack almost killed Stella, too. She was shattered by the event. I don't believe she left her apartment for nearly two years.

About fourteen months after Mitch died, I got permission to see Stella and went up to the apartment. She was in bed and looked dreadful. Exhausted, haunted, grief-stricken. When I left, I doubted that I would ever see her again. I thought she really wanted to die, and would probably succeed. It seemed to me that Mitch Wilson's early passing broke Stella's heart because she realized he had been the love of her life. Both regretted how little of their lives they had had together. Often, over the many years after Mitch's death, Stella would refer to him in loving ways. When I would mention Robert Graves—who by the early eighties had become my favorite writer—she would invariably say that Graves had been Mitch's favorite writer, giving the impression that Mitch's endorsement was the one she valued above all others. Stella remained close to Wilson's children, and it was at Stella's Los Angeles house one year in the early nineties that I met editor-writer Victoria Wilson, who became my treasured editor at Knopf. Vicky shepherded my *Who the Devil Made It* (companion to the present volume) into a success.

After Mitch, Stella seemed to lose interest in men and I saw her in only one brief dalliance years later with a California university professor about three or four decades her junior. I think he was entirely bewildered by her, and she chewed him up and spit him out in about three and a half minutes. And that was that.

In her later years, Stella spent more and more time in Los Angeles, though she didn't really like it there. But it was easier: the weather generally was mild, and walking was far less necessary. This became of particular importance after Stella fell in her early eighties and broke her hip. The doctors who operated and installed a replacement did not do a good job and she never mended right, which made walking increasingly difficult for her—the only real impediment Stella had physically as she aged. It angered and frustrated her and made her sad. When I tried to console her once by pointing out all the positives in her situation, she would have none of it. But she couldn't *walk,* she responded in essence, and so her freedom of movement was profoundly compromised. For the first time she became dependent on other people and she did not like any of this at all. There was the invariable jockeying for position around the circle of people who took care of running her life and schools (on both coasts), and she was, by turns, aware of it, irritated and bored by it, or knowingly in denial. (Luckily, her beloved daughter Ellen Adler and Ellen's son Tom Oppenheim have kept the New York school going since her death; Irene

Gilbert has supervised the L.A. school.) She had a lot of friends in Los Angeles but found the place culturally stagnating. One time, while I was still living there, I complained of being depressed and Stella said, "Darling, if you drive and drive and everywhere you look it's *ugly*, darling—of course that is very depressing."

In the eighties and early nineties, I had a number of severe setbacks in my life and career, but Stella was always there for me. She kidded about it once: "Peter, darling, your life is very difficult on your friends!" I remembered a significant anecdote she told about her being sick one time while married to Harold Clurman. Over a period of three or four days he went from being deeply concerned and solicitous to being utterly irritated with the whole matter. Stella concluded: "You can only be ill for a short while, darling, before people get bored with you!"

So she didn't really complain about her inability to walk properly, though it irked and infuriated her. I phoned a few of her old students and suggested that a call from them would certainly cheer up Stella. She was lonely. Harvey Keitel said he would call; Bobby De Niro said he wouldn't. He was annoyed at Stella, said she never knew who he was. Stella did tell people in class she never knew who De Niro was because every time he did a performance he immersed himself so completely and successfully in the role that he became unrecognizable. Therefore, she never recognized De Niro. Instead of realizing that this from Stella was a compliment, Bobby was insulted, which seemed to bother Stella. Warren Beatty was quietly livid with Stella after she attacked him in front of his new wife, Annette Bening. It was at someone's Hollywood party, to which Warren—who had been a student of Stella's just before me in the fifties—had brought Annette specifically to meet his old teacher. Stella had decided to castigate Warren on the *Golden Boy* issue, about the loss of integrity. According to others who were there, Stella delivered an unnecessarily brutal tongue-lashing in fairly loud tones. At one point, when Annette tried to say something, Stella supposedly snapped at her to "Shut up!" Within ten minutes of delivering this speech, however, Stella was apparently laughing with Warren again and talking animatedly about other things.

Warren eventually forgave Stella. When telling me about the incident, however, he was clearly upset and trying to pretend that he wasn't; he minimized his time spent as her student. I remembered meeting him for the first time at Stella's around 1958, after he had come into her studio one afternoon, embraced her in a bear hug, and chatted briefly. I felt jealous of his apparently earned intimacy with Stella. Another time, in Los Angeles years later, Warren came into one of Stella's classes with his then current

Stella Adler (billed as Ardler) in her single Paramount vehicle, Love on
Toast *(1938), a screwball comedy directed by E. A. Dupont, and co-
starring John Payne; she is brilliant in it.*

amour, the Russian ballerina Maya Plisetskaya. Again, much embracing
and a brief chat. Afterward, Stella told me Warren and Maya's relationship
was perfect: "He speaks no Russian, and she speaks no English—of
course, they get along wonderfully."

Toward the end of her life, Stella received some acclaim for her
achievements. There was a TV special on the Group Theatre which featured her prominently, her first book on acting was published (though she
had only approved it, rather than writing and constructing it), and the
prestigious PBS series *American Masters* devoted one of their programs,
entitled "Awake and Dream," to Stella and her legacy. There were articles
in the *Times,* both New York and Los Angeles. She herself seemed most
impressed by the couple of honorary university doctorates she was given.

The last time I saw Stella was one late summer afternoon in 1992 at her
Los Angeles house. She was worried about me because my financial situation was terrible—I had declared bankruptcy, things hadn't yet started
improving at all—and my personal life wasn't in good shape, either. She

offered to loan me some money. Though I felt badly, I took her up on it. Naively, while opening her checkbook, she asked how much I needed to pull myself out of the mess I was in. I told her honestly it would take about half a million. Well, she didn't have that kind of money, she said without blinking, but she would do what she could. I said that anything was a big help and she wrote out a check for five hundred dollars. This was terrific, I said, and would be paid back as soon as possible. She told me not to worry about it, that she knew I was good for it eventually, that I should stay in touch, that she loved me. As usual, I kissed her on both cheeks when I said so long. We spoke on the phone a few times—I called not too long afterward to tell her I'd gotten a studio directing job, would now, therefore, be OK, and sent back with many thanks the five hundred she had loaned—but I never saw Stella again. The film I did took me out of town to Nashville for a while and we came back to Los Angeles shortly before Christmas. I was going to call Stella and see her during the holidays. She died peacefully in her sleep on December 21st.

A little girl who once saw Stella's grand entrance at a Manhattan cocktail party—and Stella Adler had such size in life as we shall never see again—turned to her mother and asked, "Mommy, is that God?" To so many of us who knew and worked with her, of course, she was.

Born Stella Adler, February 10, 1901, New York, NY; died December 21, 1992, Los Angeles, CA.

Features (with director):

1938: *Love on Toast* (E. A. Dupont)
1941: *Shadow of the Thin Man* (W. S. Van Dyke II)
1948: *My Girl Tisa* (Elliott Nugent)

5

MONTGOMERY CLIFT

A Rolls Silver Cloud pulled up in front of the New Yorker movie theater one afternoon around four, and a tall, stately woman got out, followed by a thin, frail man whom I immediately recognized as Montgomery Clift. As though in somewhat of a trance, the two of them—the lady, we found out later, was Mrs. Walter Huston—made their way into the theater, where we were running a couple of Hitchcock pictures. One of them was *I Confess* (1953), starring Clift, and I guess that was the reason they had come all the way up to 89th Street and Broadway that gray spring day in 1961.

I had been working there for about a year, having started shortly after Dan Talbot acquired the theater, renamed it and changed its policy. Under Talbot's management, it became the first theater in New York City—and among the first anywhere in the States—regularly to revive good American movies. I was then just twenty-one, having directed one play, and what I didn't know, as Clift and Mrs. Huston went in to see *I Confess,* was that Monty Clift was near the end of the line.

Clift had been a kind of unacknowledged leader. His performances in Hawks' *Red River* (his first movie, though Zinnemann's *The Search* was released earlier), in Wyler's *The Heiress,* in Stevens' *A Place in the Sun,* heralded a new acting style. It came to be known, inaccurately, as the Method. After Clift came Brando, and after Brando, James Dean. Clift was the purest, the least mannered of these actors, perhaps the most sensitive, certainly the most poetic. He was also remarkably beautiful. Over eight years he acted in eight films, became a teenage heartthrob as well as a popular star with older audiences. He was nominated for Best Actor Oscars three times in six years and should have won each time. He gave at least four performances—in *Red River,* in *A Place in the Sun,* in *I Confess* and in Zinnemann's *From Here to Eternity*—that remain among the finest

Montgomery Clift as Pvt. Robert E. Lee Prewitt listens while AWOL in Pearl Island to radio reports of the bombing in Fred Zinnemann's film, based on the superb James Jones novel, From Here to Eternity *(1953). Clift received his third Oscar nomination as Best Actor (he lost to William Holden in another WWII story,* Stalag 17*).*

anyone has given in the movies. Hawks would tell me: "He *worked*—he really worked hard."

In the middle of shooting his ninth picture (*Raintree County*), he was driving home one night from a party at Elizabeth Taylor's house in the Hollywood Hills when his car went out of control on one of those narrow, absurdly winding roads and crashed. His face was shattered by the windshield. Plastic surgery did what it could, but those heartbreaking eyes now looked out from behind a mask that could only approximate what his actual visage had been. He finished the movie he'd begun (it is a chilling experience to see both faces in the same picture) and made another eight films, never once giving a performance without the same riveting intensity, the same soulful integrity, but the mystery had been tampered with and the magical perfection of pitch was gone.

Here it was about eight years after Clift had acted in it, and *I Confess*

John Wayne as Tom Dunston and Montgomery Clift as Matthew Garth
in the finale of Howard Hawks' classic Western Red River *(1948),*
the first movie Clift acted in. Hawks would say that Monty worked
diligently on all aspects of the role, including the learning of a little
hop into the stirrup on mounting. This performance was actually
the first in pictures of what came to be called "Method acting,"
later popularized by Brando, and then James Dean.

was on the screen; I was standing at the back of the theater watching. About halfway through, I saw Clift come up the aisle, slumped over, weaving a little. At the back, he lit a cigarette and turned to look at the screen again. I came up and said I worked there. He was polite. I said I liked the picture and asked if he did.

The huge image on the screen at that moment of his pre-accident beauty must have seemed to mock him. He turned away and looked at me sadly. "It's . . . hard, you know." He said it slowly, hesitantly, a little slurred. "It's very . . . hard," he said. I nodded. He looked back at the screen.

A few steps away was a "request book" Talbot had set up for his patrons. It was a large lined ledger in which audiences were encouraged (by sign and trailer) to write down what movies they would like to see. I told Clift about the book and said I wanted to show him something. He

Clift with Elizabeth Taylor in George Stevens' memorable drama A Place in the Sun *(1951), adapted from the Theodore Dreiser novel* An American Tragedy. *Clift received his second Oscar nomination as Best Actor.*

followed me over, puffing his cigarette absently. I leafed through the book quickly and found the page on which I had noticed a couple of days before that someone had scrawled in large red letters: "ANYTHING WITH MONTGOMERY CLIFT!"

The actor stared down at the page for several moments. "That's very . . . nice," he said, and continued to look down. "That's . . . very nice," he said again, and I realized he was crying. He put his arm around me unsteadily and thanked me for showing it to him. Then he turned and walked back down the aisle to his seat.

When the picture was over, he and Mrs. Huston came out of the theater. I was standing outside. He waved to me gently and they got back in the Rolls-Royce and it was driven away. He made only two films more before he died five years later at the age of forty-six—a lost poet from Omaha, Nebraska, the most romantic and touching actor of his generation.

Born Edward Montgomery Clift, October 17, 1920, Omaha, NE; died July 23, 1966, New York, NY.

Selected feature films (with director):

1948: *The Search* (Fred Zinnemann); *Red River* (Howard Hawks)
1949: *The Heiress* (William Wyler)
1951: *A Place in the Sun* (George Stevens)
1953: *I Confess* (Alfred Hitchcock); *From Here to Eternity* (Zinnemann); *Stazione Termini/Indiscretion of an American Wife* (Vittorio De Sica)
1958: *The Young Lions* (Edward Dmytryk)
1959: *Suddenly, Last Summer* (Joseph L. Mankiewicz)
1960: *Wild River* (Elia Kazan)
1961: *The Misfits* (John Huston); *Judgment at Nuremberg* (Stanley Kramer)

6

CARY GRANT

"President *Kennedy* called me once from the White House for *precisely* that reason!" Cary Grant was answering a question of mine, grinning broadly, buoyant as a kid. We were in his Beverly Hills living room toward the end of January 1985, soon after he had turned eighty-one; though in no way looking much over sixty-five, he had only another year and a half to live. "My secretary told me the *President* was on the *line*," Grant went on, cheerily, "so naturally I was curious why he was *calling* and picked it right up—said, 'Hel-lo!' The President said he was *sorry* to bother me—I said not at *all*—and he told me that his brother, the Attorney General, was on the line with us, *too*. So I said 'Hel-lo' to the Attorney General as well, and then I asked what I could *do* for them. 'Well,' the President said, 'Bobby and I were just sitting here in the Oval Office talking, and we both decided that we wanted very much to hear Cary Grant's *voice*—we wanted to *hear you speak*!' "

Personally, over the twenty-five years I was fortunate enough to know this even then legendary star, I would phone him often on some pretext or other, sometimes with only the same motivation as the two Kennedys in the Oval Office. Not just his voice and Bristol-born English accent, but also his unique way of speaking, had an enormously invigorating effect—made you excited and happy—which generally was how he always sounded. I rarely heard him down, rarely negative.

He was quick, too, and extraordinarily self-aware. I remember the night of March 31, 1973, at the Beverly Hilton Hotel, when another President, Richard Nixon, was about to bestow the Medal of Freedom for the first time on a U.S. film artist, John Ford, during the American Film Institute's first Life Achievement dinner—and Grant, Cybill Shepherd and I were standing on line at the ticket tables. Cary had come stag that evening—a nasty divorce from his fourth wife, actress Dyan Cannon, had

Cary Grant, moving like a cat, as he escapes from the hospital in Hitchcock's greatest innocent-man-on-the-run chase picture, North by Northwest *(1959), among the most purely entertaining movies of all time. Hitchcock would say, "It's a complete fantasy."*

finally quieted down—and so he appropriated my date, at least for the pleasant walk we had all just taken from a large hotel conference room, where a group of about two hundred luminaries shook hands with the President.

Cybill and I had arrived on that long receiving line coincidentally right after Grant, and I had introduced her to him. "Hel-lo, you beautiful girl!"

he had said as only he could, and from that moment I lost her—for the next twenty minutes or so while we waited, and they talked to each other animatedly, mostly Cary being his most charming. Which was beyond words, because of the amazing sparkle of joy mixed with mischievousness he had in his manner, in his catlike movements, in his tears-of-mirth-filled eyes.

We had shaken hands with the President, not all of us gladly—it was in the late stages of Vietnam and the early stages of Watergate—though none of the people in the room that night talked politics. There seemed to be a tacit understanding that it was Jack Ford's night, period. So there was a general air of congeniality, and no one was more congenial than Cary Grant. He looked great, as always, ever young—though now almost fully gray and wearing dark-framed glasses—too dark and too narrow, I thought, but it didn't matter. Hadn't he worn much thicker lenses and less flattering frames in *Bringing Up Baby* and in *Monkey Business*? It was impossible for him to look bad, because he always had those darkly intriguing eyes, and especially that laugh, both intoxicating and infectious—with something remarkably naked about its joyful pleasure—more than he had ever revealed in movies.

We'd been laughing by the ticket tables where three middle-aged women sat to collect the invitations or tickets—and as Cary stepped up for his turn, he smiled while saying, in that inimitable (though much imitated) way, "I am *terribly* sorry, I forgot my *tick-et*—may I get in, please?" One of the ladies, still looking down, said, "Name." Grant leaned slightly closer, bending more—he was a couple of inches over six feet tall, though he always slumped his shoulders a bit: "Ca-ry *Grant*," he said. Now the woman looked up, frowned just a touch as she appraised him and said: "You don't look like Cary Grant." To which he replied, quick as a wink, leaning closer still and shrugging his shoulders, "I know—nobody *does*." Both Cybill and I burst out laughing and Cary turned to us briefly as he stood straight and then looked back sympathetically at the lady.

Of course, he knew what she meant; he had had the same problem throughout his life—ever since he had adopted that name, Cary Grant, in exchange for his own, which was Archibald Alexander Leach. He once said even *he* wished he "could be Cary Grant," by which he meant that there was no way on earth anyone could possibly embody all that his screen roles and screen persona exemplified or promised. (I would make that mistake with him a couple of years before he died, almost ruining our friendship.) Of course, he knew better than anybody how much of his image was created for him, or through him, by others. Directors, writers, photographers, co-stars, were all somewhat responsible—in lesser and greater ways—for what Cary Grant came to mean and be.

He conveyed his awareness of this to me in several ways, most memorably perhaps that time I pressed him about the reason why he would never tell me when one of his staged interviews, *An Evening with Cary Grant,* would be scheduled so that I could go to see him telling anecdotes to a large audience and answering questions about his career. He had been about to do one of those in Iowa in late 1986 when he died suddenly of a stroke. For a few years I had been after him to invite me; he always said he would but never did. Finally, I mentioned it with light exasperation and he respected me enough to finally tell the truth: "Well, the thing is, I don't really want you *there*! Because I would be telling some story about making a pic-ture and it would be *difficult* for me with you sitting there knowing the *truth* of what *really happened*! I just don't want you *there*!"

How many actors with such a distinctive voice and manner are there for a President to call today? After Clint Eastwood, Jerry Lewis, Barbra Streisand, Jack Nicholson or Marlon Brando, who's left? Back in the original studio system (c. 1912–1962), Cary Grant was made to order to be a movie star: tall, devastatingly handsome, and he talked funny, with some kind of English accent you couldn't ever quite place. His unmistakable voice and large, expressive dark eyes ("It's all in the eyes," Orson Welles used to say), were born to be recorded and photographed. Then a lot of very talented, creative, brilliant, clever people went to work with, and on, Cary Grant. A handful of superb picturemakers—among them Leo McCarey, Howard Hawks, Alfred Hitchcock, George Cukor—and a great many writers, had an enormous impact on this persona that came to be world famous as Cary Grant. As an actor, which was all his own, he had the remarkable ability to incarnate entirely what numerous different viewpoints asked for, to become a virtually seamless, ideal romantic, comic, and dramatic leading man of amazing versatility. A career like Cary's, from start to finish to forever, is totally impossible today. To examine the shape of it, is to understand why.

The first important film director who picked out Cary Grant, in the actor's first year as a Paramount contract player, was the legendary, enigmatic Josef von Sternberg, discoverer and "creator" of Marlene Dietrich. Sternberg cast Grant opposite Dietrich in the director's fifth collaboration with her (out of seven), *Blonde Venus* (1932), only Cary's own fifth role in features. I asked if Sternberg had directed him much. "Not really," he answered, saying he could see what Sternberg and Dietrich "were up to" (they had a complicated Svengali-Trilby relationship) and he "wasn't going to get mixed up in that," then added that there *was,* however, one memorably useful direction Sternberg gave him. "The first day of *shoot-ing* he took one look at me and said, 'Your hair is *par-ted* on the *wrong side.*' " What had Grant done? "I parted it on the *other* side and wore it that way for the *rest* of my *career!*"

The next person to have a constructive impact on Grant's image was Mae West—just then getting started in films, having conquered Broad-way long before. She saw Cary on the Paramount lot and requested him to co-star in her second and third pictures, both of which she essentially wrote herself, *She Done Him Wrong* (1933) and *I'm No Angel* (1933), the actor's eighth and twelfth feature in less than two years. It was to Cary Grant that Mae West made her most famous (and often misquoted) sex-ual invitation, "Why don't you come *up* sometime—an' *see* me?" To which Grant's missionary character responded that he didn't really have the time, and West countered with, "Hey, what're ya trying to *do—insult* me!?" Being the object of her attention gave him not only confidence but a cer-tain air of inaccessibility and distance he would effectively exploit through the years.

It wasn't until his twenty-first movie, in 1935 (on loan from Paramount to RKO Radio Pictures), that Grant gave a truly solid and distinctive per-formance; until then he had been simply a very good-looking though fairly bland leading man. But for George Cukor on *Sylvia Scarlett*—the first of four times he would appear opposite Katharine Hepburn, three times directed by Cukor (and once by Howard Hawks)—Cary "felt the ground beneath his feet," as Cukor described it to me. Playing a cockney con artist, Grant suddenly had a character for which he could draw from his youth, sink his teeth into, and with Cukor's enthusiastic encourage-ment, he went all the way with the role, effectively "stealing the picture," which is how *Variety* put it in their original review. However, the film was a dismal box-office failure; though it's an interesting, quirky piece with Hepburn masquerading as a boy through much of it. Nevertheless, Grant's confidence rose measurably.

Five films later (his seven-year Paramount contract having run out), he had his first modest success in what is actually a pretty flat and labored, if popular, movie, *Topper* (1937)—with only one somewhat charismatic scene in which he sings a bit in a bar. But that same year came his tri-umphant breakthrough in the picture that gave birth to the Cary Grant persona we all came to know and love: director-producer Leo McCarey's enduring comedy classic, *The Awful Truth,* co-starring Irene Dunne and Ralph Bellamy. The film was Grant's twenty-ninth, and it turned him overnight into an A-list leading man, yet he had tried desperately to buy his way out of doing it.

After only a few days of shooting, Cary was so thrown by what McCarey was asking him to do, and by the director's unorthodox work habits, that he panicked, went to Columbia Pictures' studio-head Harry Cohn and offered $5,000 to be let out of his contract or be allowed to switch roles with Bellamy, who had the square "other man" part. McCarey's method was to improvise each scene, dialogue and all, shortly before shooting it, inventing all the moves and words as he went along. If he had a problem, he would sit down at the piano and play for a while until the solution came to him. As McCarey told me in 1969, shortly before his death, "A lot of times we'd go into a scene with nothing." He gave Grant slapstick falls and numerous urbane and sophisticated moments, grunts, moves, bits.

The late director-writer Garson Kanin, having worked with Grant and McCarey (who was producer-writer) on *My Favorite Wife* three years later, explained to me in the mid-seventies that most of what Cary did in *The Awful Truth* was to play aspects of McCarey himself. Leo had told me this in his own way by referring to the picture as "in a way, the story of my life." Both McCarey and Grant were tall, dark and good-looking, McCarey being noted for his sophisticated wit and comic dexterity. He was, after all, the man who had paired Stan Laurel with Oliver Hardy to create the first great (and perhaps still best) comedy team in pictures. Before *The Awful Truth,* he had also very successfully directed such legendary screen comedians as Charley Chase, W. C. Fields, George Burns and Gracie Allen, Eddie Cantor, Harold Lloyd, the Marx Brothers (in their best, *Duck Soup*), and Mae West, as well as having guided Charles Laughton two years earlier to his first great comic success, *Ruggles of Red Gap.*

When I asked McCarey why Grant had wanted to get out, the director replied, "He had no sound judgment," but since the performance is so superb, and since the two would work together three more times (most notably in the classic 1957 comedy-romance *An Affair to Remember*), the experience for Cary must have been something like the metamorphosis a caterpillar goes through to become a butterfly; and had to be scary in its way. Though McCarey on his deathbed seemed not really to have forgiven Grant, Cary always spoke fondly, if a little sheepishly, of McCarey. And when I expressed some misgivings to Grant about McCarey's negative

In the role that made Cary Grant one of the top leading men in light comedy pictures: Jerry Warriner in Leo McCarey's perfect screwball comedy The Awful Truth *(1937), co-starring Irene Dunne and Asta, the dog that made Grant suffer again the following year in* Bringing Up Baby.

comments to me being published in a couple of places, Cary just said he understood how the director had felt, and didn't contradict him.

The fact is that McCarey was perhaps chronically irritated because to his mind Grant essentially had appropriated everything McCarey had given him on that picture as part of his continuing screen persona, made it his own, so to speak, and became the foremost star in pictures of sophisticated yet physical comedy. Perhaps McCarey—who received the Oscar as Best Director for *The Awful Truth*—felt that Grant never gave him enough of the credit for basically handing him the characteristics he would play variations on throughout the rest of his career.

But Cary—having found his footing, finally recognizing what he had been given, liberated now—never looked back. His very next two pictures, both 1938, both with Katharine Hepburn—*Bringing Up Baby* and *Holiday*, though neither hugely popular at the time and now considered classics—solidified and expanded brilliantly what McCarey had started. Never one to miss a trick, Howard Hawks (in his first of five films with Grant) pushed him even further with farcical business in *Bringing Up Baby,* suggesting he bray like a donkey when angry, having him wear outrageously thick lenses, do numerous falls, and put on ridiculous costumes, including one of Hepburn's negligees. In *Holiday,* George Cukor also capitalized on Grant's physicality, had him do a couple of acrobatic moves, and emphasized the sophisticated yet unpretentious side of his persona, his ability to be earnest, witty, vulnerable and debonair all at once.

The following year brought the final strokes that made him among the most sought-after stars in pictures: George Stevens' popular comedy-adventure *Gunga Din*—which had been largely developed for Grant by Howard Hawks, who was replaced before shooting started—and then, the *coup de grâce,* Hawks' aviation drama, *Only Angels Have Wings,* in which Cary finally had a huge hit doing the lead dramatic role and getting the girl—or, since it was Hawks, the girl getting him. In this case it was Jean Arthur, though he also had some heated scenes with a newcomer called Rita Hayworth. Her name in the movie was Judy, and the way Cary pronounced this came out, "*Ju*-dy." The film's popularity, and Grant's success in it, can be measured by the fact that impersonators from then on started doing Cary Grant by saying, "*Ju*-dy, *Ju*-dy, *Ju*-dy," though he never actually said this in the picture. In the seventies, he once told me he'd never figured out where the "Judy, Judy, Judy" business came from and when I told him my supposition, he got excited and said I was probably right.

For the next twenty-seven years, from 1939 until he retired after his last film was released in 1966, Cary Grant was the epitome of sophisticated comedy while possessing as well the darker range of an expressive dramatic actor. With his matinee-idol looks, and despite a unique voice and accent, he became universally accepted as some kind of an American even though he never remotely sounded like one. Cary's versatility within his own persona was striking. The bravura panache of his newspaper editor in Hawks' classic comedy *His Girl Friday* was followed soon after by the ambiguously dangerous, possibly homicidal character he played in *Suspicion,* his first of four movies for Alfred Hitchcock. In 1940, he received top billing over Katharine Hepburn in her own hit stage comedy vehicle, *The Philadelphia Story,* and in 1941 was nominated by the Academy for the first time as Best Actor in his heavily dramatic performance for George Stevens' sad love story *Penny Serenade,* again with Irene Dunne. I remember mentioning this picture to Cary one time in the late seventies and his saying, "Oh, yes, I just got a check on that one." It was amazingly early for

*With Rita Hayworth as "Ju-dy, Ju-dy, Ju-dy" (though Grant never
actually says that in the movie) for Howard Hawks' moody and
exciting flying picture* Only Angels Have Wings *(1939). Though he
was a star in romantic comedies, this was Grant's first dramatic success
and established him securely among the top leading men in pictures.
One of the (rarely acknowledged) great American films.*

a star to have a piece of the movie—this didn't become common until
more than a decade later—but Grant was always a good businessman and
never signed a long-term deal again after his one with Paramount.

Forming the arch of his own career, Cary made just a few real clinkers
(like *The Howards of Virginia* or *The Pride and the Passion*, both unfortunate costume pictures), and only rarely did conventionally glossy Hollywood product (like playing Cole Porter in *Night and Day*, having been
Porter's own choice). He could be equally believable and vivid as the
crooked gambler/con man in the underrated crime romance *Mr. Lucky*, or
as the cockney drifter in Clifford Odets' poetic and touching family
drama, *None But the Lonely Heart*, for which Grant received the second of
his two Oscar nominations. Grant and writer-director Odets remained
close friends, despite the film's lack of financial success, and it was through
Odets that seventeen years later I would meet the actor.

Generally, Cary Grant's career was divided between films he did for directors he admired, like Hitchcock, Hawks or McCarey, and family/romantic comedies he chose or, later, initiated (like *The Bachelor and the Bobby-Soxer, Mr. Blandings Builds His Dream House, Room for One More, Houseboat, That Touch of Mink,* or *Father Goose*). During World War II, he was as convincing as ever in naval uniform as the commander of a submarine for *Destination Tokyo,* agreeing to allow writer Delmer Daves to direct his first of numerous pictures. Grant did the same for Richard Brooks, in whose first directorial effort, *Crisis,* Grant is extraordinarily believable as a brain surgeon: watch him in the operation scenes and you will believe he has done it a thousand times. Some years later, Grant was also the first superstar-producer to hire Blake Edwards—a troubled relationship that produced the biggest box-office hit of Cary's career, *Operation Petticoat,* a service comedy with Grant again commanding a submarine.

Among other highlights: Frank Capra's adaptation of the hit Broadway farce *Arsenic and Old Lace,* a picture Cary always disliked, saying his performance was over the top, but the film remains a classic; arguably Hitchcock's best films, the dark love story *Notorious* with Ingrid Bergman and the quintessential chase saga *North by Northwest* with Eva Marie Saint, not to mention the entertaining, glamorous *To Catch a Thief* with Grace Kelly; for Hawks, there was the hilarious *I Was a Male War Bride* with Ann Sheridan, and the less successful *Monkey Business* with Ginger Rogers and Marilyn Monroe, though his scenes with Marilyn are vintage stuff; with Stanley Donen directing, Grant produced four comedies—two misfires and two both likeable and popular—*Indiscreet,* reunited with Ingrid Bergman, and *Charade* with Audrey Hepburn, which was released two years after I first met him.

That encounter happened in early January 1961, on my maiden visit to Hollywood. The previous season, I had revived Odets' Hollywood drama, *The Big Knife,* and had corresponded with the playwright but not met him. Clifford would later tell me that the lead character in *The Big Knife*—the troubled and doomed movie star—had, in fact, been conceived by Odets with Cary Grant in mind. I was preparing to do an article on my impressions of Hollywood, and anxious to meet Odets and also as many other picture professionals as possible. I phoned him a couple of weeks before to confirm my arrival. I was a little nervous as I'd never been in a plane before. Clifford said he was at that moment sitting with a person who'd flown all over the world his whole life and never had a problem—Cary Grant. I could vaguely hear a man's voice in the background, and then Odets said, "Cary says to be sure and take a jet plane, not a propeller-driven one; he says the jet engines are *simpler.*" It was the first, but by no means the last, piece of advice I got from Grant, and not the last I heeded, either.

Odets arranged a meeting for me at Grant's bungalow-office on the Universal lot. It was an odd experience, walking into an office and confronting a man who didn't know me but whom I'd known for as long as I could remember. He'd just come out of a long story conference, his hair was messy, he hadn't shaved for a day or so, and his dark slacks and white shirt looked as though he'd slept in them. We talked about Clifford for a while, and I don't remember a word of what was said. My mind was flooded with images from all the Cary Grant movies I'd seen—and I had this uncanny desire to be terribly honest and open with the man, at the same time realizing this might easily put him off. It's a feeling I've had with several movie stars I've met—knowing them so much better than they could ever know me—and finding it impossible to satisfactorily bridge the gap. All I could think about was how like his movie self he was: the same charm, humor, the totally uncalculated yet unmistakable air of mystery. I kept thinking, He's just like Cary Grant.

It wasn't his celebrity that impressed me; I can think of several stars who wouldn't have affected me one way or another, but Grant has always been among my two or three favorite actors, and certainly one of a handful of the great movie personalities. Because Cary Grant became synonymous with a certain character, a kind of cockney directness combined with impeccable taste and a detached and subtle wit. What made him so desirable as a player and so inimitable (and there've been many counterfeits through the years) was a striking mixture of farceur's talents and matinee idol's looks. He became such an accomplished master at comedy, both high and low, that his dramatic talents have been generally overlooked. Each of the great directors he worked with brought out different facets of Grant's fascinating personality; I asked several of them about certain particularly delightful moments in their Grant films, often getting the same reply: "That was Cary's." Hitchcock, whose (not entirely justified) reputation is of a director who cares little for actors, told me, "One doesn't direct Cary Grant, one just puts him in front of a camera. . . ."

I remember how complimentary and warm Grant had been about Hitchcock that first time I met him: "Oh, Hitch is *great!*" he had said. "You walk on his set for a scene and the set is *everything* you thought it *would* be, just as you envisioned it—never *anything* out of place or *wrong.*" He smiled. "And he's so *patient.* I'll never forget when we were shooting *Notorious* with Ingrid. In the morning we started a scene that was quite *difficult* because, you see, Ingrid had to say some of her lines a certain way so that *I* could *imitate* her readings. Well, anyway, we started," he went on, leaning forward, acting out the situation, "and Ingrid just couldn't *get* it. We went over and *over* the scene and she was in some sort of *daze.* You know, she just wasn't *there*! But Hitch didn't say anything. He just sat there next to the camera, pulling on his cigar." Cary laughed slightly at the memory. "Finally around eleven o'clock, I began to see in Ingrid's *eyes* that she was starting to come *around.* And for the first time all morning, the lines were coming out *right.* And just then Hitch said, 'Cut.' " Grant stopped and did a fast downward take to the left, as though looking amazed at Hitchcock, yet leaning his body backward slightly as he'd done in a score of films. "And I thought," he said, looking back at me, "what on *earth* is he stopping for *now*? Hitch just sat and looked up at Ingrid and said, quietly, '*Good* morning, Ingrid.' " Grant's eyes were wet with amusement as he broke up at the recollection.

The perfect leading man or zany, the most admirable dandy, the most charming rogue: except perhaps in his earliest years at Paramount, he was never allowed to die at the end of a film and with good reason—who would believe it? Cary was indestructible. Yet, by 1965, he had never won an Academy Award. That year, accepting the Oscar for co-writing a Grant vehicle called *Father Goose,* Peter Stone was perfectly succinct: "My thanks to Cary Grant," he said, "who keeps winning these things for other people." Five years later, when the Academy finally gave him an honorary award for his whole career (it was the evening's highlight and one of the rare TV appearances he made), Grant gave an especially gracious and spirited thank-you speech, prominently mentioning most of the best directors he had worked with. It was quite a list, and no accident either, but rather a monument to his good taste as well as his ability—since he worked with more good directors than any other star in pictures.

Grant didn't make a film after 1966, when he did *Walk, Don't Run,* in which he let Jim Hutton and Samantha Eggar have the love interest, while he played their matchmaker, a role that had been done originally by (heavyset aging English character man) Charles Coburn in the first version of that story, *The More the Merrier,* directed by George Stevens. The remake was not an unlikeable movie, but audiences didn't care to see Grant in that sort of part. There is a moment in the movie when Cary gives Samantha a glass of champagne and a kiss on the hand that must have made everyone yearn to see him go further—it was certainly the most romantic bit in the picture. But Cary had decided he was too old to play opposite young women and, in fact, I would guess the relative failure of *Walk, Don't Run* prompted his unannounced exit from the movies. If people wanted him only as a figure of romance and he felt he was just too old, the only thing to do was quit. No one ever convinced him he was wrong. I remember Howard Hawks complaining to me in the early sixties that Cary wouldn't do the comedy *Man's Favorite Sport?*, which Howard had conceived and written for him. I asked why, and Hawks answered, "Because he doesn't wanna be surrounded by all those young women. 'Holy smoke,' I said to him, 'how old was that girl I saw you with last week?!' " That she was in her early twenties wasn't the point for Cary—that was life, not the movies. Pushing sixty, Grant was fearful of looking like a dirty old man.

When I told Cary that I'd love to get him into a movie again, he answered jokingly that if there were a role for an old fellow in a wheelchair, maybe he'd do it. No matter that he looked only about fifty years old then, and that most women I knew (young or old) became slightly moony at the mention of his name. Nothing to be done—he was off in the international business world and fascinated by it, he claimed. Perhaps he was happy, but the movies lost someone quite irreplaceable. Too soon. He could argue that he had done everything in pictures, and of course he had, but I always wished he hadn't stopped.

When an *Esquire* column I did on him appeared in 1972, Cary called me and said, "I want you to read *that* at my *funeral*! It's a *eulogy*!" He thanked me profusely and then, nearly ten years later, called to ask a favor regarding it. He was being feted by the Kennedy Honors (in 1981), and Garson Kanin had been asked by the committee to write the Grant tribute for the official published commemorative program, but Cary was very unhappy with the result. "You know Gar," he said ruefully, "the smiler with a *knife*." No doubt I had not been the only one over the years to whom Kanin had told of the essential origins of the comic Grant persona. But, of course, I'm sure Gar knew that Leo McCarey could have given exactly the same material and business to another actor and the fires would not have started; because it was Cary Grant doing the stuff and *making it work*. "Anyway," Cary was asking, "you remember that lovely piece you did in *Esquire* some years back? I wonder if you would *allow* the Kennedy Honors to reprint it?" I said that I'd be more than honored, and would rewrite the article somewhat to fit the occasion. He said he was thrilled and would supply tickets to the gala night if I wanted to go. I did and got three tickets.

The evening provided for me another enduring Cary Grant image. All the honorees for the Kennedys are always seated in the first balcony, so that people in the orchestra have to turn around in their seats and look up in order to see reactions from them during the staged festivities. Before these had begun, I was gazing up at Cary when yet another President, Ronald Reagan, arrived, the last one in. The honorees all shook hands but Grant was first, and as Reagan enthusiastically grasped Cary's hand, it appeared to me from that distance like a long shot in a late-fifties movie. The beloved President Grant on the left welcomes the boyishly tardy Vice President Reagan. Certainly no movie would have ever cast it the other way around. Only life could be that square.

After Grant and I first met, he would make just four more pictures before his retirement. I happened to be in L.A. on a magazine job so he invited me to a private screening of the first of those, *That Touch of Mink* (1962), and an error in show-business etiquette on my part that night is probably one of the main reasons why I wasn't invited to any of the others. (I was only twenty-two, but should have known better.)

It was a small gathering in one of the more intimate projection rooms at Universal. Cary sat right in front of me holding hands throughout with his fiancée—and soon to be fourth wife—Dyan Cannon. On the other side of the aisle, also holding hands, were Warren Beatty and Natalie Wood. A couple of days later, I typed a card about the picture for my personal movie file (a 4 × 6 index card on every picture I saw, 1952–70) that accurately encapsulates my first reaction to the movie forty years ago: "Poor. Cary Grant's superb comic talents and charm are wasted in this tasteless, silly little sex comedy with Doris Day. Most memorable aspect: sitting behind Mr. G. at screening in Universal City. Least favorite aspect: he produced it."

I should have borne that last fact in my head as I walked up to thank him for inviting me and comment on the picture. I knew he hadn't heard me laugh much but I lied and said it was funny and that I'd enjoyed it. Then I made the mistake. I jokingly said that there was only one little unimportant factual error in the picture: I had just been getting unemployment insurance in New York myself, and the way Doris Day's character got hers in the picture was not the way it worked. Grant became very agitated. "No, no! We did a lotta research on *that,* and it is *exactly* the way it's *done.*" I laughed slightly and didn't press the point. Grant repeated that the whole issue had been carefully researched and that I was mistaken. I said it didn't matter really, and moved away. He even called after me that there had been "much research" done.

Less than a year later, I heard Cary was passing through New York and I called him at his hotel. "You didn't like my picture!" he said almost immediately. I lied fervently, but he would have none of it. "No," he said, "you didn't like my picture. But that's all right, it's been quite profitable and a lotta people enjoyed it. But I know *you* didn't like it!" By messenger, I sent over the recently published Museum of Modern Art monographs I'd done on Hawks and Hitchcock, in both of which he was discussed fondly by the directors, and was featured in numerous photos. He called to thank me for them, and marvel on the extent of both men's work. *That Touch of Mink* was never mentioned again. Though I remember his somewhat irritable exasperation when he said, referring to me, "The man doesn't have a clue . . . ," regarding how much Grant did as producer of his films. Because, of course, he was right, I didn't. It turns out he was extremely hands-on, much to Blake Edwards' regret, for example, though that picture (*Operation Petticoat*) did make Edwards virtually overnight a bankable director, thanks to which he got *Breakfast at Tiffany's*, another smash and one of his signature films.

After moving to Los Angeles in the mid-1960s, my then wife Polly Platt and I were invited one time by Cary to join him and his (by then) wife Dyan, for a baseball game: the Dodgers, with the legendary Sandy Koufax pitching. Polly had first met Cary when I was sent to Hollywood for a couple of writing assignments in 1962 and she accompanied me. I brought her to his Universal office; he took a call just as we were being seated. While we waited, I leaned over and asked if she was nervous. She was terrified, she said. Just then Cary hung up and looked at us over his left hand, as he said, very dramatically, "What are you two wiseacres whispering about?" Polly stammered something, but he was gracious and disarming as always. He took one look at my jacket and said, "Brooks Brothers?" I said yes, surprised. "Right off the rack, isn't it?" I nodded. "Yeah, I do the same thing. Fits perfectly." (This reminded me that I had recognized the shirt he puts on in the hospital scene in *North by Northwest* as being from Brooks Brothers.)

Now Polly and I were parking our car on the Universal lot, as Cary had asked. He then picked us up in his Rolls-Royce and, Dyan at his side, he drove us to Dodger Stadium and back to our car that afternoon. And he bought us all hot dogs. Neither Polly nor I were fanatic baseball fans as both Cary and Dyan seemed to be—they had a very informed commentary going throughout the game—making it all the more fun for us, even if we had no idea what they were talking about.

Dyan Cannon was Cary's penultimate wife—after actress Virginia Cherrill in 1934–35 (she was Chaplin's poignant leading lady in *City Lights*); heiress Barbara Hutton, also in the thirties; and the quirky and likeable actress Betsy Drake in the late forties and fifties. I saw Cary and Dyan together only twice really, but I somehow always felt Cary was more in love with her than she was with him. He seemed to dote on her and do whatever she asked, and she appeared to enjoy showing him off: "Sing 'em that song, Archie!" she called out on the way back from the game. In his earliest theatrical days, as a London stilt-walker and in British music halls, Archie Leach had been his name; the "Cary" came from one of his first stage roles, and the "Grant" he just picked out. (In Hawks' *His Girl Friday*, there's an inside reference to this when Grant's character says to someone on the phone: "Say, the last person who called me *that* was Archie Leach, the day before they *hanged* him!") Cary's aged mother, who had never left Bristol—she was still alive as we rode back from that baseball game, and lived to be ninety-six—no doubt had once called him Archie, too.

Cary seemed to like it and did just as Dyan had asked: he sang a rowdy old British music-hall song—did it full out, with a lot of gusto and humor but without kidding it. There was great affection in the way he sang it for Dyan and she appeared to be as delighted as we were in the back seat. I felt both awed and strangely touched. It's one of my fondest memories of Cary Grant—sitting behind him in his Rolls, seeing only the side of his face and the back of his head, and sometimes his eyes in the mirror, as he lustily belted out for us a corny old comedy song.

That was early in 1965. The very next year he retired from the screen, and I directed my first picture-work. Within five years, both of our marriages would be over. His would produce one beautiful daughter, Jennifer, henceforth the main focus and love of his life, and mine would result in two terrific daughters. Both our divorces were long, somewhat loud and enduringly acrimonious. Dyan won custody of Jennifer, as Polly did of our daughters. Around that time I remember Cary saying ruefully to me over the phone: "Women always win in the end, you know, Peter, they always do win in the end. So you might as well just give up and give them what they want, they're going to get it anyway." So, although I was in my twenties and Cary in his sixties, we had a great deal in common over the next twenty years as divorced husbands and first-time fathers. Since he was experienced and I was callow, and as my career hit extremes of both highs and lows, he helped me many times with his hard-earned wisdom, his innate kindness.

All of our most intimate, and many not so intimate, conversations were over the phone. Nearly every talk had a similar feline pattern. Cary would usually sound suspicious, distrustful, but after a few minutes he warmed and then opened up more and more. Most of his helpful hints for better living came to me through the receiver. "*Ne-ver* put your *hands* to your *face!*" he would admonish, as a way of avoiding skin eruptions of any kind. One time I told him I'd stopped smoking, and he said, "That's good—that means you *like* yourself again!"

Once, before I'd made a picture (and was relatively broke), I called to tell Cary that for a magazine piece I was writing, Polly and I were going to be staying for four days in the Presidential Suite at the Beverly Hills Hotel, all expenses paid. He was delighted. "The first thing you must do," he said, "is kick off your *shoes* and let a lot of minions pick them up!" Later, when I wanted to quote him in the piece, he said absolutely not, it wouldn't sound good. In those days, you didn't say "too elitist," but that's what he meant. However, it does also convey a not unnatural human reaction to dreams of luxury. Only someone who had to earn this comfort through hard or intense labor would make that sort of comment. In 1973, I was asked to sit on a dais with a hundred others for a Hollywood celebration and Cary advised, "Never *eat* while you're on a dais." Why? "Because they take photographs all the *time,* and they'll get one of you with your mouth open, full of food, and *that's* the one they'll *use!*"

When Cybill Shepherd and I were getting a lot of bad press, Cary admonished me, "Will you *stop* telling people you're in *love!*? And *stop* telling them you're *happy!*" Why, I asked. "Because *they're* not in love and *they're* not happy." But, I protested, I thought all the world loves a lover. "Don't you believe it," he answered. "Just remember, Peter, people *do not like* beautiful people." The degree and depth of his knowledge about the destructiveness of jealousy and envy was far beyond me. I was starting to catch up when, on a tragic occasion a few years later, the only person not closely involved who called me was Cary Grant. "I'm so *sorry,* dear Peter, that you have to go through something so terrible." At that moment, his call meant much more than I could possibly ever tell him.

Once I asked him what sort of a feeling it was all these years seeing his image projected in huge proportions. He didn't really answer the question. All he did was nod (we were together somewhere for this) and say, "Yeah—you could park a car in my *nostril!*" Another time, he described an argument he'd got into on a plane in the late 1930s, and the other person had hit him with, "Who do you think you are!?" And Cary smiled cockily, and answered sharply, "I know who *I* am!" Early in 1972, I called excitedly to tell him that my new picture, a comedy called *What's Up, Doc?*, was opening at New York's famous Radio City Music Hall, in that year still America's premier showcase for family-oriented quality entertainment. As a kid, I had loved going to the Music Hall with my parents now and then as a special treat, so the venue had special resonance for me. Cary's response to the news was, "That's nice—I had *twenty-eight* pictures play the Hall." I exclaimed the number, and he added, "Yeah—*all* my pictures opened at the Hall."

For me, that opening was most appropriate, since the picture was certainly in the screwball comedy tradition Cary had pioneered in movies with Leo McCarey and Howard Hawks. In fact, I had discussed the whole project with Grant, and asked if he would meet with my male star, Ryan O'Neal, to give him some pointers. Cary agreed—gladly, he said. When Ryan returned, I asked for a report and he told me the only thing Cary had advised was that Ryan "wear silk underpants while shooting the film." We both laughed, but Ryan wore the silk underpants. And much of my direction was in pointing out to Ryan various takes or line-readings that essentially mimicked or recalled Grant. As Hawks had always said, "When you steal, steal from the best," and there has never been anyone to equal Cary Grant at romantic comedy, period. So Ryan and I were consciously creating a Grant-like, bespectacled and inhibited professor. I don't recall Cary ever saying much about the finished film except to congratulate me on its success, and he told Ryan he'd done a good job.

Talking about the Music Hall over the phone that first time, Cary said, "You know what you must do? Put on a raincoat and a pair of sunglasses—oh, well, *you* won't need those. Just go down to the Hall and stand in the back, and you listen and you watch while *six* thousand *five* hundred people laaugh at something you *did*! It will do your *heart good*!" Of course, I went (twice). And—Cary being right again—it became one of the most exhilarating experiences I've ever had. Of those twenty-eight pictures of his that played the Hall, how many, I wondered, had he himself come in raincoat and sunglasses to see, in order to do his own heart good?

In the second half of the seventies, Warren Beatty was preparing to do his version of the Robert Montgomery fantasy *Here Comes Mr. Jordan* (1941), calling it *Heaven Can Wait* (1978), with a new script by Elaine May (and later Buck Henry). In talking to me about directing it, Warren said that Cary Grant was going to play "Mr. Jordan," the messenger from

Cary Grant, in even thicker glasses than he wore for Bringing
Up Baby, *does a typically subtle take on Marilyn Monroe's pose,
in* Monkey Business *(1952), the last of Grant's five pictures
with director Howard Hawks.*

heaven which Grant's fellow Englishman Claude Rains had done in the
original film. I said to Beatty that if Grant was really doing the picture, I
would certainly be interested in directing. Warren assured me: Cary was
going to do the movie. I decided to call Grant and ask if this was true. He
wasn't in, so I left a message. The next day, a Saturday, Beatty called to say
he was in the neighborhood, could he drop by for a sandwich? Sure, I said,
and while we were in the kitchen—Warren about to cut himself a slice of
bread—the phone rang and I answered it right there: It was Cary returning my call.

I said, "Oh, hi, Cary," and proceeded to have the conversation as though I were alone. So I told Grant what Warren had said and he replied, "I'm not going to do that *picture*. I mean, Warren certainly *wants* me to do it, and I like Warren, but I'm *not* going to do that picture!" Having nothing to lose, I said, "Well, it's not really a very good part, is it?" Cary leapt on this: "No, it's *not* a very good part! All those *long* speeches and none of the jokes. Claude pulled it off in the original picture—*he* was good, but it's not really a very good *part*!" Feeling Beatty's ire behind me, I pressed on: What if the scenes were rewritten to give Grant's character the ability to appear and disappear at will? And therefore to just fade on for his line, then fade out again? And give all the long expositional speeches to the character of his assistant, letting Grant just come in for the punch lines. "Yeah," Cary said, "that might work."

With this tiny wedge in, I went on giving Grant some ideas on how to do the picture but especially how to deal with his character. Knowing he was very concerned about his looks, I suggested that before he's actually seen his voice be heard in a kind of Godlike manner throughout an entire introductory scene that plays in heaven—with Beatty in the midst of a cloud—hearing Cary's voice talking to him but not seeing Grant for quite a while. And then, eventually, we begin to see Grant through wisps of fog and cloud, but never see him absolutely in the clear for long, appearing and disappearing at will. Cary exclaimed, "That might *work!*" a couple of times, so I said why didn't we rewrite it for him along those lines and see what he thinks then? "No," Cary said, "because if you rewrite it especially for me and I don't do it, then where are you?" I assured him my vote would be to redo it for him and take our chances. Cary said, "Well, that's up to Warren and to you." He wished me good luck as we hung up.

When I turned back to Beatty, he did not look amused. He was still holding the bread knife as he said, very softly, "Do you know why I don't stick this knife in your belly and rip it open?" "No," I said, "why, Warren?" "Because," he said, "if I were you, I'd have done the same thing." Cary didn't do the movie, and neither did I, but Warren had a great success with it (as star, producer and co-director with co-writer Buck Henry), casting James Mason in the Mr. Jordan role. (Ironically, Dyan Cannon had one of her best roles in it.)

Grant wouldn't do any of the numerous movies proposed to him over the years after 1965. It just wasn't to be because Cary did not want his aged appearance to alter the essential screen image he had projected since 1932. I once complained, in the late seventies or early eighties, that here we'd known each other all these years and my two daughters had never even met him, and he said, "Well, you don't want to *frighten* the poor dears, do you? I mean, they think they're going to meet Cary Grant and in comes this *old man* in a *wheelchair!*"

In those years during which Dyan was making it very difficult for Cary to see his beloved daughter, there were times when I heard a different Grant talking about pictures. On those occasions, he had no use for films at all: just movies—who cares?—doesn't add up to much. There was contained anger and contempt behind those words, not simply in what he said but in how he spoke. There was almost a sense of betrayal in his tone.

As there also was when Sophia Loren sold to television her best-selling autobiography, which pretty candidly featured her fifties affair with Grant. Cary had fallen pretty hard for Loren on the Spanish location of *The Pride and the Passion.* Describing their affair (which occurred while she was living with Carlo Ponti), Cary said to me once, "We certainly ripped up a few bull rings in Spain, I can tell you *that!*" I said, "I *knew* there was some reason you did *The Pride and the Passion.*" Cary responded brightly, "That was it, all right." Immediately after, the two co-starred again in Grant's own production of *Houseboat,* in the last scene of which their characters are married on-screen. In the ceremony, Cary is at his most ironic since, in real life, Sophia had just rejected his marriage proposal and agreed to marry Ponti. After the TV-movie was shown, I asked Cary if it wasn't rather odd to have someone portray him in a film. "Yes," he said, "it *is* rather odd, but let her *go,* poor darling, if she needs the money so *bad-ly.*" There was more than an edge of wounded bitterness there; in Cary's life Sophia Loren seems to have been "the gal that got away."

The only time I ever heard Cary really angry, however, was when Chevy Chase, in a Tom Snyder NBC-TV interview, called Grant "a homo." Cary told me he wasn't "going to let him get away with that," and slapped Chase with a lawsuit. "I don't have anything *against* homosexuals," Cary said to me, "I just don't *happen* to be one." I remember asking Howard Hawks once in the sixties if there was any foundation to the old rumor that Cary was gay. Hawks, who had done five films with Grant by then, just snorted and wrinkled his face as though that was the silliest thing he'd heard all week. "Every time I see him, he's got a younger girl on his arm." Hawks shook his head. "No, that's just ridiculous." The Chase suit was eventually settled out of court. "Chevy didn't really mean any harm," Cary told me, "he was just stupid. He's apologized. Actually, of course, he did me a *favor.*" How was that? "I've had it all my life," Grant continued. "Guy takes his girl to a picture and there I am, and the girl says she likes me, so the fellow says, 'I hear he's a *fag!*' Now he's just done me a favor, hasn't he? Because if I ever come to that town, who do you think will be the first one around my hotel to see if it's *true*? His girl! He's done me a *favor*, you see!"

Whenever I saw Cary, or spoke with him, during his marriage to his last wife, Barbara, he looked and sounded happy and contented. He told me he was a lucky man to have found Barbara. The two or three times I saw them together, they both looked awfully pleased to be with each other. Of course, Jennifer was still the light of his life, but as teenagers will, she needed her independence, and Cary was careful in his fatherly ways, wisely allowing for space when it was required. She was only twenty when he died, but I would guess that Cary's last years were probably his most satisfying, certainly his most serene.

Not that he wasn't still suspicious or distrustful at times. He invited me to join him and Barbara at the races one afternoon a couple of years before his death. Since Stanley Donen was also invited and lived only a block or two from me, Cary asked if Stanley could pick me up and bring me out to the track with him? And that's what happened. On the way back, I remember, Stanley marveled at Cary's physique, especially considering that Grant always swore the only exercise he ever got was from making love. Donen said as far as he knew, that was true.

It was a pleasant afternoon, very civilized. Surprisingly, there was hardly any film talk, and only casual interest in the ponies. Small bets. Good food. At one point, I was talking to Barbara (who was seated opposite me, Cary beside her) about an ancient calendar-system I'd become fascinated with in a couple of nonfiction books by Robert Graves. Since it was essentially a female-oriented calendar, Barbara was quite interested but I could feel that Cary was getting increasingly distracted from his conversation with Donen and director-producer Mervyn LeRoy, who was nearby. Grant finally turned to me, with some irritation, and said, "What *is* all *that*?" I started to explain but could see that he wasn't at all interested. The impression I got was that Cary thought I was using the calendar as a kind of intellectual come-on with Barbara, and it annoyed him. I dropped the subject.

One time, when his daughter was about nineteen, I remarked to Cary that here we'd known each other all these years, and I'd never met his daughter. He responded immediately, "Yes, and knowing your predilection for younger women, I hope you *never do*!" (I didn't until seven years after Cary had died, and I told Jennifer this anecdote. She laughed sadly.)

In 1984, for Cary's eightieth birthday, Barbara had an audiotape made with all his friends saying, "Happy Birthday, Cary" however they liked. She included me, and asked me also, if I wouldn't mind, to do my impres-

*The famous kiss sequence: Cary Grant and Ingrid Bergman in
one of Alfred Hitchcock's five best films, perhaps the most
ambiguous love story ever made,* Notorious *(1946),
screenplay by Ben Hecht. It was the second of four pictures
Grant and Hitchcock did together.*

sions of Hawks and Hitchcock saying, "Happy Birthday." Since they had both died, and Cary had remembered my impressions as being accurate, she was certain it would please him to be reminded of them. So I did it, and Cary got a big kick out of the whole thing, he told me himself, and thanked me personally for all three greetings. "Come on, do Howard for me," he said, as he often did. Hawks and Hitchcock were Cary's favorite directors, and while people were always "doing" Hitchcock, hardly anyone knew what Howard Hawks sounded like. And so I would do Howard, and Cary would laugh, saying loudly, "God, you sound just like *Howard*!" It was, for both of us, a way to bring him back for a second, a kind of shock of recognition that was pleasant because he and I both were so fond of Hawks, and missed his voice and presence.

The following year, I sent Cary for his birthday a two-foot-high styrofoam figure of himself as done by a California florist. It was quite a good likeness of the older Cary, with white hair and black-framed glasses. About a week later, he called me excitedly. "Petah! Barbara and I *just got back* from Bar-ba-dos and walked into the living room where there are all these *pre-sents* I haven't *opened* yet. And, by God, sitting on the piano is this *lit-tle Ca-ry Grant*!" He stressed every syllable of the last three words with an absolutely bursting sense of amusement, thanked me profusely, and then asked if I had seen the little fellow before sending him over. No, I said. Cary wondered therefore if I'd like to drop by and see his "lit-tle Ca-ry Grant," saying those three words exactly the same way.

So a couple of evenings later, I drove to Cary's white ranch house up on top of the Beverly Hills. There was a very bright full moon as I got out of my car on the vast blacktop parking area in front of the simple, rustically designed and sprawling one-story house. In fact, the moon was so perfectly placed while I walked to the front door that I couldn't help thinking it was extraordinarily appropriate in its cinematically pictorial effect as I approached Cary Grant's home—for the first time, I suddenly realized, though I'd known him by then for twenty-four years.

The butler let me in and, entering, I looked down the corridor to the right. Coming slowly toward me were Cary and Barbara, arm in arm, and both beaming. After our hellos, they took me into the living room where the "lit-tle Ca-ry Grant" (as he called him yet again) was still perched on the piano, and did indeed look like Cary, in comic-strip terms, dressed in a tux. He posed with it briefly, doing a take for my benefit. His eyes were brimming with joy. There were so many unwrapped presents around the room that it looked like Christmas wasn't over, though it was late in January or early in February.

After a little while I asked if I could borrow his phone for a quick call. I was preparing a picture for M-G-M and was late in calling its president, Frank Yablans. Grant was on the M-G-M board of directors, and exclaimed Frank's name with affection, then said, "I'll get him on the *line* for you! That'll *impress* 'im." He laughed mischievously, then led the way conspiratorially to the phone in the foyer, dialed M-G-M, asked for "Frank Yablans, please," and then, when the secretary answered, with perfect Cary Grant aplomb, said, "Hello, I'm *call*-ing for Petah Bog-*dan*ovich—can Mr. Yab-lans speak with him *now*?" There was a pause and then Cary said, "Yes, it *is*." He winked at me; the secretary had obviously

Cary Grant and Deborah Kerr in Leo McCarey's An Affair
to Remember *(1957), which starts out with sparkling light
comedy. The film was a color and CinemaScope remake of
McCarey's own black-and-white* Love Affair *(1939), co-starring
Charles Boyer and Irene Dunne. Writer-director McCarey
preferred the original, and it is better, but for many the
later version packs the bigger emotional wallop.*

asked him if he was Cary Grant. "All right, dah-ling . . ." Pause. "Yes, *you*
can tell him it's *me* hold-ing for *Petah*." Pause. "All riiight . . ." Covering
the speaker, he told me she was seeing if Yablans could take the call, he
was in a meeting, and on another line. Cary seemed to be having a great
time, and looked genuinely disappointed when she came back and told
him that Yablans would phone back because he couldn't take the call right
now. "*Can't* he, dah-ling? All right." And he thanked her, hung up, and
told me that Yablans must be in an important meeting; he shrugged. "Too

bad—we tried," he said, and I thanked him. (Little did either of us know at the time that Yablans was under tremendous corporate pressure, and that his tenure at M-G-M would shortly be ending. Or, that I would never do the picture there, either.)

We went back into the living room; Cary sat in a large easy chair and Barbara draped herself comfortably on its arm and around him. I sat in a straight-backed chair and told them both the current mess I was in. Cary had asked me what I was up to and, privately, I thought if he knew what was going on in this matter, maybe he could help. In fact, I was a bit desperate because the studio picture I had recently finished, *Mask* with Cher, was caught in the middle of a corporate struggle, both internal and external, with another mega-company. Everything centered around using twenty-five minutes of Bruce Springsteen's music right at the peak of his phenomenal success with the *Born in the U.S.A.* album: we had several of his songs for our use when not only was that record number one, but every single other album Springsteen had ever recorded was in the top forty. And, at that point, Springsteen had almost never allowed anybody to use any of his music in a movie, much less so much of his best and most famous songs.

Cary listened very closely. Because the movie studio was Universal— where I had first met him and where he and his company had a production deal for years—and because Lew Wasserman was still top man there, and still the most feared and respected man in Hollywood (and who actually liked my picture), I hoped Grant might ultimately intervene in some way on my behalf. If the situation had occurred in a movie of his—*Holiday*, for example, or *The Talk of the Town*, or *People Will Talk*—Cary Grant would surely have gone to bat for the artists against the money.

But this wasn't a movie. Cary had a remarkably empathetic expression on his face, and by the end of my tale of woe, anger and frustration, his look was sad, his eyes tearing, but not out of happiness now. I could see that both he and Barbara were affected by the absurdity of the situation, yet when I had finished, all he basically said, apart from a touch of genuine commiseration, was: "Well, I am *cer*-tain that *com*-mon sense *will* pre-*vail.*" In the agitated state I was in, looking for crumbs, I took "common sense" to mean the studio would have to eventually see the light; I took it as a vote for our side. (And Cary proved right again, though it took twenty years: in 2004, Universal finally put out a DVD of my Springsteen version.)

But at the time, everything couldn't have gone worse. At one point, in a last ditch letter to Wasserman, I invoked Cary's name and quoted his remark, using it to bolster my point. Nothing helped. Later, I felt badly about having used his name at all, especially without his permission. Whether or not he definitively knew of my letter to Wasserman, he certainly didn't ask me what I was talking about when I eventually called and apologized to him for using his name in the matter. He simply took a positive note and said he'd heard the picture was terrific, but underneath his letting me totally off the hook was a feeling that he still wished he could have helped me, saved the day. Soon after, I sent him the most valuable thing I could possibly give: one of my late father's paintings, each of them a treasure to me. He took it in kind and responded by doing something he had once told me that he never did unless it was really important: he wrote me a letter. It was neatly typed on his personal blue stationery, his name in very small type at the top; in ballpoint, he had written the salutation, "Dear Peter," himself, and signed "Cary" at the bottom. Between were two paragraphs of praise for my father's work, saying what a pleasure it was to wake up each morning to the painting's "vibrant colors." He wrote that while he understood why I had sent the gift, it had not been necessary in any way. Nevertheless, he was happy to receive it and appreciated the spirit in which it was sent. His signature was under the word, "Gratefully."

We spoke after that, of course, and he even told me once that he was having it put into his will that when he died, my father's painting would be returned to me. I objected to this and told him the present was for him and for whomever he wished to leave it. He thanked me again, even more enthusiastically.

Yet the last time Cary and I were together in person was the evening I went over to see "the little Cary Grant" and told him my troubles. He and Barbara had walked me back to the entrance, both of them sympathetic and gracious. Cary seemed a little more tired and was a trifle more slouched over than usual, but warmer than ever. Barbara moved back into the house and, with the full moon now directly over the house, Cary gave one final wave from his doorway. By the time I pulled my car out, the big white front door was closed and I never saw Cary again.

When I heard, eighteen months later, that he had died in Iowa, preparing to do one of his *Evening*s, it seemed somehow touchingly appropriate. The death of Cary Grant came in the heartland of the country that had adopted the Bristol boy named Archie and for over fifty years had taken him to its heart, as the rest of the world had, too. Barbara would tell me they had just been saying that if Cary lived to be as old as his mother, they had at least another thirteen years together. And then suddenly, backstage in Davenport, ready to go on, he had a stroke. It was over very fast. He held her hand.

Thinking of all the laughs, human insights and sheer pleasure he has given millions across the planet through those pictures in the dark, it adds up to something pretty substantial as a legacy. Looking back now, nearly two decades since his death, there is a lovely irony in his remark that even *he* wished he "could be Cary Grant," because, of course, that was exactly who he did become, and will remain. And there will never be anyone like him again, not even close.

Born Archibald Alexander Leach, January 18, 1904, Bristol, England; died November 29, 1986, Davenport, IA.

Selected starring features (with director):

1932: *Blonde Venus* (Josef von Sternberg)
1933: *She Done Him Wrong* (Lowell Sherman); *I'm No Angel* (Wesley Ruggles)
1935: *Sylvia Scarlett* (George Cukor)
1936: *Big Brown Eyes* (Raoul Walsh); *Suzy* (George Fitzmaurice)
1937: *Topper* (Norman Z. McLeod); *The Awful Truth* (Leo McCarey)
1938: *Bringing Up Baby* (Howard Hawks); *Holiday* (Cukor)
1939: *Gunga Din* (George Stevens); *Only Angels Have Wings* (Hawks); *In Name Only* (John Cromwell)
1940: *His Girl Friday* (Hawks); *My Favorite Wife* (Garson Kanin); *The Philadelphia Story* (Cukor)
1941: *Penny Serenade* (Stevens); *Suspicion* (Alfred Hitchcock)
1942: *The Talk of the Town* (Stevens); *Once Upon a Honeymoon* (McCarey)
1943: *Mr. Lucky* (H. C. Potter)

1944: *Destination Tokyo* (Delmer Daves); *None But the Lonely Heart* (Clifford Odets); *Arsenic and Old Lace* (Frank Capra)
1946: *Notorious* (Hitchcock)
1947: *The Bachelor and the Bobby-Soxer* (Irving Reis); *The Bishop's Wife* (Henry Koster)
1948: *Mr. Blandings Builds His Dream House* (Potter)
1949: *I Was a Male War Bride* (Hawks)
1950: *Crisis* (Richard Brooks)
1951: *People Will Talk* (Joseph L. Mankiewicz)
1952: *Room for One More* (Norman Taurog); *Monkey Business* (Hawks)
1955: *To Catch a Thief* (Hitchcock)
1957: *An Affair to Remember* (McCarey)
1958: *Indiscreet* (Stanley Donen); *Houseboat* (Melville Shavelson)
1959: *North by Northwest* (Hitchcock); *Operation Petticoat* (Blake Edwards)
1963: *Charade* (Donen)
1964: *Father Goose* (Ralph Nelson)
1966: *Walk, Don't Run* (Charles Walters)

7

JACK LEMMON

First meeting Jack Lemmon in January 1961, on my initial trip to Hollywood, I interviewed him briefly in the Beverly Hills Hotel's famous Polo Lounge, at that time the epicenter of glamour. Jack then had been living in Los Angeles only about seven years. I remembered seeing him on New York television in the early fifties in a little daytime serial he was doing with his first wife, and then on Broadway in a not very successful revival of the classic farce *Room Service*. Lemmon was virtually the ideal comedy juvenile. There was only a small section on him in my first *Esquire* article, but a couple of years later, the magazine assigned me to do a profile on Lemmon, so I spent two weeks watching him work on Billy Wilder's adaptation of *Irma La Douce* with Shirley MacLaine.

Of course, by the time we did that piece, Lemmon had acted in seventeen pictures in eight years, among them such highlights as his very first, *It Should Happen to You,* in which he is "introduced" opposite Judy Holliday, original screenplay by Garson Kanin, directed by George Cukor. There was also *Mister Roberts,* starring Henry Fonda, directed by John Ford and Mervyn LeRoy, for which Lemmon—in only his fourth picture—won the Oscar as Best Supporting Actor. Other popular and challenging works included the zany *Operation Mad Ball,* written by Blake Edwards; Wilder's two comedy classics, *Some Like It Hot* and *The Apartment;* and an achingly painful and moving portrayal of an upper-middle-class drunk in Blake Edwards' film version of *Days of Wine and Roses,* a role that evidently mirrored Jack's own problems with alcohol during a certain part of his life.

The funny thing is that I had seen Jack in person for the second time (after the Broadway play) one night in 1959 when he and Wilder were doing a scene in Manhattan's theater district for *The Apartment.* They had a call out for a bunch of theatrical extras; I was one of them, but didn't

Singing at the piano, Jack Lemmon in his first movie role, opposite the divine Judy Holliday, in the poorly titled It Should Happen to You *(1954); writer Garson Kanin originally called it* A Name for Herself, *which is only what the picture is all about. It was directed beautifully (with locations in Manhattan) by George Cukor.*

even get close to Lemmon, who was standing outside waiting while we all went inside. (Worse, I never could find myself in the finished film.)

Jack was one of the last major contract players in picture history, starting out with a seven-picture deal at Columbia. When we sat down at the Polo Lounge, the first thing he talked about was why he thought his Columbia contract films (this was at the tail end of the old studio star system) had not been as successful as those (*The Apartment, Some Like It Hot*) he had made on loan-out. He said, "Some of the Columbia pictures were damned good, too, but I think what screwed them up were the titles. No, really, titles are important. Look at the ones I've been stuck with: *It Should Happen to You, You Can't Run Away From It, Phffft.*" He smiled. "When we were shooting *Phffft,* they stopped production right in the middle of the day so they could discuss that title. Everyone waited while they went into a two-and-a-half-hour huddle upstairs. When they broke, I asked the director about it, and he said they'd decided to take out one 'f.' "

Esquire never got around to running my profile of Jack, but this is pretty much how it went:

"When I first got out here, I thought they were pulling my leg," Jack Lemmon said, excitedly. "*Private* dressing room. *Mister* Lemmon. This is your *chair.* This is your stand-in. Stand-in for *what?* And, of course, your private bungalow is outside. I was a New York actor. For me, the theater was *it.* What did I know about being a movie star?"

Angrily: "I get livid when people call me a comedian. I could no more get up in front of a microphone and do jokes . . ."

Warmly: "Andover's really a great school. I'm hoping to send my son Chris there. Had a lotta fun, too. In the senior year, we put on a revue—I'll never forget a lyric some nut wrote: 'I'm going into the Army / And if Hitler ever saw me / He would never, never harm me now . . .' And he graduated, too!"

Wistfully: "My parents both came out here when I did. Pop was retired, so they just came. They were very close—they just weren't living together when Pop passed away."

Broadly: "I was born in Boston, but I never got that accent because my parents both came from Baltimore. But I remember while I was at Harvard—I was in the Ritz Bar—and this college girl came in. She was wearing bobbysox, a camel's-hair coat—you know, the whole thing. One of the guys knew her and asked her to sit down. And she said, and I quote, 'No, ay cahn't—Mums, Dad and Poopoo are waiting in the car . . .' I fell out of my chair. 'Mums, Dad and Poopoo . . .'? It's classic."

Reverently: "Alec Guinness wrote me a letter after *The Apartment*—at least four pages, handwritten—about his attitude toward acting, talked about my work. I was delirious with happiness and shock at what this man had taken the time to do. That letter is as valuable to me as anything I've ever received."

Earnestly: "Used to play an awful lot of squash. Two or three hours a day when I was at Harvard. Just can't find anybody around here who knows how to play."

The *Irma La Douce* set took up all of Stage 4 on the Samuel Goldwyn lot, being a realistic re-creation of a Paris street. The fabled Alexandre Trauner designed it. This was October–November 1962. In the film, Lemmon plays a French policeman who gets fired and inadvertently becomes the pimp for the best whore on the block, a role taken by Shirley MacLaine. Bruce Yarnell plays her former pimp, who is bested in an extensive fight sequence which the company was in the process of shooting at the "Chez Moustache" bistro.

Wednesday afternoon. The shot: Lemmon, sitting on a billiard table, was to get sprayed from across the room by Lou Jacobi holding a seltzer bottle. Revived, he was to pick up a (latex) billiard ball and, after a couple of lines, to come over to Yarnell and shove it into his open, laughing mouth. Whores, pimps, and gamblers stood about as spectators. Rehearsal: "I don't have anything to tell you," said Billy Wilder. "I should, because I'm the director, but I can't think of anything. Somevon should write material for me." Lemmon was tossing the ball in the air and glowering at Yarnell. A bell rang signaling silence. "OK, let's try it vonce," Wilder said and imitated a seltzer bottle: "Spritz-spritz-spritz-spritz-spritz . . ." Lemmon (angrily tossing the ball in the air): "Now I'm mad. Now I'm really mad. And when I'm mad, I'm like a tiger." Yarnell (laughing): "Did you hear that, boys, he's a tiger." Wilder (interrupting): "Yeh, vell, dat's da *line,* Bruce."

Lemmon stopped tossing the ball and wiped his face nervously. Actress (playing whore): "Are we supposed to laugh, Billy, when he sticks the ball in his mouth?" Wilder: "Are you *kidding?* The *audience* is supposed to laugh. Ve hope. I have a thing like Hitchcock—I try to put *von joke* into every movie." The crew laughed. Lemmon (dropping the ball): "Oh, oh, wait, I lost the prop." Wilder: "Yah, make it a little dirty before you shove it down his throat." Lemmon took a sponge from Harry Ray, his makeup man, and wet his hair and face with it.

The takes: Wilder called for another ball. "Magic time," said Lemmon, anxiously. The seltzer-spray missed Lemmon's face and hit his stomach. "All right, hold it," said Wilder. Two short bells rang. Wilder turned to a particularly busty actress: "Susan, you gotta breathe out, ozzervise ve don't see Harriet's face." For the next eight takes, the spray continued to fall short of Lemmon's face; his clothes were soaking but he did not seem to notice.

"You know the difference between falsies and the real thing?" Yarnell asked of no one in particular. "Falsies taste like rubber." Take 12: "C'mon kids," said Wilder. "It's the usual siphon shot we've done before." The bottle finally worked right. "Print dat von," said Wilder. Four or five of the whores began screaming and chasing each other about the set. "Vish ve had dat kind of audience at a preview," said Wilder.

Lemmon meandered out of the bistro; one of the male extras came up to him and began a conversation. The actor was telling Lemmon some of his problems and he listened with concern. When the young man mentioned that he thought Lemmon might win another Oscar for his performance in *Days of Wine and Roses,* Jack pantomimed picking up a telephone receiver. "Hello, operator," he said, "this is a bad connection— I can't hear a word you're saying. . . ." The extra laughed quietly. Lemmon excused himself hesitantly and moved away. At every opportunity, Lemmon retired to an upright piano outside his portable dressing room and practiced for a television appearance he was to make on *The Dinah Shore Show.* "Where was I?" he said, resting his cigarette at the edge of the piano top. Nearby, several actresses hummed along with the music.

Lemmon put the cigarette back in his mouth and, squinting through the smoke, played a refrain easily, gently. His eyes watered because of the smoke and, taking the cigarette from his mouth, he rubbed them. "I've always wanted to play the piano with a cigarette in my mouth," he said, still rubbing. "Only Hoagy Carmichael can do it, though. He must have glass eyeballs."

The shot: Yarnell, with the ball in his mouth, was to get punched repeatedly in the belly by Lemmon. Rehearsal: "All right, Bruce," said Wilder. "Put the ball in your mouth, as the sailor said to the lady." Lemmon (eagerly, nodding at Yarnell): "He didn't read for this part, you know, he just sent in his mouth measurement." Then, to Wilder: "I'm not going to go full steam here, Gadg!?" (A reference to director Elia Kazan's nickname, short for "gadget.") Wilder: "Gadg!? Thanks a lot, Mr. Tony Randall!" Shirley MacLaine stood off-camera watching. "All right," said Wilder. "Let's get it on celluloid." The takes: Lemmon punched Yarnell, who made loud noises of frustration trying to get the ball out of his mouth. On one of the takes, Lemmon twisted his wrist; he covered the pain with his other hand. Wilder asked if he was all right and whether he wanted to stop for a while. Lemmon vehemently said no and joked awkwardly about the injury. The work went on. MacLaine broke up loudly and stumbled around the set trying vainly to stifle her laughter. Several abortive takes later, she was still laughing, her hand cupped over her mouth. "That's the funniest thing I ever saw, Billy," she said, wiping her eyes. "Are you *serious?*" Wilder said. "Please, Shirley, go on another set. Go watch *Toys in the Attic*" [shooting next door]. Then: "Do it right this time, Bruce, and I give you Lizabeth Scott's phone number." MacLaine (still laughing): "It's hysterical, Jack. Just hysterical." Lemmon (abstractedly): "Thank God. It better be." Just before the eleventh and final take, Lemmon stood by himself at a corner of the set, preparing. "Sonofabitch," he mumbled. "Sonofabitch."

Tuesday afternoon. Election Day, '62. The shot: At the bar—Lemmon and MacLaine in front, Jacobi behind. After several drinks, Lemmon was to ask her to take the night off from her streetwalking duties; she refuses and leaves. Rehearsal: Lemmon checked over his lines with the script boy; he tried several different readings. Nearby, Wilder flirted with a Japanese stripper, Tura Satana: "It vould be impossible betveen us," he said, "because at some point I vould remember Pearl Harbor." Lemmon took Wilder aside to discuss the scene, telling him he preferred not to kiss MacLaine because it didn't fit with his character's mood. After a few minutes of debate, they found a way to do the kiss that satisfied them both. The actor tentatively suggested a bit of business and before Wilder could give an opinion, he himself negated it. "No, huh?" he said. "OK."

Lemmon told the director he was excited because there were dialogue scenes coming up. "Oh, you delightful little clown, you," said Wilder, smiling. Lemmon did a little tap dance. MacLaine arrived and stood out of camera range waiting to enter. I asked Lemmon if he felt frustrated watching himself on the screen. He nervously lit a mentholated cigarette. "Sometimes I'll laugh at myself in a scene—but very rarely," he answered. "And even then I'm not really laughing as much as I'm saying, 'Yeah, it's working.' " He puffed on his cigarette. "Did you ever watch one stand-up comedian telling a story to another?" Lemmon asked excitedly. "When he hits the punch line, the other guy doesn't laugh, he says, '*That's* funny, that's *funny.*' He's analyzing." He nodded his head twice. "Excuse me," he said politely, and went to take his position in the scene. The bell rang.

Dean Martin abruptly turned up and visited for a while, to which Lemmon remained essentially oblivious, even when Dean slapped him on the back, smiled weakly when Martin kissed MacLaine loudly (see Martin

Lemmon as a gendarme *and Shirley MacLaine as a* poule *in Billy Wilder's adaptation (without songs) of the hit musical* Irma La Douce *(1963), the director's not very successful attempt to duplicate the magic of Lemmon and MacLaine in his* The Apartment *of three years earlier*

chapter). Joe La Shelle, the director of photography, asked Lemmon whether he was going to wear his hat at that angle for the entire shot. Lemmon turned to him vaguely: "I'm sorry, Joe, would you repeat your question? I wasn't listening." The bell rang.

Wilder asked Jacobi to practice pouring the drink. Nervously, the actor complied. Wilder: "Too soon, Lou. Count to four and then pour. Can you do that?" Jacobi nodded. "Let me hear you do that." Jacobi counted to four. "Brilliant!" cried Wilder. "But *slower*." Lemmon smiled sympathetically at Jacobi: "Now take three giant steps forward." Jacobi grinned appreciatively. "All right now, Jack Lemmon," said Wilder. "Are you ready, Academy Avard Vinner—thrice nominated, tvice screwed by very inferior talent?" Lemmon nodded.

The first three takes were spoiled by MacLaine, who had trouble with props and lines. "I don't know what the fuck I'm doing," she said, flippantly. Lemmon gave her a blank look. After several more takes, Wilder declared: "This is the slowest company in Hollywood. Stevens started *The Greatest Story Ever Told* last week, and Jesus is bar mitzvahed already." The bell rang.

After two more unsatisfactory takes, Dean Martin left and Lemmon frowned, growling to himself: "I'm acting. I'm acting." Finally, the shot was completed and two takes printed, one at Lemmon's request. It was election day: "OK, kids," said Wilder, "vote for [Governor Pat] Brown and let's go home." Lemmon sauntered off the set, removing his jacket. "I'm not sure about that scene," he said, uneasily. "I'll have to see the dailies." He shook his head. "Yeah, I gotta see that one before I'll be sure it was all right."

Opposite Stage 5 is Jack Lemmon's permanent dressing room, a comfortable but sparsely furnished little apartment. Lemmon sat behind a large white desk, and Dick Carter, his press agent, and I sat on a long sofa. He called his wife—actress Felicia Farr—to make sure she was meeting us for dinner, had a couple of drinks, and spoke of the necessity of "unwinding" after a day on the set. "You can't just go home," he said. After a while, Wilder, Jacobi, an actress and an assistant director burst into the dressing room. They were all seated, had drinks and crackers, made jokes, told stories (most of them lewd). Lemmon listened quietly, leaning back in his chair; he contributed one story. A half-hour later, everyone left. Lemmon showered ("Just take me a minute—don't want to keep Feleesh waiting alone"), put on a sport shirt, khakis and a sweater ("We could go to Chasen's or something but I haven't any other clothes here"), and we went outside. He got in his beige XKE Jaguar, adjusted his cap with flair and, the top down, drove to Chianti's, a little Italian restaurant not far from the studio. I followed in my car. When we arrived, he suggested I park at the curb instead of in the lot because, he said, his car had once been broken into while it was in the lot. The restaurant owner came out and advised us not to park at the curb because there was a sign forbidding it. "I've been parking there for weeks," said Lemmon quizzically, "never noticed that sign."

We went inside. The employees treated Lemmon like a regular customer and Lemmon treated them as old friends. At one of the front tables, a little girl stood up in her place. "There goes Jack Lemmon, Mommy," she said in an awed whisper. Her parents looked around; Lemmon didn't see this. We were seated in a back booth. We ordered drinks and after a short while, Felicia Farr Lemmon, a tall, slender, determined-looking woman with soft amber hair, arrived wearing a two-piece beige dress with a string of pearls around her neck. Jack kissed her and told her she looked lovely. We ordered pepper steaks. Jack told me they had just been married about a month ago in Paris; Wilder was their best man. More drinks—martinis—were ordered. We discussed people's names; Jack telling me that Felicia's real first name was Olive. "Olive Lemmon," he grinned. "What d'ya think of that?" The food was served. We got on the subject of reading; the Lemmons both said they read a great deal. Felicia said that when she was small she used to take books with her whenever she had to visit relatives because she got so bored. Lemmon looked at her with surprise and then kissed her gently on the cheek. He mentioned that he read very fast and often worried therefore how much he retained. "I do everything too fast," he said. "Read, talk, smoke, eat, everything. I read in the bathroom every morning," he said mischievously. "Mums, Dad and Poopoo taught me to go every morning, without fail; sometimes I just pretend, but I always go."

We got on the subject of articles written about the actor. "I'm very bad copy," Lemmon said, taking a bite of his steak. "People are always making things up about me so I'll sound more interesting. They write articles like 'Jack Lemmon's 17 Rules for Bachelorhood' or something. Let's face it, I'm an actor, I love my work, and that's the story." Felicia grinned. "Yeah, we're not interesting. Why don't we do an article about you?" Jack laughed and said that was a great idea.

I asked him about his late boss, Harry Cohn, for years the head of Columbia Pictures, and one of the most feared men in the industry. "We got along," Lemmon said, finishing his drink. "He was fantastic. Crude. Rude. But he was tough—and he was honest." Felicia looked at him skeptically. "He'd never knife you in the back," Lemmon went on. "He'd show it to you and then let you have it. And I don't think he respected anyone who treated him like a boss. I never once saw him with a riding crop, never once saw him with a clenched fist." Felicia asked Jack to order another drink. He did.

After dinner, Jack told Felicia that he thought Lou Jacobi was having a hard time on the set and what did she think of going over to his hotel and maybe trying to cheer him up. She smiled and said she thought that would be nice. Jack excused himself to call. His wife looked after him for a moment, and then turned to me with a tough smile. "Jack can't believe there's evil in anybody," she said. "He forces me to be the cynical one, just by refusing to see anything really bad in a person. He's kind of like a child that way." She sipped her drink. "Jack's always desperately hurt when someone does something cruel. And surprised. He never thinks someone might be trying to take advantage of him. My friends are amazed at how sensible I've become. I didn't used to be so practical."

On our way to Jacobi's hotel, I drove behind Lemmon, and his wife, in a Lincoln Continental, drove behind me. Nearing the hotel on Sunset Boulevard, a car with two women turned left unexpectedly. Lemmon braked quickly and so did I, but Felicia was caught unaware and bumped me slightly. We drove up the hotel driveway, followed by the two women. When we had parked, Lemmon strode over to them. The driver stuck her head out the window and apologized. "You know you could've caused a bad accident turning like that," said Lemmon. "Yes, I'm awfully sorry," she repeated. "Well, you should be," he answered testily. The women pulled away sheepishly. Lemmon grinned and walked over to me. "I don't know if it's because of the picture or what," he said, laughing giddily, "but I could swear those two were hookers."

Upstairs, Jacobi and his wife, a bit sleepy-eyed, were dressed, and had ordered champagne. Lou poured out drinks all around; his wife said it was a real pleasure to have Jack there. Felicia sat moodily on a sofa; she sipped her drink once. Jack did an impersonation of Jacobi and everyone laughed. Felicia quietly mentioned a woman's name and asked Jack who she was. Jack looked at her dimly and asked her to repeat the name. She did—twice. He remembered then and told her she was an actress he had worked with once. Felicia nodded. Jacobi talked about an experience he'd had on Broadway. Felicia got up suddenly and said thickly that she'd have to be going now. Lemmon looked up and asked what was wrong. She said nothing and that we should all stay; she headed for the door. Jack stood and quickly drained his glass of champagne. Jacobi and his wife were standing. "Wait a minute," said Lemmon, "I'll go with you." Felicia shook her head. "No, it's all right, John, you stay." Jack grinned. "We're going the same way, you know," he said, lamely. Felicia was out by the elevator. Mrs. Jacobi asked if they'd said something to upset her. Jack assured them they hadn't and that he'd see them tomorrow. He closed the door behind him. The Jacobis looked at each other. "I hope it wasn't something we said," Mrs. Jacobi repeated.

*Jack Lemmon with Marilyn Monroe and Tony Curtis in Billy Wilder's
enormously popular screwball comedy of the twenties,* Some Like It
Hot *(1959), released only three years before Marilyn's sudden
death. It was Lemmon's first of six pictures with Wilder.*

The next morning. Thursday. Jack meandered over to me on the set
and I asked if Felicia was feeling better. He explained, simply, that it had
all been a minor misunderstanding. She had seen someone's name in his
appointment book and mistaken it for an old girlfriend. He shrugged his
shoulders slightly. "It wasn't anything," he said, evenly.

The shot: In a cutaway police van—camera was to start on a close-up
of Lemmon, standing at the rear of the van, and then pull back to reveal
about eighteen prostitutes in various states of undress, all trying to
rearrange their clothing.

Rehearsal: "As the camera goes back," Wilder instructed, "I'd like to see how clever you are vith business. Let me see now vhat you're going to do." The girls writhed and wiggled into their clothes. Lemmon reacted appropriately. Wilder (to a buxom girl in a clinging dress): "Susie, you look like a schoolteacher. We vill have to invent some business for poor Susie. Can't you pull the dress over your head?" The girl shrugged. "Sure I can," she said, pulling her dress up past her thighs. "But I gotta put some clothes on—I mean, I haven't got any panties on." A couple of makeup women appeared and climbed into the van; they applied body makeup to the ladies' exposed backs, legs, arms. Wilder (watching): "This is the most expensive pornographic film ever made." Then to Lemmon: "Are you vith it, Jack?" Lemmon (from inside the van): "I'm gettin' in the mood, D.W. [a reference to film pioneer D. W. Griffith]. My image is that I'm in a candy store, right? And I can't make up my mind." Shirley MacLaine's double left the van and the actress took her place.

The takes: The bell rang. Wilder: "All right—babble! And action!" The girls wiggled, squirmed and babbled into their clothes. Two bells. Wilder: "Julie! Are you doing anything back there?" Lemmon: "Is she ever! And mind your own business." A tray of dixie cups filled with water was passed back into the van; Lemmon helped distribute them. There were five takes, after which everyone left the van. A few minutes later, Mrs. Lemmon, the actor's mother, a short, gray-haired lady with pale blue eyes, came on the set accompanied by several other women. "Hi, doll," she said as her son came over. "How are all your little whores?" She introduced him to her friends and Lemmon shook hands politely with each of them.

The shot: Inside the van again, Lemmon was to react to one of the girls (Tura Satana) adjusting her bra. The takes: While doing the shot, the stripper (on Wilder's whispered suggestion) tried to help the reality of Lemmon's reaction by pulling down the front of her bra for a second, exposing herself to the actor. Lemmon reacted with a tiny squeal and then started laughing and so did everyone else. Crew members craned their necks to get a peek at what was going on, but by then all was concealed again. The shot was completed without further incident. Lemmon undid his jacket and jumped from the van. "You were very quiet in there, Jackie," his mother said to him. Lemmon looked at her and shook his head. "I don't have any lines in this scene," he said.

The following Saturday afternoon at the NBC-TV studios in Burbank, Lemmon rehearsed for the show he was to tape the next evening. Wearing khakis and a green sweater, he doodled alone at a grand piano. After a while, he decided to have some lunch and Dick Carter and I joined him. Walking toward the "Artists' Entrance," a uniformed male receptionist asked if any of us knew how to spell the French word "derrière." Lemmon stopped. "Yeah. Wait a minute," he said. "It's D-E-R-I-E-double-R-E, isn't it? With one of those doohickeys over the second to last E. I think that's it." The man thanked him and we continued out of the building. As we stepped into the parking lot, Lemmon stopped again. "Wait a minute," he said. "Is it D-E-R-I-E-double-R-E or D-E-double-R-I-E-R-E?" Carter shrugged his shoulders. "I think the double-R comes first," Lemmon said, turning. "I better tell him. Be right back." He trotted up to the door and went back inside. Carter grinned at me. A few seconds later, Lemmon reappeared and nodded his head once. "Done," he said.

The restaurant was dimly lit and occupied by about a dozen men, most of them at the bar watching a football game on television. "What's the score?" Lemmon asked as we came in. One of the men told him. The three of us sat at a center table. "What were the final odds goin' in?" he called to the group at the bar. Someone gave him the information. From where he sat, Lemmon could see the TV set and he watched the game for a few moments. "I love football," he said, turning toward me. "Probably because I could never play it. Too light. Broke my nose twice trying." He ordered a martini and a hamburger with onion. "Who's got the ball?" he called out again. Someone told him. The drinks arrived and then the sandwiches. Carter asked Jack what he'd done that morning. "I woke up early," he answered, biting into his hamburger. "And I read a very good article on Shakespeare in *Realities*. It's really incredible, you know, that possibly England's most fantastic man is also probably its least-known man. This piece debunks the possibility that Shakespeare was ill-educated. It says that being a brilliant man, you really can't find Shakespeare himself through his characters, but only out of certain recurring images. Like the snail, for instance. Interesting, huh?"

A phone call came through requesting Lemmon to return to the TV studio. He hurriedly finished his meal and we got up to go. Coming out of the restaurant, we passed a middle-aged couple on their way in. As the actor walked by them, they both turned and stared after him for several moments. Lemmon didn't notice this. Going back through the artists' entrance, the receptionist looked up from his book. "D-E-double-R . . ." said Lemmon, without stopping. The receptionist laughed.

On Sunday evening, just before the taping of *The Dinah Shore Show*, Lemmon's wife and mother came to visit him in his dressing room. Felicia wore a beige mink coat over a black wool dress, topped by a knitted wool-fringed hat that hid most of her hair; Jack kissed her gingerly as she came in. Mildred Lemmon wore a low-cut, blue satin dress and a brown mink stole; "Hello, Minnie," he said, kissing her. He was called out of the room for a moment. His mother sat at one end of a long sofa and his wife, after picking up a pair of socks from the floor and hanging them over a lamp-shade, sat at the other end. By this time, the elder Mrs. Lemmon was excitedly telling me a story about the first time she had gone to the Motion Picture Mothers' Club, soon after her son had come to Holly-wood. "I was very nervous," she said. "I was sure no one would know who I was. And all new members had to stand up and give a speech. Well, I've got more guts in my little finger than Jackie has in his whole body. So I stood up and I did it." Lemmon returned at this point and closed the dressing room door. "And afterward," Mrs. Lemmon went on, "Lou Costello's mother came over to me and introduced herself. She asked me whose mother I was and I said, 'I'm Jackie Lemmon's mother.' 'Oh,' she said, 'what movie is she in?' " Felicia and Jack smiled and exchanged looks. "Jackie said that's what I get for calling him Jackie."

Lemmon looked at me. "Ya—and she still does it," he said, making a face. "My father was Jack, too, so to distinguish between us she always called me Jackie. But, my God, after thirty-seven years, it's a little tough to take. Every time she does it I cringe." Mrs. Lemmon turned from her daughter-in-law. "What did you say, Jackie?" Lemmon raised his voice. "I said after thirty-seven years you could stop calling me Jackie." Mrs. Lem-mon laughed. Jack turned to his wife. "Dinah's got twenty-eight numbers in this thing—she's the whole show." Felicia smiled. "And you told me you were the whole show, John," she said.

"You look very pretty tonight, Feleesh," said Lemmon. She touched her head. "You think anybody'll be able to see over this hat?" He assured her they would, and then noticed the socks on the lampshade. "Hmmm," he said, grinning, "I wonder who could've put these socks up here." Feli-cia smiled. "You're pretty calm, John, for an old man," she said. Her mother-in-law, meanwhile, had started telling me of her TV-viewing habits. "I use earphones," she said. "And I won't answer the phone. People call me the next morning and ask why I didn't answer. 'I have news for you,' I say to them. 'I'm deaf. And when I watch television, I can't hear anything else.' "

A bearded crewmember stuck his head in the door and told Lemmon something. "Beaver!" exclaimed Mildred Lemmon. "Did you ever play Beaver?" she asked me. "Every time you see someone with a beard you yell 'Beaver'—first one to do it gets a buck." She smiled mischievously. "We used to play it all the time. One day, Jack, my husband, took a bunch of us to see *The Man Who Came to Dinner.* And when [white-bearded actor] Monty Woolley came on, I yelled 'Beaver!' " She laughed giddily. "Jack didn't speak to me for a month." She paused. "But I got my buck." Felicia was looking critically at her husband's attire. "Aren't you worried about your pants falling, John?" she asked quietly. "No belt or suspenders?" Jack tugged comically at his trousers. Someone knocked at the door and told Lemmon it was time to get ready, and the two Mrs. Lemmons left to take their seats in the audience.

The show was taped. Afterward, in the corridor, Lemmon's wife and mother congratulated him. "Was it really all right?" he asked his wife. She nodded approvingly. A small boy came up next to the actor and waited there tentatively. After a few moments, Lemmon noticed him. "Hi, there," he said. "Could I . . . Mr. Lemmon, could I have your autograph?" He handed over pencil and paper. "Sure," Jack said, smiling. "Thought you'd never ask."

Over the years, Lemmon and I didn't ever spend any real time together again; he was discussed for some movies I made but it never worked out. However, the couple of times we ran into each other he was kind, pleasant and hugely complimentary. The night I didn't win the Directors Guild Award as Best Director for *The Last Picture Show,* Jack passed me after the ceremony and out of the corner of his mouth, he said, "It's all a crock of shit! You made the best film in twenty years," and patted me on the back as he moved past. He echoed the compliment with a gesture and a look on the night I didn't win the directing Oscar.

After *Irma La Douce,* the highlights in Lemmon's career continued to come for Billy Wilder and Blake Edwards: *The Great Race* for Blake, with Tony Curtis, Peter Falk and Natalie Wood; and, for the first time with Walter Matthau, in Wilder's *The Fortune Cookie.* This was followed up two years later with their second pairing, the hugely successful film of Neil Simon's Broadway smash *The Odd Couple.* Lemmon directed once— Matthau in *Kotch* in 1970. But his biggest triumphs in the seventies were both dramas: *Save the Tiger* (won Best Actor Oscar), at the start of the decade and *The China Syndrome* at the end. In the eighties and nineties, Jack plowed right on with quality work such as *Missing* and *Tribute* (both Oscar nominations), Edwards' *That's Life, Glengarry Glen Ross, Grumpy* (and *Grumpier*) *Old Men*—both with Matthau again. The two were great friends and did ten pictures together. Walter's death was very hard on

*Jack Lemmon destroys a greenhouse in frustration over his and his wife's
(Lee Remick) alcoholism in Blake Edwards' Days of Wine and Roses
(1962), among Lemmon's best and most personal performances.*

Jack. He had a great triumph on television with a dramatization of the
best seller *Tuesdays with Morrie.* As he got older, the slight hunch to his
shoulders off-camera gave way to a pronounced stoop that got worse and
worse. A coworker in Jack's last years remembered that Lemmon would
walk around slumped over terribly and then when they said, "Action!"
he'd rise up to his full height and play the scene. As soon as he heard,
"Cut!" he stooped right over again. He and Felicia stayed together
through thick and thin, their son Christopher is a good actor, and Jack
just kept working right to the end, which I'm certain is how he wanted it.

Especially certain when I remembered something from our first youth-
ful conversation at the Polo Lounge forty years before. In front of the
hotel, waiting for our cars to be brought from the parking lot, Lemmon
had looked at me, smiled, and said, "You know, I'll tell you something.
Here I am at thirty-five and—though, believe me, everything's wonderful

that's happened—I can only play *two* parts a *year*. I yearn for those days when I was doing a *different* TV role every *week*. You know, I'm an actor, I like to *work*."

The cars arrived, we said good-bye, and both of us drove away in the night. We met again at the first red light. From his convertible sports car, he yelled, "Driving is wild in this town, isn't it?" And we raced down Sunset Boulevard until a red light separated us and he raised his fist in the air with the middle finger extended in a gesture of comic defiance as he sped away from me down the dark, empty boulevard.

Born John Uhler Lemmon III, February 8, 1925, Newton, MA; died June 27, 2001, Los Angeles, CA.

Selected starring features (with director):

1954: *It Should Happen to You* (George Cukor)
1955: *Mr. Roberts* (John Ford and Mervyn LeRoy); *My Sister Eileen* (Richard Quine)
1957: *Operation Mad Ball* (Quine)
1959: *Some Like It Hot* (Billy Wilder)
1960: *The Apartment* (Wilder)
1962: *Days of Wine and Roses* (Blake Edwards)
1963: *Irma La Douce* (Wilder)
1965: *The Great Race* (Edwards)
1966: *The Fortune Cookie* (Wilder)
1968: *The Odd Couple* (Gene Saks)
1973: *Save the Tiger* (John G. Avildsen)
1979: *The China Syndrome* (James Bridges)
1982: *Missing* (Costa-Gavras)
1986: *That's Life!* (Edwards)
1992: *Glengarry Glen Ross* (James Foley)
1993: *Grumpy Old Men* (Donald Petrie)

8

JERRY LEWIS

When Jerry Lewis and I met in January 1961, he was at the peak of his career, the king of the Paramount lot, among the biggest box-office attractions in the world. He was as misunderstood during this golden period—which had already lasted for more than a dozen years (people forget that Lewis was a huge star by the time he was twenty)—as he was misunderstood when some of his home country turned on him with savagery by 1970, as if his earlier success had all been some sort of clerical error. As though he hadn't been wildly, outrageously funny, first in nightclubs, then on television, radio, films; even comic books featured Lewis in the fifties, and to his mainly young fans (age seven to twenty-five), he had the sex appeal and personal charisma of today's rock stars.

I loved him right from the moment I was first exposed to him in *At War with the Army* (1950), his initial starring-role picture opposite his partner Dean Martin, which was—not insignificantly—an independently produced movie, only distributed by Paramount. Lewis always made smart deals. What is now a common practice was anything but normal in Hollywood at this very early date in the history of the picture business's huge upheavals between 1945 and 1962, around which time the original long-term-contract studio system finally collapsed. Stars had declared their independence from the studios, which had been, of course, exploiting the talent. So what else is new? (Now the situation is reversed.)

This is another of the reasons why Lewis' career is so interesting—it spans seismic re-orderings of the vast entertainment industry. Also—unlike all but two others in this book: Chaplin and Cassavetes—Lewis very successfully starred in pictures he wrote, directed and produced. One of the biggest of the mindless jokes about Lewis—or France—is the supposed aberration of the French loving Jerry Lewis. Well, the Germans, the Italians, the Spaniards do, too, just for starters. No, we're very good at

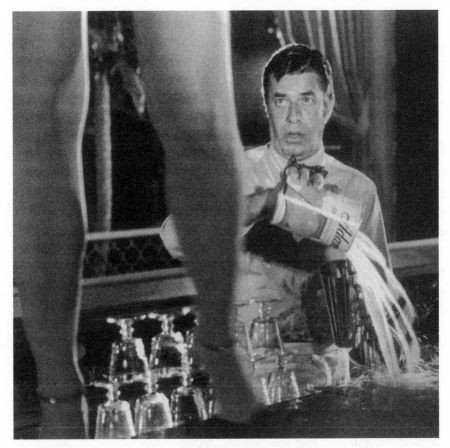

Jerry Lewis is an out-of-work circus clown trying to make good as a bartender in Lewis' popular return to the big screen (after a decadelong absence), Hardly Working *(1981), which he co-wrote and directed.*

turning on our own popular culture, dealing with it as disposable and constantly having to renew itself through degrading last season's product. It took the French to explain jazz to us, as well as mainstream American movies (circa 1912–1962), genre by genre (a French word). Yet what seems to be forgotten here is that jazz, mainstream American movies, and Jerry Lewis were also extraordinarily *popular* in the United States *before* the French explained them to us. Indeed, the explaining often happened after these had stopped being popular, had gone out of fashion—a word which resonates in the U.S.A.

That Lewis was misunderstood during two long eclipses (1970–80, 1984–95) is at least not surprising in revisionist times; but that even in his glory days he was almost equally misunderstood—by critics, reviewers, even most of the audiences which loved him—is more unique. What the huge public recognized almost immediately—on an unconscious level—was that Jerry Lewis represented the frightened or funny nine-year-old in everybody, most especially the male, adult or not. As life gets tougher perhaps in one's second half-century, you sometimes find yourself wanting to have, or resorting to, a private Jerry Lewis moment: some "MAILEEE!" scream; translation: "HELP!" Lewis touched the truth in every guy, no matter what age, but as his audience got older, they often turned on their own youth, and rejected it as kid stuff. The truth is they were actually hiding a secret desire to resort to some form of infantilism in order to survive the knocks of life. Men are taught to keep their deepest feelings always in check. How refreshing if more guys copped to being scared: there is humility to that. Which is why Jerry was so appealing to women—they recognized his vulnerability in themselves. At his peak, Lewis was often referred to as a spastic, a retard, The Idiot (but a little sexy); never admitting that the reason you laugh at his openly expressed fears is because you've felt them, recognize his reactions as ones you've had inwardly yourself. That's why the Lewis laughs were often so gut-busting: Jerry's behavior touched some true identification. Yet who would own up to it?

That Lewis did all this instinctually is both true and not. Right from the start, he knew exactly what to do to be funny; and when he saw what could be done with a partner like the conventionally handsome, dry, wry, older, suave and satiric ladies' man that Dean Martin was, together they struck a vein of gold that was never fully mined, yet yielded during its initial decade billions of dollars, and billions of laughs. What he did with himself alone for nearly fifteen years was another gold mine (as was Dean's alone). And Lewis knew that, too: when the twosome should leave 'em laughing. Dean took a major part of Jerry's act—breaking up the joint—to his Rat Pack days.

Here's most of the first thing I ever wrote about Lewis (part of a long piece on Hollywood), published in *Esquire* in August 1962:

> One morning at Paramount, I was taken to *The Ladies' Man* sound stage where Jerry Lewis was directing, producing and starring. The area was buzzing with technicians, actors, actresses, signs, props, television cameras and electrical equipment, TV monitors, motion picture cameras, cables, booms, chairs, and other paraphernalia. . . .
>
> Atop a huge crane, with an added extension, at the end of which was the camera, sat Jerry Lewis, screaming instructions, insults, jokes, and exchanging quips with the cast and crew. Painted in

large white letters on the side of this mountainous piece of equipment was the notice: Jerry's Toy. Next to the camera was an old-fashioned car horn that Lewis intermittently sounded as a sign of approval or anger. When he wished to get down to the ground, he screamed to a man at the rear of the machine, who controlled the crane's raising and lowering. Whenever Lewis was making a movie, I was told, it was "a free-for-all set," and yet *The Bellboy,* made under even more haphazard circumstances, was one of the studio's biggest money-makers.

I watched Lewis throw cigarettes down at technicians and then demand them back. Almost at the opposite end of the stage, facing the vast four-story boardinghouse set and running from one wall to the other, was a huge banner colorfully lettered: Very Happy Holidays from the Lousy Producer-Director, followed by a caricature of Lewis' profile, which, I noticed, was also to be found on walls, pieces of equipment, instruments, and even on the shirts of some of the personnel. Suddenly Lewis screamed: "That's no damn good! Two demerits for Jim!" On the side of Lewis' portable dressing room there was a bulletin board marked with a sign, Little Bits of Information We Couldn't Do Without, surrounded by a jumble of ads, press layouts, stills, and so forth, from Lewis' last two comedies. Near the set were two rows of bleachers where, someone informed me, children were allowed to watch shooting; two or three small children were there now along with a couple of bewildered parents. Nearby was a large display cabinet filled with old comedy and vaudeville props, each separately labeled. On a side wall were some hundred-fifty coffee mugs, each with a person's first name under it; at Lewis' request, each member of the cast and crew had his own cup.

After a while, Lewis dismounted his crane, changed his shirt, and was ready for a take. He called for quiet, climbed the spiral staircase in the boardinghouse, entered a second-story room, and comically began cleaning with a feather duster. The camera recorded his moves. Suddenly he stopped. "Cut!" he screamed. "What the hell is this crap doing here?" he demanded, indicating a little table on which stood a small spray bottle. "Hey, Jim," he yelled, "what are you, some kind of a nut?" A heavyset technician lumbered into the room and Lewis started squirting him with the contents of the atomizer. Running away, the man cried, "Hey, come on, Jerry, cut it out! Hey, cut it out, Jerry!" Instead, Lewis chased him zanily around the set as other technicians and actors chuckled wearily. Then, hiding behind a jog in the set, he waited until the winded man rounded the corner and gave him a good squirt full in the face.

This attended to, the comedian repeated the scene, expressing satisfaction with the take when it was completed, and went into his dressing room, followed by an entourage of five or six. A bit later, he reappeared in an insane Indian disguise, which, I was told, was not for the picture but for the general amusement. After checking a new setup, he took the costume off, and looked at some rushes of the previous day's shooting on a large screen behind his dressing room.

I asked him why the three or four TV sets were on the stage. "We use them to set up the shots," he answered seriously. "We can see better what the shot'll look like with them."* Then, grabbing a baseball, he began tossing it around the area with some technicians. I lingered long enough to see him mischievously set up an inflatable toy clown behind a large carton and amuse the company, as, seemingly on its own rubber legs, he made it rise and fall from behind the box like a grotesque dwarf. Exchanging some droll comments with it, he called him Melvin. (Lewis' shrill "Melvin!?!" had become a catch-phrase with Martin in the early fifties.) A moment later he was screaming instructions again, and climbing aboard his expensive "Toy," from where he could survey his make-believe kingdom.

The prescient, legendary editor of *Esquire*'s peak years, Harold Hayes, called me after he read that (in the lengthy article it was part of) and said that not only was he going to publish the piece, but he would be interested to see what would happen if I did a full-blown portrait of Jerry. This resulted in only my second visit to Hollywood, where I spent nearly three weeks following Lewis around.

It was the beginning of a friendship that happily survives to the present, as ever-young Jerry—unbelievably—nears his seventy-ninth year. Having been a hopeless fan of Martin and Lewis, as a teenager, I built up a 300-page scrapbook, for God's sake. Here's a shorter, revised version of the Lewis profile *Esquire* published in September 1962:

*This became known as the Video Assist, now standard equipment on the shooting of nearly every picture made; see pages 148 and 192 and the photograph on page 187.

"Before you meet him," Jack Keller said, "I better tell you there's a couple of things he's sensitive about." Keller had been handling Jerry Lewis' publicity for more than sixteen years. "One of them is Dean Martin, though the antagonism is all on Dino's part. Jerry's always a little shocked, even now, when Dean lams into him. He's got a scrapbook called 'Dean Shoots His Mouth Off.' " Keller lit another cigarette. "I was there the day they split up in 1956—July 25th, ten years to the day. They did their last show at the Copa and that was it. It was a traumatic experience for the kid, and to make it worse, he could never understand Dean's antagonism." Keller paused. "But Dean's a tough one—I'll tell you a weird story.

"A couple years ago, Jerry and Patti, his wife, were in a Las Vegas club. And Dean was filling in for somebody that night. They hadn't spoken, remember, for about four years, not a word. Suddenly Dean sees Jerry sitting at a table, comes over and sits down. He's very friendly, and they talk about old times. He tells Jerry he's got a train to catch, and asks him whether he'd fill in at the end of the show. Jerry says sure. Anyway, comes time for Dean to go on, he gets up there and announces, 'Ladies and gentlemen, there's a fella sitting in the audience I'd like you to meet, my partner, Jerry Lewis.' Not my former partner, 'my partner.' Well, it's a pretty moving scene—everybody's bawling. He and Jerry re-create some of their old routines; you know, they ask each other, 'Did we really do this shit,' they do a soft-shoe. Then Dean leaves to catch his train and Jerry finishes the show. Now get this. Not long afterward, in a U.P.I. interview, Dean slams into Jerry like crazy. So go figure."

He smiled. "But Jerry's a pussycat. Not that it's always waltz time. Like sometimes he'll call me up at two in the morning. 'Listen,' he says, 'I want you to hear something.' He wrote a new proverb maybe, and he wants me to hear it. Jesus! What do I want to hear at two in the morning!" He chuckled. "Jerry and me are like water and oil—we don't mix. I guess that's why we like each other."

After a quick phone call, Keller turned back to me. "I'll tell you something you people in New York don't realize about Jerry. He is the only star in the history of the industry who's never had a flop. That's a fact. Take any of our big stars—Cary Grant or Gary Cooper or Clark Gable, any of them—they've all had at least one picture in their careers that didn't make money. Jerry's made twenty-six films and not one has grossed less than five million dollars. Deedle-dee. You know what he gets for an hour on television? $400,000. For a week in a nightclub, his minimum is $40,000. And you can't even talk to him for less than that." Keller paused to let the facts sink in.

"In 1960," he continued, "they had this picture, *CinderFella*, and they were a little worried about it. Jerry wanted to release it for Christmas—the fantasy angle and all that, he thought would be good for the holidays. Well, Paramount wanted to release it in July, and Jerry said it'd die in the summer. See, they always release one Lewis picture for the summer holidays and one for Christmas vacation, the best timing for the pre-teenage audience. Only this time they didn't have any product for the July slot. Anyway, Jerry was on his way to Florida to appear at the Fontainebleau, and on his way he stopped in New York to see Barney Balaban, the head of Paramount. Jerry told him how he wanted *CinderFella* released in December, and Balaban said he needed a Lewis film for the summer. So right there Jerry stands up and says he'll make Balaban a picture while he's down in Florida; he says he's got the story and everything. And right there he made up the basic outline for *The Bellboy.* On the spot. He had nothing when he walked in." Keller chuckled at the recollection.

"Anyway, I'm sitting here in Hollywood, resting, when I get a call from Jerry. He says to me, 'Jack, you better come down here right away, we're starting a picture on Monday.' I said, 'Where are you?' He says, 'I'm in Florida.' I say, 'What picture? We ain't got no picture!' 'We do now,' he says. 'The trucks are already on their way.' So that's how he got to direct his first picture—he produced and wrote it as well. You shoulda seen that production. I asked him, 'Who's gonna be in it?' He says, 'What's the difference? We'll cast it from Celebrity Service.' Every scene was written the night before he shot it—for whomever was in town. That's Jerry. I gotta hand it to him, he's really got guts. The picture was made for $900,000. To date it's grossed 8 million. Isn't that a pussycat?!"

Frank Tashlin* had directed Jerry Lewis in five films, including the last Martin-Lewis movie, and one of their best, *Hollywood or Bust.* "They didn't speak to each other during the whole picture," he told me. "It was a bitch." Tashlin was in the process of directing his sixth Lewis picture, *It'$ Only Money,* when I met him lounging on a couch. "There's a side of Jerry Lewis you probably don't know about," he said. "He's really an electronics genius. You see those television monitors over there?" He pointed at two TV sets near the camera. "That's really a marvelous thing Jerry made. At the side of the movie camera he mounted a small-size TV camera. It's lined up with the movie camera so that when you're shooting a scene you don't have to look through the viewfinder; you just look into one of the monitors and there's the shot just as it'll appear on the screen—it's like

*See Tashlin chapter in *Who the Devil Made It.*

seeing your rushes as they happen. Jerry's used it since *The Bellboy*, and when he told me about it I said I didn't want to bother with it. He begged me to try it just one day on this picture. Well, the first day I didn't take my head out of that thing." The director put a stick of gum in his mouth. "Another thing is the boom mike." He frowned slightly. "This is a real horror—such an antiquated thing. For *Ladies' Man*, Jerry bugged his whole set with fifty or sixty mikes and cut his shooting time tremendously. You see, a director actually works maybe one hour out of eight—and four of those other seven hours are literally spent lighting for the boom—so there won't be shadows and so on. Jerry eliminated this problem. Paramount says that it worked and still they refuse to let us have it on this picture. It's ridiculous; this is 1929 sound."

Tashlin's secretary came over with a gin drink she gave him. "Jerry hates to do serious scenes. I think he'd rather jump off a bridge to get a laugh. In *CinderFella* we had a scene where he's all alone and he sings a kind of serious little song. He was so nervous about doing that goddamn thing, he procrastinated one day from nine in the morning till four in the afternoon. Then at four he did it, one take, and it was beautiful."

For a moment, Tashlin looked over his script, then said, "Jerry never rehearses. Just one take and that's it. You rehearse with Jerry and you'll die. So you can't really do anything interesting with the camera—his habits dictate your style. Sometimes when I have to repeat a scene, he'll change it around and do something completely different. And that's his charm, you see—you never know what he's going to do next. He doesn't look at his dialogue until he walks on the set, and then he never sticks to the lines anyway—usually he makes them better. I just tell him roughly what the scene is and he does it, kind of hit-and-run, and it's very successful. But you get no credit for doing a Lewis picture."

The director was called away to check a camera setup, then returned, and said gently, "But there's no dreaming for Jerry—all he has to do is think of something and he can go out and buy it. Up in Vegas once he bought a hundred cashmere sweaters—he wears them a few times and gives them away." He sipped his drink. "Wait till you get out to his house—it's Louis B. Mayer's old mansion out in Bel Air. Jerry left all the décor just as Mayer had it. All he did was change the initials on the ashtrays." Tashlin smiled. "When you drive up, you'll think there's a crowd there, but it's all his cars. He's got something like fourteen of them. And you've never seen so many leather-bound books in your life—it's a complete record of everything he's ever done, like the Pharaohs." The director chuckled. "His wife, Patti, she's a rare woman. They've been married eighteen years. She's like a person in a cyclone holding on to the kite—that's how strong she is."

Tashlin looked around him abstractedly. "Comedians always have an entourage. It's the need for constant laughter, even though you're paying for it. But don't misunderstand, Jerry's compassion is as large as his extravagance. It often gets him in trouble, too: I'll tell you a story. Somewhere, Jerry met this guy who really needed a couple operations. Jerry felt sorry for him, paid for his trip to the Coast, paid for the operations. And then he gave the guy a job as a gagman. The stuff he turned out was no good, but Jerry kept him on the payroll anyway. One day he's on the set, kidding around, and this guy suddenly appears, rushes over to Jerry, puts his hands on Jerry's throat and literally starts choking the kid—he's trying to kill him. It took four guys to pull him off. Jerry was white; he was shaking. And this guy is screaming, 'I'll get your kids, I'll kill your kids.' Well, from then on there's been a policeman guarding his home twenty-four hours a day. You know what Jerry did? He paid this guy's plane fare back to his hometown and, I swear, to this day Jerry doesn't understand why the man did that." Tashlin looked sadly around and finished his drink.

Jerry Lewis was born Joseph Levitch in 1926 in Newark, New Jersey. In 1962, he was a millionaire a few times over. On the door to his private office at Paramount the sign reads: "Jerry Lewis—The Chief." The office itself was spacious, simply furnished in modern style; on its oak-paneled walls hung hundreds of photographs of his wife, his five sons, himself with various friends and personalities, mementos, plaques, awards, and the Gold Record he received for "Rock-a-Bye Your Baby with a Dixie Melody." When I met with him the first time, he was sitting behind a long, wide desk, surrounded by a typewriter, phones, Dictaphone machine, and assorted gadgets, tanned and looking at least ten years younger than he was. He wore a powder-blue sweater, white shirt, gray slacks, white socks, heavy dark suede shoes, and a pair of black thin-rimmed glasses that he took off a few minutes after we began our conversation and never put on again. When he talks or listens he looks directly at you, and uses his professional high-pitched voice only rarely for an effect; his normal speaking voice, still nasal, is a good deal lower.

Jack Keller was sprawled on a couch nearby, and Lewis was discussing certain journalists with him. "Those guys have got chutzpah," he was saying. "You know what chutzpah is, don't you?" he asked me. "Chutzpah is a man who kills his mother and father and then pleads mercy to the court 'cause he's an orphan." He shook his head twice. "If I've been unkind and I know the other fella knows it, I wanta go bury my head in the sand." I asked him why no one had thought of his TV-monitoring system before. "Too simple," he answered. "Same thing with the boom mike. On *Errand Boy* I used the boom very little. The sound department came in here— four very tall heads. 'We hear you're rebelling,' they said. 'When I'm through,' I said, 'you will, too.' " Lewis tore a sheet of paper with his caricature on it from a memo pad and took a sharp pencil from one of the four glasses filled with them on his desk. He made a drawing to illustrate his points, explaining as he went along. "Now watch how sweet this is," he said. "If you're told not to open a door on the set twenty-five feet away from where we're shooting 'cause the boom'll pick it up—why shouldn't a mike, held eight feet away from the actor, out of camera range, be able to pick up the actor's voice as clearly as the boom over his head? We took a test and I showed them how well it worked—they still won't buy it. I use it on my own productions though, which *It'$ Only Money* ain't." He folded the piece of paper neatly in half, then tore it in half again, threw it in a wastebasket, and replaced the pencil in the glass.

"In order for people to justify their position," he continued seriously, "they have to complicate it. Comes from thirty or forty-five years of working one way. Whenever I'm ready to roll a scene, some poor guy will run on to put something in the scene that he could've put in before; it's quite sad. It's his way of calling attention to his little duty. People gotta learn." He took a drag on his cigarette. "I say if I pay you from Monday to Friday and if you can deliver in three days, you got the other two off. They'll stretch it out to five days." He shook his head. "One of my biggest peeves is fear. If everyone figures they can't do something, they'll never do it. You gotta try." He paused. "I know what you're thinkin'. You're thinkin' it's easy for somebody who's well off like me to talk. But I was fired from every job when I really needed bread. And I feel this way: a person can tell me to go to hell, that's OK, but he better know what he's talkin' about."

Keller sat up slowly on the couch, got up, and quietly left the office. Lewis glanced at him as he closed the door. "I think that in this day and age," he went on suddenly, "considering all that's happened in the industry, what we need is peace of mind. I want people to leave my movies with a happy heart. I think when you depict the ticket buyer, it's sad. Two and a half hours of cold-water flat and then he leaves and goes home to his cold-water flat—that's unfair, it's unjust, it's a terrible rap." He paused to pour himself a glass of water from a plastic pitcher nearby. "I have a dedication to the people I make my pictures for. I make a picture without a plot so the kids can come down the aisle with mommy or uncle anytime. They don't have to worry about gettin' there at the beginning. A thin plot, OK, but otherwise it gets in the way."

Keller returned and sprawled on the couch again. Lewis put his feet up on the desk. "Did you ever read *The Catcher in the Rye?*" he asked. I told him I had. "Well, you never saw a more Holden Caulfield guy than you're sittin' with right now." He grinned slightly. "And Salinger's sister told me she used to call him 'Sonny.' That's what my grandmother used to call me. It's frightening."

Keller began practicing golf strokes as I asked about Tashlin. "Tish," Lewis said, smiling warmly. "Frank Tashlin made me understand the use of the word 'friend.' I hear his name and I get tears in my eyes. I hate him and he's a son of a bitch." He drank the rest of the water. "Frank's my teacher."

The comedian went on to discuss the duality in his own mind between his screen personality and the man who plays him; he spoke of the person on the screen as "him." "Sometimes I write a memo in the morning," he explained, "and then later on the set when it's carried out, I rebel against it—I've forgotten that it was me who asked for it." The intercom buzzed, Lewis flicked a switch, and his secretary's voice informed him that Mrs. Lewis was on Two. Quickly reaching for the receiver, he fumbled it, dropped it on the desk, retrieved it, and said, "Did you hear Graceful pick up the phone?" On the wall behind him I noticed an autographed photo of President Kennedy.

After a few moments of quiet conversation, Lewis hung up and smiled. "That's the third time today we've talked. She'll probably call twice more." He lit a cigarette. "Patti calls me the Jewish Sir Lancelot. I derive pleasure from giving happiness to people. She always asks me, 'Who'd you give an apple to this morning?' " The comedian went on to say that when he was busy he ignored people, even his friends, and that he knew he was ignoring them. "If you turn your back on me when I'm busy, don't come around when I'm havin' fun," he said. "And if a person ain't genuine, I know it. I can spot a dirty, lying, phony rat—I can smell 'em." He smiled.

When I asked whether he ever thought he'd do a dramatic picture, he said, "Why?" and paused. "Five thousand people are far more capable of it than me," he explained rationally, putting out his cigarette. "Why should I compete with them? But there's only eight guys who do what I do. Ha-ha-ha, that's my responsibility. Why should I do Sammy Glick or something like that? For what? So dat four Park Avenue dames can go see it and say, 'Didn't I tell you, John?' " he mimicked effeminately. "They can go see Charles Laughton belching at Elsa Lanchester if they want, but when they come to see me, they come to see the Idiot, and they're rootin' for me 'cause I'm the underdog." He paused and blew some ashes from a memo pad, tore off the top piece and threw it away. "I gotta lot of loyal people," he continued. "There're three-year-olds that grew up and now they bring their three-year-olds to see my pictures. There's this seven-year-old kid and his mother called me up this morning—he's deaf, but he reads me and he laughs. How can I take that away from him?" he asked rhetorically. "You're sayin' to yourself, 'Can this *schmuck* be genuine?' Well, if not, I'm foolin' myself."

"This is not a Closed Set. Come On In. You're Most Welcome," reads a sign on the entrance door to whatever sound stage Jerry Lewis works on. On the set every day is a man hired by Lewis to play electronic mood music or sound effects on a huge tape machine.

Tuesday: An extended fanfare resounded through the set. "That's his music," said Frank Tashlin, and Lewis walked jauntily in, saying hello to everyone, wearing sky-blue pants (a hundred dollars a pair) and a tan windbreaker. Drums sounded and he walked to their beat. A bed had been placed on a waist-high platform for a close-up of Lewis underneath, snoring. Tashlin took him aside and quietly explained the shot to him: while he was under the bed, someone would sit on it, out of camera range; the someone was supposed to be an actress, but would actually be one of the heavier technicians so that the mattress springs would sag lower and hit Lewis. This explained, Tashlin attempted to get Lewis under the bed, but Jerry began imitating a monkey and jumping all over the director. "Did ya ever see a Jewish monkey?" he asked, a cigarette dangling from his lips. Tashlin coaxed him: "C'mon, Jerry. C'mon, little boy. Get under the bed and make your funny little faces. C'mon, be funny." Finally under the bed, Jerry suddenly yelled, "I'm hooked. Lift the bed up, ya guinea faggot!" A couple of technicians lumbered over, lifted it, and Lewis unhooked himself from a spring. The lighting man put a light meter near Lewis' face to gauge the reading and Lewis bit his hand. "C'mon, Jerry," said Tashlin quietly, "get your little arm out of the way so it won't cover your little face." Lewis asked sarcastically whether the bed would collapse on him: "If the whole goddamn thing comes down, I'm outta business." Tashlin assured him it wouldn't. "From where you're standing you're very confident," yelled Lewis. "Why don't you get under here, you big giraffe!" Tashlin told him again to put his head under the bed. Lewis made faces at him. "How far did you read the director's manual after it says 'Roll'?" "Page one," Tashlin replied and Lewis chortled. The director fixed Lewis' hair so that it was more comical looking. "That's the first affection I've had from you all day," said Lewis. Tashlin called for the take to begin; Lewis started a symphony of snores. Some onlookers laughed quietly. The technician was poised to sit on the bed, but Tashlin held off giving the cue and Lewis continued to snore. "You're going crazy waiting, aren't you, you little bastard," said Tashlin. Lewis laughed and continued his snoring. The director gave a hand cue, the technician sat, Lewis reacted comically. "That's it, cut it," Tashlin said, and Lewis tried to scramble out from under the bed, but some crew members had tied his shoelaces to the bedposts. "You shits! Who did that?!" he screamed. "Who tied my shoes to the bed? Chained! Like a goddamn Jew mouse!" Someone untied the laces and Lewis crawled out. "You're through for today," Tashlin told him, and Jerry imitated a monkey again. "Put me on my bar," he said, climbing onto Tashlin.

Wednesday: Wearing sunglasses, Lewis stood in a corner conferring about script changes with Tashlin and Zachary Scott. On the first take, the action was off its mark and the camera missed some of it. A bald-headed makeup man applied some tan to Lewis' nose. The second and third takes were spoiled because the boom mike threw shadows. "Everything's gonna be fine technically," said Lewis testily. "And the only thing that'll be no good will be the actors. I'm getting stale."

Thursday: "Jerry raised a stink about the boom mike," Frank Tashlin told me. "So you'll notice there's no more boom mike."

Friday: Paul Jones, producer of *It'$ Only Money*, was talking to Keller. A short, kind-looking man with a bulging stomach and an always-worried expression, Jones wore an outsize suit and a large felt hat. The fanfare sounded, and Lewis arrived dressed in an eggshell-white suit. "Hiya, Jerry," said Jones. Without a word, the comedian walked over to him, took off his hat, squashed it, and replaced it on his head sideways, then went on to untie the producer's bow tie and pull his jacket back over his shoulders by the lapels. This done, he gave away four baseball tickets to members of the crew, and then picked up two medium-sized boxes that were tied together and tossed them across the set to Tashlin. They landed at his feet. "That's your Care package for the week," Lewis announced. "It's filled with one dirty sock, some rusty razor blades and a couple of broken shoelaces, and a lotta dirt." Tashlin grunted quietly; Lewis wheeled and left, three people in tow. "Yesterday he gave me a pair of sweat sox," the director told me later. "I'd never worn them before, and he told me they were very comfortable to wear on the set. First thing this morning he pulls up my pants leg to see if I've got them on. I did, and I made the mistake of telling him they really were comfortable. You know what's in those boxes? Ten or twelve dozen sweat sox he went out and bought. That's the way he is."

Monday: Lewis arrived wearing false buck teeth. "My mother," he said, "was scared by a beaver during the pregnancy." The comedian's father, Danny Lewis, who looks a bit like his son, came on the set wearing a blue blazer, white shirt, dark tie. He went over to Jerry, who sat in an armchair drinking a chocolate malted, told him that he had a spot on Ed Sullivan's television show next week, then asked advice on lighting and camera angles for the show while he stood in front of his son. Jerry slumped lower in the chair and answered the questions politely and quietly between sips of the malted.

"So how you been, Jerry?"

"All right."

"Everything all right?"

"Yeah, everything's swell."

"That's good."

Lewis sipped his malted.

"Watch me on the show," said his father.

"Yeah, Dad."

"So everything's OK, huh?"

"Sure."

"Well, I'll see you."

"Yeah, Dad."

Danny Lewis walked away from his son and left by the nearest exit. Jerry sat silently drinking his malted. After a few minutes, Tashlin came over, smiled gently, and asked him what he knew about painters. Lewis' face brightened. "Everything," he said.

"What about Van Gogh?" asked Tashlin. "Why'd he cut off his ear?"

"He didn't wanta hear all the crap on that side of the room." Two women and a little girl came on the set. "Hello, little missy," said Lewis, and immediately began to play with the child. He offered her some of his malted. "Can I give you a hug, huh?" he asked her. She nodded shyly and he put his arms around her. "Oh, God," he said. "So that's what they feel like. Boys are harder." The unit photographer came over and started snapping pictures of the comedian with the little girl. "Hey, come on, cut it out," Lewis said to him seriously. "You take pictures and all this looks like a phony bit."

Tuesday: The whole company moved out to the ocean for some location sequences on a pier at Paradise Cove. The sky didn't clear until after lunch, and Lewis amused himself playing football. At one o'clock the fanfare sounded and he drove to the end of the pier in a little red golf cart. "Hiya, Tish," he called to Tashlin. "Another big day! Yes, sir, this activity is drivin' me crazy. When I got loot involved, no sun." He walked over to the director, who was sitting in a canvas chair, patted him on the head and sat in his lap. "Kiss me on the lips. Try it once. You never tried it." Tashlin snorted, and called, "Hey, Carl, bring out the fish. You know, the big one." Four technicians brought out a huge crate filled with ice and a gigantic dead sea bass weighing 500 pounds; they pulled the fish out onto the pier. Lewis was to put his head into its mouth, and he walked over to look at it, leaned over, pulled the fish's mouth open and looked inside. "John L. Lewis says the strike is over," he yelled into it. "You men can come out." He stood up and surveyed the fish critically. "There's enough fish here to feed 300,000 Catholics," he said and shook his head. "This poor schmuck had to get killed to be in a picture." After two short takes, Lewis got into the golf cart and sped around the pier, chasing crew members who jumped madly out of his way. "This all started," Tashlin remarked, "because someone asked him to move that car out of the way." Finally, Lewis stopped the cart, jumped out, picked up a broom and hurled it at a technician, who ducked; Jerry ran after another, pulled off his cap and threw it over the railing into the water. Running flat-footedly over to Tashlin, he kissed him on the cheek. "Good night, Tish," he said, walked bouncily back to the golf cart and got in. The crew was gathered around him, smiling. "Good night, Jerry," they said in unison. "There's too many good nights!" said Lewis, jumping out of the cart. "What'd you do, you bastards? What'd you do to the car?" He got back in tentatively and turned on the ignition. The wheels began to turn, but the car didn't move—the men had put it up on blocks. After Jerry had driven away, zigzagging crazily down the pier, Tashlin meandered over to me. "How'd you like to have his energy?" he said. "This morning golf, then baseball, then football, then the car, and he's not through yet." All the way back to Hollywood in his Lincoln Continental, Lewis drove sixty to seventy miles an hour with one hand and spoke on the phone with the other. Passing through the Bel Air shopping district, he pulled over to the curb. "I'm stoppin' at the florist's," he said, "to get Patti violets."

On the door of the Jerry Lewis home on St. Cloud Road was a mezuzah on a gold plaque with an inscription: "Our House Is Open to Sunshine,

Friends, Guests and God." A maid opened the door and led me into the library. As Frank Tashlin had said, there were six or seven shelves of different-colored leather-bound volumes in the library, each with gold lettering, detailing the contents. The top shelf began with the scripts of Lewis' films, starting with *My Friend Irma* (1949) and continuing to the present. There were books of photographs, whole picture-stories of performances Lewis had given, with Martin and alone, as well as volumes devoted to his wife and children, a complete record of his life and career since around 1946. Behind the couch on which I sat were glass cabinets overflowing with awards, plaques and gold and silver cups that spilled out onto shelves in the room. On the wall opposite me was a framed painting of Lewis dressed as Emmett Kelly, the clown. One whole wall was a sliding glass door that looked out upon the pool, and further back was a recreation area with pinball machines, tennis, Ping-Pong, sun chairs; trees were everywhere. Facing each other, at opposite ends of this area, were statues of St. Anthony and of Moses. On a little table in front of the glass wall lay a silver-covered copy of the Old Testament in Hebrew, a copy of the complete Bible, and a leather-bound autographed script of C. B. DeMille's *The Ten Commandments*.

"Jerry and Jack will be down in a couple of minutes," said Patti Lewis, coming into the room. A petite, effervescent woman, she wore a simple red dress, and her dark hair flecked with gray ("It started to gray when I was twenty") was casually combed; she sat in an armchair near the couch. "People always say I'm the rock of this marriage," she told me after a while. "Jerry says that, too. But I don't feel that way at all. Jerry has provided everything for me and my family and I receive from him just as much as I give. Believe me." She smiled. "Jerry was playing at the Waldorf one time," she said, recalling the days before Lewis made it. "All I had to wear was this one brown maternity dress—that was when I was pregnant with Gary. I washed that thing so many times it was all shiny by the time Gary was born; there was no nap to the fabric anymore. I used to go down and watch Jerry do his act and I'd look around and envy the other women's clothes. The first present Jerry gave me was this secondhand fur coat—I think it was dyed squirrel. Well, I just thought it was the most elegant thing I'd ever seen and I wore it, you know, with great pride." She smiled warmly. "One night we went to a nightclub and I was wearing the coat and I caught some woman looking at it and kind of making a face.

Well, I don't know, it just ruined the coat for me. Not because of her attitude or anything, but because it reflected on Jerry. It destroyed his gift."

During dinner, Ronnie Lewis, twelve, came into the spacious dining room (also overlooking the pool), sat next to Jack and began talking with him about guns; Jack promised to take him duck shooting the next week. Jerry was on a phone that stood on a chair next to his place at the head of the table. Scotty Lewis, six, came down and shyly handed me a ballpoint pen (with a Lewis caricature on it) wrapped in paper; Jerry kissed him for that. The governess appeared carrying Anthony Lewis, three, who wore fire-red pajamas, followed by a slightly bewildered-looking Christopher Lewis, soon to be five, also in pajamas. Anthony was whimpering. He looked at Mrs. Lewis and said, heartbroken, "Mommy." Jerry jumped up. "Oh, God. When he says 'Mommy' like that I'm destroyed." He went over to the child and talked him out of his tears. Then the three younger children were taken to bed and, a little later, Ronnie finished his discussion with Jack, said goodnight and went quietly upstairs. During the roast beef, Gary Lewis, seventeen, came into the room and showed his father a comedy sketch he had just written. Jerry looked it over, laughed several times, and then asked us to listen to it; he and Gary read it. Jerry congratulated him and told him to retype it, double-spaced. Gary nodded and left. By this time everyone but Jerry had finished the main course, and the black maid came in to collect the plates. Jerry ran over to her and kissed her comically on the cheek. "She's so beautiful," he announced. "She does something to me." The woman laughed, embarrassed. "We'll kiss in the kitchen later," he said conspiratorially, "like before." Patti smiled and Jack said, "Deedle-deedle-deedle."

After the apple pie, Jerry took me on a tour of the house, and later, in the L-shaped stereo room ("The Jerry Lewis 'Loud' Sound Studios. If It's A Jerry Lewis Recording, We Dare You To Hear It"), Lewis spoke of his annoyance with visitors to the set who pretend not to be impressed when they are standing next to a movie star; he thought it hypocritical. "If John Wayne walked on my set, I'd shit!" he said. "I'd be impressed." Discussing money, he told me he always carried a thousand dollars with him in hundred-dollar bills, that he loved shopping and going through stores. Concerning his extravagance: "I discovered a few years ago that I can't buy what I really want, so I buy everything else."

And then, suddenly, he was speaking of Dean Martin: "The only contract we ever had," he said, "was a handshake. That was it. 'Cause I always say if I can't trust your handshake I can't trust you." He talked of the "complete emotional breakdown" between the singer and himself. "After the breakup, I asked Patti why she'd never said anything against Dean, and she told me that Dean was like a second wife to me and that she had no right to speak against him. Isn't that something?" And later: "I still love Dean, but I don't like him anymore."

Concerning his ego: "When I wake up in the morning," he remarked, "I think of me first and then my wife and then my children. I'd like to meet the guy that can honestly admit he does differently." He paused. "They say to me, I'm an egomaniac; what do I wanta do four things for? Why do I have to direct, produce and write, too? D'ya think it's so easy? D'ya think it's such a pleasure? For each cap I wear, it's eight hours work. So I'm doing four things, that's thirty-two hours a day—there ain't that many. Why do I do it? 'Cause I'd rather work that way than work with incompetents. I'm gettin' the best people I know for the job. I can't get Frank all the time."

And much later, around three in the morning, over a can of beer, Lewis talked of his birth, his youth, his parents, his grandmother whom he adored and who died when he was eleven; his eyes watered when he spoke of her and how she had called him "Sonny," and how, when the hospital told him she had "expired," he asked if that meant she was going to be all right. He spoke of his reluctance to hate anyone ("I always say, do you love 'em enough to hate 'em"), of the various aunts he had lived with while his show business parents were on the road, of the way his grandfather had searched curiously for him behind the TV set the first time he was on, of his love for children, particularly his own ("they're nice people"), and how he would always have a baby in the house. "When I'm ninety and in a wheelchair, we'll still have babies in the house. I'll adopt them." And finally: "If you're deprived of love when you're young," he said, "you can never have it given back to you. And that's what I don't want to happen to my kids."

It was after four-thirty in the morning, in front of his house, that Lewis said goodnight to Keller and me. And at six he was in his office at Paramount, ready for another big day.

One Saturday afternoon around four, Lewis was to go to a rehearsal at UCLA for a benefit he was to give that evening to raise money to send needy children to summer camp. I was to meet him at his house and shortly after I arrived he walked into the library in a black mood: he had a migraine. "I'm such a sucker," he grumbled about the benefit. "I can't turn my back on anybody. And people know it." Parked in front of the house was a brand-new maroon Lincoln Continental, with the dealer's invoice still taped to a side window. Lewis surveyed it critically. He opened the door and looked in. "Well, what the hell did they do," he said, annoyed. "Nothing. No initials, no phone." He grunted and pulled off the invoice. "They couldn't even take this off." He walked around to the rear, opened the trunk and gazed into it for a few minutes. "There's nothin' more beautiful than a new car," he said. As we drove to the university, I asked whether the car had been custom-built for him. "No," he answered. "Harry Ford, Jr., is a good friend of mine and he always sends me what I like."

The rehearsal in the 2,000-seat auditorium consisted of Terry Gibbs' seventeen-piece orchestra playing a couple of numbers, and some half-hearted clowning. As Jerry was leaving, Gibbs told him the band had to be at a recording date that night by nine-thirty. Lewis nodded and said he would start exactly at eight and do forty-five minutes. "If they ain't ready and if they don't like it," he said, "that's tough."

That evening, at seven-fifty-five, the auditorium was filled to capacity, mainly with college students who had paid $1.50 to get in. At eight sharp the curtains parted to the tune of a loud song that Gibbs' band played with gusto; there was a Lewis caricature on the bass drum. An offstage voice came through the loudspeakers. "Ladies and gentlemen," it announced, "Jerry Lewis." The band struck up "When You're Smiling," a follow spot hit Stage Left, and into it stepped the performer, wearing a shiny black tuxedo with a red handkerchief, a red bow tie on an eyelet lace button-down dress shirt and black suede Romeos. The applause was loud. He did impersonations of folk singers, boxers who sing, made cracks at the audience ("How can you look so clean and laugh so dirty"), sang "Rock-a-Bye Your Baby with a Dixie Melody" in honor of Al Jolson, donned funny hats and threw out one-liners, played a tiny trumpet, conducted the orchestra, sang "Come Rain or Come Shine," looking occasionally at Patti Lewis, who sat in the wings, did a tap dance, jumped in the air and fell on his side with a crash, threw ten or twelve twirling black canes in the air, missed them and, when he wanted to, caught them. Then the lights dimmed except for a pinspot on him sitting on a high stool, cigarette in one hand, microphone in the other, singing a melancholy song called "What Kind of Fool Am I." As he finished, he laid the mike down on the stool, the spot moved to it, and he walked off the blacked-out

Director-writer Frank Tashlin in a characteristic look
of dubious amusement as Jerry Lewis does some
pre-shooting shtick on the set of The Disorderly Orderly
(1964), one of their funniest collaborations

stage. The applause was thunderous. All the lights came up. Lewis
returned, bowed twice and waved good-bye. The applause continued as
the curtains pulled slowly together. It was eight-fifty and he still had a
migraine.

Lewis, Tashlin and I sat in the comedian's portable dressing room on the
set of *It'$ Only Money:*

> PB: What do you think of television, Jerry?
> JL: Television is an infantile medium trying to do in eight years
> what we've done in fifty.
> FT: Let's get the years right, Jerry, it's not eight years. It came in in
> '48 . . .
> JL: . . . In fourteen years what we've done since 1920.
> FT: Since 1910.

JL: You would remember. It was when you and McKinley were there. Go ahead, Mr. Bog-Bogavin . . .

PB: What do you think of psychoanalysis?

JL: For myself, I think it's dangerous: someone who has inner sad feelings about certain things which—instead of them burying him—can be put to better use. If I were to find out that these sad things are truly not sad, I think people would no longer find me funny, 'cause funny had better be sad somewhere.

PB: What do you think of Hollywood?

JL: It has to be what it is. It's everything it's supposed to be. 'Cause if you had five thousand Abe Lincolns living in Hollywood, you'd have no lovely Hollywood—then you'd have Greensboro, North Carolina. But you gotta have a lotta phonies, and a lotta liars, and a lotta brown-nosers, and a lotta yes-men, and a lotta the crap we hate, or you haven't got Hollywood. And it's the very crap that makes everyone wanta come here. 'Cause nobody wants to go to Greenland, where God built a beautiful substance—they wanta go to where all the crap is.

PB: What is art to you?

JL: Art? A man with a brush, a man with a theme, a man with a song, a woman with a cry. I think a puppet, a puppy, anything tender. A woman is art . . . a man's desire for her is even more arty . . . and when they do it together is the most art!

FT: How do you feel about being a director as well as an actor?

JL: I love it. It's me, ain't it?

FT: Which end of the camera do you like most?

JL: Dependin' upon what end I'm at. When in front of it, there's nothin' better. When I'm on the other end, the actor's a schmuck.

PB: Who've you been most influenced by in your direction?

JL: Mr. Tishman, spelled T-A-S-H-L-I-N. He's my teacher.

PB: What kind of pictures do you like, other than your own?

JL: I like good entertainment, nothin' sordid. I keep all the sordid things in the confines of a room with a broad; nobody sees that. I don't wanta go sit with two hundred people and watch someone do what I think I'd like to do sometime alone. Because it not only embarrasses me, but then I won't do it alone for fear that she saw that same movie. . . . And I ain't gonna sit in a theater for heartache. I can go into my own room and close the door and look at myself and cry.

PB: What do you think of money?

JL: Money's a pain in the ass. And I can prove it if you stay with me a few days. You'll see how I love it.

FT: You love what it gives you.

JL: No, not really. Money completely disallows me to contribute and give what I have inside, 'cause the moment money's involved I'm being paid to deliver it.

PB: Why, for instance, do you have ten to fourteen cars?

JL: I don't know, it's just a lotta cars. I like to have a lot of anything, 'cause it's proof that you're doin' swell. I used to have two cars. Then I heard a lotta guys have two, then I hadda have four. Then, when I found out there were fellas that had four, I hadda have what they don't have. So now that I got it, they're enjoying their four and I'm stuck with ten.

FT: If you like having a lot of everything, how do you feel about having one wife?

JL: Because I have all of the wives in the world in the one. I picked the best. I have very good taste. I went into a store—you know where it says "Jewelry" in a store, this one said "Wives." I went to every counter, and then there was one that had guards around it, and you couldn't look into the case 'cause it was covered. And I asked the man, "Would you let me see?" and he unrolled this velvet and there she was, smiling. And there was a big price tag that said "Two Billion Dollars." And she took the tag off and she looked at me and she said, "You can have me for free if you'll love me." All the other wives lyin' around, they were all bulldogs.

"You know, Jerry got a Gold Record for 'Rock-a-Bye Your Baby,' " said Keller after Lewis had gone. "It sold over a million copies. But the first time he ever sang that song publicly was the turning point in Jerry's career." Keller sipped his coffee. "Three weeks after his separation from Dean was final, Patti, Jerry, my wife, and I went to Las Vegas for no other reason than to get away from Los Angeles because, as I told you, the split was a traumatic thing for Jerry. He was floundering. He'd spent ten years with a partner. He was thinking what the hell would he do. Well, it was delightful in Vegas; we went to shows, kibitzed, lay in the sun, had a ball. The last day we're all packed, ready to take the eight o'clock plane back, when Sid Luft, Judy Garland's husband, calls Jerry in the afternoon and says, 'Judy's got laryngitis; you gotta bail us out tonight.' Jerry says he'll call him back. He turns to me and says, 'What d'ya think?' I said, 'What d'ya mean, what do I think? You haven't got an act. You haven't done a single for over ten years.' Still, we talk about it and Jerry decides, against my better judgment, to help Garland out. He calls Luft and tells him he'll do it on one condition. 'I realize she can't sing,' he says, 'but people paid to see Garland. If she'll come out and sit on the stage—she doesn't have to say a word—I'll go on for her.' They agreed, and that night Jerry played the whole show to her." Keller lit a cigarette and went on. "I was pacing the aisles like a father in a maternity ward. Suddenly I stop. I realize we forgot one thing. You can have a great act, but you gotta have something to get off with. Jerry was extremely funny for a whole hour. He was a real pussycat up there. Came the moment of truth: How's he gonna get off? Well, he leaned over to the bandleader and asked him Garland's repertoire. He looked through it and the only song he knew the lyrics to was 'Rock-a-Bye.' So he sang it, and in her key yet. Well, he pulled out all the stops, he belted it out, got down on one knee, he was really flamboyant. It was the greatest thing I've ever seen. Even gave me shivers, and you know what a cynical son-of-a-bitch I am. Well, when he was finished nine hundred people stood up and applauded like the Third World War had just been won." Keller paused. "And I'll tell you, that night when we were flying back home, you can't imagine how we all felt. We knew he'd made it. We knew he'd be all right."

Not too long after this article was printed in 1962, Lewis came to New York for two weeks to host *The Tonight Show*. Jerry invited me and my family to one of the broadcasts. I introduced my tongue-tied young sister Anna to him after the uproarious show that she and Polly Platt and I had watched. It was that way every night, and Lewis became the talk of the town again. For the first time since his early days with Dean Martin at the Copacabana, Jerry was suddenly chic in jaded New York. (It didn't happen again until the mid-nineties when he appeared on Broadway, a smash replacement as the Devil in *Damn Yankees*.) Polly and I visited him and Patti in his suite at the Essex House. He was still in bed, invited us to the bedroom and made a couple of lewd jokes that were outrageous and funny, as usual.

Shortly after the *Tonight Show* gig, ABC signed Jerry to a huge deal for his own weekly two-hour comedy series, which, unfortunately, was a big flop. But the president and founder of ABC, Leonard Goldenson, threw a large dinner party in New York to celebrate the signing. Jerry invited us to sit at his table—along with Mr. and Mrs. Goldenson, and the president (and Mrs.) of Gillette, and the then president of Pepsi-Cola, Joan Crawford. At the end of the meal, Polly went to the restroom and Joan Crawford came over to the empty seat beside me, sat and looked intently at me, then picked up a teaspoon, took some of the bubbles of coffee at the cup's side into the spoon, saying, "Good luck!" and started feeding this to me. Jerry, who watched the whole thing, explained later that the bubbles *meant* good luck.

After we moved to Los Angeles in mid-1964, we became frequent guests at the Lewis mansion in Bel Air, and Jerry was, as always, wildly generous. At one point, just as the first Mustangs were selling like hotcakes, Lewis bought three of them and insisted on lending us one. We were broke and had a terrible 1952 Ford convertible, originally yellow, badly spray-painted black, with a cracked block. He said to me one evening, "I don't want that filthy car of yours coming through my gate and sitting in my front yard anymore, so will you please take one of the fucking Mustangs? You need a phone in it? You don't need a phone—I'll take that out—and you can have the red convertible." I couldn't believe what he was saying. "But you need your car," I protested. "What're you talking about," Jerry yelled, "I got fourteen cars. I can afford one so I don't have to see your goddamn broken-down piece of shit drive in here again."

Generosity was very much Jerry's thing. I was trying to see as many older films as possible by directors I was interested in, or featuring noteworthy performances, so I asked Jerry if he could arrange for me to see on the big screen some of the great stuff Paramount had in its vaults. Jerry did indeed set it up and I ran original studio prints—nearly all on nitrate stock—of almost every classic that Paramount had in its vaults; several a week, for quite a while. Finally, Jerry called me explaining that his production people were on his ass and we had to quit running films, because we had screened eighty-two movies on the account of Jerry Lewis Pictures. I apologized but he cut me off, apologized, said it wasn't my fault, and he wished we could go on screening films forever. I thanked him profusely. Later, he asked if I wanted to direct a documentary about him. Of course, I did, but the studio wouldn't approve it. At that point, before I'd ever directed a film, the offer from Jerry was in itself an enormous encouragement.

That was another of Lewis' great virtues—he knew how and when to give encouragement. After I had directed and produced my first picture in 1968 (*Targets*), he asked Polly and me over—she had worked on the story and was production designer—and screened a 35mm print for his family in his living room, where he had state-of-the-art projection facilities. When the lights came up, Jerry spent two hours with us going over the work in detail and praising it to the skies. This kind of selfless generosity to a young artist remains unique in my experience.

Our lives and careers pulled us apart. While the seventies became my most illustrious decade, the same period became Jerry's worst. Significantly, the last time I saw him for more than twenty years was when he visited me on the Warner Bros. set of *What's Up, Doc?*, which I produced and was directing. Everyone was happy to see him, but he didn't really look happy at all. By then, it had already been over a year since he'd had a picture released. After twenty years of starring in an average of two pictures a year like clockwork (and through the sixties also directing, producing or writing as well), he had for the entire seventies only one release—in 1970.

Another was unfinished—a famous debacle—*The Day the Clown Cried*, about a clown in a Nazi concentration camp, which got a lot of play when the 1997 Italian Oscar-winner, *Life Is Beautiful*, covered similar ground. Lewis had been savagely criticized—without anyone ever seeing one foot of the film—for the very idea itself. Drugs, ulcers and a heart condition, plus a couple of huge business reversals, plagued Jerry for two decades. Except for one surprise hit, *Hardly Working* (1981), and his dramatic triumph in Martin Scorsese's *The King of Comedy* in 1983, Lewis' picture work really didn't pick up again until the nineties, and that was mainly fueled by remakes of pictures he had written, produced, directed and starred in, like Eddie Murphy's hugely successful version of *The Nutty Professor* and its sequel. But he never has missed the Annual Muscular Dystrophy Telethon—for more than fifty years now.

Seeing him on Broadway in *Damn Yankees* in 1995 was an emotional experience for me, and I knew it would be, but not to the degree that it was. By then, I hadn't actually been with Jerry for more than two decades. Of course, we had both of us lost many of those years in sadness—and show business is like that anyway, in its normal divergence of lives—yet when we saw each other backstage, we both were excited but certainly not strangers. Within moments, the years melted away. His hair was a little less abundant on the very top and it was finally graying a bit, and he was slightly more slumped over, but it was still Jerry.

On stage, he had been mesmerizing and given a brilliantly calculated star turn that was still within the confines of the well-crafted musical comedy of which he was only one part. His character doesn't even sing until the second act—but then, of course, he has two surefire show-stoppers. With Jerry Lewis, these weren't just that, they *became* the show! Yet when he first appeared and for virtually the entire first act, Lewis stayed completely in the guise of the supernatural character he was playing—the Devil in red socks. He effortlessly got all the laughs written for the part, but did not for a moment play with Jerry Lewis mannerisms or shtick. Indeed, so clever was his calculation that by mid-point of act one, you're privately wishing that maybe he would do a little of the old Idiot routine. And then—just at the perfect moment, near the end of the first act—he suddenly let out a big, familiar Jerry Lewis, "La-a-a-a-a-dy!?" and the whole place fell apart.

In the second act, he let himself go a little more and the audience adored each second. Virtually every night he would purposely set out to break up the other cast members at least once, and never failed. I saw two of them go to pieces and lose it over a slight look of Jerry's, and naturally the crowd joined right in and stopped the show yet again. When he sang his two numbers, while everyone was cheering, I was moved to tears. It was Jerry Lewis on Broadway—twenty-five years after being dismissed in his own country—proving once more that his phenomenal early success was no coincidence. And to me it seemed like a vindication for our generation—all of us who had fallen in love with Martin and Lewis, and then Jerry and Dean separately. We were right: the kid was a thrilling entertainer and a comic genius.

Backstage, I told him all this. With slightly shaking hands, Jerry showed me some of the amazingly positive press he had accumulated on *Damn Yankees*. He was proudest of the reviews that pointed out how understated the performance actually was, what restraint he displayed. The hugely successful Broadway run was coming to an end, and he had just turned seventy-one, though looking ten years younger. I knew he was taking it on the road but I made a special trip to New York because I wanted to see Jerry in a Broadway musical, which he would tour in successfully for over a year, both in the United States and Canada, and finally in London, where he was an equal smash. After this we stayed in touch again. He told me he wouldn't mind doing this show for ten years and he wasn't kidding. And he probably could have, but after London, business troubles and producers' disagreements sabotaged all the company's plans and Jerry had to say good-bye prematurely to one of the greatest triumphs of his career. As he went along, he knew exactly how many performances they had done, and he thanked God that it eventually reached something over nine hundred.

We kept talking about getting together. He wanted me to meet his second wife, Sam, and his daughter, Dani. They had saved his life, he said. Finally an assignment—this time from a weekly German newspaper—did the trick in the spring of 2000, and filled in so many things that had happened since he was the clown prince of Hollywood. By the time I got to Las Vegas, Jerry was suffering from walking pneumonia. Nevertheless he did his final show (of four) at the Orleans Hotel, where he has a twenty-year exclusive Vegas deal. He did two hours without a break and all the old magic was still there, if a trifle feverish from the pneumonia. He was right now probably the last of a show-business tradition that encompassed Jolson and Sinatra and Garland, Laurel and Hardy, and Chaplin.

On April 25, Jerry and I talked for several hours in the office at his Las Vegas home, the inside of which looked very much like his old Bel Air mansion—lots of leather-bound scripts and pictures, awards, photos, plaques, and a lot of paintings of clowns. He drove us himself to a restaurant for dinner—popping jelly beans coming and going. Then, in Los Angeles, at CBS Television City, as he was preparing his annual Muscular Dystrophy Telethon (this was year fifty-one), we spoke again for an hour in his office there, on August 28. He was feeling pretty good and made me laugh as hard as ever. A shortened, though still extremely long, version of our talks appeared as an entire issue of the weekly magazine section of *Süddeutsche Zeitung*.

PB: *Do you remember when you got your first laugh?*

JL: Yeah. I was five years old.

You remember it?

Yes. I was in a tux—how do I not remember the first time I was in a tux? My mom and dad had my tux made—I worked in the borscht circuit with them—and I came out and I sang, "Brother, Can You Spare a Dime?" which was the big hit at the time. I was five, it was 1931, and I stopped the show—naturally—a five-year-old in a tuxedo is *not* going to stop the show? And I took a bow and my foot slipped and hit one of the floodlights and it exploded and the smoke and the sound scared me so I started to cry. The audience laughed—they were hysterical. That was my first laugh. So I knew I had to get the rest of my laughs the rest of my life, breaking, sitting, falling, spinning.

Was your father supportive?

All he had to do was walk out on the stage. That was my college education. I just watched him. People used to ask my mother why I was so intense that I never laughed, never reacted. She said, Because he's studying. Eight, nine years old I'd sit in the front like this [*totally engrossed expression*]. I watched his skin, I watched the gooseflesh when they would sing a great song, that's how close I was. I mean, I had Brandeis, I had Northwestern, I had Colgate, Columbia, Purdue, it was all in front of me: an education of what to do in front of an audience.

Did your mother perform with him?

Oh, sure. She was his conductor.

Your parents toured all over the place and you were with them all the time.

All through the thirties; 1940, I was fourteen and my mom and dad didn't take me on this trip—they were working the Coconut Grove in Boston—in the big Boston fire. And they survived because my dad was the kind of man he was, which I'm happy to say I've got a lot of his traits—very curious. He had to see everything, had to know everything, had to check everything. He had a voracious curiosity. The only thing I thought was negative was that he was *obsessed* with having information. But he gave himself a hell of an education that way. Having not ever finished school, he made himself a brilliant man. I followed his lead. I learned what I learned by being curious. So, because of his curiosity he saw where the help came in. The performers came in from a specific street entrance and the workers at the Coconut Grove came in another place. He knew both places. And when the fire broke out, he took my mother by the arm and took her to one of those exits, otherwise they would never have made it. [Silent cowboy film star] Buck Jones was killed in that fire— my mom and dad met him that night. And I'm home with my grand- mother and she comes to me in the morning and tells me there was a fire and that Dad called and they're OK, I shouldn't worry. That was a won- derful gig for them, a step up from burlesque.

Did you perform with them during the thirties? Did you go on?

Sure. My mom and dad would get a gig and they would play other hotels. We stayed at Brown's Hotel and we would work out of there. My dad would do his show at Brown's on a Saturday night at 7 o'clock, and do Kutsher's down the street at 8 o'clock, and Grossinger's at 9 o'clock, and at 10 o'clock he would do the Luxor. So he had four gigs on a Saturday night. That's how you survived. And he'd always book whoever the hell had a car on his show—a juggler, a dancer, if you had a car—because my father didn't drive, he didn't *have* a car. Meanwhile he got to all of the gigs. Now, with him and my mom going to Kutsher's to do a show, my dad would get $20 for the two of them. But they got $25 when I was in the show. That's an extra twenty bucks in four gigs. My dad would do good on a Saturday night—almost a hundred dollars. Because what the hotel provided for him and the services were for an entire sum of ten to twelve weeks, room and board for his wife and child, and that's all he cared about, that they were covered. And with the right to do other shows. So, in a summer of ten weeks, he'd do an extra forty shows. It was nothing to have saved a thousand bucks.

Big acts that came up to the Catskill Mountains were good for $200 or $250 for a show. And they would do two or three. When the Concord wanted Dean and me, they offered us $75,000 for the night, I told them to shove it up their ass.

So you really never had any kind of formal schooling?

Oh, I did, up until second year high school—I quit.

Where were you for those years? Where did you go to school?

In Irvington, New Jersey. I went to Union Avenue school. Kindergarten through eighth year—you graduated the eighth year—you went into junior high, which is high school, you did four years of that. I only did two and quit.

And they didn't mind that you quit?

Well, I was legally allowed to quit at sixteen.

Why did you quit?

Because I couldn't wait to go and *do*. I'm going to sit there and watch them cut a frog open so I understand the anatomy of a frog. I'm not going to need to know about a frog in my lifetime. But it was part of the curriculum. I said, fuck you, I'll meet Tarzan and Jane and discuss a frog. They tried to talk me out of quitting. I said, I'm bored, I'm not productive here, I want to go out and work, I want to help my family. The *week* after I left high school I was in a burlesque house in Toronto as an act on the show. You know, in between strippers, when the guys in the audience stop with the newspaper, I'd go on. And most of them were like this when I came on [*expression of total lack of interest*].

And what did you do?

Record act.

Put a record on and you mouth the words. What did you sing?

They were recordings that you could buy. "Largo al factotum," from *Barber of Seville.* I did Sinatra—"All or Nothing at All." I did Beatrice Lillie, "A Bird in a Gilded Cage."

And you didn't really speak, you just came out and did your thing.

There was no talking.

How many songs would you do?

Three. Until they yell, "Get off!" you stay out there.

How many years did you do that?

Professionally, from sixteen when I was allowed to be professional until Dean and I got together when I was eighteen and a half. But I had been doing it in the borscht circuit with my dad for ten years.

Whenever you could.

Yeah, whenever I was with them.

And your grandmother took care of you when they were on the road. How was that? You loved your grandmother.

Yeah. She was incredible. My mom's mom. She was the only one who thought that I shouldn't be put away. One aunt said I need a keeper. Another aunt said he's retarded. Another aunt said he's insane, he should be put away.

A lot of your comedy is based on taking an established situation and destroying it. When did you discover that?

When Dean and I played the Havana Madrid together. We weren't a team, yet, but I was working as the emcee of the show and for the first time I had to talk. And that's when I was really making my bones talking, learning. And Dean and I had great fun during that four- or six-week engagement. But when I started to establish it—when I wrote "Sex and Slapstick"—which is what Dean and I were . . .

When you say you "wrote" it, what do you mean?

Well, when I started to write for us. The title of what I was writing was "Sex and Slapstick." [Feature magazine writer] Leo Rosten took the title for a *Life* piece, and I teased him and said, "You can't take my material and use it and say it's yours. I demand to be paid!" So a messenger came to the hotel room, brought me three dollars. He said, "Mr. Rosten said this is all it's worth." But in the writing process, the first thing that I did was to give Dean a kid brother, or give Dean the monkey. And the premise in my mind always was that I'm going to dig in and get the child within me alive. I cannot see two *men* standing on the stage and doing what I think we should do together, and be adults and do it. *Dean* must be the adult, but Jerry has to be the kid—the little guy—I loved that. I was as tall as Dean, except I worked in a crouch and I had his shoes lifted. Just so that I could work the crouch better. He always looked that much taller than me on the stage because I'd shrink. When I stood upright introducing him or something, I was six feet.

The Havana Madrid. Broadway and 50th. It was a great gig. I was in there for two or three months, and then Dean came in for four weeks.

You were there doing your record act, and then what happened?

Dean came in and we started to cock around, just have some fun. Which gave me the germ of the idea when I went into the 500 Club in Atlantic City. This was like, December '45 or January, February of '46. So we leave, we part, he goes away, I go away, then I'm in Atlantic City. They needed a replacement for a kid that got sick. I talked to [club owner] Skinny D'Amato about Dean. He said, "I don't want another singer." I said, "He's not another singer. He and I do a lot of bits together." So he brings him in. Dean comes in opening night, sings his three songs and leaves. I do my three records and I leave, and Skinny comes back to the dressing room and says, "Where's the fucking silliness? If I don't see it in the second show, you've got cement feet." So, we had ordered hot pastrami from across the street—the kid brought it over in a brown bag—the grease is still on the brown bag and it's now in my safety-deposit box here. I can show you the brown bag . . . We went out, and the two guys—who together did thirty minutes the first show, doing their two acts respectively—the second show was two hours and forty minutes. Playing to four people: two over here, two over there. By the third night we had a thousand people around the club. Spread like wildfire. And in less than eight weeks we were at the Loews State Theater for $5,000. I had no idea what to do on that stage. I couldn't do the shit we were doing at the 500 Club. So I had to start to re-create. See, I was a very good creator from where the geography was. Take me to where you want me to be and I'll create with that in mind.

You mean, the actual location.

Yeah, that's how I wrote *The Bellboy.* I've always been very good at that. So when we went into Loews State for two days, I sat at Nola Studios

briefing Dean on the bits I thought we should do. He was fucking brilliant. I mean, he brought such shit to the table. Incredible.

How did you get the idea for the act? Did you have a moment of inspiration?

I cannot in good conscience say to you that I knew what Dean would
bring. I didn't. So I was really writing generically: straight-man/comic.
Then, when I sat him down and I said, "Let me tell you about what the
comic must be—he's got to be your kid brother. He's got to be the nine-
year-old that's an annoyance—means well, but fucks up," Dean understood immediately. I said, "You can't waver from that position of
authority. Because what you are is, for all intents and purposes, the bank
president with the top hat that I'm throwing snowballs at."

Oh, God, we had such fun, it was ridiculous. He's doing a number one
night and he calls me up. He said, "I hope I didn't interrupt you when
you're busy." I said, "No, I was just standing around, listening to you." He
said, "In the middle of the song I thought to myself, I miss him." I said,
"That's why you called me up, because you missed me?" He said, "Yeah—
now we're together—isn't that wonderful?" I said, "What the hell are you
talking about? There's people here! What are you, a fag?" And like that
would develop into incredible shit that we'd do. For no reason he'd call me
up. "Why'd you call me?" "I missed you." But never did anyone ever bend
the material or the ideas that we were having. They all knew exactly what
we were doing.

You mean, nobody took it as a homosexual thing.

You see, the one thing that [newspaper columnist Walter] Winchell
told me that night—he saw us at the Havana Madrid—and I was sitting
having a drink with him after the show and he said, "You know what's
wonderful about what you two guys are doing?" And he's talking like
we're an act. We're not an act. He said, "I love the way you look at him." I
said I didn't know it was that evident. "You know, that's part of the
magic—and the way he looks at *you*."

You mean the affection?

Yeah. Oh, God, yeah. It was difficult not to show that.

You were just over eighteen and Dean was ten years older.

Yeah.

Had he already recorded?

He was on a sustaining [not sponsored] radio program, and he wasn't going anywhere. It was just the beginning, the embryo stage. So when he got the call, he came like it was a job. He came to earn a few bucks. He was getting two hundred and a half and I was getting two hundred and a half.

This was at the 500 Club?

Yeah. And I was so enamored by him and so thrilled that I could work with him that I saw more and more deeply. He will never ever *ever* be given his due for how fucking brilliant he was.

There was an enormous amount of wit behind him.

Oh, yeah. A brilliant sense of humor. But remember, anyone with a sense of humor and anyone that does shtick and bits—that's a cover.

You recognized in Dean a kind of kindred spirit. He did it his way, you did it your way.

Without question. Now the interesting thing is that nobody could ever get close enough to Dean to confer with him on anything.

He wouldn't talk seriously.

He procrastinated on brushing his teeth in the morning. But not with me. If I said, "Sit down," that meant I wanted to talk. He'd sit down. He knew it was going to be meaningful because he respected me. He knew I knew him so well. And he appreciated that. Because no one else knew it but me. And then he would open up a little bit. Knowing that nobody would ever hear our discussions. And then I would see the change on his face, I would see his comfort develop more. When I was offstage, I saw the discomfort of his being alone. Many shows I saw him getting into a funk a little bit. Somebody yelled something, something someone did distracted him, and I'd pop out on stage, unrehearsed, and just do some crazy shit just to take him back. He never said a word to me about it, but he was grateful for it. He always knew that I knew when.

A lot of times on the [TV] Colgate Comedy Hour *he'd sing and you'd do shtick while he was singing, which was hysterical.*

Right. We had wonderful times. If he didn't feel like really singing straight from the heart one show, we'd fuck with it. I would just create something. And the most wonderful thing about the two guys was that I could write anything at any time, or create anything at any time with anything. And I was fearless about it. "Let's go for it!" "Yeah, but you're on the air live now—there's like fifty million people tonight." "That's right, let's go for it!" "You mean, you're going to do this thing live without . . ." "It's ready. And what's going to happen to me if I fall on my ass? I'll be here next week." "Oh, OK." Now, the brilliance of Dean was that he would expedite it like he rehearsed four years. He wouldn't get in the way of it, he knew how to hold on to it, he knew where to take me, when to back off. And I'm on the stage and my mouth drops open sometimes because I'm watching this excellence, and 97 percent of it was that he wasn't even aware of how good he was.

Because he worked on a totally instinctual level.

Oh, yes. Because he always told everybody, "I can go out and drift, he'll always pull me back." And visa-versa. Jerry can get as crazy as he wants and who's the best judge of what Jerry does but Dean. And Dean knew when to pull me back if I was getting in trouble or something. So, we never sat and discussed the enormity of our emotional ties together. But it was always underlined. It was always underneath it all. I would reprimand him sometimes: "Would you sing one, just *straight*!? You've got a marvelous voice. Go out in the Copa and let the honeymooners hug while you sing a love song." "I do." "No, you don't." "Yes, I do." "No, you don't." *"Yes, I do!"* *"No, you don't!"* He felt his oats really good and clean and solid when we split up. Then he didn't *have* to do what I thought he did all those years, and that was cop out. Have me as the cop-out. "Well, that's not what got us here—singing." "No, but it was *part* of it. So you should do it. I mean, honor those who think you're a wonderful singer, that buy your records and so on." He said, "You know what we'd be getting if we were two singers?" I said, "What's that got to do with it?" He said, "Tell me, what if we were two singers and we were hot in the business. Do you think we'd get a grand a week?" I said, "Oh, that's fucking ridiculous. We wouldn't be. Two singers wouldn't have made it." He said, "How about *that*?" Now, July 25, 1946, the team legally started. And we ended July 25, 1956, to the night.

Was that a coincidence?

Yeah. Just an accident. But if I could ever describe the Copacabana that night, I'm sure I can't.

Orson Welles told me in the seventies that he saw you guys at the Copa, and he said people peed their pants.

Yeah, it was insanity. See, I forced Dean to break every barrier. . . . There were two sensual peek-a-boos at the guys. One was Dean as such a sexy-looking guy, but the kid got most of the women because they mothered him. They were there to protect him. They were there to free him up from this tyrant. Dean's reading comic books in the suite and I got a chick in the room.

I would guess since Dean was older that he was romantically more experienced than you.

Oh, God, yes.

Was that part of the affection between you—that he initiated you or he taught you about women in some way?

No, he was not a teacher at all. I brought my own education. I taught *him* a couple of things. Oh, I loved that he was a jock. Then when he's reading the comic book and I know there's girls down there and he's not in any mood, I look at him: "You crazy!? There's girls there!"

He wasn't interested.

He did it in his own time. He was not anywhere near what I was. I was a fucking animal. And they were coming in by the numbers—29A is the blonde; no. 29B is the brunette.

You mean, as soon as the act caught on, it was like rock 'n' roll groupies?

It was. Later, on pictures, it started in the morning in my dressing room at a quarter to eight, before I went to the set. And I'm directing a movie, so I'm there early with my crew. Quarter to eight I give a little hump, nice. Good to get started, get rid of the poison.

When you guys got together at the 500 Club, when you were officially a team, was that just like wildfire?

Yes, absolutely. There's no way to describe it—no way.

Did you guys ad-lib an enormous amount?

Oh, sure. Well, what I had written on the greasy brown paper bag was what I thought would be a marvelous formula. 1) Intros and acknowledging the players. That meant my introducing Dean. In other words, I would come out first and establish that I am part of a team and that I do the silly stuff: "So, I implore you, ladies and gentlemen, please don't be bored during his three songs because I'm getting ready to come out. It's not that long. Clap a lot because he's very sensitive." But that would establish where the kid was coming from. Then I would introduce him and then he would do his three songs, so we knew he was now the singing straight-man. Established. Then, I was very strong about our doing a "runner" right away. And that was: He'd be singing his third song and I come out and I'd say, "Mr. Martin, I hope you don't think I'm disrespectful, you know every night it's a strange thing, when you do that number I have to go to the bathroom. So, when you see me leaving the room that's where I'm going. It's not that I'm not liking your number. You know what I'm saying? It's just that I had to go to the bathroom." Now that starts the "runner." Because like eight minutes later Dean will say, "By the way, did you go?" "No, but it's OK. I've got great control." And we'd pass it. The third or fourth time I'm starting to weaken. "I think I can now—" and Dean would say, "I just want you to hold this music for me."

The "runner" is that you would have to go to the bathroom?

Once the "runner" was established, then you go into "bits and pieces." "Bits and pieces" were little quickies. Large number would come down in about thirty minutes. We had to do a substantial number together to show that we are indeed an act.

What did you do?

I wrote a parody on [the old song] "Side by Side," which was wonderful. "Oh, we ain't got a barrel of money. / That's why we're tryin' to be funny. / And we'll travel along, singin' a song, side by side." And it was a nice number, and you knew it was rehearsed. The music was playing. It was arranged. It had body. I was a stickler for it. He hated it.

Why?

Because he'd rather have fun. It was important to establish that we rehearsed and worked. This is business, it's not bullshit. And because everything we did had that air of spontaneity, how do you let an audience know that this is hard work and it's well prepared and so on, and he would give me, "Ah, you're flag-waving again." I'd say, "No, no, no, no. We got to where we are because of what you call a flag-wave." Yeah, I used to say to him, "When Sophie Tucker comes into the room, it's not flag-waving to introduce her. You have to acknowledge the excellence of that performer. And we have to acknowledge when they're there. Now, what looks like a selfless act on our part is very selfish. We want to be tied to the names we introduce. I want them to know that Sophie Tucker knows *us*.

That's why I make that introduction." Then he got clear on it and then it was OK. We worked in gray suits at the 500 Club. I said, "This will never do." He said, "Why?" I said, "You don't want to get dressed in a tux because it's uncomfortable. Being homeless is also uncomfortable. You've got to wear a tux." "Why?" "Because when I take a fall in a gray suit, there's nothing too fucking funny about it. 'Cause you can go down on the Bowery and see a hundred gray suits laying in the streets. You fall down in a tux, when you get up all of the dirt is on a tux, it's funny. And you're the balance of who I am and you need to stand there and be clean when I get up dirty. It's that simple." And he respected my knowledge and respected what I knew about the business and went for it. All the time we were fitting him for the tux, "You and the goddamn fucking tux! I gotta wear a fucking tux!" He hated it. But then, after we broke up, he worked some twenty years by himself, always in a tux. And always wore the watch that I gave him—it was never off his wrist—the watch I gave him in 1950.

So you knew that he loved you, in his own way.

He had wonderful ways of showing it. Because he knew I had to see it. I remember one night somewhere—I remember the subject matter but I don't remember the why of it—I said to him, "You know, you have a responsibility and obligation to me, and you never mean to pay off on it." He said, "What are you talking about?" I said, "Whenever I talk about you, I tell people how much I love you and how strong that affection is and all that. You never tell that to nobody." He said, "Maybe I don't love you." "That's horseshit. I couldn't love you if you didn't love me." He said, "Is this Freud?" I said, "No, it's not Freud. It's the truth." It's the same truth that I've been pontificating since I was twelve years old: You cannot love anybody unless you can hate. Now the person that says to me, "I hate nothing," I say, "Do you love your wife?" "Oh, yes." "You can't have only *one* of those—you have to have both. You have to have the capacity to hate so that you have the capacity to love as deeply as you say you do." And everything would always come true and he'd come to me a year or two down the pike and he'd say, "You were right about that. I hate that you were right about that but you were right about that." And what we were doing was, we were giving one another two educations. He was educating me in the world of society, the structure, the place where we lived, and I did it with him with theatrics. We were constantly teaching one another. I was on him about taking the bow, about cutting the number, about doing this bit. And he was on me constantly with "Stop being naive." You know, I took everyone in—whoever was around—I would be there to help him. And because of his upbringing, he was against my doing any of that. "Why are you giving him money?" I said, "He's a man in trouble, that's why. What's it your fucking business?" "But you don't have to do that." I said, "I don't do what I *have* to do, I do what I *want* to do." I never could crack that—never.

What was it like those first four years, before the movies? From '46 to '49?

It was wonderful. It was the Katzenjammer Kids. We had so much fun, it's ridiculous. We played football in a suite in Philadelphia, broke windows, lamps. Like two monkeys on a fucking high. We just played. And he played golf and I'd write. Then I said to him, "I've written some wonderful shit here, we've got to work on it." "Later." Uh-oh. "No, no later—because I'll quit and then you won't have any good shit to do." "Later." And I knew not to push him. He wanted to play golf during the tournament in Philadelphia, I didn't push him. We left there, we went to Chicago, I said, "Now you're going to practice." And he did. But the thing of it was this— impossible to understand was—I would write him a bit that would run four minutes, spotting the positioning on the stage and the geography within that bit. I would do it that night and he was right on the fucking money. And he had a favorite line, he said, "You only have to tell me once."

But there were certain things that you always did, right?

Oh, yeah. We had a foundation. We had a nucleus of thirty-some minutes that were locked. And we were doing an hour and twenty.

So the thirty minutes was not consecutive. You started that way and you might go off and you come back.

Which was necessary. Well, the two of us watched one another very carefully. And that *wasn't* something we sat down and agreed to do—it was something that was instinctive. He watched me like a hawk.

I see that in the Colgate Comedy Hours. *You can see him watching you.*

Yeah, so that he knew where I was going, and he knew when . . . Did you ever see the "Ventriloquist" sketch on the *Colgate Comedy Hour*?

Where you're playing the dummy? Yeah.

I looked at it the other day—I had a reason to see it—and I'm watching the timing between the two of us. I'm supposed to have incredible timing—that's what I worked my whole life to hone—but his is up to that level, instinctively. With me, it's in my bones. My dad had it—he put it in my bones: you can't do it bad. There were times when Dean laid back in a sketch because we'd gotten some mail that berated him about picking on Jerry. I said, "Dean, you know who writes these letters? Some lady from Denver who lives on a farm and raises bat guano. What is the matter with you? The secret of what we do is the beauty of the heavy and the innocent, or you can call it Romeo and Juliet for all I give a shit. But it's two factions working as one or pulling apart. It's a comedy procedure that in research we can show you: we can do a lobotomy on the nature of comedy and I'll show you how it works." "Oh, well, I don't want that." "So, don't do it. So that one fucking woman is going to be served? You're not going to do it? The stronger you are, the funnier the kid is. Then, when you make up with the kid, there's a wonderful feeling of fulfillment in the audience that's good. We're touching a lot of emotional buttons here. There but for the grace of God go I. There's a man sitting in the audience who interprets you as his boss and me as him. If he identifies with me, it's funny. *He's* getting it, not *me*. And there's a very, very fine line there, but we can't fuck with it. We have to be very careful." And, after about seven years of pontificating, he was getting very tired of me challenging the work.

He felt challenged?

Well, when I'd say, "You gotta get stronger in that bit tonight," he knew I was right. He never said I was wrong about our work. I might have been wrong about something personal, something emotional, something passionate. But not about the work.

Are you saying, he kind of got tired of it? Not resentful, but tired of your being right?

He was tired and resentful. Because he was never given his due. . . . If the tables were turned and I had to succumb to the value of this team effort, I wouldn't have made a *year*, no less ten.

How exactly do you mean, Jerry?

Meaning that if it were physically switched. If, when you got up in the morning, you opened the Copacabana and the whole thing's about the silly, fucking crazy Jerry? Wait a minute. The silly, fucking crazy Jerry was only there because of him. And he wasn't *mentioned*? Oh, "He sang three songs and they were OK." He got that *all* the time. I don't know how he *ever* dealt with it. With the exception of him saying to me, "I know where my bread-and-butter is. Don't worry about it." I said, "But Dean, if you don't deal with this, if we don't get it fixed or in some way pat you on the shoulder, it's going to fall apart. You need it, as I need it. And don't you resent the guy that got this whole column who you work with? He wasn't entitled to that whole column or review." I would always speak in the second person, or third person. I did a movie because of that. I wrote *The Caddy* [1953] so Dean would have a substantial movie of his own. That's how it happened, and it worked very well. It worked for him psychologically. I never said a word to him. We just went ahead and made a movie, that was it. I told him it was about golfing—he was thrilled. But I repeat, he took ten years of sucking hind tit. But he became a big star in that decade—a big fucking star. Demanding all kinds of money and everything was wonderful for him. But I never could have made it.

With Stan Laurel and Oliver Hardy, there wasn't a clear differentiation. Hardy often was very funny, too.

There was no split. It was always both guys were funny.

But nobody wrote, "Oh, Laurel is the genius!" Even though people didn't know that Laurel actually wrote the material.

Never—Stan and I talked about that many times—it never happened. You couldn't say "Laurel and"—you had to say "LaurelandHardy" as one word. And Martin and Lewis became that. And Stan and Ollie, interestingly, had the same relationship that Dean and I had: Ollie was on the golf course all the time. But if you took one without the other, without changing any of the other elements—structure, wardrobe, preset, practice—all that had to be the same. And you take one out of the mix, nothing works. And Stan told me that Ollie was the happiest at the country club, drinking at the bar, playing poker, doing all the things that Dean loved to do. But when Stan called, Ollie was there, on his fucking mark, and knew the material. He never gave Stan one bit of angst. He was just a consummate professional when he got on that set. But it was almost like Stanley had a piece of himself cloned into Ollie. For that matter, the reverse as well. Because Stan had this infinite time, the breathing time, the beating time, to fill all of Ollie's motion and movement. You never saw Stan just look at Ollie. His body movement was like a great juggler.

What was it like, coming to Hollywood for the first time?

Frightening.

You came to Hollywood when the studio system was still at its height. How was that?

It was just like you think it would be. It was like Cagney and Bogart, Robinson, Claire Trevor, Jane Wyman, Joan Crawford, Bette Davis. I mean, it was Clark Gable, Spencer Tracy—it was movie time!

Were you a movie fan?

Oh, God, yes. I wrote Lana Turner a love letter, eight pages.

When you were a kid?

Yeah, I was about eleven or twelve. So now I'm dancing with her at Ciro's and I can't believe my fucking eyes. I'm dancing with Lana Turner and I can't say anything. "Hi, how you doing, sweet?" "Nice to see ya." "Hi, kid." Scared shitless—peeing in my pants—holding her close to my body. Oh, my God. And I didn't do her—that's what pisses me off.

I didn't come out there until '61 and it was really ending by then.

Well, from '50 to '60, we were royalty. We were taking over the Crosby-Hope mantle. All of the stuff being made was incredible work when we went out there. *The Heiress* [1949; William Wyler] was just being completed. Great work. *All About Eve* [1950; Joseph L. Mankiewicz] was just being completed. I became very friendly with Joe Mankiewicz and we had a great friendship for all the time until he died. And he was like you are—he did interviews with his friends—if he was enamored by something or someone. He only wanted me to tell him about comedy, then he married my secretary. We were there when, on Monday night, it was [George] Burns and [Gracie] Allen's house; Wednesday night, Danny Kaye; Friday night, Jack Benny—all year long.

Who went?

Van Johnson and [his wife] Evie, Keenan Wynn and his wife, Clark Gable, Bette Davis, Olivia de Havilland—which you shouldn't have both in a room at the same time, but it was OK—Danny Kaye, Leo Durocher, Astaire, Judy Garland, Mickey Rooney—all of the Metro people. I mean, it was nothing for Jack Benny to have a twenty-eight-person dinner party. It was like every Friday night.

Did you go with Dean?

Dean and I socialized in that Hollywood swing for the first two or three years.

With your wives.

Right. And then we started to get a little annoyed with having to go to parties all the time, so I started to back off, and so did he. We were happier being home. We were working very hard.

You guys were doing two movies a year.

Yeah, and nightclubs and concerts and *The Colgate Comedy Hour.*

You were working pretty much all the time.

I was having a wonderful time. I was never tired, per se. But it's pretty tough, you know, getting up at four in the morning, you're at your office at the studio a quarter to five and you go until maybe eight, or I see rushes and I give my cutter all of my information. I'm home at nine and I'm at a party at someone's house at ten. And you don't leave there until twenty to four. And I'm at the studio in twenty minutes. Many times I've left the party and went right to the studio. And it was great fun until you get a little tired of it. But the education that I got in those first ten years was just absolutely incredible.

The first ten years in Hollywood, or the first ten years with Dean?

The first ten years at Paramount—from the end of '49. I was in the camera department more times than I was on the set making the movie—miniature department, editing, scoring, dubbing. I was in every department making friends with all the right people so that I could sneak and hear and watch and listen and learn.

You obviously wanted to make your own pictures.

Oh, yeah. I don't think I knew it at the time. What I think it was, was my bones that my dad gave me—just so curious. Little did I know that what I was doing was preparing myself—I didn't *know* I was doing it.

But didn't you make some home movies?

Home movies, oh, classics! *The Re-enforcer* was also good. *Watch on the Lime*—um-hum.

But how did you do those?

I stayed up at night writing a screenplay to shoot on a Sunday. Now I would write it on a Monday night and I've got Tuesday, Wednesday, Thursday, Friday, Saturday at the studio to get all the props and cast it. By

Saturday night I knew I had Jeff Chandler in it, Janet Leigh, Tony Curtis, Dean, Sammy [Davis, Jr.]. Sammy was so cute—he said, "Why do I always have to play a black guy?" "What would you play? A tall, white, fucking Wasp? What would you play?" Oh, we had such fun. What I was doing was, I was spoofing what we did all week in the studio. I shot my own main title.

You must have known you had some interest in doing it for real.

I loved it. I still didn't know the depth of it until around 1959.

The Bellboy *didn't have much dialogue, right? Wasn't it all pantomime?*

No—the kid was pantomime.

When I think about the picture, it almost seems like a silent movie.

There's a lot of talking and a lot of everything, but nobody knew that *he* didn't talk. That was something that I devised and didn't think I could pull off. And it worked. But Frank Tashlin said, "Do it yourself. You got a great piece of material here. Go with it. You know what to do." I said, "Frank, I *don't* know what to do." We shoot the first day in Florida and I call Frank after the shoot. He said, "Well?" I said, "Frank, I was doing things I never knew I knew. I was terrific. I got great stuff. I must have six fucking minutes of screen footage, and I shot wonderful stuff and I *knew* what to do, Frank." It was incredible, because I did. I have no idea how I knew it. And then that night I'm sitting with my production team and I'm telling them what I'm gonna do tomorrow. I'm giving them setup for setup . . . You know that my greatest education came from learning what *not* to do. Did I learn? Whew.

You mean, from some of the directors who weren't so hot?

Oh, yeah. But I also learned the psychology of them being not so hot. They don't know they're not so hot. They think they're hot, and that's when it's like a magnet that draws me to them to watch very closely. I remember saying to one director, who has to remain nameless, I said, "When you say 'Print,' do you have any fucking idea what that means?" He didn't half understand what I was talking about. I said, "When you say, 'Print it,' do you know what that means?" "What are you trying to say?" "I'm trying to say that when you say 'Print,' you open the optic of a billion children around the world. You can't dog it. You can't just say 'Print' because it's expedient, or you want to get on with the day. You had no right to print that—it was inadequate material." "I thought it was

*Classic Martin and Lewis: Dean and Jerry in a typical moment from their
original nightclub act—and as they would appear at the conclusion of
each of their TV shows—re-created as the finale of* The Caddy *(1953);
Martin's first hit recording, "That's Amore," was introduced in this. Jerry
suggested golf as a subject because Dean loved the game.*

funny." I said, "Yeah? Do you have a sense of humor like your rectum?" I
could have killed him. But I had to get through it, because it was a [pro-
ducer Hal B.] Wallis picture and I had to do it. But did I learn from that?!

Were all those films that you and Dean made big money-makers?

Oh, God, yes. *Sailor Beware* [1951] did 72 million dollars when tickets
were a quarter. We made more money for Wallis and Paramount than they
had made in fifty years before that.

Right up to the end?

Oh, yeah. *Hollywood or Bust* [1956; last Martin and Lewis film] was a
very big picture.

When did you start really getting involved with rewriting and changing?

I would have to say I wrote and collaborated on *Pardners* [1956] and
Money From Home [1953], and collaborated with Frank on *Artists and*

Models [1955]. I mean, doing a lot of visual stuff. The great story was *Sailor Beware* when Wallis said, "I need a block comedy scene." I said, "I could have told you that the day I read the script." He said, "Can you help me?" I said, "Yeah, let me think about it." So I said, "I'll help you, Hal, but it's gotta be my way. I don't want to get into a shouting match. I don't want to get into I've-done-this-for-forty-years horseshit. Because you could have been doing wrong. But I'll give you a hunk for the picture." And I wrote the whole boxing sequence. This became the highlight of the film. When I handed it in to Wallis, though, he looked at it and said, "Jesus Christ, that looks like it could be terrific." I said, "It will be terrific if I do it my way." He said, "Well, you wrote it, I didn't bother you." I said, "Yeah, but now we're gonna shoot." "Well, what did you have in mind?" I said, "Seven cameras." "What?" All he saw was dollars. I said, "Hal, I'm gonna use two slaves [less crucial cameras] that I probably won't take a frame from, but I need them. And I need A, B, C, D and E [cameras] in absolutely critical positions, which will enable me to just go on through the whole sequence. I got a six-inch [lens] on that fucking camera and I know when to turn to it. I got a deuce [another lens] there that's gonna cover the ring. I got a three-inch there I know I'm going to take him[self] into a waist shot." We shot it, and it was a wonderful hunk.

So you played it in one piece.

Yeah. We did the inside of the scene in the locker room, with Dean and I. And I covered that with just two cameras, but we got it. Because I wanted spontaneity in it. So Wallis has the material, he looks at it, he loves it, and I said, "Now we have to talk about your owning it." We're having lunch at Lucey's [restaurant across from Paramount lot]. He said, "What do you mean by 'owning it'?" I said, "Well, you haven't paid for it. And my contract with you is as an actor, not a writer, and if you're going to use this material, you have to talk to my agent about a figure that I'm gonna want." I said to [agent] Herman Citron, "Get fifty thousand for it—just get it." A lot of money then. Wallis balked. "What!? Fifty thousand!" Herman said, "Don't use it—it won't cost you anything." "What are you talking about? We shot it. It's great, it's wonderful." "Yeah, but you don't own it. You had no right to shoot it." And what I did, in my little cagey thought-process in writing it, I wrote the cover page to read "Augmented Material for *Sailor Beware* requested by Wallis, Inc., by Jerry Lewis." And that made it mine. It had nothing to do with the script. It came as an augmented blue page, an appendage to the script. So he knew I had him. He

Jerry Lewis setting up a shot for The Ladies' Man *(1961),*
which he directed, co-wrote, produced and starred in. Note the
RCA TV-camera mounted onto the 35mm camera, a device
now installed within the camera and known as the
Video Assist, invented by J.L.

said, "Tell him I'll give him forty." And Herman said, "Listen to this: it's not negotiable. He wants fifty thousand dollars." And he went back to him a week later, he said, "Listen, Jerry sent you a message. You can make the check out to Muscular Dystrophy Association, but you're going to make the check out. If it makes you feel any better that he's not going to get any of it, make it out to the way I told you because he's gonna give it to them anyhow." Wallis is balking. It's now November. He's got 680 theaters booked for *Sailor Beware* on New Year's Eve. If he doesn't ship in the next five days, no theater will have the picture. He went up to the last day, that son-of-a-bitch.

And then he paid?

He paid me the fifty thousand.

How did you first sign with Wallis? How did that come about?

He saw us at the Copa and he was in that mix between Joe Pasternak and L. B. Mayer and Sam Goldwyn and Zanuck.

He had a long history at Warners and at Paramount.

And I wanted Paramount. I told Dean, I said, "We're not going to go anywhere but Paramount."

Why did you feel that way? Because of Hope and Crosby?

No, I was an usher at the Paramount [theater originally on Broadway].

Oh, you liked the sound of that.

I loved Paramount. And I also loved what [founder] Adolph Zukor represented, and Barney [Balaban, studio head]. They were like a *hamisha* group, I thought, and they were. I was right.

Did you do some research on that, or you had instincts?

I just knew about it. So when the Paramount deal came up, I said to Dean and [agent] Lew Wasserman, "This is good for us. I want to go there." And Dean, of course, heard what I had said and said, "Fine." So we went to Paramount.

Was your deal with Wallis or was the deal with Paramount and Wallis?

No, it was strictly a Wallis commitment that developed into my Paramount deal following that. But it was always Wallis.

And when you guys broke up?

We had to disseminate the material, as it were.

You owed Wallis some pictures and so did Dean, separately?

Right. Dean owed two and I owed two.

Was the dynamic between you and Dean the same when you first got into features? Did it change?

No. The change in the relationship started to fester in '54.

Do you know why?

Yeah—outside factions. I've had a philosophy all my life: if you have something that's whole, you can either take a knife and cut it in half or have outside factions ruin it. And that's what happened. We had outside factions that were envious of our relationship. Whatever mean-spirited people do, we were getting the ass-end of it.

You must have had a lot of that.

Yes, we got a lot of it. But now, Dean's pain was compounded by the fact that they're not writing about him anymore. They write about Jerry all the time. I couldn't see it ending, theoretically. We had every chance to go on for another ten years—theoretically. But if we couldn't inject into it for the next ten years the same energy and the same passion that was there the first ten years, it won't work. So I thought, Let's quit a winner. Let's go out way ahead. And I, literally, motivated the break.

How?

I went to Dean one day at the studio, I said, "You know what? I think we should go out like champs and not like bums. And if we keep up with what we're carrying on now we're going to be bums."

What did you mean?

Nitpicking. Our being uncomfortable with one another. His not wanting to talk to me and my being hurt so desperately by it. And I just said, "I don't think we can fix what's happened to us and we should go our separate ways. You'll be happier, 'cause you'll be able to do the stuff that you are capable of doing. And I hope I can do something on my own. I don't know. I don't know what's going to happen to either one of us. But I know that we should not stay together."

What had precipitated his not speaking to you and you being so hurt by that? The outside factions?

Because he heard some shit that I was supposed to have said about him. I never spoke about him negatively. Even in the feud time. I loved him.

So somebody was putting poison in him.

Absolutely. I would say to him, "How do you listen to outside forces? How do you listen to outside people that don't know who we are, what we're about, and then they can come and poison your mind?" And he, of course, would deny hearing anything. But that's his point of view. I said,

"You don't think that way, Dean. I'm sorry, I'm not going to buy that."
And I said, in this discussion—which was the one that broke the back of
the team—when I said to him, "Look, after all is said and done, you've got
to remember how we got here. Meaning, two guys that love one another."
And he said, "Look, Jerry, let me tell you something. You have always
been and you are now, and always will be, a dollar sign to me." There was
a long pregnant pause. And I'm twenty-eight years old now. A mind of my
own, have a point of view, pride—'cause he didn't mean it.

Did you know he didn't mean it?

No, not at the time. It killed me.

What did you say?

I just walked away after a long pause. I just walked out. But I contributed to the break by not challenging him. "What the fuck are you
talking about? You're not that good an actor. I been a dollar sign to you?!
Bullshit! I'm your best friend. And you love me like I love you and you're
full of shit and somebody's telling you shit." Which is what I would normally have done. But I knew that we were getting to that time when we'd
better just wrap it up. But it chilled me for six months. I couldn't look at
him. We had to do a movie yet. So we did *Hollywood or Bust.* We never
said a word to one another.

Frank said you never spoke to each other, except in scenes.

It was terrible. I even took off on Frank one day. He was *there,* that's
why. But I let a toilet-bowl mouth come out, disrespectful and ill-
mannered, and all of the pain came out in that tirade I gave Frank. When
I got all through—there were 180 people on the set—Frank said to me,
"Try this scene." And I gave him a reading like, "Why don't *you* do it? See
if you know how." Something like that. And the rest of my life I'll remember his saying, "That's it!" He came over to me and took me by the arm,
walked me into the key light, stood me there, he said, "Stay right here."
And he brought everyone around the set and he said, "Let me tell you
something—you spoiled, untalented prick—what you put people
through and what you've done these last three months to all of these people, and me: 1) You don't have the right to do that; 2) Your life is not the
only one that's meaningful on this earth." And he went on for ten minutes. Dagger, dagger, dagger, dagger, bazooka, dagger. And I'm paralyzed,
I can't move. And he ended with, "Now get your fucking, unfunny ass off
my set." And I turned and I walked, with all eyes on me, everyone in

shock, everyone knowing I had it coming, but everyone feeling badly that I got it.

I go home and I call Frank—I get him on the phone. He said, "I have nothing to say to you," and he hung up. I called back, I said, "Frank, I need your help." So he stayed on the line. I said, "I need your help—I've got to see you—I've got to talk to you. Will you meet me in my dressing room tomorrow morning?" He said, "What time?" I said, "Six o'clock." He said, "I'll be there." I meet him the next morning and I said, "I want to thank you for what you did. I'm sure that you were thinking I'd fire you, which I can't, because you were right and I was wrong. And I think I really needed what you did for me because—I'm not making any excuses but whatever I did, I didn't mean to do. And I think whatever I did was a human response to the pain that I'm in, and I have no right to give other people pain because I'm in pain. And I think I can be better if you give me another chance." He said, "OK, be on the set, know your words, nine o'clock, and we'll see." And he left my dressing room. I went on the set at nine o'clock and worked. I've never berated anyone again since that day, about anything. And he saved my life, because if I had continued with the thought-process I'd have gotten in terrible trouble.

Did you know right away when you met him on Artists and Models *that he was the best director you had worked with?*

Right away. Come to me with a cartoon brain and I'm in heaven.* And how he'd laugh! We would talk it down and he'd sit there, and I said, "If you close your eyes, you're not gonna be able to say 'Print.' " I'd get him crazy. The most fun he ever had was having me come in a door 'cause any time he'd yell "Action," I'd have a black guy come out instead of me; I'd come out with a pig; I'd have flowers; I'd throw water at him. And maybe on take 9 I would come out to do the scene. I've got some of those outtakes—they're hysterical.

I notice you still use an electric typewriter [on a side table by Lewis' desk].

Hey, I wrote *The Nutty Professor* [1963] on that thing. I've got this terrible loyalty to equipment. You know why I'm a dichotomy? I'll tell you why: because I love progress but I hate change. It's the truth. I mean, I'm the first guy to run to you and tell you about a technical aspect of our business and I'm thrilled. And then I don't want them to put a hotel in Hyde Park—a fuckin' Hilton?!

---

*Tashlin had been a cartoonist *and* a cartoon director.

Speaking of technology, how did you come up with the Video Assist—which now everybody uses?

When Frank said to me, "You, director—go, boy," I knew that day was going to happen. In 1956. Not literally that script, but in '56, 'cause Dean and I had just broken up, and I decided if I am going to direct, I'm going to need a couple of tools. And the best tool in the world, for me, would be a Video Assist, so I could be on both sides of the camera. I was able to direct myself. On *The Bellboy*, there was no videotape, but I had twenty-five monitors on the set. Anywhere I would work, there's a monitor. Any actor I'm talking to, there's a monitor. I turn to do the bit with the lady over there, there's a monitor. I could see exactly that the camera was stopping on the mark I gave them.

All the spinal injuries you've had were from your work—from all the falls.

Everything from my work.

Occupational hazard.

You see, there's an old comic theory: if you get in trouble, take a fall. I learned that early on: if you're in trouble, go for the fucking fall. My dad was so cute—he'd watch me take a fall on the set while making a movie: "You know what that fall's gonna cost ya? Wait till you're fifty-one or fifty-two—will you pay for that fuckin' fall!" He was right. I've been doing nothing but paying for them all.

You took a lot of falls.

Peter, I was in such bad shape with pain that when I was in London, which was 1977, and I'm still eating thirteen Percodan a day. Well, you can't get Percodan in London so when I meet Moe Green, who owns Green's delicatessen in Soho, I told him of my plight. He comes out of his office and he says, "Be here at midnight tonight—outside, right by the lamppost." I said, "With a little fog, we're doing Sherlock Holmes." He laughed; he said, "He won't meet you inside. He needs air. He needs space." I said, "For a buy of Percodan?" He said, "That's right." So he's bringing me ten of them, OK? For a thousand dollars. A hundred dollars a tablet. Hey, I'm thrilled to death. I did my show, I'm off the stage at the Palladium at eleven, I got there at five to twelve, and I'm standing outside Green's delicatessen. A little fog came in, I said, "Fucking Sherlock Holmes—I swear to God." The guy comes up. "Hey, how ya doin', mate? Are you the buy?" "Yes, I'm the buy." "OK, let's see your loot." I give him ten one-hundred-dollar bills, he counts them, then he hands me a brown envelope. That's how I got fixed that night. But meanwhile, it didn't get me through the whole day tomorrow because I only had ten. That was how bad it was. You become very, very strategic with your bullshit—knowing you're not supposed to be doing it in the first place. But, yeah, let the next man talk—let him have my pain—you go through all that denial shit. And then, when he cleaned me out, Michael [Dr. DeBakey] said, "Now it's up to you—your head's gonna take you from this point on." Bad addiction—bad. I was taking Quaaludes to get up. I was taking Nembutal to get down. It's a vicious system.

And all that was going on for about thirteen years?

Yeah—from '65 to '78.

How'd you work, then?

They tell me I did five telethons from '73, '74, '75, '76, '77—I don't remember one of them. They told me I did three movies. I don't remember that either. I don't remember anything. From '73 to '77—black. I run into my library and look up '77 once in a while, I pull a tape out, put it on. Yeah, that's me, I was there, I think.

Do you remember when you see it?

No!

What about the telethon you did when Dean came on?

That was '76. I was starting to come around pretty good. Because, you see, in '76 I was already immune to the Percodan. I'm taking it, but it wasn't doing nutsy, crazy shit to me. And there was no alternative except shooting up. And I would never do such a thing. I figured I'll handle the pain. And, thank God, Michael says that I've got the highest pain tolerance of anyone he's ever known. That I can take pain longer, and more brutal pain, than he's ever seen with anybody.

That means when you were doing those falls, you probably were in pain, but you just . . .

When the laughter's there, you don't know anything else. There's no ham in my family, I got it *all.*

When did things get difficult in terms of making pictures?

I don't know—1970, I guess. Around 1970 I started to see the decline of quality thought-processes. They were gone. I made *Which Way to the*

Front? [1970], which was a goddamn good movie, and Warner Bros. flushed it in the toilet because they had *Woodstock* [1970]. I was very debilitated by what they did to the movie. I mean, my children didn't see it! And because I made a movie for four and a half million—well, you can't put that in competition with a movie that costs thirty million. So [studio head] John Calley and I—we had at it. And he said, "Jesus Christ, you're the most hostile man I ever met in my life." I said, "I am, John. When I'm fucked, I'm hostile." I said, "But, Jesus Christ, John, this is your gig—who would you have me come to, to be hostile? Are you running this studio or not?" Then he had compassion for me; he said, "I know where you're coming from. You know, what could I tell you—New York said . . ." "OK." Then it started to get iffy. When I did *Cracking Up* [1983], which was twelve years hence, even then I could feel the shake in the industry—it was going a crazy way.

The industry had become very different.

Fortunately for me, I had so many other things to fall back on, so many other things that I was doing. I feel badly for someone whose only area of revenue is their work as an actor. They don't get work, they do nothing. I do everything. I mean, I've been doing lectures for the last four, five years: I get $75,000 for a night. I did ten in the fall. It's nothing: I get my book [*The Total Filmmaker*], I get on a plane, I go, they pay for everything. And this year I'm doing fifteen. It's wonderful fun. It's great for your mind. You know, when you speak, you walk away with more information than when you came. It's a learning process. And remember something else. A lot of people would discuss this with you and give you a variety of terms as to what was happening. I'm going to tell you exactly what it is: it's a young boy—basically still nine years old—standing before an audience that is treating him as someone special. And that's all that's about. All of the guys and women out there whose parents told you you'll amount to shit, are having to listen to you because you're the qualified speaker that night. That's how it starts—that's where it's coming from. Now, when you take pride in accomplishment . . . I mean, I've spoken to everyone—from the United States Glass Association to the United States Marine Corps Association to the AMA [American Medical Association] community. I talk on subjects and on things that, at one point, I get into the lecture and I say, "I want you ladies and gentlemen to know that I could ask you all to leave, all you caregivers, you people in medicine, and then bring in here the entire airline corporate syndrome as we know it, and I wouldn't change a lot. When we get rid of them, I would bring in probably the most important CEOs in the country, representing some of the biggest corporations, and I would change nothing I'm saying."

It's basically the same speech?

No.

It changes each time?

Oh, yeah.

You do shtick?

Oh, God, yes—absolutely. I get very serious and they get into it pretty good. I run the gamut: I talk about everything from my daughter to nuclear physics. And I miss nothing. They want to do Q&A, I say, "Let me tell you something, I'll stay here with you as long as you want to do this, as long as I feel not insulted by someone yelling, 'Was Marilyn Monroe a good piece?' So if you're gonna go there, don't go there. Here's what I'm gonna do with you: Ask me about my racket, ask me about my friends, ask me about things that truly create a curiosity within you, and I'll bust my ass for you." Well, I did it at Northwestern on the tenth of November two years ago, and I stood before that audience for seven hours. Seven hours, after I had talked for two. Four hundred and seventy-five people stayed seven hours. Hey, the questions kept coming. I said, "You keep coming," and I sent out for sandwiches. And I say to them, "Remember this, any subject you want to talk about—go! If I'm not clear on it, I'll make something up. But you'll never hear me say, 'I don't know.' " They loved it—they love the truth.

Then I went to Texas A&M [University] to talk to the medical community there, and there's like 700 of the top researchers, psychiatrists, clinicians, pathologists—mostly white coats. And at one point I said, "How many of you people here tonight, I'm just curious, came here thinking—because it's called 'Laughter and Healing'—you came here tonight assuming I was going to help you to create laughter in your work?" All the hands went up. I said, "Let me tell you something, ladies and gentlemen, the patients are fine. *You're* the people that need to lighten up. *You're* the problem in this country. You take your work too seriously. Everyone knows we live and die and you people are carrying on like we shouldn't. We're going to. Lighten up!" I said, "Don't you know that a terminally ill woman knowing that she's going to die in three months is better than you and me? We don't know when we're gonna get it. She's been blessed. She's got a game plan. She's fine with it. You're the problem. You're tiptoeing in her life. You're reminding her she's gonna die because you're allowing it to affect *you*. It's serious business, but it doesn't mean you have to be serious about it. *Lighten up.*" I really reprimand them.

And they like it?

Oh, they love it. I said, "One of you nurses, why don't you go up to the head man of this administration and just walk up to him tomorrow and go—[makes a rude sound]—you won't be working here Wednesday but at least . . ."

How did The King of Comedy *come about?*

I did that just before my open-heart surgery. Marty [Scorsese] sent me the script, asked me what I thought. I said, "It's great, I love it." He said, "Will you do it?" I said, "Yeah, I'll do it." He said, "But there's a provision that I have to mention to you." I said, "Wait a minute, I'm not doing it yet—how am I getting a provision?" He said, "When you read the script I'm sure you saw what it was about." I said, "Yes, of course." He said, "Well, you see, Bobby [De Niro] and I—we don't understand that kind of celebrity." And then he went on to tell me, you know, Bobby walks in the street, nobody recognizes him. But this is the time he had just made *Taxi Driver* [1976], he made *Raging Bull* [1980], and no one knew him. Bobby had complete anonymity at that time, and so did Marty. So the *provision* was that I come to New York for six weeks before we shoot to tell them about celebrity and to talk about it. I did: for six weeks we had a wonderful time. Then we did a couple of rewrites, injected a couple of things that I told them. Paul Zimmerman [the screenwriter] was very good, very helpful. And it was a wonderful movie. It would have been better if they had a finish.

They didn't have one?

No, and I gave them one. I *wrote* a finish. Bobby was nervous about it.

What was it?

The finish was that Rupert [De Niro] escapes, Jerry returns to the program, and Rupert gets him, kills him.

Kills Jerry?

Yeah, kills Jerry. Bobby was concerned that *Taxi Driver* was rough, *Raging Bull* was rough—and he was seriously thinking that people would think of *him* as the people he portrays. Well, that's childlike. But they passed on the idea. I said, "It's a very exciting, dramatic finish." I said, "He's *got* to kill him. You've got to make it clear that these are the people that are out there." No, they weren't looking for statements and messages, and that was OK. In the shooting process, Marty came to me about the fourth week in, he said, "You know, I have to do this whole internal television sequence—I don't know a fucking thing about television. Will you direct it for me?" I said, "Yeah, am I going to get a credit? Martin Scorsese and the Jew?" He begged me. I said, "Marty, of course I'll do it." So we went into the studio for three days, I gave him all of his background material, I shot everything necessary that was scripted. He was sitting up in the bleachers watching me and at one point I walked over to him, I said, "Marty, both cameras do the same thing here. The electronic camera takes the stuff and sticks it in someone's house. The other one is film and we go to the lab. But they both point the same way. They both must be sharp and you pan this way if the person's walking! What's the fucking problem?" He said, "Meanwhile, I just got out of three days—just continue." It was a very quality time.

Was any of it ad-libbed? Improvised?

Yeah. The last scene when he comes to my house and I'm so pissed at him, we ad-libbed that whole thing. We did like a ten-minute spontaneous screaming at one another.

Was that a difficult period for you, from '70 on?

I don't know that it was difficult—I was pretty active and busy, I was working. I think I was in flux from '70 to '78: "Yeah, I'll do that, OK." Go to Europe, do ten concerts, get a lot of money, and it's terrific and wonderful. And I'm like royalty when I go to Europe—it's just incredible—Germany, Italy, France.

But it always comes back to Sam [Lewis' second wife]. When I met her, she brought a spirit into my soul that made everything important from that point on. It was February '79. And because of her presence, I had to reevaluate everything that had gone by. And I'm sitting there wondering: Why am I reevaluating? It's gone, it's done—that's the past. I just have to remember it so I don't repeat it, that's all. And, of course, Sam and I, we were like two lovebirds. I mean, people got nauseous: "Get a room!" And I'm twenty-four years Sam's senior. Now she's pushing twenty-nine years old, and one day I said to her, "Would you like to think about a family?" She said, "Well, every woman thinks about a family. I didn't know how *you* felt." I said, "I'll do anything you want. A woman needs to feel fulfilled. And that's the way that gets done." "OK." We go for it. We're up now, three years later, in vitro fertilization. We get her pregnant and she loses the baby. Get her pregnant again, she loses the baby. The third time she was pregnant, they find out that she had an enzyme in her body that didn't allow foreign matter. It killed the baby, this enzyme. Now she's shattered—it's five years later. She sits me down upstairs and she says, "I know that I'm asking a lot of you, but could we adopt a baby?" I said, "Under one condition. That when it comes, it's put into my arms and then I can present it to you. And it has to be a girl."

We went for it. We got a baby in less than a year and a half later. We had that little cupcake in my arms and my tears were dropping on her little cheeks. What it did for us! We got tired of saying we're so blessed. "He heard you already—enough with the bless." Now Dani [his daughter, Danielle] comes to us a few months ago, she says, "Will I ever meet my real mommy?" This takes us aback a little bit. And we sit her down and say, "Yeah, one day, maybe—if you want to." "No, I don't really care. Mommy, why didn't you have me from your belly?" And Sam says, "Because Mommy's belly was broke, and Mommy couldn't *have* a baby in there. So we went to a lovely lady who *could* have a baby and we said, 'Could you make a baby for us?' And they made you for us. And you're our baby girl." And she's satisfied with that. She's fine. See, I had an adopted son—I know what the ground rules are. Yeah, Ron—he's great. Fifty years old this week. So I bought a house in Florida, established residence, did everything: voting rights, driver's license, living there for six months. We got the baby, and in Florida, in three months you're given the right to keep it. It's tougher in California. I'll never forget the day with the judge: I'm holding Dani in my arms three months after she was born, and the judge said, "I've been doing this for a lot of years but I cannot remember ever feeling as good about granting a child to a man who does so much for so many children." He started to cry—the judge; the bailiff cried, my attorney cried, Sam cried, I cried. And Dani peed in my hand. She was watching my show at the Orleans last night—the first-night video we gave to her. She wasn't coming closing night because she had school in the morning. So we come home and Sam says, "She's running the show from the Orleans and she's mesmerized." She loves it.

You tape all the shows?

Oh, we always do.

You've been taping your live shows for years.

Just for reference. If I need to clean up something, I need to change something—I gotta know I did such and such. Sometimes I look at it and I say, "Jesus Christ, that's old hat, it's three years old." And it's interesting how it gives you another place to go. The negative aspect will give you a positive aspect most of the time. At least with me. And here [on shelf], these are the four shows I just did. So I got a backup audio and a master video. We then put it into the film computer and I can call on it any time I want.

When did you first meet Chaplin?

Oh, Charlie. It was the year he was cutting *Limelight* [1952]. I was in Chasen's [restaurant] and so was he. I'm having dinner with my wife and my children and Dave Chasen comes over to me and says, "I know you don't like to table-hop, and you don't like to meet people, and you're here for dinner, but I thought that since this is an extraordinary case that you might want to come over and meet this person." And I said, "There ain't no extraordinary cases, David, I come in here to relax. I really don't want to go meeting people." He said, "What if it was Charlie Chaplin?" "What? What are you saying to me?" He said, "I know who you are and what you are—I knew how you'd react—now get off your ass and come over with me." I go. My whole life flashed before me. "Charlie, this is Jerry Lewis." "How do you do, Mr. Chaplin." He said, "Charlie." I said, "Hi, Charlie." That's when I did my first gag with him; I said, "You call me Mr. Lewis."

Did he laugh?

Oh, God, yes—broke him right up. He asked me to sit down. And Oona's with him. And, to the best of my recollection, it was around ten to ten at night. We were finishing our dinner when Dave called me. I sat with Charlie till three-thirty. We talked about his beginning, my beginning. He talked about the wonderful work that Dean and I are doing that will ultimately gain the mantle of Laurel and Hardy as one of the greatest comedy teams, and so on.

It must have meant a lot to you.

Oh, God almighty.

Had you been an abject fan from the time you were a child?

Five years old, sure. So we talked and it's late, we have to go. But I have to tell you that the last half-hour was about cutting a scene in *Limelight*—

and he'd like my opinion. He's gonna give me two versions of the scene. And I'm sitting like I'm trying not to look like I'm nine, you know, half-crossed legs, smoking my cigarettes. "You're gonna ask about an edi . . . an edi . . . edit?"

Then I got to be with him in 1959 in Lucerne. I spent two days at his home, as his guest. You can't talk education—I had it *all*. I got a four-year discussion from Charlie on how to really make movies. We talked and talked and talked. [*Pointing across to the opposite wall:*] That's his picture over there, you know? That's his last Christmas card to me—I got one every year—that was his last one. To make a long story short, I revisited Charlie in '63 in Lucerne and I said, "You know, I wanted to ask you this the night we met, but I didn't have the courage. But now, since we're such good friends, I figure you're not gonna throw me out of your house, because, I don't know how to talk Switzerland." He said, "What is it?" I said, "I love *Modern Times* [1936] more than I do breathing. And if I could get a print of *Modern Times* so I could show it to my children every Sunday. . . ." He said, "You'll have it." "That's it?" He said, "Yeah, you'll have it." "How do I know you're not lying?" He says, "I'm not lying to you. I love that you *want* it. I'm gonna call New York and draw a mint print from the negative and send it to you. With one provision." That's if I'll send him *The Bellboy.* Well, I called New York the next morning and got it done. I get home and on my front step at Bel Air—remember the entrance to the house?—there's a can delivered from United Artists Los Angeles with a tag: "To Jerry—Love, Charlie." I never touched the tag. It's in my vault.

Now, here's the *best* of Charlie in the four or five wonderful experiences I had with him. When I opened at the Olympia [in Paris] in 1970—if you could have seen *that*—it was a once-in-a-lifetime thing. Because, in the front row was Jean-Luc Godard and François Truffaut and [Jacques] Tati, Fernandel, and anyone you want to think, including Catherine Deneuve, Jean-Pierre Cassel. Name it—every actor, every director, every actress—were in that opening night at the Olympia. Maria Callas was in the third row. The world of Paris was at my opening night. I just paralyzed that fucking city.

It was the first time you played there?

Yeah. There were like 20,000 people around the block of a theater that seats 2,100 and I'm doing one show a night. It was incredible. If I had to name one thing that was my whole life, it was *that* night. . . . Now, we're at Maxim's for an after-theater party. And Geraldine Chaplin couldn't

Jerry Lewis walks the hotel guests' dogs as The Bellboy *(1960), the first
film he directed (and co-wrote and produced and financed), one of
the biggest box-office hits of its year. Though a talking picture,
Lewis doesn't speak at all.*

stop telling me how much she loved the show. Also, Geraldine and I were
establishing a terrific fund for the poor children of Paris that she brought
to my attention—I was going to help her by doing a couple of shows for
her—so she reminded me we were having breakfast the next morning.
The next morning she's in my suite at the Hilton, we're having breakfast,
and I said, "I haven't asked you, how's your dad? How's he doing? Is he
well?" She said, "He's terrific—and he thought *you* were terrific." "What
do you mean, he thought I was terrific?" She said, "He was there last
night." "What!?"

Now, after the show, I forgot to tell you, Jean-Luc and everyone were
backstage in my dressing room. My dressing room sat four people—I had
thirty-five people back there with chairs outside my dressing room and
I'm holding court till six in the morning. So I said, "*Where* was he?" She
said, "He was in the light booth. He didn't want to steal your thunder on
an opening night." He stayed for the whole performance and couldn't tell
her enough about how much he was enthralled about what he saw. He

was leaving that afternoon and I asked Geraldine if I could call him. She gave me his number. I said, "Charlie, Jesus Christ, I would never stand in a spotlight booth when *you* were onstage!" He says, "Don't worry about it. You'll never see me onstage. Ha, ha, ha. You were just wonderful. I loved every minute of it." That was Charlie. He was so delicate—he had a delicate frame—kind of a ballerina. I loved him. I was working him—loved to make him laugh—and anything I could do or say that was irreverent . . .

Would make him laugh.

Fred Karno, who Chaplin worked for at the beginning—I told him that Karno called me, and he started to laugh hysterically because Karno's been dead for fifty years. I said, "Karno called me and wants me to do a transvestite in Liverpool . . ." and he's banging on the table.

How did you meet Stan Laurel?

It was after Ollie died. Dick Van Dyke was at a party with me and he told me about Stan hearing over the telephone that Ollie died. And the arm that he was holding the phone with just went paralyzed. They had to pull the phone out of his hand and then work his arm to get it down. Paralyzed—stroke—at the thought of Ollie's death. I said, "I'd love to meet him." He said, "He'd love to meet you." So Dick arranged for me to meet him at his apartment. And I flew that Sunday morning—did I get there! And for the last five years of his life I was there like twice a month, three times a month.

What did you talk about?

Work. We talked about his five wives. One he married twice. We talked about the film process. He taught me to thread the BMC and the Panaflex [cameras]. I learned to load. Then all through my first ten or twelve pictures, when I was just the actor, the crews and the people who worked on the lot—I mean, I was their kid. The first day I loaded a BMC was the thrill of my life.

Why did you want to learn that part?

Because I had to know everything. I had to know it all.

Did you do a lot of European gigs?

Yeah. I did the Berlin Film Festival. I did the Opera House in Rome. Stockholm was a big gig. Oslo.

Which audiences were the best? Which country?

They were *all* incredible.

And you spoke only English? Or you did shtick in . . .

Cracked. [*Performing voice:*] Swedish people, they sing when they talk—[*sings*]—they would love it. You know, when I am in France [*doing French accent*]: "I would like to do zis number—I hope you like eet." But in Germany [*Prussian accent*]: "I VILL DO ZIS NUMBER! YOU *VILL* LOVE IT! SIT DOWN!" They loved that shit—loved it. And, of course, everything I did was primarily visual. They understood everything they *saw*. And then when I bend the language a little bit, I'd pick up words that worked for me.

Words that sounded funny to you?

Yeah. Like "schnapptelefoncouplingbox"—you know what that is? A schnapptelefoncouplingbox is an extension from this phone to that one. "JERRY! YOU GIVE ME YOUR AUTOGRAM!" "My autograph? Who the fuck you yelling at?" It was great.

It must have been an amazing thing to go to Europe and have the kind of reaction that maybe you'd expect in Florida.

I mean, you should see what happened in Cannes—I thought I was going to get swallowed up. The first time I went to Cannes, which was probably around '78: pandemonium. They sent runners to tell them where I was located at the time. I made speeches from the Carlton Hotel. I had all the people down the street. [*French accent:*] "STOPPING THEM! WE HAVE TO DO SOMETHING ABOUT THIS! THE FRENCH DON'T GIVE YOU BUTTER IN THE MORNING!" And I would carry on and mobs would congregate, laughing and carrying on.

That reminds me of the story about when you and Dean had to do a free performance on 44th Street because they wouldn't leave the Paramount theater.

And we were doing eight a day. Each show was an hour and some. At one point, Bob Weitman [of Paramount] came up to the dressing room to see me. He said, "We got a problem, Jerry. Jesus Christ, I need ten minutes." I said, "Ten minutes?" He said, "Yeah, with eight shows, that totals eighty minutes. Can you give me ten minutes?" I said, "What do you want me to *do*?" He said, "Make a cut in the movie." I said, "I'll do that for you." I made a cut—I eliminated a thousand feet [equals 10 minutes].

Which picture?

My Friend Irma [1949]. That was on the screen and we were on the stage. I gave him the eighty minutes he needed. We then, on a Saturday, did NINE! This was 1950 and Dean and I took out $299,000 for the week. The Paramount did good, too. But that was our cut in 1950: three hundred grand! In a week. Fifty-six shows. Then we went to the Chicago Theater, did the same thing.

Did you realize at the time this was a phenomenon? Or were you too much a part of the whirlwind?

It was hard to tell. I think your perspective changes. It's not really all "on the money." You're being torn from every which way—there's so much going on. So *much.* The extensions at the Copacabana: two weeks, four weeks, three months. It's like principal and interest—the principal creates so much interest—and then there's no time. There's *really* no time to think about what's happening.

Was there a moment when you stopped and said, "What the hell happened?!"

I guess I thought about it all the time—on some level—because I needed to justify the kind of work I was putting in.

You were working all the time.

But at this kind of money, that's enough to justify this kind of work, this kind of input. We're at NBC, we're at Paramount, we're at the concert venue, we're at the goddamn supermarket opening! All that stuff had to be examined and calculated and you're in the foreground of all of that. I think there were nights when I'd lay down and say, "I don't fucking believe this is happening." I didn't have a car payment, you know.

You weren't just a hit—you guys were a phenomenon. Then when you went on your own, it was the same, actually.

Yeah. You see, there was an interesting thing, Peter. When we split, the people took umbrage. This country was very upset with us and our conduct. We took something away from them that they loved. And all they questioned was, "Why couldn't you just continue? You didn't hurt anybody."

So they felt as if they were penalized in some way—did you feel that from the audience?

No, you never felt it. But when you get into intellectual discussions about the growth of the career and so forth and so on, you ultimately get to that place where, Jesus Christ, we made so many enemies by quitting—quitting one another—and it was tough for them to re-acclimate. But they did. Once others said we're OK, then they fell into line and it was OK. But I had people come up to me in the airport and say, "Do you know what you did to my life in July of 1956?" I said, "No, I don't really know, but I know where you're coming from." "Everything was perfect. And then you two guys had to break up and then, I didn't have that Sunday night anymore." Our problem is, we don't take the word "fan" too seriously—the word comes from fanatic. And it's a time and a place where you are made to recognize—this is not a fucking joke—fan. Like, for example, the other day security came back to my dressing room and said, "There's a bunch of stuff at the box office for you. Someone sent a baseball—please sign your name. A photograph—please sign your name." And so forth and so on. And I looked at the security guy and I said, "No, I'm not signing anything. Take it back." He said, "Yeah, I thought you'd say that." I said, "Yeah, but you don't know *why* I say it." He said, "No, why?" I said, "Because I cannot allow them to believe that since they bought a ticket I am now locked into them as a commitment to do more. No. I'm gonna give them my heart and my soul and sweat for the ticket they bought, but they can't have anything else." I don't know how to put it except that it feels like you're like a fuckin' whore. It offends me.

Of the pictures you directed, which was the most successful?

Bellboy, I think—a lot of goddamn money.

You also made it for nothing.

Nine hundred thousand dollars is not nothing. And then when Paramount decided they don't want to be my partner, I said, "OK, I'll do it alone." I did.

You funded the picture?

Uh-huh.

Why? Didn't they want to do it?

They were afraid of a silent movie. I said, "If you look at it, you'll see it's not a silent movie." So, to this day, the word "bellboy" is *verboten* at Paramount. 'Cause to today I made a fortune on it.

During that period when you were directing the pictures, would you say that was your happiest time?

Creatively, uh-huh. '60, '63, '65, '67, up through '70, it was a great time—a great time.

Of that period, what would you say was the high point, The Nutty Professor *or* The Bellboy?

The Bellboy was the first high point because I found out I knew more than I thought I did. So it was a very exhilarating period, which only helped me then go to *Nutty* and write it and finish it. And I trusted myself then. I think I had written five versions and shot the first.

Went back to the first one.

First one. I tried to look it over and edit and—why'd I go to two? What the fuck do I need three for? I was scared, that's why. I didn't like what I felt. I was feeling uncertainty and yet I knew if it was going to be right it would be big. And I think that kind of kept me at bay.

It was such a departure—you hadn't done anything like that. You really went far out playing Buddy Love.

And the terrible thing is that the cunts in the newspaper racket would write, "Oh, he did a homage to Dean." Oh, hell, they didn't know. They didn't get it.

You weren't thinking of Dean on that picture?

Oh, God, no.

What would you say the two sides—Professor Kelp and Buddy Love—were?

Buddy Love was a conglomeration of mean-spirited people. The man who pushes inside of an elevator—a lady and a child be damned—he'll push. The ill-mannered people that we come in contact with every day. The mean-spirited people that really are the ugliness on the planet and they think everything else is. I watched guys in bars, I watched people function.

He was very much a show-biz type.

Well, I made him a show-business type only because I had a glamour thing going that way. But I could have easily made him the president of the bank. I literally sat for days trying to think of what he would look like. And I ran the gamut from the grotesque . . .

Because you were doing Dr. Jekyll and Mr. Hyde . . .

So I'm writing and thinking, "What does he look like? What's at the end of that long walk where people are doing that kind of thing?" So I'm thinking about Julie Podell [owner of the Stork Club], Joe Bananas [gangster], I know goddamn well I was thinking of Alexander Cohen [theatrical producer] throughout. Alexander Cohen was a house number: he was a clone of all of the bad fuckin' people in show business. He was beneath contempt. Hal Wallis was in that mix. The dichotomy of that man who could be so wonderful personally, socially. And such a motherfucker when it meant fifty cents. So when I put all of these people together—if I were to do this in a cauldron—what's gonna come out? Well, what has to come out is someone who can get through on the planet, either not noticed at all, or noticed terrifically. And as I kept going, I kept seeing the manifestation of the fluid—the ugliness, the terrible last cut of that fucking transformation. It was diabolically terrible. And so I made Buddy anything but what you think is coming up.

It was interesting that you went with a very attractive-looking guy for the monster.

He was one of the people that was out there, with bad manners. Anyhow, we were named [by the American Film Institute] one of the one hundred best comedies of the century.

How did the character of the professor evolve?

I had met him on a train from L.A. to New York. Dean and I were gonna play the Copa and this: "Are you show people?" In the parlor car. I thought, Oh, dear God, let me just keep him for a few minutes. "Yes, we are, sir." "Well that's good—good. We need it, we need it. This world is a terrible fog without laughter." And I said, "I fucking got him."

And you stored him away for all those years.

For a long time. I called on him because I had his face—he wore the glasses I wore and I got him down perfectly. On the train, I spent the next two days feeding off him—buying him drinks, talking to him. He was going to New York, too. And then for fifteen years I stashed it. Then, that summer I was writing *Nutty,* I took my boat and dropped the hook—I just wanted to relax—I was by myself sitting at the typewriter. "What should I name the professor?" And I was sitting topside on my boat and other boats are passing by pretty closely and they're watching me: "He's fucking talking to himself." "Julius. Yes. Julius." And I'm looking in the water and there's all that kelp. "Julius Sumner Kelp."

Where did the Sumner come from?

Summertime.

What about the Eddie Murphy remake and the sequel—you get a piece of that, too?

Oh, God, yes.

So if they do it again . . .

They're doing it right now. I got a check this morning would blow your head off.

You get a piece of the gross?

Oh, God, yes, of course.

That's because you got the rights back to all your pictures after thirty years.

Also, I wouldn't let them have *Nutty Professor* unless they guaranteed me we'd get either Eddie Murphy or Robin Williams. And Eddie was wonderful. I don't particularly care for what they did with it because they took it so far afield there's nothing to connect it—why'd you buy this?

Why did you leave Paramount in '65—what happened?

Well, the suits arrived with contracts and papers.

You had no contract up till that time?

I said, "I'm not signing anything. I don't want to stay here." Frank Freeman had died, and a bunch of others died, and I felt like there was nothing to keep me there anymore. They were very sad about it—they were very unhappy. I said, "I don't know this new company, Gulf & Fuckman." [The conglomerate Gulf & Western had bought Paramount.] Bob Evans came over, fucked a cookie, then whatever happened, I don't know. The studio was off its foundation . . . I'm now shooting up Lavoris—it's safer.

Did you have a spinal break?

March 20, 1965.

From what?

*Jerry Lewis in the Dr. Jekyll role of Professor Julius Sumner Kelp,
with Stella Stevens as a tantalizing coed, in Lewis' original*
The Nutty Professor *(1963), probably his most personal film.
There were apparently no photos released of Jerry in his
Mr. Hyde character, Buddy Love, the evil Las Vegas hipster lounge
performer–seducer. Lewis also directed, co-wrote, and produced.
He was extremely proud of the film's inclusion in an American Film
Institute poll of the top one hundred comedies of all time.*

I did a flip off the piano. At the Sands [in Las Vegas]. I went on with
the band, and came off with 911. It was terrific. And they did an MRI of
my spine last month and the doctor put it up and said, "Take a look—it's
the funniest picture I ever saw." It's like gnarled—unbelievable. He said,
"What did you expect? You know what you did for sixty-eight years? The
falls you've taken?"

Do you have a tape of all the falls you've done?

Yeah. We call it "The Combined Oops." I'll show you falls, incredible.
I came off a two-story building into corrugated boxes. I did all my own
stunts.

Didn't you know you would injure yourself?

Nah. You're immortal at thirty years old. I raced a horse in *Pardners*
that was doing forty miles an hour and I couldn't get him to ease up—he

was *going*. And I had no recourse, I had to jump because he was fucking nuts, he lost it. We were riding up in this canyon and fortunately for me the canyon growth at the base of the mountain was all of this fern kind of foliage that grows at the base of the rock. And I threw myself into it.

At forty miles an hour?

Yeah—you can miss, you know. I could have gone into the rocks. But I had to get off. I was riding sidesaddle for a while before I took my body off the horse to eliminate any stress. So I'm riding on the right side, looking for where I can dump. When I saw that stuff coming up, I said it's like God planted it—very soft material.

But at that speed you could have easily misjudged it.

And I went down in a sub, four hundred feet, for *Sailor Beware*. I was on the deck and I rehearsed with the captain a couple of times so that he could take her down while I'm on the top of the deck. So he threw ballast to take the sub just to break the water for me, and they over-ballasted it so that it swirled. It's supposed to just sit, but the ballast was wrong and it swirled like that [*gesturing*], and I went whoosh with a fuckin' whiplash. I'm in the middle of the ocean now, and the sub is trying to find its way back to me . . . I was on an Air India, and the captain knew I'd flown and he said, "You want to ride shotgun?" and I said, "Yeah, I'd love it." So I'm sitting there—375 people on this 747 should only know Jerry Lewis is flying this fucking airplane. I said, "Captain, could I announce to the audience that I'm flying?" He said, "I don't think that would be wise." Flying a 747.

You've flown before?

Oh, yeah, sure. I had a ticket [license to fly]. I was flying until they stopped me. So I'm at the outer marker of Heathrow [London], and he says, "Take it down to 18,000," and we're at 32,000. So I just proceeded to move it down and I was halfway and he said, "Move it to 132 degrees." I'm still declining, and I move it, and you feel this fucking moose just like it was a piece of paper on a table. I moved it to the new heading, took it down to 18,000, locked it off, hit the automatic. I said, "Thank you, God bless you, I'm leaving," I'm so fucking nervous. But getting off that flight, there was an overzealous fan that wanted my autograph so he pushed into me and I went down the steps with my spine hitting most all of them. . . . I sprained my back doing basic training for *Jumping Jacks* [1952]. Then, when I made my jump and I got my wings—I made an actual jump out of a plane—it's a wonderful feeling. I went up the next day, they let me jump again.

What pushed you in that daredevil direction?

I love to challenge things. Playing ball with the major-leaguers is a much bigger challenge. It's much more dangerous than anything I'm talking about. I went to Phoenix in '54 and stayed the whole ten weeks spring training with the Giants. Played first base in all the exhibition games. It was incredible. I walked, I hit a single, I made ten unassisted plays at first base, four double plays. It was great.

I didn't know you had prostate cancer.

It was rough. There's so much mental involved. I mean, I came around in twelve days after the surgery—I didn't need any diapers anymore. I'm a quick recoverer. And I was having sex with Sam like four weeks later.

With the open-heart surgery, did you feel like you were dead for a while?

Well, I was—I was gone for seventeen seconds. I went into V-tach [ventricular tachycardia], which is a lock-off to the heartbeat. It stops. And the nurse in the hospital hit me a shot in the chest that brought me around. I was in surgery six minutes later.

You were conscious?

I was in intensive care under observation because I had a chest pain early that morning. DeBakey and his team were flying from Houston to operate.

Where are you?

I'm at the Desert Springs Hospital. And Michael would be landing in an hour and we couldn't wait, 'cause I went into V-tach, so they had to rush me in. Fortunately, the man who did the surgery on me was one of Dr. DeBakey's primary students who learned from Michael. So I was very blessed. This was Christmas '82.

What was the psychological stress? Was there a feeling of having lost yourself in some way?

You go through a series of devastating nightmares after the surgery. People don't understand that in order for them to save your life they have to kill you. You must be dead before they can go in to get your heart to work. You're put on a pump. So Michael said, "You're gonna have some devastating moments in the next three or four months. You just cannot let them bother you. They're going to annoy you and frighten you." And the first thing I dreamed the night I came home from the hospital was that I was lying on a bed in a clinic with nothing on. The walls and the floors were all made of glass, and my grandmother's coming over to me in the bed with a bread knife and sticks it into my chest and rips my chest open. I wake up soaking wet, trembling. That was one. And there is no way to recount the others that I had on and off for three and a half, four months. But the fourth month I was on stage in Atlantic City doing my act.

Looking back over your whole career, do you have very specific high points you remember?

In '77, the nomination for the Nobel Peace Prize was about all you need in your life. If you're looking for trophies, as we all do, if you get *this* trophy, you don't need anything anymore. It dwarfs everything else. But that was about the best time for me. I was just coming out of all of the drugs and shit. I had a better sense of myself. And, you know, I can't discount opening night at the Copa with Dean. It always pops up as one of the fucking incredible nights. It was an incredible time. The ten years with him—nobody would ever understand it that way. Because we had the fun in the dressing room waiting to go on to have the fun. And then, of course, the third section of fun was counting the money. Like two fucking chimps in a zoo.

I picked up a copy of that book about Dean [Dino: Living High in the Dirty Business of Dreams, 1992] by Nick Tosches. It's not a bad book.

No, it's not a bad book—but it wasn't accurate. It made him look like a *putz*. That's not Dean. See, Tosches couldn't write as a postscript: "I wasn't good enough to get the balls of the character—" I called him when I got the book, and I said, "Does a cunt have trouble sleeping at night? You fucking hack!" And the answer I got from him made me doubly pissed. He said, "Well, I didn't say anything about you." I said, "Is that the only reason you think people'd get upset? I'm upset because this is my partner, you fucking moron." And I hung up on him.

In that book, there's a time which I think was Dean's seventy-second birthday . . .

At Bally's [Las Vegas casino].

You brought a cake out. The book says Dean got choked up about it.

He did. And so did I. We were both choked up. See, if I ever wrote *Dean and Jerry* and what they were from an outer look—staying away from the internals—it would make a hell of a book about two men who were in love with one another.

Are you going to write it?

Yes, I'm three-quarters on the way. And it's an incredible book, because when I think of anything we did I sit down and write. So I started the book twenty years after we were over. I had to start it with what happened on the stage that night [in Las Vegas] when Frank [Sinatra] brought him out on the telethon. That was 1976 and I'm into the book and then I'm into 1949 with Dean and me. So it jumps back, and then on up to 1970. So whatever I remember at the time, I put it in—that's the order. And it feels wonderful because you're bathed in this glitz and then you're shattered at what happened there—but that happened way after. And this happened way before that. I find it's not important to be chronological. I know that I would diminish the book by trying to make it chronological. It doesn't make any sense. Because in '76 we were already theatrical professionals; 1947, these two putzes were hoping to have a burger for dinner.

How did the cake happen on his seventy-second birthday?

I was picked up at the airport and my driver said, "You know it's Dean's birthday?"—driving me from the airport to my home. I said, "No, I didn't know that. But I do know that he's at Bally's." So I ran home and I said, "Sam, I gotta get a tux on." And while I'm changing I'm telling her what I'm gonna do. She said, "That's wonderful. Just go and do it." This was three in the afternoon when I got home from whatever that trip was. So I called Claudia [Stabile], I said, "Get a fuckin' cake made. They're probably doing it at Bally's, but tell 'em what we're gonna do and we'll do it together. Whatever. Just get it to be a nice cake. And I'll wheel it out at the end of the show."

He had no idea.

No, of course not.

Was that after his son had been killed?

Uh-uh.

Nobody really saw him much after that.

No. I was about the only one who talked to him after that. We talked twice a week. He needed to communicate but didn't have anything to say. He just let me talk. Because he did respect that I knew about the human condition and communicating with people. The thing that he didn't want to do. He could probably have been very good had he wanted to.

If somebody asked, "What advice would you give in terms of living?" what would you say?

What I would say, off the top of my head, is, "Reach for the child within. The child has never died within you, you've just abandoned him, that's all. Dig him out. Give him some wings and some air and you'll fly with him."

Back to innocence.

It's really back to wisdom. The *real* wisdom. See, the nine-year-old hasn't learned yet to be deceptive. The nine-year-old doesn't understand why he should circumvent his feelings or why he should cap the emotions that spring from a nine-year-old. He doesn't understand why he sees grown-ups do that. I don't do it. I let out a yell when I'm happy [*a huge yell comes out!*] and I don't give a fuck who says, "Is that man crazy?" I do it on airplanes. Sometimes I get so happy I scream out like that. And Sam looks at me and says, "Are you happy again?" But I do it. I do it downtown, in any city we go to—like in City Hall, and when visiting museums, and things are beautiful, and if I get that surge of happy, I just let it out [*another gigantic yell*]! And I scare half a dozen people. The other day, I'm coming out of the mall in San Diego and it's Friday so it's jammed with people. And walking in the mall is this sweet little lady—you never saw anything so cute in your life. She looked like [actress] Kathleen Freeman, only three times as wide. And she looked at me so I knew she knew something—was I? And I went [*sings loudly, song from* Camelot]: "NO, NEVER IN SPRINGTIME . . ." And a thousand people see it's me, and they start laughing. And she's just paralyzed. "NO, NEVER SHALL I LEAVE YOU." And I gave her a kiss and I went to my car. . . . I do that every once in a while because it's good for *me*. I'm not doing it for *them*. That keeps the child within me alive. . . . I think it would be so sad if someone that was as blessed as I am—having grown up with most of this country—if I grew up old and crotchety, without humor, without fun. That would be a terrible, disastrous thing to see. I've seen certain comedians that've gone off that way and it's been terrible. No, before they close the box let me do one [*yells, mouth wide open*]: "MAILEE!!" Now close it. I couldn't stand them closing it without one "MAILEE!"

Exactly that kind of scene played over the phone with me in Jerry's seventy-fifth year. He'd had a bad bout of pulmonary pneumonia, for which it took Dr. DeBakey again to pull him through. He had just returned from Houston a couple of days before I called him at home in Las Vegas to hear how he was doing. When he got on the line, he sounded a little breathless but otherwise with the same usual energy and cheer. He said they wouldn't let him talk for long—did I want to hear a joke? And he launched into a lengthy setup for the punch line, and as usual with Jerry, the way he built up to the big laugh was through an increasing number of little laughs along the way. These were largely based on his performance— readings and intonations—how much or little he stressed each word.

"Late at night, in New York, this fellow comes into a subway and stops dead in his tracks. Sitting across from him in this empty car is a youngish guy in tie-dyed shirt and pants—many colors in those pants and shirt— and his hair is several colors and the guy wears it in spikes. It goes straight up—it goes dooown, it goes up—it goes dooown. He's got about ten rings in each ear, a ring through his nose, a ring in each lip, and a spike in his tongue. On his feet he's got multicolored socks and sandals. So the fellow's staring at him, and the guy on the seat says, 'What's a matter—didn't you ever do anything just for fun?!' And the fellow says, 'No, I'm sorry, I was just thinking—I remember a long time ago I *fucked* a *parrot* once, and I was wondering if you were my *son!*' "

With his delivery, he got me completely, and I laughed loud and long. Jerry said, "Isn't that a great one?" As I was catching my breath, he said, "OK, I gotta go now. They've got me on oxygen and they say I gotta get back on it." I cried out, "They've got you on oxygen and you just told me that whole long story?! What're you doing?" "I thought you'd get a kick out of it. I love you. 'Bye now." That was Jerry.

While he was getting better (which took three grueling years, and a great deal of attention and love from his devoted wife, Sam, and his adoring daughter, Dani, as well as his sons), Lewis continued working nearly full time on his detailed and vivid memoir of his days with Martin. I've read a couple of hundred manuscript pages and it is riveting, funny and touching. Never before has someone right smack in the eye of a show-business cyclone written about the experience, much less with such candor and narrative skill. It's like hearing Jerry tell you the whole thing from the inside. For someone who was growing up in the late forties and early fifties, these memories are like black jelly beans or cherry Life Savers—you can't get enough. It's also a unique opportunity to share again that magical friendship they had. Recently I saw nearly all twenty-eight of their *Colgate Comedy Hours* (soon to be released on DVD), and a lot of the stuff is still fall-down-on-the-floor hilarious. Usually, it's Lewis who ad-libs a line or some piece of comic business that makes Martin laugh, which in turn often causes Jerry to fall apart, too; he always got a big kick out of breaking up Dean. These moments are not only infectiously funny, they sparkle with a delightfully unfettered sense of loving camaraderie and joy. When I mentioned this to Jerry, he said quietly, "Yeah, if you could bottle that, you could change the world."

Born Joseph Levitch, March 16, 1926, Newark, NJ.

Selected starring features (with director):

1950: *At War with the Army* (Hal Walker)
1951: *That's My Boy* (Walker)
1952: *Jumping Jacks* (Norman Taurog)
1953: *The Stooge* (Taurog); *Scared Stiff* (George Marshall); *The Caddy* (Taurog)
1954: *Living It Up* (Taurog)
1955: *Artists and Models* (Frank Tashlin)
1956: *Hollywood or Bust* (Tashlin)
1958: *Rock-a-Bye Baby* (Tashlin); *The Geisha Boy* (Tashlin)
1960: *The Bellboy* (Jerry Lewis)

1961: *The Ladies' Man* (Lewis)
1962: *It'$ Only Money* (Tashlin)
1963: *The Nutty Professor* (Lewis); *Who's Minding the Store* (Tashlin)
1964: *The Disorderly Orderly* (Tashlin)
1965: *The Family Jewels* (Lewis)
1966: *Three on a Couch* (Lewis)
1967: *The Big Mouth* (Lewis)
1969: *Hook, Line & Sinker* (Marshall)
1970: *Which Way to the Front?* (Lewis)
1981: *Hardly Working* (Lewis)
1983: *The King of Comedy* (Martin Scorsese); *Cracking Up* (Lewis)
1995: *Funny Bones* (Peter Chelsom)

9

DEAN MARTIN

When Dean Martin died, on Christmas Day 1995, at the age of seventy-eight, it seemed strangely inconceivable. Dean was such an integral part of our youth, our coming of age, our idea of cool and funny, how could he die, he who always seemed so impervious to care or age? But there was also the question of our own mortality. If Dean, who not? Since I first saw all the Dean Martin and Jerry Lewis movies and live TV shows in my preteen to late teen years when I was an unequivocal fan of theirs, I do admit to nostalgic sentimental attachments. Yet that is what pop culture has always been, and always will be: what gets to you as you age is eternally about who and what you grew up with. You ache not just for the performers' past, but for your own.

Only once did I sit alone with Martin—for about a half-hour in his dressing room on the M-G-M lot in January 1961—when he was forty-three and shooting *Ada,* among his most forgettable pictures. I had seen him in person one time before, during the second half of 1953 at New York's old Paramount Theater on Broadway at Times Square. He and Jerry did about a half-hour version of their act between showings of a terrible Glenn Ford picture (*Plunder of the Sun*). It was so unspeakably boring that, although I had intended to sit through it twice in order to see their show twice, I just couldn't face even another five minutes of the thing. (In those days, unlike today, one ticket automatically bought you as many consecutive shows as you cared to watch.) Certainly, that movie was carefully selected to be a chaser, the trade term for an act or film that will automatically empty a house—chase the audience out—in this case, allowing room for a fresh set of ticket-buyers.

With Martin and Lewis, Paramount was learning from their mistakes. The first time (late 1950) that the team had appeared live at the Paramount, with Dick Stabile and His Orchestra, they couldn't get the audi-

*Dean Martin in the opening sequence of his twelfth starring vehicle
with Jerry Lewis,* Artists and Models *(1955), not only among their best,
but one of Martin's most likeable performances, bringing out what director
Frank Tashlin called his "Cary Grantish qualities"*

ence out. Kids would just sit through the movie over and over; it, too, featured Dean and Jerry. Finally, in desperation, Martin and Lewis
announced from the stage that they would do a free show off the fire
escape outside their dressing room window on West 44th Street. That
did it.

However, while the houses emptied, the Times Square area became gridlocked with thousands of fans on the street outside, extending onto Broadway, snarling traffic up to 59th Sreet. Dean and Jerry did their impromptu bits, tore off clothes and ripped newspapers, dropped them into the crowd, scattered thousands of fan photos! It was a sensation and became part of the show-business lore around Martin and Lewis—how they literally stopped traffic on Times Square.

When they came back to the Paramount and I saw them less than three years later, the bloom was off the rose, and there was not the wild crowd or the need for a fire-escape show, though a dedicated little group of fans did wait hopefully outside the fabled 44th Street window, but to no avail. Infrequently some photos would come flying out. Between the first Paramount appearance and this one, six more Martin and Lewis musical comedies had been released to huge box office, each among its year's top grossers. By the time of the Paramount engagement I attended, they had had two top grossing films in both 1951 and 1952; they had three in 1953. My own personal exposure to Martin and Lewis throughout 1953 was like so many others' in the United States and abroad: I went to first runs of *The Stooge* and *Scared Stiff,* then saw the boys in person, plus watched them live once a month on TV's *Colgate Comedy Hour,* and then the first run of *The Caddy* (twice) as well as seeing their cameo appearance in the Bob Hope–Bing Crosby hit *Road to Bali* (twice), and listening to Dean's numerous recordings, among which "That's Amore" (from *The Caddy*) went to number one.

What I saw them do onstage at the Paramount was much like what they are seen doing at the end of *The Caddy,* and for the last ten minutes of each of their *Colgate Comedy Hour*s: the boys in tuxedos (even during Paramount's morning and afternoon shows), their bow ties untied, fooling around in front of Dick Stabile's orchestra, their caricatures displayed throughout the band. Dean sings—Jerry disrupts. They sing together. They throw things into the audience or Jerry runs into the auditorium. They do jokes putting each other down. Dean sings as if he's sending up crooners and doesn't mean a word, Jerry screeches hysterically for attention and his outrageousness becomes contagious. For a privileged minority, Dean was as funny in his own dry way as Jerry was so obviously. In fact, even Frank Sinatra had originally missed the self-deprecating wit behind Dean's comedy. When Frank saw the act the first time at New York's Copacabana, he reportedly said, "The wop's not much, but the Jew's funny."

When I sat down with Dean, he had had ten years (1946–1956) of unparalleled success as half of the most successful comedy team in history, a rocky moment or two as a solo (1957), and then three major Hollywood pictures in a row that proved he could act as well as play straight or funny, *and* sing. With Marlon Brando and Montgomery Clift in *The Young Lions* (1958), the demands on him were not too taxing—as an entertainer who becomes a soldier—he had already been in uniform for three early Martin and Lewis hits. Again, with *Some Came Running* (1958)—superb as he is—the role wasn't far from his Vegas-gambler persona (he had been a dealer in his youth). Nevertheless, Vincente Minnelli's widescreen production of the James Jones novel is one of Dean's best and among the finest of fifties American films—Martin's first with Frank Sinatra, and his second with Shirley MacLaine (he had starred with Lewis in one of her first movies, *Artists and Models*).

However, for Howard Hawks' *Rio Bravo* (1959), with John Wayne, Ricky Nelson, Angie Dickinson and Walter Brennan, Martin had to stretch as an actor, and did, with considerable grace and conviction. Strictly from an acting point of view, *Rio Bravo* was the pinnacle for Dean—he never got the chance to do better. That same year he took a risk starring alone in a drama based on a successful little off-Broadway play, *Career,* but it fizzled, and 1960 saw the release of three unabashed entertainments: a wild farce with Tony Curtis, *Who Was That Lady?,* the kind of material Dean was born to do; co-starring with charm and aplomb opposite Judy Holliday in the big-screen adaptation of her hit Broadway musical and, unfortunately, her swan song, *Bells Are Ringing,* also directed by Minnelli; and the first so-called Rat Pack movie, the infamously poor *Ocean's Eleven* with Sinatra, Davis, Peter Lawford, etc.

When Martin and I met, these were all the films of his that had been released. Although he would make another twenty-seven movies, except for Billy Wilder's vicious satire *Kiss Me, Stupid*—in which he played the ultimate bad-Dino legend—Martin never again did a really challenging film role that worked. He tried, but was sabotaged by his associates on *Toys in the Attic* (1963), poorly adapted from Lillian Hellman's Broadway drama. After that failure, he never even tried much, phoning in most of the acting work—quite amusingly as detective Matt Helm in three James Bond–like spy spoofs (starting with *The Silencers*), but with the most noticeable enjoyment in the Westerns, which he loved watching and doing (eight in ten years).

In his portable M-G-M dressing room—a small, moveable bungalow on the sound stage—Dean sat very politely with me and was quite forthcoming. He had been told that I was writing a piece on the state of Holly-

*Dean Martin hanging out in Vincente Minnelli's riveting,
vastly undervalued adaptation of James Jones' novel*
Some Came Running *(1958), one of the last substantial
star vehicles of the golden age*

wood for *Harper's Magazine* (it ultimately went to *Esquire*), so I assume he thought of this interview as fairly weighty stuff, answering my questions with a kind of uncharacteristic earnestness and little kidding around. Which doesn't mean he was pretentious or less than candid. Since he had just done *Bells Are Ringing* the year before, I asked if he would ever consider doing a musical on Broadway. He made a face. "Doin' the same thing ev'ry night?" he asked rhetorically. "*Jesus,* how borin'." He shook his head once. "I wouldn't mind tryin' it for about *three* nights," he said, "but I'd sure as hell hate to be in a *hit.*"

We got on the subject of acting drama, as opposed to comedy, and how he prepared for a serious role. "I just kinda think the way the part is, you know?" He leaned forward in his chair. "I kinda think back to some-thin' that's happened to *me*," he continued. "Like in *Rio Bravo*—there was a scene I was supposed to be very sad in, supposed to cry even. So I thought about a time I was unhappy—time my son, little Dino, was very sick—and that helped me. I kinda used those feelin's I had then." He sighed deeply. "Before I started that picture, I went to Brando and he helped me out a little bit. Told me to listen. Actin' is reactin', you know? Think that you're thinkin'."

Martin went on to tell me that *Rio Bravo* director Howard Hawks had so correctly sensed the actor's anxiety about this key emotional scene—to be played in a stable with John Wayne—that he saved it for the last one Dean did on the movie. A little over a year after interviewing Martin, I first met Hawks, who confirmed to me that the scene had purposely been held for last. "And he did a hell of a good job of it," Hawks said. "He really found out he could act in that thing and it was a great scene. He worked so hard—practiced handling a gun and got real good at it. The ones who are good, work."

In the same conversation, Hawks told me how he had happened to cast Martin in what would remain the finest dramatic performance of his career. "I always liked him," Hawks said, "I'd met him personally." Martin's agent had asked if Hawks would consider Dean for the role of the drunken deputy and talk with him. Hawks said, "OK, nine-thirty tomorrow morning." When the agent said he wasn't sure Martin could get there quite that early, Hawks just closed him off: "Look, if he wants to get here at *all*, have him get here at nine-thirty." Hawks grinned, remembering that Dean had come in the next day right on time and said, "Well, I'm kind of shufflin'. I did a show till midnight over in Vegas—got up early, hired an airplane to get down here and I've had a lot of trouble gettin' 'cross town." Hawks shook his head. "You went to all that trouble to get here at nine-thirty?" Martin answered, "Yes," and they talked for a few minutes until Hawks abruptly said, "Well, you'd better go up and get your wardrobe." Dean looked confused. "What do you mean?" he asked, and Hawks replied, "Well, you're going to *do* it—go get your wardrobe." Howard went on to me, "And that's what we did. I *knew* that if he'd do all that, he'd work hard, and I knew that if he'd work we'd have no trouble because he's such a personality. And he did—he worked *hard* over that drunk."

It shows—yet only in the best way—never labored, remarkably natural. Clearly, Martin never worked that hard over a role again, nor did he ever have as layered a part to play. Apart from a cowboy burlesque with Lewis (*Pardners*), *Rio Bravo* was also Martin's first Western, which was by

The last scene Dean Martin shot, in the stable, for Howard Hawks' Rio
Bravo *(1959), the most dramatic one and the actor's best serious
performance. It was only his fourth film after the breakup with Jerry Lewis.*

far his own favorite kind of entertainment. Especially John Wayne Westerns. In his last tragic eight years, supposedly all Dean ever did was sit in
front of the TV and watch Westerns. Therefore, to co-star with John
Wayne (of all cowboy stars, the most popular), and to be directed by
Howard Hawks—for the director's first Western since his triumphant
debut epic with Wayne, *Red River*—must have been for Dean one of the
crowning moments of his career. The performance he gave was a kind of
committed investment proving to doubters that if he wanted to, Dean
could, within his range as an actor, do just about anything.

A year after my brief talk with Martin—while preparing a monograph
and retrospective on Hawks for the Museum of Modern Art and Double-
day—I wrote to several of the director's stars for comment. Dean was one
of them, and he responded with a succinct note: "Every day he would say,
'Dino, don't worry about the next scene. We'll make one up. . . .' I think
he's great."

Many years later, Martin's comment to me on using the unhappiness
about his young son Dino's illness for the sad scene in *Rio Bravo* would

take on a terrible, tragic irony. In 1987, as a captain in the California Air National Guard, Dino (known by then as Dean Paul Martin) was killed at age thirty-six when his F-4 Phantom jet fighter crashed during a training mission. Dean Paul was the apple of Martin's eye and the death devastated him, leading quite soon to his almost total retreat from life. All reports are that he never recovered from this unimaginable blow, and his own death less than eight years later was a kind of relief to him.

Yet, in 1961, he was still not at the peak of his solo popularity—which was to come after the mid-sixties while he starred in his own weekly TV variety hour, *The Dean Martin Show* (1965–74)—not to mention the weekly TV roasts that followed, and the *Golddiggers* shows, or the numerous hit singles and albums he had throughout the sixties and seventies. As popular as he was when officially teamed with Jerry, he became hipper and nearly as popular both alone and when unofficially teamed with Frank Sinatra (countless gigs in Vegas, recordings for Reprise, numerous TV appearances, and eight movies). In our brief conversation, the last thing I asked Martin was about the many jokes already then being made about his drinking. He shrugged. "They don't bother me, but they're a little silly. If anyone drank that much, how long you think people'd keep hirin' him?" He paused, but not for an answer. "Oh, don't get me wrong, I *drink*. But I hardly ever get drunk. I don't mind the jokes though. Matter of fact, they kinda help the image, you know what I mean?"

Of course, through television, this eventually became the entire image, and Dean milked it all the way to one of the biggest of show-business fortunes. In the seventies, I saw Martin in person twice in Las Vegas. Booze was the one running joke. He would sing "Drinkin' Again" right at the start, and spin countless references to being drunk. The word in the business was that it was largely an act, and that he told me the truth about rarely getting drunk; certainly he never let anything come in the way of his performances. He was hilarious in a Vegas nightclub, owning the place very differently from Sinatra, but as completely. Onstage, he always kidded the singing, virtually never singing a song straight through without some shtick. He used to announce that if you wanted to hear him "sing serious," you'd have to "buy an albeoom." In the clubs, it was mainly about getting laughs—which he certainly did—with casually impeccable timing.

In 1969, Orson Welles told me that he'd been backstage in his own *Dean Martin Show* dressing room when, before the taping, Dean knocked, then came in, drink in hand. "Hey, Orson," he said, holding up his glass, "*you* want one of these before we . . . ?" Orson shook his head.

"No, no, Dean, I'm fine, thanks." Martin looked shocked. "*You* mean you gonna go out there *alone*?!" Welles roared with laughter when he told me the story. " 'Alone!' " he repeated loudly. "Isn't that great!?" Orson went on, "That's the best definition of addiction I've ever heard."

A couple of years after our M-G-M visit, I was doing a piece for *Esquire* on Jack Lemmon, who was shooting *Irma La Douce* for Billy Wilder on the old Samuel Goldwyn lot at Formosa Avenue, where Martin was filming *Toys in the Attic.* Wilder had noticed a familiar figure leaning against one of the Parisian sets toward the back of the stage; it was Dean. "Vait a minute!" yelled Wilder. "Get the hell out of there, Dino." Lemmon looked around, glassy-eyed. The extras laughed as Martin strode, smiling, into the bistro, wearing makeup and costume—a tan suit. He clapped Lemmon on the back and shook hands with Wilder. It was Election Day. "Hey, Billy," Martin said, "*I* voted 'No' for governor!" Turning, he embraced MacLaine and gave her a loud kiss. Lemmon watched, smiling weakly as Wilder said, halfheartedly, "Get the hell outta here, Martin." Smiling, Dean took a seat next to the director. After watching for a little while, and seeing eight aborted takes, Dean suddenly yelled out loudly, "C'mon, Shirl, Jack—let's do it right! Speed it up! OK—roll 'em!" Lemmon ignored him and Wilder said, turning to Martin, "Vhy don't you go to visit dat set of *The Nutty Professor*?" referring to the Jerry Lewis film shooting at Paramount. Dean laughed, and after the next (unsatisfactory) take, he quietly left.

That was in 1963. I would be in his presence only one other time—on a sidewalk in Beverly Hills—about six months before he died. But in 1976, I was just a few blocks away from the Las Vegas Sands Hotel where, on Jerry Lewis' Muscular Dystrophy Telethon, Frank Sinatra made history when he brought Dean Martin onstage with him and—live on national television—for the first time in two decades, Dean Martin and Jerry Lewis embraced. Ten years before, in 1966, *Esquire* editor Harold Hayes had called to ask me to use my access to Lewis to help bring about a cover photo they wanted for their fat special year-end Christmas issue: Martin and Lewis hugging each other, under which they would run the words "Peace on Earth." I *did* call Jerry at the time and he said, "Forget it—it'll never happen." And here it was happening at the Sands, just down the strip from my suite at Caesar's. As part of a subsequent column for *Esquire,* I wrote about this—for some of us—momentous, memorable event:

Jerry gave an elaborate introduction for Sinatra and out he came, sang a quick, up-tempo number and told the audience that, unbeknownst to Jerry, he had brought a friend along to help him. He pointed off left and the camera panned over to see Dean Martin walk out from behind the set. Only someone who grew up in the late forties and early fifties could appreciate the sentimental value of what happened then . . .

"I thought it was about time," Sinatra shouted over the tumult of the studio audience. Without prompting they had risen to their feet and stood applauding for several long minutes. Jerry buried his head in Dean's shoulder on the far side of the camera. Martin clasped him warmly in his arms, but just a trifle patronizingly, too. *He* was the one, after all, making the charitable gesture—for the M.D.A. drive. They came out of the embrace and looked at each other. Sinatra stood between them, beaming. The cameras went to various angles of the two. Dean looked a little embarrassed as the ovation continued, slightly ill at ease. Jerry was savagely chewing his lower lip; to Sinatra, from the side of his mouth, he could be seen (though not heard over the noise) saying, "You son of a bitch." Sinatra laughed and got each of them a microphone. The applause continued in expectation, Jerry still chewing his lip, his mind racing, it seemed to me, in an attempt to come up with a good opening line. As the applause finally died down, he looked at Martin sheepishly, raised his voice to that familiar squeaky adolescent pitch he always used around Dean and said, "You workin'?" It got a big laugh and a hand. Suddenly, anything seemed possible—the past really could be recaptured, perhaps there was a Santa Claus somewhere if Martin and Lewis, like the two old comics in *The Sunshine Boys,* could team up again and enjoy a splendid last hurrah.

But when Martin spoke, the mood began to evaporate. He answered Jerry with an overly dry, slightly defensive line about doing his two weeks every so often at the MGM Grand; in hip Vegas style, he called it "the MeGuM," which only baffled the audience, and looked upstage toward Sinatra and the band. If Jerry looked almost like the princess who had awakened after a long sleep, Martin was perhaps beginning to feel he was back in a nightmare he had stopped having. He was a straight man again.

Not that he'd ever been that, really, but it was what the media and the soothsayers had proclaimed all through the partnership: Jerry was the talented and funny one, Dean was just a fair singer and a reasonably attractive foil. Except, perhaps, in their worst movies, this simplification had never been the case, since Martin's zany timing and spontaneous wit were apparent long before his solo appearances made it obvious to everyone. But the old bad dream couldn't be denied, and suddenly Martin seemed to want out of this situation into which Jerry had welcomed him with open arms. Sinatra must have sensed it, because he stepped forward quickly and sent Jerry away with exaggerated majesty so that he and Dean could sing. Jerry couldn't have wanted to get off—their moment had been so brief—yet he played what he felt for laughs, walking away in a flat-footed dejection to another scream from the crowd: "Well, there he goes *again*!"

But the event wasn't over. Sinatra and Martin now began a duet during which Dean started breaking up the routine in much the same way Jerry used to do when he and Dean were working. He screwed up the lyrics, walked purposely out of camera range, made dirty asides to the orchestra (it was live, so no bleeps), pretended to trip, all the while glancing over to see if Jerry was watching. He was. Wearing a severe pair of metal-frame glasses, he looked on with a wistful, if strangely analytic, expression. He knew what Dean was doing and, surprisingly, he seemed to admire it. Martin was funny, one could say, with a vengeance. Sinatra kept breaking up, the audience roared, and all the while Jerry looked on quietly. But Martin's message was clear: if there was ever going to be any comedy team in his life again, Dean would get all the laughs. Those long, wide-eyed glances he kept giving Jerry during his funniest moments spoke of pride and victory. . . .

Not long after this was published in February 1978, I got a message I have treasured from Dean's second and beloved wife, Jeanne Martin, saying that as someone who had known Dean the longest, she felt my sketch had portrayed his thinking accurately.

Despite the televised embrace, Martin and Lewis did not instantly resurrect their close relationship. There was little contact until nearly a decade later. Although, in the mid-eighties, I did almost manage to get them together for a movie, again with Sinatra's involvement. It was to be a dramatic comedy shot in Las Vegas about a group of degenerate gamblers led by Sinatra, with Dean and Jerry as two guys in the group who had had a falling-out and hadn't spoken directly to each other for years, but communicated by having others in their gang speak for them to the other. Frank loved the idea and said that I should talk to Jerry and he would talk

Martin and Lewis (with Anita Ekberg and Pat Crowley) in the last sequence from their last picture together, Hollywood or Bust *(1956), directed and written for them by Frank Tashlin; such was the tension between the two that the team spoke to each other only during scenes.*

to Dean. When Sinatra phoned Martin to propose the idea, Frank would tell me later, Dean immediately thought it was funny and accepted. Frank then asked if he didn't "have a problem working with Jerry?" Martin replied, "Aw, who gives a fuck!" Unfortunately, Sinatra's lawyers and reluctant producers screwed things up.

A few years later, when Martin's son Dean Paul was killed, Jerry came, uninvited, to the funeral. He sat way in the back, and left after the service was over without making any attempt to speak with Martin. He ducked the press. According to son Ricci Martin's recent memoir of his father (*That's Amore*), Dean was so touched by Lewis' gesture, and its self-effacing method, that he called Jerry to thank him and this contact led to more frequent calls back and forth until Martin's death.

The last time I saw Dean was one evening in front of the Beverly Hills restaurant La Famiglia, less than a year before he died. This popular Italian restaurant was nearly always where Dean ate when he went out. Just as I was walking past, Martin started to come none too steadily out the front door. He looked alarmingly thin, face gaunt and pale. As he stepped onto the sidewalk, it seemed as though one of his knees gave out, and he had to catch himself by the door to stop from falling. He made a funny surprised expression and, looking down, said with a touch of dry irony, "Oops. . . ." Right up to the end, I thought, he'll go for the laugh. Then Dean straightened himself to full height, shoulders back, and slowly moved toward a waiting car, weaving only slightly. The image had become the reality.

Or had the reality always been different than we thought? Five years after Dean died, I said to Lewis once that I had always had the feeling (right from the start) that Dean was usually kidding the whole crooner thing, that he was never really serious about it. "There's a lot of truth in that," Jerry said right away. "See, Dean could never ever sing and do it with a full heart because he wasn't clear about his worth. He did not have self-esteem. He didn't have self-esteem of any kind. So he would kid his singing and he would never allow it ever to get serious so that people would compare him to anybody. I don't think he knew this." I asked why did he think the self-esteem was so low, and Lewis said, "I heard about his demons, his fears, talking about his mother. She was a two-fisted Italian woman who gave him one credo to take through life. And that was: you take money into your pockets, you never take it out. Take. You never give. You cry, you're worthless. You have emotional feelings, you're a fag. And all of that was ground into his head. In just one year, I *un*-ground it all. He was talking to me like a kid that needed to get it out . . ."

During their partnership, Lewis told me, Martin surprised him one day while they were performing at the Fox Theater in San Francisco: "I'll never forget this," Lewis recalled. "Dean said, 'Don't you think I know that people go for popcorn when I sing? Don't you think I know that?' I said, 'What are you talking about?' He said, 'I'm talking about us. Don't you think I know that?' I said, 'Well, to be perfectly honest with you, I was hoping you didn't know that.' He said, 'But I do. And it's OK. I have committed to this and that's part of it. It's OK.' He was brilliant about it. He said, 'I'm making a fortune. I'm a big star because they're going to popcorn during my singing . . .' " But it nevertheless irked Martin eventually and Lewis remembers the breakup in painful detail (see Lewis chapter).

When I asked Jerry to take me behind Dean's supposed coolness, he said, "Dean had a wonderful device in his life. 'Recluse' was wonderful for him. 'Above the crowd' was wonderful for him. The best thing he ever had working for himself was his way of standoffishness. And I think throughout all of it, he must have peeked through the door to see what everyone was doing. I never knew that he did that, but I always wondered if he did. And did he come away from the door saying, 'Whew, I don't need that.' Or did he come away from the door saying, 'Why can't I be with them?' If you know about his background, you'll see the complicated is simple. He came from a Mafia-like upbringing—an insensitive set of parents. And certainly sad to have to say they were also incredibly dumb. They were coal people. Father was a barber—started out in coal. And Angelina, his mother, wanted so much to appear like [charming TV personality] Betty Furness when she was really Jack Palance."

Lewis paused a beat for the laugh. "Then," he went on, "at his twenty-ninth birthday, he put his arms around me because I got my arms around him. And he liked it. And then he would push me away like I'm the kid brother: 'What's with the hugging?' And he loved it. He used to do what my grandmother did. He pushed me with this hand and pulled me with that hand. Because I was the only human on God's earth that he would communicate with then. He was kind, he was generous, he was silly, he was simple. He read comic books because that was easy. And I used to say to him, 'Will you stop sending people for comic books? Go yourself and buy them. What are you hiding?' He said, 'Aw, you know, Jer.' I said, ' "You know, Jer"? my balls! This is something an individual, who has the inalienable right to live as a human being, with the pink slip on himself, won't go over to a stand and buy what the fuck he wants with his own hard-earned money?' He said, 'Can I please send out for them?' And I said, 'OK.' He was so fuckin' cute. He loved sitting in the corner and having a beer and he had his fuckin' comic books. And if a Western was on, he tabled that and the Western is on!"

That Dean Martin died on Christmas Day was the kind of black joke he might have made. It didn't seem real to me until I heard that all the casinos on the Vegas Strip had turned off their lights for one minute to commemorate Dino's passing. You could almost hear Dean saying, in amazement, "One whole minute!? I must have been a big shot." He was.

Born Dino Paul Crocetti, June 7, 1917, Steubenville, Ohio; died December 25, 1995, Beverly Hills, CA.

Selected starring features (with director):

1950: *At War with the Army* (Hal Walker)
1951: *That's My Boy* (Walker)
1952: *Sailor Beware* (Walker); *Jumping Jacks* (Norman Taurog)
1953: *The Stooge* (Taurog); *Scared Stiff* (George Marshall); *The Caddy* (Taurog)
1954: *Living It Up* (Taurog)
1955: *Artists and Models* (Frank Tashlin)
1956: *Hollywood or Bust* (Tashlin)
1958: *The Young Lions* (Edward Dmytryk); *Some Came Running* (Vincente Minnelli)
1959: *Rio Bravo* (Howard Hawks)
1960: *Who Was That Lady?* (George Sidney); *Bells Are Ringing* (Minnelli); *Ocean's Eleven* (Lewis Milestone)
1963: *4 for Texas* (Robert Aldrich)
1964: *Kiss Me, Stupid* (Billy Wilder)
1965: *The Sons of Katie Elder* (Henry Hathaway)
1966: *The Silencers* (Phil Karlson); *Murderers' Row* (Henry Levin)
1967: *The Ambushers* (Levin)
1968: *Bandolero!* (Andrew V. McLaglen)
1970: *Airport* (George Seaton)

10

SAL MINEO

"You know what day they killed me?" Sal Mineo said with his usual macabre amusement. "The same day as Kennedy—November 22nd [1963]. We're all up there in Monument Valley—and the Old Man likes the weather." He is talking about John Ford on a picture called *Cheyenne Autumn,* in which Mineo played an American Indian, Red Shirt. "So he says, 'Let's kill Saul.' He always called me Saul—I don't know why—and they get the camera set up and old Ricardo Montalban shoots me. I fall down. Ford says, 'That's well!' and they do something else. A couple of hours later we hear the President's been murdered and Ford calls a wrap for the rest of the day. Somebody figured out that at the same time Ricardo was shooting me, Oswald was shooting Kennedy. Is this weird?" Having riveted everyone's attention, Sal suddenly dropped his head to the left, closing his eyes as he did, and snored softly in a mock sleep. This sleeping bit was an old number of his which never failed to get a laugh from me. At that moment it was a significant gesture of self-deprecation, a trait of Sal's. But he could as easily use the snoring to demolish pretense and ease boredom by pointing it out.

The bizarre irony of the shooting story, however, was in no way clear that cool evening in Manhattan when Sal told it in the spring of 1964. None of us had enough perspective at the time to realize how much Kennedy's death would come to represent the end of a generation's brief, perhaps even illusory, moment of political inspiration. Certainly Sal was far too unpretentious to make any serious connection between Kennedy and himself, yet both, in vastly different ways, became American symbols: Kennedy of the sixties, Mineo of the fifties. Nor could any of us have guessed that Sal's death scene in *Cheyenne Autumn* was to be his last film appearance of note, though he was to live another twelve years. But we

Sal Mineo as Dov Landau, the sympathetic Jewish terrorist, here with Jill Haworth (who fell in love with him) in Otto Preminger's Exodus *(1960), a profoundly relevant film about the birth of Israel, based on Leon Uris' best seller. Mineo received his second Academy nomination for Best Supporting Actor, and gives probably his finest performance.*

both were only twenty-five then (he was six months older) and there were a lot of things we didn't know.

Of course, Sal knew a great deal more than I did—he'd been out in the world so much longer. A child actor on the Broadway stage—in the original productions of Tennessee Williams' *The Rose Tattoo* (with Maureen Stapleton and Eli Wallach) and Rodgers and Hammerstein's *The King and I* (with Gertrude Lawrence and Yul Brynner)—Sal was a beautiful little boy riding the subways home alone to the Bronx while my parents weren't allowing me on the streets after dark. But Sal was from a large Sicilian family, and if his paycheck could help everyone out, where was the harm? He told me he'd seen enough John Garfield movies to sustain him in nervous situations, particularly after he started carrying around a pistol loaded with blanks.

One time in a deserted subway car, a heavyset, smarmy man in his mid-thirties tried to pick him up, only to discover that Sal's big, innocent brown eyes were deceptive. When the guy wouldn't leave him alone, Sal pulled out the gun and made the fellow drop to his knees, keeping him there at bay until Sal's stop came up and the train slowed down. Then he pulled the trigger. "Jesus, the sound was so loud it scared the shit out of the guy. He thought he was dead. There was nothing wrong with him, but he started yelling. The doors opened and I ran like hell. I ran all the way home."

By the time he was fifteen, Sal was in Hollywood making pictures. Not much more than a year later, in 1956, he received an Academy Award nomination for a supporting performance in what was only his third movie, *Rebel Without a Cause,* directed by Nicholas Ray and starring James Dean, a good friend who had died in a car crash two weeks before the movie was released. Sal was seventeen. Jack Lemmon won Best Supporting Actor that year for *Mister Roberts,* but the teenage hearts went out to Sal, a survivor of the Dean tragedy and an heir to much of the posthumous adulation that followed.

It was Mineo, after all, who had played out the surrogate death scene in *Rebel:* he is senselessly gunned down by police who do not know that the revolver he is brandishing has already been emptied by his friend Dean. "I got the bullets!" Jimmy yells out desperately, but too late. "I got the bullets!" he sobs, but Sal is dead. Were the public's tears for the character Sal played or for the futility in Jimmy Dean's cry, transfixed in the audience's view by the knowledge of Dean's own death? If it was reassuring that Sal was just acting—after all, it's only a movie—what thought could ease the sadness that Dean's offscreen fate was no fiction? For a generation of otherwise complacent American children, death suddenly became an early reality.

No character could have been more unlike Sal than the withdrawn, insecure and neurotic teenager he played in *Rebel.* Indeed, I never saw any movie that even remotely captured his essentially sunny, easygoing qualities, his quick wit and infectious self-mockery. The rest of his teens were spent mainly in a succession of juvenile-delinquent roles both on live TV and in pictures. Before he died, Jimmy Dean had got him a small role in the Rocky Graziano biopic, *Somebody Up There Likes Me;* when Dean was killed, Paul Newman took over and Sal kept his role, in which he was excellent as usual. Especially so in *Dino* (a hit play on TV for Sal, then repeated for the big screen). He showed real charm in Raoul Walsh's forgettable but likeable service romance, *A Private's Affair.* To play the title role in *The Gene Krupa Story,* Sal spent days perfecting his drumming, studying Krupa. Again, unfortunately, he was a great deal better than the

*Mineo (second from left), with Mark Rydell, John Cassavetes and
James Whitmore in yet another juvenile-delinquent picture,*
Crime in the Streets *(1956), based on a TV drama, and
adroitly directed for the big screen by Don Siegel*

picture. In George Stevens' *Giant* he had a tiny role, thanks once more to
Jimmy Dean, but he is entirely convincing in Don Siegel's hard-edged
Crime in the Streets—another TV play transferred to the big screen—with
a superb cast including John Cassavetes and Mark Rydell.

His finest, most enduring film performance, however, came as Dov
Landau in Otto Preminger's hugely successful *Exodus,* now considered
among the last masterpieces from the movies' golden age. On the film, Sal
met fifteen-year-old Jill Haworth, and the two fell in love. As *Exodus*
opened, they made the cover of *Life* together. He received another Oscar
nomination for an extraordinarily intense, heartbreaking performance as
the tortured young Israeli terrorist, certainly a rebel *with* a cause. But the
old establishment snobs in Hollywood could never quite forgive him his
teenage popularity and gave the award to Peter Ustinov for an infinitely
less challenging role in *Spartacus,* a considerably inferior film as well.

This was symptomatic of the prevailing critical winds around Sal
Mineo in the early sixties; they were anything but favorable. The best

gauge of unspoken antipathy is my own reaction to finding him among the cast of the John Ford picture I had been sent to cover (*Cheyenne Autumn*). Not even my idolatrous admiration of the director could counteract a vague sense of distress at finding Mineo listed with the players when I arrived on the Navajo Indian reservation in Monument Valley. Preconceived notions of what celebrated people are like must account for a good measure of all the misunderstanding and hostility in our ever more informed society. It is a lesson—do not make personal judgments based on hearsay—that cannot be learned often enough, and Sal taught me first.

Not that he was particularly aware of any instruction going on. He could tell we were similar in age, and since there were very few twenty-four-year-olds around—the majority of the cast and crew were well over thirty, forty or fifty, and Ford himself was in his late sixties—I would guess Sal was pleased to see a contemporary, especially one from his hometown. We were seated next to each other at one of my first meals on the location, and he immediately struck up a conversation.

I've still to meet anyone quite so instantly disarming as Sal was. Inhibitions and prejudices dissolved in the heady rush of his good humor and his happy conspiratorial manner. No one took himself less seriously than Sal, which is not to say that he was frivolous; he'd just drop off into that funny snore of his at any hint of pomposity in himself or others. His nature was generous—from the $350,000 Mamaroneck home he bought for his parents in the first flush of success—to the many kindnesses he showed me both before and after I moved to California in mid-1964.

Indirectly, he even paid for the trip. Enthusiastic about him when I returned from the Ford location, I talked Harold Hayes into letting me do an *Esquire* piece on Sal. Harold was more than a little reluctant, but a few of the funnier Mineo stories convinced him. Sal and Jill Haworth and I spent some time together in New York—along with my first wife, Polly Platt, and a young singer Sal had discovered and was promoting named Bobby Sherman. We all had a few meals, hung out at a recording studio most of one day while Sal made a single. He didn't feel comfortable with his singing (though he had some hit singles and a popular album in the fifties), and preferred to encourage and sponsor Bobby. I met Sal's parents, his two older brothers and his younger sister Sarina, of whom he was especially protective. Only Sal and Sarina looked related, like dark Mediterranean angels come to earth—you could instantly tell they were brother and sister. Neither of the other siblings nor the parents resembled them.

Sal brought the first Beatles records over to my tiny Riverside Drive apartment and played them loudly late into the night, joking compulsively, listening to dreamy aspirations, telling some of his own. On opening night of an ill-fated production I directed and produced off-Broadway, I received one telegram from the Coast; it read: "Zzzzzzzzzzzzzzzzz. Love, Sal." Hayes bought the article (I used the money to buy an old car and move to California), had it set in type, had photos taken, but never ran it (the original has been lost). After several postponements, he admitted finally: "I just couldn't stand the idea of having Sal Mineo in the magazine."

It was the dominant attitude. Sal had somehow become an anachronistic reminder of the teenage fifties—which chic people now preferred to forget. That he was also widely acknowledged as a talented actor seemed beside the point. In some circles, his name had become a punch line. As my fortunes improved in the late sixties and early seventies, Sal's deteriorated. When I first arrived in Los Angeles, the car Sal drove was a giant four-door Bentley, and the Santa Monica home he rented was grand and spacious. But the movie jobs stopped coming while the debts remained: in particular, over a quarter of a million dollars in back taxes. Mineo's houses kept getting smaller, and so did his cars, though it took a while to notice because one thing Sal never did was complain about anything. One afternoon, when he asked if he could have some run-down old furniture we were getting rid of, I began to get the picture.

As a favor, he did a walk-on for me in my first movie, *Targets,* but the shot was eventually cut out. Sal hung around all day to watch. He had been the first person to offer me a job in pictures, writing a script for him. We talked a lot about it but he never could get the rights to the novel he had suggested we do, William Maxwell's *The Folded Leaf.* Maxwell did not want to sell them. Sal directed me one afternoon in a home-movie thriller we started but never finished. We kept breaking up too much. I would start to peer over a sand dune, as he had instructed, and as I appeared over the rise, I heard him trying to suppress laughter. I broke up and so did he. This happened about ten times before we finally stopped for lunch. One time we were hanging out in a beach house he had rented, and Bobby Sherman was listening to Sal and me discuss Michelangelo's work. After several minutes, Bobby said, "Michael Angelo—is he the guy who directed *Around the World in 80 Days?*" Sal looked so shocked that he actually put one hand on top of his head, as though fearful that it was going to fly off. "No . . . that's Michael Anderson," he said wildly. "Michelangelo is only one of the greatest artists that ever lived!" And then Sal and I completely broke up.

I came to the rehearsals of a controversial prison drama he was directing in Los Angeles, John Herbert's *Fortune and Men's Eyes*. He yelled in exasperation at the actors, then turned to me and winked. One day he gave me a paperback of a novel he said he had always wanted to buy and make into a movie, but felt he was now too old to play the lead; he thought I would like it. The book, by Larry McMurtry, was called *The Last Picture Show*. I invited Sal to the first New York running of that movie, at Columbia's projection room on Fifth Avenue, and he sat next to me. I was a nervous wreck, so he kept squeezing my hand and whispering what I wanted to hear. When the picture turned out to be a critical and popular success, nominated for eight Oscars, Sal never even took a small bow for being the one who gave me the book. I always credited him but this was rarely printed.

The months flew by—and the busy, giddy years—for me one film after the other. We weren't in touch so often: somehow we rarely seemed to be in the same city at the same time. Once we had lunch at Claridge's in London. Sal talked openly of his troubles then, but never with any remorse or even a hint of resentment at my improved circumstances. We spoke of an important part I wanted him to play in a picture, *Bugsy*, from a script by playwright Howard Sackler; Sal would do the gangster Bugsy Siegel's closest friend, who is nevertheless killed by Bugsy. The picture kept getting postponed. He was doing dinner theater around the States, had optioned a novel of Robin Maugham's which he wanted to direct, did any television part he could get, was promised a lot more than anyone ever delivered. He never railed against the system, never even questioned why the studio powers considered him so undesirable. The audiences that came to see him on the little stages across the country still loved him, still cheered his perfectly erect, strutting figure, his soulful brown eyes.

On another picture of mine, an ill-fated Cole Porter musical (*At Long Last Love*), Sal came to visit one night while we were shooting Burt Reynolds and Cybill Shepherd in a heated Beverly Hills swimming pool. Sal just hung around quietly and watched; I would go over and stand beside him and talk as often as possible. He was smiling a lot.

The last time I saw him, in 1976, when we bumped into each other at 2 a.m. in an all-night news and magazine store on Santa Monica Boulevard, he still looked like a teenager. We embraced. He was rehearsing a new play, James Kirkwood's *P.S. Your Cat Is Dead!*, a comedy that would open in L.A. soon; I was shooting a picture. Somebody waved at him, yelling, "Hey, Sal Mineo!" as we walked out to sit for a while in the car I had then, a big old Rolls-Royce. His Volkswagen Bug was parked in front of it. The jokes he made were at his own expense. You never felt any awkwardness around Sal—he made sure you were at ease—and somehow it never seemed like more than a day or two since we had seen each other.

A couple of weeks later, we were filming on a Western exterior outside Los Angeles. It was early—sunny and freezing cold. As I stepped out of the car, there was a solemn little group from the crew huddled together looking forlorn. I came over with a joke about their grim looks; I said, "Who died?" The assistant director glanced up. "Sal Mineo," he said.

That Sal was stabbed to death in an alley was so horribly in keeping with many of the movie deaths he died that its bitter irony on some level no doubt must have amused him. After all, he had a black sense of humor and a firm grasp of the absurd. How could he not? A teenage symbol in his late thirties who never had a childhood. To see that newspapers plastered his murder in banner headlines around the world—especially in Los Angeles, the town in which he couldn't get arrested—probably would have made him drop his head to the side and snore: "A lotta good that does me."

A Hollywood cynic was heard to call Elvis Presley's death "a smart career move," but Sal's more violent passing did not give rise to similar demonstrations of concern or grief. Usually, when confronted with anything especially unpleasant—such as the Manson killings—respectable members of the community look for ways to place the blame on the victim. Odd sexual habits or drug-taking or whatever peculiarity might come to light posthumously would invariably lead to the conclusion that the victim was just asking for it in the first place and such are the wages of sin.

That comfortable rationale makes it easier to live—not only in Hollywood—and any guilt which could momentarily be felt about the job that might have been given or the call that could have been returned can pass quickly and painlessly. Soon after the murder, a close friend of Sal's, public relations advisor Eliot Mintz, sent out letters to some of Sal's old friends and associates asking for contributions toward a $10,000 reward he wanted to raise for information leading to the arrest of the killer. Only a tiny fraction of that amount was sent in: virtually none of the letters, he told me, were even answered.

In this racket, when you're not hot anymore—when you're cold—you're dead anyway, so a lot of movie folk turned the page on Sal's murder and shrugged: he wasn't up for any picture.

Sal's murderer was caught in 1978, and a year later, found guilty of second-degree murder (and ten armed robberies); the sentence was fifty-one years to life. A light-skinned black from the South, he was nineteen when he stabbed Sal, who was thirty-seven. In passing sentence, L.A. Superior

Sal Mineo with James Dean and Natalie Wood in the empty-mansion sequence of Nicholas Ray's Rebel Without a Cause *(1955), released two weeks after Dean's fatal auto accident. All three actors suffered shockingly violent, early deaths.*

Court Judge Ronnie Lee Martin said, "I don't think he's susceptible to rehabilitation, considering his escalating conduct of committing [since age fourteen] more and more serious crimes." Nevertheless, the man who brutally and senselessly ended Sal Mineo's life was paroled in 1990, after serving eleven years. Sal would have been forty-eight. Soon after, this killer was again arrested and convicted of robbery and murder.

With all the filmland speculation about Sal's death involving sexual gangs or cults, and the media's pontifications on the wicked ways of Hollywood, the most brutal irony was that his assailant had no idea at the time of the murder who the victim was, that Sal had been killed for his money, and that the $38 he had on him was about all he had.

I remember my mother didn't approve of *Rebel Without a Cause,* indeed thought it was a dangerous picture. She said it painted *all* the teenagers as poor mixed-up kids and *all* the parents as insensitive simpletons, without showing any responsible alternative behavior. Certainly *Rebel*'s huge success led to countless spin-offs on that same theme, of misunderstood childhood and "teendom," leading to an ever more tolerant and therefore ever more permissive society. Sal's killer had been born two years after *Rebel* first hit, and was thus a direct product of the society the film helped to spawn. All three stars died young, and violently: Mineo by knife; Dean by car; Natalie Wood by drowning, after falling off her yacht five years after Sal's death.

During all the lurid media speculation following the murder and until his killer was caught, only Mineo's family and friends knew the truth. Because they understood that Sal was a talented artist, and also the kind of generous pal you are lucky to find once in a lifetime.

Born Salvatore Mineo, Jr., January 10, 1939, Bronx, NY; died February 12, 1976, West Hollywood, CA.

Selected starring features (with director):

1955: *Rebel Without a Cause* (Nicholas Ray)
1956: *Crime in the Streets* (Don Siegel); *Somebody Up There Likes Me* (Robert Wise)
1957: *Dino* (Thomas Carr); *The Young Don't Cry* (Alfred L. Werker)
1959: *A Private's Affair* (Raoul Walsh); *The Gene Krupa Story* (Don Weis)
1960: *Exodus* (Otto Preminger)
1964: *Cheyenne Autumn* (John Ford)
1965: *Who Killed Teddy Bear?* (Joseph Cates)

11

JAMES STEWART

James Stewart's wife, Gloria, told me over the phone—before I visited their home early in 1994, for what I didn't know would be the last time I'd see or speak with either of them—that Jimmy always enjoyed my visits, and so did she. By then I had known them both for about thirty years. Within what seemed like maybe two or three months, with virtually no warning, Gloria Stewart died of cancer and Jimmy Stewart disappeared from sight or sound until his own death about a thousand days later at age eighty-nine. I spoke with his daughter Kelly a year before he died, and she said he had seen no one but family and maybe five of his closest friends, and those only briefly. Mostly he just stayed upstairs in his bedroom, ate hardly at all, refused to hear any suggestions of maybe going out for a walk or stopping by the office. "You know my dad," she said, ruefully, "he's a Taurus—he's stubborn." Clearly, after Gloria's sudden death, following a close public and private marriage of more than forty-five years, Jimmy felt his life was over, too.

There was perhaps more than grief involved, but of course we'll never really know. Certainly a complicated tension existed between Gloria and Jimmy that last time I saw them. She had just returned from seeing a doctor and slightly visible near her neck were some doctors' X-ray markings which she clearly had not had time to wash off. I believe I happened to have a date with them for a drink around five in the afternoon on the day Gloria was told she might have, or in fact did have, cancer, but she hadn't informed Jimmy yet. After I heard about her illness and then her death, I have often thought about that final time with them, and the emotions which the Stewarts seemed to have boiling just below the surface.

Jimmy hadn't been feeling well for a while—nothing very specific, just a kind of weakness and exhaustion. When I asked Gloria about this on the phone, she said, "Oh, Jimmy's always got something wrong with him,"

James Stewart as Junior Senator Jefferson Smith at a low point toward the end of his Senate filibuster during the famous conclusion to Frank Capra's masterful and hugely successful political drama, Mr. Smith Goes to Washington *(1939), which at the time the real members of the Senate hated. Everyone thought Jimmy should've won the Oscar, so he did the following year for* The Philadelphia Story.

with the clear implication that he was also a bit of a hypochondriac. I then remembered asking Stewart once, maybe ten years before, how he was feeling and he said, "Aw, Payter, I'll tell ya, after seventy, it's all patch, patch, patch." Of course, as always, the Jimmy Stewart delivery made this memorably funny, but it also speaks to a general attitude about his aging.

Now, a certain stoic fragility was very much a part of his mystique and of the ambiguous heroes he sometimes played. Especially in his five

Anthony Mann Westerns where it's most apparent that no other male film star was ever better at showing the real pain and fear caused by violence. Or, indeed, the crushing anguish of lost love. You can see it crystallized in the few (brilliantly shot and edited) moments of the frantic tussle at the end of Alfred Hitchcock's *Rear Window,* when villain Raymond Burr throws him out of his own rear window: searing pain and terror in a few seconds. And there is simply no better lost-love–anguished performance in picture history than his in Hitchcock's *Vertigo.*

In no way did this honest commonality compromise his stature as a leading man; it showed a vulnerability that average people in those cir-cumstances would identify with. His ability to overcome the fear and pain made him therefore even more of an everyman hero, as he was for his cur-rently most often-remembered role, in Frank Capra's small-town-America fantasy *It's a Wonderful Life* (1946). Average American guy, in fact, is how he was cast in his first Western (the most American of genres), *Destry Rides Again,* released in 1939, the same year as his breakout performance of the naive Midwestern senator in Capra's then-controversial *Mr. Smith Goes to Washington.* In *Destry* he was cast opposite Europe's world-weary Marlene Dietrich, as a way of accentuating the extreme polarities of their personas. The picture (adroitly directed by George Marshall, an amiable studio journeyman) is a perfect example of what made the old star system in its heyday work so well—both stars' parts being expertly styled for what these two actors could do best. Because their innate personalities have such appeal and scope, the characters instantly achieve a mythic size impossible to attain only with good actors.

The sizeable success of *Destry Rides Again* (in a year that also saw the release of *four* other Stewart pictures, including *Mr. Smith*) led to nearly twenty (all postwar) Westerns. He was rivaled solely by John Wayne for hit cowboy pictures throughout the fifties and early sixties (Wayne's first successful A-Western, John Ford's *Stagecoach,* also was released in 1939). *Destry* set a particular image of Stewart that he and others exploited for the rest of his career (as did *Mr. Smith,* in a much more learned mode). Stewart's Destry was the book-reading, nonviolent Eastern dude in the West who must learn to use a gun when necessary. Ford cast Stewart in precisely that same role twenty-three years later for what would turn out to be both the actor's and the director's last great Western, *The Man Who Shot Liberty Valance* (1962). Dietrich told me that she and Jimmy had a blazing affair during the shooting of *Destry,* and the electricity is notice-able. During one love scene, Marlene said, Stewart's "interest" in her became so "apparent" that director Marshall called an early lunch, at the

James Stewart and Marlene Dietrich in Stewart's first Western (of some eighteen), Destry Rides Again *(1939), directed by old pro George Marshall. Stewart and Dietrich (whose first Western it was, too) had a blazing affair during shooting.*

same time wagging his index finger reproachfully at the actor, "Jimmy . . ." Orson Welles once told me he had taken Dietrich "to have an abortion after Jimmy knocked her up."

The shy, retiring character Stewart generally played around women evidently was like catnip to them (my mother always said she wanted "to mother him") and Jimmy was a well-known ladies' man prior to his marriage to Gloria Hatrick McLean in 1949 at the age of forty-one. The popular image of Stewart from that point on was as "an exemplary husband" and family man. Since they soon had twin girls and Gloria had two sons from her first marriage, he was suddenly a responsible father of four. What was known only among a few people in the business was that Jimmy did continue occasional dalliances with his co-stars in the fifties. He once joked very obliquely about this around the time of *Rear Window* (1954), when asked how he felt about being married while kissing Grace Kelly. "Waall," he said, "I'm married, but I'm not *dead*!" The common wisdom is that Ms. Kelly had already been through Gary Cooper (*High Noon,*

1952) and Clark Gable (*Mogambo,* 1953), and that Stewart had no escape. Hitchcock hinted to me that Stewart also could not resist Kim Novak on *Vertigo* (1958), and the director's longtime assistant and dear friend, Peggy Robertson, confirmed this romance; and a good friend of mine heard about it directly from a still fond Kim Novak. Evidently the affair continued, because immediately after *Vertigo* the two of them co-starred in a pretty weak *Bell, Book and Candle* (1958). Of course, this occasional occupational hazard could have caused some private grief to Gloria, which Jimmy would no doubt have profoundly regretted after her passing.

Ironically, it was Stewart's involvement with his first postwar Western, *Winchester '73* (1950), that eventually changed Hollywood beyond recognition, certainly far beyond where either Jimmy or I could see at the time we first met in January 1964. *Winchester '73* also marked the beginning of his extremely fruitful relationship with its director, Anthony Mann, and was among the first and best of the genre's darkening trend, a kind of noir Western with complex and ambiguous reverberations. Since its subject, in essence, is the uniquely American obsession with firearms—in this case a highly prized rifle—the picture tragically retains a contemporary significance and an ominous quality perhaps not nearly as resonant, nor as grimly intended, on its initial release. Since one of the key uses of art is to illuminate, *Winchester '73* continues to serve that purpose.

Although Cary Grant had flourished since the end of the thirties as an independent star, not signed to any studio's long-term contract, and although by the end of the forties such stars as Humphrey Bogart and James Cagney had their own production companies, it wasn't until Jimmy Stewart's percentage deal on *Winchester '73*—negotiated for him with Universal by his agent Lew Wasserman (whose own company, MCA, within a decade would buy this same studio)—that the notion of a star's receiving a hefty piece of the action in lieu of salary began to gain wide acceptance. As a direct result, by the time the sixties had barely started, the old studio star system had crumbled, and soon all stars were getting a piece *and* large salaries. What was initiated as a name-actor's honest sharing of the gamble with a film's financiers deteriorated into a no-lose situation for the talent, and a deep crisis for the business and the art of pictures. And roles for Stewart and his contemporaries dried up after the mid-sixties because there were no studios to look after the talent and design roles as they aged.

Mann and Stewart would eventually work together on eight other movies, most memorably four more of the finest fifties Westerns—the last full decade of the genre's classic period—with strikingly photographed exteriors and generally hard-edged stories of greed, ambition and vengeance: *Bend of the River, The Naked Spur, The Far Country* and *The Man from Laramie*—the last featuring an especially violent and frightening sequence in which Stewart is tortured and maimed. His edgy, chip-on-the-shoulder performance in *Winchester '73* set the standard and remained one of his most intriguing. Stewart used these tough, somewhat neurotic frontiersmen he played for Mann to help radically alter his original image as all-American dreamer and whimsical man of integrity (though he still mined that area occasionally with pictures like *The Glenn Miller Story*, also directed by Mann, and *Harvey*). As a result of these, and his three extraordinary Hitchcock movies during the same years (*Rear Window, The Man Who Knew Too Much* and *Vertigo*), it's not surprising that the fifties were by far Stewart's most popular decade, concluding in brilliant high form with Otto Preminger's *Anatomy of a Murder* (1959), the best film ever made about the American judicial system.

Five years later, Stewart and I met, when I interviewed him in his suite at New York's St. Regis Hotel while working on a profile of John Ford for *Esquire*. Less than two years later I did a long piece on Stewart himself for the same magazine. We spent a week or so together in Los Angeles— where I first met Gloria—and after the article came out in 1966, he wrote me a lovely letter of thanks on behalf of himself and his family. I began the profile with a parody of John Dos Passos' biographical portraits in his *U.S.A.* trilogy, to introduce the mythic persona Stewart had already long ago achieved (all references are from actual Stewart movies):

William Smith Jefferson Smith Ben McKenna Jeff McNeal was bornandraised
 in LansingMichigan Muncie MiddletownOhio FortDodge
 grew to sixfootfour but had a way (which wasn't easy) of keeping his head down and looking up at you; stuttered, stammered; was great at basketball, better at baseball; a Boy Scout leader; wore his hair slicked down ("Jus' like a kid goin' t'Sund'y School"); hemmed, hawed; had a nasal stuffed-jaw voice that shook when he whispered, that you could tell a block away ("I don't s'pose you'd . . . m'by . . . shlow down on your way through Fort Dawdge an' m'by . . . drawp by?"); took his hat off coming into your house.
 Reticent ("Never been much of a talker"), bashful ("Always took a team just to drag him to a dance"), innocent ("Jus' a country

boy"), easily hurt ("Ya gotta put some pants on that guy"), awkward (kept his fingers together when holding a girl, as though if he opened them, she might slip away), he

became a lawyer, doctor, reporter, shop clerk, flier, sheriff, teacher, was appointed to the Senate, never left the hometown.

His Dad used to tell him: "The only causes worth fighting for are lost causes . . ."

That sank in—deep.

But the bigguys—fat pokerplaying moneygrubbing graft-taking guys with bigcigars—they didn't think he looked like much: "The simpleton of all time—a big-eyed patriot—knows Washington and Lincoln by heart . . . collects stray boys and cats . . ."

"This boy's honest, not stupid."

"Dreamer!"

"He'll be good—when his voice stops changing."

"Don Quixote!"

"He wants to go it alone—but we'll get him."

Thought because he was too shy to look at the marriage bed, this sap was a pushover, a twentyfourkarat sucker.

They didn't know Willie Johnny Scottie Jeff. Didn't know you could fool him just so long. Didn't know what his Dad used to tell him.

"Dope!"

"Idealist!"

That he could go from: "*Who!* Miss—! Is that—? Why didn't you—? Holy smoke. H-hello . . . Yes, Miss Paine . . . How—how are you, Miss Paine . . . ? What . . . Escort you—gee—I mean—*sure*—*yes*! I'd be— Reception for a *princess*! Gawsh!"

to a twentyfourhour filibuster culminating in: "You think I'm licked. You *all* think I'm licked. Well, I'm *not* licked and I'm going to stay right here and fight for this lost cause even if this room gets *filled* with lies like these."

At his lowest ebb, he wished he'd never been born till a fellow showed him what his town'd be like if that were so—all those people he'd helped, all those lives he'd saved. Always fairandsquare never belowthebelt where the bigguys hit.

The kids knew about him—no matter what anyone said or what lies they printed. Not fooled. Knew about this dreamer-dope. Knew what his Dad had told him.

Then the war came.

And it changed Slim Mac Joe Skinny. No longer the wide-eyed boy in the bigcity, shocked by corruption, outraged by deceit. Knows now that the world stinks; what men are capable of; that fighting fair doesn't always win. Had seen his fellows fall with the flag; knows it takes more than ideals and a stoutheart to win.

No more the simplesucker the easytouch the fallguy; tough now, skeptical, worldly, cynical ("I'm only a reporter—I just *write* the story").

"The only causes worth fighting for—"

"That an' a dime'll buy me a cup of coffee!"

But the kids know, can see beneath the hard shell. Just convince him. Make him believe. Show 'im it ain't phony. The kids know, without knowing . . .

". . . are lost causes."

that the toughness hides a view of the way the world oughta be but never is but—*oughta be.*

Better fighter now, stronger, can tell the fatguy's move, more stubborn, knows about bending the rules of the game; would use his fists now (though he still looks even in the midst of fury sad-dened at the violence sick because of it); let them kick his insides up, drag him through the fire, shoot him in the hand—they could not equal what he'd seen *before* he

fought this battle.

Though settleddown with wifeandkids; sourly ridingtherange; bitterly coveringthestory arguingthecase drawingfaster—aging— the old words and the hometown come back to haunt him still

THEmuncieONLYdodgeCAUSESlansingWORTHmiddle-townFIGHTING . . .

Still wears his hair slicked down; still stammers near the girl; still takes his hat off in the house;

Still the American.

"That's just the way Jimmy was," Henry Fonda told me. "It was all part of his character—his way of talking, everything." They met in 1932— Fonda was doing stock on Cape Cod—and Stewart, just out of Princeton, came up for the summer to do bits and play the accordion. They became friends—for life. "You know, he just kinda *fell* into acting," Fonda went on. "When we got back to New York, he took the part in *Carry Nation* just for a lark. An' when that was over he was set to go home but some-thing else came along—he took that—an' then when *it* was over he was goin' home—an' something just kept *happening*. Till, finally, it started dawning on him that he was getting good at this. An' he *was*. He'd had no training, no background. I'd been at it ten years an' . . . I saw him in *Divided by Three* with Judith Anderson, 1934, and as far as I was concerned—this *punk*! this sonofa*bitch*! what right did he have to be so *good*! And he just fell into it really. . . ."

" 'S true," Stewart said. " 'Cause if I hadn't become an actor, I think I'd a been mixed up in flying . . . I took my B.S. in architecture, but I was always wrapped up in flying. It was . . . acting was getting bit by a malaria mosquito—but flying . . . When I was about nine or ten, right after World War I, I was working in my fawther's store, just . . . just savin' up so's I could take a ride in one of those barnstorming planes used to come around. Fifteen dawllars for fifteen minutes. That was a *hell*ova lawta money. . . . It was. . . . But I saved it up and finally . . . finally, I talked my fawther into it. Dad was good about things like that . . . he was . . . and we gawt in the car . . . but on the way we stawpped so's he could pick up the family *dawctor*! I thought it was nice—the tremendous faith my dad had in this new invention."

"He's one of the great guys I've ever known," Fonda said. When the two came to Hollywood they shared a house for a time. "He was such fun company to be with—life was just too *much*—laughing all the time."

"We were both too skinny," said Stewart. "An' one time we d'cided to . . . to gain a little weight . . . a little . . . so a fella told us for breakfast every morning we should drink an eggnawg with brandy. But the thing was . . . we noticed that the eggnawg kept getting darker an' darker—and by eleven a.m. we were both *pissed*! So we . . . we said, There's . . . there's gawta be a better way . . . I was always a big fan of Garbo's, you know—we were at the same studio—at M-G-M—and I never *saw* her . . . never . . . Then she . . . she moved in next door to us and I thought, Waall, now I'll . . . now m'by I'll—but she moved in and she built this eight-foot stone *wall* around the place! Waaall, noow, we . . . gawt pretty sore about that—and one night, we . . . one night, we gawt drunk and we d'cided to . . . that if we dug a hole under the wall . . . we could just . . . just dig right up into her front *yard*! And we gawt just far 'nough down to hit a water main . . . and . . ."

"Seems to me we got drunk and *talked* about digging a hole," said Fonda.

"And then . . . we had *cats*! When we moved into the house there was a mother cat there and she'd just had a litter. We said . . . waall, that's . . . that's *fine*. But they . . . these weren't *ordinary* cats—they were *wild*! And they started to attract other wild cats in the neighborhood until . . . we had cats all . . . all around . . . in the trees, under the house, on the . . . you'd hear them at night walking on the tile roof. You'd come home in the dark and . . . and you'd go up the walk to the front door . . . fumbling for the key . . . you'd hear this *noise*—right under your feet . . . it was . . . *hhhrrrrrrr*!! *sssssss*! One time I came home . . . and I found Fawnda in the front yard with a . . . he had a bow an' *arrow*! He was . . . he said if he could just shoot an arrow through the cat sideways—it would get stuck goin' through a narrow place and he could *catch* it! He could . . . Didn't work. We called the ASPCA. They said, '*Sure, sure,* we'd love to take your cats. Just . . . just put 'em in a bawx and we'll take 'em . . .' Waaall, then, I had a cousin of mine—senior at Princeton—came to visit one summer, and I said, 'I'll make a deal with you, I'll . . . thirty dawllars to get rid of the cats.' Nooow, he had an idea—it was a fine Princetonian idea—he caught one of the cats and painted it *purple*! The idea was—that when the other cats saw it, they'd all say, 'Look at that—purple—let's get outta here!' Didn't work . . . didn't . . . We just had a purple cat around the place, that's all!"

"And the *fleas* they had," Fonda said.

"Yeah . . . Wonderful days."

When I asked how he had felt at the start about being in pictures, Stewart said, "I loved it. Right away—didn't miss the stage at all. Loved it. All that stuff ya hear 'bout how the big studio was nothing but an enormous factory—this just isn't true . . . it's nawt . . . It was wonderful—you were doing something all the time—if you weren't shootin' a picture, you were working out in the gym or doing a test with someone or taking singing lessons or . . . Picture-making was . . . it was more *exciting* in the old days . . . it was more fun. And the big studios had a lawt to do with generating that excitement . . . An' this stuff 'bout no freedom! Nobody told [Ernst] Lubitsch what to do, or Frank Borzage, or John Stahl. An' you could . . . you could bargain about parts—you didn't have to take *everything* they offered—you could make deals."

"Well, Jim had it pretty good at M-G-M," Fonda said. "His experience was quite different from mine at Fox. He really enjoyed it."

"When I first gawt out there," Jimmy remembered, "one o' the things they tested me for was a part in *The Good Earth* . . . it was . . . as a *Chinaman*! They gawt me all made up—took all morning—an' gawt me together with Paul Muni and . . . there was just . . . just one thing . . . wrong . . . I was too *tall*! So they dug a *trench* and I walked in it and Muni walked alongside . . . an' I . . . I didn't get the part. I didn't . . . They gave the part to a Chinaman!"

"Jimmy had a kind of specific inarticulation," said George Stevens. "This film we did was about inarticulation . . ." It was Stewart's fourteenth picture—and his first of any distinction—a 1938 comedy called *Vivacious Lady*, which Stevens directed, and in which he played a timid college professor who disrupts the staid atmosphere of the institution by getting engaged to a nifty nightclub singer acted by Ginger Rogers. Stevens was an unhurried, thoughtful man, who sounded as though he had gone to an Eastern prep school, and who directed such memorable pictures as *Alice Adams, Gunga Din, Woman of the Year,* and others more famous, like *A Place in the Sun, Shane* and *Giant.* "The boy and the girl had no business getting together—so the movie was really about the pleasant frustration of non-communication. This was very *close* to Jimmy Stewart's vein of expression—this struggle to get anything said. Now, to overcome disbelief is the most difficult thing to do in films. And Jimmy, with this extraordinary earnestness he had, just walked in and *extinguished* disbelief."

"He had some of the same qualities that Gary Cooper had," Frank Capra said to me. "That indefinable personal integrity—awfully hard to make Jimmy look bad." Capra—a small, sad-eyed man who spoke in a clipped yet hesitant manner and seemed most at ease when he was laughing, which he did with abandon—first directed Stewart in a supporting part in *You Can't Take It with You,* which they made in 1938. The next year, Capra gave him the title role in *Mr. Smith Goes to Washington,* and in 1946, the lead in *It's a Wonderful Life,* which always remained Stewart's favorite among all his own films. The Capra hero, of course—from his silent Harry Langdon comedies to such great successes as *Mr. Smith, Mr. Deeds Goes to Town,* and *Meet John Doe*—was an innocent dreamer who came up against hard reality, yet managed not only to keep his illusions but to triumph with them. Because that was the way Capra wanted it to be. "When *Mr. Smith* came along, it was either Gary Cooper or Stewart, and Jim was younger and I knew he would make a hell of a Mr. Smith—he looked like the country kid, the idealist—it was very close to him. I think there's no question but that this picture shaped the public image of him, of the real Jimmy Stewart."

"Yeah, that was a good picture," Jimmy agreed, "that was the first time I felt I was really getting across."

"Cyclically speaking," Cary Grant explained to me, "Jimmy Stewart

James Stewart and Donna Reed are small-town newlyweds who have to change their honeymoon plans when Stewart's father's building and loan company gets into trouble in Frank Capra's now perennial (originally unsuccessful) comedy-drama-fantasy, It's a Wonderful Life *(1946).*

had the same effect on pic-tures that Marlon Brando had some years la-ter. We did one picture together in 1940 called *The Philadelphia Story . . .*"

"I never thought that much of my work in *The Philadelphia Story,*" Stewart mentioned once. But the Academy awarded him an Oscar for that performance, though it's probably true, as the story goes, that they gave it to him that year mainly because they had passed him up the year before on *Mr. Smith Goes to Washington.*

"Jimmy had the ability to talk naturally," Grant said. "He knew that in conversations people *do* often interrupt one another and that it's not always so *easy* to get a thought out. It took a lit-tle while for the sound men to get used to him, but he had an *enormous* impact. And then, some years la-ter, Marlon came out and did the same thing all over again—but what people forget is that Jimmy did it first. And he affected *all* of us really."

"Isn't that interesting!" Stevens said in response to this. "Of course, it's true. Jimmy did it with a kind of emphasis and Brando did it with a kind of reticence."

"We did a scene together," Grant said, "in which he was drunk . . . and I got absolutely *fascinated* with him—watching him—you can see it in the film—he was so *good*!"

"He was good in anything," John Ford told me. "Played himself but he played the character. . . . People just liked him."

Then the war came. And Stewart, who had had over four hundred hours of civilian flying time, joined the Air Force. He moved from second lieutenant to colonel, commanded twenty bombing missions over Germany, was awarded the Air Force Medal, the Croix de Guerre, the D.F.C. with Oak Leaf Cluster, came home when the war was over. His experience of World War II was something he didn't talk about. But once, in a conversation about the tragic, disastrous low-level bombing raids on the Ploesti oil fields—in which he himself did not take part—Stewart remarked to me, "Everything's planned . . . it's all set . . . it's all—and then you're over the target—and it's . . . nothing's the way . . . it's all *different*! *Every*thing's different from the way you'd planned—everything's *wrong*. And you're nawt supposed to—but everybody gets on the radio and starts yelling!"

"After flying those B-29s," Capra remembered, "Jimmy didn't feel quite right being back in pictures. In the middle of *It's a Wonderful Life*, which was his first film after the war, he told me—he said he thought maybe being an actor was not for decent people. That acting had become silly, unimportant next to what he'd seen. Said he thought he'd do this picture and then quit. Lionel Barrymore was in the film, and he felt, you know, that acting was one of the greatest professions ever invented—very outspoken about it, too. One day he said to me, 'That Jimmy Stewart is good.' 'Yeah,' I said, 'but he's thinking of quitting.' 'Really? Why?' So I told him what Jimmy'd said. A few days later, Lionel Barrymore talked to Jimmy. 'I understand you don't think acting is a *worthy* enough profession,' he said, and then he gave Jimmy a pitch on acting as I've never heard. 'Don't you *realize*,' he said, 'you're moving millions of people, shaping their lives, giving them a sense of exaltation . . . What other profession has that *power* or can *be* so important? A bad actor is a bad actor. But acting is among the oldest and noblest professions in the world, young man.' Jimmy never said anything to me about it, but I think it must've had an effect on him. He never *said* it, but I think Jimmy decided if he was going to be an actor, he was going to be the best there was."

"I realized after the war that I wasn't going across anymore," Stewart recalled, "after a couple of pictures. I remember on *Magic Town*, one critic wrote, 'If we have to sit through another picture while that beanpole stumbles around, taking forever to get things out. . . .' The *New York Times* sent a guy out here to do an article on me, and he said, 'Now, I'll tell ya right off, the title of this thing is gonna be "The Rise and Fall of Jimmy Stewart!" I realized I'd better do *some*thing—I couldn't just go on hemming and hawing—which I sometimes overdid too . . . I looked at an old picture a mine—*Born to Dance*—I wanted to *vawmit*! I had t' . . . toughen it up . . ."

"When he's doing those tough characters," Frank Capra said, "he's *not* playing himself—fundamentally, Jimmy is an idealist."

"I gawt . . . tougher—and I found that in *Westerns* I could do it an' still retain what I was. People would accept it."

People did. "You can't knock a Western," John Ford used to say as late as the sixties, "they have kept the industry going." A look at the (now defunct publication) *Fame* annual exhibitors' poll of the Top Ten Money-Making Stars confirms this remark: on the list for eighteen years, predominantly Western star Gary Cooper; for sixteen years, John Wayne; for ten years, James Stewart. His initial appearance (fifth place) was in 1950, the year his first two postwar Westerns were released. He remained in the Top Ten throughout the fifties—hitting first place in 1955; of the score of pictures he made in those ten years, a third were Westerns. Three extremely popular non-Western fifties films—Hitchcock's *Rear Window* and *The Man Who Knew Too Much,* and Preminger's *Anatomy of a Murder*—did not exactly hurt his standing either. In 1960–64, Stewart dropped out of the Top Ten but was back in eighth place in 1965: the picture that did it was *Shenandoah,* a Western. (Besides the westerners, in that decade Stewart also played two other distinctly American heroes: Glenn Miller and Charles Lindbergh.)

"Casting the film star is, in many respects, a compromise," Alfred Hitchcock said to me. "Now, Stewart can play all the scenes, and in character, but what I mean is epitomized in those film reviews—you read the résumé they give of an adventure story: 'Well,' they say, 'Jimmy Stewart rides in on a horse and comes face to face with a hundred Indians. But Stewart is very clever and he outwits them . . .' You see, it's always 'Stewart,' never the name of the character he's playing." Hitchcock first cast Stewart in 1948 as the professor in *Rope,* and they did four films together (three in financial partnership), including his devastating performance as a guilt- and love-haunted ex–police detective in *Vertigo.* "But the *enormous* advantage in casting the star is because of familiarity," Hitch concluded. "His *face* is familiar. . . ."

"I've always felt, from people, that it was a friendly attitude," Stewart commented, "which has been very *nice*. 'Geez, I *know* that fel-low.' . . . They're . . . you can feel the *concern*—the friendliness—they come up an' say, 'I feel like I *know* you.' Some of it has resulted from the kind of parts I've been in. But the important thing *is* that they should be concerned for your welfare up there on the screen. 'Cause I've always felt, through the years, although they're . . . they're always sure everything's going to come out all right—they're nawt *quite* sure in my case. . . ."

"You see, the moment he gets into jeopardy," Hitchcock explained, "the audience reaction is much stronger than it would be if the actor were a character man, who might be more right for the part. So your story is helped enormously."

"People used to ask Spencer Tracy," said Stewart, " 'Don't you ever get tired of playing Spencer Tracy?' An' he'd say, 'Who the hell do you *want* me to play!?' I'm against people who yell the star system is dead. I've never agreed with that—ya talk to people an' they can't put it into words—but a star is just someone to root for. . . ."

"Stewart is a perfect Hitchcock hero," the director concluded, "because he is Everyman in bizarre situations. I mean, let's look at his pri-vate life—Princeton, Air Force colonel—he's not an uneducated oaf, you can believe him as a professor, a doctor, family man . . ."

"I always wanted to live on a hill—I don't know why," Jimmy remi-nisced. "An' I used to. But when I gawt married . . . and the kids . . ." The family of six lived in a large Tudor house on Roxbury Drive at the foot of the Beverly Hills. One of Gloria's sons, whom Jimmy raised, was killed in Vietnam in 1970 and buried at Arlington National Cemetery, to which Jimmy and Gloria made regular pilgrimages. "I thought m'by it'd be good to go back to the old way, where there was a *sidewalk* an' you could go 'round the corner to the grocery store. And the twins . . . I think now that if they have pills to stawp babies, they oughta be able to have pills that make *twins*! Because . . . I think it's . . . the most wonderful . . . They're never lonely . . . they're . . . and they have a bond between them that's . . . They . . . they hold secret *meetings* in the cellar . . . and I can't go—no one's allowed down there—no one . . . but the *dog*! The only thing I wish . . . is . . . I think they've gawt too much work in cawl-lege . . . the boys are in cawllege and *I* never coulda gawtten through the stuff they've gawtta do. They . . . I guess the teachers would kill me, but I wish they were given a little more time to dream. . . ."

Coming out of a restaurant one evening, Stewart was approached by a man and his wife. "I don't guess it means anything to you," the man said, "but I just wanted to say we've seen your pictures many times and have enjoyed you very much." Stewart, holding on to the man's hand, said warmly, pointedly, "Why, it means *everything* to me." Afterward, I asked how he really felt about being a star.

"I take it as a sort of respawnsibility," he answered. "Ted Healy once told me, long time ago, he said, 'Treat the audience as a partner, nawt as a customer.' Good advice. You know, I gawt an awful lawtta letters after *Anatomy of a Murder:* 'Ya let us down, I'm nawt goin' t' your pictures any-more—I took m'family to see a Jimmy Stewart picture an' you're up there in court talkin' dirty and holdin' up women's panties . . .' An' . . . I have to take these things into consideration. Now, I didn't think *Anatomy* was offensive—or in bad taste. An' if anything like it came along again, I'd have to take it—parts like that just don't come along every day . . ." he concluded firmly. The New York Film Critics Circle agreed and gave him their Best Actor Award for his superbly personal, definitively archetypal performance in *Anatomy.*

"But, ya see, I think our business is to tell stories—that involve people emotionally—and if the story gets so far away from what people can understand, then you're nawt . . . you've lost your audience . . . Now, I've seen actors 'n' actresses who do a realistic, technically beautiful jawb in a scene of, say, withdrawal from heroin addiction—it's frightening, very effective. Later on, the same person comes in an' says, 'Hello, were there any messages for me?' an' you don't *believe* it . . . *That's* it . . . that's . . . *believability!* The withdrawal thing is a sort of an exercise in act-ing realism, but as far as believability is concerned, the audience doesn't know what the symptoms of withdrawal are—he could stand on his head—that . . . that might just as well be the way you do it. But *every*body knows about 'Hello, were there any messages.' Believability—so the audi-ence can understand—so they can believe what you're doin' up there."

The whole world believed James Stewart. They never caught him act-ing. He was a very particular American—though his accent and intona-tions were undetectable geographically—therefore all the more uniquely himself. He was also eighty movies, eighty different views of him, millions of magnified images combined to create one image called—whether you were from the Midwest or Europe (and despite his James billing)—"Jimmy" Stewart: at whatever age, the name for a boy.

"Funny how that caught on. There w'd no pattern to it—my mom called me *Jimsy!* And with my fawther it was Jimbo, and my teacher called me Jamie . . ."

"People just like him," Ford had said.

Stewart himself summed it up best: "This is the great thing that the movies have . . . the potential to really press things home *visually*—they come closer than anything else, the people can see your *eyes* . . . they can—I remember we were up in Canada, in 1954, in the mountains shooting a picture called *The Far Country*. We were havin' a bawx lunch—the usual terrible bawx lunch—and this old guy came into the camp . . . and looked around . . . he looked . . . and he came over t'me . . . nawdded at me. 'You Stewart?' 'Yeah . . .' 'You did a thing in a picture once,' he said. 'Can't 'member the name of it—but you were in a room—and you said a poem or something 'bout fireflies . . . That was *good*!' I knew right away what he meant—that's all he said—he was talking about a scene in a picture called *Come Live with Me* that came out in 1941—and he couldn't remember the title, but that little . . . tiny thing—didn't last even a minute—he'd remembered all those years . . . An' *that's* the thing—that's the great thing about the movies . . . After you *learn*—and if you're good and Gawd helps ya and you're lucky enough to have a personality that comes across—then what you're doing is . . . you're giving people little . . . little, tiny pieces of *time* . . . that they never forget."

Although I never saw Stewart working on a picture, I did actually direct him one afternoon when we shot an interview in his Beverly Hills backyard for *Directed by John Ford* (1971), a feature-length documentary I made for the American Film Institute. We had audio-taped a long conversation about Ford in October 1968; this was transcribed, and then I pulled out the sections I wanted Stewart to tell me on camera, and gave those pages to him on the day we shot, about a month later. Since I filmed Wayne and Fonda for this work, too, the major differences between the three actors were noticeable, all having to talk spontaneously—though knowing which stories they would be telling—but without any set script. Both Wayne and Fonda stumbled here and there, lost or flubbed their words a bit, repeated themselves, but Stewart was absolutely flawless.

In the one most extended take, the lens was over my shoulder onto Jimmy, fairly tight so that you couldn't see my arm or hand. The camera was on a dolly track, and at a certain moment I was going to signal the cameraman and the dolly would slowly bring the camera into a single close-up of Stewart, excluding me in the process. Overall, Jimmy talks for several minutes without a break, the camera moving in during this, and he finishes perfectly. Seeing the film over the years with various audiences, the one certain reaction is to this speech of Stewart's, during which he gets about twenty huge laughs.

*James Stewart and Kim Novak in the first of their two pictures together,
Alfred Hitchcock's tragic love story,* Vertigo *(1958); the nearly palpable
chemistry between them was real. Long after his death, friends said that
Kim would speak lovingly of Jimmy Stewart.*

It gives a hint of his brilliance one-on-one as a raconteur. He was hilariously funny, with his slowest, driest delivery. None of his television
appearances, even on the Johnny Carson show, quite duplicate the devastating humor Stewart had in private conversation. Because he felt no
time-pressure, as there always is on radio or TV, he could relax and take as
long as he wanted. This slow timing was actually funnier than any
sped-up version, because Stewart could get laughs from pauses, hesita-
tions, half-finished thoughts. His sense of humor was prodigious, very
much in the American country grain, and often complemented beautifully
by Gloria's more urbane personality, and her quick Rosalind Russell–Eve
Arden delivery, which invariably amused the hell out of Jimmy.

That documentary we did was the only time I got him into a film,
though I tried on at least three other occasions. After seeing *On Golden
Pond* on Broadway in the late seventies, I called Jimmy, who was then in
his early seventies, and asked if he'd seen the play. Yes, he had, he said, and
thought it was very good. Enthusiastically, I said I thought it would make
a terrific little movie or television special and that he would be *perfect* for

the part. "Thanks a lot," he said, somewhat irritated, "the guy's eighty years old!" The irony was that a year or two later, his best pal Fonda did the role as a feature film when he was seventy-five and won an Oscar for it just before his death.

Other times I tried to cast Jimmy: for a comedy with Ava Gardner in the mid-eighties just before Ava had a stroke, and then the producer finally preferred not to pay for any names; as a degenerate gambler for a comedy-drama set in Las Vegas with Frank Sinatra, but the deal fell apart (see Sinatra chapter); and a large-scale elegiac Western that Larry McMurtry and I conceived at Warner Bros. in 1972, for Wayne, Fonda and Stewart to co-star, featuring a large supporting cast including Ben Johnson, Cloris Leachman, Cybill Shepherd, the Clancy Brothers, and Ellen Burstyn. At the time it was titled *Streets of Laredo*. Both Fonda and Stewart agreed to do it, but Jimmy was somewhat less enthusiastic. "Waall, there's one big thing I just . . . I don't understand," he complained to me. "Why do I let the horses go!?" A key climactic sequence was precipitated by Stewart's character (Augustus Clay) deciding to free the horses they've all been herding northward for months. I told Stewart that the motivations would be shored up and clarified in the subsequent draft, this still being only a first pass. When Wayne was strongly discouraged from doing the film by Ford and backed out, Jimmy did, too. "Waall, if Duke's not gonna do it . . . ," he paused, "and besides," he went on, grouchily, "why do I let the *horses* go!?" After McMurtry broadened and hugely enlarged the 150-page screenplay into his epic 850-page (bestselling, Pulitzer Prize–winning) novel, *Lonesome Dove*, the work was dramatized into an enormously popular mini-series, with lots of sequels and prequels.

In the original series, Tommy Lee Jones played Jimmy's part, Robert Duvall played Wayne's, and they were both terrific, but, of course, in my head Jimmy and Duke had to be better. McMurtry had captured their cadences perfectly and the fit of the words was tailor-made. I've done impressions of Stewart and Wayne since I was a teenager, and would occasionally read Larry's dialogue back to him in their voices to considerable amusement for us. One time I "did" Stewart on the Carson show in the course of telling a Stewart anecdote and called him the next day to ask if he'd seen it. All he said—sounding amused by my moxie—was: "Pratty *gud*, Payter . . ."

Stewart had been fascinating and incisive in his taped remarks about Ford, and although we spoke briefly of certain other directors, for some reason I never really had a chance to ask in detail all the questions I would have wanted to pose about so many of the other memorable pictures he made with such classic masters as Lubitsch, Hitchcock, Capra, Preminger, Stevens or Mann. He once compared Hitchcock to Ford: "I think they're a lot the same. Two entirely different personalities, but they're very similar in their emphasis on the visual, and in their actual sort of *dislike* for words and long scenes. Hitch really doesn't *listen* to scenes. I've always felt that you could get up and read the phone directory, and if Hitch sort of liked the way it moved, and liked the way you looked and reacted and everything, he would say . . ." and Stewart nodded as if to say "that's fine," shook his head and grinned.

Ben Gazzara had told me that on *Anatomy of a Murder,* the main thing he remembered about Stewart was that he always wanted to rehearse. When I had brought up the subject to Jimmy in regard to Preminger's rehearsing, he said, "The one I did with him . . . *nobody* rehearsed. I couldn't go to Lee Remick, Ben Gazzara . . . I couldn't get *any* of them to rehearse. They said they had all this Actors Studio stuff . . . and I don't know much about 'em, but I must say that they're *damn good.* . . ." He shook his head. "God, I had a helluva lotta lines in that thing, you know. I would say: 'Would you just go over that . . . ?' Waall, they'd sit and they'd *sort* of go over it, and I'd get closer and closer to them and try to *hear* the cues and then I found myself doin' . . ." and he mumbled something as though following their lead. "And they'd say, 'OK?' And I'd say, 'Waall . . .' and they were gone. But this gets you on your toes. This gets the sweat in the hands." I asked him how he had liked Preminger's technique of shooting long, uninterrupted takes of entire scenes, and he said, "I never minded that too much. There again it gives you a chance to sort of go through the *whole* thing and *get* it, and fool around with it . . ."

Stewart's memory for specific scenes and sequences from his movies dimmed over the years, but that last time I saw him, when he was eighty-six, he remembered vividly the difficulties he had with the café scene in Ernst Lubitsch's sublime *The Shop Around the Corner* (1940). The complicated and crucial dialogue with Margaret Sullavan evidently gave him a lot of trouble, and took quite a few takes to get it right. Lubitsch, he said, "told you exactly how he wanted the thing played, but of course you had to make that work for you, and I had a devil of a time with that scene. Isn't it funny, I can remember *that,* and I can't remember half the other stuff I ever shot."

Now, the word was that he had been in love with Margaret Sullavan— perhaps she was for Stewart "the gal that got away." They did three other pictures together, remaining good friends until her tragic early death, not

Stewart with Margaret Sullavan in the café scene that, he remembered, had given him a lot of trouble in Ernst Lubitsch's most memorable human comedy, The Shop Around the Corner *(1940), among the movies' finest treasures*

long after he married Gloria. His friendship with Fonda even endured the fact that Fonda and Sullavan were married for a time, not too happily.

The relationship with Fonda was a teasing kind, a lot of kidding each other, which extended to the way Jimmy spoke of Hank when they weren't together. I never became that friendly with Fonda, but I usually asked Stewart how his pal was doing. One time he answered with mock irritation that "Fawnda" was in Europe doing a picture (*Ash Wednesday*) in which he was playing Elizabeth Taylor's husband. "Waall," he summed up, "*that's* a lawta shit!" This was meant to signify a kind of jealous envy, but of course there was the joke, because Jimmy didn't feel that way at all, he was happy for Hank to be working. Everything was in the nuances of how he made the comments, the subtle intonations of which naturally Stewart was an absolute master.

And he could do this, not just in the relatively short pieces films are generally made up of, but for a two-and-a-half-hour stage production. In the second half of the seventies, when Jimmy was in his late sixties, I saw him do Elwood P. Dowd in *Harvey* in London's West End and he was entirely remarkable. Stewart always felt he could improve on the performance he'd given in the lackluster 1950 movie of the famous stage comedy about a man whose best friend is a large invisible rabbit, and so returned to the play a number of times in his career, doing it first on the New York stage (replacing the original Elwood, Broadway's Frank Fay), then later for a not very good television production with Helen Hayes. The London version came in-between, and Stewart always felt it was the best he had done the role. He was right.

The supporting cast and staging were of a typically high London quality, but Jimmy bestrode the show like a colossus. I told him afterward in his dressing room, and repeated it when we had dinner another night at the Connaught Hotel's restaurant, that his size on the screen had been undiminished by the stage, that he still seemed bigger than life, yet as real as ever. The performance had been perfectly modulated for the dimensions of the house, and retained both his usual amazing intimacy and his brightly spontaneous freshness. There were bits he obviously had developed which got big laughs, laughs only Jimmy Stewart could have gotten because they played into the audience's familiarity with him. When asked how tall the invisible pooka Harvey is, Stewart got a stream of laughs by tentatively holding his hand up to indicate Harvey's height, altering this approximate measurement several times until he felt it was exact. Another time, he topped a series of laughs by taking a terrific pratfall, slipping right off a bench to the floor. The audience screamed. Certainly it is among the handful of great star performances I've seen on the stage.

At dinner in London, Jimmy was quietly funny, but seemed very lonely. Gloria was off in Africa on safari with some of their children. They did that quite often together, but he'd had to miss this trip. He looked happy to have some company—I was with Cybill Shepherd—and he definitely enjoyed making her laugh, which he did. His tweedy Ivy League way of dressing fit right in with the quiet Old English atmosphere of the Connaught. His suite, which I saw briefly, was tiny, but all the rooms at the Connaught are small. He was never in any way ostentatious—only polite, wry.

In the latter half of the eighties, I accompanied Stewart to Washington, D.C., and went around the Senate with him. It was a pretty strange live-action *Mr. Smith,* and the sad irony is that he was in the nation's capital trying to see if there was some legislation the senators could pass that would make it against the law for black-and-white movies to be colorized—films like *Mr. Smith Goes to Washington* and *It's a Wonderful Life.* Jimmy and Burt Lancaster were representing the Screen Actors Guild, and I was there for the Directors Guild. Lancaster took most of his meetings separately, but Jimmy and I did most of ours together. He was pushing eighty by then, and certainly no longer so spry, but he walked steadily and not slowly. There he was in the halls of the Senate, as in the movie, with people occasionally coming out of offices to see him or wave as word spread that he was around.

In the senators' offices, his hat quite literally in his hand, his overcoat by his side—it was wintertime—I saw Jimmy Stewart plead for help to preserve his life's work from being destroyed. He would explain that the colorization was extraordinarily distracting and severely altered the performances, the lighting, everything the director, actors and writers had spent their painstaking time achieving. "Just paint right over it!" He shook his head, and with a world of meaning in each pause, and the classic Jimmy Stewart intensity, he said, "It's . . . it's just . . . it's . . . *terrible!*" Sometimes I would present the essential argument—to save Jimmy his breath—and then he would come out with a final, heartbreaking, "It's just . . . it's . . . *terrible* . . ."

All the senators seemed to agree, if not with much indignation or even real concern, but they were happy to meet Jimmy Stewart, and a couple even asked for autographs—for their wives or daughters, of course. Lancaster, Stewart and I went on Larry King's CNN show together to spread the word. I did a paragraph or two. Lancaster did his best Lancaster, with hand gestures and teeth, through several solid and impassioned paragraphs, and Jimmy summed it all up with, "It's . . . it's . . . just . . . it's . . . *terrible!*"

Eventually, there was a lot of hoopla in the media against colorization—everyone essentially agreeing with Jimmy—plus the success of Orson Welles' original RKO contract in squelching Ted Turner's vow to colorize *Citizen Kane.* All this led to the demise of colorization. However, since it remains much more difficult to sell black-and-white DVDs or videos, which is what brought about the lousy idea in the first place, there's no guarantee it won't come back.

Stewart could be a bit icy if he didn't approve of something, or felt boxed in on a point after he'd made up his mind. I recall a frosty conver-

James Stewart is the news photographer who suspects his Greenwich Village neighbor across the way has committed a murder, and Grace Kelly is the model who's mad about Jimmy and gets dangerously involved, in one of Alfred Hitchcock's most likeable masterworks, Rear Window *(1954).*

sation when I was checking out his availability for a picture and he told me rather stiffly that he had retired from acting, that he was no longer doing pictures. He reiterated this and seemed to take a little pleasure from my declarations of regret. Obviously it was a very sore subject, but he made it clear he wasn't about to change his mind and, as it turned out, he didn't act again, except for a couple of voice-overs. Of course, by then he had suffered the humiliation of having had not one but two television series in which he starred go under fast (comedy: *The Jimmy Stewart Show,* 1971–72; drama: *Hawkins,* 1973–74). That neither were really what the audience wanted from him, or good enough for him, had much more to do with their failure than with public indifference to Stewart. There was simply no studio to help keep his persona alive into old age and, on top of that, since the sixties, the big commercial appeal in America has moved ever more rapidly to youth.

So, in 1994, when I came to see Gloria and James Stewart for the last time, he had, over the previous fourteen years, done exactly one voice-over for a cartoon feature released three years earlier, and two years prior to that had published one book (*Jimmy Stewart and His Poems*). Of course, there were his Johnny Carson TV appearances—which led to the poetry book in the first place since he would read hilariously the often-amusing verse—and many honors: the American Film Institute Life Achievement, 1980; the Kennedy Center Honors, 1983; Special Academy Award, 1985; the Medal of Freedom (America's highest civilian honor), 1985; the Film Society of Lincoln Center Tribute, 1990. There were also a number of biographies and picture-books published about him, retrospectives all over the world, and at least two or three exceedingly warm and laudatory television specials on his career and life, one of which was titled *Jimmy Stewart: A Wonderful Life.* That late winter afternoon in Beverly Hills, just months before her death, and little more than three years before his, any observer would have called it the opposite way: Jimmy seemed weak though relaxed and Gloria seemed strong but edgy.

Indeed, I had never seen Gloria edgy before. Usually she was the bubbling life of a party. Jimmy could be laid-back and reticent, but Gloria was always out there, bright, spunky, forthright, pushing him along to tell a story. Not today. There was some hard, unspoken other truth behind everything she said, but I couldn't understand any of this subtext then. At one point, Jimmy leaned forward on the couch and then suddenly let himself fall back on the cushions and said, exasperated, "I don't *feel* well!" Gloria barely looked up, and said something curt and slightly impatient, though couched humorously, to the effect that this feeling of his was not an uncommon occurrence. I had never seen her cut him off quite like that, and she clearly wasn't kidding, either. He took this in his stride, but didn't complain again. Later on, he looked around for a book he had been reading, and had misplaced. Gloria told him exactly where it was, but with a touch of impatience. The book, after he found it—where she said it was—turned out to be one of those popular biographies on him that basically go through his career, picture by picture, in the most rudimentary fashion, with press-release information and prose. He said it was helping him to remember some of the pictures he'd done. Gloria confirmed that Stewart couldn't recall much about his films, that I probably knew them better than Jimmy did.

They both had a couple of glasses of white wine while I was there. Jimmy opened the bottle as soon as he came down to the family room, which was around five in the afternoon. Gloria had welcomed me warmly, and then encouraged Jimmy to get to the drinks as soon as possible. This amused Jimmy, who complied happily and said, "We usually wait till six!" The ritual first drink seemed to be a fondly welcomed daily event. When I asked about their twin daughters, Gloria said they were both doing fine now, especially considering that each had been through her share of problems with substance abuse.

Jimmy looked a little surprised that Gloria had so casually said such a personal thing in front of me, but then he picked up on her tone, and made some kind of small dark joke about their own drinking. Neither of them had ever been this unbuttoned with me before, and it made me comment on how long I'd known them. There were several laughs, and Jimmy's spirits seemed considerably improved after he'd had half a drink. I spoke a good deal about my admiration of River Phoenix, who had died recently, and they commiserated, agreeing that it had been a tragic loss, spoke of the insidiousness and pervasiveness of drugs in the world. Most of the time, Gloria listened with some degree of intensity and sort of refereed but said little. Eventually, I got up to leave and hugged Gloria goodbye, thanked her. She told Jimmy to show me their garden on the way out, and waved good-bye, still looking strangely preoccupied under it all.

We went to the vast garden—which famously had been created by knocking down the adjacent Roxbury Drive house and expanding their large existing one—and Jimmy, in rather a good mood by then, launched into one of his long, extremely funny anecdotes, which he proceeded to tell all the way through Gloria's beautiful vegetable and flower garden, with a couple of stops, right back to the front door.

The story was about the only time he had taken Katharine Hepburn flying. She had come over to him on the set of *The Philadelphia Story* and said, in her evidently typical terse way, "You *fly*." Telling it, Jimmy did a take as though startled, and then looked around, glanced down and back up before he said, a bit tentatively, with a gesture as if to indicate it wasn't any big deal, "Yeah . . ." With the same kind of military dispatch, Hepburn then told him that she would meet him the next morning, seven-thirty a.m., at the Santa Monica Airport (where Stewart used to keep his small plane). He practically saluted as he told this. He said she absolutely terrified him, which he certainly exaggerated for effect; but it was hilarious, in that liquid way Stewart had of tickling you with a constant barrage of nuances beneath the words, gestures, stammers. Everything always meant more than he ever really said, and his nostrils flared as he knifed through pretension or pomposity. In person, every Stewart story had a satirical edge.

The Hepburn tale continued with Kate arriving punctually, and then, while airborne, leaning forward over his shoulder and asking him peremptorily why he did every single thing he did. "Why did you *do* that!?" Patiently, he would try to explain. "Why!?" More patient explaining. He flicked a switch. "Why did you do *that*!?" Further polite explanations, funnier each time. Eventually, they land, she exits, says thanks, and never even mentions flying to him ever again. " 'Course, she did a lawta flying with Howard Hughes," he concluded, with the self-deprecating, slyly sexual, implication that Stewart obviously couldn't match up to Hughes. Smiling, he opened the door for me after I'd finished laughing and thanking him for his hospitality. I hoped he felt better. "Oh, I'm OK," he said. I waved back as he swung the door shut, and was still smiling as I walked up the path to my car. That was the last time I saw or spoke with him. I often wondered later if when he went back inside, Gloria had perhaps told him about the doctor, or waited until the possibility of cancer was confirmed. In any event, our brief visit was probably one of Jimmy's last tranquil evenings.

I was in East Hampton at a friend's house in July 1997 when the Charlie Rose TV show called for my reactions to, and comments on, the death of James Stewart. That was how I found out he had died. Overcome with emotion, I asked them to call me back in a little while. There was so much attached to the name Jimmy Stewart, whom I'd known of since I was about five years old, and whom my parents both loved. One of the memories that came flooding back so vividly to me was how kind he had been to my younger daughter Sashy at the wedding reception for Sean Ferrer, Audrey Hepburn's son. Sashy was only about fourteen then, but growing up around our house, she had seen an awful lot of James Stewart movies, and he was her favorite actor, so it was a big deal when I introduced her to him that night. She poured out her admiration so fulsomely that Jimmy seemed touched. She was very specific about certain films, and he responded by thanking her profusely and telling her it meant a lot to him that someone as young as she was would be so familiar with his work and like it so much. Then Sashy teared up, thanked him again for all his movies, and gave him a kiss on the cheek. He smiled warmly.

Later, the first dance of the evening was led out by the bride and groom, joined only by the groom's mother, Audrey Hepburn, and her partner just for that dance, Jimmy Stewart. Gloria was there, and danced with him afterward, but for obvious dramatic and strangely romantic reasons—it being Hollywood, after all—the star team that night was Stewart and Hepburn. And it certainly was a memorably electric, mythic moment: two of the last classic movie stars, who never did a picture together—*but should have,* you're thinking as you watched them—both tall, trim and graceful, dancing cheek to cheek to a slow tune in the misty light. Something from the lost films of James Stewart, the ones he didn't make after the system fell apart. But the beautiful work he did leave behind—just the final heartbreaking sequence from *Vertigo* alone would be enough to immortalize him—is right up there with the best acting anyone did in the twentieth century.

Born James Maitland Stewart, May 20, 1908, Indiana, PA; died July 2, 1997, Los Angeles, CA.

Selected starring features (with director):

1938: *Vivacious Lady* (George Stevens); *You Can't Take It with You* (Frank Capra)
1939: *It's a Wonderful World* (W. S. Van Dyke); *Mr. Smith Goes to Washington* (Capra); *Destry Rides Again* (George Marshall)
1940: *The Shop Around the Corner* (Ernst Lubitsch); *The Mortal Storm* (Frank Borzage); *The Philadelphia Story* (George Cukor)
1946: *It's a Wonderful Life* (Capra)
1948: *Call Northside 777* (Henry Hathaway); *Rope* (Alfred Hitchcock)
1950: *Winchester '73* (Anthony Mann); *Harvey* (Henry Koster)

1951: *No Highway in the Sky* (Koster)
1952: *Bend of the River* (Mann)
1953: *The Naked Spur* (Mann)
1954: *The Glenn Miller Story* (Mann); *Rear Window* (Hitchcock)
1955: *The Far Country* (Mann); *The Man from Laramie* (Mann)
1956: *The Man Who Knew Too Much* (Hitchcock)
1958: *Vertigo* (Hitchcock)
1959: *Anatomy of a Murder* (Otto Preminger)
1961: *Two Rode Together* (John Ford)
1962: *The Man Who Shot Liberty Valance* (Ford)
1964: *Cheyenne Autumn* (Ford)
1966: *The Flight of the Phoenix* (Robert Aldrich)
1968: *Firecreek* (Vincent McEveety)
1976: *The Shootist* (Don Siegel)

12

JOHN WAYNE

John Wayne and I first met in 1965 while he was on location at what used to be called Old Tucson in Arizona for the making of Howard Hawks' *El Dorado*. I was there for more than a week avidly watching Wayne, Hawks, Robert Mitchum and James Caan, among many others, work on a kind of unofficial sequel to Hawks' and Wayne's popular *Rio Bravo* of six years before. They were night-shooting and on my first evening there, one of the shots took a particularly long time to light, so Wayne—who had been introduced to me by Hawks himself and knew that John Ford had sort of "approved" me—spent over an hour talking with me about the making of movies, and various directors. When he was finally called away for a shot, he said, enthusiastically, "Jeez, it was good talkin' about—*pictures*! Christ, the only thing anybody ever talks to me about these days is—politics and cancer!"

Almost forty years later, at the start of the twenty-first century, and twenty years after Wayne's death—in a public poll on the popularity of all favorite movie stars ever—Duke Wayne stood at number one. This is based solely on his acting in pictures and not at all on his politics or cancer. Yet during his lifetime too many people either endorsed or deplored Wayne because of his right-wing political views, which still strikes me equally as dull as those people in charge of the gold stars on Hollywood Boulevard who refused (for a long period) to allow Charlie Chaplin's name in because of his left-wing politics. Neither actor's views really matter very much in terms of their creative work or what they left behind. Wayne isn't remembered today for winning his first bout with lung cancer—or very painfully losing his second—or for endorsing certain national political candidates, or even for acting in a few easily forgettable fifties anti-Communist movies. (The whole country was lurching out of control at that time, why blame Duke?)

John Wayne as Tom Dunston, a character more than twenty years older than the actor was at the time (and one that continued to define him), in Howard Hawks' first Western (and first of five films with Wayne), the classic Red River *(1948)*

Wayne remains popular as a remarkably charismatic and effective personality actor whose unique qualities and limited but expressive talents were explored and mined by at least four key American film artists (Ford, Hawks, Raoul Walsh and Allan Dwan), and have thereby subsequently enriched the work of a host of other directors with varying degrees of ability (from Cecil B. DeMille, Tay Garnett and William Wellman to Henry Hathaway, Nicholas Ray and John Farrow; even, once, rather amazingly, Josef von Sternberg). In a lifetime of almost thirty years as a top-ten box-office attraction (plus twenty before that as a not unpopular star actor),

Wayne's accumulated persona had even before his death attained such mythic proportions that by then the most myopic of viewers and reviewers had finally noted it. He brought to each new movie (good or bad) a powerful resonance from the past—his own and ours—which filled the work with reverberations above and beyond its own perhaps undistinguished qualities. That was the true measure of a great movie star of the golden age.

There's a moment in *Rio Bravo*—which features, I think, Wayne's most genuinely endearing performance—when he walks down the steps of the jail/sheriff's office toward some men riding up to meet him. Hawks frames the shot from behind—Wayne striding slowly, casually away from camera in his slightly rocking, graceful way—and the image lingers a while to let us enjoy this classic, familiar figure, unmistakable from any angle, America's twentieth-century Hercules moving across a world of illusion he had more than conquered.

Among the most revealing things about Wayne on a movie set—and probably the most charming—was how much he himself still relished that world. Old Tucson itself, where Wayne so often shot, was created for illusions. It used to be right outside Tucson, Arizona, and was a quite elaborate, labyrinthine, period Western town with numerous streets built in 1939 by Columbia Studios especially for a misbegotten, long-forgotten epic, *Arizona*. Hawks and Wayne shot all of *Rio Bravo* and *El Dorado* there, as countless Westerns did before and after (until the place burned down).

For a week at Old Tucson, I saw Duke playing around with his six-shooter off-camera, or with that repeating rifle he often carried in pictures—as Wyatt Earp himself had told Ford he had done in life—with all the enthusiasm of a kid with a new toy. He was always ready, always prepared, did not go off to his trailer between shots—as Mitchum and Caan did, as most stars do, unfortunately—Wayne clearly enjoyed watching the process take place, loved the crew, the atmosphere. For Duke Wayne, this was home. Certainly he had spent the great majority of his life on movie sets, often five or six pictures a year.

The very breadth and longevity of Wayne's career has become impossible to achieve ever since the original star system died forty years ago. Fewer and fewer movies are made, the audience therefore unable to attain the familiarity of repeated exposure that personality stars used to have (which explains why so many of today's stars began with the weekly intimacy of TV series, from Clint Eastwood to Tom Hanks). While a contemporary star is lucky to have two pictures released in a year, audiences of the thirties or forties could see Cagney, Bogart, Gable or Tracy on giant screens four, five or even six times a year.

Wayne had already acted in about a hundred Z-budget Westerns in those ten years before Jack Ford saved him from the Monogram and Republic treadmills in 1939 with *Stagecoach.* Of course, Ford had first put him in pictures more than twelve years before that. Wayne was going to USC, playing football—Marion Michael Morrison was his name—and he used to go to the movie studios in the summer looking for work. In 1927, Ford gave him a job as an assistant propman and a goose-herder at Fox Studios on *Mother Machree,* then bits, small roles in several other late silent and early sound films. Among them was *Hangman's House* (1928), in which Ford gets his first laugh with Wayne's size, as young Duke stands out, cheering with a crowd, and eventually stomps down a picket fence before him in his innocent enthusiasm. For Ford's early talkie *Salute* (1929), Wayne speaks (characteristically) his first line, razing a rookie cadet: "What do they do in the movies, mister?" (The answer: "They neck.") In 1930, Raoul Walsh decided he so much liked the way Marion M. "Duke" Morrison walked and behaved that he cast him under his new name—Walsh helped him decide on "John Wayne"—as the romantic lead (hardly usual for a newcomer) in an expensive Fox talking epic called *The Big Trail.* A giant dud at the box office in its day, the film is actually quite a likeable movie. I first saw it around the same time that I ran two popular, critically acclaimed, Oscar-winning Westerns of similar vintage, *In Old Arizona* (1929) and *Cimarron* (1931), and the Walsh-Wayne film was infinitely superior. (The other two are virtually unwatchable.)

Right from the start in Walsh's picture, Wayne had an engagingly natural quality, and this kept him going through the endless poverty-row Westerns he turned out after the failure of *The Big Trail,* and until Ford's *Stagecoach* finally made him respectable. Even then, it took almost another ten years of pictures for Wayne to find the character that really immortalized him: the gruff, tough, often mean, often bad-tempered, sometimes sentimental, but certainly unregenerate and lonely older man he first played while still quite young in Howard Hawks' first landmark Western, *Red River* (1948).

Until then, all his best movies had been for Ford (*Stagecoach, The Long Voyage Home, They Were Expendable, Fort Apache*), and another good one with Walsh (*Dark Command*), but his roles had all been likeable, decent leading men—not without charm and color—yet definitely without the later complexity and spirit. After *Red River,* not to be outdone, Ford cast Wayne as an even older (though kinder and more honorable) man in *She*

Wore a Yellow Ribbon (1949). But the Wayne prototype had been established and Ford's was the first of many variations on the theme, the character aging and deepening as Wayne and his two favorite directors aged and deepened their art. A remarkable series of films followed: from Hawks, the quietly revolutionary *Rio Bravo* and the rollicking African romance *Hatari!*, plus the darker *Rio Bravo* variation, *El Dorado*. From Ford, the more diverse and increasingly complicated beauties of such fifties and sixties treasures as *Rio Grande* (an ambiguous story of love, duty, parenthood), *The Quiet Man* (Wayne's and Ford's most romantic picture), *The Searchers* (perhaps their best), *The Wings of Eagles* (their most misunderstood), and *The Man Who Shot Liberty Valance* (the final masterwork with all the deceptive simplicity of a classic woodcut).

His performances in these pictures rate with the finest examples of movie acting, and his value to each film is immeasurable; yet none of them was recognized at the time as anything much more than "and John Wayne does his usual solid job," if that—more often he was panned. The Academy nominated him only twice; first for Allan Dwan's excellent *Sands of Iwo Jima* (1949), an effective and archetypal John Wayne Marine picture of non–Ford/Hawks dimension. Yet I remember that Wayne's sudden death from a sniper at the end of *Sands* was the first real shock—and one of the most lastingly potent—I ever had at the movies. The reason why this worked so powerfully for me at age ten, as well as for millions of all ages, was because of Wayne's even then accepted indestructibility. In fact, *Sands of Iwo Jima* was the first of only three films in which Wayne dies. Still, it wasn't until twenty years later, when he put on an eye patch, played drunk, and essentially parodied himself in *True Grit,* that anyone thought he was acting, and so with this over-the-top performance Duke Wayne got his second nomination and finally won his Oscar.

The particular quality in a star that makes audiences instantly suspend their disbelief—something men like Wayne or Jimmy Stewart or Henry Fonda naturally bring with them when they enter a scene—is an achievement which normally goes so unnoticed that most people don't even think of it as acting at all. To a lot of people, acting means fake accents and false noses, and a lot of emoting. Although Paul Muni gave his finest movie performance in Hawks' *Scarface,* he became "Mr. Paul Muni" (literally—that was his billing) with the theatrical posturing of his Pasteur-Zola-Juarez series at Warner Bros. Bogart was inimitably Bogart in quite a number of films, but the establishment insists on remembering his most "acted" performances in *The Treasure of the Sierra Madre, The African Queen* and *The Caine Mutiny.* A career of roles like that, however, might perhaps have garnered more awards, but certainly no Bogart cult. Similarly, John Wayne was at his best precisely when he was simply being what came to be called "John Wayne."

And after forty years in films, Duke had more excitement about the job than most people just starting out. He liked working with newcomers, too, and was generous with advice; those who didn't let ego stand in their way could learn quite a few good tricks. And all of this came without a note of pomposity or pretentiousness. In fact, he always seemed genuinely surprised, even slightly embarrassed, by praise. Without ambiguity, Hawks had said to me that "when you have someone as good as Duke around," it became "awfully easy to do good scenes" because the actor helped and inspired everybody.

Wayne was also a colorful storyteller, punctuating his sentences with numerous expletives and profanities. In personal conversation, they rolled off his tongue almost without pause. Everything was "goddamn," there were many "shit"s and quite a few "fucking"s. At one point, he was illustrating to me how he had resolved an argument with John Huston. He grabbed me by my shirt front, and threw his arm back as though to throw a punch, at the same time saying, "I took that sonofabitch by the—" His face was suddenly close to mine, his teeth clenched fiercely. Evidently, on the single Huston-Wayne film, *The Barbarian and the Geisha* (1958), the two did not get along. Wayne was in the process of reenacting the climactic moment in their relationship when I got that unexpected Wayne close-up. I laughed and said, "Jesus!" Then Duke laughed, shook his head once, and let go of me. "Sorry," he said. "That guy really sets me off." It's difficult to describe the impact of the moment; remember, Wayne was every bit as big a guy as he seemed, over six-foot-four, wide-shouldered, with small feet and huge hands. When we shook hands it felt as though my own disappeared in his grasp.

On a Howard Hawks set everyone called him "Mr. Hawks," including Wayne; only in private was the first name spoken. Hawks was the most laid-back director I've ever seen and yet in total control. During the making of *El Dorado,* I often saw or heard Wayne giving other actors a word or two of direction. He would tell Jimmy Caan how to do this or that. Caan seemed to mind more than Hawks. Five years later, I would see Wayne and Hawks on a Hollywood sound stage during their last (and least) film together, *Rio Lobo,* and watched as Wayne directed Chris Mitchum (Robert's son) in how to pick up a chair or a gun, always turning to Hawks afterward and saying, "Isn't that right, Mr. Hawks?" And Howard, standing in the darkness outside the set, would reply, "That's right,

Duke." During a break I finally asked Hawks if he didn't mind Wayne directing the actors like that. "Oh, hell, no," Hawks said. "Duke and I have done so many pictures together, he knows what I like. It just saves my breath." As Wayne recounts, one of the actor's proudest memories was that Hawks had told the press he couldn't have made *Red River* without John Wayne.

It was often reported that Wayne also had a tendency to be generous with advice to some of the younger directors he hired, but evidently they didn't seem to mind too much, either, since at least two I can think of continually did pictures with him. They may have been totally intimidated or perhaps realized that his interference came from exuberance and a real passion for the work rather than simply from some desire to bully. (Nevertheless, the two movies Wayne signed as a director, *The Alamo* and *The Green Berets,* are hardly among his best.)

In 1967 and '68, I went a couple of times to Wayne's home in Newport Beach, California, preparing and shooting an interview with him for a documentary which the American Film Institute (with the California Arts Commission) had asked me to make on John Ford. As Duke was walking me back to my car, he took me on a shortcut through his sizeable garage. Entering, I was greeted by a virtual sea of 35mm motion picture canisters—large, octagonal specially-built metal cases to hold the heavy 2,000-foot reels of film—two or three reels per canister; this is how movies had always been shipped and stored. Suddenly, here before me, were original prints of an awful lot of vintage John Wayne movies; mostly brand-new–looking cases, boldly marked RED RIVER, THE QUIET MAN, SANDS OF IWO JIMA, RIO BRAVO, SHE WORE A YELLOW RIBBON, etc.

For a movie buff, it was a heady moment. I said something like, "Jesus Christ, Duke, do you have 35mm prints of *all* your pictures!?" He said, "No, but just about. It's been part of my regular deal for a long time—the studio's gotta give me a print off the original negative." A light went on in my head. I looked around and saw quite near me a print marked STAGE-COACH. Knowing that the original negative of this film had been lost or destroyed, I was excited: "Is that print of *Stagecoach* from the original negative?" Wayne answered, "I believe it is—don't even think it's ever been run."

This was golden news for film lovers because, as I told Wayne, his print—which did turn out to be a mint copy—could be used to create a new negative, producing a better result than anything known to exist. If he would actually contribute his *Stagecoach* print to a nonprofit institution like the American Film Institute, I told him, he would get a very good tax write-off. After a new negative had been made, a new copy could then be sent to him. Duke was enthusiastic, especially about the tax break. What I outlined in the garage did in fact happen, and just that accidentally is how *Stagecoach* was saved.

The day I came with a crew, and while they were setting up on a large terrace overlooking the bay, I chatted inside with Wayne as he sat in front of his dressing-room mirror putting on his toupee. When I admired it, he agreed, "Good one, isn't it?" I asked if it was true that he often directed Andrew V. McLaglen's direction on their films together. Wayne said no, but that of course Andy, the son of Victor McLaglen, a great Ford regular, had grown up on Ford-Wayne sets and was given his first feature-directing job by Wayne. It was true that he occasionally made "suggestions" to Andy, but, Duke said, "there's only one captain on a ship—and when Andy's the captain, he's the captain." I let it go and went to check the setup.

When it was ready, Wayne came out and, looking around, immediately began issuing orders excitedly. "Move that light over a little bit," he said, "and take that one to the side. Better give me a higher chair to sit on—bring that stone elephant over—that'll do—" After several moments of this—my tiny crew had jumped into action on his first word—he glanced over at me. I'd been watching him and I guess I looked amused. Our eyes met, held a second, then he grinned broadly. "Oh," he said, "sorry, Andy . . ."

PB: *How did you start out in pictures?*

JW: Well, I've naturally studied John Ford professionally as well as loving the man. Ever since the first time I walked down his set as a goose-herder in 1927. They needed somebody from the prop department to keep the geese from getting under a fake hill they had for *Mother Machree* at Fox. I'd been hired because Tom Mix wanted a box seat for the USC football games, and so they promised jobs to Don Williams and myself and a couple of the players. They buried us over in the properties department, and Mr. Ford's need for a goose-herder just seemed to fit my pistol. So I went on the set, and he said, "Ah, you're a football player, huh?" This was the time when USC was first getting football teams of renown, so everybody was starting to get interested in football. Well, Mr. Ford had played a little ball and he said, "How do you get down?" So I got down and just braced myself on all fours, and he just kicked my arms out from under me and rubbed my face in the plastic mud, and when my nose hit, it wasn't the sod of old Ireland, I'll tell ya. And then I said, "OK, let's just try that

Wayne tells Easterner James Stewart he had better learn to use a gun in John Ford's final Western masterwork, a kind of moving woodcut, The Man Who Shot Liberty Valance *(1962), among the most ironic of movie titles once you know the film's outcome. It is the penultimate Ford-Wayne feature of the twenty or so they did together.*

again." The next time he tried to go around me, and I whirled and kicked him in the chest, and he went right on his ass. He sat there and for a minute it was a case of whether or not I had a future in the motion-picture business—I didn't realize how important it was then. But he took it humorously and laughed like hell—and the crew laughed. When he laughed, they laughed—they waited their turn. But that started our association.

Didn't you have another run-in with Ford on Four Sons *[1928]?*

Oh, yeah, Jesus, that was the *next* time I pretty near left the business. I was just working vacations, wasn't really interested in the business as such, but I really liked Ford. He had this wonderful woman, Margaret Mann, who had never done anything before, and he was talking a performance into her—taking two, three hours to talk her into the right mood for this scene. It was the fourth son bringing the letter from the third son she's lost in the war. It's fall, and when the door opens, my job as property man was to throw up the maple leaves, and they had a fan there to blow them out—it was a silent picture, remember. The fan turned on, and down came the breeze into the middle of the set and the door closed and I relaxed. Then I'd go out and sweep the leaves away and get ready to do another take. We kept doing this over and over, and it got to be fairly monotonous for one who wasn't as interested yet in the business as he should have been. So this one time, they opened the door, the son went in, I threw up the leaves, the leaves wafted in, I figured the scene was over, you know. The fellow turned off the fan and I picked up the broom, went in, and started to sweep. And I looked up and I'm looking right into two cameras—and they're *turning*! And looking at me are the cameraman, and John Ford, and the wife of the man who was head of the studio then. Shit, there I was. I just threw down my goddamn broom and started to walk off. There was that moment of tension and then, again, he broke up laughing, so they all laughed. They said, "Whoa now!" They had Arch-duke Leopold's Serbian heir working on the picture, and a lot of German guys, so they played a martial piece of music and marched me around, and then took me to the Archduke and bent me over in front of him and he pinned the Iron Cross on me. Then they took me back to Ford and he bent me over and kicked me in the ass. And *then* they sent me off the set, because this actress laughed every time she looked at me—she couldn't stop laughing. I was never so goddamned embarrassed in my *life*. My God, it was awful . . . But after *Mother Machree,* they'd put me on every summer.

Was that only for Ford?

Well, there were two other fellows that used me: a director named Benny Stoloff, who was an old baseball player, and then the fellow in the electrical department there. You could belong to one union then and it took care of everything. I don't know how kids can learn their business today. Jesus, in those days it was wonderful. You'd work as a prop man part of the time, maybe you'd do some stunt work, then you'd work in the electrical department, and you'd get the feel of your business, like they do in summer stock, where they build their own sets and everything. It's a shame that all the guilds don't have a pool out of which new people could work and find their place—but they don't. I guess the only ones that have an apprentice program are the makeup men.

I saw Ford's Hangman's House *[1928] and—*

Oh, Jesus! There was the *third* time! That one pretty near *really* cost me my career—and I thought it *had.* I was at school, and the prop man Lefty Huff called me up and said, "Pappy Ford says there's a young Irish boy got to be hung in this picture. He's got to be in the prisoner's box, and we're gonna do it tonight. If you wanna pick up seven and a half, fine. Come on over." So I went over, and they had me standing in the prisoner's box. And a very *dramatic* actor—Christ, I can't remember his name—played the judge [Hobart Bosworth]. Anyway, he was telling all the cowboys how he used to do his own stunts—he was really carrying on—and I'd had quite a bit of listening to this fella talk—as the young always have, I guess, when older people tell about their past glories. So this fella begins his line: "And ye shall hang by the neck until you are dead, dead, dead!" And as he points, the camera moves up to a close-up. Well, about the third time they were doing this I said, "AAAAMEN!" And all the noise on the set—still silent pictures, remember—stopped right then, so this "AAAAMEN" came out like a bullhorn! Jesus, I got all the attention in the room, and Jack says, "Get that sonofabitch out of the prisoner's box! Get him off the stage! Get him off the goddamned lot! I don't *ever* want to see him again!" Well, shit, I went over and got out of my clothes, started out the front gate, and old Lefty Huff stops me; he says, "Come here." And I says, "What?" "Stay the hell out of sight—Jack doesn't want the old sonofa-bitch to see you because you'd ruin the guy's performance. Just stay the hell out of sight." So that's the way it was. I thought I was through.

You also played a spectator at the—

Oh, that was a Saturday thing where I broke down the fence.

It was very funny, you walking over the fence.

Actually, I think that was before school started. I was propping at that time.

And he just put you in.

He just stuck me in there. He did that in *Men Without Women* [1930]. And I don't think Jack really started appreciating me until *Men Without*

Women, one of his first sound pictures. They needed a fella talking to the divers, and he looked around and said, "All right, you, get in there." He had fifteen actors, and we were out between San Diego and Catalina—all the destroyers are finally coming back at the right time—and I have an air hose out into the water, and each actor is supposed to go out, duck down in the air bubbles, and be picked up. But I want to tell ya, this was one of those gunmetal-gray days—the swells were about the size of this house—and these guys took a dim view of what they were supposed to do. Well, here comes the fleet with that black smoke comin' out of the destroyers, and the light just hitting everything right, and I knew: "Jesus, what the hell is the matter—why don't they go?" I was up on amidships deck with this hose, and I turned it over to somebody else and ran to the edge. Ford said, "Duke!" I said, "Yessir!" and I hit the goddamned water and swam out there, went down under, and came up for *all* of 'em! All except one guy, an old bald-headed guy, J. Farrell MacDonald. He was a wonderful actor; he got drunk on wine the night before and felt so guilty that he jumped in the water.

Well, Ford appreciated that. 'Cause *I* appreciated it. That was the time I started looking at pictures with a different view. I was beginning to enjoy this work, and thinking about how long it'd be before I'd get any place if I took the law course I had been planning on. I was going to school with kids whose fathers and uncles all had law firms and I started thinking I'll end up writing briefs in the back room for these bastards for ten years. I tell ya, the picture business started lookin' pretty good.

Were you thinking specifically of being an actor?

No. I wanted to be on the production end of the business, and so naturally I wanted to be a director. Now, let's face it, I just looked up to this man Ford—he was a big hero to me. He was intelligent and quick-thinking. Had great initiative. It was just wonderful to be around him. He kept you alive and on your toes. Of course, I started watching *what* he was doing, how he was working on people.

Somebody said that you walk like he does, but I don't think that's quite accurate.

Oh, Christ, no.

You have a great walk.

That's how Walsh first noticed me.

Did Ford recommend you to Raoul Walsh for the lead in The Big Trail?

I understand he did, though I didn't hear about that until after I had made the picture. I believe the first time Walsh saw me was during a Fox picnic. We were out there having a few bottles of beer—I was gettin' over a horrible hangover. It was a hot day, and I had on a Harris tweed suit—I remember that. Finally this electrician says, "Jeez, we haven't anyone in any of these picnic events—Duke, you go in." I said, "OK, what's the next event?" A walking contest! Well, how are you gonna walk and keep the heel down and the toe down! There was this little sonofabitch about five feet tall, and he was right on my ass all the way around. I'd taken off the coat, I had on suspenders and those hot tweed pants, and I'm trying to beat this fuckin' little grip that's just right on my ass!

Walsh was going crazy at the time because, with talk in pictures, they were sendin' out all these New York actors in these phony outfits with phony whips and phony shoes—and he had to see their tests every day. Now that there was sound, these old motion-picture directors of the silent days were supposed to be out, but fellas like Ford and Walsh still had the great prestige, so they couldn't put 'em down *too* much. Walsh still had to go through all this crap, though, and he just got sick and tired of it one day, and he saw me run across the street with a table on my head. It must have reminded him of the picnic. Actually, I was goin' to a Ford set, and Walsh asked [producer] Eddie Grainger who I was, and Eddie yelled to me. I came over, we were introduced, and then Walsh came over to the set; I guess he talked to Ford then. That night, as I was leaving, Eddie came around: "Jesus, don't cut your hair—Walsh wants to take a test of you for this picture."

And you hadn't thought about being an actor?

It was the furthest thing from my mind. But a funny thing happened with Ford after *The Big Trail*. He was a strange character, you know. After I did that picture, I came back, and he was making *Up the River* [1930]. I went over and said, "Hi, coach." Nothing. I thought he didn't hear me. So I figured, Oh, well, he didn't see me. The next time I saw him I went, "Hi, coach, hi." And *again* I didn't get anything. So the next time I just went right up in front of him and went, "Hi, coach." And he turned and talked to somebody else. I thought, That's that—he won't speak to me. I don't know how the hell I can communicate. About two years later, I was in Catalina with Ward [Bond], having a belt, and Barbara [Ford], his daughter—she was a little girl then—she ran in and said, "Daddy wants to see

*John Wayne as Sheriff John T. Chance and Angie Dickinson as Feathers
in Howard Hawks' supremely laid-back town-Western,* Rio Bravo *(1959).
An entirely character-driven film, it's the shortest 141 minutes in
picture history, and among Wayne's most likeable performances.*

you." I said, "Whoa, wait a minute, Barbara, you got the wrong boy—
must be Ward." She said, "No, it's you, Duke." So I said, "Yeah, honey,
run along, you know this is a bar." So his wife, Mary Ford, came to the
door and she said, "Duke, come here. Jack is expecting you out there." I
said, "All right." So I went out to the *Araner,* his boat, and I go aboard—I
remember Jim Tully was there and four or five guys—and Jack was in the
middle of a goddamn story, and he looked up at me and said, "Hi, Duke,
sit down." And to this goddamn day I don't know why he didn't speak to
me for two years.

Everything was OK from then on.

He acted like he'd seen me the day before.

And you saw quite a bit of him before making Stagecoach.

Well, then, for ten years we were very close. Whenever I had vacations
or he had vacations we usually took 'em together and actually I went to

the Isthmus [of Panama] a lot and they were always over there on his *Araner*. As a matter of fact, the sightseeing boats used to go by and say, "That's John Wayne's boat." And Jack would stand up and say, "Yeah, this is John Wayne."

But it was almost ten years before he cast you in Stagecoach.

Yeah, he was talking to me one day, and he said, "Jesus, I've got a great story here—you want to read it?" I read it—it was just a little short story—"Stage to Lordsburg." He said, "Who the hell in this business could play that part?" I said, "There's only one guy." He said, "Who is it?" I said, "Lloyd Nolan. He played in *Two for Texas*—have you seen that picture?" He said, "No. For Chrissakes, couldn't *you* play it?" Jesus, it knocked me out. *Now* I was afraid he'd go see the Nolan picture! And that was three years before he finally settled down to make it.

The wonderful thing was that he really fought for me to play the part. Most people say they'll do things like that, but he really did. Goldwyn wanted him to make it with Gary Cooper. The studio I was at, which was Republic, had no idea of the value of my doing a thing like that, so they weren't very cooperative. It was touch and go as to whether I'd make it.

For ten years I had been making these quickie Westerns, and I just thought I was stuck there. 'Cause, you know, they thought if they put John Wayne in a picture, they can get him down the street for five bucks in any one of those hundred Westerns I'd made before I made *Stagecoach*. So I didn't really expect anything like that—it turned out terrific, for *me*.

What was it like to make?

Well, having been a prop man, I think I knew more about props. I mean, I don't profess to be the greatest actor and here I was working with Tom [Thomas] Mitchell, you know, and a top cast. After we'd been on the picture for a couple of weeks, Ford said, "Would you like to see some of the stuff?" I said, "Oh, yeah." He said, "Well, Lovey, the cutter [Otto Lovering], he's running some of it, why don't you go up and ask him if he'll let you—you're not going to work here for a couple of hours." So I went up, and I saw quite a bit of it. Now, during the picture, Old Gravel Throat Andy Devine is driving the stagecoach. And I had found out that in order to make it look natural driving those things in close angles, you had to put one of those rubber exercisers—a shock cord—on the other end of those lines to give it tension. Otherwise it looked monotonous. Of course, only to someone who's really technically interested in how a fella drives a six-up [coach with six horses]. This I didn't realize then as I do now. But I wanted to be of some help, so I told the prop guy to get it, he didn't get it, and I was sore as a sonofabitch. So now I see the picture, and Ford says, "Well, how did you like it?" I said, "Well, it's just magnificent, coach, I've never seen anything like it in my life." He said, "How do you like Mitchell?" "Oh, he's great!" "How do you like Claire [Trevor]?" "Great!" "Well, how do you like yourself?" I said, "Well, hell, I'm playing you, so—you know what I'm doing." He said, "Well, Jesus, Duke, you've looked at the whole goddamned thing, isn't there one criticism, one constructive criticism you can give me? You're acting like a schoolboy." I said, "All right, that sonofabitching prop man—that thing with Andy . . ." I'd noticed that, and I told him. He said, "Oh. Wait a minute. All right, everybody, down here!" He brought the goddamned electricians down off the lights, he gathered everybody around in the center of the stage, and he said, "Well, I just sent our young star in to see his first effort. And he's very well satisfied with himself, and with the rest of the cast, but he thinks Andy Devine stinks!" Well, Christ, what do you do?

Luckily, I knew Andy very well. As a matter of fact, when they were making *Noah's Ark* they called our school and wanted kids over six foot to come out for $15 a day and swim while they broke the temple down on top of us. Another fella and I were standing together and Andy came up beside me and he says, "Hey, give me a hand, will you?" And he put a hand on my shoulder and a hand on this other guy's shoulder, and he's that big around, he's the first one they picked, you know. So that's how far back I went with Andy Devine, and I could explain to him what happened. But, Jesus Christ, what a dirty, miserable, mean, Irish, frigging trick.

That's typical of him?

Yeah. That's the way he keeps you in your place.

What did you mean when you said you were playing him?

Well, obviously this was a character Jack liked very much, and he was careful to put him in a good light professionally—I don't mean in a spotlight. Any time there was a chance for a reaction—which is the most important thing in a motion picture—he always took reactions of me, so I'd be a part of every scene. Because I had a great deal of time in the picture when other people were talking, and all my stuff was just reactions. They become very important throughout a picture, they build your part. They always say I'm in action pictures, but it's in *re*action pictures that they remember me—pictures that are full of reactions, but have a background of action. Well, Ford treated me with great care, so I knew he liked that particular character as well as me, and I think this is what he would have wanted a young man to be. So it's *him*.

How would he direct you?

Well, I remember one of the ways—he made sure that all the cast were on my side. I'm not sure whether he did it for that reason or not, but it worked out that way. I had a scene—they're all talking about what they're gonna do about the Indians and all that shit—I'm washing my face and I say, "I'll go with you, Sheriff." And he'd say, "Cut!" We were about halfway through the scene. He said, "For Chrissakes, *wash* your face! Don't you ever wash at home?" He says, "You're daubing your face, you're *daubing* it!" Shit, I was so fucking mad I wanted to kill him. And he got the whole cast hating him for doin' that—until finally even Tim Holt, the young kid, was saying, "Goddammit, quit picking on Duke like that." Shit, I had the whole cast on my side from then on.

You think he planned it that way?

Yeah, I do. I think mainly he pushed me there because although I *was* part of the scene, I was in the background. So if he pounded on me there, it wasn't too important. But when I had a scene to do, he left me alone.

The character everybody associates you with really began with Hawks' Red River, didn't it? Before that, the characters you were playing were straighter, not so ornery.

That's right. I had found kind of a niche that I fit into rather well, and it was a character that the public liked.

You weren't worried about playing old too soon?

No. Hell, I was young, and this was a challenge. The only thing that I worried about with Hawks, I was afraid he would make me petty. In one scene, two fellas decide to leave and I tell them they can't. And the kid [Montgomery Clift] and Cherry [John Ireland] back me up. Well, ahead of that Hawks wanted me to be nervous and irascible and frightened and now the kid steps forward and saves my life. I didn't take too kindly to that. And it was best for the picture that I didn't. But I tell you, one of the nice things about Howard on *Red River*—and one of the things that struck Ford—is that Howard told every news conference that he couldn't have made the picture if he hadn't had John Wayne, which was a wonderful compliment.

*John Wayne as Sean and Maureen O'Hara as Mary Kate
near the conclusion of John Ford's beautiful comedy–love
story set in Ireland,* The Quiet Man *(1952), Wayne's most
romantic movie role; this was the second of three
Ford-Wayne-O'Hara pictures, and the actors appeared
together in two other non-Ford films. O'Hara would
call Wayne her best friend in show business.*

Is it true Ford said he never thought you could act until he saw Red River?

When we did *She Wore a Yellow Ribbon,* he gave me a cake with one candle on it. You see, I was just part of the family. He never thought of me as an actor, and then he saw *Red River,* and he wanted to top it, and he did. He gave me that part in *Yellow Ribbon,* where I play a sixty-five-year-old guy. I wasn't forty then, and I think it's the best thing I've ever done. Outside of this one—*True Grit,* I think, is such a colorful part. The hard things to do are the things like *The Quiet Man* [1952], where you have to stay alive for eight reels before you really come into a part.

What was the candle for?

Actor. I had finally arrived.

What was Ford's direction to you about playing a Swede in The Long Voyage Home *[1940]?*

Well, I was on another picture right up to the night before I went to work. So they hired a girl—she was actually a Dane—to talk to me about these lines and things. But I went onto the picture cold. I had no chance to see anybody or even talk to a Swede so I had no real feeling for it. And he tried to give me a couple of lines at the beginning. He realized I wasn't any good, so he got this girl. Then I had quite a long scene with Mildred Natwick and he had me work with this girl on the scene and he never heard it or anything until the day we were going to shoot and he said, "Well, sit down here and read the lines." I read the lines. He said, "All right, put the camera here." And he shot the scene. But that was the only really hard scene to do. Because with any kind of an ear you can—Christ, those first couple of days, it didn't sound like Swedish to me.

I'm surprised John Qualen didn't do it for you. He does such a great Swedish accent.

Well, I had to be careful because Qualen's a comic, humorous thing and he has a tendency to put that kind of a reading on things. So I had to be really careful not to pick that up at all.

It's been said that when Ford worked with you, particularly in the early days, he didn't let you talk too much. He liked to have you react rather than talk.

He didn't like *anybody* to talk. If he had anyone talk he'd like to have a [John] Carradine talk who could display great histrionics and he could stay away from him and cut to reactions of other people throughout the man's story. This is what in his mind makes for good pictures and I agree with him. He taught me that a reaction is the most valuable thing you can have on a picture. Having made so many cheap quickie pictures, I'm in a position to know the difference between the two. The quickie things they imagine that I do, and I have done them certainly, are those kind of pictures in which you tell the audience what you're going to do, then you go do it, and then you tell them what you've done, then you tell them what you're going to do next. So any time you walk into a scene, the only person who has a chance is either the comic—they might stop the picture long enough to give him a funny line—or the heavy, whom you're telling the audience how you're going to catch.

One of the most memorable moments of any picture I've seen you in is a silent moment in The Searchers *[1956]. After you see what's been done to the white women, there's a close-up of you, camera moves in—*

I turn back. Terrific shot. Helluva shot. And everybody can put their own thoughts to it. You're not forced to think one way or the other.

Your gestures in pictures are often daring—large—and show the kind of freedom and lack of inhibition you have. Did you get that from Ford, or did you always have that?

No, I think that's the first lesson you learn in a high school play—that if you're going to make a gesture, make it.

You also use gestures in your Westerns as though you've learned an Indian language.

That's right. You know, I have fooled around with that just for that sake. There's something about it that I know is attractive to people. Because they have a feeling that you're—

It gives depth. There's that wonderful scene in Yellow Ribbon *when you talk to that—*

Indian. God, that Indian was wonderful.

That was Chief Big Tree, wasn't it?

God, he must have been eighty years old then and was working in a defense plant back east.

He had been a stuntman on The Iron Horse, *hadn't he?*

Well, he wasn't exactly a stuntman. We also used him on *The Big Trail.* There was a group of those Indians from up in that area, all magnificent-looking men.

On The Quiet Man *I heard that Ford laid down horse manure for you to drag Maureen O'Hara through.*

Well, he didn't have to lay down horse manure. There was pig shit all over. And actually, there was nothing we could do. I had to drag her through it.

On Liberty Valance *did he ever discuss who Vera Miles was really in love with at the end of the picture?*

I don't remember—he really made it tough on me on that picture, I'll say that. Hawks does it all the time, he just says, "Oh, well, Duke will get by," and he gives everybody else everything to do. Well, Ford was doing that with me. Thank Christ, he thought of me kicking that steak out of the guy's hand. And then he was going to cut out the scene at the end, of me coming back to Stewart and saying, "Get in there, you sonofabitch." He said, "The scene isn't important, and then you're walking out." And I said, "Oh, God, Jack—." He said, "Well, we'll ask Jimmy," and thank Christ he asked Jimmy and Jimmy said, "Oh, Jesus, Jack, he needs this scene." And I don't know why he was doing that. Because I'm sure he knew that he had to do the scene. Maybe he was doing it to get a feeling or maybe to make me work a little harder to make that a valuable scene. I don't know.

That's one of my favorite Fords. I know you don't like it as much.

Liberty Valance? I love it. I don't know how the hell I lasted through the picture. The kicking the steak and the last scene gave me enough strength to carry him [Wayne's character] through the picture.

Actually, Ford talked to me about how everything revolved around you.

Everything revolved about me, just like I was the lead in *The Quiet Man,* too, but for Christ's sake everybody's got the jokes around me and I'm standing there all the time and had to try to find some way to be alive and to be sympathetic.

Ford knows you have such presence that you don't have to do much.

In *Liberty Valance* he's got the flamboyant heavy—a wonderful guy, Lee Marvin—he's got Eddie O'Brien doing the intelligent humor, he's got two or three other guys doing the jokes and Andy [Devine] and Jimmy kicking the horseshit and the girl [Vera Miles] playing "I can't be in love with Duke because the girl's in love with Jimmy," so what the hell? Where do I go?

Yet in Rio Bravo, *everybody had the scenes but it was your picture anyway.*

I would have been lost in *Rio Bravo* at one point; we took a whole day—when Dean [Martin] goes in and discovers the blood and shoots the guy down and I stand back as the father image. I was a pain in the ass. You know, I'm just the father image then and that woulda wrecked me. I finally thought of a thing—when we first come in and the guy says, "Nobody came in here."

When you hit him with the rifle.

So I said, "Nobody came in here, huh?" Not even the hitting him with the rifle. But Martin says, "Easy there." And I said, "Aw, I'm not gonna hurt him!" Shit, now this put me back in the picture. But I would have been out of it too long if I couldn't find something for right there.

It was a huge laugh. I said to Ford that by the end of Liberty Valance *it seemed that Vera Miles was still in love with Wayne. He said, "Well, we meant it that way."*

I don't know for sure what he wanted. I think he was so afraid that Jimmy's part was so colorless, even though, Christ, he had everything to do, you know. But it was still a kind of a weak character—let's say an ordinary character—that I think he was afraid to portray it any more that the girl was still in love with a dead guy.

Were you kind of unhappy during the making of Liberty Valance?

No, I was never unhappy. Don't misunderstand me. I knew when it was all over that I would have been protected because Ford's too dedicated to his own work to not protect me. Even if he didn't like me. His own sensitivity would not allow that. I worried a lot. Because I couldn't see where he was going to do it. But he always managed to find some little thing that he stuck in.

Your entrance is terrific—you ride in and the music becomes "I'll Take You Home Again, Kathleen."

Yeah. Well, you see, it's a sentimental thing that I don't think many young people have today. And it's too bad because they've lost a wonderful feeling that I'm sure you get when you look at something like that. And that *I* get. And it's sad that they don't have it. But I don't know what the hell it is about family life today. I just don't get it anymore, in life. Fathers are not strong enough. Something has to make an impression on you to have a deep feeling. Ford knows how to put that on the screen better than anybody in the business. He can handle terribly sentimental situations without being maudlin.

Was Donovan's Reef *[1963] mostly improvised on location?*

Yes. That's what I mean about Ford being impatient with writers.

It's an enjoyable film.

Well, he might as well have used a young, nice-looking leading man. Me, I was useless in the goddamn picture—I figured I was too old to play this part. I was never satisfied with it. I don't know, just something lacking. But not for the picture, for me. I didn't give something to the picture that I should have been able to give. And I don't know what the hell it is.

How did you like Hawks' Hatari! [1962]?

There was only one thing wrong—he let his production manager do the second-unit work. Shit, we did everything the second unit did. They didn't come up with any new values in action or anything. I did all the crap that you see in the picture. We should have done something so two or three sequences would have been different. You know, you just can't ride out and catch animals the same frigging way all the time. Even though it's more dangerous, it still needs to have a variety of approaches and he let the second unit do it and they didn't know how to handle action. It's too bad he didn't hire a good man.

Well, didn't you and Howard do a lot of the action in the picture?

I looked at the stuff—they'd been over there for three months when I got there—and I said, "Christ, Howard, there isn't anything there that we can't do." And he said, "Riding out like that?" And I said, "Yeah, that's all right." So we went out and I got on the thing [catch-car] and rode around and you know before long he's putting his kid on it. At first he thought that was going to be too dangerous, but I said, "Bullshit. There's nothing to it." Why, then all the second-unit stuff went out the window. We didn't need it. But there should have been some stuff made that was more hazardous than that to add to the picture. What I did was exciting, but it wasn't dangerous.

Well, the rhino almost got you at one point.

The rhino was a little rough. The fucking kids let the rope burn out of their hands and didn't scream "Look out!" or anything. I just looked up and see this sonofabitch is loose and they're just standing there.

It's a great moment.

Yeah. It's a pain in the ass when it's you. His head is right there and I'm riding his ass. Here I am trying to throw a line clear around his legs and I look up and he's loose. Now, the Mexican doesn't see this and I say, "He's loose." Shit. The truck was right over here and I went *hssssh* and I was in the truck. He says, "What?" And I said, "He's loose!" And the fucking

*John Wayne himself helps to catch the giraffe on location in
Africa for Howard Hawks' comedy-adventure* Hatari! *(1962);
the title means "danger." It was Wayne's third film with Hawks.*

thing turned around and looked at the side of the cab and went "yuunk"
and stuck that horn right through the metal just like it was paper. And
then he stood there a minute and then he started to move his head and
goddamn he tore that cab all to hell and then he started charging both
cars. And finally—Red [Buttons] was sitting by the window when it starts
and the girl's over there, when it finished the girl was over here and Red
was over there. I don't know how that little sonofabitch got over, but he
got over and got [Elsa] Martinelli on the side and then we just eased our
truck out and teased the rhino away and then let him go. He was going to
kill himself beating into the metal.

Where was Howard during a thing like that?

He was up on the camera car.

Didn't you direct some of the horse race in The Quiet Man?

I did the whole goddamn race for him.

Was he sick?

Yeah, he had three days that he was really down over there. The first day we went out and shot—just in the afternoon—shot a couple of fight shots. And we told him about it that night, so then he let us go out the next day and shoot some more and then in the meantime they set up for the horse race and I got lucky that day. I had second-unit cameraman Archie Stout, who's a terrific outdoor man. And everything was working just right. There were about 400 spectators. So I got Arch, and we ran down a cliff there. We jumped on a little cart we had and got down the cliff. I held the horses back on the beach. And the people spread out coming up toward where we were, and finally I said, "Hold still, everybody!" And so I had about 400 people in there where we only had about fifty extras. And we shot down through grass—I had some really nice shots in it. And he appreciated it, too.

Do you think you picked up any of Ford's mannerisms?

Possibly—I think so. I can't recall one at the moment, but I'm sure there's no doubt. You approach a situation, maybe, like he would approach a situation, rather than a personal, physical gesture. That might be true. There's one thing he always told me. He said, "A lot of scenes are corny, Duke. *Play* 'em. Play 'em to the hilt. If it's *East Lynne, play* it! Don't avoid 'em, don't be self-conscious about 'em. *Play* 'em!" And he's right. If you try to play a sentimental scene with your tongue in your cheek, or kidding it, you lose size and the scene loses everything. Another thing I learned—if *you* cry, the audience won't. A man can cry for his horse, for his dog, for another man, but he cannot cry for a woman. A strange thing. He can cry at the death of a friend or a pet. But where he's supposed to be boss, with his child or wife, something like that, he better hold 'em back and let *them* cry.

While we were shooting the documentary, it started to rain, so Wayne and I took a break while the crew moved the equipment inside and reset the camera. Duke was eating a grapefruit and showed me around the huge living room, filled with mementos, awards, photos, and Western paintings.

He was on a grapefruit diet and I watched him demolish both sides of one, using his teaspoon as a kind of bowie knife to get every last morsel of liquid and pulp out of the fruit, right down to the skin. At one point, a long-haired teenage son of his strolled gingerly through the room with an equally long-haired contemporary. They didn't say a word as Duke watched them like a hawk while they crossed, gouging the grapefruit even harder. Under his breath, as they were disappearing, he muttered, "Goddamn son-of-a-bitch . . ."

He showed me his tattered old cowboy hat under glass. He had worn the wide-brimmed trooper-style hat in *Stagecoach,* and virtually every Western he made after it, right through *Rio Bravo* exactly twenty years later, by which time the hat already showed considerable signs of terminal wear. Duke told me he retired the hat after *Rio Bravo* and put the soft felt memento under glass to preserve it. He pulled a prize Remington rifle off the wall to show me, just as the teenagers crossed back through the room. Duke froze, rifle in hand, glinty-eyed, watching them go. Then he looked at me and grinned, putting the weapon away.

Though having been only slightly humorous at Ford's expense in the filmed interviews I had shot, Wayne, Stewart and Fonda were all nervous nevertheless about Ford's reaction when the documentary was finally screened in the second half of 1971, more than three years after we had started. Ronald Reagan was then governor of California, and he introduced the picture at a special showing for Ford and his actors. I was sitting near Duke when the picture ended and as he stood I heard him saying, "I'm not goin' near him! Not me."

About a year later, I saw Wayne out at President Nixon's "Western White House" for a Hollywood party the Republicans threw in celebration of Nixon's re-election campaign (described in Introduction: Stars and Politics). I was standing a few feet from Wayne as the President made a speech in praise of Hollywood; at one point, he said, "The other day at Camp David we were looking over the movie list, and there wasn't anything that had been made recently that particularly appealed, so we wanted to get something that could be shown to younger people safely, and consequently, we ended up selecting a John Wayne movie. I asked Manolo [Sanchez], my very wonderful aide, I said, 'Manolo, do you think this would be a good movie?' He said, 'Oh, yes, sir. I saw it thirty years ago in Spain.' " Big laugh there. I looked at Wayne, who nodded once, lifted his drink in a toast, and said quietly, "Keep those *comin'*."

It was around this same time that Larry McMurtry and I were working on an original screenplay for a Western we planned to offer Wayne, Stewart and Fonda; our working title was *Streets of Laredo*. When we finished a first draft, I sent it to Duke and he turned down the project. Quite upset, I asked him why. He answered, "Well, it's kind of an end-of-the-West Western, and I'm not ready yet to hang up my spurs." I protested, "But *you* don't die at the end." Wayne answered, "Yeah, but everybody *else* does." And that was that. For a while I thought I could talk him into it, but I was wrong. As a last resort I said that Ford had endorsed the script, and Wayne responded, "That's not what he told me." I asked what he meant, and Wayne said that Ford had told him he didn't like the script at all. Years after both Ford and Wayne had died, Ford's daughter Barbara confirmed that Ford had indeed told Wayne to turn down the script. Larry would later adapt and vastly expand this story into his best-selling, Pulitzer Prize–winning novel, *Lonesome Dove*. One of the several sequels he later wrote was named *Streets of Laredo*.

Just to show it wasn't personal, around this same time, Wayne offered me the directing job on *The Train Robbers*, offering one of my *Last Picture Show* stars, Ellen Burstyn, the female lead. We both turned him down. Still pushing, I said, "You gotta do mine first." He just laughed. Two years later, he asked if I would direct *Rooster Cogburn*, the sequel to *True Grit*, which he was to do with Katharine Hepburn. Ironically, the picture turned out to be Duke's penultimate work, and naturally, I now wish I had done it. The only other he would finish was decidedly an "end-of-the-West" Western, *The Shootist* (1976), in which Wayne is dying of cancer, and finally gets killed in a bloody shoot-out.

The last time I saw him was in October 1978 and, like all the other times, we talked mostly about Jack Ford. It was especially appropriate this time because, a couple of weeks before, the Utah Film Festival had given out its first John Ford Medallion for outstanding contributions to Americana on the screen, and they had given it to Wayne. Because of one illness after another, Wayne had been unable to accept the Utah award in person, and had suggested two alternatives—former President Gerald Ford or me, and since Mr. Ford was unavailable, I went. That was the reason for our last meeting—I brought the award over—though it was anything but a formal presentation. He was in his pajamas, watching a USC football game on television at a bungalow of the Beverly Hills Hotel, where he was staying for several days.

Before calling me about the award, we had last been in touch a few months earlier while I was in Singapore making *Saint Jack* with Ben Gazzara. Benny and I heard that Duke was having trouble with the cancer, and we had sent him a get-well-soon, thinking-of-you telegram that we know he liked because he responded quickly and warmly, saying he wished he was there with us in Singapore, wishing us luck with the picture, and thanks for the thought.

Now, here I was at the hotel bungalow, giving him the Utah award. His son Pat came over with a couple of the grandchildren and, as usual with Wayne, it was all very casual, very easy—he made you feel at home. We drank iced tea and talked about movies—Hawks and Ford, mainly. He told me he missed them very much. "Christ, everybody's gone," he said. Then he asked me if I'd direct his next picture, a period piece called *Beau John*. He didn't know if he could make it, but I said of course he could and that I'd be pleased to direct it for him. He thanked me, said it'd be fun. Of course, he didn't make it.

Hawks was talking to me about Wayne one time, and he said, "The thing about Duke is—he's like a big kid. I don't think, with all that's happened to him over the years, that he's ever really come to terms with it. Almost as though all of it was just a little over his head." And Ford, when I told him that I was planning on giving Wayne a birthday present of a book, said, gruffly: "He's *got* a book."

Strangely, perhaps what they were both driving at was Wayne's remarkable quality of innocence. He was, indeed, always a little childlike—bewildered, enthusiastic, generous, impatient, excitable, easily moved to laughter, and just as easily to tears. When he read a transcript of the interview we did, he roared with delight at every profanity, like a boy who'd just seen dirty words in print for the first time: "Jeez, isn't it too bad you can't talk like this in pictures!"

The Duke "went West," as Ford used to say, eight months after our visit at the Beverly Hills bungalow. The fatal cancer, I learned, caused him excruciating pain. In 2004, Maureen O'Hara published her autobiography (*'Tis Herself*), which contains a moving account of Wayne's last days. They had done five films together, including Ford's classic *The Quiet Man;* she adored Wayne, and referred to him as probably her best friend in show business.

And Lauren Bacall was very fond of Duke, having co-starred in two films with him, two decades apart, the second being his last, *The Shootist*. On *Blood Alley* (1955), while Bacall was married to Humphrey Bogart and despite their polar opposite political views, she got along extremely well with Wayne (she would tell me in 2002). She referred to the "chemistry" they had, saying one of the things that made him so appealing was how uncomfortable he seemed to be much of the time. When Wayne was asked for an autograph, he produced a card with a stamped autograph on it.

*The final memorable image of John Wayne, just before that door
closes on the outsider walking away from the home, in John Ford's epic,*
The Searchers *(1956), which is now universally accepted as being among
the best of American films.*

Duke brought Bacall home on the final night of shooting *Blood Alley,* after
they'd had a few drinks and he'd got somewhat drunk. Bogart was waiting,
and Wayne was noticeably awkward around him. It was hard to imagine
the two of them in a movie, much less in the same room. Bacall called the
moment "ridiculous." Wayne quickly excused himself, saying his wife
Pilar would be *on* him if he didn't get home soon. A tabloid story said that
Bacall and Wayne had fallen in love on *The Shootist,* though the paper had
commented that they were the least likely couple on earth. Bacall told me
she had known of his cancer during shooting, and how bad it was. The
first locations were at high altitudes, and Wayne had breathing difficulties,
often requiring oxygen. A few times he had to be held up. Duke never
spoke of these things, however. One day on the set, while waiting for a
setup, Wayne reached out and held her hand, saying nothing. Another
morning, a crew member arrived remarking on what a beautiful day it was.
Wayne's response, Bacall said, made her understand what he was thinking:
He said that "every day you *wake up* is a beautiful day . . ."

To me, Duke had always seemed slightly out of breath, as though he hadn't yet caught up on the last twenty years, not to mention the last twenty minutes. Both Ford and Hawks truly loved him, of course, and even knowing him a little, as I did, it was pretty difficult not to like him. All this, and a lot more, obviously communicated itself to the public— still the top American star more than seventy years since his beginning. His visual legacy has defined him as the archetypal man of the American West—bold, innocent, profane, idealistic, wrongheaded, good-hearted, single-minded, quick to action, not given to pretension, essentially alone, ready for any adventure—no matter how grand or daring; larger, finally, than life or death.

Born Marion Michael Morrison, May 26, 1907, Winterset, IA; died June 11, 1979, Los Angeles, CA.

Selected starring features (with director):

1930: *The Big Trail* (Raoul Walsh)
1939: *Stagecoach* (John Ford)
1940: *Dark Command* (Walsh); *The Long Voyage Home* (Ford); *Seven Sinners* (Tay Garnett)
1942: *Reap the Wild Wind* (Cecil B. DeMille)
1945: *They Were Expendable* (Ford)
1948: *Fort Apache* (Ford); *Red River* (Howard Hawks); *Wake of the Red Witch* (Edward Ludwig); *3 Godfathers* (Ford)
1949: *She Wore a Yellow Ribbon* (Ford); *Sands of Iwo Jima* (Allan Dwan)
1950: *Rio Grande* (Ford)
1952: *The Quiet Man* (Ford)

1953: *Hondo* (John Farrow)
1954: *The High and the Mighty* (William A. Wellman)
1956: *The Searchers* (Ford)
1957: *The Wings of Eagles* (Ford); *Jet Pilot* (Josef von Sternberg)
1959: *Rio Bravo* (Hawks); *The Horse Soldiers* (Ford)
1962: *The Man Who Shot Liberty Valance* (Ford); *Hatari!* (Hawks)
1963: *Donovan's Reef* (Ford); *McLintock!* (Andrew V. McLaglen)
1965: *In Harm's Way* (Otto Preminger); *The Sons of Katie Elder* (Henry Hathaway)
1967: *El Dorado* (Hawks)
1969: *True Grit* (Hathaway)
1970: *Rio Lobo* (Hawks)
1975: *Rooster Cogburn* (Stuart Millar)
1976: *The Shootist* (Don Siegel)

13

HENRY FONDA

Henry Fonda was the star of the first Broadway stage production I ever saw; it was the summer of 1952, and I had just turned thirteen. The play, *Point of No Return,* was a kind of drawing-room drama, adapted by Paul Osborn from a novel by John Marquand. I went by myself and sat in the last row of the balcony for a Saturday matinee, and still recall the excitement of seeing (albeit from a considerable distance) a movie star whom I had seen a couple of times on the screen, one my parents were especially impressed with as an actor and as a person. I can't now recall anything much about the play or the production except that I enjoyed it so much that going to the theater became a regular event in my life.

There was, however, one transfixing moment which came about because of my youth and the extreme differences between that time and the present. Somewhere in the middle of the play, Fonda's character said, "Goddamn it." I remember blushing deeply and glancing around quickly to see if anybody else had been as shocked. No one seemed even remotely troubled. In those days, and for about another decade and a half, there was no swearing on the screen, radio or television, and hearing a star of Fonda's magnitude speak that way had an unforgettable impact. How tough it would be to similarly shock even an innocent teenager today!

Although I didn't actually meet Henry Fonda until fourteen years later, I did see him on the Broadway stage in five other (more memorable) productions, two of them new works: as the defense attorney in Herman Wouk's *The Caine Mutiny Court Martial,* directed by Charles Laughton, and with Anne Bancroft in the two-character play *Two for the Seesaw,* by William Gibson, directed by Arthur Penn. Fonda had a remarkable ease on the stage, a commanding presence though always as understated as he was on the screen. And a particular way of phrasing and speaking that was quietly mesmerizing, with a kind of raw beauty. I also saw him in revivals

*Henry Fonda as Sheriff Wyatt Earp on a bustling Sunday morning
in Tombstone for John Ford's first postwar Western* My Darling
Clementine *(1946), among his finest works of Americana, and among
Fonda's most personable performances*

of William Saroyan's *The Time of Your Life* and Thornton Wilder's *Our
Town,* in which he was the quintessential Stage Manager; and in his
enthralling one-man interpretation of the famous trial lawyer for an
eponymous evening called *Clarence Darrow.* All by himself, for two hours,
he filled the huge stage with the utmost simplicity and grace. Long before

anyone was saying it—both on stage and screen—Hank Fonda was a national treasure.

Now if Fonda would have run for President or governor, you could have been *sure* he'd have won, and no one would've been unhappy about it, either. Was there ever a more reassuring President on the screen than Fonda in *Fail-Safe?* He was the definitive Lincoln (*Young Mr. Lincoln*), the most likeable presidential candidate (*The Best Man*), and the most convincing Secretary of State (*Advise and Consent*), having a quality most politicians lack—true solidity. When Henry Fonda said something, you believed it—whether spoken as a country boy or a playboy, college professor or criminal, sheriff, outlaw, architect, fisherman or hillbilly—whether he was supposed to be Wyatt Earp or Frank James or Teddy Roosevelt, Jr.

Believability is a special quality of real stars and no one had it more than Fonda; see him, for example, in some potboiler like *Battle of the Bulge* (which he wins single-handedly) and note how scene after scene is made convincing by his presence, his subtle playing. He was, in fact, a consummate actor who was able to project facets of his own unique personality into an amazing variety of characters. Too many of his good movie performances over the years were wasted on bad projects—first, from his home studio, 20th Century–Fox—later, from a great deal of bread-and-butter work. Having started acting in the theater, first in Nebraska (where he was born), later on Broadway, Fonda returned to the New York stage with noteworthy results (first with more than 1,700 performances of *Mister Roberts*) more often than any other American star of his stature, and pictures were the poorer for his absence.

Yet his Lincoln, his Mister Roberts (though he didn't like the movie version of it), his Earp (in *My Darling Clementine*), his Tom Joad (in *The Grapes of Wrath*), have immortalized him—with such few others as James Stewart, Gary Cooper and John Wayne—as a somehow more learned, yet equally individual aspect of The American. Because it was the Nebraska upbringing that kept him accessible to the heartland of the country, right from his first movie (in a part he originated on the stage), the title role in *The Farmer Takes a Wife* (1935). This one picture made him a star. His second film was the first shot outdoors in Technicolor, *The Trail of the Lonesome Pine* (1936), and Fonda's personification in it of a young mountaineer gave syndicated cartoonist Al Capp the inspiration for his popular, now immortal American hero, Li'l Abner.

It was this country boy–city boy duality that was perhaps Fonda's most tantalizing and ambiguous aspect. He could effortlessly switch from simple rural to civilized urban or some enormously attractive combination of

*After doing the title role on Broadway for more than 1,700 performances,
Fonda's portrayal in* Mister Roberts *(1955) was brought to the screen by
John Ford and, after Ford became ill, by Mervyn LeRoy. The last of
seven films Fonda did with Ford, this one ended in acrimony,
not resolved until late in the sixties.*

the two, and did throughout his career, from his first great film perfor-
mance as Lincoln in one of John Ford's finest, most inspiring pieces of
Americana, *Young Mr. Lincoln,* to the illiterate ex-con Okie, Tom Joad, in
Ford's version of John Steinbeck's *The Grapes of Wrath,* and on. Indeed,
Tom Joad (and therefore Bruce Springsteen's song "Ghost of Tom Joad")
became synonymous with Hank Fonda as the great outlaw Spirit of
America, yet the following year the same actor could play a hapless, book-
ish scientist in a wild screwball comedy, *The Lady Eve.* In 1942's *The Male
Animal* (based on the stage play by James Thurber and Elliott Nugent),
Fonda could be as entirely convincing as the college professor who
believes in the freedom of ideas and risks his position for that principle, as
he was playing a simple, honest cowboy in 1943's *The Ox-Bow Incident,* or
as the more complicated western lawman in Ford's and Fonda's first
postwar film, *My Darling Clementine* (1946).

If John Ford at his best is probably the finest American director, Henry

Fonda played in more Ford pictures than any other star actor but Wayne, and holds the record for three in a row that couldn't be more different: *Young Mr. Lincoln,* in the same year as the New England farmer in *Drums Along the Mohawk* (Ford's first in color), and the following year as Joad in *The Grapes of Wrath.* Through Ford's most poetic Western (and among his most personal), *My Darling Clementine,* then expressive if miscast as an outlaw priest in *The Fugitive,* on to Ford's complex (and essential) *Fort Apache,* in which Fonda gives a brilliantly ambiguous portrayal of a proud, strict, very intelligent but racist cavalry colonel who leads his men into an Apache massacre.

Fonda's innate quality of overriding intelligence, a kind of inborn faith and wisdom, with an entirely liberal spirit (which was certainly true of the actor's own politics) runs through all his work, whether in Ford's (and Mervyn LeRoy's) somewhat misbegotten version of *Mister Roberts,* through Alfred Hitchcock's nightmarish drama *The Wrong Man,* based on a true story, with Fonda quietly magnificent as the Stork Club musician arrested for a robbery he did not commit. One of Hitchcock's key works, and among Fonda's finest performances, it came out the same year as *12 Angry Men,* Sidney Lumet's powerful first theatrical feature, starring Fonda as an architect who is the lone dissenting juror in a murder trial. If there is an archetypal "Henry-Fonda-as-he-was-thought-of-in-life" movie, it is *12 Angry Men.* No coincidence that it was one of the very few pictures Fonda himself produced. In Gore Vidal's *The Best Man,* Fonda is as much the quintessential thinking-man's liberal Democrat as he was in *12 Angry Men,* and Vidal's provocative script about a presidential convention conveys obvious parallels between Fonda's character and Adlai Stevenson, another quintessential egghead Democrat.

All this makes even more impressive Fonda's amazing facility as a light comedian in what is probably Preston Sturges' greatest screwball comedy, 1941's classic *The Lady Eve,* certainly among the top five in that treasured, long-lost genre. That's the one in which Fonda (at age thirty-five) played an ale-heir millionaire who studies snakes and, after a long while in the jungle, finds himself on an ocean liner with the sexiest, smartest, most attractive card-shark con artist you could ever imagine, played by Barbara Stanwyck (at age thirty-four). Strangely, *The Lady Eve* was the single time in Fonda's long, valuable career that he played this sort of absentminded innocent professor–type, or did the kind of slapstick-pratfall business he does repeatedly here, and so wonderfully that you'd think he would have made a specialty of these roles. If you doubt his range, compare the Sturges work with his Lincoln and Joad which immediately preceded it.

When Fonda finally got the Best Actor Oscar, it was for one of his most obvious (yet beautifully calculated, if a bit exaggerated) performances, in *On Golden Pond;* the release had been held up over a year, and by the time of the Awards ceremony, Fonda was too weak to attend. Jane Fonda (producer and co-star of the picture) accepted in his name. That was in 1982, the same year Hank died. Sixteen years earlier, when I met him, however, at age sixty-one, he looked no more than forty-five, quite boyish still, and indestructible. When he finally aged, it happened very quickly. Our first meeting was in 1966 as part of the James Stewart profile I was doing; I interviewed him for an hour or so at his Bel Air home on Chalon Drive. The same place in Los Angeles where we spoke on January 3, 1969, his last wife Shirlee letting me into the house for taping an interview with Fonda, parts of which we would later film for the documentary, *Directed by John Ford.* It was a pleasant afternoon, talking casually on tape.

HF: I'd been on the set when Ford was doing *Stagecoach,* because I was under contract to Walter Wanger [producer of *Stagecoach*] but I sort of snuck in the back and watched a couple of times. I'd never met him and was a fan.

PB: *Weren't you under contract with Fox?*

Not yet. *Grapes of Wrath* started that—a long story. Because *Grapes* was the bait they dangled in front of me to get me to sign the contract.

You were with Walter Wanger . . .

And when Wanger dissolved his company, I became a freelance and, among a lot of pictures, I did several at Fox: *Jesse James* and *Farmer Takes a Wife.* Anyway, Lamar Trotti and Kenneth Macgowan [writer and producer of *Young Mr. Lincoln*] first told me about it, and I said, "Are you kidding? I can't play Lincoln." The idea was like playing Jesus or something—I just didn't want to try it, didn't want to think about it, didn't want to read it. They eventually came to my home and Lamar read *Young Mr. Lincoln* to me and my wife, sitting in our living room, and it was a beautiful script. But I said, "Fellas, I just don't see myself playing Lincoln. And if I can't *see* it, then I don't see *how* I can do it." Well, eventually they persuaded me to make a test of it. I agreed to do that because I wouldn't be committed—I could just do the test—I could let them put the makeup on me and then look at the rushes and decide. So I did. It was a good, important test, took most of the day. It took them three hours just to put the makeup on me. And subsequently, they call me and I come in and I see it, and this guy on the screen—right away—it was Lincoln. But a minute later he opens his mouth and my voice came out and I was destroyed again. Because that didn't fit—my voice. I can't stand the sound of my voice anyway. I rarely go to my movies because I can't stand the sound of my voice. I'm not the only one—there're many people don't like to hear themselves—it isn't what they think it sounds like. Anyway: "Don't bother me, boys—I can't do it—so forget it!"

Then, months later, they finally assigned Ford to the picture, and I get a call to come in and see him. I had still never met him. So I go into his office at 20th Century, and Ford's sitting there, with a slouch hat. This is the first time I see the whole bit—the cigarette and the handkerchief in the mouth, and the pipe and the handkerchief, chewing on both back and forth. And I stood there [*standing up at attention to illustrate*] like a sailor in his white hat in front of the admiral. That's really the way I felt. I mean, I was Henry Fonda and this was John Ford! And one of the first things he said was something like: "What the fuck is all this shit about you not wanting to do Lincoln?!" The admiral, God here, was using dirty words to make me feel that I was a stupid son-of-a-bitch. "What the fuck you think this is?! You think he's the goddamn emancipator? He's a jack-leg lawyer in Springfield, for Christ's sake!" Anyway, he went on and on like this, and I don't think I said anything, my mouth was just hanging open. But before it was over, I agreed to do the picture.

He was making Lincoln human for you.

That's all, yeah. He knew—and it was perfectly true about me—the reason I didn't want to play it was because Abraham Lincoln to me is next to God, Jesus, you know—he's an image. And I didn't think I could do justice to it, and he had to show me that it wasn't the great emancipator, it wasn't the image of the martyred President, it was a jack-leg lawyer in Springfield. He did, if you remember the picture, sort of give you intimations [of Lincoln's future] in the last scene as Lincoln walks up the hill and the storm starts to come in and the music plays ["The Battle Hymn of the Republic"] . . . It was a great, great experience for me working with him and it's still—he says—one of his favorite pictures. It's still good, it still holds up. And it started this wonderful love affair, as far as I'm concerned, with Ford. I did three in a row. Nobody had ever done three back-to-back with Ford. Not even Duke or George [O'Brien]. And I had done all three inside a year, I think. *Lincoln* was in the spring, *Drums Along the Mohawk* was in the summer, and *Grapes of Wrath* was in the fall.

Henry Fonda as Abraham Lincoln in John Ford's Young Mr. Lincoln *(1939), the actor's first picture with the director, who had to bully Fonda into playing the role*

You did that funny polka in several Ford pictures . . .

Well, I did that same dance in three pictures.

He thought you were funny doing that.

Oh, yes—he just loved it. I did it just joking the first time and he laughed it up and embroidered it . . .

For the same scene in Lincoln, *where you're first dancing with Mary Todd . . .*

It wasn't supposed to be good, of course. Because it's easy to do this step—but to do it with a knee way up like that [*holds leg up high*], I'm not sure whether he told me to, or whether I did it joking, but in any case he just loved it.

[Talking of Ford's well-known penchant for shooting in bad weather—rain or lightning storm—Fonda described a number of incidents he had observed on Ford films; summing up:]

And he's so right. I've used it myself. Sidney Lumet was in Central Park on his second picture [*Stage Struck*], and [Christopher] Plummer and I had a dialogue scene on a park bench. We had been working outside the park and then broke at lunch—I lived about eight blocks away—and I went home for lunch. When I came back, it had started to snow—one of those great big-flake lazy things so that in an hour the snow was this deep [*knee-high gesture*] and it was still snowing. When I got back, they were all standing around, the unit manager and everybody saying, "Jesus Christ, what do we do now?" I said, "What do you do now? Shoot it! You haven't committed the scene. You haven't started that scene!" Lumet had already in his script imagined like seven setups. I said, "Put it on a tripod and get the whole goddamn thing fast. If you don't get it, at least you got the establishing . . ." Well, he did it and, of course, that was it—that's the scene. It wasn't a good picture—but that scene was good because you could see the snowflakes come down and hit your eyelash and melt. But that's what you learn with Ford.

Your first distant location work with Ford was on Drums Along the Mohawk.

It was in Utah. It was way up—nine, ten thousand feet altitude—in a valley that was high above the cedar breaks. I don't remember any town. You drove forever up past the breaks, then when you got on top drove *forever*—like hours to get to this area where they set up a camp. It wasn't near any kind of civilization. We were there three weeks. Which meant that you can get rock-happy, to use an army expression, in that kind of isolation. Nothing to do at night. So Ford set up things to do. And it was so typical. He's always done something like this, never quite the same way. But the first day he had workmen and the crew get big logs and put these logs as seats, all the way around in a big circle in which would be a campfire. And every night there was a campfire. Every night there was some different kind of entertainment. I was made camp director. And it was kind of a joke, we called it "Camp Junalusca—Camp for Boys Between the Ages of Fourteen . . ." It was all with humor. Oh, we'd sing if somebody could play a guitar, and there would be somebody; and, of course, there was always Danny [Borzage] with the accordion for music. And Ward [Bond] and I, and maybe two or three other guys, worked up three-part harmony to some old barbershop-type songs. I'm not going to be able to remember specifics but there was always something. It got to be a thing that was so much fun. Anybody could have an idea and say, "Can I, tomorrow night? I got an idea!"—so you would. And they'd work up wardrobe. It was something you'd look forward to. And it always ended by . . . There was a bugler who, on a cue—and he was off in the woods someplace—would play taps. There's usually some sort of group singing toward the end, and then taps coming from the woods.

You really got to be like a kid is at camp: having a loyalty toward your camp and a loyalty toward your tent and this kind of thing—keep your own tent clean. You really got to feeling like you did when you were youngsters at camp. Or games of Pitch [a card game]—always the loudest, most raucous games, and most fun. I never had more fun in my life than on locations with Ford. Whether it was playing Pitch or the campfires or whatever. But that was always at night. During the day it was making the picture, you weren't horsing around.

How did you get the role of Tom Joad in The Grapes of Wrath?

I don't know whether it was Ford's idea or not, but I know that [20th Century–Fox studio head Darryl F.] Zanuck had been after me to sign for a long-term contract, from the time I did *Jesse James* [1939]—which is the first picture I did for him—and I wouldn't. I was happy being a freelance until *The Grapes of Wrath* and he held that out as bait. I remember having scenes with Zanuck in his office where he'd pace up and down and hit himself with a small mallet that he carried around. He'd whack his leg with it and curse and say, "I don't want to put you in a big fuckin' part like this and then have you go over to M-G-M and play something with Joan Crawford." He had to protect his investment. And, of course, first thing after the war, I did a picture for him with Joan Crawford, right at 20th Century [*Daisy Kenyon,* 1947; directed by Otto Preminger].

Anyway, he held *Grapes of Wrath* out for bait. He said, "You know, I can't put you in this picture if I can't control you. I've got big plans for you." And, of course, it was a lot of shit because once I signed, I did a whole mess of them and the only good picture that I like to remember was *Ox-Bow Incident* [1943; directed by William Wellman], which Zanuck had nothing to do with.

How did you come to play that Spanish priest in Ford's The Fugitive?

I was on one of our junkets down in the Mexican waters on the *Araner* [Ford's yacht] and it was during this time that Ford read the Graham Greene book *The Labyrinthine Ways* [a.k.a. *The Power and the Glory*], and

Henry Fonda as Tom Joad, with father (Russell Simpson) and uncle (Frank Darien), a family of Okies pushed off their land in the Dust Bowl of the thirties, for John Ford's version of the John Steinbeck novel The Grapes of Wrath *(1940), among the darkest studio pictures ever made, superlatively photographed by Gregg Toland*

gave it to me. "Read it," he said. "Oh, God, wouldn't this make a hell of a picture?" and talked a lot about it when we were fishing down on the *Araner.* And I read it and liked it but I said, "You're out of your mind. I can't play that part. It's just not fair to ask me to." And I just used Robert Montgomery—who in those days was an image, a recognizable face, an American man—or Gary Cooper: "You shouldn't ask us to play this Mexican Indian priest. It's putting too much of a burden on the audience." We argued about it. And then the war came along and we were away for four years and when we'd come back, by God, he hasn't forgotten. He's going to do it and he wants me. And we had the argument again—argument meaning it was friendly. I just didn't agree with him.

You thought you were too American.

Not only American, but an American face, that to be asked to put dark makeup on and the wardrobe and be accepted as a Mexican Indian particularly, not just Mexican—I thought it was too much to ask an audience. At least that's the way I felt. If I was producing, I wouldn't cast it that way.

Anyway, we were having this discussion about it and in trying to talk about who should do it—to make my point, I said, "A guy like Joe [José] Ferrer. He's a hell of an actor, he happens to have the kind of a face that could be—he *is* Spanish. But mostly, the audiences don't know him, they're not going to have any burden to change identity, lose an image and so forth." And by chance, Joe Ferrer was out here at that time looking for a Roxanne for [a New York City stage production of Edmond Rostand's] *Cyrano* [*de Bergerac*]. I'm an old friend of Joe's and I called him and I said, "I want you to come with me." And I took Joe over to Ford's office and introduced them and they sat and had a conversation. At the end of that meeting, Ford bought him and Joe was going to do it. But he had to go back [to New York] to do *Cyrano* first. He didn't dream that *Cyrano* was going to have any kind of a run . . . After Joe had gone back and rehearsed it for the four weeks and tried it out and then opened in New York—this was several months later—Ford is getting close to production, and *Cyrano* was doing well enough that Joe couldn't afford to close it. It wasn't fair to his backers; he had to keep it going as long as it was making a buck. So Ford was ready to go and Joe couldn't. So Ford turned to me and it went like that, and there wasn't anything more I could do. I went into it not thinking I should have played it. But we went down there and, as you know, it was an all-Mexican location and studio—did the whole thing down there with Gabby the cameraman [Gabriel Figueroa], who was an artist . . . I didn't fit and belong in this one, and it may be for that reason that there were arguments. They were friendly arguments. But for the first time in however many movies I had done with him, I found myself in dissension sometimes about how to do a scene . . .

You went with Ford quite often down to Mazatlán on his yacht—[Jimmy] Stewart told me something about a boa constrictor . . .

Well, Ford stayed on the boat that night. He could still ambulate but he didn't come up to shore that particular night. Duke and I came ashore and went to the Hotel Central in Mazatlán and we had some drinks at the bar. Later, we were sitting in an area of small tables for four people, and there was a young American couple on their honeymoon. Everybody else was Mexican so you could spot them as Americans, and we were Americans, so eventually we got together—we invited them, or Duke did—to sit at our table and we were talking to them. And at this point somebody brought in a boa constrictor. Now, I didn't know about it and I don't think Duke did then, but this was a house pet at the hotel. And it was tremendous. I mean, it was about that big around [*gestures two feet wide*], and probably twelve feet long. It was a pet, like a house cat, and it would go through the lobby, any place; it caught rats and it was harmless. Well, either it crawled in or somebody brought it in. Anyway, my back was toward where it came in but Duke saw it.

I'm getting a little ahead of my story because what had happened was that I was getting drunk—we'd been drinking for three or four days—and Duke, as you know by now, is a very forceful, dynamic guy. Dirty words, "shit" and "fuck" would come out of him, and now we've got this young married couple with us, and he's telling a story of some kind and he said "fuck" or something, and he heard himself say it and he said, "Oh, shit, I'm sorry." Well, that was too much for me. I just collapsed laughing and I was close enough to being ready to pass out—or at least so tired or drunk—that I laughed myself, not sick, but into like a pass-out. There was another empty chair there and I laughed until I was weak and I collapsed, and just let myself stay collapsed for a while. And I was like that when the snake appeared and Duke got this idea. He went to the guy who knew about the snake, and the guy was paid, and he came in and draped the snake over me while I was down in this position. Of course, I felt something happen and I got up and here's this snake. And instead of leaping—'cause I'm not afraid of snakes and Duke didn't know this—I said, "Duke, look what I got." And I had my arms on it and I got up like this [*standing*] and Duke got up and ran through the lobby clear outside. He didn't want any part of it.

That's really the end of the story, except the next day when we went back to the *Araner*, we told the story to Pappy [Ford] and he came in with us about noontime and I wanted to find the snake to show Pappy. And I looked all over the hotel and finally went into the kitchen and I found it curled up in back of the stove. There was about that much space [*gestures very little*] between the back of the stove and the wall and it got back there—which was its favorite spot because it was warm evidently—and there was just a loop of it sticking out just beyond the edge of the stove. And I got my hands in this loop and I'm tugging, trying to get it out, and I was having a hell of a time. Finally, one of the Mexican cooks came and said, "I wouldn't do that if I were you." In other words, it may be a pet but it doesn't like to be jerked around.

Colonel Thursday, your character in Fort Apache, *is basically a heavy, yet he's very sympathetic in a certain way. Did you and Ford work for that?*

No. He wasn't written to be unsympathetic. It wasn't something that I had to do. It was in the part.

As the square ale-heir scientist, Fonda is quite literally overwhelmed by the slickness of cardsharp–con artist Barbara Stanwyck in Preston Sturges' surpassingly brilliant screwball comedy The Lady Eve *(1941); Fonda's only real foray into slapstick, he seemed to the manner born.*

He was quite ambiguous.

He was a martinet son-of-a-bitch that had some human moments. At least when you got to know him. The idea was he was supposed to be Custer, and there were probably men who knew Custer who liked him. I'm not a student of Custer and I don't know how close it is to him.

Ford implicitly says in the final scene that Colonel Thursday's errors—and we've seen he was terribly in error—were not as important as the tradition of the army. That seems to be one of the major points of the picture.

I'd forgotten that, and you know that's the point of *The Caine Mutiny Court Martial,* the play? And people took exception to that play's epilogue. But that was the reason why Herman Wouk wrote the play—that epilogue in which the character of Greenwald [Fonda's stage role] makes the point that it was the Queegs who saved the country . . . By the way, I'll be curious as to how people react to the Leone movie [*Once Upon a Time in the West,* not yet released] because I'm an all-out, flat-out sadistic son-of-a-bitch in that. Even in *Firecreek* [with Stewart], he [Fonda's character] had some humanity—a little bit—he was a heavy but not like the guy in Leone's picture.

From a transcript of the tape, my immediate response to Fonda on the Leone film might seem presumptuous: "I probably won't like that. I only like you when you're a nice guy." But it was said with a smile and I could see that Hank took it the way I had meant it, as a compliment on his own personality—which is how he always was with me—terribly nice. A trifle distant, but that was his natural reserve; yet he could reach out, which made those moments all the more meaningful. He gave me a compliment I've always treasured, coming as it did after I'd directed only a few plays and one picture, none of them especially successful. We were shooting the 35mm Ford documentary in the beautifully sun-dappled backyard of Fonda's modest Spanish-style home in Bel Air. When he had first told me the above story of his initial office meeting with Ford, Fonda had leapt to his feet to demonstrate how he had stood in fear, virtually at attention, in front of Ford's desk. So I had some dolly tracks laid down and told him that when he got to that part of the story—if he wanted to stand up as he impulsively had when telling me—he could; and the camera would dolly back to accommodate him. His face lit up and he said, "I'll *do that!*" Then he leaned in a little, tapped my hand on the table once and said with a smile and slight surprise in his tone, "You're a good director." He was about sixty-four by then and I was just thirty—what a kind and encouraging gesture it was!

During our filmed interview, I noticed that Fonda was not as confident of himself as Wayne or Stewart were in the same circumstances. As a storyteller, he tended to repeat himself more often, the right words eluding him; of the three, he was the only one to betray a kind of insecurity in just being himself, a vulnerability that was strangely touching. His screen persona, too, never became as firmly fixed in the audience's mind as Wayne's or Stewart's, yet of the three he was the most versatile actor, if not the most charismatic. As a result, perhaps, his last decade on the screen was generally disappointing, certainly not memorable. As a whole, his postwar film career never quite lived up to the extraordinary promise of the years just before he entered the Navy for the duration of the war.

During the sixteen years I knew Fonda, we saw each other very little: the business, and life, took us in such different directions. But we almost worked together once in the early seventies when Larry McMurtry and I prepared a Western script that was to star Fonda, Wayne and Stewart. Of the three, Fonda was the first to commit and remained steadfast to the project, even after Wayne, and then Stewart, backed out. I talked over the phone with Hank a couple of times, and he loved his part and commented on McMurtry's dialogue, characterizing it as "awfully damn good." This was long before McMurtry's dialogue or books had attracted the attention they have since received and always deserved. Eventually Larry created his best-selling novel, *Lonesome Dove,* based on parts of the script, and the even more popular television mini-series that followed starred Tommy Lee Jones in the "Wayne part," Robert Duvall in the "Stewart part" and Robert Urich in the role originally conceived for Fonda: the loverboy gambler who became an accidental killer and wound up on the wrong side of a rope. Overall, the character—like Fonda—was the most ambiguous, the most difficult to neatly define.

To Lauren Bacall, Fonda was " very funny," though when they first met in 1955, doing *The Petrified Forest* on live TV together with Humphrey Bogart, he barely said a word. But they would eventually become good pals, both doing Broadway shows at the same time; they shared many suppers together. The two co-starred on-screen in *Sex and the Single Girl* (1964) and, Bacall told me, she "loved" her experiences with Hank Fonda. She recalled him sometimes asking if a scene or a piece of dialogue was really funny, she'd say it was, and he'd nod. "I adored him."

The story of the boa constrictor and the hijinks of his early days with best friend Jimmy Stewart (see Stewart chapter) suggest a very different kind of Fonda than was ever shown on the screen. Also, that Fonda was an outspoken liberal all his life while his closest pal was a staunch Republican suggests a man whose personal feelings considerably outweighed his political positions. When I once asked Fonda about this situation and how it affected his relationship with Stewart, he just said, "It's easy—we never talk about politics."

During the making of *Mister Roberts,* Fonda and Ford had a major falling-out. Since Fonda had done the play for so many years and knew how extremely well it worked, he was dismayed when Ford began altering construction, cutting dialogue, muddying well-defined characters, adding service-comedy slapstick. Ford, who didn't like too much talk in pictures, felt he was making a movie, not photographing a sacred text, and became incensed at Fonda's questioning his authority in any way. This eventually led to a showdown that was to be refereed by the producer of the film (and of the original stage production), Leland Hayward. Both Hayward and Fonda would tell me the same basic series of events: Ford and Fonda sat on opposite sides of a table. Fonda started to explain his position. Before he had said more than a sentence or two, Ford stood up and socked the actor on the jaw, knocking him off his chair to the floor. "There I was on my can," Fonda said, "looking up at him. What was I gonna do, get up and hit this old man back?" (Ford was about sixty, Fonda around forty.) The meeting was over. Soon after, Ford seems to have had a gall bladder attack—or so he always said—and was replaced by Mervyn LeRoy. Fonda and Ford didn't speak for more than a dozen years.

What Fonda didn't know at the time was that when Jack Warner signed Ford to direct the hit play as a movie—this was circa 1954—the studio head had been insistent that either Marlon Brando or William Holden (both coming off very popular films) play the title role. Fonda hadn't even been in a picture since *Fort Apache* in 1948 and therefore—though he had triumphed on Broadway—was not considered movie box office. Ford had just had two huge successes with *The Quiet Man* (1952; winning his sixth Oscar) and *Mogambo* (1953), starring Clark Gable, with Ava Gardner getting a Best Actress Oscar nomination. Ford told Warner he wouldn't even consider anyone other than Fonda for the role he had originated onstage. Nobody ever told Fonda a word of this, however, until Barbara Ford passed it along as part of a request for him to participate in the documentary we were doing for the AFI. Fonda agreed, called Ford, and the two were speaking once more. But by then Jack Ford had made his last film, and the two never worked together again. The movie of *Mister Roberts*, unfortunately, fell between two stools: although a financial success, it wasn't a great picture, and it wasn't really the play. Despite its vividly reintroducing the actor to the screen, and while he never really stopped working, Fonda never did get the great picture roles again.

But everything he did on Broadway was a hit, and like so many serious actors, he very much preferred doing plays to movies. What Fonda enjoyed was getting "into the role"—what athletes call being "in the zone"—and sustaining it for the length of a full act at a time, instead of the usual film method, which breaks short scenes into numerous camera angles, rarely even these played straight through, and almost always done totally out of any sequence with the characters' development. Ford and Preston Sturges, among others, had a tendency to allow scenes to play through in long pieces, but that sort of directing was rare (and today nearly nonexistent), and even Ford had to follow schedules that generally paid no attention to the order of events in the story.

The theater, finally, is a real actor's medium: once the curtain goes up, it's just you and the cast and the audience—and this is what an artist like

Fonda relishes—getting into the role and playing it for an hour or two without interruption. As Otto Preminger (especially notorious for letting an entire scene play in one shot) used to say, "Every cut is an interruption." He meant not simply for the audience but especially for the actor trying to become lost in a part. I once mentioned to Gena Rowlands that I had directed a certain actor to just "be himself." She warned me that it wasn't necessarily a good thing to say since many actors didn't *like* themselves or *know* who they were, this often being the very reason they became actors. Maybe Hank Fonda was in this category. Certainly in life he did not have the kind of self-confidence in who he was or, at least, who he had been created into, that stars like Grant, Stewart or Wayne had.

Yet he possessed a kind of rough-hewn but literate American poetry about him that remains unique. There is possibly no more touching utopian speech in pictures than Tom Joad's vision of a better world at the conclusion of Steinbeck's and Ford's *The Grapes of Wrath,* but it is Fonda's extraordinarily beautiful incarnation of this man and those words that makes the moment both transfixing and ultimately transcendent. "I'll be there," he concludes; and Springsteen is right that the ghost of Tom Joad will always be there to haunt America for its broken promises—the ghost of Henry Fonda as well, having merged seamlessly into that outlaw mystic. As smoothly as he became the single convincing Abe Lincoln we'll ever see. That Fonda could within his persona embody such different kinds of Americans also resonates mythically—Tom and Abe as twins—and confirms the deepest contradictions of the country.

When I heard that he had died—in 1982, soon after his seventy-seventh birthday—the first thing I remembered was a summer night in Manhattan a few years earlier, when it happened that the Fondas and the Stewarts and I were all staying at the same hotel, the Pierre. As I was waiting for a cab at the 60th Street entrance, the two couples came bursting out the door all dressed up in formal evening clothes, bubbling with excitement and enthusiasm, obviously joyous to be together and going out on the town. Everyone was beaming and seemed to be talking at once. I waved, and said hi. The guys and Gloria and Shirlee all responded gaily, warmly said hello—commenting on what a coincidence it was that we were all at the same hotel—and I could suddenly see Hank and Jimmy as young, eligible bachelors in the late thirties sharing that house in Los Angeles. They didn't really seem much older at that moment, as they waved so-long and piled into a waiting limousine, all talking at once again, and laughing.

Born Henry Fonda, May 16, 1905, Grand Island, NE; died August 12, 1982, Los Angeles, CA.

Selected starring features (with director):

1935: *The Farmer Takes a Wife* (Victor Fleming)

1936: *Spendthrift* (Raoul Walsh)

1937: *You Only Live Once* (Fritz Lang)

1938: *I Met My Love Again* (Joshua Logan, Arthur Ripley); *Jezebel* (William Wyler)

1939: *Jesse James* (Henry King); *Young Mr. Lincoln* (John Ford); *Drums Along the Mohawk* (Ford)

1940: *The Grapes of Wrath* (Ford); *The Return of Frank James* (Lang)

1941: *The Lady Eve* (Preston Sturges)

1942: *The Male Animal* (Elliott Nugent)

1943: *The Immortal Sergeant* (John M. Stahl); *The Ox-Bow Incident* (William A. Wellman)

1946: *My Darling Clementine* (Ford)

1947: *The Fugitive* (Ford); *Daisy Kenyon* (Otto Preminger)

1948: *Fort Apache* (Ford)

1955: *Mister Roberts* (Ford, Mervyn LeRoy)

1956: *War and Peace* (King Vidor)

1957: *The Wrong Man* (Alfred Hitchcock); *12 Angry Men* (Sidney Lumet); *The Tin Star* (Anthony Mann)

1958: *Stage Struck* (Lumet)

1962: *Advise and Consent* (Preminger)

1964: *The Best Man* (Franklin J. Schaffner); *Fail-Safe* (Lumet)

1965: *The Rounders* (Burt Kennedy); *In Harm's Way* (Preminger)

1967: *Stranger on the Run* (Don Siegel)

1968: *Firecreek* (Vincent McEveety); *Madigan* (Siegel)

1969: *Once Upon a Time in the West* (Sergio Leone)

1970: *Too Late the Hero* (Robert Aldrich)

1973: *Ash Wednesday* (Larry Peerce)

1981: *On Golden Pond* (Mark Rydell)

14

BORIS KARLOFF

"The Monster?" Boris Karloff confirmed with his famous lisp when I asked him how he felt about the role in James Whale's 1931 production of *Frankenstein* with which he is immemorially identified. "I'm very grateful," Karloff said with no irony or condescension. "The Monster not only gave me recognition as an actor but created for me a certain niche, which has given me a career."

Through four decades during his lifetime, and now more than thirty years later, the name Boris Karloff has not only identified a star actor, but conjured up a certain sort of character as well, a very particular representative image. The identification certainly began with the sensation of *Frankenstein,* but this was deepened through the years by equally intense, brilliant performances in horror movies that most often were less than inspired. Yet he brought the same concentration and sense of responsibility to things like *The Haunted Strangler* (1958) as he did to more complicated roles in films like John Ford's *The Lost Patrol* (1934); or, on the Broadway stage, with wickedly funny self-parody in *Arsenic and Old Lace* in the forties, or in the fifties with children's story-book menace as Captain Hook in *Peter Pan* and with poetic realism as the Dauphin to Julie Harris' Joan of Arc in Jean Giraudoux's *The Lark*—a beautiful performance I was fortunate to see—and for which he received a Tony nomination. In 1966, his superb narration for the brilliant Chuck Jones feature cartoon of Dr. Seuss' *How the Grinch Stole Christmas* helped to make that work an abiding classic.

Considering the majority of the movies in which he was cast (about 140 in all, including 40 silents, starting as an extra in 1916), it is not so remarkable that he almost always transcended his vehicles; but that audiences the world over still treasured him after so much screen junk is unique. They knew that Karloff's star presence in even the worst of these

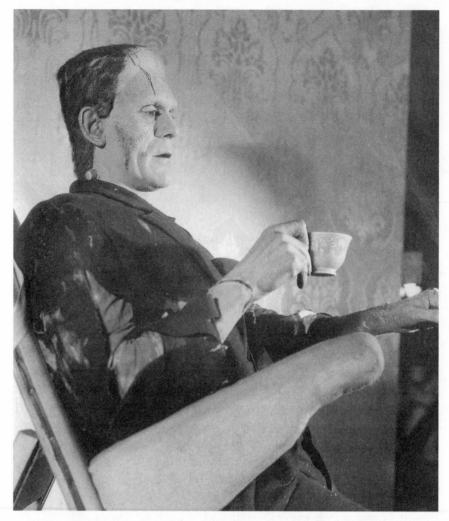

Boris Karloff, as The Monster, takes a tea break during the making of
James Whale's The Bride of Frankenstein *(1935), a superior sequel.*

gave them a measure of his considerable talent, grace and wit. Therein, of
course, was the great irony of his horror image: it was absolutely nothing
like the man, any more than the sinister-sounding stage name which
William Henry Pratt chose for himself, the surname Karloff by itself sending chills up the collective spine throughout the thirties, forties, fifties and
sixties. It still does.

Yet the audience also knew in some way that this consummate
beyond-evil heavy was actually a tasteful, knowledgeable British gentle-

Boris Karloff in the brief but memorable role of the gangster who gets
killed while throwing a perfect bowling strike ("Watch this one," he says)
in Howard Hawks' murderous original Scarface *(1932), no doubt*
the most violent film of its time.

man—shocked by unkindness and never less than polite—with a sense of
humor about himself and his roles, and only genuine gratitude to the
public for their long-lasting affection. It was one of the reasons he kept
working right through his eighty-first year. He was just an actor, he
would say, who had been lucky enough to find a particular place on the
screen and, as long as people wanted him, what right did he have to
retire?

Actually, he had plenty: a shattered knee and another injured leg, the
two necessitating separate braces at least, and sometimes a cane or
crutches, together with a severe case of emphysema that badly constricted
his breathing. It was difficult for him to move about and speak both at

once, but he never complained, was always prepared, and never held up shooting. Throughout his career (which included hosting a popular TV series called *Thriller*), he was known always as the quintessential professional.

Over the years, I talked to a number of directors who had worked with Boris, and each of them spoke glowingly of him. On *The Black Cat* (1934), director Edgar G. Ulmer told me that Karloff occasionally would turn to the camera and say, "Boo!" Ulmer said, "Every time I had him come in by the door, he would open the door and say, 'Here comes the heavy.' He was a very lovely man . . . very charming—and he never took himself seriously. My biggest job was to keep him in the part, because he laughed at himself." Chuck Jones got the idea to have Karloff narrate *How the Grinch Stole Christmas* from hearing his superb recording of Kipling's *Jungle Book*. "What a nice man," Jones said to me. "His passing is a great loss."

Karloff was the star of my first film as a director (*Targets*, 1968) and also the only reason the picture ever got made. Roger Corman had called me in 1966 with his producer hat on. I had just worked for director Corman as (uncredited) writer–second unit director on his then-current success, *The Wild Angels* (the first biker movie to work at the box office, making Peter Fonda a star, setting the stage for *Easy Rider*). And he was now offering me a picture of my own which he would finance, but only on the following conditions: since Boris Karloff owed Corman two days' work, I was to shoot twenty minutes of new Karloff material in those two days, then take another twenty minutes of Karloff footage from another Corman horror epic, *The Terror* (1964), which, combined with my own material, would equal forty minutes of Karloff; then, over ten days, I was to shoot an additional forty minutes with other actors; therefore, with only twelve days of shooting, Roger would have a new 80-minute Karloff picture. Would I do it?

The film that eventually resulted—with Karloff working five days and my shooting for an additional eighteen—was the one Boris himself liked to call his swan song. Though soon after ours, he did, in fact, do some scenes in four Z-budget Mexican-shot movies few ever saw, both he and his delightful last wife Evie always referred very warmly to *Targets* as Boris' "last film."

What a lovely couple they were—Boris and Evie—a real love match as I came into the story, with Boris nearly eighty years old, Evie about thirty years younger. They were married for twenty-four years, since 1945. The day before the wedding ceremony he was divorced from his fourth wife, librarian Dorothy Stine, to whom he had been married for fifteen years.

They had one daughter, Sara, his only child. Prior to 1930, then, his biographers seem to agree that Boris was married three other times.

From March 20 through 24, 1967, we filmed all his scenes—nearly half the script—five long, consecutive days and nights. He immediately went off to Mexico, shot all of his stuff back-to-back for the four programmers, then went home to England. *Targets* was released in 1968 to considerable praise, especially for Boris. He died in England the following year, 1969, about ten months after a private L.A. running of the movie for him and Evie.

Targets is inconceivable without Karloff. The film's story evolved directly from Karloff's very existence, from his amazing longevity as a star of horror films. In trying to figure out what to do with the specifications Corman had set for the work, Polly Platt (my collaborator on the screen story, production designer of the picture, and my first wife) and I asked ourselves repeatedly what Karloff could play that would be relevant to a sixties audience. And how this would connect to the Karloff footage we were supposed to use from *The Terror*—a fairly lame Victorian-style horror film set in post-revolutionary France and co-starring a very young and callow Jack Nicholson as a pretty unlikely Legionnaire.

We didn't want to do a period film, and so kept trying to imagine what sort of a heavy Karloff could play in a contemporary setting. All sorts of bad ideas were floated between us until one morning the solution came to me out of a frustrated joke. Since *The Terror*—which had been shot by Corman and several of his protégés (including bits by Francis Coppola)—was such a poor movie, in my mind I pictured running the end of that film, having the lights come up in a projection room where Karloff would be seated next to Corman; he would turn to him and say, "Roger, that is one of the worst films I have *ever* seen!" Suddenly, I realized the idea of Karloff essentially playing himself, an aging horror movie star, would enable us to use the *Terror* footage as a film within a film and therefore not have to be part of our story. This was liberating.

Then we recalled that Harold Hayes—the editor of *Esquire,* for which I had been writing since 1961—had suggested once that perhaps a film could be built around a character like Charles Whitman, the young Texas man who a year or two before had, with an arsenal of weapons, climbed to the top of a tower on the campus of the University of Texas in Austin and started shooting people below at random, killing many, wounding more, before turning a gun on himself. What if Karloff in our movie wanted to retire because his own sort of Victorian horror had been rendered considerably less horrible compared to this sort of modern horror: a clean-cut

Boris Karloff (with Wallace Ford) as the religious fanatic in John Ford's
The Lost Patrol *(1934), an art picture of its time, with a screenplay by
Dudley Nichols and co-starring Victor McLaglen*

American boy suddenly turning sniper and randomly killing strangers. We could cross-cut between the two characters—two seemingly unrelated stories—until fate finally brings them together. After writing a draft like this, I met with director-writer Samuel Fuller—a good friend—and he solved most of the other problems, at the same time suggesting a far better ending. Corman liked the script, we sent it to Karloff in England, he liked it, and we had a picture.

The character Karloff would play was named Byron Orlok—quite obviously founded on the actor himself—and his reasons for wanting to quit had to do not only with a feeling of being old-fashioned and out-moded, but also with a general disgust with the sort of films he had ended up doing. One speech of his went: " 'King of Blood,' they used to call me, 'Mr. Boogie-Man'! 'The Marx Brothers make you laugh, Garbo makes you weep, Orlok makes you scream.' And once I thought I'd be an actor . . . It's not just the pictures that got bad—*I've* got bad." Boris called me from outside London and, after praising the basic script, said, "But since I'm playing myself, Peter, could I possibly not say such *terrible* things about myself?" I argued that the more wretched the self-criticism was, the more the audience would say, "No, no, it's not true," that they would be all the more on his side, wanting him to be all right with himself. Boris didn't sound entirely convinced, but never again brought up the point. He did all the self-castigation with relish, and did indeed become only more sympathetic.

He and Evie didn't arrive in Los Angeles for the filming until just a few days before shooting was to begin. We invited them for dinner to our first home, a modest rental out in the smoggy San Fernando Valley, the night after their plane landed. During the meal, Boris all of a sudden said to me, "You know, you have written the truest line I've ever read in a script. I was reminded of it as we landed yesterday and drove about." I was amazed and asked what line that could possibly be. Boris answered, "The one when I'm looking out the car window at the city streets and I say, 'God, what an ugly town this has become.' My Lord, it's never been truer."

Boris had several old friends in L.A. but never stayed any longer than he absolutely had to, anxious to return to his country home in Sussex. He was every bit as self-effacing as I had written, but without the bitterness, or rancor. Unlike Orlok, Karloff had no intention of retiring.

We shot his five days' work first—all in one long week. Every day he would go uncomplaining into heavy overtime, never charging Corman— though he made a point of saying he did this only for me. Almost every day began around seven-thirty a.m. and ended well past midnight. One time the scene we were doing required us to get drunk together (I was playing the role of a young director) and for us both to pass out on top of a bed beside each other. The next time we would be seen, the script said my character woke up, sat up, rubbed his eyes, glanced down, saw Karloff, was startled and then began to laugh. Laughing on cue I found to be one of the tougher things to do, so I screwed up a couple of takes. Finally, Boris said, "You don't *have* to laugh, you know. Just because you wrote that in the script doesn't mean you *have* to do it." It was pretty difficult, I said, and he replied with a touch of exasperation, "Then by all means don't *do* it!" I followed his direction and we got the shot on the next take.

In a hotel room set, where the characters get to drinking too much, we watch on TV a scene from Karloff's "first really important part," as he called it, in Howard Hawks' version of a successful play, *The Criminal Code*. Boris repeated a memorable small role he had done on the Broadway stage. I wrote a line for my character about Hawks: "He really knows how to tell a story," and Boris ad-libbed, "Indeed he does," so we kept it in.

The night we filmed his scenes on location at a drive-in theater went very late and it was, as usual, chilly at night in L.A. Boris never complained once. The final day with him started at eight a.m. and went until two-thirty in the morning at a little studio on Santa Monica Boulevard in Hollywood. Evie Karloff stayed the whole time and helped Polly with various set decorations, hanging curtains, moving props. Among his last scenes was a two-minute fable he would relate—a great many words to learn—and I told him I would like to try doing it without cutting, which meant he would have to say all of it straight through. There were three others in the scene with him (besides me) and when I was first explaining the shot to him, I said I thought perhaps we could start on his face, then slowly pan the camera across everybody listening and end on him again. I could tell from his expression that he wasn't very keen on that plan, but he didn't say anything.

The little story he told was taken from a play by Somerset Maugham (quoted as an epigraph to John O'Hara's novel *Appointment in Samarra*) and told of a merchant from Baghdad who sees Death in the marketplace make a "threatening gesture" at him and so rides off to Samarra to escape his fate. When Death is asked why the threatening gesture had been made, Death replies that it wasn't a threatening gesture at all but a "start of surprise." Death explains: "I was astonished to see him here in Baghdad, for I have an appointment with him tonight—in Samarra." The reason the fable had been inserted—a late addition—was because I had seen on television *How the Grinch Stole Christmas* narrated so eloquently by Boris that I decided I could not make a film with Karloff and not have him tell some sort of extended tale. Then why, his expression seemed to say, was I panning the room while he was speaking? So I said, "Or maybe we could just start way back, holding all five of us, and then slowly, as you're talking, dolly into a big close-up of you." Boris nodded. "That sounds better," he said.

While the camera and the lighting were being set up, I asked Boris if he perhaps wanted some cue cards set up off camera so that he could read the speech. "You mean, Idiot Cards?" he asked, using the trade term. I nodded. "No," he said confidently, "that's all right. I *have* the lyrics." He always called his dialogue either "the lyrics" or "the jokes." When we were ready, I called action and Boris started, but we had to stop after a few lines because the crew had messed up floating a table out of the path of the oncoming camera. We began again. Everyone was tired—it was around one in the morning—yet this time, the table was moved without a hitch and Boris did the speech beautifully all the way through. Just before we rolled, I had whispered to him that after he finished the fable—and by

Boris Karloff (age seventy-nine) rehearsing a scene with me for Targets
*(1968), my first film, which Karloff and his wife always referred to as his
last. He lived less than two more years after we shot this.*

then we would be well into his close-up—he should give me a moment in
which the character silently thinks about his own death. Boris just nodded, and then did this superbly, too. I called out, very enthusiastically,
"Cut. Print! Great!" Suddenly the crew broke out in spontaneous
applause—something crews very rarely do—and I could see that Boris
was touched by their most genuine reaction. I thanked him profusely and
he seemed pleased. A moment later, I walked over to Evie, who was wiping her eyes and still looking a bit teary. "Do you know how long it's
been," she said quietly, "since a crew has applauded for Boris?"

The last time I saw Karloff was when we had a special screening of the
picture for him and Evie. Afterward, I could see they both had been
moved by the inherent tribute to him, and they thanked me very graciously and warmly. I thanked them. They were heading back to their
beloved home in Sussex, where a few months later, Boris died. I will
always be grateful to him: he showed me the finest example of true profes-
sionalism and grace I've seen to this day, now thirty-seven years later. As
actor or man, Karloff was a tough act to follow.

Born William Henry Pratt, November 23, 1887, Dulwich, England; died February 2, 1969, Sussex, England.

Selected sound features (with director):

1931: *The Criminal Code* (Howard Hawks); *Five Star Final* (Mervyn LeRoy); *The Yellow Ticket* (Raoul Walsh); *Frankenstein* (James Whale)

1932: *Scarface* (Hawks); *The Old Dark House* (Whale); *The Mask of Fu Manchu* (Charles Brabin); *The Mummy* (Karl Freund); *Night World* (Hobart Henley)

1933: *The Ghoul* (T. Hayes Hunter)

1934: *The Lost Patrol* (John Ford); *The House of Rothschild* (Alfred Werker); *The Black Cat* (Edgar G. Ulmer)

1935: *The Bride of Frankenstein* (Whale); *The Black Room* (Roy William Neill); *The Raven* (Lew Landers)

1936: *The Invisible Ray* (Lambert Hillyer); *The Walking Dead* (Michael Curtiz); *The Man Who Changed His Mind* (Robert Stevenson); *Charlie Chan at the Opera* (H. Bruce Humberstone)

1938: *The Invisible Menace* (John Farrow); *Mr. Wong, Detective* (William Nigh)

1939: *Son of Frankenstein* (Rowland V. Lee); *The Man They Could Not Hang* (Nick Grinde); *Tower of London* (Lee)

1940: *The Ape* (Nigh); *Before I Hang* (Grinde)

1941: *The Devil Commands* (Edward Dmytryk)

1942: *The Boogie Man Will Get You* (Landers)

1944: *House of Frankenstein* (Erle C. Kenton)

1945: *The Body Snatcher* (Robert Wise); *Isle of the Dead* (Mark Robson)

1946: *Bedlam* (Robson)

1947: *Lured* (Douglas Sirk); *The Secret Life of Walter Mitty* (Norman Z. McLeod); *Unconquered* (Cecil B. DeMille)

1953: *Abbott and Costello Meet Dr. Jekyll and Mr. Hyde* (Charles Lamont)

1958: *The Haunted Strangler* (Robert Day)

1962: *Corridors of Blood* (Day)

1963: *The Raven* (Roger Corman); *Black Sabbath* (Mario Bava); *The Comedy of Terrors* (Jacques Tourneur)

1967: *The Sorcerers* (Michael Reeves)

1968: *Targets* (P.B.)

15

JOHN CASSAVETES

Although I'm not quite sure where John Cassavetes and I met—probably it happened with a brief encounter in director Don Siegel's office at Universal Studios in the late sixties—he would over the next two decades evolve into one of my closest friends, especially during the last few years of his tragically short life. He died at age fifty-nine, in February 1989, and I have missed him terribly ever since. In most cineaste circles, John would more properly belong in a book about directors, but I have included him here because he was not only among his generation's most intelligent and individualistic actors, but because as a filmmaker, his work was really all about the actors' performances. Cassavetes' last name in Greek means "old house" (or "old home"), and though nobody was more profoundly modern in his approach to making pictures, John in life was a very old soul.

The first time I became aware of him was in 1955, seeing a taut little thriller called *The Night Holds Terror*—his first movie lead—in which he played a psychotic who holds a family hostage in their own home. To me then, he looked like a murderous Jerry Lewis, and I was riveted by the intensity and subterranean wit of the portrayal. The second time I saw him was in *Edge of the City* (1957), and I was even more impressed by his terrific work opposite Sidney Poitier, with whom he became lifelong friends. (He was always trying to get Sidney to do *Hamlet* onstage.) Then, three years later, suddenly he was the director-producer of a supposedly improvised (it wasn't entirely), decidedly offbeat independent film, *Shadows*, which became quite controversial in New York. Some loved it, some denounced it, no one seemed to be impartial. It was the second American feature to be self-financed, only Orson Welles' *Othello* (1952) having preceded it; both Welles and Cassavetes used their acting salaries to finance their films. But *Shadows*—in which John did not act—is officially considered the start of the independent film movement in the United States. As

John Cassavetes lines up a shot for Husbands *(1970), the first film
he directed, produced, wrote and also acted in. The first great film of
the seventies, it was generally either dismissed or misunderstood on its
initial release.*

it turned out, Cassavetes would become one of the most exciting and
influential of filmmakers, and the only one of his generation who could
really be called a poet.

As the sixties rolled on, my interest in him as an actor kept increasing:
I caught up with Don Siegel's modest juvenile-delinquent drama *Crime in
the Streets* (1956), and then saw Siegel's disturbing *The Killers* (1964) when
it came out, with its reverberating moment of Cassavetes socking Ronald
Reagan (in his last film). Unfortunately, by this time, John had in real life
socked producer Stanley Kramer for his re-cutting of Cassavetes' third
directorial effort, the uneven but poignant *A Child Is Waiting* (1963), and

had become quietly blacklisted in Hollywood circles. Both of John's studio movies (the other was 1962's forgettable *Too Late Blues*) had been deeply unpleasant experiences for him and he never really went back. For three years, he didn't work, and his wife, the beautiful and brilliant Gena Rowlands, brought home the bread for their burgeoning family of three children ("Don't let them outnumber you," John once warned me). Another Hollywood maverick, Robert Aldrich, broke the blacklist by hiring Cassavetes as one of *The Dirty Dozen* (1967), a huge box-office success which got John an Academy Award nomination as Best Supporting Actor, his only acting nomination. The role had started with only a few lines but Aldrich gladly allowed Cassavetes to improvise and expand his speeches, and when it was done, John pretty much stole the picture. Today his performance still seems remarkably fresh and unexpected at every moment, existing on a level of reality no one else quite gets near.

The following year, 1968, saw the release of the most popular movie John ever acted in—Roman Polanski's version of the best-selling horror novel *Rosemary's Baby*—as well as Cassavetes' own fourth film as director-writer-producer, his first mature work, and an extremely successful one too, again self-financed. *Faces* was not only his breakthrough picture, it had enormous impact and in effect started what came to be called the New Hollywood. An independent, grainy black-and-white (16mm blown up to 35mm), decidedly offbeat movie about middle-class people and their quietly desperate relationships, the work received three Oscar nominations, including one for his original screenplay. Though Cassavetes did not get along with Polanski (whose extremely hands-on direction of actors went totally against John's grain), he now could easily have had a lucrative career as a leading man in studio pictures. Instead, Cassavetes did not act in any other director's movie for eight years, devoting his time solely to his own films.

Before *Faces,* he had formed a production company with director Robert Altman for the two of them to make independent movies. Not long before he died, Cassavetes himself told me why this had fallen apart. It seems that Altman's secretary, despondent over an affair that went badly, had tried to commit suicide, and Altman had subsequently fired her. John said this so disturbed him that he essentially ended the business relationship, and then hired the young woman as an actress for *Faces*. This was Lynn Carlin and she received an Academy Award (Best Supporting Actress) nomination for her performance. And *Faces* today remains an electrifying experience.

It wasn't until *Husbands* (1970), Cassavetes' next film, that he combined all his talents, directing, writing and acting, in one picture—about three middle-class Americans' extreme reaction to the death of a buddy—and the result is one of his best, co-starring Ben Gazzara and Peter Falk, two equally quirky, gifted and essentially underrated actors with whom he would work memorably more than once. The interaction between them is exhilarating, each so vividly different from the other; also, revealingly, Cassavetes as an actor is always in peak form in his own work. *Husbands,* financed and distributed by Columbia, was not a box-office success, and neither was 1971's *Minnie and Moskowitz,* which Cassavetes wrote and directed for Universal, co-starring Gena Rowlands, Seymour Cassel (who had been nominated for Best Supporting Actor in *Faces*), and John in the small, brutal role of an ex-boyfriend of Gena's. Both *Husbands* and *Minnie and Moskowitz* only get better as the years go by.

Playing Minnie, Gena has a monologue in a drinking scene with an older woman friend (in reality Seymour Cassel's mother-in-law) which obliquely underlies a lot of what Cassavetes was doing in his pictures, and why. After the two women have discussed lovemaking and their continued desire for it, and men who crave to possess rather than love, Minnie comments that "the movies are never like that." She goes on:

> You know, I think that movies are a conspiracy . . . because they set you up. . . . They set you up from the time you're a little kid. They set you up to believe in everything . . . in ideals and strength and good guys and romance—and, of course, love . . . So . . . you go out, you start looking. Doesn't happen, you keep looking. You get a job . . . and you spend a lot of time fixing up things—your apartment and jazz. And you learn how to be feminine—you know, quotes: "feminine"? You learn how to cook . . . But there's no Charles Boyer in my life . . . I never even *met* a Charles Boyer. I never met Clark Gable. I never met Humphrey Bogart . . . I mean, they don't exist—*that's* the truth. But the movies set you up and no matter how bright you are, you believe it.

In essence, then, John was making movies that did not "set you up," that were attempting to be honest about the way people behave, that purposely tried not to be like all other movies in terms of construction, subject matter or execution. Cassavetes used to talk fondly about Frank Capra's pictures—he said, "Maybe there never *was* an America, maybe it was all Capra"—yet his own work could be called most decidedly anti-Capra.

It was around this time that I began to get to know John and Gena.

Cassavetes (with Lee Marvin) as a member of The Dirty Dozen *(1967),
an international success directed by Robert Aldrich, who encouraged
Cassavetes to improvise his own stuff, which got John his single
Oscar nomination (in acting) for Best Supporting Actor*

They were at an early running in New York of *What's Up, Doc?* and Cassavetes gave me my favorite one-line review of the film, but a lot of the
impact had to do with exactly where and how he said it. There were a few
celebrities in the audience, including Shirley MacLaine, I recall—a
slightly hard-to-please group. Less than a half-hour into the picture, when
it became clear that we had made a flat-out, unashamed, totally unredeemed slapstick farce, John's laughter rose boisterously above everyone
and he said, quite loudly, choking slightly on the words, and with considerable affection: "I *can't believe* he's *doing* this!" Everyone heard him, and
laughed. I thought the remark made the screening.

A couple of years later, John invited Cybill Shepherd and me to one of
the first showings of *A Woman Under the Influence* [1974], when it was still
a work in progress and the running time over four hours (final release version was 2 hours and 27 minutes). I always told John I liked all four hours
and never felt it was too long. The film was the most emotionally devastating experience I'd had since seeing the original Broadway production of
Eugene O'Neill's harrowing *Long Day's Journey into Night* in the late

fifties. I remember coming out of the screening room at what was then the American Film Institute (they had loaned John the room), having been terribly moved—both Cybill and I—and feeling the real world was somehow not nearly as real as what we'd just seen; squinting from the lights in the lobby, fighting to get some sense of equilibrium after an event that had rocked us in some very fundamental way. And there were John and Gena, both smiling expectantly. I couldn't understand why they were smiling. It was everything I could do not to burst into tears. I embraced John for a long moment, not able to speak; I think all I said was, "Oh, John—Jesus Christ . . ." And John said, brightly, "Did you like it?"

Slowly, I tried to say that there were no words to describe what an extraordinary work it was. Gena and John both looked pleased. Cybill tried to say something about Gena's transfixing, annihilating performance. Words were inadequate. They both smiled even more. Since it was among the most heartbreaking stories I'd ever seen, without it being depressing, I somehow felt their smiles inappropriate. But then, of course, they had made it. For the artists, the work could never be the wrenching emotional torrent it would be to viewers. Naturally, they had had to experience it in order to make it, but then couldn't possibly feel it as a movie the way an audience would. That's one of the ironies of being a picture-maker, and it was borne in on me that night in a way I had never quite understood before. When I could finally say something coherent, it was the same thing I would say after most of Cassavetes' movies: "I don't know how you do it, John. I just don't know how."

When he couldn't get a distributor interested, Cassavetes went out on a dangerous limb and self-distributed *A Woman Under the Influence,* laboring as passionately on that aspect as he had on the picture itself, designing ads, booking theaters all across the country, talking percentages. The film became one of the more successful art-house pictures in history, grossing an unheard-of $11 million. Perhaps his finest movie, it was nominated by the Academy for two major awards, Best Director and Best Actress, though they did not win. In the nineties, the film was correctly designated a "national treasure" by the Library of Congress.

Contrary to the common perception that Cassavetes improvised all his scripts with the actors, he actually did that just once, on *Shadows,* and then only partially. All the other films he directed were written (or, in two cases, co-written) by him. When asked once about the matter of improvising, Peter Falk—Gena's superb co-star in *Woman*—answered: "Who the hell can improvise lines that are that good!?" Actually, John elicited performances which seemed to be caught in improvisation because the lines were remarkably well written—in fact, Cassavetes dictated the first drafts of most of his scripts—to capture the cadence of regular people talking; and because he inspired amazing kinds of naked truth from his actors.

Another of the reasons why the improvisation myth has clung to Cassavetes is because of the deceptively haphazard construction of the pictures themselves. They seem not to be constructed at all, but rather to have grown out of a kind of daily free-floating inspiration. Yet this, too, is part of his remarkable ability to catch an uninhibited freshness; his unique genius at making what might be called life studies—personal, moving, necessary, strangely poetic, and among the finest achievements of the American screen—virtually alone in their insistence on artlessness as antidote and restorative.

The title character of *A Woman Under the Influence* is a perfect embodiment of the kind of person Gena's character was describing in *Minnie and Moskowitz,* one who had been "set up" by movies—who has, in fact, been driven to insanity by expectations—her own, and others' of her. There has never been an American film that more devastatingly reveals the terrible underside of a middle-class housewife-mother's existence.

After *Woman,* Cybill and I invited John and Gena over to our house for dinner a number of times, and they had us over to theirs. We met John's exuberant, outspoken mother, whom he adored (she acted awfully well in a number of her son's movies), and his quiet, self-effacing father (who died not long after), and Gena's witty, laid-back mother Lady Rowlands (who also was a player in a few of John's films). And their three rambunctious children—Nick (now a successful writer-director, and dedicated father), Xan (short for Alexandra, a feisty writer-director and devoted mother), and Zoe (an insightful writer and actress). Also, a number of close regulars, like actor Seymour Cassel, and Al Ruban, who photographed or co-produced, or both, most of John's films. Cassavetes often used his own home in his pictures—a rambling, comfortable, two-story New England–style old house off Mulholland Drive near Laurel Canyon. Often, he mortgaged it to pay for his movies; afterward, it was usually a cliffhanger if he'd ever pay off the mortgage. He always managed to. Like most real artists, money to John was not the goal in life, it was the means to certain ends, mostly his own work.

In the mid-seventies, while Orson Welles was staying at our house in Bel Air, I invited John and Gena over for an intimate dinner with him. Cassavetes later admitted to being totally intimidated by Welles, but you certainly never would have known: John completely monopolized the

John Cassavetes directs Gena Rowlands and Peter Falk during the shooting of probably Cassavetes' greatest film, A Woman Under the Influence *(1974), for which both he and Gena were nominated for Oscars they didn't win, but should have.*

conversation, a good deal of the time telling Orson in great detail the plot of his next picture, *The Killing of a Chinese Bookie* (1976; starring Ben Gazzara). The two of them had a lot in common, but their styles and approaches were so different that somehow the combination didn't quite take. They liked each other but neither seemed in a hurry to meet again; I don't think they ever did.

Unfortunately, *Bookie* was as big a flop in his self-distribution manner as *Woman* had been a hit. So much so that John blew all his reserves and went into heavy debt to make the next one: *Opening Night,* which he then could not quite afford to open. The picture languished on the shelf until after John's death when it eventually came out on home video, in a few festivals, and in theaters for special runnings.

Early in 1977, John had called me to say he was shooting *Opening Night* in some legitimate theater down on Wilshire Boulevard. It was supposed to be a Broadway opening, and he needed a few celebrity faces, so Peter Falk was going to come down as an extra—could I? "Anything for you, John," I said. The picture, he told me, was about theater people bringing a new play to New York, again starring Gena Rowlands—as the play's star on the verge of a nervous breakdown—and Ben Gazzara as the director, Joan Blondell as the playwright, Paul Stewart as the producer, Zohra Lampert as the director's wife, and Cassavetes himself as an entirely self-absorbed actor playing opposite Gena.

A Broadway opening probably meant fall or winter in New York, so I brought an overcoat. When Peter Falk spotted it, he said, "Where'd you get the coat?" I told him my thinking. Peter immediately called John over to say that I had a coat, and so he needed one. John whirled away, calling to an assistant to get Peter a coat. For my big shot backstage behind the curtain, all Cassavetes told me was to go on over to Gena, give her a kiss on the cheek and "tell her how great she was in the play." Then he did a little yelling to get everyone on their toes, pointing out that every single screwup was costing him personally. There was no rehearsal. Once he called out, "Action!" everything went quickly, in a kind of blur, a slew of people moving and talking at once. While I was having my intimate moment of praise for Gena, suddenly—without anyone having prepared me—Gazzara's character was introducing Zohra Lampert's character to me. "You know Peter Bogdanovich . . . ?" The joke was that Zohra is so stoked by Gena's opening-night performance that she's totally uninterested in meeting me; she just ignores the introduction and only gushes at Gena. And that's how the picture ends, though I didn't know when we shot it. (It was during the shooting of this sequence that I first met Ben Gazzara and, as a result, cast him in my next two films.)

Later, knowing John's financial situation with the movie, I offered him the use of my projection room at home so that he could screen dailies for himself and his crew and any actors he felt like bringing. He took me up on this and for a while they all came over; I sat in once or twice and it was fun. Then I called and asked if there was any second-unit work I could direct for him, and he said, yes, it'd be great if I could shoot a couple of shots of Gena and Joan Blondell in a car pulling into a garage. We knocked off three little setups in an hour or two at a garage in downtown L.A., and John used to praise me by wildly exaggerating and saying it would have taken him half a day.

Cassavetes has said, "I won't make shorthand films, because I don't want to manipulate audiences into assuming quick, manufactured truths." *Opening Night,* which is still one of his least-known pictures, is a perfect example of this credo. There are certainly neither quick nor manipulated truths, and what dominates is the mystery of personality, and the often unfathomably complex motivations of artists. The struggle to open the play depends on these intangibles. This could be called Cassavetes' anti–*All About Eve*. The adoring fan who becomes a threat in that picture, shrewdly calculating her way to stardom, here turns into a weirdly troubling, clearly disturbed fanatic accidentally killed in an auto accident on a rainy night while trying to maintain contact with Gena's character.

This tragic encounter haunts her throughout the rest of the movie, the young woman's troubled ghost even appearing to her, fighting with her— only one of numerous obstacles Gena's star has to overcome to make it through opening night. Others include her fear of aging, discomfort with the role, even active dislike of the playwright's creation, conflicts with the director and especially with her co-star (played by John). The terrible whirlpool of emotions that swirl around a theatrical production are beautifully evoked. The main obstacle, of course, is a paralyzing fear, and the picture eloquently dramatizes John's comment: "You can defeat fear through humor, through pain, through honesty, bravery, intuition, and through love in the truest sense."

Again, all the performances are not so much acted as caught. Everyone feels absolutely real, and Gena is magnificent in an extremely challenging role, her characterization as naked and memorable as her amazing work in every one of Cassavetes' masterpieces. If any other director and actress have together repeatedly achieved such emotional depths, I don't know about them. That John cast himself as the least understanding or sensitive character in the picture—and that he plays it so convincingly—is probably the slyest inside joke in this singular, distinctive look at show business people. One of the biggest kicks is the extended sequence of Gena and John acting together brilliantly onstage, supposedly improvising on the opening night, altering the play and making it work better than the written text: a Pirandello-like box within a box—the actor as author.

A year or two later, John called and asked me to come over for the reading of a script he'd written called *One Winter Night*, in which an entire Spanish-American family, except for one little boy, is wiped out in a mob hit, and an ex–gun moll reluctantly finds herself saving the kid as the killers go after him. But Cassavetes felt the basically melodramatic thriller material wasn't really his thing, that he had written the script to make some money by selling it, not to make it himself. So he tried to persuade me to direct it. He said I knew how to do this sort of thing. Besides being flattered, I replied that actually he was the only one who could make its complicated dualities work. He still tried for some time to convince me I was better for it and then, eventually, not very happily, he gave in and

*Gena Rowlands and John Cassavetes as actors who can't stand
each other, during one of their extraordinary stage sequences in*
Opening Night *(1977), the last of John's own productions,
finished but unreleased for more than a decade*

agreed (when Columbia bought it) to shoot the picture himself if he could
use Gena in the lead. The studio said he could, but only if Barbra Streisand
wouldn't do it. As it turned out, Barbra was still annoyed at John for turning down her offer for him to direct the rock 'n' roll *A Star Is Born* (1976)
and also, justifiably, felt nobody would believe her as a mob doll, so she
passed, Gena was cast and, fortunately, John made one of his most financially successful and expressively subversive works, finally titled *Gloria*.

Long after John died, Gena would tell me that the main reason he
hadn't wanted to do the movie was because of the terrible massacre of that
whole family which sets the picture's story in motion. But one of the
things that makes the final film so effective is precisely this tension
between Cassavetes' poetic temperament and the devastatingly violent
material he was treating. Ultimately, the picture is one of a kind in the
way it turns upside down everything the normal gangster shoot-'em-up
does. That an attractive woman is the strongest yet most deeply compas-
sionate figure in the whole piece—a kind of feminine variation on John

Wayne, Humphrey Bogart and James Cagney combined—is also what gives the work its unusual distinctiveness and resonance. It might well have been adopted as a centerpiece for feminism: in a cold and out-of-control universe—an increasingly urban jungle without rules or honor—the woman as a kind of prehistoric archetype of both destruction and salvation is certainly a vivid statement.

And nobody could have portrayed this better than Gena Rowlands. Her "Gloria" and her "Woman" (. . . *Under the Influence*) are the quintessential two sides—strong and broken—of the modern female psyche. In *Gloria,* John presented a New York City never seen quite in this way: ominous, dangerous, unpredictable, a microcosm of the world at large. From the six-year-old boy, played by John Adames, he elicited a striking performance. Director-actor Vittorio De Sica (*Bicycle Thief, Shoe Shine*) once said you're not a director until you've directed a child. Well, without doubt, Cassavetes was a director like no other.

As it happened, John was shooting *Gloria* in New York as I was preparing to shoot *They All Laughed* there with Ben Gazzara and Audrey Hepburn. I came to one of their last cast and crew dinners, which was rollicking, and also met John one night for a few minutes while he was still shooting and before I had begun. His driver invited me out of a restaurant and into John's waiting limousine for a few intense minutes. Mainly, he complained viciously about his "lousy" crew, called them all the names in the book, cursed them a number of times, and then laughed his most diabolical Cassavetes laugh, and said, "Fuck 'em!," that he would prevail over them all in the end, "the bastards!" Of course, he did.

Not long before this, John and I had almost made a picture together, another one he'd written called *Dancing,* about two sailors on the town in Las Vegas with two showgirls; the sailors were going to be John and Peter Falk, the showgirls, John proposed, would be Cybill and Raquel Welch. For some probably obscure reason, I didn't feel that I should direct this, and suggested producing it instead, with Ivan Passer directing (he'd recently done a film with Cybill called *Silver Bears,* and she had liked him a lot). John, Ivan and I had a couple of script meetings at my place, discussing sometimes heatedly the various permutations of the story, but we didn't agree, any of us, on a couple of central issues, and, finally, I could tell that John and Ivan were not a good mix. Looking back, it's one of my major regrets that I didn't just direct the film myself; with that cast alone, it could've been awfully interesting and probably a lot of fun.

It was during a long script conference for *Dancing* that I noticed John

John Cassavetes himself photographs a scene with Ben Gazzara for his production of Husbands *(1970), among his best and most personal works, co-starring Peter Falk.*

finish off by himself a fifth of whiskey. Never having been a drinker, I had no idea what this indicated, but the key thing I remember is that John never even slightly slurred his words as the evening progressed into the small hours, nor in any other way seemed inebriated. He would tell me a few years later that this was one of his biggest problems with booze—he couldn't *get* drunk—which is why he drank too much; and eventually developed the cirrhosis of the liver which would kill him.

In 1981, Cassavetes took his first turn at directing for the stage. He mounted three productions in repertory at a small ninety-seat, odd-shaped theater in Hollywood, starring Peter Falk in a kind of courtroom drama John had written called *Knives;* Gena in a drama, *The Third Day Comes;* and Jon Voight and Gena as brother and sister in a lovely play by John's close friend Ted Allan, *Love Streams,* rewritten with numerous suggestions by Cassavetes. Because of a tragedy in our family—my fiancée, Dorothy Stratten, had been murdered in August 1980—seeing two of these productions were the first times I'd ventured out of my house in months, and they were quite astonishing. And strangely beautiful. John's direction in this medium was every bit as unorthodox and original as his work in the movies. Gena, Peter and Voight were all superb. *Knives* was mesmerizing, with Peter never off, and you can never get tired of Peter Falk. I missed *Third Day*, but *Love Streams* was one of the most exciting productions I've ever seen in the theater: a powerfully moving dramatic piece but with an enormous amount of laughter—even a large furry dog played by an actor in an animal suit. Instead of being ridiculous (the dog player was exceptional), this worked within the highly stylized, yet also somehow realistic, conception John spread brilliantly across a Cinema-Scope-shaped stage. Voight acted with more than a touch of characteristically neurotic Cassavetes intensity, which I had never seen him quite do before, and it increased both his charm and his danger. A few years later, when Cassavetes was already very sick, he directed his last work of any kind, another stage piece he had written, *A Woman of Distinction*, starring Gena Rowlands, more amazing than ever as a bag lady. John had to direct most of it lying down on a cot; nevertheless, the production was uniquely moving.

During the early eighties, John did a lot of acting in other people's movies so as to earn back what he'd lost on *Bookie, Opening Night*, and the first three plays. A number of artlessly fascinating performances ensued in more mainstream, though still offbeat, pictures like *Whose Life Is It Anyway?* (1981; John Badham), based on a Broadway success; *Tempest* (1982; Paul Mazursky), loosely based on Shakespeare; and *Marvin and Tige* (1983; Eric Weston), perhaps his most touching portrayal until his acting swan song in the movie version of *Love Streams* (1984). I remember phoning him while he was on location in Philadelphia for *Marvin and Tige* and he admitted feeling kind of lonely, watching TV in his motel room. I had called to tell him the basic plot for the first movie idea I'd had since Dorothy's death. Because I trusted him as an artist and friend, and wanted him to play the lead role, John was the first person I tried the idea on, and he was enormously encouraging. The central part is a self-involved, somewhat self-destructive, but talented filmmaker-actor who has been married a number of times, has several daughters, and has been brought low because of the sudden death by plane accident of his current, and favorite, wife.

John and I talked for over an hour that initial time, and he kept saying, "Just write it down, for Christ's sake, will ya? Will you write it down as you told me?" Which I did eventually, though he had to prompt me two or three more times. We would speak of this comedy-drama-fantasy—there were ghosts involved—until he died. Long after it was apparent that he could no longer play the part, he read a couple of poor early drafts, and made a key suggestion: I should find a way to remove as much of the responsibility for exposition from the actors (and there was quite a lot of it necessary). "Take the heat off the actors," John wisely advised; there's nothing duller for an actor to play than expositional dialogue. One of the last things John said to me before he died was that I had "better *make* that picture" because, alluding to the ghosts in the story, "I'm going to *be there!*"

John and I started talking more often after the call in Philadelphia, but we didn't see each other because I rarely went out, and he was shooting a lot. As the film production of *Love Streams* geared up at a low budget—again to star Gena Rowlands and Jon Voight as sister and brother—I went through his frustrations with Voight, who suddenly had become difficult after being, as John put it, "a pussycat" during the play's production. The final straw came, John would tell me, when Voight told Cassavetes he would do the picture only if he, Voight, could direct it. Very reluctantly and unhappily, then, John had to let Voight go and, at this late stage, play the part himself. He does give, however, one of his subtlest, most brilliantly lucid and layered performances; and he and Gena as brother and sister are magical. When they dance together in long-shot to the tune of "Where Are You" (one of John's favorite popular songs), it is an indelibly heartbreaking image of filial affection, and of the two actors' transcendent, ardent love for each other.

While he was filming *Love Streams,* John called late one afternoon to ask if I could come in the next day and help him with a scene he was going to shoot with himself as an actor. I said, with obvious disbelief, that he certainly didn't need *my* help in directing himself. No, John said, it was a difficult dialogue scene between him and Diahnne Abbott, and he really wanted me to please come over tomorrow to help him with it. I protested yet again, and his voice dropped several degrees as he said, "You mean to tell me, you, as a friend, are *not* going to come down here and help me out tomorrow?" There was disappointment, discouragement, and incredulity in his tone. OK, OK, I said, I'll come down, but you don't *need* me, or words to that effect. I was so confused by the request, both flattered on the one hand and still disbelieving that he had any real problem with the scene, but thinking maybe he was just feeling insecure, or God knows what; yet when he put it the way he did, I simply couldn't refuse. I realized driving over that it was going to be the first time I had been on a movie set since Dorothy's death, a month after we finished shooting *They All Laughed* in July 1980. It was now 1983.

The next morning, arriving at his home on Woodrow Wilson Drive, I was immediately confronted with a small, bustling film crew getting ready to shoot in John's driveway. I had to be parked out of the shot, which was supposed to bring Diahnne Abbott in her car up to the front of the house, where she would stop, get out, walk to the front door and ring the bell. Al Ruban saw me first and yelled out, "Jesus, now we can finally get some work done quickly around here!" Cassavetes and the rest of the crew gave a warm greeting—John introducing Diahnne as he handed me the two or three pages for the scene at the door, when John's character opens it in answer to her ringing. They stand there and talk for a couple of pages—a good, clear scene, obviously with a lot of subtext and innuendo, which I, of course, couldn't grasp entirely because I hadn't read the script. John asked me to set up the shots necessary for Diahnne's arrival while she and he started rehearsing inside. Having looked over the area, I told Al I thought we could do it all in one panning shot. He was happy about that, and set up the camera and lighting while I joined John and Diahnne in his living room. The three of us rehearsed for a while, but they seemed to have it down perfectly, as far as I could see. I can't remember suggesting much of anything, but gave out some praise, saying the scene played for me. John asked how many angles I thought we could do it in, and I said it seemed to me like four—two different sizes of John at the door and two of Diahnne.

John nodded. "See, that's why I needed you—I'd have said we needed seven or eight or something." He was very affable and sweet, if slightly preoccupied by the scene he had to play. I noticed his stomach seemed a bit bloated, though the rest of him wasn't fat at all. For a long while, John would tell people this was some kind of hernia, but actually it was an early indication of the cirrhosis. Eventually, while the rest of him shrank, his belly would balloon out to the size of a nine-months'-pregnant woman. On this lovely day of *Love Streams,* though, we didn't think of such things; or maybe John already knew, I don't know. Personally, I was feeling a trifle tentative directing *his* material, but when I suggested Diahnne pick a flower for him as she walked to the door, John leapt on it and endorsed the idea. After doing a couple of takes of the pull-up, both good, we moved to the doorway and shot first Diahnne's side, then John's. They were both excellent, of course, the crew was swift; it was over before I knew it, and painless. Much as I had felt slightly superfluous, everyone was very sweet to me as I departed. I embraced John and he thanked me. I thanked *him* for getting me out of the house.

Only later did I realize that this was exactly why he had done the whole thing—to get me out of my house. We had been talking quite a bit over the last couple of years while I wrote a painful memoir about Dorothy. Not until I saw the completed movie, about a year after he finished it (I had meanwhile been shooting *Mask*), did I realize fully what John had done for me. He had brought me back to the world of the living that I understood—a movie set is a kind of second home to a directing veteran.

From the last part of 1985 to February of 1989 when Cassavetes died, we saw a great deal of each other. We almost made a picture together. I had first heard he was ill while prepping *Mask*, which led me to remember that his son Nick was now a good actor and would be right to play a biker, so we hired him; he had a few scenes opposite Cher, and was awfully good, and easy to work with, too. Unfortunately, I had a lot of problems with my picture in post-production, and at the same time John did Peter Falk a favor and came in to finish *Big Trouble* (1985) when the original director had to be fired. The film was a follow-up in the same vein as the hit comedy *The In-Laws* (1979), both co-starring Falk and Alan Arkin; the studio wasn't happy with the result and re-cut it. John regretted doing the movie at all, though he got much-needed bucks. Later, he would say the film shouldn't be listed among his works. Still, I thought parts of it were hilariously funny, and somehow felt a lot of John's dark yet exuberant humor, despite the screenplay and the poor re-editing, like some strange mix of Martin and Lewis and Molière. In fact, John loved silly humor, slapstick, and low comedy, and admitted to be a sucker for Jerry Lewis, with whom he hung out a few times in John's early days at Paramount. Jerry would recall, fondly, "John was a pushover for a laugh—one of the great laughers."

Over the phone, John told of getting his routine checkup for insurance on the picture. For many years, it was the same doctor at every studio, and he had examined Cassavetes often. "When he saw me," John said, "the doctor broke down!" He imitated the man's anguished, tearful tone: "Oh, no; oh, no, John, not you! Oh, God!" John broke up laughing. "This is what the doctor says to me: 'Oh, God, John, not *you*!' " He laughed even louder. I did, too, but then said, "That's not funny, John." Though I'd heard he was ill, I didn't know the seriousness of it; this was John's way of telling me. "I don't know," John insisted, "it's pretty funny," and laughed infectiously again. Supposedly, the doctor covered for John, and didn't report the gravity of his condition. The rigors of shooting didn't help, though he had conclusively stopped drinking and smoking.

Toward the end of 1985, after I'd had a rough time—for a number of physical, professional and personal reasons—I went for a while on a strict diet of raw fruits and vegetables, and drinking only distilled water. So the next time John and I saw each other was lunch at his place when I brought over two honeydew melons for myself to eat and my own water in a half-gallon glass bottle. Gena and John teased me about that from then on (and we had lunch several times): "Bogdo came over with two melons and water!" Bogdo was John's and Gena's nickname for me. Only they and their children have ever called me that.

We would sit out on his covered porch or in the living room and talk up a storm. John looked terrible—emaciated body, bloated stomach—but was always fun to speak with; the conversation was forever real and never bullshit. We were like a couple of underground conspirators in a war that had been going on for decades out there, a war of which we both were veterans by then. So our talks invariably picked up in the middle, as if we had just left off speaking minutes before. There was such unlabored spontaneity with John that although the exact substance of our conversations may fade, what remains is a sense of having gone through life with him those last three years, and of the time being full and enriching.

John was always planning several pictures at once and writing scripts to the end. He would excitedly tell me the plots. One or two he almost made. There was the play *Begin the Beguine* (he loved that song and the title), about a couple of guys—to be played by Gazzara and Falk—who spend most of their time in a hotel room ordering up hookers over the phone. The girls come in, one after the other, but the only thing the guys want to do with them is talk. That was the play (and maybe a movie): two guys and various hookers speaking about all their lives. They read it a couple of times, went to New York, but things didn't work out.

Soon after, I had dinner with the three of them, and Gena, and Ben's wife, Elke, and my then-wife, Louise Stratten, at an Italian restaurant in Hollywood which John used to love. We went there together a number of times, Cassavetes totally unperturbed walking around with his stomach glaringly distended. What a riotous, lovely meal it was, with the stars of *Husbands* together again, all three picking on each other in traditional ways, always a trifle edgy, the humor sardonic or just silly for a second. John kidded them on the square about not "being available" to start *Begin the Beguine* as a picture till next winter or something. The implication that he didn't really have all that long to wait around hung in the air unspoken, but Peter and Ben both took it in with sheepish looks. Yet, of course, John understood: they had to earn a living.

The really sad experience was on *She's DeLovely*, another Cassavetes script. John had Sean Penn ready to play the lead role of a pretty violent young man who loves the girl far too much and she him—a kind of street-wise tragic romance which led to trouble, and a passionate redemption. One afternoon, John called to ask a favor. He was prepping this picture with Sean Penn, but knew he couldn't get insurance as director, unless another director was there as backup in case of emergency. Would I be that guy? Certainly, I said. John thanked me profusely, while I told him it would be an honor and I was confident I wouldn't be needed. We made a date for him to pick me up in his car and drive over to where Penn was rehearsing a play so the two of us could meet. A day or so later, he drove himself over in his long, old Lincoln convertible, his belly touching the steering wheel, the rest of him now gaunt; he had allowed his hair to go completely gray for years. (John used to color his hair black for pictures and let it go gray in-between. When I asked him about this once, he said, "Of course I do, I'm an actor!") He insisted on driving, and took us way downtown as we spoke enthusiastically about his movie. Sean Penn acted a bit suspicious of me, and was less than communicative. John did most of the talking. Rehearsals had to go on, so we didn't stay very long. Driving back, the talk was mainly about how he was going to get the money for the picture.

Further meetings ensued—with agents, and a couple of production outfits, especially Norman Lear's, which expressed a lot of interest. But everything fell apart when Sean decided he was going to do *Casualties of War* (1989) first, because it was big money, and off he went. It was a long shoot and by the time he'd get back, it was unlikely Cassavetes would be fit enough. To me, John was just disappointed with Sean. What I didn't know at the time, and didn't discover until long after John's death, was that Penn's decision to take *Casualties* was at least partially because John wouldn't consider anyone else but me as his backup. Evidently, Penn wasn't thrilled with my being the one to take over a Cassavetes picture, John got angry and told him it was me or nobody, and Sean preferred nobody. So John never made the film. After he died, Nick Cassavetes eventually concluded a deal with Penn and directed him in John's script, re-titled *She's So Lovely* (because of exorbitant costs to the Cole Porter Estate on the use of the word "DeLovely," which Porter had coined for his song, "It's DeLovely," another of John's favorites). Sean had wanted to direct the movie himself but Gena and Nick owned the rights to the script. Reportedly, Nick and Sean had a rocky time of it during the shooting and all through post-production. Perhaps the result didn't please either of them, I don't know, but I never could bring myself to see it. I remember a reading of another Cassavetes script, with Richard Dreyfuss, that was funny and promising, Richard being brilliantly skillful in his rendition of the lead. But nothing ever came of that, either, and John didn't make another film. Except in his head and on paper.

Cassavetes was amusingly stoic about his terminal illness. One time, commenting on this in relation to his drinking, he said, with aggressive ambiguity, "Fuck 'em if they can't take a joke!" And then he laughed, mischievously as ever.

Sometimes we would talk for a long time over the phone, especially while Gena was away in New York doing Woody Allen's *Another Woman* (1988), an obvious reference to *A Woman Under the Influence*. The shooting schedule kept lengthening, and both John and Gena were miserable apart, counting the days, and then, repeatedly, having to re-count them. They spoke for hours at a time. John would tell me how miserable they both were about the delays and postponements. One time, after she finally got back, I went over for lunch again. While John was washing up, Gena took me on a tour of her vegetable and flower garden. I'd never seen Gena thinner, or more anxious, though she was covering it well by proudly showing me her plants and how well they were doing. She smiled quite often but there was a sad desperation in her eyes. Walking around the side of the hill on which the garden lay, she moved quickly, like a teenager; glad to be out of the house a moment, yet wanting to go back soon.

Except about Gena's absence, John never once complained to me or in any way expressed suffering. He was always feisty, and his voice never sounded any different. On a visit to the dentist, he had a bad reaction to the treatment and, because of his condition, almost died. He told me about it the next day as though it had sort of happened to him but more to another guy. "That was a close one," he said with a mixture of awe and astonishment at the danger he had passed.

Less than a year before his death, I invited him to an early screening of my worst film, a comedy starring Rob Lowe, mangled on top of everything else by the producers; with Gena and others from the family, John came. I could tell he was trying to like it—they all were—but the film just didn't really play. Afterward, John walked over, hugged me and said it wasn't my "best work," but not to worry. I appreciated his candor, and behind that John knew I'd agreed to the picture only for the money, and that it had been pure hell to make. Shortly after, there was a writers' strike and Cassavetes encouraged me in my decision to quit a picture because of the producer, and focus on doing a screenplay based on Larry McMurtry's 1987 novel *Texasville,* a sequel to *The Last Picture Show,* book and movie. He was the first to read the initial draft and the next revision, very encouraging and enthusiastic about each pass. What a rare pal he was, always honest, without even a hint of envy, jealousy, self-pity, competitiveness, judgment—or any of the other things that ruin friendships.

Early in 1989, John called to say that *Opening Night* had been invited to open Holland's popular and prestigious Rotterdam Film Festival in the first week of February. They had offered all expenses for John or Gena or both, but he couldn't go and she wouldn't leave him. Might I fly there for him, and represent him after the screening, explain why he wasn't there, and thank them? Of course, I'd go. John said the festival would pay for Louise to go along. We had just got married, having caused quite a stir in the press.

We spoke a few more times before Louise and I went to Rotterdam. The night before we left he asked me to give his regards to both Rotterdam and Amsterdam—where he had suggested we go after the festival and take a long weekend at a hotel, also on the festival. John had arranged this little vacation for us, he said, because festivals themselves are usually work for someone representing a picture, with so many interviews to give. This was especially so for a new Cassavetes film, John being generally very highly regarded as a filmmaker all over Europe (far more than in America), certainly among the Dutch. We said so-long, we'd see each other as soon as we got back.

On the night, to a packed house—some people seated in the aisles and many standing in back—I gave a little introductory talk about *Opening Night,* and said I'd be happy to answer questions after the screening. The picture played terrifically. I couldn't wait to tell John how "with it" the audience was all the way through, and that the weird sequence where Gena fights the fan's ghost also had worked, that he was right to keep it in, though I had once told him I thought cutting it wouldn't hurt. John had asked me, abruptly, "You think I should cut the ghost scene?" And I had said I thought that might be a good idea, might make things simpler for people. There was a beat or two and John said, "No, I'm gonna keep it in . . ."—almost as if he'd been testing me. I was going to go on to him about why this sequence, in fact, worked so well to put us in Gena's shoes, to better understand her fear and guilt. When the picture was over, there was tumultuous applause, and I felt a little silly going up there, having

*John Cassavetes and Gena Rowlands as brother and sister in the
last of Cassavetes' own films as director (and co-writer, with Ted Allan),*
Love Streams *(1984), a deeply human drama of some lost people
in an out-of-control universe. In John's amazing stage version,
the large dog was played by an actor.*

been in the movie for about two minutes; but I did, and applauded with
the audience, answered as many questions as I could—nobody left—told
a few Cassavetes anecdotes, all through a translator, though a lot of the
people understood English quite well. It was all very pleasant. Right after
I stepped down, and the audience started to leave, the festival director
took me aside and said they'd just been notified that, a couple of hours
ago, John Cassavetes had died.

The news was so shocking that I didn't really react for quite a while.
Apparently, he had gotten very ill, couldn't breathe, was taken to the hospital, where things got only worse. He was in considerable pain. Gena was
with him until the end. He had died right around the time we started to
show the film. So maybe his ghost had made it to the screening after all.
Certainly I felt his presence throughout, as everyone did, as everyone
always does when seeing his films, because only John could've made them.

The private memorial would be in a couple of days but it would have meant missing the weekend Cassavetes had arranged for us in Amsterdam. I could hear him telling me, for Christ's sake, to stay there and have a good time, the memorial will all be funny stories about him! So we stayed in Holland, and heard what happened at the memorial from Gena, Peter, Ben and Al, that it was a lot of very funny anecdotes about John, everyone breaking up. I was asked to host, and help put together, an official tribute to John at the Directors Guild of America, which I did, and again, it was mostly laughs. Gena didn't go to that one. She said she couldn't handle seeing the clips of John. Some years later, I would be behind Gena as she entered one of many profoundly deserved tributes to her; on the screen were she and John in their first TV drama together, both very young, thin, gorgeous. Gena froze in her tracks, and stared at the screen in amazement. "God!" she said out loud. "We were both so *young*!" and she turned her back to the screen and waited till it was over. "I can't look at that," she said.

In Amsterdam on the weekend he died, of course, like a lot of people from there to Los Angeles and around the world, we were thinking of John Cassavetes, each of us in our own way. And from February 1989 on, as Nick Cassavetes put it to me in the summer of 2002—"Jesus, thirteen years!" And he continued, "The world's sure a darker place since then, isn't it?"

Referring to my ghost picture, I always remember that John had promised to be around, and since he always kept his promises, I *have* indeed felt his presence now and again. Once was in the morning prior to the DGA tribute when I could hear John's voice telling me some things I should be doing during the presentation. I said, out loud, "You're still directing!" and in my head I could hear him say, "What'd'ya think!?"

Born John Cassavetes, December 9, 1929, New York, NY; died February 3, 1989, Los Angeles, CA.

Selected starring features (with director):

1955: *The Night Holds Terror* (Andrew L. Stone)

1956: *Crime in the Streets* (Don Siegel)

1957: *Edge of the City* (Martin Ritt)

1958: *Saddle the Wind* (Robert Parrish)

1964: *The Killers* (Siegel)

1967: *The Dirty Dozen* (Robert Aldrich)

1968: *Rosemary's Baby* (Roman Polanski); *Machine Gun McCain* (Giuliano Montaldo)

1970: *Husbands* (Cassavetes)
1971: *Minnie and Moskowitz* (Cassavetes)
1976: *Mikey and Nicky* (Elaine May)
1977: *Opening Night* (Cassavetes)
1981: *Whose Life Is It Anyway?* (John Badham)
1982: *Tempest* (Paul Mazursky)
1983: *Marvin and Tige* (Eric Weston)
1984: *Love Streams* (Cassavetes)

Other films he directed:

1960: *Shadows*
1962: *Too Late Blues*
1963: *A Child Is Waiting*
1968: *Faces*
1974: *A Woman Under the Influence*
1976: *The Killing of a Chinese Bookie*
1980: *Gloria*
1985: *Big Trouble*

16

CHARLIE CHAPLIN

Told once that as a director his camera angles were not very interesting, Charlie Chaplin responded, "They don't have to be interesting—*I am* interesting." If ever there was an actor's remark, that's it, and so Charlie Chaplin is included in this book, though, of course, he also wrote, directed, produced (and even scored) virtually all his own work. At the peak of his success, from about 1917 through the mid-thirties, Charlie was the most popular, deeply beloved human being on earth, maybe in the history of the world. His silhouette as the Tramp is one of the most famous images of the twentieth century.

On the screen, I was first introduced to him by my father, who took me to see some of his shorts (1914–18) at the Museum of Modern Art in the mid-forties when I was about five, but I didn't meet him in person until 1972, when Charlie was eighty-three and had only five more years to live. We had a few exchanges, and I even visited him and his beautiful last wife, Oona O'Neill (Eugene O'Neill's youngest daughter), at their imposing villa in the hills above Vevey, Switzerland, and would ultimately direct the shooting for a documentary that included what was probably the last shot of him walking off (with Oona) into the sunset.

Chaplin had walked off into his own final cinema sunset way back in 1936 with the by-now legendary ending of *Modern Times:* the Little Tramp and the Gamin (his third wife, Paulette Goddard) heading away from us, hand in hand, down the long, long road into the future, and the past. Charlie had invented and developed his immortal Tramp character during the first two years of his life in movies, having started in pictures in 1914, with Mack Sennett's resonant Keystone company (after coming to America with a popular British vaudeville troupe). Within the initial year—either as actor or, rather quickly, actor-director—he was seen in thirty-five two-reel (twenty-minute) comedies, though sometimes in supporting

*Charlie Chaplin and six-year-old Jackie Coogan in one of the climactic
sequences of* The Kid *(1921), Chaplin's first feature and the most
successful picture made since D. W. Griffith's landmark* The Birth
of a Nation *six years before*

roles. By 1915, he was already popular enough to be wooed away with
much more money by Essanay—from $175 a week at Keystone to $1,250 a
week at Essanay (plus a $10,000 bonus). In one year he made fifteen
shorts—including gems like *The Bank, A Night at the Show, Carmen* (his
first to exceed two reels), and, announcing what was established by then,
The Tramp.

Just over a year later, his success had become so great that the ante
went up again when Mutual gave him an as yet unprecedented $10,000 a

week (plus a $150,000 bonus) to make twelve two-reelers yearly with complete artistic control. This resulted in his first masterpieces, including such classics as *Easy Street, One A.M., The Pawnshop, The Cure, The Rink,* and *The Vagabond* (1916–17). In 1918 First National hired him for eight films at one million dollars; most of those ran to three or four reels, memorable for things like the World War I satire *Shoulder Arms,* and *A Dog's Life* and *The Pilgrim.* His first feature, *The Kid* (1921), became the second-biggest-grossing film of all time after the epoch-making *The Birth of a Nation* (1915), which more people saw in theaters than any film in history. In 1923, Charlie became co-founder—along with Douglas Fairbanks, Mary Pickford, and D. W. Griffith—of United Artists, for which he produced all his subsequent feature masterworks, such as *The Gold Rush* (1925), *The Circus* (1928), *City Lights* (1931), and *Modern Times,* the four final Tramp movies.

Using dialogue for the first time, he made only three more, progressively less popular, pictures before being asked not to come back to America: *The Great Dictator* (1940), *Monsieur Verdoux* (1947) and *Limelight* (1952). Orson Welles used to say it was not until *after* the poor reviews had come out on *Monsieur Verdoux* (and equally bad box office) that Chaplin added, following his own screenplay credit: "Based on an idea by Orson Welles." My parents always used to say—echoing a popular European sentiment—that if only Chaplin had made *The Great Dictator* three or four years earlier, Hitler might have been laughed out of existence and World War II prevented. In fact, Chaplin had been showing off his Hitler impression at Hollywood parties for years before he ever did it for the camera.

In 1952, informed by the State Department (while traveling by ship to Europe) that because of moral and political reasons—he was a suspected Communist and had just been married for the fourth time, to a teenager (Oona O'Neill)—he would not be admitted back into the country which had made him rich, but of which he had never become a citizen, Chaplin vowed never to return. Having sold his share of U.A. in 1955, Chaplin made—ten years apart—only two more pictures in his life, both shot in England (where he'd been born in 1889), and both not really worth including in the canon: *A King in New York* (1957), his last starring role, and *A Countess from Hong Kong* (1967) with Marlon Brando and Sophia Loren obviously trying to mimic Chaplin much as child-actor Jackie Coogan had in *The Kid;* they were not successful at it.

For twenty years, from 1915 through 1936, Chaplin held his audience—which was the whole world—captivated and bewitched to laughter and tears. *Modern Times* was his last great success, after which he steadily lost touch with the very pulse of the people. Even when he re-edited and re-issued two of his greatest silent successes (with both critics and public), Chaplin essentially destroyed the artistic integrity and brilliance of his original work: the 1942 version of *The Gold Rush,* with music and added commentary by Chaplin, is dreadful, and the 1969 revised version of *The Circus,* with Chaplin singing a terribly corny ballad, is no better. Unfortunately, these are the only authorized forms the Chaplin Estate lets us see. And it's ironic that this essentially silent movie star made two of his best features after sound had well taken over and he had bravely refused to conform: *City Lights* and *Modern Times.*

Only Chaplin's fifth feature-length film, *City Lights,* was released early in the third full year of all-talking pictures, and though it had numerous sound effects, a synchronized score, several sound jokes including some sardonically squeaky babble at the beginning, it is essentially a silent movie, the second to last one made. His own *Modern Times* (1936) takes honors as the last—although some dialogue is heard, and Charlie does sing one entire song—albeit of French-accented gibberish. Everybody had warned Chaplin that *City Lights* was a terrible risk, since, while he was shooting it over a period of nearly three years, the craze for sound films had exploded and entirely transformed the picture medium.

But Chaplin's gamble worked. Released just as the novelty of talking films was wearing off, *City Lights* became a huge box-office success, prompting *Variety* in 1932 to note that the picture's grosses showed "that Chaplin was right about silence on the screen," and, indeed, comparing the overall figures for sound films versus silents, concluded: "Silence in pictures, after all, *was* golden. It represented in money from some individual pictures much more for their makers than any talker to date . . ." The reason, the trade paper argued, was "the gigantic possibilities of silents, with the world market to pick from, as against talkers with outlet narrowed." The article's headline, "SOUND FILMS SHY BIG SILENT SUMS," was prophetic, for although there was no turning back for the industry, movie attendance, after rising precipitously in the first year of full sound, soon dropped just as sharply, and never again reached the extraordinary peaks of the silent era, during which Charlie Chaplin had been and would always be the golden boy.

There are pangs of nostalgia for the lost Eden of the silents below the surface of *City Lights* that still are palpable today. Since talkies had so definitively taken over, Chaplin felt the need to subtitle his movie: "A Comedy Romance in Pantomime." Like most of his stories, *City Lights* has the Dickensian-Victorian sentimentality Chaplin so often recalled. The blind flower girl central to the plot was a pretty dated concept even then, but within the atmosphere of fable evoked, and the dreamlike quality natural to silent movies, it still works now. And this is tempered by the sharply satirical element of the millionaire who only when drunk recognizes and loves the Tramp; when sober, he wants nothing to do with "the little fellow." Both Virginia Cherrill as the blind girl (the lovely actress would later become Cary Grant's first wife) and Harry Myers as the millionaire are exceptionally believable.

I first saw *City Lights* in Manhattan when I was twenty-four and the picture was already thirty-two years old. On my movie-file card, I gave it the highest rating and raved: "One of the sublime achievements in the history of the movies. Perhaps Chaplin's greatest work, certainly the one in which he alternates comedy and tragedy with the most incredible facility and success. Several times it is achingly funny, and at least twice truly heartbreaking. Of course, the ending—the final close-up—far surpasses its reputation, and sequences like the boxing match are unparalleled hilarity. A great and beautiful film, certainly among the best dozen ever made." This was long before I saw Buster Keaton's *Battling Butler* (1926), in which Buster does a boxing match that is definitively funnier than Chaplin's, and from which Charlie definitely "borrowed." Nevertheless, the concluding scene in which the blind girl—her sight now restored thanks to the Tramp's sacrifices—first sees her unknown benefactor is still extraordinarily touching. Writer James Agee called the concluding shot of Charlie looking at her hopefully, with a flower to his mouth, "the greatest piece of acting and the highest moment in movies," which certainly remains a valid judgment.

Personally, I think *The Kid* is his best feature. This now eighty-three-year-old example of Chaplin's unique genius with pathos comedy still retains its magic glow, as the Tramp tries to bring up a six-year-old orphan, in an exhilaratingly fresh performance from newcomer Jackie Coogan, carefully coached, maneuvered and manipulated by Chaplin. The reason the picture was such a resounding success in its day is still quite evident: the potent mixture of irreverent slapstick comedy with a profound sense of squalor and tragedy remains an unbeatable combination. On the screen, Jackie and Charlie will always remain wonderfully larcenous as they, often hilariously, brave the cruel world. In his own grim childhood, Chaplin had been a poverty-stricken kid—his father dead, his mother driven insane—dancing and clowning on London streets with his half-brother for a few shillings. These horrific beginnings are nowhere

Chaplin in his first Tramp movie of the talking era, City Lights *(1931), though it was essentially a silent film; he buys a flower from the blind flower girl (Virginia Cherrill, Cary Grant's first wife) whose sight he eventually helps to restore. It was such a box-office success that* Variety *made a point of its having out-grossed most talkies.*

more sharply drawn than in *The Kid,* one of the glories of the silent era, and among the great American movies.

We met at the 1972 Academy Awards presentation, when Chaplin returned to America for the first time in twenty years in order to receive a Special Oscar. It was his second Special Oscar; the first was for *The Circus* at the very first awards ceremony in 1929. I had been asked to supervise the editing of a montage of clips from Chaplin movies that would precede his appearance on the TV stage. Bert Schneider, one of the producers of *The Last Picture Show* (for which the picture, four actors, the script, the photography, and my direction had been nominated that year), had partnered in a company that was going to reissue all the Chaplin films in America, and Bert wanted to know what I needed in order to cut together the sequence. Just an editor, I said, plus a list of the specific Chaplin pictures I would use; I'd seen almost all of the work by then and was pretty familiar with it. We hired the young man who had been my editor on the AFI John Ford documentary we'd finished a year before: Richard Patterson and I were used to working together, and the montage took shape very quickly.

We covered all phases of Chaplin's career—from the classic two-reelers of the teens through the feature masterpieces of the twenties and thirties. These were not cut in chronological order, but rather with a kind of emotional flow, and the concluding big chunk was four and a half unedited minutes from one of the very moving last sequences of *The Kid,* as Jackie is taken away from the Tramp by the law, and Charlie chases over rooftops to steal him back, finally wrapping him into his arms. The concluding image in our montage was from *The Circus* (released during 1928, the last year of silent movies), and kind of an extended metaphor not only for Chaplin's own particular art—both broad and subtle comedy, and pathos, born out of calamity or dire tragedy—but for the whole of show business. We ended, therefore, with probably the most poignant image in all of Chaplin's movies: the circus wagons gone, the Tramp alone, with only a torn paper star blowing off as he turns and walks away while the sun sets on the silent screen.

Our montage ran thirteen and a half minutes and after it was submitted to the Academy, Bert was notified that while they liked it, they couldn't possibly run such a long section of film on a live show. Bert called me into his office to tell me and asked what I thought we should cut. I said we'd made it as tight as possible and that we needed all of it for the impact I felt certain it would have. But, he said, they were refusing to run it at this length. "Bert," I said, with heavy emphasis, "it's . . . *Charlie . . . Chaplin.*" Bert thought a moment, nodded, called the Academy president, and told him we couldn't cut any of it. The response was that they simply couldn't run it that way, to which Bert replied, "OK, then Charlie won't come." They ran the full version. And during those final few moments of *The Kid* and *The Circus,* there wasn't a dry eye in the house. At this point, Chaplin had not been able to walk down a lot of stairs, so when the montage was over, the screen went up and Charlie was discovered standing there, with his bowler hat. The audience went wild.

Afterward, at the Academy Governors Ball—the annual dinner that followed the ceremony—I went over to Chaplin's table and introduced myself to Oona, who was seated at his right. He and I had as yet had no personal contact. When he was shown the montage for approval, the only comment of his sent back was that he wanted a clip added from *The Great Dictator,* which I'd left out since it's not among my favorites of his. We added a short bit of him in the Hitler caricature playing with the globe as a huge balloon. Now, Oona turned to him and got his attention, saying, "Charlie, this is the man who put your clips together." Chaplin looked up at me. He was certainly quite frail by now, and somewhat distanced—his speech on TV had been pixieish and charming—but also overall a bit feeble. He had become an old man with a kind of childlike, somewhat dimmed manner. Chaplin looked interested, though, and gazed up at me with a sad smile, and said softly, "Oh, thank you, thank you—good job." Then, he leaned in closer, his eyes watering; I bent lower to hear him better. "Jackie *Coo*gan . . ." he said to me. Coogan was there that night—I'd seen him at the ceremony—tall, heavyset and graying. Chaplin leaned in more, repeated "Jackie Coogan . . ." and nodded slowly twice. His tone went up an octave as he continued, incredulously, "He used to be a little boy . . ." He paused, and I nodded some form of understanding, I thought, but he went on, ". . . and now he's an *old, fat* man!"

That stopped me. I didn't know how to react or what to say exactly, so Oona jumped in and said that the choice of *The Kid* sequence for the montage was terrific, and Charlie looked over at her, a little vacantly, then turned back, smiled at me slightly, and nodded. I said it had been great to meet them, and excused myself. Of course, I was about thirty-three at the time—he had fifty years on me—so the profound ache of lost youth was a trifle above my experience level. But also mingled into my reaction was his peculiar, slightly disgusted attitude, his emphasis on the "old, fat" part. Today, he still has twenty years on me, and I probably will empathize more sharply the nearer I get to Charlie's age at that time.

Yet there was another part which no one on earth could empathize with because there was only one Charlie Chaplin; and what he had experienced by the time I met him at the Governors Ball in his eighty-third year—fifty of them as an icon—no human had ever experienced before. That sort of virtually instant world affection and adulation had not before been granted even to a religious icon. There have been many gods and goddesses, but never the same deity for the whole world. Charlie Chaplin had made people the entire globe over *one* in their laughter and tears for him, all achieved without a single spoken word. And, being silent, Charlie spoke in all languages; the Tramp was poor and oppressed like *most* people, so he was Everyman; also feminine and sensitive enough to be Everywoman, too, in some cockeyed way the movies have of transforming reality. Yes, the world thrilled to the adventures of brave Doug Fairbanks and sweet Mary Pickford (both of whom also could be funny), but laughed out loud from the belly with Charlie, yet cried as well. What did all this do to the actual human being below the hugely magnified and manipulated image? As opposed to Charlie—or the Tramp or Charlot, or any one of the score or two of nicknames the world had for him—what happened to Charles Spencer Chaplin, the person, the manipulator and manipulated in one?

Jerry Lewis had an insight. He first met Chaplin in 1951, after Lewis and Martin took Hollywood by storm, a couple of years before Chaplin was for all intents and purposes deported, and then saw him repeatedly until Charlie's death twenty-eight years later. He said he had made Chaplin laugh by being outrageous. In 2002, I screened for Jerry my new film, *The Cat's Meow,* which featured Charlie Chaplin as a character on William Randolph Hearst's yacht for a weekend in November 1924. At that time, Chaplin had just had his first failure with *A Woman of Paris* (1923), also the first picture (and the only one but for his last) in which he did not star. He was embroiled in a romance with sixteen-year-old Lita Gray, whom he had unwisely cast as the lead girl opposite him in *The Gold Rush.* The picture was running way over budget, and he would eventually have to recast Lita, and re-shoot all her scenes with Georgia Hale; plus he had to marry Lita because she was pregnant. They had two sons, and got divorced after three years. In our film, played by the extraordinarily brilliant English comedian Eddie Izzard, Chaplin is embroiled in all this, and spends most of the picture trying to get his host's mistress, Marion Davies, into the sack, and succeeds. Izzard, having had similar experiences to Chaplin as a child performer on the streets, did an excellent analysis of exactly where he thought Charlie was at this point in his stardom and glory: having had the biggest hit of his career and the biggest flop, and most women at his feet. When I asked Jerry after the screening how well Eddie had captured the Chaplin he had known, Jerry said, "He nailed it! You guys nailed it! Charlie was *very* laid-back." Jerry paused for a moment, and then said, more quietly, "In life, Charlie didn't give you much."

That was also my experience with him. It was as though he had used up everything of himself for the screen, and now, except maybe when he was alone with his wife (and perhaps with his children), Chaplin was very reserved, withheld. Maybe on some level, he felt that people had essentially eaten him up, and therefore he had little left except for the muse (his young wife Oona) who kept him going. To everyone else, was there some touch of resentment and distrust? Hadn't the people betrayed him, stopped coming to see him? (Remember the deeply self-pitying finish of the aging comic Chaplin did in *Limelight.*) Did Charlie, on some level, still feel like that lost and lonely child of the London streets whose only salvation was to make people laugh so they'd throw him haypennies?

Charlie Chaplin as the Little Tramp, standing out among the Yukon multitudes for a scene in his memorable comedy The Gold Rush *(1925), among his costliest (he had the leading lady replaced well into shooting) but greatest successes*

A day or so after the Oscars, in a hotel conference room, Chaplin gave several brief audiences, and I brought Cybill Shepherd to introduce her to him. Of course, he perked up quite a bit more than when looking at me, and was charming, though brief. Later, Cybill and I shot part of Henry James' *Daisy Miller* (1974) in and around Vevey, and visited once for a short while with the Chaplins; a couple of his kids came on the set to watch. Charlie seemed out of it. A year or so earlier, Cybill and I had been in his home shooting film of Chaplin for a documentary, eventually called *The Gentleman Tramp* (1975). The photographer-cameraman was the legendary and lovely Nestor Almendros (who shot so many of Truffaut's films). We started by trying to interview Chaplin in his den. I was sitting off-camera asking questions and he was looking at me pleasantly but essentially not answering them. There were strange non sequiturs; nothing seemed to really make sense. At one point, he went over and showed me this large doll he had and sort of flew it through the air, trying to explain a movie he had in mind to make. Oona watched him devotedly, and everyone else was confused but pretending as though it all was clear. None of this interview was useable.

We went outside into the partially sun-dappled backyard, high in the mountains overlooking beautiful, ancient, isolated Vevey and Lake Geneva. There we made a couple of shots of Charlie and Oona walking slowly around the picturesque landscape. As it got later, I said to Nestor that we should get them walking away from us into the sunset, and Nestor leapt at it while I asked Charlie and Oona to walk in a certain direction, explaining what we were doing. This seemed to delight them both, and we made the shot of Charlie and Oona, hand in hand on their sacred mount, walking haltingly into eternity.

Not long after Charlie died on Christmas Day in 1977, I became a witness on behalf of the Chaplin Estate in a celebrated and precedent-setting lawsuit against the CBS Television Network and CBS News. As part of their obituary reports on Chaplin's death, CBS had run a good part of the montage I assembled for the Oscars. The Chaplin Estate sued for infringement of copyright. CBS said it was "fair use" to run clips from an actor's films when reporting his death. But, the Chaplin case claimed, this was not what they had done; they had used the montage especially assembled by Peter Bogdanovich for the Academy Awards presentation and licensed only for that one showing. CBS argued that this was nitpicking—they were still Chaplin clips—and their usage "fair" and "customary." The Chaplin Estate was demanding something like $10 million in damages. On the witness stand, my role was to show that every single cut I had decided upon for the montage was based on years of study, learning, experience and personal vision. It was important for the jury to know that I had seen all of Chaplin's movies more than once, made a number of prominent films myself, always involved myself intimately in the editing process, and that only I would have made those particular choices of juxtaposition. All this was to help prove that CBS was wrong in claiming fair usage of random film clips. Chaplin's Estate won to the tune of $3 million.

I was glad to have helped Oona, who seemed blasted the one or two times I saw her after Chaplin died. She didn't live that much longer. Truman Capote had told me that Oona used to buy clothes all the time in Paris or London, and never wore them. "She'd hang them in the closet," Truman said, "and that's where they'd stay. She and Charlie hardly ever went out." After Chaplin's death, she stopped even buying them.

Naturally, I can't say I really knew Charlie Chaplin at all. I just met very briefly a part of what was left of him toward the end of his reign.

Chaplin and his last wife, Oona O'Neill, as he
returned to America in 1972 for the first time in two
decades to receive a Special Academy Award. This is
how they looked when I met them.

Belatedly, the Queen knighted Chaplin a year or so before he died; as though he hadn't long ago been exalted far beyond knighthood by an adoring multitude. Sir Charlie. I wonder how it felt on his lips, bitter or sweet, or both, or neither. There were those I knew and admired who loved him, like Jean Renoir, who adored both the man and his work; and those like Orson Welles, who didn't find him funny and couldn't stand him personally. Charles Lederer, the brilliant screenwriter, and Marion Davies' nephew, used to tell about having been in the dressing room as a child when Chaplin was introduced to the great Russian opera singer Fyodor Chaliapin. Supposedly, the fabled and famous bass, noted also as a superb actor of opera, had gushed over Charlie in a thick Russian accent: "Graaate arrteest! Chaarles Chaapleen!" Chaplin didn't even get up. He just sat on the sofa, looking up timidly, modestly smiling, and quietly saying "Thank you," and nodding. A towering, massive man, Chaliapin evidently tried a couple of times to get some further rise out of the diminutive Chaplin but to no avail. Eventually, repeating "Graaate arrteest . . ." he retreated, a trifle bewildered. From the other room, Lederer watched Chaplin sit there for a while, then rise and cross to a full-length mirror. He stood for a moment, taking himself in, then put one hand to his breast, and, opening his mouth wide, sang one pure but very quiet operatic note.

This perhaps apocryphal anecdote nevertheless speaks to an amazing insecurity and fear under the surface, and a blinding self-absorption that often comes as a by-product of extraordinary fame and power. If everyone is that interested in you, how can you not be equally interested, both in maintaining and contemplating? One way or the other, a life and career like Charlie's will never happen again. And, as the twenty-first century begins, the icon's work is being brought back on DVD for another welcome pass our way. That's the only Chaplin anyone will ever know, just as in *The Kid,* of course, Charlie and Jackie are still and forever young—the "old, fat man" forgotten—and the frail, jangled old man, too.

Born Charles Spencer Chaplin, April 16, 1889, London, England; died December 25, 1977, Vevey, Switzerland.

Selected starring shorts and features (all directed by Chaplin):

1914: *The Masquerader; His Trysting Place*
1915: *His New Job; A Night Out; The Tramp; A Woman; The Bank*
1916: *The Floorwalker; The Fireman; The Vagabond; One A.M.; The Count; The Pawnshop; The Rink*
1917: *Easy Street; The Cure; The Immi-grant; The Adventurer*
1918: *A Dog's Life; Shoulder Arms*
1919: *Sunnyside; A Day's Pleasure*
1921: *The Kid; The Idle Class*
1922: *Pay Day*
1923: *The Pilgrim*
1925: *The Gold Rush*
1928: *The Circus*
1931: *City Lights*
1936: *Modern Times*
1940: *The Great Dictator*
1947: *Monsieur Verdoux*
1952: *Limelight*

17

JAMES CAGNEY

Early in 1972, I met the real James Cagney. Right at that time there had been a bearded guy going around passing himself off as the actor. I was in Miami when this fellow was there—they made him honorary mayor of Hollywood, Florida—and a paper printed pictures of him; he didn't look like Cagney to me. When Barbra Streisand was singing in Las Vegas around Christmas 1971, they told her Cagney was in the audience so she introduced him from the stage and when this same bearded chap stood up, she thought he didn't look like Cagney to her. Cagney himself seemed rather amused by all this the one time I got to meet him, at a small dinner party in the Brentwood section of Los Angeles. He was six months older than the century, so he was already seventy-two, and lived to be eighty-six. There were four couples, including Cagney and his wife, nicknamed Billie, and Cybill and me. He told us several similar imposter incidents that had occurred over the years—people pretending to be him, or his son or his daughter. By then, Cagney hadn't made a new movie in more than a decade and was rarely if ever seen in public, so the pretenders must've assumed no one would know the difference.

An incredible impudence, I thought, since Cagney was one of the most inimitable actors who ever appeared on the screen. Though, of course, everyone did the standard Cagney impersonation, hiking up their pants with their wrists while saying, "Aaall riiight, yoou diiirty raat . . ." But I don't think anyone in pictures ever had his energy or his theatricality. The year before, I had run for Orson Welles a 16mm print of Raoul Walsh's devastating gangster film starring Cagney, *White Heat* (1949); Welles had never seen it and was a very enthusiastic admirer of both Cagney's and Walsh's, so we looked at it one night. Afterward, Orson got to musing on the absurdity of all those theoretical writings about the supposedly huge difference between movie acting and stage acting. "Look at

*James Cagney with platinum bombshell Jean Harlow in the Warner Bros.
gangster picture that made him a star,* The Public Enemy *(1931), directed
by William A. ("Wild Bill") Wellman*

Cagney!" Orson exclaimed. "Everything he does is *big*—and yet it's never
for a moment unbelievable—because it's *real,* it's true! He's a great movie
actor and his performances are in no way modulated for the camera—he
never scaled anything down."

Even in a likeable early programmer like Mervyn LeRoy's *Hard to
Handle* (1933), with a plot that spins dizzily from one maniacally contrived
situation to another, Cagney's breakneck delivery and elaborately embroi-

dered gestures never for a moment seem labored or unconvincing. The portrayals he gave were always like that—walking a dangerously narrow line between gimmicky caricature and unique eccentricity with the sureness of a ballet dancer—he never fell to the wrong side.

There were many superb Cagney performances—not always in the best films. He said they'd shoot three pictures at the same time in his early Warner days, and told of director Lloyd Bacon asking him to quickly rehearse a phone-call scene for one picture while he was actually finishing another movie. He ran from one stage to another, did the speech and then heard Bacon yell out, "Cut. Print." Cagney said, "Hey! I thought we were *rehearsing.*" And Bacon said, "No, it's OK, Jimmy, we got it!" I remember with special fondness his reckless race-car driver in Howard Hawks' *The Crowd Roars* (1932), and his vulnerable daredevil flyer in Hawks' *Ceiling Zero* (1936); the ebullient, love-struck dentist in Walsh's nostalgic *The Strawberry Blonde* (1941); his doomed "big-shot" gangster in Walsh's *The Roaring Twenties* (1939), and that psychopathic mama's-boy killer in *White Heat,* which also features two of my favorite Cagney scenes. In the first, set in a prison mess hall, he is told that his beloved mother has died, and Cagney slowly builds an astonishing reaction from disbelief through sorrow, grief and, finally, complete hysteria—among the most chilling sequences in movies. At the end of the picture, fatally wounded and trapped by the law on top of a huge globular gas tank, he grins malevolently, laughs, then fires his pistol into the tank itself and, as flames shoot up around him just before the blinding explosions begin, he screams, maniacally happy, "Top of the world, Ma! Top of the world!"

One critic wrote of *White Heat* that only a hard-boiled director like Raoul Walsh could get away with having Cagney—during a terrible migraine attack—sit on his mother's lap, a moment of startling intimacy. But I think Cagney could probably have got away with almost anything, because he had as a performer such amazing intensity and conviction. Whether it was shoving a grapefruit in his girlfriend's face—in William Wellman's highly prized if a bit overrated *The Public Enemy,* the 1931 gangster film that made him a star overnight—or doing a little dance step down the stairs of the White House after meeting F.D.R. (in 1942's *Yankee Doodle Dandy*), Cagney's indisputable authority as a film personality and his flawless sense of honesty as an actor could transform even the most improbable material into something totally believable. His one-sentence advice on movie acting was profoundly succinct: "Look in the other actor's camera eye"—meaning the eye closest to the lens for more direct contact with the camera and therefore the audience—"and tell the truth!"

*In the prison mess hall, James Cagney as the murderous Cody
Jarrett hears of his mother's death and goes berserk in one of
the most memorable scenes from Raoul Walsh's annihilating
masterpiece* White Heat *(1949), probably the last great
gangster film of the golden age.*

He was different from most of the great stars of the golden age in that
he often played villains—even late in his career—comically in *Mister
Roberts* (1955), with unsentimental pathos in *Love Me or Leave Me* (1955),
with complicated and disturbing psychopathic ambivalence in *White
Heat.* His essential persona was as fixed in the public's consciousness as
Bogart's or Cooper's or Gable's but—being a more resourceful and versatile actor—he could express ambiguities in a character even if they weren't
written into the script or featured by the direction. Because he was
innately so sympathetic, his heavies created an intriguing, even alarming,
tension in the audience. As a result, *White Heat,* as an example, contains a
decidedly subversive duality: in the glare of Cagney's personality—though
his character is in no way sentimentalized—the advanced, somewhat
inhuman technology of the police and the undercover-informer cop
(Edmond O'Brien) become morally reprehensible. As a result, I remember Welles and I hissing the law and rooting for Cagney like schoolboys.

That rarest of actors—who could totally transcend their vehicles—and in common with a number of other stars of the movies' greatest period, he was indisputably one of a kind.

During the course of my single evening with him, Cagney also proved to be an absolutely brilliant, riveting, and often hilarious raconteur. He didn't just tell a story, he got up and acted it out, playing all the parts with remarkable precision and an economy of movement that was as subtle and revealing as his screen appearances. He gave us that night some memorable impressions of people he'd worked with, like the gentle Hungarian director Charles Vidor, who had directed him in the Ruth Etting biopic, *Love Me or Leave Me* (1955), and whose accent Cagney had down perfectly; he pantomimed holding a cigarette very thoughtfully from below with thumb and forefinger, which immediately caught the flavor of the man.

Then he did the anything-but-gentle Hungarian director Michael Curtiz, a tyrannical martinet of the old school, who directed him in two of Cagney's biggest successes, *Angels with Dirty Faces* (1938), and the Oscar-winning *Yankee Doodle Dandy;* this involved a couple of outrageous anecdotes, and one that summed up the director's apparent heartlessness. On a period seafaring picture called *The Sea Hawk* (1940), Cagney described how Curtiz had been working on the deck of a huge mock-up of a ship that rose high above the sound-stage floor. Everyone was scared of his rages, so all the actors and extras tried to stay out of his way as much as possible. Unfortunately, Cagney explained, during one setup, a bit-part player in the role of a minister found himself behind Curtiz as the director moved this way and that, trying to decide where to put the camera, his right hand up to his face like a frame, stepping quickly backward and forward and sideways. Cagney played this all out quickly and vividly, doing both roles, the minister fearfully dodging Curtiz's erratic movements. The poor guy eventually became so rattled that he accidentally backed off the edge of the deck and fell twenty-five feet to the cement floor below. When Curtiz heard the commotion and glanced downward over the edge to see what the problem was, grasping it in a second, he rapidly turned back to his task, Cagney said, yelling out as he did with slight impatience and strong accent, "Get me another minister!"

In another sharply observed story, Cagney played out the absolute essence of John Ford, also a famously crusty and truculent director, during the filming of a sequence from *What Price Glory* (1952), in which Cagney starred along with veteran supporting actor William Demarest. Ford, Cagney said, was standing on a small hill overlooking a road on which Demarest was supposed to drive off in a motorcycle with Cagney in the

sidecar. Ford was puffing on his pipe and, at one point, called Cagney, gesturing for the actor to join him. Cagney did, he said, pantomiming Ford
on his pipe: "Puff, puff, puff, puff, puff." Then he imitated Ford's gruff
delivery, "You gonna ride in the sidecar with Bill?" Cagney looked puzzled, answered, "Yeah. Sure." Cagney imitated Ford with the pipe again,
"Puff, puff, puff, puff, puff," after which the director had asked, "Why?"

Cagney told us he was confused. "Well, that's what it says in the
script," he said to Ford, "I get in the sidecar and Bill takes off." Cagney
again did Ford puffing the pipe, then imitated his terse, "OK." The actor
looked even more puzzled, then was called to shoot and so, he said, got
into the sidecar and Demarest took off. "Took off!?" Cagney exclaimed.
"The motorcycle careened up the road at full speed, went off onto an
embankment, swerved around, and smashed into a wall. I was thrown
out, and Bill walked away, just limping slightly. When I looked up the
hill, Ford was still there, puffing away on his pipe. So while they were getting another bike ready to try it again, I walked back up to him. I was a little dazed, but he just stood there—puff, puff, puff, puff, puff—and then
he said, 'Didn't I *tell* ya?' "

We all laughed, and Cagney tied it up for us: "There's *one* word that
sums up Jack Ford—*and* the Irish," the actor said with a dark smile, being
Irish himself, and enunciating the one word with great relish, letting the
final syllable hiss for a beat: "*mal-ice.*"

Cagney played out several other memorable characters for us that
evening, including a "hop-headed pimp" he had observed in his Yorkville
(Manhattan) childhood (a section of East 91st Street is named after
Cagney) standing on a corner, nervously cracking his knuckles and jack-
ing his pants up with the sides of his arms—a mannerism the actor would
immortalize in *Angels with Dirty Faces.* One of the guests asked how he
had developed his habit of physically drawn-out death scenes, probably
the best coming at the conclusion of *The Roaring Twenties,* where he runs
(in one continuous shot) along an entire city block, and halfway up, then
halfway down, the stairs in front of a church before finally sprawling dead
onto them. In answer, Cagney described a Frank Buck documentary he'd
once seen, in which the hunter was forced to kill a giant gorilla. The animal died in a slow, "*amazed* way," Cagney said, which gave him his inspiration, and which he played out for us in a few riveting moments of
mime.

It was a strange feeling to watch him being so brilliant and to know
that he had given up acting. I asked what it would take to get him into a
movie again. He leaned back on the couch, smiled gently and said, in

*James Cagney with Gladys George on the church steps where he falls dead
in Raoul Walsh's memorable gangster film* The Roaring Twenties
*(1939); to the cop's question about who Cagney was, she answers,
"He used to be a big shot."*

characteristic fashion, with a tiny shake of his head, "I have *no* in-ter-est."
Then he sat up and leaned forward. "That's not a line ei-ther—I really
mean it." So Jimmy and Billie Cagney divided their time between Los
Angeles, where they had a house, and Martha's Vineyard, where they had
a farm; he owned a lot of land and cattle, and they seemed contented. The
Cagneys had been married for something like fifty years and still seemed
very much in love. Billie looked at him with great affection while he told
stories she must have heard numerous times. After eighty pictures, I suppose there were very few things left to challenge him, but still I couldn't
help feeling he was just too good not to be acting all the time.

Yet there were probably a lot of reasons why, which Cagney couldn't—
or wouldn't want to—put into words: so many of his old pals had passed
away and certainly Hollywood was no longer the fresh, exciting and intimate place it once had been. If some of us who hadn't lived through the
golden period felt a keen sense of loss for those incomparably better and

James Cagney as George M. Cohan in the actor's own personal favorite among his pictures, Yankee Doodle Dandy *(1942), one of the great star-turns in movies. Michael Curtiz directed efficiently, and Don Siegel supplied the tight and effective montages. Cagney dancing, however, simply requires the camera to be turned on, and he becomes uniquely electrifying.*

more creative times, how could we calculate the feelings of people who had actually experienced them? Late in the evening, Cagney gave a hint of this: "When I drove through the studio gate, and the thrill was gone," he said, "I knew it was time to quit."

As it turned out, Cagney broke his retirement about a decade after our dinner, on doctors' orders to be more active, by accepting a small role in Milos Forman's *Ragtime* (1981), and then doing the lead in a TV-movie, *Terrible Joe Moran* (1984). Neither added much of anything to his legacy. In 1974, he became the first actor to receive the AFI's Lifetime Achievement award; in 1980, a similar salute from the Kennedy Honors; and in 1984, the Medal of Freedom from the U.S. government. Three years after our dinner in Brentwood, he published his autobiography, *Cagney by Cagney,* in which he said the "best directors" were the ones like Walsh, who, "If I don't know what the hell to do, can get up and show me."

At dinner, Cagney had told us that only once in the ten years since his retirement had he been tempted to return: when director George Cukor offered him the Stanley Holloway part in *My Fair Lady* (1964). "That was inviting," he said, "but I'd made up my mind." It's not insignificant that this was a song-and-dance role because, although he won his only Oscar for playing George M. Cohan in *Yankee Doodle Dandy,* Cagney is associated by most movie fans with gangster roles. But when someone asked during dinner which of all the movies he'd done was his favorite, he answered without a moment's hesitation: "I guess it'd have to be the Cohan picture."

Of course, he was like no other dancer: his straight-legged, cocky, constantly surprising way of hoofing—which is how he started in show business—was seen only in a couple of other films, not really very good ones. *Footlight Parade* (1933) is the best of these, yet his manner as an actor and his grace as a performer no doubt owe quite a lot to his dancing days. He just moved eloquently, and therefore could easily have been a great silent star. However, he arrived with the talkies, and gave even the least of them a large measure of his boundless panache.

Born James Francis Cagney, Jr., July 17, 1899, Manhattan, NY; died March 30, 1986, Stanfordville, NY.

Selected starring features (with director):

1930: *Doorway to Hell* (Archie Mayo)
1931: *The Public Enemy* (William A. Wellman); *Blonde Crazy* (Roy Del Ruth)
1932: *Taxi* (Del Ruth); *The Crowd Roars* (Howard Hawks)
1933: *Hard to Handle* (Mervyn LeRoy); *Picture Snatcher* (Lloyd Bacon); *Footlight Parade* (Bacon); *Lady Killer* (Del Ruth)
1935: *"G" Men* (William Keighley)
1936: *Ceiling Zero* (Hawks)
1938: *Angels with Dirty Faces* (Michael Curtiz)
1939: *Each Dawn I Die* (Keighley); *The Roaring Twenties* (Raoul Walsh)
1940: *City for Conquest* (Anatole Litvak)
1941: *The Strawberry Blonde* (Walsh)
1942: *Yankee Doodle Dandy* (Curtiz)
1945: *Blood on the Sun* (Frank Lloyd)
1947: *13 Rue Madeleine* (Henry Hathaway)
1949: *White Heat* (Walsh)
1950: *Kiss Tomorrow Goodbye* (Gordon Douglas)
1952: *What Price Glory* (John Ford)
1953: *A Lion Is in the Streets* (Walsh)
1955: *Run for Cover* (Nicholas Ray); *Love Me or Leave Me* (Charles Vidor); *Mister Roberts* (Ford and LeRoy)
1956: *Tribute to a Bad Man* (Robert Wise)
1960: *The Gallant Hours* (Robert Montgomery)
1961: *One Two Three* (Billy Wilder)

18

MARLENE DIETRICH

"Marlene Dietrich's taken your seats." The assistant director was a little out of breath. "You don't care, do you? She likes to sit in the first two on the right. They moved you guys behind her." It was September 1972, and Ryan O'Neal and I were at Los Angeles International Airport with a few others of the cast and crew of *Paper Moon,* which we were flying to Kansas to shoot. I said we didn't mind.

Ryan was incredulous. "Marlene Dietrich is on our plane going to Kansas!?"

No, it turned out she was flying to Denver (we had to switch planes there) to give six concert performances at the Denver Auditorium. Hard to believe, but sure enough, there she was, sitting across from us at the gate, all in white—wide-brimmed hat, pants, shirt, jacket—looking great and also bored and a little suspicious of the noisy good spirits around our group.

We went over to say hello. I introduced myself. Ryan said, "Hello, Miss Dietrich, I'm Ryan O'Neal. *Love Story*?" He grinned.

"Yes," she said. "I didn't see it—I liked the book too much. I won't see *The Godfather* for the same reason—Brando is too slow for it anyway—why didn't they use Eddie [Edward G.] Robinson?" She had that deep voice and distinct German accent.

There were several people I knew who had worked with and loved her, and I mentioned a few of them, trying to get a conversation going, but she was a little frosty, so we slipped away after a few moments. Ryan said, "I think we did great," but I didn't.

She was right behind us as we waited to have our hand baggage searched, not a common event then, and I can't recall why it was done. We tried again; she was nicer this time. "I saw *The Last Picture Show,*" she said

*Marlene Dietrich as Lola-Lola, the role that made her an overnight
international star, in Josef von Sternberg's Berlin-made* The Blue Angel
*(1930), shot simultaneously in German and English. This was the
first of seven Dietrich-Sternberg collaborations; all but the
last two were very successful.*

to me; the film had opened a year before. "I thought if one more person
stripped slowly, I would go crazy."

"Did you see *What's Up, Doc?*" Ryan said. "We did that together." The
picture was still in theaters at the time.

"Yes, I saw it," she said and nothing more. I changed the subject—told
her I'd recently run a couple of her older pictures—Ernst Lubitsch's *Angel*
(1937) and Josef von Sternberg's *Morocco* (1930). She made a face at the
first and said the second was "so slow now." I said I assumed Sternberg

wanted it that way—he'd told me he had. "No, he wanted *me* slow," she said. "On *The Blue Angel* [1930], he had such trouble with [star Emil] Jannings—he was so slow." For some reason the luggage inspector was especially thorough on her bag—and she looked disgusted. "I haven't been through anything like this since the war."

On the plane she sat in front of us, with her blond girl Friday, and by now, she had obviously decided we weren't so bad; she spent almost the whole flight turned backward and leaning over the top of her seat, on her knees, talking to us. She was animated, girlish, candid, funny, sexy, with her baby-talk "r" (that becomes "w") and everything.

I told her I was trying to stop smoking again. "Oh, *don't,*" she said. "I stopped ten years ago and I've been miserable ever since. I never drank before—and now I drink. I never had a cough when I was smoking—now I cough. *Don't* stop—you'll get fat and you don't want to do that."

We talked about movies she had been in and directors she had worked for. After a while, it became apparent to her that I had seen an awful lot of her pictures. "Why do you know so much about my films?"

"Because I think you're wonderful, and you've worked for a lot of great directors."

"No," she said dubiously. "No, I only worked for two great directors—Sternberg and Billy Wilder."

"And what about Orson?"

"Oh, well, yes, Orson—of course."

I guess she wasn't so impressed with Lubitsch or Alfred Hitchcock or Fritz Lang, Raoul Walsh or Tay Garnett or René Clair or Frank Borzage. She looked amazed when I told her I liked Lang's *Rancho Notorious* (1952), amused that I enjoyed Walsh's *Manpower* (1941), confused that I was fond of *Angel.* I had read somewhere that her own favorite performance was in Welles' *Touch of Evil* (1958).

"You still feel that way?" I said.

"Yes. I was terrific in that. I think I never said a line as well as the last line in that movie—'What does it matter what you say about people . . . ?' Wasn't I good there? I don't know why I said it so well. And I looked so good in that dark wig. It was Elizabeth Taylor's. My part wasn't in the script, you know, but Orson called and said he wanted me to play a kind of gypsy madam in a border town, so I went over to M-G-M and found that wig. It was very funny, you know, because I had been crazy about Orson—in the forties when he was married to Rita Hayworth and when we toured doing his magic act [*The Mercury Wonder Show,* benefits exclusively done for servicemen]—I was just crazy about him—we were great friends, you know, but nothing . . . Because Orson doesn't like blond women. He only likes dark women. And suddenly when he saw me in this dark wig, he looked at me with new eyes: Was this Marlene . . . ?"

"Well, he certainly photographed you lovingly."

"Yes, I never looked that good."

Welles had once told me, I remembered, that Marlene was a lifelong worshipper of Greta Garbo but had never met her, so Orson arranged the meeting to happen at a little party at Clifton Webb's house. He drove Dietrich there and she was as nervous and excited as a young girl. Garbo was about an hour late and when the two were introduced, Dietrich praised her, but Garbo just nodded blandly and moved on. Marlene, Welles said, was crushed but said nothing. Driving back, Dietrich was silent for a long time and then, finally, said, "Her feet are not *soo* big . . ."

"You have great legs," Ryan suddenly said.

"Yah—great!" She grinned. "Great thighs!" She slapped one of them behind the seat.

"I dream about your legs and I wake up screaming," said Ryan.

"Me too," she said.

I asked her if she'd been upset about Sternberg's acerbic autobiography, *Fun in a Chinese Laundry* (first published in 1965), in which he'd said that he had created her, and implied that she would have been nothing without him. (He had once said to me, "*I* am Miss Dietrich—Miss Dietrich is *me*.")

She pursed her lips, lifted her eyebrows slightly. "No—because it was true. I didn't know what I was doing—I just tried to do what he told me. I remember in *Morocco,* I had a scene with [Gary] Cooper—and I was supposed to go to the door, turn and say a line like, 'Wait for me,' and then leave. And Sternberg said, 'Walk to the door, turn, count to ten, say your line and leave.' So I did and he got very angry. 'If you're so stupid that you can't count slowly, then count to twenty-five.' And we did it again. I think we did it forty times, until finally I was counting probably to fifty. And I didn't know why. I was annoyed. But at the premiere of *Morocco*—at Grauman's Chinese Theatre"—she said the original name of the L.A. movie palace with just the lightest of mockery—"when this moment came and I paused and then said, 'Wait for me . . .' the audience burst into applause. Sternberg knew they were waiting for this—and he made them wait and they loved it."

I asked if Jo had gotten along with Cooper. "No—they didn't like each other. You know, he couldn't stand it if I looked *up* at any man in a

Marlene Dietrich with Gary Cooper in her initial Hollywood-made feature, Josef von Sternberg's Morocco *(1930), shot after* The Blue Angel *but released in America first. Much to Svengali Sternberg's misery, Dietrich and Cooper had a torrid romance during shooting.*

movie—he always staged it so that they were looking up at me. It would infuriate him—and Cooper was very tall—and you know, Jo was not. I was stupid—I didn't understand it then—that kind of jealousy." She shook her head lightly, but at her own folly. (She did not mention that during the picture—as I heard some time later—she'd had an affair with Cooper.)

Which of her seven films with Sternberg was her favorite? "*The Devil Is a Woman* [1935] was the best—he photographed it himself—wasn't it beautiful? It was not successful and it was the last one we did together—I love it."

Ryan said, "I hear you're a good cook."

"I'm a *great* cook."

"When'd you have time to learn?"

"Well, when I came to America, they told me the food was awful—

and it was true. Whenever you hear someone in America say they had a great meal, it turns out they had a steak. So I learned. Mr. Sternberg loved good food, and you know . . . So I would go to the studio every day and do what he told me, and then I'd come home and cook for him."

I mentioned *Song of Songs* (1933)—the first American picture she had done without Sternberg—and said I didn't like it very much. She agreed. "That was when Paramount was trying to break us up. So they insisted I do a picture with another director. Jo picked him—[Rouben] Mamoulian—because he'd made *Applause* (1929), which was quite good. But this one was lousy. Every day, before each shot, I had the soundman lower the boom mike and I said into it so the Paramount brass could hear me when they saw the rushes, I said, 'Oh, Jo—why hast thou forsaken me?' "

What a remarkably dedicated Old World artist she was! The only German superstar, the one European with the longest international appeal—and this despite two World Wars that made Germany not exactly the most popular country to be from. In a brand-new medium for which no one really knew the rules of the game, Dietrich—which means "passkey" in German—had to make them up for herself. There was no way to predict the price she would have to pay: her last ten-plus years in seclusion so as not to destroy the legend she had created, the myth that was a part of her art, both of which—though pretending otherwise—she took very seriously. Her unique qualities and upbringing, and fate, gave her the remarkable ability and opportunity to express—through the first six decades of women's official emancipation (the right to vote)—the many faces of Woman: sacred to profane, victim and killer combined, nurse, bohemian artist, siren, vamp or love goddess to Great Earth Mother.

Marlene's German-born mother—"the good General," she called her—had told daughter Dietrich repeatedly: "Do something." And to her European sensibility, implicit in that injunction was: "Do something well." Marlene did everything extremely well, made it all look so easy that many people eventually took her for granted. Many still do: separating her always from the "serious" actors of the time, as opposed to "personalities." But personality-actors were those star-players whose actual personae were uniquely appropriate to the closely analytic eye of a camera: the character and actor merge into one—a seminal difference about this new performing-art form.

Growing up as a would-be artist in the Weimar Republic, first a violinist, Marlene (a contraction of her own making, from her given names, Maria and Magdalene) had her first affair when she was sixteen, with her (considerably older) violin teacher. She had affairs from then on—kind of a one-woman freedom brigade—with both men and women, long before and long after her one official marriage in the twenties to a chicken farmer (Andy Scriber). In Berlin, in that same roaring decade, Dietrich used to explain: "In Europe it doesn't matter if you're a man or a woman. We make love with anyone we find attractive." She used to say—this was, remember, also only the first period of female emancipation in several millennia—"Women are better, but you can't *live* with a woman." For living together, she preferred men.

Of course, Marlene Dietrich did grow up in probably the most open city of the world in that era—Berlin being the home of Kurt Weill and Bertolt Brecht, of Lubitsch, Lang and George Grosz—with its burst of creative artistry, and its uninhibited social mores. Marlene's first job was as a violinist in a small combo playing for silent movies. She was fired because her legs kept distracting the other musicians, all of them male. As various Berliners and Viennese quickly began to point out, Dietrich had "Those Legs," also "That Face," and on top of everything else, "That Voice." Long before she did *The Blue Angel* (1930), Marlene became very well known in prewar Berlin as "the girl from the Kurfurstendamm," the name of that city's main drag.

Starting out in small stage roles, working her way up, studying at the Max Reinhardt school, playing more than thirty parts in the theater; she had also acted in nearly twenty German movies—seven of them leads— before her European "debut" in *The Blue Angel*. Her introduction to general U.S. audiences came with *Morocco,* shot after *The Blue Angel* but released before it in America. She was even a singing star in Berlin (with numerous recordings) before Sternberg "discovered" her for the Lola-Lola part in *Der Blaue Engel*—a supposed vehicle for the great German star Emil Jannings, which Dietrich stole with a vengeance. After that, she stole nearly every movie she was ever in—there were thirty-seven of them— often with material and collaborators of infinitely lesser quality.

The first Sternberg-Dietrich collaboration, a classic drama of passion and betrayal, *The Blue Angel* was photographed in German with sections in English—a not uncommon practice in the early sound era—though the English-language version was lost for years. Most recent generations (including mine), therefore, have seen only the subtitled version, which was universally considered better because the cast of German actors were naturally more comfortable in their mother tongue. Jannings, among the most distinguished and popular of German actors, and an international silent star, had been the first ever to win a Best Actor Oscar (for the 1928 Sternberg silent masterpiece, *The Last Command*). Because of this, Jan-

The infamous couple: Josef von Sternberg with his most famous "creation" in the early thirties, when their romance created a scandal and broke up his marriage. Dietrich would break his heart, too.

nings specifically asked for Sternberg to come to Germany to direct the star's first talking film, never suspecting that his little-known co-star and ultra-sexy nemesis in *The Blue Angel* would shortly eclipse him in stardom and popularity, or that the film would be his last success in America.

However, *The Blue Angel* instantly set Dietrich among the immortals. Her chair-straddling portrayal of cabaret singer Lola-Lola defined her essential image in certain irrevocable ways. She would forever sing the song she is doing (in German) the first time we see her: "Falling in love again . . . never wanted to—What am I to do? Can't help it . . ." She too, then, was a fool for love, like all the men who fell for her. Talking with Sternberg one time, I said that among the pictures he made with Dietrich, *The Blue Angel* was actually the only time she really destroyed a man, to which he replied: "She did not destroy him—he destroyed himself. It was his mistake—he should never have taken up with her. That's what the story is." Was he speaking of himself a bit or only of the prudish boys'-school teacher Jannings played, who fell madly in love with a loose, bawdy, compulsively unfaithful performer? The strain breaks him down to ultimate degradation. Like that line in Jacques Brel's masochistic love chant, *"Ne me quitte pas,"* Jannings becomes content to be to Dietrich "the shadow of your dog . . ." The moment when Marlene humiliates Jannings by making him crow for her like a rooster is one of the most chilling in picture history. It was a scene Sternberg added.

That Dietrich (married by then, already a mother of a little girl) and Sternberg (also married) were "an item" was a big issue in its day and the cause given for Sternberg's divorce from another actress. Of course, Dietrich broke his heart long before they made their last picture together. Indeed, Sternberg's career never recovered from the initial success (of the first four) and then the fairly dismal failure (of the last three) of his Dietrich pictures. Marlene had a lengthy professional life, while Sternberg's never really caught on again. His "creation" long outlived him, but Dietrich always spoke of her Jo with the kind of reverence one generally reserves only for God.

According to her biographers, Marlene was not faithful to any of her lovers, not even the one with whom she seems most to have been in love, French working-class star Jean Gabin—the only one who wouldn't forgive her for straying. When Gabin died, shortly after her own husband, Dietrich said: "Now I am a widow for a second time." The man she most wanted to please, however, was still Sternberg—who seems to have withheld his total approval to the end of his days—as she withheld from him the constancy he no doubt hoped for from her. But he had to understand—as he did in some of his films with her—the need Marlene had for freedom at all times to be herself.

Certainly she always dressed as she pleased, was in fact the most famous cross-dresser of all time: white tie, top hat and tails, and (apparently) see-through dresses, were an equal portion of her legendary concerts. And this in-person aspect of Dietrich was perhaps the most amazing—though, sadly, the least available to experience: only one (barely adequate) TV special and a few live record albums to give evidence of one of the few truly electrifying theater experiences. Dietrich's command of her ethos, her style and technique, and her personal magic— everything merged for those mystical times Marlene not only took over the whole stage, but owned the people out front as well.

. . .

The day after our plane flight—in my Hays, Kansas, motel room—the phone rang. It was Marlene. "I *found* you." She said it silkily and low. It was lovely and a little unnerving. We hadn't told her where we were going so she must have done some tracing. "I got to my hotel last night," she said, "and I missed you."

"Me too. How're you doing?"

She told me about a press conference she had been through at the airport after we left. "I don't think I made them very happy—but they ask such stupid questions. One old woman there—old—older than *me*—asked, 'What do you plan to do with the rest of your life?' I said to her, 'What do you plan to do with the rest of yours?' "

We talked several times during the week, and she sent me a couple of warm and funny notes thanking me for the opening-night telegram and flowers, and supplying anecdotes about the Denver performances: "I sang fine last night," she wrote, "but I don't think it was necessary. . . . Lights are bad! They have no equipment. Poor country, you know!"

"How were the reviews?" I asked her on the phone.

"Oh, the usual—'the legend' and all that—you know—fine."

On Saturday, Ryan and I and six others from our company flew to Denver for the night to see her show. I have never seen as mesmerizing a solo performance. She sang twenty songs and each was like a one-act play, a different story with a different character telling it, each phrased uniquely and done with the most extraordinary command. No one has ever teased and controlled an audience better. "I'm an optimist," she told them, "that's why I'm here in Denver." They loved her. How could they not? How could anyone not? Here was a woman of seventy-one, looking forty, by turns sexy in all ways, and witty about it, maternal, cool, fragile, dominating, stoic, intimate, inspiring.

Everything she did was done completely—there were no half-gestures or unfinished thoughts in her performance. When she said Sternberg's name, you knew she was really thinking of him. And she never repeated an effect, didn't move much, just stood there and sang for you. Though meticulously rehearsed, everything appeared spontaneous, as though it were the first time she had done it; a great showman—very theatrical—yet subtle beyond praise.

She always transcended her material. Whether it was a reliable old standard like "I Can't Give You Anything But Love, Baby" or "My Blue

Heaven," a schmaltzy German love song, "Das Lied ist Aus," or a French one, "La Vie en Rose," she lent each an air of the aristocrat, yet she was never patronizing. She transformed Charles Trenet's "I Wish You Love" by calling it "a love song sung to a child" and then sang it that way. No one else could sing Cole Porter's "The Laziest Gal in Town" (which she had done in the 1950 Hitchcock thriller, *Stage Fright*)—it belonged to her by now, as much as *The Blue Angel*'s "Lola" and "Falling in Love Again" always have. She kidded "The Boys in the Back Room" from the Western *Destry Rides Again* (1939), but with great charm.

For Dietrich, *Destry* had been a huge change of image—done with that end clearly in mind. Despite her numerous successes with Sternberg, several failures followed, and toward the end of the thirties Marlene had become "box-office poison" to exhibitors—the exotic pedestal on which Sternberg had put her obviously having lost its allure with Depression audiences. *Destry* ripped her right off any sort of pedestal and, significantly, it was Sternberg himself who convinced her to take the role of a tough, brawling, saloon chanteuse/woman of easy virtue. The extended catfight between her and Una Merkel is justly famous, and the novelty song she sang, ". . . Oh, see what the boys in the back room will have, And give them the poison they name . . ." became a popular Dietrich standard throughout the rest of her career. Marlene told me that she and co-star Jimmy Stewart had quite an affair during the making of the film (see Stewart chapter), and the heat is apparent.

At the Denver concert we saw, Marlene sang more than one song in German; in her rendition, "Jonny" became quite frankly erotic, including the way she handled the mike. A folk song, "Go 'Way from My Window," never had been done with such passion, and in her hands, the famous American song "Where Have All the Flowers Gone?" became not just an antiwar lament, but a sort of tragic accusation against all of us in the audience, sitting there doing nothing. Another pacifist song, written by an Australian, had within it a recurring lyric—"The war's over—seems we won"—and each time she sang this line a deeper ironic nuance was revealed.

Of course, she saw World War II at close range, entertaining the troops for three years with "benefits"—more than any other star performer ever did, for which she was awarded America's highest civilian honor, the Medal of Freedom, as well as France's most valued order of distinction, the *Légion d'honneur*. And the experience was all brought back through her touching introduction to "Lili Marlene"—an old German song, forbidden by Hitler in her own country—which was comprised mainly of a

*Marlene Dietrich among GIs near the front lines during World War II,
where she performed tirelessly and in many countries*

recitation of the names of all the countries in which she had sung "Lili
Marlene" during the war. It called to mind what Hemingway had written
in his World War I novel, *A Farewell to Arms:*

> . . . There were many words that you could not stand to hear and
> finally only the names of places had dignity. Certain numbers were
> the same way and certain dates and these with the names of the
> places were all you could say and have them mean anything.
> Abstract words such as glory, honor, courage, or hallow were
> obscene beside the concrete names of villages, the numbers of
> roads, the names of rivers, the numbers of regiments and the
> dates . . .

And that was what Marlene conveyed; as she said, "Africa, Sicily, Italy,
Greenland, Iceland, France, Belgium and Holland"—here she paused—
"Germany, and Czechoslovakia," her inflection carried with each a different untold story of what she had seen, what the 500,000 soldiers she sang
for had seen. It was all there, too, in the way she then did "Lili Mar-

lene"—and terribly moving. Suddenly you understood another thing Hemingway had written—this time about her (in *Life* magazine)—and you knew that the soldiers must have understood it as well when she sang to them over the course of three very long years:

> If she has nothing more than her voice she could break your heart with it. But she has that beautiful body and that timeless loveliness of her face. It makes no difference how she breaks your heart if she is there to mend it.

Privately, Dietrich would tell friends, she felt somehow guilty about World War II. Hitler had wanted to sleep with her, and she had refused him. Later, Marlene often said that if she *had* slept with him, she might have altered his views on life, and history would have been different.

After the show, still onstage, she saw that all the musicians and technicians got a drink, and thanked each one personally. She was particularly effusive about the local soundman. A short, middle-aged fellow, he came up shyly to say good-bye, and she embraced and kissed him lovingly, not the way I would guess it is usually done in Colorado, or anywhere. The guy looked bewildered, thrilled, overwhelmed all at once; speechless as Marlene Dietrich hugged him to her and told him it was the best sound she had ever had on the road. He wandered away with glazed eyes and a foolish grin, the happiest man in Denver.

In the dingy dressing room, her helpers were packing up. "Closing night is my favorite," she said, "because I can call and cancel the insurance." She sipped champagne, then picked up the only photo on her makeup table—a framed picture of Hemingway, the glass cracked, an inscription on it that read, "For my favorite Kraut." She spoke to the photo. "Come on, Papa," she said, "time to pack up again, huh? OK, here we go." And she kissed it. Hemingway had been a lifelong friend but never a lover. Proudly, she showed off a pair of ballet slippers she had been given by the Bolshoi troupe, a sentiment in Russian carved on one sole; and a stuffed black doll she picked up gingerly. "Remember this—from *The Blue Angel*?"

We all ate at Trader Vic's and she told stories and unwound from the show. She called Ryan her "blond dream-friend" and said she would have to look at *Love Story* now. The next morning she came downstairs to see us off, stood at the hotel entrance in her slacks and shirt and cap watching us pull away.

She gave me an envelope as we left. In it were two pieces of hotel sta-

*Marlene Dietrich and Cary Grant (in his fifth movie role) in von
Sternberg's* Blonde Venus *(1932), in which she plays a loving wife
(to Herbert Marshall) and mother (to Dickie Moore), and becomes a
nightclub star to support her family. Grant said he saw what the director
and star "were up to" and "wasn't going to get mixed up in that."*

tionery—on one she had written out a quote from Goethe: "Ach Du warst
in löngst vergangenen Zeiten meine Schwester oder meine Frau." On the
other, her own "literal" translation: "Oh, you were in long passed times
my sister or my woman." You too, dear Marlene, for all of us.

We saw each other only one more time. For the first public screening of
Paper Moon in New York, she had accompanied Cybill Shepherd and me.
Of course, she knew that Cybill and I were living together and I had told
her there would be three of us, but I guess the actual experience did not
thrill her. We had picked Marlene up at her apartment house in a limousine and she spent the entire brief ride sitting in the middle, her back
completely turned to Cybill, talking only to me. Naturally, it created quite
a stir when I walked into the screening room with Cybill on one arm and

Marlene Dietrich on the other. But Marlene had not only been icy to Cybill, she had been a bit snippy, too, and after the screening told me that "an old friend" (veteran *Vogue* editor Leo Lerman) would escort her home. The next day, a gigantic bunch of flowers arrived at our Waldorf Towers suite addressed to Cybill. The floral arrangement was so tall and large that it took two bellmen to bring it in, sideways. Inside the envelope marked "To Cybill Shepherd" was a note card which read simply, "Love, Marlene." As it turned out, neither Cybill nor I ever saw her again.

We spoke on the phone, however, and one time she told me she didn't know why, but she loved me. I was so thrown that I said something stupid about being "flattered." She hated that and threw it right back in my face: "Don't say you're *flattered*!" During this period, she did her one television special—for producer Alexander Cohen, whom she hated. She complained bitterly about his cheapness and bad taste, and thought the show was dreadful. She wasn't wrong; it certainly did not do her justice or come close to approximating the amazing concert I had seen. A couple of years later, she had her disastrous fall. She had just finished a live performance somewhere and, as usual, went to shake her conductor's hand. He had lost his balance and inadvertently pulled her into the pit. Her legs were terribly hurt, and the wound never healed. She thought it would be all right eventually and didn't immediately have the proper attention or care. Things got worse. Eventually, she holed up in her Paris apartment and never went out again.

I spoke to her a few times while the trauma of her leg injuries was going on, but we lost touch at the end of the seventies. In 1980, my life was shattered by personal tragedy, and about a year later, Marlene's Hollywood agent, Paul Kohner, had called to say that Marlene had personally requested me to direct a documentary about her life and career. Her first choice had been Billy Wilder but he had politely declined. I was her second choice. Again, I said I was flattered, but told Kohner that I was not in any shape to take this on, that I simply couldn't accept such a difficult and important responsibility. This was the last connection I ever had with Marlene. Though I wrote to her a couple of times and did a TV tribute to her on CBS's morning show in the late eighties, a tape of which I sent to her, she never responded. The documentary *Marlene* was finally done by Maximilian Schell and Dietrich was quite vocal about hating it.

Almost immediately after she died in 1992, two biographies were published—the one by Stephen Bach being exceptionally good (I reviewed it very favorably for the *Los Angeles Times*)—but both were overshadowed by her daughter Maria Riva's voluminous memoir. Orson Welles, who had

*Dietrich, in a black wig, as Tanya the Gypsy in Orson Welles' originally
dismissed (in the United States), now widely
treasured crime thriller,* Touch of Evil *(1958); in this scene, she reads
co-star Welles' cards and tells him his future is "all used up." Welles'
first studio picture in ten years, it was also to be his last.
Dietrich especially liked herself in the role.*

been rather ambivalent about Marlene—affectionate at times, quite cutting at others—told me long before his own death in 1985 that Marlene's daughter "hated her" and was "just waiting for Marlene to die" so she could publish a devastating portrait. Dietrich died seven years after Orson—ironically, on Welles' birthday—and his prediction turned out to be quite accurate. Clearly, being Dietrich's daughter was a tough life. Nevertheless, what the artist in Marlene left behind was haunting and unique, and personally I prefer to recall that part of her legacy together with the brief good times and conversations we had together. Being Marlene Dietrich couldn't have been very easy, either.

Years later, I would remember that Marlene always carried with her— "for good luck," she had said—a little plastic bag of Scottish heather, which she had shown me in Denver. "If you carry this with you," she told me in her cramped little dressing room more than thirty years ago, "it means you will come back." Perhaps Dietrich knew (as I certainly didn't then) that in the Celtic Scottish Highlands, heather was the sacred plant of the Queen Bee, the Summer Goddess, known in Rome as Venus Erycina, "Love goddess of heather," and in ancient Greece as Urania, meaning Queen Heather or "Heavenly One" or "Earthly One" or "Queen of the Winds." This same deity's original symbol was the Sphinx, as both Dietrich and her only rival, Greta Garbo, were sometimes pictured during their careers. Of course, like the Sphinx, Dietrich's own riddle would always be tantalizing and probably unsolvable. But, like the winds, Marlene would be forever; she would always come back.

Born Maria Magdalene Dietrich, December 27, 1901, Schöneberg; died May 6, 1992, Paris.

Selected starring features (with director):

1929: *Ich küsse ihre Hand, Madame/I Kiss Your Hand, Madame* (Curtis Bernhardt); *Die Frau nach der man sich sehnt/Three Loves* (Bernhardt)
1930: *Der Blaue Engel/The Blue Angel* (Josef von Sternberg); *Morocco* (Sternberg)
1931: *Dishonored* (Sternberg)
1932: *Shanghai Express* (Sternberg); *Blonde Venus* (Sternberg)
1934: *The Scarlet Empress* (Sternberg)
1935: *The Devil Is a Woman* (Sternberg)

1936: *Desire* (Frank Borzage)
1937: *Angel* (Ernst Lubitsch)
1939: *Destry Rides Again* (George Marshall)
1940: *Seven Sinners* (Tay Garnett)
1941: *Manpower* (Raoul Walsh); *The Flame of New Orleans* (René Clair)
1948: *A Foreign Affair* (Billy Wilder)
1950: *Stage Fright* (Alfred Hitchcock)
1951: *No Highway in the Sky* (Harry Koster)
1952: *Rancho Notorious* (Fritz Lang)
1957: *Witness for the Prosecution* (Wilder)
1958: *Touch of Evil* (Orson Welles)
1961: *Judgment at Nuremberg* (Stanley Kramer)

19

ANTHONY PERKINS

The first time I saw Anthony Perkins was on the Broadway stage in 1953. I went alone to a Saturday matinee of *Tea and Sympathy,* a successful new play by Robert Anderson, directed by Elia Kazan and starring Deborah Kerr and John Kerr. However, for this particular performance John Kerr's role was taken over—said a little note slipped into every *Playbill*—by an understudy named Anthony Perkins. The coming-of-age drama was about a confused, sensitive teenager who is helped to find himself, as well as initiated finally into the mysteries of sex, by his school headmaster's wife, and Perkins was absolutely riveting, extremely touching. He reminded me of a very young, slightly more neurotic Jimmy Stewart, and had amazing intensity, skill and charm. If this was the understudy for the highly-praised portrayal by John Kerr, how good must Kerr have been? I found out when I saw the Vincente Minnelli movie version (1956) starring the leads from the original stage cast: John Kerr wasn't nearly as good as Anthony Perkins had been—not by a long shot. Of course, Kerr never became a major actor, either, eventually drifting out of show business and ending up as a lawyer, while Tony Perkins became a star, in the theater and in pictures.

It was my good fortune to see him at his brilliant best twice more on Broadway: later in the fifties, as the surrogate character (Eugene Gant) for writer Thomas Wolfe in Ketti Frings' popular adaptation of Wolfe's autobiographical novel, *Look Homeward, Angel;* it was a beautiful, poetic, natural, yet towering performance. In the seventies, when we already knew each other, I saw him do the complicated lead role of the psychiatrist in *Equus,* and felt that he made the character and play more believable than anyone else could ever play it. In the sixties, I became friendly with two directors who loved working with Perkins: one who generally loved actors, Orson Welles, on *The Trial* (1962); and one who said he often didn't,

Anthony Perkins in his first movie role, playing Jean Simmons' boyfriend in George Cukor's amusing, sensitive and touching small-town film The Actress *(1953), based on Ruth Gordon's autobiographical play* Years Ago, *and starring Spencer Tracy and Teresa Wright as her parents*

Alfred Hitchcock, on *Psycho* (1960). When I finally met Perkins around 1972, I found him awfully likeable, really a terrific guy, with such a great sense of humor that to work with him must have been a joy.

The first director ever to cast Tony in a movie was George Cukor in *The Actress* (1953), shot right before I saw him in *Tea and Sympathy*.

(Cukor certainly had an eye; just four others among the many he started in pictures: Katharine Hepburn, Judy Holliday, Jack Lemmon, Angela Lansbury.) *The Actress* is a beautiful small-town period film based on actress-writer Ruth Gordon's teenage years dreaming of being what she did in fact become: a Broadway star (plus a great screen- and memoir-writer). The lovely and touching Jean Simmons played Ruth, with Spencer Tracy and Teresa Wright as her parents, and Anthony Perkins in a small role as her first boyfriend. He was gangly, slightly awkward, and immediately appealing. The picture was a modest one the studio did little to promote; essentially, it was an art film before its time. I didn't see the movie until a decade after its release—long after Perkins had become a star—indeed, he had already peaked with *Psycho.*

In 1953, however, with the studio system starting to have problems, Tony went back to New York to work in live television and on Broadway until his next film appearance three years later in William Wyler's extremely popular Civil War family drama *Friendly Persuasion* (1956), starring Gary Cooper and Dorothy McGuire as Perkins' Quaker parents. Playing their sensitive and troubled teenager fraught with conflicting emotions about the war, Tony was superb in that role, nearly stealing the picture from Cooper, and receiving the one Oscar nomination of his life, as Best Supporting Actor. This set him up to play the psychotic baseball star Jim Piersall, in a low-budget biopic based on Piersall's autobiography, *Fear Strikes Out* (1957). In my movie-card file for the picture, which I saw when it came out, the first thing I noted was "Tony Perkins' exceptionally fine performance," and ended with the effusive paragraph: "It is a very powerful document with a splendid performance by Mr. Perkins." The picture, sensitively directed by Robert Mulligan, was a critical, if not a commercial, success.

After that, though, Perkins never stopped working, and through the remainder of the fifties I saw most of his pictures when they came out, but none of them hit the mark, despite Perkins' being never less than excellent in them. Yet, except for Anthony Mann's little Western *The Tin Star* (1957) with the still indestructible Henry Fonda, and René Clément's re-cut and truncated *This Angry Age* (1958)—and just the fact of co-starring with Audrey Hepburn in *Green Mansions* (1959), weak though it was—none of his other fifties pictures really worked. Unfortunately, Anthony Perkins had started to become established just as the original studio system was falling apart; it was essentially over by 1962. Thus Perkins signed no long-term contracts, and the notion of guiding star-actors into their particular niche and mining it soon vanished completely. If he had become a star

As Eugene Gant in the 1957 Broadway stage production of
Thomas Wolfe's autobiographical first novel, Look Homeward,
Angel, *adapted by Ketti Frings, with Jo Van Fleet as his*
mother. Perkins' performance was magnetic and had great size.

before 1950, his own special American characteristics would have been
exploited and turned to far better advantage.

Ironically, it took Alfred Hitchcock to synthesize Perkins' qualities in
Psycho—and turn them to striking dramaturgical effect—as directors and
screenwriters had always done with star personalities in movies, of course,
for the previous fifty years. Tony's essential persona of troubled, sensitive
and neurotic young all-American boy (which was not unlike Tony himself, but largely without his humor) had been firmly established in
Perkins' first two sizeable movie roles. So Hitchcock took advantage of

that and completely threw initial audiences for a loop. Not Tony Perkins! It couldn't be! The shock of his turning out to be the killer in *Psycho* nearly equaled the shock of star Janet Leigh getting murdered a third of the way through the picture. The double irony, however, was that the film was both Anthony Perkins' making and breaking. Suddenly, he became in many ways so identified with the character of Norman Bates that people had trouble seeing him any other way.

Yet Perkins was in the Brando tradition of the fifties, not wanting to be typed; otherwise he might have stayed in Hollywood and done horror pictures for a while. Instead he went to Europe and attracted challenging work on both continents throughout the rest of his career. Overseas, he seemed to be more respected than in his own country. Tony was something of an actor's actor; other players could see how brilliant he was, but it was completely organic to him, without any grandstanding, and therefore largely invisible: the *best* kind of acting, but too effortless for prizes. He was awfully smart, too, and, as Robert Mitchum used to say, he "brought a lot to the party."

One time, I was discussing Perkins with Hitchcock and repeated to the director what Tony had told me about his bringing in the bag of candy corn to eat during the memorable scene with private detective Martin Balsam, and said that Hitchcock, as always, had encouraged him. "Yes," Hitchcock responded, "and Balsam, too. I said, 'Fellows, you both do a lot together in this scene. Now, why don't you both go in a corner and have a go.' After all, there are limits. You can't direct good actors in a scene that should come naturally—hesitancies and so on. No, people like Tony and Balsam are intelligent men and you leave them to it." Which translates to mean that the totally real, seemingly spontaneous, absolutely perfect interaction between the two actors came out of those rehearsals together and that Hitchcock just shot it—from all the correct angles.

Orson Welles cast Perkins as the perfect guilt-ridden Joseph K. (giving the character thereby an American spin) in his version of Franz Kafka's nightmare novel, *The Trial,* photographed entirely in Europe. It was never my favorite Welles picture, but I eventually came around to the work when Orson made me understand that a lot of the film was meant to be very black comedy; and then I saw it with him in Paris and he kept laughing at moments which made his intention clear. "Tony and I," Welles would recall, "spent a good deal of the time convulsed with laughter! What a treat he was to have on a picture."

Perkins used to say of Welles that there wasn't anyone better in the world to be directed by or to hang around with. (We had that in common,

Anthony Perkins as Norman Bates with Martin Balsam as Detective Arbogast in the ambiguously suspenseful interrogation scene for Alfred Hitchcock's Psycho *(1960). The director said the two actors worked out all their complicated moments together while rehearsing by themselves.*

because I'd been directed by Welles and hung around with him, and I agreed.) Tony felt the greatest pride of his career that he had played the lead in an Orson Welles picture. (Again, I felt similarly, mine being the still unreleased *The Other Side of the Wind.*) We used to talk about Welles, exchanging stories about him, experiences with him. I was with them together once in the early eighties, Perkins' abject admiration of Welles being obvious. And Orson treated him with undeniable affection and a considerable sense of intimacy and trust. Tony and I could barely exchange hellos and we were then separated by the party—a gallery opening of sculpture by Oja Kodar, Welles' constant companion since *The Trial,* so, of course, she and Perkins were friendly. As it turned out, that was also the last time I actually saw Tony or Berry Berenson Perkins, who had been his wife by then for about a decade.

Son of the stage and screen character-actor Osgood Perkins (after whom he would name his first son), Tony hardly knew his father, whose most memorable screen role was in Howard Hawks' *Scarface* (1932), as the gangster who loses his girl to the Al Capone prototype (played by Paul Muni). Perkins *père* is exceptional, and the movie is way up at the top of the list in the gangster genre. In 1937, when his son was just five, Osgood Perkins died. So Tony followed in his father's footsteps, but reached a level of success and fame that quite eclipsed his dad's. In other words, Perkins was from an actor's family, show business was in his blood, and he worked right to the end of his life when AIDS killed him in 1992 when he was only sixty.

He left behind two sons, Osgood and Elvis, with their beautiful mother Berry (for Berinthia) Berenson, sister to actress Marisa Berenson, both granddaughters of famed designer Elsa Schiaparelli, grand-nieces of art collector–historian Bernard Berenson. The two had married in 1973, after years of rumors that Tony was gay. Berry and Tony were virtually an ideal couple—obviously adoring each other—fun to be around. The two boys (very young when I knew them in the seventies) were a source of pride and happiness. I remember hanging out with them all in their Manhattan apartment a few times while Tony was doing *Equus* on Broadway—just the two kids, Tony, Berry, Cybill Shepherd and me. Cybill and I loved both of them. Berry was a beautiful blond angel, a talented and serious still photographer, a patient, loving mother and a supportive, often selflessly caring wife. She took an unusual and evocative photo of Cybill alone in a New York diner for the cover of a jazz album Shepherd recorded with Stan Getz (*Mad About the Boy*).

We had first met, Tony and I, on the set of *Catch-22* in Guaymas, Mexico, early in 1969; Welles introduced us between shots on the Mike Nichols picture. (Orson and I had just begun our marathon interview sessions which eventually became the book *This Is Orson Welles*.) I barely had time to tell Tony how terrific I thought he had been a year or so before in a little-known but enthralling picture he had done with Tuesday Weld called *Pretty Poison* (1968), one of his best performances, though the direction and script unfortunately were not up to the basic material or the two superb stars. The first chance we had to really talk a little was probably about three years later at a Hollywood party hosted by the agent Sue Mengers. Sue's first two clients after her switch from agent's secretary to agent were Anthony Newley and Anthony Perkins. I was her third. Pretty soon she had just about everyone else, too, from Barbra Streisand and Ryan O'Neal to Mike Nichols and Arthur Penn. Tony and I, therefore, had Sue in common, too. Welles and Mengers alone could cover a year of conversations, and so whenever the two of us met over the precious few years we knew each other, we always picked up where we had left off.

On the sunlit porch of an afternoon party somewhere in L.A., I recall sitting with him while he told me with great glee the plot of the murder-mystery screenplay he was writing with Stephen Sondheim, which eventually became *The Last of Sheila* (1973), in which Tony did not appear. All the characters in the film were based on people he and I both knew—various Hollywood movie people, stars and filmmakers of all kinds—and Tony excitedly elaborated at length on who the prototypes were. He was very funny and wonderfully charismatic as he conspiratorially let me in on the whole thing. Tony also loved movies. That was the third thing we had in common, and the fourth was that he *knew* pictures, was very film literate, thus there were numerous allusions to movies we both liked, as Tony sketched in the story line of his script.

When we later saw each other in New York, where we had more of a chance to relax and just talk casually, have a meal, keep talking—something of a luxury in Los Angeles or New York show-business circles—Tony and Berry were so easy to be unbuttoned with, to be candid, unafraid of being judged or misunderstood, or used. Even more of a luxury elsewhere. That's what they were like individually; together, it was almost too good to be true.

Most of the pictures he did after *Psycho* and *The Trial* were not up to the caliber of the Hitchcock and Welles, though none of these subsequent films were totally without interest and, sometimes, had considerable merit. He even acted for French master Claude Chabrol in two pictures, *The Champagne Murders* (1967) and (with Orson) *Ten Days' Wonder* (1972), but they weren't necesarily Chabrol's finest hours, though intriguing, and in the latter a unique chance to see Welles and Perkins together. Sidney Lumet's very smoothly done all-star Agatha Christie piece, *Murder on the Orient Express* (1974), was probably Tony's only real hit until the two *Psycho* sequels he did, in 1983 (*Psycho II*), and in 1986 (*Psycho III*), the second of which he directed as well. There was even a *Psycho 4: The Beginning* in 1990 for cable TV. In show business, it's hard to get away from your *primary* success (maybe it's hard in any business). Perkins also directed *Lucky Stiff* in 1988, a bizarre black comedy about a guy who falls prey to a modern family of cannibals. Tony's humor was always pretty dark, filled with irony and an ability to see several viewpoints at once.

Four years later, Tony died. Afterward, there was some talk about the AIDS question, of course, but who cared? He was gone. I heard that Berry and the boys were devastated, naturally, even having lived for well over a year with the knowledge of where Tony's illness was going. I wasn't really

Anthony Perkins is brilliant as Joseph K. in Orson Welles' haunting adaptation of the Franz Kafka novel The Trial *(1962), shot all over Europe but especially at the then-deserted Gare d'Orsay in Paris.*

filled in on all this until nine years after the fact, when a catastrophic tragedy brought Berry's lovely sister Marisa Berenson and me together again. We had known each other in the seventies; I had been with Cybill to Marisa's wedding; she was as darling as her sister. Berry was on one of the planes that crashed into the World Trade Center on September 11, 2001. When I heard that sweet Berry was a part of this horror, one of my first thoughts was that now she and Tony would be reunited. Marisa told me she felt the same way, while on a plane ride we coincidentally shared just a week later. Marisa was still in shock, cried on my shoulder for a while, told me that Berry and Tony had had a very tough time, Berry nursing him to the end. In 1992, Tony had died on September 12; precisely nine years later, Berry was killed. My prayer is that they *are* finally together again, and are watching over their sons, as I remember them doing in their New York apartment thirty years ago.

Born Anthony Perkins, April 4, 1932, New York, NY; died September 12, 1992, Hollywood, CA.

Selected starring features (with director):

1953: *The Actress* (George Cukor)
1956: *Friendly Persuasion* (William Wyler)
1957: *Fear Strikes Out* (Robert Mulligan)
1958: *This Angry Age* (René Clément); *The Matchmaker* (Joseph Anthony)
1959: *Green Mansions* (Mel Ferrer)
1960: *Psycho* (Alfred Hitchcock)
1961: *Goodbye Again* (Anatole Litvak)
1962: *The Trial* (Orson Welles)
1965: *The Fool Killer* (Servando González)

1966: *Is Paris Burning?* (Clément)
1967: *The Champagne Murders* (Claude Chabrol)
1968: *Pretty Poison* (Noel Black)
1970: *Catch-22* (Mike Nichols)
1972: *Ten Days' Wonder* (Chabrol); *The Life and Times of Judge Roy Bean* (John Huston)
1974: *Murder on the Orient Express* (Sidney Lumet)
1978: *Remember My Name* (Alan Rudolph)
1979: *Winter Kills* (William Richert)
1983: *Psycho II* (Richard Franklin)
1984: *Crimes of Passion* (Ken Russell)
1986: *Psycho III* (also directed)

20

FRANK SINATRA

One of the first things I remembered when I heard that Frank Sinatra had died was his parting wish to a concert audience at the Royal Albert Hall in London one of the two times I saw him perform there in the seventies and eighties: "May you be happy and wealthy, may your children prosper, may you live to be one hundred," he had said, "and may the last voice you hear . . . be mine!" And something like ten thousand British people cheered wildly, as though death surely would lose its sting were it to be accompanied by the sound of Sinatra. Certainly his voice had been present the world over at so many of what the French call *les petits morts:* how many fervent kisses, passionate embraces and epiphanies had been achieved with Sinatra singing in the background! His songs formed not only his own autobiography but served as similar touchstones for millions the world over, from the early forties to the present. Yet, as things turned out, the man who had kept company with and for so many, who had most feared and dreaded loneliness—and therefore, by extension, dying alone—had sadly gone out with great conflict and without the comforting companionship for which he had so yearned. The ultimate singer—the cocksman personified—who wooed and won all the world's beauties, had, according to his youngest daughter, ended his life in an unfulfilling relationship, one that his last road manager said he endured because he felt he was deserving of punishment. His old pal Jerry Lewis, who phoned Sinatra often in his last years, agreed: "Yeah, Frank was pretty good at beating himself up."

Sinatra's epoch-making theme albums of 1953 and 1954, *Songs for Young Lovers* and *Swing Easy,* happened to coincide with the start of my own serious teenage dating. We didn't notice at the time that these mood-sustaining "concept" albums (with which he had experimented in the forties) essentially invented the long-playing record as an art form. In 1954,

Frank Sinatra is superb as Frankie Machine, the heroin addict, in Otto Preminger's adaptation of the Nelson Algren novel The Man with the Golden Arm *(1955), the first major U.S. film to deal with drugs.*

when Sinatra won his Oscar for *From Here to Eternity,* many experienced the most jubilant reaction they would ever have to any Academy Award; listening to the radio (television still not quite ubiquitous), I myself leapt up with such excitement that the rug slipped out from under me and I almost broke my neck. After that (twenty years before I finally met Sinatra), I made sure to see any movie he was in, though he wasn't in too many good ones. There had been the very young and innocent Sinatra of the three early Gene Kelly musicals—*Anchors Aweigh* (1945), *Take Me Out to the Ball Game* (1949) and, best of all, the wonderful and joyous Kelly–Stanley Donen–directed *On the Town* (1949)—in which Frank's essential sweetness was most guilelessly represented. Then came the somewhat dangerous, loose-cannon Sinatra of pictures like *From Here to Eternity* or *Suddenly* and *Young at Heart* (both 1954) or *The Joker Is Wild* (1957); the romantic, wise-guy, swinging Frankie of *Guys and Dolls* or *The Tender Trap* (both 1955), *High Society* (1956) or *Pal Joey* (1957). And, most arresting, there was the dramatic, sensitive and complicated loser of his finest picture-work in Otto Preminger's *The Man with the Golden Arm* (1955), Vincente Minnelli's *Some Came Running* (1958), Frank Capra's *A Hole in the Head* (1959), and *The Manchurian Candidate* (1962), directed by John Frankenheimer.

Those kind of Sinatra memories, however, were very much like countless others' around the globe, but the few encounters I had with the man himself between the mid-seventies and the start of the nineties came rushing back when I heard of his death—as well as memories of things I had heard about Frank from others who had known him. From Barbara Ford, John Ford's daughter, for example—her father having directed the strikingly beautiful and talented Ava Gardner in probably her best performance, in *Mogambo* (1953), shot in Africa during the lowest ebb in Sinatra's life. Though he was madly in love with her—and she with him (he divorced the mother of his three children to marry her)—his career was at its absolute nadir, his vocal cords having hemorrhaged, his records no longer selling, his movie and recording contracts canceled. Sinatra came to Africa, in desperate shape, to visit Ava. Ford used to order him around jokingly: "Make the spaghetti, Frank." And he did, rather happily, Barbara Ford remembered. Ava Gardner, at her hottest then, called Columbia studio chief Harry Cohn and asked him as a favor to cast Frank as Maggio in the Fred Zinnemann movie of James Jones' novel *From Here to Eternity*, John Ford seconded the idea, and Sinatra got the part—at $1,000 a week for eight weeks. That's after being a huge recording and picture star only four years earlier. Such are the perils of American fame.

When Sinatra had left Africa to start *Eternity*, and Ava had finished the only role in her career for which she was nominated by the Academy for Best Actress, cinematographer Robert Surtees and his wife accompanied her to London, where she had an abortion. Evidently, her fateful decision (she never had children) was somewhat in retaliation for his chronic fooling around. Sinatra didn't know about this until after the fact, and he was devastated. The two were divorced—she left him—within a couple of years, but both seemed to carry the torch for each other through their lives. I met Ava in the mid-eighties, and she still spoke very warmly of him, just as there was always an especially tender sound to Frank's voice whenever her name came up.

The first personal contact I ever had with Sinatra was a nasty telegram he sent me. Cybill Shepherd and I were living together then, and I had just produced for her (not very well but I didn't know that at the time) a Cole Porter album, and sent copies to several performers we both admired, hoping for some endorsements which could be used as liner

The innocent Frank Sinatra: with Gene Kelly, Jules Munshin and the real Statue of Liberty on location for On the Town *(1949). Sinatra's favorite song from the original Broadway show, "Lonely Town," was never shot—much to his angry disappointment—but he recorded it definitively seven years later on the album classic* Where Are You?

notes. We got a few (Fred Astaire, Gene Kelly, Orson Welles), and then came Frank's wire:

Heard the record. It's marvelous what some guys will do for a dame. Better luck next time.

Sinatra

Well, Cybill and I tried to pretend to each other that there was a missing period after "marvelous," and let it go. I finally met him not too long afterward—to be exact, on February 9, 1975—when he hosted the American Film Institute's Lifetime Achievement tribute to Orson Welles. Actually, I thanked him for his telegram. He looked slightly bewildered, but when I added that we thought it was funny, he smiled a bit uncomfortably and said, "Yeah, I thought you'd get a kick out of it." The subject never came up again.

That year, the AFI's Welles gala—only their third such affair—was not really a popular event in Hollywood since a lot of people thought there were *many* others who should have been honored before Orson. (It had come about because George Stevens, Jr., had the noble idea that perhaps the prize could be used not only to commemorate past achievement but also to attract future work, especially for the not exactly studio-friendly Welles. It didn't.) So the dinner was not as star-studded as everyone would have liked, and therefore Sinatra's participation was all the more important.

Of course, Sinatra had always been extremely fond of Welles—they were born the same year, 1915, only seven months apart: Orson on May 6, Frank on December 12—and Welles had always spoken very warmly of the singer. Sinatra had been the first investor for Welles' ill-fated, never-completed modern version of Cervantes' *Don Quixote:* in 1956, he gave Welles $25,000 with which to start the work. Frank's enduring nickname for Orson was "Jake"—Welles claimed he never knew why, but perhaps it's because "jake" is a slang synonym for "good" or "great" or "fine," as in "everything's jake," and that was certainly Sinatra's opinion of Welles. In any event, Welles named the leading character in his last film Jake—the still-to-be-edited *The Other Side of the Wind*—with John Huston playing the part, a legendary macho film director called Jake Hannaford: certainly an inside tribute to Sinatra. The night of the AFI fête, Frank sang with great gusto a special version of Rodgers and Hart's "The Lady Is a Tramp," rewritten to proclaim that Orson was "a Champ!"—at that time still a quite controversial opinion not only in Hollywood but in America as a whole. Yet "controversial" never bothered Sinatra: he had often championed unpopular causes, fought for the underdog. His presence that night had deeply touched Welles.

They had known each other since the 1930s in New York, when Sinatra was with Harry James and then with Tommy Dorsey. After Sinatra's false retirement (1971–73), when he returned with an album (and TV special) titled *Ol' Blue Eyes Is Back,* Welles had laughed: "Where did that 'Ol' Blue Eyes' come from I wonder?! No one's ever *once* called him that before!" It had always been "Frankie" or "The Voice." "The Chairman of the Board" came later, from New York deejay William B. Williams. In the forties, on radio's *Your Hit Parade,* it had been "F.S. for L.S., Frank Sinatra for Lucky Strike, saying . . . 'Put Your Dreams Away' . . ." After Humphrey Bogart died in 1957, Sinatra eventually took over Bogie's title as "Leader of the Rat Pack," or "the Clan." But with "Ol' Blue Eyes," Sinatra had reinvented himself again, as he had when he went from being the almost femininely vulnerable mama's boy–crooner of the forties to America's top swinger of the fifties and sixties.

A year or so after the Welles tribute, Cybill and I were invited to be guests at the Sinatra table at Caesar's Palace in Las Vegas, where he was performing. "The show starts at midnight," his secretary had said, "but Frank will be on the Jerry Lewis telethon at eleven-fifteen, if you want to watch." It was early in September 1976, and Cybill and I were in our suite, with both television sets on as we dressed for Sinatra's second show. In those days, there was only one fellow who brought the high rollers to town, and that was old Caesar's countryman from Hoboken, New Jersey.

Jerry Lewis, live from the Sahara down the street, had been exhorting viewers to pledge money to the muscular dystrophy campaign, and now Jerry gave an elaborate introduction for Sinatra, who came out, sang a quick, up-tempo number, and then told the audience that, unbeknownst to Jerry, he had brought a friend along to help him. He pointed off left and the camera panned over to show Dean Martin walking out from behind the set. After the phenomenally successful Martin and Lewis team broke up with acrimony twenty years earlier, the two had barely seen each other, much less been seen together, so this was quite an event (see Lewis and Martin chapters).

"I thought it was about time!" Sinatra shouted over the tumult of the studio audience, which had risen to its feet and stood applauding for several long minutes as Jerry and Dean embraced. Finally, when they looked at each other, Sinatra stood between them, beaming, while Jerry could be seen (though not heard over the noise) saying to Frank, "You son of a bitch." Laughing, Sinatra got each of them a microphone, and after they exchanged a couple of lines, Martin seemed to cue Frank that he wanted out of the moment. Sinatra stepped forward quickly and sent Jerry away with exaggerated majesty so that he and Dean could sing a duet.

Whatever Sinatra may have felt was covered by a kind of magnanimous, even paternal, amusement. With no attempt to compete, he played straight for Martin and had a good time. Was he remembering that precisely when Dean and Jerry were on their first giddy waves of popularity, between 1948 and 1953, he had toppled to the bottom? When those swooning bobby-soxers of the war years had stopped following him, and he was counted out? When the Sinatra craze—a tumult we would see repeated for Elvis Presley and then for the Beatles, with Frank's the first of its kind and the most fervent—was over?

But, of course, that end had been only the beginning. The Oscar came, the fabled comeback began. Suddenly, there were two or three Sinatra movies every year (five released in 1955, his film peak), and the new, remarkably mellow theme albums for Capitol—before him, LPs had been

Frank Sinatra as Pvt. Maggio, with Montgomery Clift (who helped Sinatra with a little coaching), in the picture that began Sinatra's legendary comeback, From Here to Eternity *(1953), winning him the Oscar for Best Supporting Actor*

only collections of singles—not only revolutionized the recording industry, but became the most conspicuous and popular alternative to rock and roll throughout the fifties and early sixties. Brilliantly conceived and executed mood pieces, most of the albums became classics, from "quarter-to-three" torch songs for *In the Wee Small Hours* (with an unheard-of sixteen songs) or *Only the Lonely,* to swinging make-out entertainments like *Come Fly with Me* or *Nice 'n' Easy.* All of these Capitol albums would remain in print and continue to sell until his death—and will, long after. Toward the end of the fifties, Dean Martin, having gone solo, became one of the mainstays of Sinatra's Rat Pack of friends, always playing the Joker, their informal slogan echoing the late founder Bogart's favorite maxim: "The whole world is three drinks behind and it's high time it caught up."

When Sinatra retired in 1971, no one quite knew why—he was only fifty-five. Maybe he had discovered that you can have everything you ever wanted, even your own record company (Reprise, as of 1961), and still not be happy. On the other hand, maybe he was just trying to attract attention while he took a few years off. His last movies had not been very good or very successful. Of the seventeen starring roles he had done in the preceding decade, only three or four were even worthy of mention: besides Frankenheimer's and Richard Condon's engrossing *The Manchurian Candidate* (which Sinatra also produced), there was the ultimate, though quickly dated, Rat Pack vehicle, *Ocean's Eleven* (1960), prosaically directed by Lewis Milestone; the uneasy Robert Aldrich Western, *4 for Texas* (1963); and Mark Robson's reasonably effective World War II film, *Von Ryan's Express* (1965), in which Sinatra is extremely personable in the title role. His recordings for Reprise, though profitable and sometimes quite adventurous (like *Watertown,* a sort of pop opera, or the Antonio Jobim albums), and occasionally on a level with the fifties classics (like *Moonlight Sinatra*), never quite achieved the popularity of the Capitol catalog. Maybe Frank also remembered that exits and entrances are often the most rewarding parts of any performance.

Yet, by 1971, Sinatra seemed to have completely lost what little interest he ever had in pictures, which is not to say that he hadn't given some deeply resonant performances: I'm thinking especially of his complex portrait of a failed writer in Minnelli's *Some Came Running*—excellently adapted from another James Jones novel—in which Dean Martin also was superb and Shirley MacLaine easily broke your heart in perhaps her greatest performance. As a portrait of a troubled American artist in his provincial hometown, this is one of the last important films of Hollywood's golden age, and probably Sinatra's most subtle, layered performance. The picture also was a favorite of the French New Wave, Jean-Luc Godard making a relevant and textured reference to the Minnelli movie in his masterfully ambiguous Brigitte Bardot picture, *Contempt* (1963). Overall, *Some Came Running* is probably Sinatra's best movie.

Still, in all the unprecedented outpouring of tributes to, reminiscences of, and commentaries on Sinatra after he died (and the best published was Pete Hamill's lovely *Why Sinatra Matters*)—though everyone naturally mentioned *From Here to Eternity*—hardly anybody singled out *Some Came Running* for special attention, though his role in the second was far more complicated and challenging, and he is better in it. Very convincingly he plays a sometime writer—clearly Jones' surrogate—who after World War II returns to his Indiana hometown, where he deals with the intensely conventional middle-class hypocrisy of his brother (Arthur Kennedy); falls in love with a schoolteacher (Martha Hyer) who can explain artists to students but can't understand the one she sleeps with; has an off-and-on affair with an ex-hooker (MacLaine); and becomes fast friends with a local gambler-boozer-playboy (Martin, in the first and best of the numerous films he and Frank would do together).

Knowing that Sinatra as a serious singer always did his recordings with full orchestra, singing each song straight through, normally requiring only one or two takes, Minnelli wisely staged nearly all the most important scenes in *Some Came Running* in single continuous shots. The players really had to be good to work in this way, and they all were. In fact, Sinatra has the least showy role, but its central weight and complexity had to be dead-on or the whole thing would have collapsed, and as an actor Sinatra has rarely been as focused or committed as he is to the uneasy, never-black-and-white truth of the character he played. His commanding presence here totally suspends disbelief, and carries with it a troubled unspoken inner gravity which only a star-actor can bring with such seeming effortlessness.

Sinatra also did a shattering job as a heroin addict in Preminger's groundbreaking, Production Code–busting *The Man with the Golden Arm*. Though some of the fake Chicago sets and Eleanor Parker's overheated acting hurt its effectiveness today, Sinatra's work has enduring integrity and the pain he conveys remains palpable. As it does in his often searing impression of alcoholic comedian Joe E. Lewis in *The Joker Is Wild*, overpolitely directed by Charles Vidor. He makes a perfect Joey in the otherwise watered-down, weakly made *Pal Joey*, though his rendition of "The Lady Is a Tramp" could not be improved upon. Nor could his honest, touching job as a once-brainwashed returning Korean War veteran in *The Manchurian Candidate*, or his sadly tarnished modern-day Capra anti-hero in the ambiguous *A Hole in the Head* (in which, unfortunately, Eddie Hodges' performance and the "High Hopes" song are now both awfully hard to take).

Yet it was about his singing that Sinatra always appeared to be most serious, in person and on records. Will Friedwald's amazingly detailed and fascinating 1995 book about Sinatra's recordings (*Sinatra! The Song Is You*—subtitled, more to the point, *A Singer's Art*) reveals at length how closely Frank was involved in every stage of these productions, no matter who the arrangers or producers were. Though Friedwald ranks Nelson Riddle's arrangements the best fit Sinatra ever had—and I doubt anyone could seriously disagree—quality and musicianship were hallmarks throughout the bulk of this singer's art. The personal hands-on touch is obvious, for example, in *Sinatra & Company*, his last album before the temporary retirement. One side featured a group of complicated Jobim songs, beautifully rendered; on the other were several new popular tunes,

*Frank Sinatra and Dean Martin during a break in the filming
of their first and finest picture together,* Some Came Running
*(1958). Sinatra was not inherently funny, while Martin was,
which delighted Frank and encouraged Dean.*

none of them to become standards but all evocatively performed. One
selection, "Lady Day," was an homage to Billie Holiday, from whom Sinatra certainly had learned some important things not only about phrasing
but about acting a song, and it comes as close as a popular song can to an
operatic Italian aria—Sinatra's other big musical heritage—with emotional resonance. Years later, when I mentioned the Italian opera connection, he nodded, pleased at the comment. "Yeah," he said, "that's what we
had in mind."

Usually, Sinatra would knock off three or four, sometimes five, songs
in a single recording session. But on "Lady Day," before being satisfied, he
did the song on several dates, months apart, with three different arrange-

ments. There is an asterisk next to this one title on the album, and down below it's explained by the footnote: "Produced by Frank Sinatra," a credit he rarely ever took. The song is placed as the last cut on side two so as to stand as his own unofficial farewell, too. He prepares you for it with the previous song—a tough, jaunty (not very appealingly arranged) rendition of "Leavin' on a Jet Plane" that concludes with a melancholy ad-lib coda:

> Don't know when I'll be back again—
> Oh, babe, I hate to go . . .

Then, at the close of "Lady Day," with the whole orchestra playing the melody-line behind him so that his voice seems to be riding a series of soaring ocean waves—in opera it's called *sono voce* (one voice)—Sinatra took his leave:

> And then the evening comes,
> And now she doesn't cry.
> And it's too late to say—good-bye . . .

As it turned out, of course, three years later he returned. But the *Ol' Blue Eyes Is Back* TV special flopped. Performing before a group of Hollywood names in a small studio, Sinatra seemed ill at ease and out of shape. Several months after that, however, he came back with the proper panache. Broadcast live over national TV—the same way he would stage that reunion of the two other most popular entertainers of his generation—Sinatra appeared in a boxing ring at Madison Square Garden and, before twenty thousand delirious fans, he requested another chance—his way, in a song: Though he had told them he was "leaving," he "just couldn't say goodbye." This would simply be "self-deceiving . . ."

> Let me try again!

Who could deny him? From "Nancy" and "All or Nothing at All" and "Polka Dots and Moonbeams" through "The Wee Small Hours of the Morning," "All the Way," and "I've Got a Crush on You," "Nice 'n' Easy," "You Go to My Head," "New York, New York" and "My Way"—these songs and scores of others indelibly charted the days and nights of his life and ours.

And so, three more years after that, in 1976, I was at his table with Cybill in Las Vegas. It was the first time either of us had seen him sing in person, and especially memorable because we were seated (across from each other) with one of our shoulders quite literally leaning against stage center. He also not only introduced us to the audience from our seats, but played much of the show directly to us (especially Cybill), even slanting some of the songs to the kind of attitude he thought we might like, often kidding the cornier material. When he got to the words "my way" for the first time, he sang instead, "I did it . . . sideways!" Being physically so close to him was literally overwhelming—he towered directly above us— and the intensity of his dramatic numbers was impressive. Through age— he was now sixty-one—Sinatra seemed to have regained with a vengeance the kind of valiant vulnerability he had as a young man. More than that, he had achieved a remarkably old-world flavor in his performance, the sophistication and stature of a fine classical musician. He would tell me that for him each song was something like a one-act play for one player and, together with the expressive brilliance of his phrasing, and that voice, he was the most superb *actor* of songs.

After that, I would see Sinatra perform in person five more times: twice in London, once at New York's Carnegie Hall, twice at the Universal Amphitheater in Los Angeles. Each time, he was subtly different, modulating the performance, altering it slightly for the differing audiences, because they each affected him in different ways, changing the songs or their order. Overall, I thought he was at his best in London, but he was never less than strikingly charismatic. Most sentimental with the L.A. crowds, he would salute the American flag and sing "The House I Live In" with an awful lot of strings. (He had received a Special Oscar in 1946 for the short film based on that song of tolerance, an ideal for which he fought enduringly in his career.) After one of these shows, in the mid-eighties, when I had just had a success with the movie *Mask,* he greeted me afterward, saying with a small grin of admiration, "Look who's back from the dead."

At the time of the Carnegie Hall concert, in 1980, I had been shooting *They All Laughed* and arrived with Dorothy Stratten in the middle of his first song, "The Lady Is a Tramp." We had the misfortune to time our entrance with the song's line, "She loves the theater and never comes late," which Frank, of course, directed pointedly right at us as we came down the aisle.

In the early eighties, Sinatra and I almost did a picture together. It was a Las Vegas comedy-drama called *Paradise Road* (loosely based on a novel by David Scott Milton), which I had envisioned to star him and James Stewart, Lee Marvin, Charles Aznavour, Dean Martin and Jerry Lewis, all playing degenerate gamblers. Although Sinatra had brought Dean and Jerry together briefly on that telethon night, they had, nevertheless, not bonded again. So when I suggested to Frank that in the film they would play two guys who were in the same group but spoke to each other only through intermediaries during the entire movie, he thought this was funny but would not be easy to achieve. Still, he said he'd try to get Dean, and I should try to get Jerry, who had been a friend of mine for many years (see Lewis chapter). One afternoon, Frank called me, excited. "I spoke to Dean," he said. "He'll do it!" I was amazed and thrilled. "Yeah," said Frank, "I asked if he wasn't bothered about Jerry, and you know what Dean said? He said, 'Aw, who gives a fuck!' " Sinatra laughed delightedly. Jerry agreed, too, but as often happens, business people and middlemen got in the way and, sadly, things never did work out.

In 1981, I went to Sinatra's compound in Palm Springs to talk about this project and to screen for him my film with Audrey Hepburn, *They All Laughed*. (While we had been shooting this in Manhattan, Sinatra had taken Audrey and me and a few others to dinner one night. Reagan was running for President, and when I said I wasn't for him, I'll never forget the patient, strangely innocent way he said, "Why, Peter?") He allowed me to use on our *They All Laughed* soundtrack four cuts from his latest album, *Trilogy* (having sent me one of the first copies, signed "Francis"), including his rendition of our title song by the Gershwins as well as his last top-ten single, "Theme from *New York, New York*," arranging for us to get all known publishing and performing rights in perpetuity to the four for an unheard-of $5,000 total. Normally, each song could have cost ten times that, so he must have bent the composers' arms, too, I guess, to get me that whole package for practically nothing. It was a lovely and touching gesture as well—prompted, I believe, by the tragedy of Dorothy's murder.

He had a few Palm Springs friends over to dinner, then we ran the picture, which takes a while to reveal what sort of movie it is. But at a certain point, Frank called out, "It's a romantic comedy!" and everyone relaxed. Later that evening, he played for us a just-completed mix of his new (and penultimate solo) album, *She Shot Me Down*. It was an unusually challenging saloon-song collection, in that sad mood of "wee small hours" loneliness which he's such a master of. Before each cut played, Frank would tell us (just as he did in all his concerts) who the composers and arrangers were. And it was oddly moving to see, after all those decades of recording and performing, how vulnerable and excited he still was when playing for others a brand-new work of his. At least two of the songs on this last personal collection of his became Sinatra classics for me: "I Loved Her" and "Monday Morning Quarterback."

The next day was a Sunday and I came over in the morning for a talk about our proposed picture. We sat across from each other at a card table in the den, and he seemed as up about the project as I was. At one point, talking about returning to form with a vengeance, we coincidentally both at the exact same moment moved our chairs forward with happy intensity. It spoke of a kind of uncynical enthusiasm on his part that delighted me. We both noticed and grinned at each other. During this conversation, I asked him who was his favorite composer and he answered, "Mozart." After a while, his wife, Barbara, came into the room and, walking behind me, clearly made a high sign to Frank. He nodded, then asked me, "Are you Catholic?" I answered that I didn't belong to any religious group. He said, "Well, we're going to mass—you wanna come?" I said OK and he smiled and, standing up, said, "Sure, what the hell—it's only an hour."

Soon after, the three of us piled into their station wagon, Frank dressed in tie and tweed sport jacket; he drove to the ultramodern-looking church which had been dedicated to his late mother, Dolly Sinatra, who had been killed not many years before in a plane accident, flying to her son's open-ing in Las Vegas. The mass did indeed take about an hour, both Mr. and Mrs. Sinatra eating the wafer at the end. Afterward, we drove to his stables where Barbara Sinatra rode her Tennessee walking horse around the corral while Frank and I talked. Hearing that I rode, she invited me to join her but I felt he was rather relieved when, politely, I declined.

After I brought up his legendary dislike of doing more than one take per movie scene, he quickly said he certainly would do more for me. Yet, upon my saying that I understood his desire to keep things fresh, he responded, "Yeah, otherwise it's like singing a song twice for the same audience." Sinatra used to come to a recording session, let the musicians rehearse the arrangement, and then he'd sing the song down once, maybe do one more take straight through, and that would be it. Shooting a movie scene over and over—and from numerous different angles—was anathema to him, and so it's no wonder that two of his best picture per-formances were both for directors who often used to photograph an entire scene in one continuous take, with no additional coverage at all: Pre-minger on *The Man with the Golden Arm*, Minnelli on *Some Came Run-ning*. Speaking once about Minnelli, Sinatra told me with warm amusement of the time Vincente—who was known to be very artistic but somewhat dreamy and absentminded—had come on the location and been very upset about the placement of a huge Ferris wheel: he wanted it moved a few feet. Frank quietly had suggested he simply move the camera instead, and Minnelli had been delighted with this solution. As he told the story, Sinatra smiled affectionately.

Frank Sinatra and Ava Gardner, during their tumultuous
marriage: both always spoke of each other to the end with
the same soft look in their eyes and tone in their voices.

The next day, we were talking about the casting of his female love
interest for our *Paradise Road;* the woman's character arrives in Las Vegas
looking for him, and Sinatra's character is extremely troubled when he
sees her, tries to avoid her. It turns out the two had been very much in love
some twenty years before, she had left him, and he had been heartbroken,
was still quietly carrying the torch. So, with perhaps typical director's
moxie, discussing who should play that part, I said, "What about Ava?"
There was a slight pause, during which Frank looked at me coolly but
with a sadness behind it and a kind of respect that I'd put it out there.
Then he said, quietly, "Too close to home, kid." I quickly said, "How
about Sophia?" He had already done a picture with Sophia Loren but
they'd not had an affair. He relaxed. "Sophia's OK," he said.

Sinatra often had a kind of surprisingly lost quality when he wasn't acting a song or a role. In moments of banter with Dean Martin, he was

never quite as fast or as comfortable as some of the others in the Rat Pack; he wasn't as quick with the improv, but he did love to laugh at it. One of the things I remember most was that often cool yet nonetheless sad look in his eyes. Just a couple of weeks before he died, I acted in two little movie scenes with Mia Farrow (Frank's penultimate wife) and, of course, we spoke of Sinatra. She said that during his last illness she had been talking either with him or one of his two daughters nearly every day. When they were married briefly in the late sixties, there had been a thirty-year difference in their ages, Mia was saying, which of course had its shortcomings. "Frank would be talking about his days with Tommy Dorsey," Mia told me, "and I'd say, '*Who's* Tommy?' " She shook her head. "And he'd be so patient and sweet and explain to me who Tommy Dorsey was and everything." And that was one of the characteristics I remembered about him, too, a quality of tough kindness.

I never really saw the mean Sinatra, though at dinner once he let out a little irritation at Barbara because the food wasn't being served right or something, and during his concerts a couple of times, there was a bitter, ugly sting to a few comments about the press or other people he didn't like. As Lauren Bacall told me a few years after Sinatra died, he decidedly had a Jekyll and Hyde quality. She said that she "loved" her good times with Frank but that he could become "ice cold"; she admitted that it was "quite terrifying to be a victim of that." In 2003, an extremely close look at Sinatra was published that confirmed this: *Mr. S.: My Life with Frank Sinatra,* by George Jacobs, a young black man from New Orleans who became Frank's right hand from 1954 to 1968, and then had the curtain lowered and never saw him again. Extremely readable and unpretentious (co-written with William Stadiem), it is perhaps the best many-sided portrait of Sinatra that's been printed, and underscores what Bacall referred to as "that fucking mercurial personality," both the highs and lows.

Of, course, Bacall had known Sinatra for some years as a friend of hers and Bogart's, a charter member of the original Holmby Hills Rat Pack, which was not in any way like the later Sinatra Rat Pack, the name appropriated after Bogart's death (see Bogart chapter). Sinatra also, for a time, appropriated Bacall. Bogie had been the Head Rat and Frank was dubbed sarcastically—because of his well-known antipathy for the press—The Rat in Charge of Publicity. Sinatra, she said, was "in awe of Bogie," not comprehending how a person could possibly combine such talent, such intelligence, with a loving family life, no screwing around, and "still be fun." Less than five months after Bogart died, Bacall told me, Sinatra had called her and immediately started listing what they were going to do on

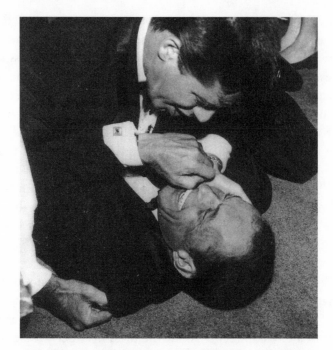

*On the night Frank Sinatra won his Oscar, Jerry Lewis
tackled him backstage and yelled out, "I'm so proud
of you, I'm going to kiss you on the mouth!" Sinatra said,
"No, no, don't kiss me on the mouth!" This moment
was caught by a nearby photographer.*

every night of the coming week starting with a championship boxing
match. Still grieving, she remembered being happy to have someone take
over and plan her time for her. And since they were such "good friends,"
there was, along with the fun they shared, a sense of his concern for her.
She added that in those days, of course, Sinatra was "not unattractive."
Their relationship did not turn romantic, however, until some time later,
after a July Fourth yacht cruise down to Balboa Island, even though Frank
became drunk and abusive with a waiter, which, Bacall shrugged, was par
for the course.

In her grief, as she put it, she simply wanted her "life to go on," and
Sinatra was a help, not only because he was so "attentive, caring, very
lovely," but also because of his special sweetness with her two young children. He would bring them gifts, she remembered, even though this
seemed somehow alien to his persona and he was awkward in the role.
They had an unpleasant split on New Year's Eve while at his Palm Springs
home. He had asked her to be there a few days before him to shop, send-

ing a list of things. She got a kick out of this, "playing house." After Frank arrived, they had dinner with friends at a popular restaurant and he was more than complimentary and kind, yet a couple of days later, he behaved "like a maniac." They had a New Year's Eve party, Bacall said, and Sinatra got drunk and became abusive, bringing her to tears. The next day she hardly spoke to him, he drove her home and there was no communication for two weeks.

Out of the blue he called while both of them were in New York and asked if they could meet. She agreed reluctantly, not wanting any repeat of the New Year's Eve humiliation. He was sweet to her, however, and not long after, when they were in L.A. again, he called once more and this time he asked her to marry him. "Crazy!" Bacall exclaimed. Sinatra was not only charming, he seemed extremely sincere, and without thinking things through, she agreed. They went to celebrate and ran into agent Swifty Lazar; Sinatra told him the good news, and soon after left for Florida. In his absence, Lazar took Bacall to an L.A. theater opening where, unbeknownst to her, Lazar gave gossip columnist Louella Parsons the hot tip. The next morning, it was all over the front page of the *Los Angeles Examiner*. Bacall was horrified, figured it out, and insisted Lazar tell Sinatra what he had done. Lazar called, laughing, Bacall said, with lingering irritation at the agent's cavalier attitude. Toward the end of the next day, Sinatra had phoned her and complained that he had to hole up in his hotel room because of the media hullabaloo. She said she had never said a word. He replied that perhaps they had better cool it, not see each other for a little while. They never spoke again. A few years later, when she ran into Sinatra at a Palm Springs event, he looked at her as though she were "a wall."

The kind of stardom Frank Sinatra enjoyed comes with such an inherent built-in aggravator of megalomania—everyone is all over you all the time and you yourself are so much the product of what you do—that equilibrium is not easy to maintain. Finally, I could somehow understand why it was so hard for him to end his nights, why he was usually up very late, especially after performances. That extraordinary rapport he always had with the crowds—how do you come down from that? He was, after all, an interpretive artist—he could not get his fulfillment from the joy of creation, writing new songs, scripts or books for himself—and so perhaps there was a certain hollowness to the achievement, no matter how tumultuous the audience's reaction. Along those lines, therefore, it's no coincidence that he loved to paint. That was all his own. I had an oddly pervasive sense that, on top of the lonesome emptiness, the loss of Ava

Gardner never quite left him, that the heartbreak of "the gal that got away" was somehow always there, even at the height of his later triumphs, the feeling perhaps that what he had most wanted in life had been denied him after all.

His last road manager, Tony Oppedisano, affirmed some of this—as did Tina Sinatra's popular and touching memoir of her dad (*My Father's Daughter*)—that the marriage with Barbara wasn't happy. Eventually, there was no real communication between them, or companionship. After his final illness got worse, she would leave him alone evenings to have dinner out with friends. It was on one of these nights that he had his fatal seizure. Barbara made it to the hospital but she didn't let his children know about the crisis. They weren't there for him at the end, as they so wanted to be, as he would have wanted. Tony O. (as Sinatra and other friends called him) told me that Frank could never forgive himself for what he felt he'd done to his children by leaving his first wife, Nancy, Sr., with whom he continued to stay in touch to the end of his life. Tony would ask if he hadn't realized his kids had all forgiven him long ago, as had Nancy, Sr. But Frank couldn't forgive himself, and so the unhappiness of his last years was his punishment. That was how he felt, Tony said, trapped in his own house.

One night Frank got Tony to drive him over to Nancy, Sr.'s house but he couldn't bring himself to go inside. He became afraid, and told Tony to drive him back before Barbara returned. Tina's memoir relates how angry she had become over this situation, her father's seeming inability to confront Barbara, so she didn't speak to him for the last year or so of his life, and, of course, she deeply regretted this afterward. The breach between Sinatra's last wife and his children could never be repaired, as Tina's book made clear. Barbara has made no response; she remains the last Mrs. Frank Sinatra.

During Sinatra's last years, Tony O. told me, Jerry Lewis would call Frank at least once a week "no matter where in the world he was." Sometimes Sinatra would be so physically weak that it took considerable effort to pull himself together enough to get on the line, but he always did. He would ask Tony to have Jerry hold on, then he would summon "all the strength he had" and eventually answer as though everything was fine with his usual, "Hello, Jew!" They would talk, Frank would laugh, and then he would hang up exhausted and have to sleep for an hour. One time, as a joke, Lewis sent Frank a note with a check enclosed. He wrote that he was thinking of them and wanted Sinatra to buy "something special" for Barbara and himself. The check was for $27.50. Frank broke up.

Mrs. Sinatra, Tony said, wanted Frank to endorse the check so she could cash it, but Tony had it framed instead.

In our final conversation, around 1991, I told Frank I was planning a comedy-drama with several ghosts in it, and that I wanted him to play one of the ghosts. He said, "I can do that." Of course he could. Wasn't that an aspect of what he had played most of his life to most people? Only a fraction of the world had ever really met him, talked with him, sat with him—compared to the countless millions for whom he was a shadow on the screen, a ghost image on the tube, a voice in the air. And he would be all of these forever, but especially that voice—the most honest and naked in its romantic vulnerability—more so than any other popular male singer of the twentieth century. Certainly, all the audiences I had ever been a part of watching him in person would have agreed; I remember the joyous acclamation they gave him when he altered Bruce Johnston's lyrics to Barry Manilow's pop hit, "I Write the Songs," into his own wildly immodest but nonetheless quite accurate summation of what he has meant to six decades of lovers:

> I sing the songs
> That make the whole world sing . . .
> I am music, and I sing the songs.

One of the things that moved me most during the world's first reaction to his death on May 14, 1998, was when the Empire State Building, an unofficial symbol of New York, New York, on the night of his passing turned its lights blue: a strangely poignant tribute from a city to a seventies incarnation of Sinatra's, only the last in a career that began as The Voice of the forties. I was just as touched as I had been when I heard that all the lights on the Las Vegas Strip had been turned off for one minute on the night Frank's pal, Dean Martin, had died. Each was a gesture more potent than lowering the flag to half-mast—from both the private sector and the public—a bow of respect to say in silence that someone we would always remember with pleasure had gone from us.

Born Francis Albert Sinatra, December 12, 1915, Hoboken, NJ; died May 14, 1998, Los Angeles, CA.

Selected starring features (with director):

1945: *Anchors Aweigh* (George Sidney)
1949: *Take Me Out to the Ball Game* (Busby Berkeley); *On the Town* (Stanley Donen and Gene Kelly)

1953: *From Here to Eternity* (Fred Zinnemann)

1954: *Suddenly* (Lewis Allen); *Young at Heart* (Gordon Douglas)

1955: *Guys and Dolls* (Joseph L. Mankiewicz); *The Tender Trap* (Charles Walters); *The Man with the Golden Arm* (Otto Preminger)

1956: *High Society* (Walters)

1957: *The Joker Is Wild* (Charles Vidor); *Pal Joey* (Sidney)

1958: *Some Came Running* (Vincente Minnelli)

1959: *A Hole in the Head* (Frank Capra)

1960: *Ocean's Eleven* (Lewis Milestone)

1962: *The Manchurian Candidate* (John Frankenheimer)

1963: *4 for Texas* (Robert Aldrich)

1965: *Von Ryan's Express* (Mark Robson)

1967: *Tony Rome* (Gordon Douglas)

1968: *The Detective* (Douglas); *Lady in Cement* (Douglas)

1980: *The First Deadly Sin* (Brian G. Hutton)

21

BEN GAZZARA

The first review I ever wrote or had published dealt with the smash off-Broadway success by Calder Willingham called *End as a Man* (based on his own novel), with a brilliant Actors Studio cast headed by a newcomer who was clearly a major new star, Ben Gazzara. I raved about him in my first column in the high school paper (*Collegiate Journal,* 1953); I was fourteen. Everyone else who published a review raved about Benny that year. Indeed, virtually overnight, Gazzara became a certified Broadway name. Director Jack Garfein's production, featuring such other beginners as George Peppard, Pat Hingle, George Kennedy and Arthur Storch, soon moved to a Broadway house. Gazzara was electrifying in the role of a somewhat psychotic bad rich-boy bully at a Southern military academy. He was also, everyone said, the sexiest, most hypnotic male actor anyone had seen on or off Broadway since Marlon Brando in *A Streetcar Named Desire* about six seasons earlier. While Brando was passively brilliant, Gazzara was aggressively so. And funny. Playing essentially a sadistic heavy named Jocko de Paris, Benny got a lot of big laughs that emerged solely from his amazing charisma onstage, and the wit behind it, and a consummate control over himself and the audience.

Within the next few years, I would be lucky enough to see Gazzara on Broadway three times more: as Brick in Elia Kazan's original production of Tennessee Williams' remarkably successful *Cat on a Hot Tin Roof;* as the drug addict in Michael V. Gazzo's popular and critically acclaimed drama *A Hatful of Rain;* as a poet-drifter in Gazzo's weak follow-up, *The Night Circus,* co-starring Gazzara's second wife, the willowy, beautiful Janice Rule. His work in the first two of these, along with *End as a Man,* are among the top few performances I've ever seen in the theater. Transfixing is not too big a word in Benny's case. During the entire first act of *Cat,* Gazzara had been staged to stand to the side, leaning on a crutch (because

*Ben Gazzara became a Broadway star almost overnight in 1953
because of his electric (and often hilarious) performance as Jocko de Paris
in Calder Willingham's adaptation of his own novel* End as a Man,
directed by Jack Garfein. *In the same role, he made his movie debut,
retitled* The Strange One *(1957), also directed by Garfein.*

of Brick's broken leg), looking out the window and sipping a drink. His
wife Maggie, played by Barbara Bel Geddes, sits on the bed, walks
around, talks virtually nonstop. Gazzara's lines are mainly, "That's right,
Maggie," or "Yeah, that's right, Maggie," or "Uh-huh." The rest of the
time he was looking out that (imaginary) window at the Southern landscape below, and he was silent. Yet audiences could barely take their eyes
off Ben—I was no exception—he had the most astonishingly magnetic
attraction and quality of danger in his virtually total silence and lack of
movement. And his terse, disinterested or ironic responses remain the
most memorable out of an enormously effective Kazan production of one

of Tennessee's best plays. Benny stole it with dead calm and a kind of eruptive quietude.

Yet they didn't hire him for the movie—Paul Newman played Brick—and Elizabeth Taylor played Maggie in a deluxe Metrocolor Hollywood version rewritten by Richard Brooks which didn't come near the Broadway original on any level, not by a ten-foot pole. Nor was Gazzara hired to repeat his equally riveting and superb performance of the drug addict fighting his way back in *A Hatful of Rain*. For that movie, Don Murray got the part in Fred Zinnemann's fairly faithful but miscast production. Aside from Newman's obvious movie-star popularity (Murray, on the other hand, had little), is it possible Benny's ethnicity got in the way? Both Newman and Murray were fair, blue-eyed Anglo-Irish types, without the darker sexual threat of the Mediterranean Gazzara. Because of his Broadway commitments, he couldn't accept Kazan's offer to play the lead male role (an Italian) in Tennessee Williams' original screenplay, *Baby Doll,* so Kazan hired Eli Wallach instead. Gazzara didn't get to the screen until producer Sam Spiegel hired the entire *End as a Man* cast and production, including first-time (film) director Garfein, shot the play, and released it as *The Strange One* (a decidedly inferior title). Ben was as brilliant as ever in the part, but Spiegel buried the picture in pique because of Garfein's rude behavior to him during shooting. The picture got great notices but no publicity, improper advertising, and inadequate distribution. My last column in the high-school paper—four years after starting with *End as a Man*—was a review of the 1957 movie version. I praised Gazzara with equal passion, but it had taken him four years to reach the screen, essentially because of his dedication to the theater, which forever has remained Benny's first and greatest love in acting.

The first time Gazzara was starred in a successful movie was for Otto Preminger's classic *Anatomy of a Murder* (1959), one of the great American films. Ben played an extremely ambiguous role with infinite resonance and repressed violence. Here were Broadway's newest stars, Ben Gazzara and George C. Scott (only his second movie), opposite such Hollywood legends as James Stewart and Eve Arden, all on location in a small Midwestern city where the real story—which formed the basis of Robert Travers' best seller—actually took place. The score is one of only two ever done by the immortal Duke Ellington (who appeared briefly), and remains extraordinarily fresh and modern nearly half a century later. The movie is like that, too, and Gazzara gives one of his best and most charismatic performances. Benny would tell me that he was especially impressed with Stewart, who "always wanted to rehearse!"

Ben Gazzara as an Army officer accused of murder, and James Stewart as his attorney, in Gazzara's second film, Otto Preminger's brilliant and probably best movie, Anatomy of a Murder *(1959), the finest picture ever made about the U.S. judicial system*

However, Ben's movie career did not have the best of luck. He ended up doing some clunkers for money, missing out on some other important gigs, and appearing in a couple of TV series—*Arrest and Trial* and *Run for Your Life*—that were popular but which he abhorred having to do. The truth is that Gazzara is an artist, and wasn't happy at all with the profound compromises of television, or films for that matter. He kept going back to Broadway, where he has always been a sensation. Onstage, he and Colleen Dewhurst did a legendary production of Edward Albee's *Who's Afraid of Virginia Woolf?* and he was starred in a memorable version of Eugene O'Neill's *Strange Interlude;* did superbly O'Neill's one-man *Hughie* (with a terrific curtain-raiser by newcomer David Scott Milton, coincidentally an old friend of mine); was enormously touching opposite Gena Rowlands in a reading of *Love Letters,* recalling their pairing in a picture by Gena's husband, John Cassavetes.

One of the few to give Gazzara the kind of movie roles he deserved was Cassavetes, through whom Gazzara and I first met in 1977. Benny's work with John—in *Husbands* (1970), *The Killing of a Chinese Bookie* (1976) and *Opening Night* (1977)—consists, apart from his first two, as probably the most challenging and rewarding roles he has had in pictures. Each captures a different aspect of Ben's complicated persona, and showcases his versatility as an actor. Two further sides appeared to great effect in two starring roles for movies I directed and co-wrote, *Saint Jack* (1979) and *They All Laughed* (1981). We shot both on islands—Singapore and Manhattan—and they were two of the most highly charged and life-altering experiences I've ever gone through. Gazzara had an incalculable effect on both works, which are also among my own personal favorites.

During the shooting of Cassavetes' *Opening Night* in Los Angeles, I went downtown to play a bit as myself, and at the lunch break, got to know Ben Gazzara a little. His gregarious, outspoken, expansive nature immediately suggested to me what I had been trying to find in an actor to play the title role for my next picture. The script of *Saint Jack*, based on Paul Theroux's novel, had been rewritten and restructured by the Pulitzer Prize–winning playwright Howard Sackler (*The Great White Hope*), who was also a friend. The lead character was Jack Flowers, an Italian-American living in Singapore, circa 1973—while the Vietnam War still raged nearby—an equally gregarious and expansive guy, the eternal host no matter who's paying the tab. "Peter, sit over here, order whatever you want," he said to me, "John's paying!" Cassavetes would nod: "That's right, John's paying—as usual." And Benny would explode in laughter. He used to do that to me, later, in Singapore: "Go on, order whatever you want—some more satay and wine!—Peter's paying!" When I'd say, "That's right, thanks, Benny," he would merrily laugh it up. A quiet communication in a public place was generally impossible with Ben Gazzara. Especially if he'd had a drink or two to warm him up. There was little that Benny mightn't say out loud publicly—the word "irrepressible" was coined for Gazzara in a crowd.

We spent three or four months together in Singapore, at the same hotel, writing and acting together for *Saint Jack*, Ben directing me for my scenes, as I did for his. He encouraged me to play the part of the main heavy, and was hugely involved in all the rewriting of the screenplay, which went on virtually for the entire sixty-day shoot. Indeed, so inexpensive was the production crew, that it was worth it for us to stop shooting for a few days to give ourselves time to finish mapping out the remaining third of the movie. While living there, we had come to real-

*Ben Gazzara, Gena Rowlands and John Cassavetes getting ready
for a scene in Cassavetes' complicated theater drama,* Opening Night
*(1977), the last of three pictures Gazzara and Cassavetes did together.
Ben and Gena would work with each other a number of times
afterward, on screen and stage.*

ize—Benny and George Morfogen (that superb New York actor and dear
old friend of mine, serving as co-producer on *Jack*) and I—that here we
were doing a film about a pimp and his women and there were no fully
developed female characters in the script. To remedy this, both Ben and I
did a lot of what we would between us call "research," among the broth-
els, the madams, pimps, hookers, as well as the more regular men and
women of Asia. Since Singapore is a huge melting pot of the East, as New
York City is of the West, Gazzara and I came to know Chinese from
numerous provinces of the thirteen that make up the mother country,
people from Malaysia, from Sri Lanka, from Thailand, as well as from
India, Korea, Vietnam and Japan. Over the six months I was there and the
four Benny was, we certainly got to know, albeit briefly, men and women
from all these places, especially the women. And we put what we
learned—as much as we could—into the picture.

Therefore, it wasn't entirely fiction, that certain remark Ben made one
morning to his daughter, which turned into a running gag. Both of us had
been up pretty late in our separate rooms with ladies of the evening whom

we had requested from the Chinese madam, who also played a madam in our picture. Several of these women ended up being cast in roles, one or two of them substantial, and a number were able to save up enough to move back to their homes away from Singapore. Anyway, Gazzara and I had both been doing this so-called research and casting until early in the morning, and we both had a six-thirty a.m. call, so when we got to the location in the heart of Singapore's Chinatown—by today all razed and rebuilt—we were zonked, fried, exhausted. But coffee or tea and gorging on food somehow kept us going. Gazzara's eighteen-year-old daughter Elizabeth had joined the staff while we were shooting, and seeing her father a trifle pooped first thing in the morning, she asked why he was so tired. Gazzara said we had been working very late, pointing at me and shaking his head in exhaustion. Elizabeth wasn't satisfied. What were we *doing?* she asked. Benny vigorously slapped his forehead loudly, bending over as he did, and exploded, "*Think*ing and *writ*ing, darling! *Think*ing and *writ*ing!" I didn't laugh at that moment, but simply walked away. Later, alone, I imitated his line, "*Think*ing and *writ*ing!," slapping my forehead, and Benny completely broke up, as did I. That became our private catchphrase for the rest of the picture, and after.

In retrospect, our occupational hazards on *Saint Jack* had a lot to do with ending my nine-year relationship with Cybill Shepherd (co-producer and co-writer on the film), and with Gazzara ending his longtime marriage to Janice Rule. The main positive result of all this was the film we made, of which both of us were equally proud, and which won for Benny and me, respectively, the Best Actor Award and the Critics Prize at the 1979 Venice Film Festival. The picture also reinvigorated Gazzara's picture career, and garnered the best notices I'd had in six years. His price shot up from a low of $15,000 for our film to $250,000 for his next, then $500,000 and a million for the next two. The picture he got cast in directly off *Saint Jack* was *Bloodline* (1979). Michael Eisner and Barry Diller (then heads of Paramount) had come to my house and watched a screening there of *Saint Jack* with the idea of acquiring it for distribution. They almost did, but encountered internal opposition. However, the next morning Gazzara was offered a quarter of a million to co-star opposite Audrey Hepburn in *Bloodline*. This directly led to my writing *They All Laughed* for Gazzara and Hepburn, that film offering Audrey her last starring role in features.

Gazzara and Hepburn had a brief but intense affair during *Bloodline*, and when he returned from shooting, Ben was mad about Audrey and told me a lot about her life at that time and about their affair, and how

*Ben Gazzara and Peter Falk in Cassavetes' superbly acted,
resonant* Husbands *(1970), about three pals' reactions
to the death of a fourth; one of Gazzara's best performances.
Falk and Cassavetes are brilliant as the other two.*

lonely and fragile and saintlike she was. I took note of it all and used this for the character she eventually played opposite Gazzara in *They All Laughed.*

The idea for the picture in the first place was to deal with many of the personal crises and romantic dilemmas Benny and I and our friends had experienced over the years, but to hide these behind the genre-coating of a bittersweet, slightly screwball comedy about a group of private detectives who get much too emotionally involved in their cases, a metaphor for what we do in our work. So all the parts were not only written for the actors who eventually played them, but a lot of their scenes and backstories were based on those actors' personalities and their real lives.

Certainly, Benny was playing a guy totally inspired by Gazzara's actual manner, his ways of speaking, his typical phrases, like "Yeah, that's right."

Ben Gazzara and Audrey Hepburn on location on Fifth Avenue, near
Tiffany, for a scene in their second film together, They All Laughed *(1981),*
which came about because of the romantic involvement they
shared on their first, Bloodline *(1979)*

I noticed no matter how many times he might say, "Yeah, that's right," he
never said it the same way twice, there always being a slightly different
intonation. In both *Saint Jack* and *They All Laughed,* the line between the
characters Benny played and himself was erased. He existed in those roles
so that when the pictures were over, his characters could be imagined
walking on forever. To me, that's the best kind of movie acting and Gazzara gave me the gift of this sort of golden performance twice.

While *Saint Jack* had been a very close experience for the two of us, life
got in our way on *They All Laughed.* While filming *Inchon* (1981), shot
right after *Bloodline,* he had fallen in love with Elke Stuckmann, the German woman who would become his third wife. This situation obviously
created some tension between Ben and Audrey, which doesn't show in the
picture but was nevertheless another obstacle for Gazzara (and Hepburn)
at that time. The shooting of *Laughed* and the next period of his life were
marked by depression and anxiety, both of which he eventually licked.
Since then, he has acted in many foreign and domestic productions, never
less than excellent in all, superb in some (like Marco Ferreri's *Tales of Ordinary Madness,* 1983); was suddenly discovered at the end of the nineties by

the younger generation of American director-writers, like the Coen brothers, Todd Solondz, David Mamet and Spike Lee; had a great personal triumph off-Broadway with a one-man show about Yogi Berra, into whose persona he managed to submerge himself completely; wrote and repeatedly rewrote his autobiography, soon to be published, called *Only the Beginning*.

Both of us were terribly saddened by the death of John Cassavetes in 1989. We never see each other or speak that John's name doesn't come up. As it did while we were shooting in Singapore. Gazzara loved him like a brother and the feeling was mutual. "An artist!" Benny would exclaim about Cassavetes. "John is a *real* artist! How many *are* there?!" And John would say, "Well, Ben's an artist, you know," as a way of explaining Gazzara. I treasure the memory of Ben and John at dinner, their ways of egging each other on—with Peter Falk joining in; and Ben's love of John's wild rebelliousness, indefatigability and genius, John's delight in Ben's large-scale talent, humor and ego.

Recently, there was an AFI tribute screening in New York of *Saint Jack*, and Gazzara and I went. Watching the picture, it was hard for us to believe we had made it nearly twenty-five years before. The memory of every shot was vivid to each of us, as well as what we had been doing around it. Since we both looked a good deal younger, too, it wasn't always easy to watch. We were often moved. Afterward, the Q&A portion with the audience was rewarding, as several mentioned how much the movie wasn't like most films, because what Benny and I had tried to do was exactly that. We kept saying to each other, Let's leave out all conventional movie scenes, let's avoid anything obligatory. Gazzara had been a splendid watchdog on this vow.

At the end of shooting, for example, his character and mine had a big climactic scene running four-and-a-half pages of conversation, during which the moral underpinning of the picture is stressed. Ben's Jack has made a deal for fairly big bucks—enough to take him back to the United States—with the CIA-FBI guy I play, in order to get some incriminating sexual photos of an American senator briefly visiting Singapore. Jack takes the sensational shots, but in the concluding scene, when he brings them to my character, decides against turning them over, saying at some length why finally he cannot stoop so low and continue to live with himself. The night before we were to film this, Ben and I rehearsed it at the hotel. We read the dialogue through a couple of times and both of us felt uncomfortable with it.

Benny said, "Isn't this one of those scenes we were trying to avoid? Hitting it on the nose?" I agreed that's what it was. "What am I really saying here?" Ben went on. "Aren't I just saying, 'Look—fuck it! I'm not playing ball!'" And that's just what the scene became; neither of us caring that we'd just lost a major, heavy-dialogue sequence. Instead, Ben calls out my character's name: "Hey, Eddie!" I look up to see him across the street from me. Gesturing with both arms as if to say, "It's finished," he yells to me over the traffic: "Fuck it!" and walks away, throws those scandalous photos into the river and disappears into the Asian crowds. Gazzara's sense of truth as an actor helped give us an honest, undidactic, unmelodramatic ending. That is what happens when a brilliant actor so inhabits a part, and makes it his own, that he can do no wrong. At his best, on both stage and screen, this is exactly what you always get from Ben Gazzara—a real human being whom he finds for us within himself.

Born Biagio Anthony Gazzara, August 28, 1930, New York, NY.

Selected starring features (with director):

1957: *The Strange One* (Jack Garfein)
1959: *Anatomy of a Murder* (Otto Preminger)
1961: *The Young Doctors* (Phil Karlson)
1962: *Reprieve* (a.k.a. *Convicts Four*) (Millard Kaufman)
1965: *A Rage to Live* (Walter Grauman)
1969: *The Bridge at Remagen* (John Guillermin)
1970: *Husbands* (John Cassavetes)
1972: *The Family Rico* (Paul Wendkos)
1975: *Capone* (Steve Carver)
1976: *The Killing of a Chinese Bookie* (Cassavetes)
1977: *Opening Night* (Cassavetes)
1979: *Saint Jack* (P.B.); *Bloodline* (Terence Young)

1981: *They All Laughed* (P.B.)
1983: *Tales of Ordinary Madness* (Marco Ferreri); *The Girl from Trieste* (Pasquale Festa Campanile)
1985: *An Early Frost* (John Erman)
1988: *Don Bosco* (Leandro Castellani)
1989: *Road House* (Rowdy Herrington)
1994: *Parallel Lives* (Linda Yellen)
1996: *Shadow Conspiracy* (George Cosmatos); *Stag* (Gavin Wilding)
1997: *Farmer & Chase* (Michael Seitzman); *Buffalo '66* (Vincent Gallo)
1998: *The Big Lebowski* (Joel Coen); *Happiness* (Todd Solondz); *The Spanish Prisoner* (David Mamet)
1999: *Summer of Sam* (Spike Lee); *The Thomas Crown Affair* (John McTiernan)
2004: *Dogville* (Lars von Trier)

22

AUDREY HEPBURN

The first time it occurred to me that I might be lucky enough to make a picture with Audrey Hepburn was when Ben Gazzara walked into my kitchen in 1979 with groans of yearning, "Oh, my God, I'm in love! Oh, Audrey, my Audrey!" Ben had just returned to Los Angeles from playing opposite Hepburn in *Bloodline* and couldn't stop raving about her: "The sweetest woman I've ever known—she breaks your heart . . . Audrey's a saint." It's true that for actors one of the most serious occupational hazards of filmmaking is falling in love with each other or with the director, and vice versa, but Gazzara and Hepburn—both at the time nearing the end of failed marriages to others—had a dear and passionate relationship during the filming of that picture.

Unfortunately for the movie, their scenes together were really the only things worth watching in it, especially unfortunate considering this was Audrey's first film in three years, the last being Richard Lester's terrific (but not markedly successful) *Robin and Marian* with Sean Connery in 1976. Prior to that, remember, she had not been seen on the screen for nearly a decade, not since the smash hit *Wait Until Dark* (1967), in which she played a blind woman in jeopardy and for which she received her fifth Best Actress Oscar nomination. She had spent those intervening years bringing up her two sons. Following *Bloodline,* Audrey would appear in only one other feature starring role: again with Ben Gazzara, and shot in Manhattan, *They All Laughed* was a romantic comedy we all made together—I wrote and directed—during the beautiful spring and early summer of 1980. While shooting, on May 4, we celebrated Audrey's fifty-first birthday. Seven years later, she was lovely as ever playing the lead in a forgettable TV-movie, *Love Among Thieves,* and then—as, appropriately enough, a guardian angel—in Steven Spielberg's *Always* (1989), devoting the rest of her life to her family and the world family of children she

Audrey Hepburn as Holly Golightly has her little Breakfast at Tiffany's
*(1961), at the corner of Fifth Avenue and Fifty-seventh Street, in Blake
Edwards' charming and enormously popular film version of the Truman
Capote novel; it is the role perhaps most identified with Audrey.*

touched and nurtured through years of grueling UNICEF tours. In 1993,
she died after a short bout with cancer; she was sixty-four.

To most of the world, Audrey Hepburn had arrived fully grown, so to
speak, like Botticelli's *Birth of Venus.* Suddenly there she was in 1953, the
English princess incognito in William Wyler's *Roman Holiday,* falling in
love with the cynical American reporter (Gregory Peck) and transforming
him through her extraordinary beauty and charm, her magical innocence.

The public and the media around the globe fell in love at first sight with Audrey, and our Academy here, along with everyone else, instantly recognized the seemingly miraculous birth of a superbly accomplished actress as well as a film star of the first magnitude. She received the Oscar as Best Actress of that year. Overnight, as they say, this English-Irish-Dutch-Belgian unknown, who had previously appeared only in tiny parts in six British films (1951–52), became a world-famous and vastly popular American star. She was twenty-four.

The most respected and successful picture makers in the country all vied for her unique presence in their films; the fortunate ones who got her were: Billy Wilder (twice), King Vidor, William Wyler (three times), Fred Zinnemann, John Huston, Stanley Donen (three times), George Cukor, Terence Young (twice), Richard Quine, Richard Lester, Blake Edwards, and me. Her leading men, besides Peck and Gazzara, included Humphrey Bogart, William Holden (twice), Henry Fonda, Mel Ferrer (who also directed her once), Anthony Perkins, Gary Cooper, Burt Lancaster, Fred Astaire, Rex Harrison, Cary Grant, Peter O'Toole, Sean Connery and Albert Finney. Upon receiving numerous honors in the last years of her life, these exactly were the two groups of people she thanked.

Throughout the declining fifties and increasingly desperate sixties, Audrey Hepburn was a beacon of tasteful glamour, of sensitivity and of the integrity and innocence of youth; a symbol of unalloyed kindness, morality and goodness on a screen ever more darkened by the baser forms of life, and increasingly peopled by anti-heroes and ambiguous—or simply victimized, or eventually nonexistent—heroines. Audrey was as unlike Marilyn Monroe as she was unlike Grace Kelly or Elizabeth Taylor. It's been said that this Hepburn's appeal was a throwback to the world of silent pictures, a far more rewarding time for variety in women's roles, or to the 1930s when that other Hepburn, Katharine, dominated side by side with Shirley Temple. The great French writer Colette had first spotted Audrey crossing a Riviera hotel lobby—she was doing a bit in *Monte Carlo Baby* (1951)—and knew at a glance that this young woman must play the title role on the Broadway stage of her now-famous coming-of-age heroine in *Gigi*. Looking back today, we can see clearly that in the final full decade of the golden age of movies, Audrey Hepburn became the last true innocent of the American screen.

Robert Graves has said that a good way to understand people's lives is to put them into a mythological context. This is particularly easy with the larger-than-life, uniquely twentieth-century phenomenon of a true film star, one whose own vivid personality becomes the human basis for all the roles he or she plays. Hadn't Audrey played a princess and been entirely believable? The media certainly featured her as princess of the world from *Roman Holiday* onward. She had been the chauffeur's daughter (in Billy Wilder's *Sabrina,* 1954, Hepburn's second star-vehicle and second Oscar nomination), as well as a lowly detective's daughter (in Wilder's *Love in the Afternoon,* 1957), who grew up to be a society princess solely because of the magnificence of her glamor, charm, talent and beauty. Wasn't this Audrey herself?

There was no great difficulty in thinking of her as a dedicated nun (in Fred Zinnemann's *The Nun's Story,* 1959, her third Oscar nomination), and no great coincidence that this was among her most popular films. Audrey not only had a deeply spiritual quality that shone through her eyes, hadn't she also sacrificed herself to the sacred mission of her own children and the children of UNICEF? The best kind of movie casting is always when it is easiest to eliminate the dividing line between actor and character. With Audrey, she always—in George Stevens' apt phrase about Jimmy Stewart—"extinguished disbelief." Was there any problem accepting her as Fred Astaire's new dancing partner (in Stanley Donen's *Funny Face,* 1957)? Audrey had begun as a dancer, looked and moved like a dancer her whole life.

Nor, for that matter, was it hard for classics readers to accept her as Tolstoy's innocent yet sophisticated Natasha of *War and Peace* (directed by King Vidor, 1956), nor as W. H. Hudson's Rima the wild girl of the forest from *Green Mansions* (directed by Mel Ferrer, 1959): she was a natural for both—a striking indication of Audrey's versatility within her own persona. She could easily flow from indomitable pioneer woman (John Huston's 1960 *The Unforgiven*) to Greenwich Village bohemian (Blake Edwards' 1961 *Breakfast at Tiffany's,* her fourth Oscar nomination and perhaps most enduringly popular and resonant incarnation) to a cockney flower girl (in George Cukor's 1964 version of *My Fair Lady*) who is transformed into a mythical princess. Always back to nonhereditary royalty.

Just like Robin Hood's outlaw queen Maid Marian (*Robin and Marian*), named after one of the Old Religion's earliest deities, Marian meaning "queen mother," or "the fruitful mother of Heaven"; again, awfully close to the real Audrey, to whom her son Sean always referred privately as "The Mutti"—in German "The Mother." The same one who had lived in Nazi-occupied Holland for all of World War II, who saw at close range the twentieth century's most heinous crimes. Experiences of that nature shape you and remain with you for the rest of your life.

At the age of thirty-four, she was approved by Cary Grant, age fifty-

Audrey Hepburn, who always wanted to dance, in a musical number from
Funny Face *(1957), co-starring Fred Astaire, with classic songs by George*
and Ira Gershwin, directed by Stanley Donen

nine, to play opposite him in one of his last pictures (Stanley Donen's delightful 1963 *Charade*); Grant actually retired only three years later because he felt he was getting too old to be a leading man opposite young women. With Audrey, however, the age difference was totally acceptable: she always seemed far wiser and more mature than her years, yet at the same time retained a kind of sacred innocence. In the last twenty years of her life she was most frequently associated with the free-spirited, unpredictable and inimitably stylish Holly Golightly in *Breakfast at Tiffany's*, a girl born in the South. In the movie, when she says, "I love New York," you love it for all the magic she herself brings to the mythology of a great melting pot. Blake Edwards—one of the best filmmakers of the last fifty

years—understood this profoundly while making the picture. It's clear by
the way he brings Hepburn into the film at the very beginning: an empty,
early dawn Fifth Avenue; a single cab; a tall, striking, unmistakable figure
gets out, walks toward Tiffany's in a long shot, and Hepburn's title-card
fades in, the "Moon River" theme playing with all the utter confidence of
certain nostalgia. From start to finish, Edwards knew it: this was Hepburn's picture, and he is never away from her for long.

She is timeless. How beautifully she conveyed everything, and the subtle complications behind everything, and all with such amazing simplicity. Her silent looks, the grace and expressiveness of her movements, are a
marvel. She is comparable in all those ways to the great women of the pre-
talkie era—Lillian Gish or Mary Pickford or Gloria Swanson—in whose
eyes you could read volumes. She shared with some of the early stars that
same abiding innocence—even when her character, like Holly, had certainly been around. When she sings "Moon River" with just a guitar, she
could break your heart.

She was equally convincing as a brilliantly brave blind woman (Terence
Young's version of the Broadway hit *Wait Until Dark*) and a chic modern
sophisticate of privilege in a troubled marriage (Donen's *Two for the Road,*
1967), who somehow comes to represent an era. And she played a similar
role for another era (*They All Laughed* of 1981), but both European: Audrey
Hepburn kept internationalism going in pictures. Even when the romantic comedies fizzled a bit (1964's *Paris When It Sizzles,* 1966's *How to Steal a
Million*), Audrey always kept up her end of the bargain—she always held
out the unspoken promise of true and enduring love.

Yet what she represented on the screen and what she herself so richly
deserved was denied her in life—except from some close friends and her
two sons. Romantically, Audrey did not have such a happy time of it. On
a picture in the early seventies, William Holden told his co-star (a good
friend of mine at the time), that he and Audrey had fallen very much in
love during her second picture, *Sabrina.* But Holden was already long-
married and had had a vasectomy; Audrey very much wanted children, so
they bid each other a heavy adieu. Holden's drinking increased, and finally
killed him years later. Audrey instead married Mel Ferrer, the co-star of
her second Broadway show, 1954's *Ondine.* (She won the Best Actress
Tony for this only six weeks after winning her Oscar for *Roman Holiday.*)
Although she and Ferrer worked together again—as co-stars (in *War and
Peace*), as director and star (for *Green Mansions*), as producer and star (on
Wait Until Dark), and had one son, Sean, whom they both adored—

On location with Humphrey Bogart for her second starring film,
Billy Wilder's Sabrina *(1954), during which she and co-star*
William Holden fell in love; but he was married. Bogart liked
Hepburn but disliked Wilder and the film.

nevertheless, the union was not a fulfilling one for Audrey. Evidently, there was his temper, his infidelities.

She did another picture with Holden (*Paris When It Sizzles*), but he was in bad shape by then, ten years after *Sabrina* was shot—years that included his biggest financial success, *The Bridge on the River Kwai;* his one Oscar win, for *Stalag 17,* came while he was mad about Audrey. And he never got over her, he told my friend, and one night—in an angry fit of frustration at his fate—Holden threw his Oscar into the Bay of Naples. He died in 1981. Audrey was greatly saddened, I remember, by Holden's death. The marriage to Mel Ferrer had officially ended by divorce in 1968.

In the following year, Audrey married Dr. Andrea Dotti, an Italian psychiatrist who was nine years younger than she; they lived in Rome (and later, in Switzerland) with Sean and then with their child, Luca. This marriage also was troubled by problems similar to the first, and because Hepburn described some of these to Gazzara, her real life became the inspiration for the character I wrote for her in our picture: a woman devoted to her young son, braving a jealous, philandering husband on the boy's behalf, finding temporary respite in a brief but intense love affair.

On the movie he made right after *Bloodline,* while Audrey was still married to the doctor, Ben Gazzara met his future third wife, Elke Stuckmann. By the time Audrey was free, Ben had remarried, and Audrey had met the last man in her life, former actor Robert Wolders. Previously, Wolders had been married to Merle Oberon until her death in 1979. Soon after, he and Audrey were introduced to each other, sometime during the making of *They All Laughed*—and when she had carefully ended her marriage, Wolders eventually settled down with Audrey in Switzerland. Though they never married, the two lived together for eleven years until her death, and while there reportedly were some troubles toward the end, Audrey generally seemed very contented with Wolders. She left her home and entire estate to her two sons.

When I first met Audrey in 1979, I found she was still as determined as ever to create a home and an atmosphere of morality for her children. She had all the fame and fortune one could hope for, and considerable gratification as an artist, and felt that her first allegiance had to be to her children. She had seen plenty of show-business families (and other businesses' families, too) where this had not been the case, and she had witnessed the often sad or difficult or tragic results. The fact remains that at the height of her career, after five or six of the biggest successes of the 1960s, and commanding a million dollars a film—at the time, top dollar for a superstar—Audrey Hepburn effectively retired from the movies. She was thirty-seven.

Twelve years, and only two pictures, later, a great deal of persuasion still was required to convince her to do the movie I had by then written for her. Luca was only ten and in school in Rome, and she didn't want to be away from him for very long. I have a hunch that what finally got her into the film was not the million dollars for six weeks' work, nor Ben Gazzara as her co-star again—though both certainly helped—nor my abilities as a director, nor the script which I had tailored for her. (By the way, when I played this card in trying to woo her into the role, she said, "Oh, Peetah! don't tell me that—I'll feel so *baaad* if I don't do it . . . !") None of this did the trick until I offered to hire Sean Ferrer as my personal assistant. Sean wanted to work in films and Audrey thought this would be a good start for him. In fact, he turned out to be not only the best on-set assistant I

Audrey Hepburn with William Holden in their second film together,
Paris When It Sizzles *(1964); now she was married, too.*
The picture, directed by Richard Quine,
didn't work out either.

had ever had, but a damn fine actor in the supporting role entirely rewritten to suit him.

My first reaction after spending some time with Audrey had been to wonder how anyone of such extraordinary fragility and gentleness, with a profound shyness and self-deprecation, could possibly have been able to deal with this ruthless, often cutthroat business. How could she, in fact, ever get up in front of a camera and perform? And I kept that thought right up until the first time I watched her step in to do a shot. An amazingly subtle yet uncanny transformation then happened: this vulnerable, kind and self-effacing woman of incandescent goodness somehow could marshal all of her own sensibilities into a forceful, magical power to express all those qualities, to live and breathe even more naturally than she did in day-to-day life, with all the finest nuances of character and meaning behind her words and looks. John Keats wrote, "Beauty is truth, truth beauty," and Audrey was living proof of that; watching her in a picture was seeing beauty and truth revealed at every shimmering moment.

To make everything even harder, our picture was not done under sound-stage circumstances of comfort and ease. We shot entirely on the crowded streets of Manhattan, in real shops, hotels, restaurants. In order to achieve verisimilitude, and not able to close down part of Fifth Avenue for a week and people it with extras, we ended up trying to be as inconspicuous as possible and just "steal" the shots. Film crews and Audrey Hepburn, Ben Gazzara and John Ritter, not to mention Dorothy Stratten and Patti Hansen, were nothing if not conspicuous as hell. To be able to get these scenes, we had all but three or four crew members remain by the trucks twenty blocks away; had no chairs on the sidewalks for actors or crew, no dressing rooms or honeywagons nearby; used a handful of extras to stand casually around literally blocking the camera from sight; and asked Audrey (and the other actors) to wait in one or another of the stores along Fifth. When the camera was ready, Audrey was sent for, silent gestures gave the cues, the shot was done, and then she was sent back to wait in a store for the next take or shot. Not only did she never complain, she did not give even one second's indication that she might consider complaining. She was always gay, cheerful and encouraging. "Oh, look, Peetah," she'd exclaim, "those nice people in the store gave me this lovely haaandkerchief!" Or, "Look, Peetah, they gave me this beautiful umbreeella!" We had a joke about that: "OK, let's send Audrey over to work the other side of the street."

People gave her things everywhere—and she always seemed as pleased and surprised as a girl of ten—but it was not really a surprise to me. Audrey was a person you wanted to give things to, maybe because she gave so much of the best of herself to everyone and to everything she did, whether cooking up some pasta or risotto—which she made brilliantly—and looked breathtakingly lovely and graceful while doing so. Her risotto is my most memorable risotto. Or, revealing herself in a close-up of ineffable beauty and sadness or joy or both combined. Audrey could do anything.

Whenever the lines didn't quite suit her, she would alter them and they always sounded better her way. Often I would compliment her by saying, "That's not the line, but it's better that way." And invariably she would say, "Oh, isn't it?! I thought it was. I'll say it the way you want—I thought it was that line." And I'd always have to reassure her that her rewrite, instinctual or conscious, was an improvement. But she invariably claimed ignorance of any difference and repeatedly said she'd do it my way. I never let her.

A tragedy occurred one month after *They All Laughed* completed shooting—Dorothy Stratten was murdered—and our bittersweet romantic comedy could never again be what it had been meant to be. This horrific killing affected not only perceptions of the film but its commercial appeal, and yet Audrey's only concern was for the actress who had died and for me, who had been in love with her. She said to me that Dorothy had been like "an angel who was only allowed to come to earth for a little while and touch all of us." At a time in my life when most people turned away, Audrey did the opposite—she was there to offer hope, faith and love.

This is exactly what she gave to her own children, and to movie audiences around the world, and finally, to all the thousands of UNICEF children mired in tragic circumstances whom she visited throughout her last years. I could hear the sense of mission in her voice over the phone as we spoke of other pictures I continued to ask her to do: the only time she had now, she would say, was for the unfortunate children. Maybe she *could* do this or that movie between her tours, but probably not—her UNICEF work was too demanding, too exhausting, too painful emotionally—though she never said that, nor complained in any way.

Sean would tell me what it took out of Audrey—seeing all those starving children around the globe. She would be holding them, talking with them, Sean said, and the next day when she returned, most of them would have died. It was Audrey's last return to the pain and devastation she had seen in Europe, growing up while the Second World War raged around her—some final debt she perhaps felt she had to pay for all the privileges of the world she had been given, and which so many were not. As a child she had seen what it meant to have nothing. Her mother had kept her alive through it all, and Audrey kept her mother with her always; she died not many years before Audrey.

I spoke with and saw Audrey periodically over the dozen years between the release of *They All Laughed* and her death. Because of a couple of candid photos taken on the set of Audrey sitting on my lap, or of us hugging each other warmly, a rumor started toward the end of shooting that Audrey and I had become an item. The truth is that since Audrey was quietly dating Robert Wolders and I was trying to keep quiet my relationship with Dorothy Stratten, it was expedient for Audrey and me not to issue any kind of denial. Over the years she never ruled out all chances that we might work together again, but certainly she didn't encourage it, always being too busy with her sons and UNICEF. It was soon after she returned from one of those tours—to war- and famine-torn Somalia—that she was diagnosed with cancer.

She had come to visit me shortly after Dorothy was killed. I still had not been out of my house and Audrey brought flowers and herself. We sat in the kitchen and talked for a couple of hours over coffee. She was extraordinarily dear about Dorothy, who had been in such awe of Hepburn that she could barely say more than good-bye at the movie's farewell party for Audrey (she was finished shooting a month before the rest of us). On her visits to Los Angeles, Audrey always included me, though we crossed each other in the air a number of times. I asked her to do Noël Coward's *Private Lives* with me on Broadway. She thought that might be fun but it was too late for her; she couldn't take that much time away from her younger son. Nor would she take him out of school. We spoke of doing a movie together based on Coward's *Hay Fever*—a delightfully wicked show-business-family comedy—an idea she rather liked for a while. We talked of her doing it with Michael Caine as her husband, both philandering; talked to Michael, too. Audrey and I had several conversations about this play, but somehow we never could settle on a *time* to do it.

Personally, she had loved Noël Coward, and from all reports he had been mad about her, too. When Audrey and I talked about perhaps doing a remake of his play *Blithe Spirit,* she surprised me by saying that the part she really would rather play in that show was not the lovely ghost-of-a-wife lead, but rather Madame Arcati, the eccentric fortune-telling, bicycle-riding supporting character immortalized in the 1945 David Lean screen version by Margaret Rutherford—a far cry in type from Audrey Hepburn. What attracted her to that offbeat role? Probably that no one had ever seen her in a part like that, she answered, but she saw herself in it quite clearly.

A couple of years later, I proposed that she play the leading role of an English character actress having an affair with a younger actor and jealous of his affections, in Michael Frayn's hit stage farce, *Noises Off* (which I was filming for Disney and Spielberg's Amblin). After reading the script, Audrey called, somewhat suspicious, to ask why I had offered her that role. I said I thought she could be funny in it, even though she'd certainly never played anything like it. She said she couldn't see herself doing it at all, and wondered if I had perhaps noted some sort of parallel between her and the part which led me to offer it. (Hadn't there always been before?

she only implied.) No, I said, it was simply that since the role of the aging eccentric in *Blithe Spirit* was certainly a stretch for her, why not a theatrical diva in a slapstick comedy? It was all in good fun. She declined, politely, I think somehow still suspecting my motives. When Sean saw the film he generously said it was the only mistake The Mutti had made. But probably Audrey was right—the public could not accept her in a role so distant from the persona she had always represented.

I often told her she had so many people in the world who loved her on the screen, who missed her presence there—surely they counted for something in her equations, but her UNICEF duties outweighed all other concerns for Audrey. She always remained her own person. Although she certainly publicized Givenchy's designs through the years, she didn't dress in that high style in her daily life. She wore blue jeans, silk shirts—the cuffs always unbuttoned (because it was "more comfortable that way")—boots and pea jackets. When we came to picking out a wardrobe for our picture, I just went through her things and chose the most typical, then we doubled them all. Everything she wore in the movie was exactly like the clothes (except for public events) she wore in real life.

One of my favorite memories of Audrey happened after Sean's first wedding ceremony. The reception was held at a Beverly Hills hotel ballroom, and many of her Hollywood friends were invited, among them James Stewart, who came with his lovely wife Gloria. At one point, to initiate dancing into the festivities, Sean and his bride had their wedding dance, and were joined by mother Audrey, her partner for this being Jimmy Stewart. Both tall and casually graceful, they danced close together for one long dance. This haunting, strangely moving image—Audrey never worked with Stewart but they were old friends—could stand as a symbol for all the lost movies of Audrey Hepburn, the ones she never made because she chose not to, and then ran out of time.

In Greek myth—among the most ancient of Western religious histories—you would have to compare Audrey to Hestia, goddess of the hearth, for whom the family home was her main concern and, by extension, every home. Significantly, Hestia was the first expendable goddess; when the later Olympian religion was first revised, she was not considered essential, and was forced to relinquish her seat to Dionysus, god of the vine. We can measure by the "man's world" Audrey saw—from above, in Hollywood; from below, in the Third World countries she toured—what a terrible mistake that was.

As an artist, Audrey Hepburn also was an inspiration to artistry—all

Audrey Hepburn is a mythical princess in her first
starring role in pictures, Roman Holiday *(1953), directed*
by William Wyler, and co-starring Gregory Peck; she
became an international star overnight.

those writers and directors outdoing each other to capture the essential Audrey—like Brigit, the ancient Irish goddess of healing, patroness of poetry and childbirth, known today by Catholics as Saint Brigit. Robert Graves noted (in his *The White Goddess*): "In parts of Britain Saint Brigit retained her character of Muse until the Puritan Revolution, her healing being exercised largely through poetic incantation . . ." So it was no leap at all for Ben Gazzara to call Audrey a saint—Saint Audrey seems quite appropriate to me—for in her life and work she was born to show the world that true grace and innocence, human kindness and hope, still can exist on earth.

Born Edda van Heemstra Hepburn-Ruston, May 4, 1929, Brussels, Belgium; died January 20, 1993, Tolochenaz, Switzerland.

Selected starring features (with director):

1953: *Roman Holiday* (William Wyler)
1954: *Sabrina* (Billy Wilder)
1956: *War and Peace* (King Vidor)
1957: *Funny Face* (Stanley Donen); *Love in the Afternoon* (Wilder)

1959: *The Nun's Story* (Fred Zinnemann)
1960: *The Unforgiven* (John Huston)
1961: *Breakfast at Tiffany's* (Blake Edwards); *The Children's Hour* (Wyler)
1963: *Charade* (Donen)
1964: *My Fair Lady* (George Cukor)
1966: *How to Steal a Million* (Wyler)
1967: *Two for the Road* (Donen); *Wait Until Dark* (Terence Young)
1976: *Robin and Marian* (Richard Lester)
1981: *They All Laughed* (P.B.)

23

SIDNEY POITIER

Sidney Poitier was to the movies what Jackie Robinson was to baseball. Poitier broke the color line in leading men. He was the first black star in American films, and for many years, from the fifties through the seventies, he was also the only major one. What kind of enormous burden and responsibility must that have been for Poitier? Incalculable. When I worked with him in the second half of the nineties, I got some sense of the weight he had carried by then for nearly fifty years—ever since Joseph L. Mankiewicz cast him in his first movie role for *No Way Out* (1950). I can recall the striking impression he made on me in that picture, which I first saw at age eleven or twelve. Suddenly, there he was in the second-lead role of a doctor—his white surgical cloak emphasizing the rich blackness of his skin—and about the best-looking man on any screen. Richard Widmark plays the lead heavy, a racist who gets shot and must depend on Poitier to save his life. As a big Widmark fan at the time, I nevertheless remember being not only enormously impressed by Poitier, but wondering where he had come from (the Bahamas, it turned out—his parents were tomato farmers), and curious to see him again.

After that kind of start—even though the film was not a popular one—you'd think Poitier would never be out of work again. The fact is, over the next four years, he appeared only in three little pictures, the most ambitious an awkward if well-intentioned adaptation of Alan Paton's beautiful novel of Africa, *Cry, the Beloved Country* (1952). Now, of course, Poitier was always quite choosy about his roles, so he probably could have worked more, but there were certain parts Sidney would not do. His first (and only) agent, Martin Baum, told me that Sidney had desperately needed money when director Phil Karlson offered him a small but memorable role of a father whose child has been killed in crossfire in *The Phenix City Story* (1955). Poitier turned down the job; he told Baum he

Sidney Poitier as Porgy in the George Gershwin–Ira Gershwin–DuBose Heyward classic Porgy and Bess *(1959), directed by Otto Preminger, produced by Samuel Goldwyn and co-starring Dorothy Dandridge, Sammy Davis, Jr., and Pearl Bailey*

refused to play a victim. Later in his career, again when he could have used some popular roles, Poitier rejected both *Driving Miss Daisy* (1989) and *The Shawshank Redemption* (1994), thus effectively making Morgan Freeman's career. Sidney had not wanted to be shown being servile, nor did he think being a convict set a good example.

In any event, it wasn't until 1955 that Poitier appeared in a hit picture, when Richard Brooks' *The Blackboard Jungle* became an unexpected runaway success. Sidney played a high school senior. He was thirty. Over the next three years, he was starred in six pictures, and nominated as the Academy's Best Actor for one of them, Stanley Kramer's *The Defiant Ones* (1958), in which he played an escaped convict handcuffed to racist Tony Curtis. It was the first time in the Academy's by then thirty-year history of awards that a nonwhite had been nominated in that category. The year before, he had played Clark Gable's illegitimate son in Raoul Walsh's *Band of Angels* (1957). Mythologically speaking, for Gable, "the King" of American movies, to have a gorgeous black bastard child is potent, and echoes down the years with reverberations.

That same year he had been co-starred in *Edge of the City* (1957) with another young East Coast actor, Greek-American John Cassavetes. He and Sidney became lifelong friends, and Cassavetes kept after Poitier to play Hamlet on stage or screen. Sidney said he didn't have the nerve, but John kept badgering him for years, right up to his premature death in 1989. After Poitier's nomination for *The Defiant Ones,* there is no question that, had he been white, his career would have gone into orbit. It did not. He was next seen as Porgy—almost inevitable casting—in Otto Preminger's movie version of George Gershwin's *Porgy and Bess* (1959), his songs sung by Robert McFerrin, an accomplished singer. After two forgettable little pictures, he made his debut as a star on Broadway in the popular family drama, *A Raisin in the Sun,* by Lorraine Hansberry. I saw him in the original New York production as well as the movie that came out in 1961, which by no means carried the impact Poitier had had on the stage. His performance had great stature and Sidney proved as magnetic and mythic at a distance as he was in close-up. (It was particularly because of his work in this production that Cassavetes kept after him to do *Hamlet.*) Two years later, Poitier won the Best Actor Oscar, the first of his color to do so, for his performance in the successful comedy-drama *Lilies of the Field* (1963).

It wasn't until four years and five pictures later, however, that Poitier had another hit, though this time, in 1967, he struck with a vengeance, having three extremely popular movies released in the same calendar year: as a Northern cop in the Southern thriller, Norman Jewison's *In the Heat of the Night;* as a teacher in a London school filled with white delinquents, *To Sir, with Love;* and, the *coup de grâce* for American integration, as the fiancée of Spencer Tracy and Katharine Hepburn's daughter in Stanley Kramer's social comedy *Guess Who's Coming to Dinner.* That sort of peak

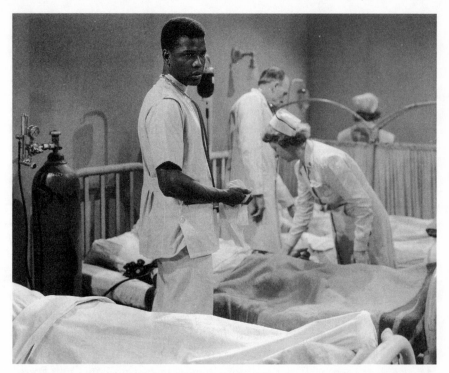

Sidney Poitier as a doctor who saves a racist's life, his first movie role, in
No Way Out *(1950), directed by Joseph L. Mankiewicz and starring*
Richard Widmark, a good friend of Sidney's since then

would be difficult to equal, and Poitier never did, but you only need to climb Mt. Everest once. And because of Sidney, black movie stars have now become not only accepted but expected. The debt owed to him is immense.

Over the next eight years, Poitier acted in at least one picture a year—two of them sequels to *In the Heat of the Night*—and began to direct some of his vehicles. (Married to his second wife, Joanna Shimkus, since 1976, he famously has six daughters; his autobiography, *The Life,* for which he had no ghost writer, appeared in 1980.) After *A Piece of the Action* (1977), he did not appear on the screen for a decade, directing four pictures instead, one of them the deservedly smash hit Richard Pryor–Gene Wilder comedy *Stir Crazy* (1980). Eight years later, he returned to acting with a couple of films, notably *Little Nikita* (1988) with River Phoenix, whom he adored and vice versa. They would work together again in *Sneakers* (1992), where Poitier kept pulling focus from the others in the all-star cast (he looked more like a leading man than co-star Robert Redford).

That same year, Poitier became the first black recipient of the American Film Institute's Lifetime Achievement Award.

Nevertheless, he did not make another picture until four years later, when he produced and starred in *To Sir, with Love II,* a sequel to his 1967 success, made for Columbia TriStar as a CBS TV-movie. I was hired to direct, with casting in New York, and in Chicago, where the story was set and mostly shot. We went to London and filmed some exteriors there for the opening sequence. I spent the better part of two months with Sidney, often in tense situations and shooting very quickly. We did the whole thing in twenty-four days, plus a few days of rehearsal, during which we discovered to our dismay that the script needed a quick rewrite. Poitier was always responsible, professional, prepared, on time, open-minded, approachable. We would disagree occasionally. He was very quick to want to replace an actor I would have given more of a chance to, but Sidney was not only the producer and the star, it was a sequel to *his* hit; we replaced the actor. At times he wouldn't budge an inch on certain speeches in the script that I thought were too long, and tended generally to go for more words than I would normally prefer. But he acted everything so well that ultimately it didn't really matter so much about the extra verbiage. He also knew the rhythm that worked for him as an actor, and I couldn't really argue with him over that, since it had worked for nearly half a century.

As an actor, on the set, he was very attentive and not temperamental at all. My main direction to him, other than in staging the scenes, was to whisper in his ear that the take he had just done was terrific but could he pick up the pace a little, talk a bit faster, put the speech together more, take out the pauses—my comments were always on this kind of point— and he always, each and every single time, did as I asked. Never seemed even mildly annoyed or exasperated with the sameness of the direction. But he knew we only had about ninety minutes of television time and that it was better to pick up the speed and get more into the picture than to have to cut things out later. As it was, we came in perfectly, with no scenes removed. Having also been a director for years, Poitier might have had to stifle the desire to decide the shots or the action; though he occasionally made staging suggestions which involved him, he never tried to second-guess me with the actors or with my camerawork. He certainly had the power to, but Sidney never once threw that around.

Yet I knew some of what I did made him quite nervous. Generally, I prefer not to cut unless it's necessary, therefore carrying scenes in one piece wherever possible or appropriate—and not filming any covering shots—to all of which I could feel Sidney's resistance. He would have preferred a more conventional, in some ways easier, approach, mainly because he was reluctant (as he said a few times) to have only one basic option on a given sequence. He would ask me, What if you *want* to cut later and have nothing to cut to? I said, I never had yet. Despite his personal anxiety over this method of working, he did not refuse or make it difficult for me, which, again, he easily could have.

This became all the more remarkable when, toward the end of filming, he finally blurted out that he did not like the kind of shots I loved—what he referred to as "walk-and-talk"—the camera pulling backward in front, or to the side, of the actors as they walk and talk. We were doing one of these and as I was explaining it, he said, with a tiny smile, "Yeah, I know—a walk-and-talk—I hate those." I exclaimed that he'd never told me that before. "It's OK, I'll do it," he said, "I just hate them because they're *harder*." Then he laughed a little. This helped me realize that at least some of his worry about filming whole scenes in one piece was simply over his perhaps not being able to do the shot well enough, remember all his lines. Of course, he was always right on, usually the first, second, or third take being the best one.

What I kept thinking all through the shooting was how enormously attractive Sidney still was; at seventy-one, he looked maybe fifty, and I couldn't quite figure out why he wasn't continually playing leads in theatrical features. Certainly his age never held him back: when he had to sprint down a hallway, it was done like a man half his age. He ate very carefully (mostly vegetarian), exercised and did yoga regularly, and never complained of the long hours or the cold Chicago winter—colder than anywhere I've ever been—or the late-night shooting outdoors. My daughter Antonia had a role in the film, and Sidney was very warm and kind to her. When people recognized him in public places, he always was affable. "Hey, Sidney!" someone would call out. Sidney would respond immediately, "Yeah, how you doing, man!"

After shooting was completed, Poitier was very anxious to see a rough cut, which I was under no contractual obligation to show him yet did anyway. He had many notes, all good, all carried out; though he seemed at the time fearful that I wouldn't listen to him. Actually, he told me later that he was concerned because I wasn't taking notes, and then amazed that I had actually addressed every single point. Well, I said, they were all perfect, like his performance. We were both very happy when the picture was finally aired, and the ratings were such that we won the time-slot.

For those two hours, more people were watching Poitier than any other TV fare in America. It was fascinating to observe corporate Amer-

Sidney Poitier as Mr. Tibbs, a Northern police detective in a Southern police chief's territory for In the Heat of the Night *(1967), co-starring Rod Steiger, directed by Norman Jewison; Poitier made a sequel,* They Call Me MISTER Tibbs! *(1970).*

ica's belief in Sidney as the commercials interrupted our movie seven times (which had been planned for in the writing and direction): just about every large advertiser you can think of had a spot that night, and all but maybe one or two were directly addressed to a black audience, with virtually all-black casts. It brought to mind what an executive at Disney had told me when I did a TV feature comedy for them with a black family in the leads. He had assured me the picture would get a very good rating; I asked why he was so certain of that. He replied that the black audience "doesn't get many shows made especially for them."

On the long flight we had taken to London, Sidney and I sat next to each other and he waxed extremely eloquent on a subject he had been studying for years—astronomy; he knew everything about planets and stars. His knowledge of, and enthusiasm for, this science was not only passionate but strongly philosophical. The reality of the heavens seemed to keep him balanced in his sense of self and the world, and with all of life's myriad unbalanced aspects. Hadn't he been living since birth with one of the worst of these—bigotry, inequality, racism—and the multiple limitations built into something as superficial as skin-color? When Sidney spoke of the planets, it was as though he could make sense of them far more easily than of the lives we were all living. To be the privileged representative of an underprivileged minority in a world of white celebrity and supremacy had to be a difficult and complicated role to endure for fifty years, all the while maintaining control of moral, psychological and emotional balance. One has to profoundly admire Sidney Poitier if for no other reason than that he carried an impossible burden with enormous grace and empowered millions by depicting beauty and hope in the face of despair, as well as conspicuous decency and courage. That he would play Nelson Mandela in a TV film about the heroic South African icon was, of course, entirely appropriate.

There was an obvious irony in the 2002 Academy Awards ceremony when Poitier was honored with a Special Oscar, and Denzel Washington won the Best Actor prize—the first to a black actor since Sidney's win nearly forty years before. Washington acknowledged that without Poitier, he wouldn't have been standing there, but further irony lay in the fact that Denzel had won for playing a role (in *Training Day*) that Sidney himself never would have even considered touching: a violent, unmitigated, unredeemed murderer. Sidney applauded enthusiastically for Denzel that night—and for Halle Berry who, the same evening, became the first black woman ever to win the Best Actress Oscar—but I wondered what he was really thinking. Did it cross his mind that Denzel had played the kind of thoroughgoing heavy that Widmark had played in Sidney's first movie, *No Way Out,* and that what Poitier had represented all his life had led ultimately to a black actor being allowed to embody a total blot on humanity? Many actors, after all, do love to play villains. Or was he thinking perhaps of those stars and planets that made sense, rather than of the fleeting honors of our brief passage through this maze of life on earth? That is the kind of stoic dignity and calm, focused introspection Sidney carries with him at every step. As a special human being he represents far more than the sum of his roles, because, finally, the part he was given to play in life, and in which he has triumphed, is among the toughest of all.

Born Sidney Poitier, February 20, 1924, Miami, FL.

Selected starring features (with director):

1950: *No Way Out* (Joseph L. Mankiewicz)

1952: *Cry, the Beloved Country* (Zoltan Korda); *Red Ball Express* (Budd Boetticher)

1955: *The Blackboard Jungle* (Richard Brooks)

1957: *Edge of the City* (Martin Ritt); *Something of Value* (Richard Brooks); *Band of Angels* (Raoul Walsh)

1958: *The Defiant Ones* (Stanley Kramer)

1959: *Porgy and Bess* (Otto Preminger)

1961: *A Raisin in the Sun* (Daniel Petrie); *Paris Blues* (Ritt)

1962: *Pressure Point* (Hubert Cornfield)

1963: *Lilies of the Field* (Ralph Nelson)

1965: *The Bedford Incident* (James B. Harris); *A Patch of Blue* (Guy Green); *The Slender Thread* (Sydney Pollack)

1967: *In the Heat of the Night* (Norman Jewison); *To Sir, with Love* (James Clavell); *Guess Who's Coming to Dinner* (Stanley Kramer)

1968: *For Love of Ivy* (Daniel Mann)

1970: *They Call Me MISTER Tibbs!* (Gordon Douglas)

1974: *Uptown Saturday Night* (also directed)

1975: *The Wilby Conspiracy* (Nelson)

1977: *A Piece of the Action* (also directed)

1988: *Little Nikita* (Richard Benjamin)

1992: *Sneakers* (Phil Alden Robinson)

1996: *To Sir, with Love II* (P.B.)

1997: *Mandela and de Klerk* (Joseph Sargent)

24

RIVER PHOENIX

Toward the end of 1992 while I was in Manhattan casting a new picture, a long-distance call came through to my hotel room from a Paramount executive on the West Coast saying that River Phoenix wanted to star in our movie. I was astonished. Had we offered it to him? No, the exec said, River's agent had called to say the actor had read it and wanted to play the male lead of James, a country singer trying to make it in Nashville. Of course, all of us involved in the project had discussed him for the role—we kidded that River's name already sounded like a country star—but we felt certain he was too big a film star by then to be part of what was essentially an ensemble picture, written somewhat more from the woman's point of view, rather than a vehicle for him. There were really four leads, two male, two female, and at least two other key roles. So none of us had even approached him. I asked how he had got the script. The exec didn't know, said I should call the agent myself. I did. The upshot was that he did do the movie and that, tragically, *The Thing Called Love* would turn out to be the last one River completed before his death on Halloween a year later at age twenty-three.

By the time I got that first call, River Phoenix had been playing leads in features for more than seven years, since he was fourteen. Born to a wandering, freethinking, vegan, "hippie" kind of family that traveled through South America for a time, River had sung and played the guitar on streets as a kid, and acted and sung on TV before he was ten. Director Rob Reiner would later report that River lost his virginity at fourteen doing his second film and first big success, *Stand by Me* (1986). River was immediately recognized as a major talent, an endlessly fascinating kid to watch who never seemed to be acting at all.

A quick succession of challenging roles in quality pictures followed, including Peter Weir's adaptation of the Paul Theroux novel *The Mosquito*

River Phoenix as a musician on the run with his political-fugitive parents
in Running on Empty *(1988), directed by Sidney Lumet, for which*
River received his one Academy Award nomination, as Best Supporting
Actor. He and Martha Plimpton were lovers in the film and in life.

Coast (1986), starring Harrison Ford (who immediately took to River and
became his pal), Helen Mirren, Andre Gregory and Martha Plimpton.
(Martha would become the first great love of River's brief life.) Also *Little
Nikita* (1988), directed by Richard Benjamin, with Sidney Poitier (whom
River adored, and vice versa), and Sidney Lumet's memorable *Running
on Empty* (1988). An extraordinarily troubling love story between River

and Martha Plimpton—while off-screen it burned even brighter—*Running on Empty* was also a fascinating political and emotional study, with Judd Hirsch and Christine Lahti, and River as a brilliant musician who gets into Juilliard. For this superb performance, the Academy nominated River as Best Supporting Actor for the first and only time. He was eighteen.

The following year he won the coveted role of Young Indiana Jones (thus playing Harrison Ford as a teenager), with Sean Connery as his father, in the enormously popular Steven Spielberg–George Lucas collaboration, *Indiana Jones and the Last Crusade* (1989) as well as a part in Lawrence Kasdan's quirky comedy-drama, *I Love You to Death* (1990) starring Kevin Kline, Tracey Ullman and Keanu Reeves, with whom River would co-star the following year in Gus Van Sant's *My Own Private Idaho*, a major critical and art-house hit, River getting raves for his rivetingly intimate portrait of a suicidal narcoleptic hustler.

Though reportedly River, like just about everyone in recent generations, had already fooled around a bit with drugs, *My Own Private Idaho* was the first time that substance-abuse played a large part in a character River portrayed. There was homosexuality, too, and there were unsubstantiated rumors that River had been pursued to experiment in both areas as preparation for his role. This would have been a rampantly misunderstood application of Stanislavski's "method." As the legendary actress/acting teacher Stella Adler—the only American to actually work with the real Stanislavski for any period of time—used to say: "To play dead, darling, you don't have to *die!*" She also always warned that it was vastly unhealthy to "take the part home with you," to continue playing a role even after work for the day is complete. Stella said, "If you do that, darling, it will drive you crazy!" River had no formal training as an actor, however, everything being picked up on the run. Talent he possessed, boundlessly, but the protective technique he lacked while expressing it instead often became "living the character," and River "lived" it for most of the time until the job was over.

Going against his own personal predilections, River did a major studio "commercial" picture next, *Sneakers* (1992), with an all-star cast including Robert Redford, Dan Aykroyd (who joked that he wanted to "adopt" River), and Sidney Poitier (a happy reunion). Back to the more avant-garde mode the young actor preferred, the next picture he took was Sam Shepard's *Silent Tongue* (produced in 1991), in which he gives a lovely performance, co-starred with Richard Harris, Alan Bates, and Dermot Mulroney, who became a friend. In fact, River was instrumental in Dermot's being cast in our film, which became River's thirteenth feature in less than eight years.

For his whole professional life, River Phoenix had only one agent, Iris Burton, who adored him, treated him as a son. When I called her from New York, Iris explained that because she knew River loved to sing and write songs, she had sent the script down to him at his family's home in Florida. (River had bought the house for his mother, Heart, his three younger sisters and younger brother; he also bought a place in Costa Rica for his estranged father.) Burton had warned River that the script needed work, but that because I was directing, she knew it would be heavily revised. After a few days, River called her. "This script really isn't ready at all," he said. She repeated that I was the director. Then she told me that River had no idea who I was. She asked him if he had seen *The Last Picture Show,* and River said no. (Of course, when that movie was originally released in 1971, River was about fifteen months old.) She advised him to go to the video store, rent the movie, run it, and then call her. He did, and enthusiastically said, yes, he wanted to work with "the guy who directed that picture," and so Iris Burton called Paramount, Paramount called me, I called Iris, and now she suggested that River call me, which he did soon after.

Significantly, as things turned out, it would be the one and only conversation I ever had with River before he officially got the part in *The Thing Called Love.* He started out by heaping lavish praise on *The Last Picture Show* and especially on the entire cast's performances. When I steered the conversation to the script of the new film, we agreed that the dialogue and construction both needed a great deal of work. I said that luckily the studio, and even the young writer (Carol Heikkinen), agreed. That meant we could essentially change it however we wanted. Since he was the same age as all the lead characters, I wanted his input throughout; not only would I welcome it, I said, but I would expect it. That excited him. I asked how tall he was. He exaggerated only about an inch or so and said, "Six feet." While he'd been brilliant in every role I'd ever seen him do, I said, he had never played a character with the strong edge of danger which this James fellow had to have. Yes, River agreed, he'd never done anything like that. I asked him, How was he going to convey this danger? There was quiet for several moments, and then River said, "Silence."

That was extraordinarily perceptive, I thought, as well as cogent and succinct. I knew just what he meant—silence from a character can be a form of power, the power of withholding—and power is dangerous. From that single word I knew he would play the role superbly, and he did. At the time, I sort of grunted and said, "Yeah, that would do it." Then River said, "Look, I want to work with you, man, so I don't have to meet you. Do you have to meet me?" I said no, it wasn't necessary, we both were professionals. "Yeah," he said, "I just want to stay here with my family as long as I can before I gotta come up there and start the picture." Which was soon enough, I answered, saying I certainly understood, and so by the time I first met River Phoenix about a month later, he was already playing the charming, talented but somewhat hard-ass role of James. What I wouldn't realize until about a month after we completed the shooting was that I didn't meet the *real* River Phoenix until then.

Prior to that, I was dealing with a kid who seemed alternately sensitive beyond words, overly self-involved, flat-out rude or jokingly abusive, moody, funny, quirky, often very likeable, dangerous. It was River's version of James, and so entirely convincing that I thought it was what River was really like and that he didn't have to act. Which clearly is what River had wanted. Throughout the working process, however, his creative side was objective, clear, and concerned not only with his own role but with each of the characters and the overall construction. During the casting, I told him we needed another attractive guy to play his buddy. He suggested Anthony Clark (later seen to good advantage on the TV series *Boston Common* and *Yes, Dear*). We flew Anthony in, and ended up using him as a secondary character we expanded to suit his exceptional comic abilities. I told River I liked Anthony but not for the Kyle part—the other male lead—we needed more of "a contender," I said. River was undaunted: "Anthony's really good with girls," he said, "he scores a lot!" I countered, "But he's not a leading man."

River stopped and looked at me for a couple of moments and then said, "Well, if you want another leading man you can't do better than Dermot Mulroney." River knew I had already met with Dermot and a number of other actors, and that Dermot was high on a short list of possibilities. River's comment cinched it, but what I found intriguing then, and even more unusual now, is that River was thinking of the overall work, and if I wanted two leading men, well, that was OK with him, he wasn't threatened; in fact, he let the other guy be more conventionally good-looking, that was OK, too.

You're supposed to be a confident old pro to have that kind of self-assurance and wisdom, but River as an artist possessed this quality in spades. Which is why I increasingly wanted him involved in all script conferences and writing sessions, every music discussion—and he was—

repeatedly making superb contributions. River was an instinctive talent of the highest caliber. When I pointed out to him once that his ideas and remarks relating to the script or characters invariably kept the full picture in mind, and never simply his own role, he said he always thought that way. I said then he would "make a good director." He said he had "thought about directing." I said, "Well, be sure and cast me, will ya?" He laughed and said he would. It became a small running joke between us. When I asked what it was that had attracted him to show business, he said his mother used to read stories to him as a kid and he "always liked stories," so he especially liked "being part of a story."

On the first day of shooting—a night scene at a mall on location in Nashville—River gave Samantha Mathis a hard time, bringing her to tears. When River's first phone call had reached me in New York, I had been there talking to Samantha about doing the film. She had been worried about the script's readiness, but when River signed, she jumped right on. Now, in Nashville, she was pretty upset, and said she didn't have to "take his shit"—he was "just rude." I asked if he was on something? She said she only knew he'd had a beer. The assistant director also told me River was acting erratically. I asked him if he thought our star was on drugs. The A.D. nodded, yes.

It's not a great idea for the director to get into a confrontational mode with an actor unless he absolutely has to, so I suggested the first thing we do is tell River he would not be driving the truck for the high angle we were preparing as the movie's final shot—of the pickup truck (with River, Samantha and Dermot in the cab) going off into the darkened streets of Nashville. (Shooting the end of a film first is, unfortunately, not an uncommon scheduling practice.) If River asked why he couldn't drive himself, I told the A.D. to say that Peter thought it was safer for a stunt driver to do it since the shot was from a good distance away—the audience would never be able to see who was at the wheel—and because the truck had to enter onto a main drag of moving traffic we couldn't control. I told Samantha I would have a talk with River later, but that my hunch was he was perhaps into playing his role a little too heavily. "Well, I'm not going to put up with it," Samantha said and went off, looking hurt but stoic. She and River hadn't fallen for each other yet, but they did soon enough, and it would be the last passionate love of the actor's life.

After a while, the A.D. came back and said River was very upset and didn't see why he couldn't drive the truck himself—he was a very good

*River Phoenix and Keanu Reeves played drug addicts in the popular
independent picture* My Own Private Idaho *(1991), written
and directed by Gus Van Sant; River was brilliant as a
narcoleptic, drug-addicted hustler.*

driver. Had he been told the shot was high and far away and no one could
possibly know? "*I* would know" was River's response, the A.D. reported. I
said I'd now go talk with him myself.

Running into Dermot first, I asked him what he thought the matter
might be with River. Dermot immediately came to River's defense,
explained that he had a rare eye problem that made him blink a lot sometimes but this had nothing to do with drugs (all true). Dermot didn't
think River was high, he was probably just "into his character"—it was
how he worked. "He's a real good guy, really," Dermot said as I moved on.

River was wandering around the parking lot, looking forlorn and agitated. I put my arm around him and we walked to the back of the mall. I
asked him if he was on drugs of some kind. He immediately said he'd
taken a pain pill, then forgot and had one beer, and the two were not mix-
ing well. He said he felt like he was being punished by not being allowed
to drive the truck. I dismissed that as "an insurance thing," and asked
what had been the problem with Samantha. He looked sharply at me.
Had she complained to me about him? Pretty much, I said, what happened? River shook his head, No, nothing, he said, it had nothing to do

with her. It was all his fault—but he didn't mean any of it. He was just try-ing "to find this character"—an edgy guy. Since the character was sup-posed to sing for an audition, "he'd be even edgier," River concluded.

I told him Stella Adler's advice about not playing the role all the time. He did that unconsciously, River said, didn't quite realize what he was doing. I said neither the studio nor I wanted James to be a druggie. River nodded and said that the character had, however, definitely "been into drugs," they've "made him edgy," made him "a bit of a bastard." I agreed in principle but since we didn't have any drug-taking scenes, this would have to be a minor element. River said we didn't need any scenes, but he had to know the kind of person he was dealing with. He himself didn't have "a problem with drugs," River told me lightly, he was just getting into the character, and felt the guy really was "pretty cool" with the stuff, too. I said he shouldn't focus on that aspect of the guy; it might be there but should by no means dominate. River agreed and then said he was sorry about tonight. I said, it just shouldn't happen again. He promised it wouldn't. We hugged. To my knowledge, with the exception of one night back in Los Angeles a couple of months later, River kept his promise; he caused me not a single further problem on the entire picture.

However, the word on what had happened immediately got back to Hollywood and a guilty-until-proven-innocent attitude toward River started to take hold at the studio. The irony was that the more brilliantly convincing River was in playing a self-involved, occasionally self-destructive, sometimes poetic, troubled, drug-savvy, arrogant and very talented singer-songwriter, age twenty-seven, the more the perception became that River was acting strange, was on something, was being unsympathetic and weird. Of course, he had never played anything remotely like this—dangerous, oddball, both brainy and macho—and some people thought this was what River had become. On the contrary, he was consciously, and as organically as possible, acting a man five or six years older than himself, who had endured just that many more embitter-ing or aging experiences. On the first night, he had for a few moments acted younger than his age—which was only twenty-two—while most of the time River seemed considerably older than his years. Back in Holly-wood, the concern about River would increase to such a degree that Iris Burton was dispatched to see about her client. She arrived, stayed a day or two—long enough to observe that he was fine and that things were going well—and then left, somewhat perplexed as to why there were any worries.

Not long after, one of the worst things that can happen to a picture happened to *The Thing Called Love:* the administration at the studio changed. Out went Brandon Tartikoff, who had green-lighted our movie. In came Sherry Lansing, who knew nothing about it. Though Sherry was very friendly and an old pal of mine, and actually saved the movie at one point from being butchered, she still had no pride of parenthood with this now orphaned product. Tartikoff had pushed us into production as soon as possible because he wanted the film distributed around April 1993, at the time of the annual Country Music Awards. That was why we had begun with a script that wasn't ready. After the change in regime, that plan would eventually change with it. But we were well past the point of no return, and so trying to stay on top of the script as we went along just became yet another given, though all the principal actors—River, Samantha, Dermot and Sandra Bullock—were deeply into it, and enjoying the process. The actors and I would meet after shooting or during breaks and work on upcoming scenes, altering many or all the lines and situations, coming up with good ideas—River more than anyone—and quite often his ideas were for the others. We found that Sandy Bullock—for whose casting we had to push the front office for a couple of months because Tartikoff hadn't liked her in some TV pilot—was a brilliant comedienne, so we built up her role, and the resulting performance helped get her the part (that made her a star) in *Speed* (1994).

Realizing some of the pressures we were under, Stanley Jaffe, who was the top executive in New York, and also an old friend, called to ask if we'd like some help with the script. Our scenarist was a first-timer. I said, yes, if there was somebody good. He proposed Allan Moyle, who was a writer-director Samantha knew, since he had directed her in *Pump Up the Volume* (1990). I hadn't seen that film, but Samantha thought he was excellent so we said to send him on down. And Allan, who couldn't have been more self-effacing, anxious only "to help, not to interfere," turned out to be of great assistance in pulling all our ideas together into scenes that could then be rewritten yet again. River took to riding Allan sometimes—as a kind of character-joke, I guessed, which seemed to me just good-natured kidding around—and Allan always looked amused. "No, Allan, not that line! Jesus!" Allan and I discussed it: River's instincts were infallible in what would play and what wouldn't.

As each scene approached, it would daily be revised or refined until all the actors and I were happy with it—which sometimes wasn't until just before the camera turned. Certainly the actors had to be on their toes, their chops in good shape, to continue relearning lines, often getting them at the last moment. An added difficulty for them was that I felt a good number of the longish dialogue scenes should be played straight through without a cut, the camera either stationary or moving.

While River and I were alone one afternoon talking about an upcoming scene, I told him that my preference was to shoot the entire sequence in one shot, with no further angles. "No coverage!?" River became very excited when I said, no, if we did the whole scene in one long piece that worked, there would be no reason to "cover" it with other shots. He said he thought that was great! I wasn't surprised at his reaction, I said, because I'd found that "all real actors" prefer this technique: not only for the challenge of sustaining an entire scene (as onstage after the curtain's up) but also for the far more easily achieved freshness. The film actor's typical grind in shooting was to repeat every line numerous times, never knowing which angle would be used for which moment, trying to be fresh on every repeat—an impossible task.

River said that Sidney Lumet hadn't shot coverage, and did numerous long takes in filming *Running on Empty*, though they had rehearsed for a while, a luxury we unfortunately never had. River became so fond of "one-ers," as film crews call this sort of all-encompassing master shot, that he would ask me on every sequence if we could "do it all in one." If I said, no, it wasn't appropriate to the scene or was technically impossible, he would push for it anyway until I laughed and said I was just as sorry, but it wouldn't work here. If I said yes he was ecstatic. Movie acting in this way requires considerable discipline and experience. River couldn't have done sequence after sequence in that way if he'd been taking drugs. Yes, he was acting differently than anyone had ever seen, but it was the first time he was playing an adult romantic lead, and a character who'd been around a bit, certainly not a Southern hick. In fact, we added a number of intellectual comments from River, ones I suggested or River asked for, which helped to define his character as a reader and thinker, not simply an instinctual artist. Eventually a few of these moments wound up being eliminated, and River's role was thereby diminished—one could not understand him as well. River loved any kind of arcane information—and when I would mention something of that sort, he would invariably want somehow to fit it into the movie. Often we did.

Our story was essentially a triangle in which the two guys—River and Dermot—were both in love with Samantha, and though she's partial to River romantically, she feels more friendship with Dermot. This particular triangle (two men, one woman)—as Robert Graves has pointed out in his studies of mythology—is the most ancient story known. Discussing that with River, we decided to add a scene to help show his character's achieved self-awareness and ability to observe his own situation with historical objectivity. It became a reconciliation scene between Dermot and River—they had fought verbally and physically over Samantha—in which River puts their relationship into perspective by describing how "the Green King and the Red King" killed each other yearly for "the affections of the Lady in White," and that this year, for Samantha, they had both "kicked the bucket." It was a scene River particularly liked and one which he and Dermot played with beautiful simplicity and grace.

River's profound understanding of this episode mirrored his own often painful relationships with the women he loved and who loved him. Martha Plimpton still speaks of River with rare fondness, as River did of her. I didn't know Suzanne Solgot, the young woman he had been going with just before we began preparing our picture. But I remember the initial evening River and I spent together, the same day we had first met face to face, and his telling me of the dismay he felt at having just heard from his girlfriend Sue that she had been unfaithful to him. Of course, he said, he had been unfaithful to her, and she had known it, but the other way around really bothered him. He went right on, however, to justify her behavior, to see it from the woman's point of view, protecting herself from the pain of his acts. I didn't say much, and River talked out his ambivalent feelings in a very mature way.

I had no idea until we were about to shoot River's and Samantha's first kiss in the film just how much River was actually attracted to Sam. It was a night scene, on location in Nashville, maybe our second or third week there. We were outside. River was to drive up in his truck, Samantha beside him, stop at her hotel, kiss her goodnight and, after she jumps out, drive off. While the first shot was being lit, River and I were talking about what sort of kiss it should be. River started out by saying he hoped I had a lot of film in the camera because it was going to be a very long kiss. He was grinning mischievously. "Oh, yes!" he said, he had been waiting for *this* scene! And then he went on—in James' sophisticated country-boy accent—to list what else he would like to do with Samantha. Mostly he kept to all the places he'd like to kiss her. He was half James–half River as he said Samantha was driving him crazy. She had a boyfriend in New York—the actor John Leguizamo—and, though River felt Samantha liked him, she was always talking about John and he didn't feel right imposing himself. But he certainly was going to kiss her tonight! And, by the way, he told me, he would be very happy to do as many takes as I wanted, and he hoped I wanted many.

I think we did about seven. I can't remember for certain which kiss ended up in the picture but I have a feeling it was the first or second take. There was intense heat on all seven. Samantha managed a pretty impassive professional look between takes, while River just loudly asked for ". . . another one—we need another one, don't you think, Peter?" Samantha would laugh. River and Samantha became closer and closer every hour after that. Not much later, John Leguizamo came to visit but stayed only one day. Samantha ended their relationship and she and River officially became an item. They were lovely together, and he treated her with the utmost respect, tenderness, humor and not one fragment of competitiveness. Most of their best scenes together—three to five pages of dialogue— were done in long continuous shots that require enormous coordination between the two players. Their closeness in life helped immeasurably to deepen their interactions in these scenes. It isn't always that way. Both were considerate and generous to the other. Unlike many male stars, River was not threatened by the woman having equally good things to say and actually often trumping him at the conclusion. Indeed, River welcomed and encouraged this. When we did the picture, I'd been in show business for nearly forty years and in my experience, a star-actor like River Phoenix was rare.

After shooting, and on weekends, River was relentless in his pursuit of Nashville atmosphere, of what it was like to be there, strive there, fail there, win there. He went all over town searching for answers. And looking for songs. *The Thing Called Love* was, after all, a picture about singers and songwriters, and the reason we had pushed all the song numbers back to the very end of the schedule (no matter where they might fall in the story) was because we hadn't set even one song. The actors, and everyone else, had been encouraged to look for new songs, or to write some for the movie. All four of the leads ended up singing a song they'd written, or co-written, for the picture during the shooting. We should have used at least one other of River's songs—a tender, melancholy ballad—but politics and compromise would force that out.

One morning, River came to the set very excited. He'd found a song in someone's office last night that he thought was "pretty damn good" for his character to perform as his first song—especially important in establishing that ambivalent character's particular talent and state of mind. In my trailer on location, River played the demo tape for me. It was absolutely dead-on. His instinct here gave me an even higher regard for him than I already had: his ear for the right sound, not only for the character but for the audience, was uncanny. It was a very sympathetic, catchy tune, but also witty and hard-driving. To get the song into the picture we would have to fight legal hassles practically right up to the day we finally shot it back in Los Angeles at the end of the schedule. With another singer, the song ("Blame It on Your Heart") would become a sizeable hit on country charts in advance of the movie's release, confirming River's popular touch.

Our shooting extended over the Christmas–New Year's holidays—a time usually avoided like the plague by studios—but we had jumped in because of the (now irrelevant) country awards date. Everyone got ill. We had to take four days off because River caught a nasty cold. He called me, worried, said he'd come in if I wanted. I said, Are you kidding, I could use a break, too. So could everybody. The studio would send a doctor to check him out, make sure he's really sick, and insurance would cover the costs. River said, OK, if I was sure, because even with a fever he'd come in for me. I said, For *me*, stay home. We were shooting nights which is also especially exhausting, turning everyone's body clock upside down. Worse, one of our primary locations was the Disney Ranch out in the wilds of L.A. where it was particularly cold at night.

River mentioned that he didn't much like Los Angeles, that it was a bad influence on him, just the atmosphere of the town itself. A few times, some of his rock-musician friends came down to the set to visit, hang around his trailer for a while. On one of those occasions, I noticed River looked drawn and strangely quiet in his intensity. Of course, it was a difficult scene, at night outside a hospital, during which River and Samantha have their first heart-to-heart talk and she tells him of her beloved father's death. As an actor, River's preference was never to do any moment in any scene exactly the same way twice. If I would say, "That was terrific—do it again like that," River would reply, "You've got it that way—let me try something different," and he would. Many actors tend to stick to one approach on a scene or a line, so it wasn't usual to see the often wildly different ways River might interpret a moment. This also fueled the drug-abuse suspicions: he's erratic, he's weird, he's inconsistent.

Since we were writing this picture as we went along, shooting out of sequence, certain reactions had to be shot a number of ways so we could decide later, once the work was edited, which best suited the character. The point was that we could use only one of each. We wound up including the straightest takes, as it turned out, which is what I thought might happen, but both River and I had wanted choices to help refine his character.

Nevertheless, on that night outside the hospital, I thought River probably had taken something. He said at the time that he was still doing his cold prescriptions but later, after the shooting ended, he admitted to having been a little high outside the hospital (he didn't say on what) and having had as a result, he thought, one of his most transcendent moments in acting. Certainly, he's pain-filled, intense, empathetic and riveting in the sequence, but it took longer to get done than it should have—though we were also rewriting as we went—and part of the scene involved two or three lines from a song of River's which he was still composing. The producers on the set, however, and subsequently some of the studio executives, were very troubled by that night, and this became the final straw for them with River: many turned conclusively against him.

In fact, there were no real problems, and his singing came off terrifically, much of it shot live. River was a very gifted musician, had a fine sense of lyrics and phrasing, worked very hard on every song, was totally dedicated to the work. I went to a recording studio while he was working with the formidable T-Bone Burnett, the arranger-producer we had hired for River's songs. River had recommended we get T-Bone and, since I was an admirer of a couple of Burnett's own albums, it was an easy sale. T-Bone and River got along wonderfully, both being deeply respectful of the other's talents and ability. Watching River in a recording studio was like seeing a painter at his easel—he was so at home there. For some reason, everybody appeared to take his singing for granted, as though of course he could just do that—but then he *did* make it look easy, which was enormously impressive.

Our having become somewhat second-class citizens at the studio, there was no wrap party scheduled by the producers, so River and Samantha decided to chip in together and throw one at a funky little Japanese karaoke club out near Culver City. It was a rainy night and a part of the club's roof started to leak, but it couldn't dampen anyone's spirits. The cast and crew all had a good time celebrating the conclusion of a very demanding job. During some karaoke singing, there was a sudden blast of enthusiasm about my getting up and doing one. I said, no, I didn't think so, but River was beside me and wouldn't take no for an answer. He cajoled and badgered, so eventually I went up, looked at the list of selections and picked Sinatra's "My Way," which I tried to personalize ruefully as I went along. A couple of times I thought, What am I doing here?! But then I would look down and see River gazing up at me with the most encouraging, sympathetic expression I've ever seen on a man. He was smiling, excited, and totally with me. At one point, there were tears in his eyes. Naturally, this made me give my all for River's sake—as you do for a good director—which is what I told him later. My performance was a hit but what I'll never forget is the entirely focused look of unconditional affection on River's face.

This was also the beginning of my introduction to the real River Phoenix. Of course, he had just completed playing James. By the time he had totally shed the character he'd been acting, there was a boyish, shaggy-haired enthusiasm and guileless charm to River. The contrast was especially noticeable a couple of months later when, having gone to Florida and then Costa Rica to be with his family, River came back to Los Angeles to do the required post-production dubbing of dialogue. Here was the sharp, brooding character on-screen, and the barefoot Huck Finn watching from the dubbing booth. River's mother, Heart Phoenix, accompanied him on this trip, and to the dubbing sessions, where we met for the first time. She had a remarkably powerful presence—a quiet, warm, sensitive and loving nature—soft-spoken yet intense and extremely in-the-moment. River's genuine deference to Heart and their affection for one another was both palpable and completely unself-conscious. I think maybe he had invited her to join him in Los Angeles to help keep away temptations he knew weren't good for him. His time with the family had clearly invigorated and cleansed him.

Redoing some of James' dialogue, therefore, was not so easy. He had let go of most of that guy, and it was a struggle to get him back. Because of a major technical error by the picture's editorial staff, in early screenings of the movie River's original sound-recordings inadvertently were not used; poorly transferred duplications were heard instead, which badly muddied his readings, made them hard to understand. I knew he hadn't sounded that way when we shot the stuff, but now it was coming out poorly. The edict became: re-record every single line of River's. Torturously, we went through it, and River kept saying the original had to be better. Whenever we asked that the original be played back, it sounded fine now, having been prepared afresh by the sound-effects crew. So why were we redoing it? I told River we had better just complete the ugly deed, but not to worry because I would use the original lines wherever possible. River begged me to use them all, because he didn't think his looping was very good—clearer, maybe, but not nearly as much in character. As it turned out, though we re-recorded all of River's dialogue, thus alleviating studio fears, we actually used virtually none of this in the final mix. Having finally discovered what the actual problem had been, we just ended up using all the original tracks, though we never told anyone, and nobody ever complained again.

The first time River saw the movie was at a rough-cut screening in the studio theater. He was excited about it, critical of some of the editing of the songs, wanting me to address these more carefully—he was right—but extremely complimentary of the overall work. During the sequence at the Disney Ranch—a line-dance party under a full moon—on River's urging, I had ridden a horse into an extreme long shot we made. When this appeared on-screen, River called out loudly, "That's Peter on the horse!" He was such an exuberant, loving kid.

Since River was very concerned about my using some different singing takes of his, I said he should come up to the cutting room and go over those with me. He loved that idea and, a day or so later, he and I ran a number of his shots in the editing rooms. I didn't realize quite how unhappy this made the editorial staff. (As a rule, post-production people tend to be suspicious of actors and all production people. And vice versa.) River and I had a great time. It was very interesting and helpful to see which takes he felt were best, especially in the crucial singing scenes, during which River did a considerable variety of different expressions as he sang: more and less arrogant; more and less mannered; harder and softer. Again, River's judgments were impressive, and I agreed with him entirely. Since the editors had in many cases chosen other takes, aggravation was only exacerbated.

The next day, I was called by one of the executives who expressed dismay and concern, having heard that I was having "actors in the editing rooms." I said River had been very constructive and I didn't see any problems. Well, the studio had a problem with it, and would appreciate keeping the editing room closed to outsiders. River and I had been looking forward to more sessions. Watching me cut was instructive for him, he told me; and I said his input as usual was terrific. It was also fun having River around on whatever pretext, but that editing session together was our only one.

A day or so later, River and Sam, Dermot and his talented wife, Catherine Keener, and Anthony Clark all came over to my Beverly Hills home to see a tape of John Ford's *The Grapes of Wrath*. River had heard me talking about the picture and Henry Fonda's performance, and was anxious to look at it. He hadn't seen many older films, he said, and felt ashamed about his ignorance of picture history. River's reactions to the movie were very fresh and uncomplicated by knowledge of either the John Steinbeck novel or much of anything about Ford. He was deeply impressed by the darkness of the Okies' true Depression story, by the striking black-and-white photography and by the transfixing brilliance of

Henry Fonda's portrayal of Tom Joad. Now River was excited at the prospect of our running many older films together, but this would be the only time we had.

One of the first things River had done when he entered the house was to spot my South American housekeeper in the kitchen. He kicked off his shoes, checked out the refrigerator for something to eat, grabbed some salad, flipped himself onto one of the kitchen counters, and struck up a conversation in Spanish with Maria, asking all about herself and her family. He was totally absorbed by this while the rest of us got drinks and chatted. River stayed with Maria until we were ready to start the movie. Maria never saw him again but she always afterward asked about "Mister River." When he died, she grieved for him.

Following the movie, River took us all to his favorite Los Angeles restaurant, Ten Masa, a Japanese family-owned establishment on the Sunset Strip. Everything was "so fresh" there, River kept saying. River was a vegetarian. The whole family worked the place—father, mother, sons and daughters—and every one of them called out to River as he walked in. Clearly, they adored him. The mother had baked special bread for his party. River went back to the kitchen, embraced the mother, was very friendly with everyone in the most openly generous way. He especially loved the Oshitashi spinach, which he ate, like nearly everything else, with his fingers.

Meanwhile, the studio was in conflict as to how to sell our picture and what its final form ought to be. There were a number of invitational previews, all with wildly conflicting reactions, none indicating a solid hit. Cuts were requested and argued and made or not. But compromise reigned. The music department was splintered into about three factions, each pulling for different songs to be on the track, over the main or end titles, and on the album. The publicity and marketing people had various terrific poster ideas yet somehow we ended up with the worst one, using neither River's nor Dermot's likenesses, only Samantha's, in a halfhearted attempt to sell the film as a young women's picture. When River saw this poster, he simply congratulated Samantha, told her the photo of her was great, and said not another word, but I knew he was hurt.

Moments showing River's erudition were requested cut, whole sequences were discussed as worthy of jettisoning. In this climate, it was all a negotiation. At one point, when things were really getting out of hand, Sherry Lansing said that in her opinion, the picture should be edited in "Peter's version," and that we should go with that. Her word became the final one, and saved a good many things from being lost, but

River Phoenix and Harrison Ford became very close while working on
The Mosquito Coast *(1986), directed by Peter Weir, based on the novel by
Paul Theroux. Three years later River played Harrison as a young man in
the beginning of Steven Spielberg's* Indiana Jones and the Last Crusade.

not everything. River and I really regretted the loss of a couple of his most
poetic moments, and one of his songs. The movie that was released wasn't
quite the picture we shot; about 90 percent survived, and sometimes 10
percent can make the difference between success or failure, mediocrity or
enduring quality. Someday I hope the version of *The Thing Called Love*
that River and I really made can be seen; it was just that much better and
more unusual.

The final distribution decision was ultimately disastrous, releasing the
film first in the South and West as a country-music picture when it was
actually closer to an art-house movie. In fact, that was the main problem:
the final picture fell between two stools, and wound up on the floor. River,
Sam, Dermot, Sandy and I all showed up in Dallas for the publicity jun-
ket preceding the opening of the film. River blazed through his numerous
press and TV interviews in a kind of intense James-like state. This was not
his favorite job—selling and promoting a movie—but he was a good
sport.

The next afternoon we all went to see River's friend Harrison Ford in
his just-released new film, *The Fugitive*. River was an ardent movie fan—

he got into the picture entirely—into the plot and into the way it was told, and especially into Harrison's performance. It was a lot of fun seeing that picture with River—his audible and physically obvious enjoyment of the work doubled the pleasure. That night, River drank a lot of beers and got a little noisy in the hall. Samantha was upset and went to bed early. My wife, Louise, and a close friend of hers from Vancouver, B.C., named Carrie Brown, and I hung out with River until it got late, and though he wasn't out of control, he clearly was drinking too much, or hyped up on something. I had to go to Arizona the next day for a promotional appearance, but Louise and Carrie stayed on with River for an extra day. He took them back to see *The Fugitive* again.

Later, Louise would tell me that River had been very sweet to Carrie. In those days, Carrie was a bit overweight, but when he first met her, River looked at her for a long moment and then said with great intensity, "You are so beautiful!" Carrie would never forget that. Louise said he was terribly funny and charming with them; referring to the Van Zant film, he called it *My Own Private Potato*. He raved about his brother Joaquin's acting talents, saying Joaquin was extraordinarily gifted, a much better actor than he himself was—he said that more than once. When River went a little over the top with the booze—at one point ordering "forty-seven bottles of beer" through room service—Carrie got angry and told him he was endangering his life and ought to be more respectful of his own great talent. River was quickly becalmed by these remarks, and swore he wouldn't touch a thing once he got home again to Florida, where he was heading next. Dallas turned out to be the last place Louise or Carrie or I saw River alive.

A few days afterward, he and I spoke on the phone. He said he was feeling good, working on a CD with his sister Rain. He said I should tell Louise and Carrie he had kept his promise—he was back to a healthy life, he told me. He had to beg off going to the Montreal World Film Festival screening of our movie because he was really into the album, into singing, and playing music. He hoped I understood. The picture had also been invited to the Vienna Film Festival, but by then he would be shooting a new film, the working title of which was *Dark Blood*. After that he was going to do *Interview with the Vampire* and there were two or three other big pictures on which Iris Burton was in negotiation. He sounded very happy to be home. Sam was there, too.

The picture was glowingly received in Montreal, by the public, the press, and by some of my peers. Several critics—all of whom were bowled over by River's transformation—said they were holding their rave reviews in anticipation of the film's imminent opening. As it turned out, *The Thing Called Love* was never commercially released in Montreal. Nor in a lot of other places. After its two-week Southwestern tryout had been disappointing, the movie was for all intents and purposes shelved, and readied for its automatic ancillary markets. As a gesture to me, people said, Sherry Lansing agreed to a winter booking in Seattle to test another marketing approach. This would be after Louise and I returned from the Vienna showing. River said he would help to promote the new opening as best he could, though he'd still be shooting *Dark Blood.* All of us hid our discouragement from one another, and hoped maybe we could turn things around in November.

In September, I agreed to do a guest shot as myself on an episode of the popular TV series, *Northern Exposure,* and called River to tell him. Because of our director-actor thing, I knew he'd be amused and enthusiastic. He was shooting *Dark Blood* on location in Utah and it took a bit of organizing to get together on the phone. Just when we finally did, his costar, English actor Jonathan Pryce, with whom he got on famously, dropped in to rehearse. River asked me to hold on and explained to Pryce that we'd been trying to reach each other, and could Jonathan come back in twenty minutes. And so River and I spoke animatedly for about half an hour.

He sounded crystal clear and completely grounded. He said he'd been clean of any kind of substance for three months, and was feeling great. The film was heavy, he said, but interesting. One of his co-stars didn't get on well with the director, which was a drag, but he loved Jonathan Pryce. As I expected, he was excited and encouraging about my TV gig. I said I'd call him after the Vienna screening and tell him how the picture had been received there. When would that be? River asked. Toward the end of October, I said, and then Louise and I were going on a short vacation. We would be arriving back in Los Angeles right around Halloween. River noted that he'd be in Los Angeles by then, finishing *Dark Blood,* and that we could see each other, and I could describe the Vienna showing in person. Since it was so hard to get each other on the phone—and even tougher with me in Europe—we just made a date to have dinner on the night of November 1. Pretty soon, Jonathan Pryce came back, so we wished each other good luck, and sent love back and forth and both said we were looking forward to seeing each other. We never did again, and that was the last time River and I spoke.

The picture was so well received in Vienna that I almost tried to reach River wherever he was by then to tell him right away what a particular hit he had been with critics and audiences. But I knew the odds were poor, and we'd be seeing each other in about ten days. So Louise and I went on our vacation, and flew back to Los Angeles on Halloween, nonstop from Genoa, where an old friend and his wife and young daughter got aboard. The noted screenwriter-director Robert Towne and I had known each other since the mid-1960s when we both were working for Roger Corman. During part of the twelve-hour flight back, he and I caught up. Mostly, I raved about River Phoenix. Bob was equally effusive about a young star he'd just been working with, Johnny Depp.

When we arrived at LAX, Bob and his family got separated from us for a while, but just as we were nearing the exit where greeters wait, we ran into each other again. Bob looked troubled and confused. He said he hated to tell me this but he'd just heard someone talking and they said, "Wasn't it too bad River Phoenix had been killed." I almost laughed—what was he talking about!? Bob said he had overheard two people talking. "But that's impossible," I said, and Louise shrugged it off, too. Some crazy rumor. Bob said he certainly hoped so. I said it couldn't be. My mind was racing: Could it be? A car accident? A fight? No, it wasn't anything. But when I saw that my longtime assistant, Iris Chester, was waiting gravely for us with the driver, I realized something had to be wrong: Iris had never before come to meet us at an airport. I asked what was the matter. Iris said she hadn't wanted me to see it on TV, but River had died tonight. Seems to have been some sort of drug overdose. It happened while we were on the plane. He had passed away on the sidewalk in front of the Viper Room, a club owned by Johnny Depp.

Louise burst into tears, and we walked her out to the ladies' room. I felt as though I had been hit over the head by a tree. Iris said that Samantha Mathis had tried to reach me a couple of times, had left a number. Louise could not stand the thought of spending even one night in Los Angeles: another senseless death just a few miles from where her sister Dorothy had been killed in 1980. She booked a ticket to Vancouver, her hometown. She wanted to see Carrie, who she knew would be devastated.

By the time I got home, it was getting late, but I called Sam. She sounded numb. It had all happened so fast, she said. She suspected River had taken some drugs earlier in the evening but hadn't been sure of it. They weren't planning to hang out at the Viper Room, only to go by, say hello, drop off Joaquin and Rain, and then go back to her house. But River had brought his guitar, knowing some friends were jamming there, and had really wanted to play with them. Reluctantly, Sam said, she conceded. After a while, she saw River with a pal of his who was a junkie—

and whom River had tried several times to get into rehab—and a bouncer was opening a side door for them. She didn't know if they were being pushed out or going of their own accord. Evidently, the junkie had given River some stuff that didn't mix with what he might have already taken. River had complained that he wasn't feeling well, but his addict friend told him he was just being paranoid. Worried, Sam followed River and the junkie out to the sidewalk to keep an eye on them, lit a cigarette, and walked ten feet away to give them privacy. When she turned around, River had started going into convulsions, then dropped to the sidewalk. His junkie friend said he was fine, to just leave him alone. Knowing that couldn't be true, Sam said, she realized something was terribly wrong and tried to get River on his feet, but he seemed to have passed out. She ran into the club to get Joaquin and Rain. Joaquin called 911 while Rain and Sam tried to help River. Then Joaquin and Rain both attempted unsuccessfully to revive River; by the time the paramedics got there—although Sam, Rain and Joaquin didn't know—it was already too late.

How was the family? I asked. Sam said that Joaquin and his sisters were overcome with grief, and that Heart was being incredibly strong, holding everybody together. How she did it, Sam said, she didn't know. We spoke a little while longer, as I tried to say something about the indestructibility of the spirit. I promised that first thing in the morning I would come over to the house where everyone was staying.

When I arrived, some friends were in the kitchen making sandwiches. The kids looked devastated. Heart, as Sam had said, was amazingly in control. We embraced for a long moment. She said her main concern right now was helping the other children through this—they were all devoted to River, worshipful—and it was so terrible for them, she couldn't really show how she felt.

Sam and I spoke for a while alone. She cried. She and River had been talking a lot, she said, looking forward to seeing each other. He had been totally clean. The minute he got to L.A., the bad influences surfaced, the temptations reached out. Because he had been off everything for more than three months, he was far more vulnerable than if he had never stopped.

Joaquin was having a cigarette in the living room. We hadn't met before but Joaquin said that River had spoken well of me. As he tried to talk about his brother, Joaquin broke down; recalling the terrible last moments, he began sobbing and couldn't go on. I embraced him. He held on to me and kept crying.

There was a memorial for River a few days later at Paramount's Studio

River Phoenix and Samantha Mathis, playing struggling Nashville singer-songwriters, fell in love during the filming of The Thing Called Love *(1993), tragically River's last completed film; co-starred were Dermot Mulroney and Sandra Bullock.*

Theater on the lot. Sidney Poitier was very eloquent and touching, as was Ethan Hawke, and numerous others. Jonathan Pryce sent a letter saying that he couldn't speak more highly of River as a great talent and a great friend, and had been looking forward to a lifelong relationship. That was exactly how I felt, like someone who had lost an enduring pal. On a TV talk-show not long afterward, the host asked veteran star Tony Curtis to comment on the death of River Phoenix. Curtis said cryptically, but with considerable weight, that it was "difficult to comprehend how much envy" there was in Hollywood. The remark resonates.

Samantha had many recriminations about the horrible final night, most particularly against the junkie, but Heart would hear none of it. There was nothing that could bring River's body back to life, Heart seemed to feel, and she focused entirely on the continuing life of River's spirit and on helping her children to overcome the tragedy and learn to live with their brother in a different way. Her strength and selflessness were inspirational. Eventually, there were lawsuits against River's estate because his death happened while a picture was in production. Corporate inhumanity knows no bounds. A few years later, River's sister, Liberty, gave Heart her first grandchild—a boy; they named him Rio, Spanish for river.

Barely a week goes by that I don't think of River Phoenix, usually wishing I could just call him up and tell him what was happening, or hear his enthusiasm as we planned another movie or he wrote another song. He was an old soul, of course, so he'll never really be gone, but that doesn't mean I don't miss him an awful lot in this life: a lovely boy, a loyal friend, a poet at heart, a true artist.

Born River Jude Bottom, August 23, 1970, Madras, OR; died October 31, 1993, Los Angeles, CA.

Selected starring features (with director):

1986: *Stand by Me* (Rob Reiner); *The Mosquito Coast* (Peter Weir)
1988: *A Night in the Life of Jimmy Reardon* (William Richert); *Little Nikita* (Richard Benjamin); *Running on Empty* (Sidney Lumet)

1989: *Indiana Jones and the Last Crusade* (Steven Spielberg)
1990: *I Love You to Death* (Lawrence Kasdan)
1991: *Dogfight* (Nancy Savoca); *My Own Private Idaho* (Gus Van Sant)
1992: *Sneakers* (Phil Alden Robinson)
1993: *The Thing Called Love* (P.B.)
1994: *Silent Tongue* (Sam Shepard)

25

MARILYN MONROE

Only one time was I in Marilyn Monroe's presence, and she never would have known it. During the winter of 1955, I was sitting a row in front of her at a Manhattan acting class being conducted by Lee Strasberg. Marilyn was twenty-nine, just about at the peak of her success and fame—with seven years left to live—wearing a thick bulky-knit black woolen sweater, and no makeup on her pale lovely face. The two or three times I allowed myself to casually glance back at her, she was absolutely enthralled, mesmerized with Strasberg's every word and breath. In his autobiography, Arthur Miller, who would marry her the following year, wrote that he felt Strasberg, though worshipped by Monroe, was a heavy contributor to his breakup with the actress, and that the acting guru's domination was self-serving and exploitative of her. From the glimpses I had of Marilyn, Strasberg certainly had her complete attention and support, but in a strangely desperate way. She didn't look contented or studious; she looked quite anxious and passionately devoted to Strasberg as somehow the answer to all of her troubles.

Miller has described her most sensitively both in his 1987 autobiography (*Timebends*) and in his 1962 drama *After the Fall*, in which he fictionalized her. Of that play's character, Arthur told me in 2001, "The idea was that if you cannot see your own handprint on your fate, you'll be destroyed." He went on: "Marilyn lived at the edge of a grave all her life. But it's understandable. I'm sure that's not an unusual situation when you're given the kind of terrible upbringing she had." (Born an illegitimate child; father dead when she was three; mother in mental hospitals all through her childhood; raised in a series of foster homes, in an orphanage, with friends of her mother; neglected, unloved, humiliated, raped; first married at sixteen, suicide first attempted the following year.) I told Miller that I felt very strongly from reading his autobiography that he was madly

Marilyn Monroe in the title role of her first comedy success, Gentlemen Prefer Blondes *(1953), a gaudy musical directed by the master-of-all-genres himself, Howard Hawks; Jane Russell was the brunette.*

in love with Marilyn and he answered, simply, "I was." And, I continued, that this love was on some profound level very beneficial to him and that he understood it at the time as a kind of truth. He replied, "It was."

Then he added, with regret, "I, quite candidly, had to realize, as many have before me, that that [motion picture] business makes human relations almost impossible—especially if you're a woman—it scars the soul."

When he said that, I recalled Orson Welles telling me about being at a Hollywood party which Marilyn attended (circa 1946 or '47) while she was still a lowly starlet, and seeing someone casually pull down the top of her dress in front of people and fondle her. She had laughed. Welles said that "just about everyone in town" had slept with her. Yet, Miller had gone on to say that the kind of mythological figure Marilyn created on the screen was all her own and a great achievement for her. But that it also helped to kill her—this movie-star disease: "They're not looking out," Arthur said, "they're looking at what other people see. And that's a crippling burden."

More than forty years have passed since Marilyn's mysterious death, but her legend and persona have survived. This is all the more remarkable because she actually made very few films, and even fewer that were any good. But there was a reality to her artifice—she believed in the characters she played, even if they were inherently unbelievable. "Everything she did," Miller said to me, "she played realistically. I don't think she knew any other way to play anything—only to tell you the truth. She was always psychologically committed to that person as a person, no matter what the hell it was, rather than as a stock figure. Because the parts she got could easily have been stock figures, which had no other dimension. But she wouldn't have known how to do that. In other words, she did not have the usual technique for doing something as a stock figure. . . . She was even that way when [director John] Huston used her the first time [in a memorable walk-on bit] in *The Asphalt Jungle* [1950]."

This went for every picture she did in her surprisingly, painfully short career as a star, barely a decade, little more than a dozen pictures. Though she managed to work with quite a number of major directors, it was not necessarily always in their best efforts; but still they *were* Fritz Lang, Howard Hawks (twice), Otto Preminger, Billy Wilder (twice), George Cukor (twice, if you count her last unfinished one), John Huston (twice), Laurence Olivier, Joshua Logan, and Joseph L. Mankiewicz (bit part in 1950's classic *All About Eve*). In my conversation with Miller, he said, "I thought she had the potential for being a great performer if she were given the right stuff to do. And if you look at the stuff she did do, it's amazing that she created any impression at all because most of it was very primitive. And the fact that people remember these parts from these films is amazing. . . . She was committed to these parts as though they were real people, not cardboard cutouts. Even though the director and author and the rest might have thought they were cutouts and would deal with them that way. The way the two men [Tony Curtis, Jack Lemmon] in *Some Like It Hot* [1959] felt with their parts; or George Raft with his part. She was real. And therefore she had the potential of being a great comedienne." (Norman Mailer, in his book on Monroe—he never met her—wrote that starting with 1953's *Gentlemen Prefer Blondes,* she *was* a great comedienne.) When I said I felt she was better than Olivier himself in *The Prince and the Showgirl* (1957), Miller told me, "With him she had trouble, there's no question. He saw it in the British fashion—they play high style. She couldn't be more ignorant of high style. Just nothing of that sort connected with her. She detected in him a certain snobbery toward her; that was absolutely accurate."

The year before her much-speculated-over death at thirty-six (rumors of presidential involvement, etc.), playwright Clifford Odets told me that she used to come over to his house and talk, but that the only times she seemed to him really comfortable were when she was with his two young children and their large poodle. She relaxed with them, felt no threat. With everyone else, Odets said, she seemed nervous, intimidated, frightened. When I repeated to Miller this remark about her with children and animals, he said, "Well, they didn't sneer at her." I said that there seemed to be a general feeling at the time that people didn't really have a clue where Marilyn was coming from. "Right," Arthur responded. "They just thought that she was cute and sexy and that's it. And she was. But she was also very real. There's a blindness to it, her beauty blinded many people."

So they basically refused to see her humanity, I said, and he nodded, "Exactly." Therefore, despite the success she created in the face of these multiple obstacles, it also did kill her, I repeated, and Miller looked sad. "Well," he said, "she was never given the dignity—put it that way—that she required. That *anybody* would want as a result of their performances. They're treated like they're some odd animal that knows how to do some tricks."

Miller paused for a moment, reflectively. "I rather think that had she endured," he speculated, "had she come ten years later, maybe it would have been different. But at that time—I mean, she came in at the height of the Hollywood system—and she was not alone feeling debased by the whole thing. It was a common complaint. Like [the way] John Garfield was a terrific actor—yet he did nothing but scream and howl. There was some demeaning aspect to the whole thing. So most of them went with it. They simply adopted the contempt with which they were treated. I think that's what happened. Pretty hard to withstand—a culture of contempt. I think it helped destroy her. Somebody like John Barrymore, he died a drunk. There are many ways of reacting to that contempt. Mitchum, who was ready to kill you at the drop of a coin. Brando is a better example."

I remembered what Tennessee Williams had called "the catastrophe of success," and said that success in America really was a killer, to which Arthur nodded, saying, "Second only to failure." He smiled slightly at the irony. "The more talent they had, the more sensitive to the lost opportunity of using their ability for some worthy purpose."

It remains amazing that Marilyn, despite her terrors and demons, managed to project her essential qualities against all odds. Fritz Lang talked to me about her only three years after her death: "It was not easy to work with Marilyn Monroe; this [*Clash by Night,* 1952] was practically her first big picture. She was a very peculiar mixture of shyness and uncertainty and—I wouldn't say 'star allure'—but let me say, she knew exactly her impact on men. And that's all. Now, just at that time, the famous calendar story came up . . ." (Marilyn had posed naked for some anonymous calendar photos in the late forties that surfaced suddenly during the shooting of Lang's picture and created a scandal that, in fact, helped make her a star. These were reprinted a couple of years later in *Playboy*'s first issue, when Marilyn was already being starred, thus fostering the mistaken notion that Monroe had been the first Playmate.) Lang went on: "I didn't mind—what a woman does with herself is nobody's business—but the thing was, because of her shyness, she was scared as hell to come to the studio—she was always late. I don't know why she couldn't remember her lines, but I can very well understand all the directors who worked with her getting angry, because she was certainly responsible for slowing down the work. But she was very responsive."

Lang hesitated a moment, then added: "One very bad thing: she asked me would I mind if her female coach was there during shooting in the studio. I said, 'No, under one condition—that you don't let her coach you.' Because when an actress has learned her lines and thinks she has caught the feeling of the part, got under the skin of the character, it's very hard to *change* it. At the beginning I had trouble—until I found out that behind the camera, unseen by me, this coach was standing and gesturing with her hands. I said to Marilyn, 'Look—either/or . . .' and told her the coach could not come on the set anymore." (Later in her career, she would insist

Marilyn Monroe in the climactic sequence of her last completed movie,
The Misfits *(1961), written for her as a present by then-husband
Arthur Miller, directed by John Huston, co-starring Clark Gable,
Montgomery Clift and Eli Wallach*

on having her new coach, Paula Strasberg—Lee's first wife—perform the
exact same function, much to other directors' now frustrated displeasure.
It had become part of her deal.)

Howard Hawks, who directed her first big success, *Gentlemen Prefer
Blondes* (co-starring established, top-billed sex goddess Jane Russell), had
initially directed her a year earlier, in a major supporting role, with Cary
Grant and Ginger Rogers, in *Monkey Business* (1952), which actually featured the first great Marilyn Monroe performance. In fact, her scenes with
Cary are the highlights of the picture and make you wish they could have
done an entire romantic screwball comedy together. The same year Marilyn died, Hawks told me, "Monroe was frightened to come on the stage—
she had such an inferiority complex—and I felt sorry for her. I've seen
other people like that. I did the best I could and I wasn't bothered by it too
much. In *Monkey Business,* she only had a small part—that didn't frighten

her so much—but when she got into a *big* part . . . For instance, when we started her singing [for *Gentlemen Prefer Blondes*], she tried to run out of the recording studio two or three times. We had to grab her and hold her to keep her there. She sang quite well, actually. I got a great deal of help from Jane Russell. Without her I couldn't have made the picture. Jane gave Marilyn that 'You-can-do-it' pep talk to get her out there. She was just frightened, that's all—frightened she couldn't do it."

Lauren Bacall, who acted with Monroe in 1953's *How to Marry a Millionaire,* remembered her fondly, saying Marilyn was "very sweet—no meanness at all," but that her self-involvement was total. Marilyn's makeup man (who had done his job even for her funeral) used to say that poor Marilyn was simply terrified of going on the set, filled with nervousness caused by low self-esteem. Her lateness was chronic. Playing scenes with Marilyn was unnerving; Monroe never looked into her partner's eyes but always at the center of their forehead. This kept her eyes more open for the camera. Bacall stressed that none of this was because of any meanness on Monroe's part. It was at this time that Marilyn was madly in love with Joe DiMaggio and used to say that all she really wanted was to fly with Joe to San Francisco and have spaghetti with him. However, Bacall said, Marilyn definitely "knew what to do when the cameras started."

Seven years after her death, when I talked to George Cukor, who had directed her in *Let's Make Love* (1960) and in the unfinished last film, *Something's Gotta Give,* he concurred with Hawks. "Marilyn Monroe had no confidence in herself," he said. "She found it very difficult to concentrate, and she really didn't think she was as good as she was. She'd worry about all kinds of things, and she would do the very difficult things very well. Sometimes she was very distracted and couldn't sustain it, and you had to do it in bits and pieces; sometimes she was in such a state of nerves that you'd have to shoot individual lines. But such was her magic that you'd put them all together and they seemed as though she spoke them all at one time. She was a real *movie* personality—a real movie queen. She had the way all these great picture personalities have. Their brains are uncensored. They could imagine all kinds of things and there was really nothing immoral about it. Quite different—and, I thought, much more subtle than it is now."

Ironically, the picture that made Monroe a sex symbol, *Gentlemen Prefer Blondes,* was intended by Hawks as "a complete caricature, a travesty on sex—it didn't have normal sex." In a 1967 interview I did with Hawks for the BBC, he said, "Their sex was a sort of a symbol, an obvious thing, which all you can do is really make fun of and enjoy, you know, and watch

*Marilyn Monroe as Cherie, the saloon chanteuse/good-time girl in
Joshua Logan's production of the beautifully written William Inge
stage comedy-drama* Bus Stop *(1956), one of Marilyn's more complex roles
and among her best performances. She would die under mysterious
circumstances only six years after the picture's release.*

them perform. You don't try to make reality. Monroe never was any good
playing the reality. She always played in a sort of a fairy tale. And when
she did that she was great—something happened. But as far as doing a real
story with her, I don't believe that she's ever done a good picture that was
a real story. They were all more or less of a fairy tale quality. Kind of a
musical-comedy sort of a thing."

Hawks had told me that when he knew her on those early pictures,
Marilyn wasn't "very sexy in real life." He said, "Monroe couldn't get anybody to take her out—nobody. A funny little agent about five-feet-two
used to cart her around. But they both [Monroe and monogamous house-
wife Russell] were sex symbols to the motion picture public . . ." Hawks

also said that while Russell peaked in one or two takes, Marilyn continued to improve through repetition: "With Monroe, the more you kept going, the better she got."

All of Hawks' work with Marilyn was, of course, a couple of years before she fell in thrall to Strasberg and the Actors Studio. Miller explained it to me this way: "She only knew one way to do a role—for real. She was trying, for example, at the Actors Studio, to formularize her approach: She didn't want to squander her energies. I'm not convinced it helped her at all. But that was her aim—to make it even more real. I was against the whole methodology. But that's not to say that she wouldn't have thought it helped her. And I think she probably did think so."

Miller commented at one point that there is one "universal truth" on the subject of Monroe, demonstrated by most books or articles written by people who never knew her, and by a number who did: "Whatever is said about her is probably not true. They use it for their own purposes."

In his autobiography, Miller speaks of the deterioration of their relationship, fueled by Monroe's paranoia, her increasing dependence on drugs, and therefore her irrationality at times, her exaggerated mistrust of everyone. Miller wrote for her the original screenplay of what would, as it turned out, be her final completed picture, *The Misfits* (1961), quite purposely a non–"fairy tale" piece. During the four years the film took to write, produce and finish, their marriage fell apart. I said to Arthur that it seemed as though he and Monroe had, concerning that project, a terrible misunderstanding which pulled them away from one another. He responded: "Well, we were out of range of each other before the shooting started." I asked if he thought she had understood what was going on in his mind—a role that could define her most sensitive and poetic nature—or if she had at one point, and then lost that understanding. He answered, "I think she understood it, but she was rejecting the whole thing anyway." Why? I asked. "I wish I knew," Arthur said. "This occurred at the far end of a long life that she had—it's a short life, but for her long. If it hadn't been *The Misfits,* it'd have been something else. She was already in bad trouble."

The fact is that Marilyn was in bad trouble from the day she was born as Norma Jean Mortenson on June 1, 1926, in the city of angels and movies, a poor bastard angel child who rose to be queen of a town and a way of life that nevertheless held her in contempt. That she died a martyr to pictures at the same time as the original studio star system—through which she

*Marilyn Monroe and Arthur Miller toward the end
of their marriage, while preparing* The Misfits

had risen—finally collapsed and went also to its death seems too obviously symbolic not to note. Indeed, the coincidence of the two passing together is why I chose to end this long book about movie stars with Marilyn Monroe.

What I saw so briefly in my glimpse of Marilyn at the very peak of her stardom (and the start of my career)—that fervent, still remarkably naive look of all-consuming passion for learning about her craft and art—haunts me still. She is the most touching, strangely innocent—despite all the emphasis on sex—sacrifice to the twentieth-century art of cinematic mythology, with real people as gods and goddesses. While Lillian Gish had been film's first hearth goddess, Marilyn was the last love goddess of the screen, the final Venus or Aphrodite. The minute she was gone, we started to miss her and that sense of loss has grown, never to be replaced. In death, of course, she triumphed at last, her spirit being imperishable, and keenly to be felt in the images she left behind to mark her brief visit among us.

Born Norma Jean Mortenson, June 1, 1926, Los Angeles, CA; died August 5, 1962, Los Angeles, CA.

Selected features (with director):

1950: *The Asphalt Jungle* (John Huston); *All About Eve* (Joseph L. Mankiewicz)
1951: *As Young as You Feel* (Harmon Jones)
1952: *Clash by Night* (Fritz Lang); *Monkey Business* (Howard Hawks); *Don't Bother to Knock* (Roy Ward Baker); *We're Not Married* (Edmund Goulding)

1953: *Gentlemen Prefer Blondes* (Hawks); *How to Marry a Millionaire* (Jean Negulesco); *Niagara* (Henry Hathaway)
1954: *River of No Return* (Otto Preminger); *There's No Business Like Show Business* (Walter Long)
1955: *The Seven Year Itch* (Billy Wilder)
1956: *Bus Stop* (Joshua Logan)
1957: *The Prince and the Showgirl* (Laurence Olivier)
1959: *Some Like It Hot* (Wilder)
1960: *Let's Make Love* (George Cukor)
1961: *The Misfits* (Huston)

Acknowledgments

My primary thanks go to all the actors and actresses in this book, for their times with me, and all their invaluable achievements. For their encouragement, guidance, and suggestions throughout the five years I worked on it: Victoria Wilson (my brilliant editor at Knopf), Sherry Arden (my deeply insightful literary agent), Iris Chester (my trusty longtime assistant, who typed every single handwritten page many times over, made numerous very useful suggestions and proofread all galleys twice); Meghan McElheny (my invaluable New York assistant, who went beyond the call of duty organizing photos and captions); and Louise Stratten (who listened and reacted most helpfully to numerous chapters when I read them first to her). For all their time and effort with the illustrations: at Photofest, Ron Mandelbaum and Tom Toth; at The Kobal Collection, Lauretta Dives. For diligent and most helpful copyediting and proofreading, John Morrone, Andy Goldwasser and Dann Baker, and for great work in the same area, Anne Fratto. For their spoken and unspoken cheering section: Anna Bogdanovich (my dear sister); Antonia Bogdanovich, Sashy Bogdanovich (my loving daughters); Cybill Shepherd, Henry Jaglom, Zack Norman, Jeff Freilich and William Peiffer (my friends).

Almost all the previously existing material herein has been heavily revised or greatly amended and expanded. Parts—some lengthy, some very short—of the Introduction and the chapters on Bogart, Cagney, Cassavetes, Clift, Dietrich, Grant, Hepburn, Karloff, Lemmon, Lewis, Martin, Mineo, Phoenix, Sinatra, Stewart and Wayne first appeared in different form—between 1962 and 2001—either in *Esquire, New York, Premiere,* the *New York Times,* the *Los Angeles Times* or the *New York Observer.* The original *Esquire* portions also were printed in my collection, *Pieces of Time* (Arbor House, NY, 1973 and 1985 editions; published under the title *Picture Shows* in England, Allen & Unwin, London, 1974).

In a shorter form, the Gish chapter was first published as a limited edition chapbook titled *A Moment with Miss Gish* (Santa Teresa Press, Santa Barbara, CA, 1995).

A small part of the Adler chapter appeared, in different form, in *Who the Devil Made It* (Knopf, NY, 1997; Ballantine, NY, 1998), as did a few small sections of the Cassavetes and Sinatra chapters in *Movie of the Week* (Ballantine, NY, 1999).

Portions of the Q&A sections in the Lewis chapter, as well as some of Arthur Miller's comments in the Monroe chapter, were first published in German translation, as entire issues of the Sunday magazine supplement for Germany's daily newspaper, *Süddeutsche Zeitung* (2000–02); no part of these conversations have appeared before in English. I am especially grateful to Mr. Miller for his time and candor.

My sincere thanks go to the editors and publishers of all these periodicals and books for their warm interest, patronage, advice and help.

P.B.
New York, NY
2004

Illustrations

Permissions Acknowledgments

Grateful acknowledgment is made to the following for permission to reprint previously published material:

BMG Music Publishing, Inc.: Excerpt from the song lyric "I Write the Songs" by Bruce Johnson. Copyright © 1974 by Artists Music, Inc. (ASCAP). All rights for the U.S. on behalf of Artists Music, Inc. (ASCAP) administered by BMG Songs, Inc. (ASCAP). Rerpinted by permission of BMG Music Publishing, Inc.

Cherry Lane Music Company: Excerpt from the song lyric "Leaving on a Jet Plane" words and music by John Denver. Copyright © 1967 by Cherry Lane Music Publishing Company, Inc. (ASCAP) and DreamWorks Songs (ASCAP). Rights for DreamWorks Songs administered by Cherry Lane Music Publishing Company, Inc. International copyright secured. All rights reserved. Rerpinted by permission of Cherry Lane Music Company.

Warner Bros. Publications U.S. Inc.: Excerpt from the song lyric "Camelot" by Alan Jay Lerner and Frederick Loewe. Copyright © 1960 by Alan Jay Lerner and Frederick Loewe (Renewed). All rights on behalf of Alan Jay Lerner and Frederick Loewe administered by Chappell & Co. Excerpt from the song lyric "Lady Day" by Robert Gaudio and Jake Holmes. Copyright © WB Music Corp. (Renewed). All rights reserved. Reprinted by permission of Warner Bros. Publications U.S. Inc., Miami FL 33014.

Index

Italicized page numbers refer to photographs and captions.

A NOTE ON THE TYPE

This book was set in Adobe Garamond. Designed for the Adobe Corporation by Robert Slimbach, the fonts are based on types first cut by Claude Garamond (c. 1480–1561). Garamond was a pupil of Geoffroy Tory and is believed to have followed the Venetian models, although he introduced a number of important differences, and it is to him that we owe the letter we now know as "old style." He gave to his letters a certain elegance and feeling of movement that won their creator an immediate reputation and the patronage of Francis I of France.

Composed by North Market Street Graphics,
Lancaster, Pennsylvania
Printed and bound by Berryville Graphics,
Berryville, Virginia
Designed by Virginia Tan